CONTAINMENT AND CREDIBILITY

The Ideology and Deception that Plunged America into the Vietnam War

Pat Proctor

CARREL BOOKS

The views expressed in this book are those of the author and do not reflect the official policy or position of the Department of the Army, the Department of Defense, or the U.S. Government.

Carrel Books may be purchased in bulk at special discounts for sales promotion, corporate gifts, fund-raising, or educational purposes. Special editions can also be created to specifications. For details, contact the Special Sales Department, Carrel Books, 307 West 36th Street, 11th Floor, New York, NY 10018, or carrelbooks@skyhorsepublishing.com.

Carrel Books® is a registered trademark of Skyhorse Publishing, Inc.®, a Delaware corporation.

Visit our website at www.carrelbooks.com.

10 9 8 7 6 5 4 3 2 1

Library of Congress Cataloging-in-Publication Data is available on file.

Cover design by Rain Saukas
Cover photo credits: LBJ Presidential Library, Library of Congress

ISBN: 978-1-63144-056-4
Ebook ISBN: 978-1-63144-057-1

Printed in the United States of America

For Jon, Amy, Matt, and Mackenzie

Be sure to check out the online resources for this book:
Facebook: http://www.facebook.com/containmentandcredibility
Website: http://www.containmentandcredibility.com

These sites have a ton of multimedia resources, including archival television footage, video, and pictures of many of the events covered in this book. And check back often! New resources are constantly being added.

TABLE OF CONTENTS

INTRODUCTION

The United States is in the grips of a new foreign policy ideology—the War on Terror. According to this ideology, Islamic extremists must be defeated abroad before they can perpetrate terrorist attacks inside the United States. This ideology was forged in the fires of the World Trade Center and the Pentagon on September 11, 2001. This ideology blossomed in the days after 9/11, as anthrax-laden letters arrived at congressional offices and newsrooms, as shoe bombers and underwear bombers boarded planes to conduct further attacks. It has reshaped what infringements the American people are willing to accept on their liberties as they board planes, talk on their cell phones, or use the Internet. This ideology has also spawned two wars, the war in Iraq and the war in Afghanistan, which have cost the United States trillions of dollars and over six thousand American lives. And, as this work is being written, the War on Terror ideology has embroiled the United States in yet another war, this time in Iraq and Syria against the heirs to al Qaida in Iraq—the Islamic State in Iraq and Syria (ISIS).

Fifty years ago, the Cold War ideology of containment was no less powerful. This ideology was forged in the fire of World War II, the bloodiest conflict in the history of mankind. It blossomed in American politics amid fear of atomic annihilation and paranoia about Communist infiltration in the 1950s. By 1964, an entire generation had grown up knowing no other framework for public debate over foreign policy; the American public *believed* that it was necessary to contain Communist expansion, using military force if necessary. President Johnson tapped into this ideology when he insisted that communists were trying to expand into Southeast Asia through South Vietnam—the so-called domino theory—and had to be opposed by force. The resulting war lasted more than eight years and cost nearly sixty thousand American lives.

Throughout the war, both President Lyndon Johnson and President Richard Nixon used the ideology of military containment of communism to justify U.S. military intervention in Vietnam. From 1965 until early 1968, opponents of U.S. military intervention in Vietnam tried to stop the war by attacking the suitability of the strategy of military containment of communism to Vietnam and Southeast Asia. Some opponents also attacked the entire ideology of military containment of communism, not just in Vietnam, but anywhere. In 1968, most opponents of the Vietnam War switched tactics and began to focus instead on the president's credibility on Vietnam. These arguments quickly became the dominant critique of America's policies in Vietnam through the end of the war and were ultimately successful in ending it.

The Gulf of Tonkin incident on August 4, 1964—in which two U.S. destroyers were supposedly attacked by the North Vietnamese—and the Tonkin Gulf Resolution were central both to the Johnson administration's use of containment to justify U.S. military intervention in Vietnam and to the change of opposition strategy in 1968 from attacking the administration's use of containment to justify the war to attacking the administration's credibility. For President Johnson, the Gulf of Tonkin incident both provided dramatic proof of the growing aggression of the North Vietnamese in Southeast Asia and provided the political impetus to overcome the private skepticism of many in Congress over whether the goal of containing communism in Southeast Asia was really important enough to warrant U.S. military intervention in Vietnam. The resulting Tonkin Gulf Resolution—the President's "blank check" to use U.S. military force in Vietnam—provided the administration with an insurance policy against congressional dissent; whatever their later misgivings, all but two members of Congress voted for the resolution. For opponents of the war in 1968, glaring inconsistencies in the administration's version of the events of the Gulf of Tonkin incident provided compelling evidence that the Johnson administration had lied to the American people, making the resulting Tonkin Gulf Resolution—obtained as a result of this incident—null and void. For the American people, revelations about the administration's dishonesty during the Gulf of Tonkin incident simply added to grave doubts they already had about the Johnson administration's credibility; the American people lost confidence in President Johnson, ending his presidency. The dramatic success of this new strategy—attacking the administration's credibility rather than its use of containment to justify the war—encouraged most other opponents of the war to follow suit, permanently altering the framework of debate over the war.

This change in the opposition's strategy—from attacking military containment as a justification for the war to attacking the administration's credibility—had a number of important consequences. First, this change in opposition rhetoric ultimately forced an end to the war. To sustain his credibility against relentless attack, President Nixon was repeatedly forced to withdraw troops to prove to the American people he was making good on his pledge to bring an "honorable end" to the war. Ultimately, Nixon ran out of troops to withdraw and was forced to accept an unfavorable compromise peace. Second, this framework for public debate of foreign policy established in the latter half of the Vietnam War—between advocates of military invention using the ideology of military containment and opponents of military intervention attacking the administration's credibility—would reemerge nearly every time an administration contemplated a military intervention through the end of the Cold War. Finally, and most importantly, because opponents of military intervention stopped challenging the ideology of containment, the American public continued to accept the precepts of containment after the Vietnam War and the Cold War consensus survived until the collapse of the Soviet Union and the end of the Cold War.

From the beginning of his presidency in November 1963 until August 1964, President Lyndon Johnson used arguments founded in the Cold War ideology of containment of communism to justify U.S. military involvement in the conflict in Vietnam, just as his predecessor, John F. Kennedy, had. Few publicly opposed these arguments or the ideology of military containment of communism that was the core of the broader Cold War consensus on American foreign policy. Still, despite a concerted public information campaign by the administration to build a consensus in Congress and among the public for the direct employment of American military force in Vietnam, the public and Congress did not support an American military escalation in Vietnam.

On August 2, 1964, the USS *Maddox* was in the Gulf of Tonkin supporting raids by South Vietnamese commandos (with American advisors in support) when three North Vietnamese patrol boats launched an attack on the *Maddox*. The attack was turned away, with one patrol boat sunk and the others damaged. On August 4, the *Maddox*, joined by the destroyer USS *Turner Joy*, reported that it was again attacked by North Vietnamese torpedo boats.

President Lyndon Johnson used this incident in the Gulf of Tonkin on August 4, 1964, to justify a retaliatory air strike against North Vietnam and to win a congressional endorsement—the Tonkin Gulf Resolution—to use military force to protect the sovereignty of South Vietnam from what his administration described as northern aggression. After the incident and the retaliation, the Johnson administration immediately returned to the ideology of military containment of communism—while occasionally evoking the tit-for-tat precedent of these initial retaliatory air strikes or the Tonkin Gulf Resolution itself—to justify "Americanizing" the Vietnam War through a series of escalations that started with sustained bombing of the North and ended with over 500,000 U.S. troops fighting in the jungles of South Vietnam.

During this same period, a growing number of opponents of President Johnson's policies in Vietnam began a dramatic broadening of the public foreign policy debate, attacking justifications for the Vietnam War rooted in the military containment of communism and even attacking the broader ideology of military containment itself. These antiwar arguments ultimately had little impact on public support for the Vietnam War, and Congress, restrained by the president's insurance policy against their dissent, the Tonkin Gulf Resolution, remained silent.

In early 1968, the North Vietnamese Army and Viet Cong insurgents initiated a massive, coordinated attack across South Vietnam in an effort to trigger a general uprising of the South Vietnamese people against their government. In the United States, this attack, initiated during the traditional ceasefire over the Vietnamese lunar New Year called "Tet," was known as the Tet Offensive.[1]

In the months immediately before this Tet Offensive—at the same time the administration was making ever more strident claims about its progress in Vietnam—a few opponents of the war began tentative attacks on the administration's credibility. Then, just as the Tet Offensive called into question the administration's rosy predictions from the previous fall, the Senate Foreign Relations Committee used the Gulf of Tonkin incident and the Tonkin Gulf Resolution as a weapon against Johnson's Vietnam policy, claiming that President Johnson had lied about the facts of the incident to deceive the Congress into passing the Tonkin Gulf Resolution. This deluge of evidence caused a collapse of public confidence in President Johnson's credibility; he was forced to withdraw from the presidential race and stop escalating the war.

Opponents of the war perceived these new, highly effective attacks on the administration's credibility as responsible for the president's retreat. Soon after, a number of prominent antiwar candidates who continued to attack the ideology of containment or its application to the Vietnam War were defeated in the 1968 elections; most on both sides of the Vietnam issue interpreted these losses as a rejection by the American public of attacks on the Cold War consensus. Thus, after the 1968 elections, attacks on the use of the military containment of communism to justify the Vietnam War or on the broader ideology of military containment itself virtually disappeared. Instead, antiwar arguments narrowed to themes surrounding presidential deceptiveness in the initiation, conduct, and resolution of the war. These latter themes became the dominant critique throughout the remainder of the Vietnam War and, in fact, were decisive in undermining congressional and public support for the war and ultimately ending it.

However, ending the war in this way—through attacks on each administration's credibility rather than through attacks on the use of military containment of communism as a justification for the Vietnam

War—had a lasting impact on public foreign policy debate in America, even after the war. First, the structure of the debate over U.S. policy in Vietnam during the latter days of the war—between the use of military containment as a justification for military interventions and questions about the administration's credibility on foreign policy matters— became the framework for nearly every future debate over military intervention abroad through the remainder of the Cold War. More importantly, however, while many foreign policy leaders in and out of government had abandoned the ideology of military containment after the Vietnam War, the American public continued to support this foreign policy framework. In other words, while the Cold War consensus among members of Congress and foreign policy experts outside of government was broken, the Cold War consensus among the broader American public survived the Vietnam War, perpetuating the Cold War until the collapse of the Soviet Union in 1991.

This book is a mass political history of the Vietnam War. The phrase "mass political" is used here to distinguish this book from an intra-governmental political history (documenting the struggle within a single branch or between branches of the U.S. government) or an international political history (documenting the struggle between national governments over the war). Instead, this book is a history of the mass politics of the war—the public struggle between supporters and opponents of the Vietnam War to influence American public opinion about the war. This public struggle was waged primarily in the print and broadcast media, but also through demonstrations, acts of civil disobedience, and even occasionally through violence. This book examines the arguments that were being made for and against the war, the people who were making these arguments, and why they were making them (i.e., what effect they hoped their arguments would have on the American public and why they thought their arguments would have this effect).

Chapter 1

CREATING A CONSENSUS ON VIETNAM

From the beginning of his presidency in November 1963 until August 1964, President Lyndon Johnson used arguments firmly rooted in the Cold War ideology of the containment communism to justify U.S. military involvement in the conflict in Vietnam, just as John F. Kennedy had before him. Few publicly opposed these arguments or the broader Cold War foreign policy ideology of military containment of communism on which they were based. Still, despite a concerted public information campaign by the administration to build a consensus in Congress and among the public for the direct employment of U.S. military force in Vietnam, Johnson failed to persuade the public and Congress to support a military escalation in Vietnam.

On August 2, 1964, the destroyer USS *Maddox* was in the Gulf of Tonkin supporting raids by South Vietnamese commandos (with American advisors in support) when three North Vietnamese patrol boats attacked it. The attack was turned away with one patrol boat sunk and the others damaged. On August 4, the *Maddox*, joined by the destroyer USS *Turner Joy*, reported that it had again been attacked by North Vietnamese torpedo boats.

President Lyndon Johnson used this incident in the Gulf of Tonkin on August 4, 1964, to justify a retaliatory air strike and win a congressional endorsement—the Tonkin Gulf Resolution—to use military force to protect the sovereignty of South Vietnam from what his administration described as northern aggression.

President Lyndon Johnson inherited much of his rhetoric for U.S. military intervention in South Vietnam—founded in the ideology of containment—from his predecessor, President John F. Kennedy. While there were a few members of Congress who were publicly skeptical, President Johnson also inherited both a press and foreign policy academia that embraced the tenets of the Cold War consensus and supported America's policies in Vietnam. Most importantly, President Johnson inherited an American public that had internalized the precepts of the Cold War consensus—a public that *believed* the expansion of communism must be contained, sometimes by military force. The Vietnam War that Johnson inherited from Kennedy primarily entailed economic aid and military advisors. And the American public was barely paying attention to the conflict in Vietnam because it did not believe it was particularly important to U.S. national security.[1]

The Kennedy administration, in turn, inherited the rhetoric and logic for supporting South Vietnam from the Eisenhower administration. And the Kennedy administration unabashedly echoed those justifications. One of the earliest arguments the Kennedy administration made was that the war in Vietnam was a defense against northern aggression. For instance, in a press conference on May 4, 1961, Secretary of State Dean Rusk said the war "stemmed from a decision made in May 1959 by the Central Committee of the Communist Party of north Viet Nam which called for the reunification of Viet Nam by all 'appropriate means'" in order to "'liberate' south Viet Nam" from the "remarkable success which the Government of the Republic of Viet Nam under President Ngo Dinh Diem had achieved." Rusk added that the North Vietnamese were violating the sovereignty of Laos to secure their lines of supply into South Vietnam.[2] In November 1961, Secretary Rusk detailed the means of this northern aggression—a "campaign of propaganda, infiltration, and subversion by the communist regime in north Viet Nam, to destroy the Republic of Viet Nam and subjugate its peoples." Rusk also argued that the threat to South Vietnam was a threat to U.S. security, though he did not explain how on this occasion.[3]

Kennedy's vice president, Lyndon Johnson, unequivocally supported his president's policies in Vietnam. In 1961, when Johnson visited South Vietnam, he hailed South Vietnamese President Diem of South Vietnam as "the Winston Churchill of Asia."[4] At the conclusion of this trip, the vice president issued a joint communiqué with President Diem that echoed the administration's arguments based on the containment of communism. Johnson stated that the sovereignty of South Vietnam was "being brutally and systematically violated by communist agents and forces from the north."[5]

Vice President Johnson's Farewell Breakfast with President Diem in South Vietnam, (roughly front to back) Ngo Dinh Diem, Lady Bird Johnson, Madame Nhu, Nguyen Ngoc Tho, Jean Kennedy Smith, Stephen Smith, Ngo Dinh Nhu, Saigon, May 13, 1961, Johnson Presidential Library.[6] Source: Republic of Vietnam

Yet Kennedy did not feel so strongly about the sovereignty of South Vietnam that he was willing to commit large numbers of U.S. troops to direct action in South Vietnam. On at least one occasion, President Kennedy misled the *New York Times* into running a story reporting that the Chairman of the Joint Chiefs of Staff General Maxwell D. Taylor and the Joint Chiefs did not support sending troops to Vietnam. He did this, presumably, to inoculate himself against charges that he was not doing enough to support South Vietnam.[7]

Foreign policy academics, by and large, supported the Kennedy administration's use of containment to justify its policies in Vietnam and Southeast Asia. In October 1954, Hans Morgenthau—esteemed professor of international relations and author of the classic *Politics Among Nations*—had argued that France's military solution to Indochina was inherently counterrevolutionary and bound to fail.[8] As early as January 1957, Hans Morgenthau had suggested that China, by virtue of its position and size, was likely to dominate Asia.[9] In July 1961, Morgenthau questioned the application of containment to Southeast Asia, based first on the contention that it was U.S. nuclear power—rather than local forces in Europe—that had deterred Soviet aggression and, second, on the argument that the undemocratic regimes of non-communist Southeast Asia could not muster the same popular support as their counterparts in Western Europe.[10] However, as America's commitment in South Vietnam deepened, Morgenthau gradually began to frame the conflict in Vietnam in terms of the containment of communism. By summer 1962, Morgenthau no longer questioned the need to contain communist China's ambitions in Asia; rather, he asked, "What is the place of the containment of China within the hierarchy of our foreign policy?"[11] A month later, in *Overseas*, Hans Morgenthau defended the United States' objective of containing communism in Southeast Asia, claiming it was necessary to maintain the balance of power in Asia.[12] In a November 1963 edition of *Commentary*, Morgenthau went further, explicitly endorsing the Kennedy administration's approach to President Diem and South Vietnam—foreign aid and military assistance to South Vietnam.[13]

Early in the war, official optimism was extremely successful in keeping Vietnam out of the headlines. By August 1962, President Kennedy could get through an entire press conference without a single question about Vietnam being asked.[14] The dramatic success of early government public information efforts on Vietnam was largely the result of a compliant, even sympathetic, press. The American press, consisting almost entirely of men who had lived through the Great Depression and World War II,[15] did not question either America's policies in Vietnam or the assumptions on which they were based.[16] The Washington press corps seldom even questioned the details of the policy. For instance, when asked in early 1962 if Americans were fighting in Vietnam, the press failed to question President Kennedy's unequivocal "no," despite the fact that Americans routinely flew combat aviation missions in support of Army of the Republic of Vietnam (ARVN) forces.[17]

This deep internalization of Cold War preconceptions that drove America into Vietnam led the American press to go beyond simply accepting the official government justifications for U.S. involvement in Vietnam to actually furthering them. The American media engaged in self-censorship, keeping the most disturbing images from reaching the American public.[18] Some members of the media, such as Joseph Alsop, even criticized the administration for not going far enough in supporting President Diem and South Vietnam.[19] Correspondents on the ground in South Vietnam were not nearly as supportive of U.S. policy in Vietnam as their counterparts in Washington, but American newspapers and news magazines filtered out the pessimism of the Saigon press corps before it ever saw print.[20]

With the press reflecting official optimism and suppressing negative news from South Vietnam, it is not surprising that the American public wasn't paying attention to the war. When the first American soldier died in combat in Vietnam on December 22, 1961, Americans, distracted by events in Laos, Cuba, and Berlin, barely noticed.[21]

Support for America's Vietnam policy was not universal. In Congress, as early as June 1962, Senator Wayne Morse was questioning America's deepening commitment to South Vietnam. In a floor speech, Morse asked that Hans Morgenthau's article "Vietnam—another Korea?" from *Public Affairs* magazine be added to the *Congressional Record*. Morse commended Morgenthau's article for raising "some very pertinent questions to which our Government needs to give heed as we reappraise American foreign policy in southeast Asia, and with particular reference to South Vietnam."[22] However, the article itself, while critical of the Diem regime and America's support for despotic regimes in Asia, otherwise supported many of the administrations justifications for U.S. intervention in Vietnam based on the containment of communism. Specifically, Morgenthau wrote, "Communist China pursues in Asia an overall military and political objective which parallels the objective of the Soviet Union in Europe. It is to remove the power of the United States from the continent of Asia."[23]

Americans were, for the first time, confronted with the grim reality of the situation in Vietnam in 1963. The battle of Ap Bac in January 1963—in which the critical assessments from U.S. troops on the ground supporting the Army of the Republic of Vietnam clashed with the glowing assessments from U.S. officials in Saigon—thrust dire assessments of the war, for the first time, onto the front pages of American newspapers.[24] As the ruling Diem regime in Saigon came into conflict with Buddhist dissidents, the American public was next confronted with images in their newspapers and on their televisions of Buddhist monks immolating themselves to protest the Diem government.[25] The Diem regime only compounded the sense of chaos by first cracking down on the Buddhist dissidents and then cracking down on the foreign press corps.[26] The episode would ultimately end in a U.S.-backed coup that deposed the Diem regime and assassinated Diem.

Yet, despite the press coverage of the worsening situation in Vietnam, no major American news sources challenged the basic premise that the United States should be supporting South Vietnam. The media came closest in September 1963 when NBC News anchors Chet Huntley and David Brinkley directly questioned the president on the validity of the so-called domino theory. The domino theory, first posited by the

President Eisenhower and his administration, held that the fall of South Vietnam would lead to communist domination of all Southeast Asia. Kennedy espoused a wholehearted belief in the domino theory and, even under cross-examination on national television, continued to support the centrality of South Vietnam to U.S. national security.[27]

And despite the dramatic events in Vietnam, the American public still took little notice. Sixty-three percent of Americans were not even paying attention to Vietnam. The majority of those who *were* paying attention to Vietnam wanted stronger action rather than withdrawal.[28]

To be sure, Americans were distracted by civil rights demonstrations in the southern United States and Dr. Martin Luther King Jr.'s speech on the national mall.[29] Still, another reason that Americans were not paying attention to Vietnam may have been that they did not see it as particularly important to U.S. security. A White House poll on Cold War issues that concluded in March 1963 found that only 34 percent of Americans believed that it was "extremely likely" or "very likely" that Vietnam would "lead to [a] major East-West 'Collision.'" By comparison, Berlin (54 percent) and Cuba (63 percent) were seen as the most likely flashpoints for conflict between the communist and free worlds.[30]

More promising for the administration's case for U.S. involvement in Vietnam, however, according to this same poll, "Communist China" was seen as a growing threat. In March 1963, 64 percent of Americans saw China as being a threat equal to, or even greater than, the Soviet Union within the next two years. When asked about the next ten years, 71 percent of Americans saw Communist China as a greater or equal threat.[32]

While most Americans did not see supposed communist aggression in Vietnam as a threat to U.S. national security, they did embrace many of the precepts of the Cold War consensus. This same poll found that 60 percent of Americans had "acute concern over National Defense, 57 percent of Americans believed that "Russia 'wants war'— now or later," 67 percent found "Cold War issues 'alarming,'" 58 percent believed that "world tensions [were] 'almost impossible' to relax," and 68 percent of respondents believed "use of nuclear weapons [was] certain in a new world war."[32]

When President Johnson took office, he wanted to continue his predecessor's measures to shore up the teetering government in South Vietnam. To sustain public support for the present level of U.S. military intervention in Vietnam, Johnson adopted the public communications strategy of his predecessor: using the ideology of containment to justify intervention. However, as the situation in South Vietnam worsened, the Johnson administration began to develop contingency plans for direct U.S. military intervention in the conflict. From the beginning, the administration believed it needed a congressional resolution of support before it could intervene. Members of the administration also realized that there was insufficient support for intervention in Congress to gain passage of such a resolution. The administration eventually concluded that it needed a pretext in the form of a North Vietnamese provocation before it could seek a congressional resolution in support of U.S. military intervention.

The American public largely favored the status quo in Vietnam when President Johnson took office, thought the public was not terribly concerned about the region. According to a Gallup poll from mid-December 1963, less than a month after the assassination of President Kennedy, nearly two-thirds of Americans believed that the United States should stay in South Vietnam. But they did not believe that the conflict should be escalated; when asked, "Do you think that we should do more than we are now doing in Vietnam," 47 percent said America should do "about the same" as it was currently doing, while 21 percent said America should be doing "less." By way of comparison, nearly two thirds of Americans supported "stronger measures including a blockade" in dealing with Cuba. When asked, explicitly, if they would support sending "more American troops to Vietnam in order to fight the communists" if "U.S. Military authorities" said they were necessary, only 47 percent said they would approve, while 36 percent said they would disapprove, and the remainder were undecided.[33]

Just days after taking office, the Johnson administration established the Kennedy administration's practice of painting the conflict in Vietnam as part of the global struggle to contain communist expansion as official government policy. A National Security Action Memo from only four days after President Kennedy's assassination, written by National Security Advisor McGeorge Bundy, stated that it was the "central object" of the nation to help South Vietnam "to win their contest against the externally directed and supported communist conspiracy." A key element of this strategy, Bundy wrote in the same document, was to "develop as strong and persuasive a case as possible to demonstrate to the world the degree to which the Viet Cong is controlled, sustained and supplied from Hanoi, through Laos and other channels."[34]

This was not just rhetoric; the president did believe the so-called domino theory—that communist aggression by North Vietnam represented a threat to all of Southeast Asia. Moreover, he believed that the United States had a commitment to South Vietnam. In a private phone conversation with Secretary of Defense McNamara, President Johnson insisted that the secretary insert comments on Vietnam into a speech that the president would give later that evening to a congressional reception at the White House. When asked what these comments should say, it was President Johnson who suggested, "I would say that we have a commitment to Vietnamese freedom. Now we . . . uh . . . we could pull out of there, the dominoes would fall, that part of the world would go to the Communists." The president also believed Vietnam was part of the West's global struggle to contain of communist expansion. In this same phone conversation, Johnson told McNamara that the United States had "kept the communists from spreading" in Southeast Asia, just as it had "in Greece and Turkey with the Truman Doctrine" and with "Western Europe by NATO."[35]

The president was the spearhead of the public communications effort on Vietnam. Throughout the first few months of his presidency, President Johnson repeatedly emphasized that the conflict in Vietnam was the result of aggression from the north. At a February 1964 speech in St. Louis, the president blamed the war on "those that are seeking to impose the Communist system by direct or indirect aggression."[36] In a speech in Los Angeles, that same month, he warned the North Vietnamese that "those engaged in external direction and supply would do well to . . . remember that this type of aggression is a deeply dangerous game."[37]

However, early in Johnson's presidency it does not appear that he wanted to escalate the U.S. military commitment in Vietnam beyond the advisors and military aid that the United States was already providing. In the same private phone conversation with McNamara, Johnson seemed reticent to send troops. He worried aloud that "[the United States] could get tied down in a third world war or another Korean action." Instead, Johnson preferred the alternative: "to advise them and hope that they stand up and fight." Johnson went on to tell McNamara that he believed the United States had made no commitment to send troops.[38]

Johnson's public pronouncements on Vietnam early in his presidency reflected this private belief that the Vietnamese were primarily responsible for fighting the war. In his Los Angeles speech, Johnson told the audience: "The contest in which South Vietnam is now engaged is first and foremost a contest to be won by the government and the people of that country for themselves."[39] About three weeks after his private conversation with Secretary McNamara, President Johnson appeared in a television interview with reporters from the three television networks. When asked by ABC's William Lawrence whether his "dangerous game" comments in his Los Angeles speech signaled direct action in Vietnam, the president rejected the possibility immediately. Likewise, when asked by NBC's David Brinkley whether the United States faced "a decision on Vietnam that's in the order of magnitude of Korea," President Johnson again rejected the possibility of sending troops.[40]

While the president did not call for direct U.S. military action in Vietnam, he did justify the present level of intervention by claiming that Vietnam was a war of communist aggression. In this same interview he explained his "dangerous game" comment from Los Angeles, he said:

> It was a dangerous game to try to supply arms and become
> an aggressor and deprive people of their freedom. And that is

true, whether it's in Vietnam or whether it's in this hemisphere or wherever it is.[41]

The president continued by reiterating the broader threat that communist aggression posed to Southeast Asia, in essence endorsing Kennedy's defense of the domino theory from a year earlier.[42]

Johnson also highlighted another idea that was central to his administration's use of containment to justify U.S. military intervention in Vietnam and would be repeatedly reemphasized throughout his presidency: that his administration's Vietnam policy was a continuation of his predecessors' policies. Johnson told Brinkley in this same interview:

> We have problems in Vietnam as we have had for ten years . . . I was only reading a letter yesterday that General Eisenhower wrote to the late [South Vietnamese] President Diem, and it was a letter I could have well written to [South Vietnamese] President [Khanh]. . . . We've had the problem for a long time and we're going to have it well into the future.[43]

Later, he reiterated this theme: "We have difficulties there, and we have had for ten years."[44]

The press was largely supportive of the administration's use of containment to justify U.S. military intervention in Vietnam. In fact, virtually the only criticism from the press was directed at the President's invocation of the domino theory; by early 1964, the domino theory had begun to take on a negative connotation in the media, implying an overly simplistic understanding of the complex international situation in Southeast Asia. In a United Press International (UPI) story about the president's television interview, the story noted that President Johnson "subscribes to the 'falling domino' theory."[45] The president had never actually used the words *domino theory*. In fact, the administration would frequently deny that it subscribed to the domino theory (and quickly follow by reasserting all of its tenets).

While the administration judiciously avoided using the term *domino theory,* they certainly made the argument that the communist threat to South Vietnam threatened more than just that country. In a speech in mid-March 1964, Robert McNamara argued that "to defend Southeast Asia, we must meet the challenge in South Vietnam." He continued that Southeast Asia had "great strategic significance in the forward defense of the United States" because of its key location in the midst of "the Indian subcontinent on one side and Australia, New Zealand, and the Philippines" on the other. Southeast Asia was also significant, he argued, as the "gateway between the Pacific and Indian Oceans." McNamara concluded: "In communist hands this area would pose a most serious threat to the security of the United States and to the family of free-world nations."[46]

In speeches in February and March 1964, Robert McNamara established another argument that would become a cornerstone of the administration's justification for the Vietnam War. In March, McNamara said that Vietnam was "a major test case of communism's new strategy," a strategy of subverting countries through wars of national liberation.[47] A month earlier, McNamara made it clear that this "new strategy" was inextricably linked to China's involvement in the Vietnam War and the domino theory. "For Peiping," he said, " . . . Hanoi's victory would be only a first step toward eventual Chinese hegemony over the two Vietnams and Southeast Asia and toward exploitation of the new strategy in other parts of the world." One of America's key goals in Vietnam, McNamara concluded, was to "prove in the Vietnamese test case that the free-world can cope with communist 'wars of liberation.'"[48]

In a speech to the National Industrial Conference Board, Secretary McNamara explicitly tied the threat of wars of liberation to the domino theory. He explained that the United States was giving aid to "11 nations on the southern and eastern perimeters of the Soviet and Red Chinese blocs," who were under threat of "military aggression from without and from attempted subversion from within." He explained that protecting these countries under the "Red shadow" was "in the interests of the United States and the rest of the free world." Protecting the rights of the people of these countries, he concluded, "strengthens our security at home."[49]

However, perhaps the most central principle of the administration's use of containment to justify U.S. military intervention in Vietnam was the idea that the Vietnam War was a result of communist aggression from North Vietnam, encouraged or aided by China and/ or the Soviet Union. Adlai Stevenson, America's ambassador to the United Nations (UN), told the UN Security Council, "The communist leadership in Hanoi has sought to pretend that the insurgency in South Vietnam is a civil war, but Hanoi's hand shows very clearly."[50] Robert McNamara insisted in a speech in April 1964 that North Vietnam was the "prime aggressor . . . encouraged on its aggressive course by Communist China."[51]

Another pillar of the administration's case for U.S. military involvement in Vietnam to contain communism was the so-called lessons of Munich: the proposition that the Second World War had taught the world that aggression must be met early and firmly or it would continue and grow. In a speech to the American Law Institute, Secretary of State Dean Rusk said that a loss in South Vietnam would result in "a drastic loss of confidence in the will and capacity of the free world to oppose aggression." He reminded his audience: "We have learned, in the course of the last 35 years, that a course of aggression means war and that the place to stop it is at its beginning." Rusk concluded that the defeat of communist aggression by wars of liberation would "be convincing proof that communist expansion by such tactics will not be permitted."[52]

Congress generally supported the Johnson administration's policy in Vietnam. Chairman of the Senate Foreign Relations Committee J. William Fulbright did not always take a hard line on Cold War issues. In a March 1964 television interview he supported thawing relations with the Soviet Union and rejected the "old myths" of monolithic communism. Likewise, he supported disarmament and acceptance of the Castro regime in Cuba as a "nuisance, but not a grave threat."[53] However, Senator Fulbright was unequivocal in his support of the administration's policy in Vietnam:

> There are only two realistic options open to us in Vietnam in the immediate future—the expansion of the conflict in one

way or another or a renewed effort to bolster the capacity of the South Vietnamese to prosecute the war successfully on its present scale. . . . It seems to me that we have no choice but to support the South Vietnamese government and army by the most effective means available. Whatever specific policy decisions are made it should be clear to all concerned that the United States will continue to meet its obligations and fulfill its commitments with respect to Vietnam.[54]

While he may have had private reservations, here Fulbright seemed to have no doubt that the United States was committed to the defense of South Vietnam, either by expanding the conflict or, preferably, by supporting the South Vietnamese military through advisors.

Not everyone in Congress agreed with the administration's use of containment to justify U.S. military intervention in Vietnam. Senator Wayne Morse lashed out at an April 1964 editorial by Secretary of Defense Robert McNamara advocating firmer action in South Vietnam. Morse warned that America would be "branded an aggressor nation," and said that the United States did not "have an iota of international law or right on our side in escalating a war into North Viet Nam." Citing Cambodia, which had rejected U.S. foreign aid in 1963 but had not fallen to communists, Morse joined those who had begun to claim that the "domino theory" was "fallacious."[55]

However, Senator Morse was not an influential senator, and his dissent was broadly dismissed. A news stories reporting on his comments also cited the State Department's response that the suggestion of U.S. withdrawal was unrealistic and that U.S. presence in Southeast Asia had acted as a shield against communism for all Southeast Asian countries, not just South Vietnam.[56]

As the South Vietnamese government became increasingly unstable, the Johnson administration came to the realization that it might have to commit U.S. military force to direct intervention in South Vietnam to save the government there. And almost as soon as they reached this realization, they also concluded that such intervention would require an endorsement from Congress in the form of a congressional resolution. In fact, this resolution was seen as an escalation in and of itself—much like the Formosa Resolution or the Middle East Resolution from the Eisenhower years—that would communicate to the North Vietnamese, Communist Chinese, and Soviets that America was committed to defend South Vietnam, hopefully convincing them to cease their aggression. The obstacle to these escalations was public and congressional sentiment; neither supported direct U.S. military intervention in South Vietnam. Thus, at the same time, the administration also contemplated a strategy to convince the public and Congress to support these escalations, and they immediately turned to the ideology of containment for this strategy.

Numerous speeches and interviews designed to convince the American public that the fate of Southeast Asia was vital to U.S. security had convinced Americans to support the present level of intervention in Vietnam. However, the American public did not yet support direct military action in Vietnam. In fact, according to another round of polling conducted on behalf of the White House in February 1964, Cold War issues had receded in importance for most Americans. Perhaps as a result of the administration's public information campaign, Americans increasingly saw China as a greater future threat than the Soviet Union, by a margin of two to one (up from a three-to-two margin in 1963). Likewise, Cuba and Vietnam were, by February 1964, seen as nearly equal in their potential to cause an "East-West Collision," with 67 percent and 64 percent, respectively. Moreover, Cuba and Vietnam were seen as nearly twice as likely to produce conflict as the next closest contender, Africa, which rated just 38 percent. Yet concern over "Cold War issues" had actually fallen behind domestic concerns (specifically the "adequacy of [the United States'] educational system") for the first time since Benton & Bowles began polling for the White House on Cold War issues in July 1960. Likewise, while three out of five Americans still said that the Cold War was serious enough to give "real cause for alarm," this was the lowest level of concern Benton & Bowles had observed. For the first time since Benton & Bowles had started polling, nearly half of Americans no longer believed the Soviet Union wanted war.[57]

Moreover, this Benton & Bowles polling data was contradicted by two separate polls—one conducted by the White House and the other by Gallup—which showed that Americans were even less concerned about Vietnam. The polls also showed Americans did not think the Johnson administration was doing a particularly good job handling the situation in Vietnam. In White House polls conducted in New York, California, Oklahoma, Ohio, Indiana, and Maryland in April 1964, pollsters found that only between zero and six percent of respondents in the surveyed regions rated "handling the problem in Vietnam" as most important. In contrast, between 9 and 24 percent of Americans in the regions surveyed rated "handling Castro and Cuba" as the "most important" issue, while between 15 and 22 percent rated "handling Khrushchev and Russia" as most important. And the president got poor marks in handling Vietnam in these same regions; only between 37 and 47 percent of respondents rated President Johnson's handling of the situation in Vietnam as "favorable."[58] A Gallup poll from the same month found similar opinions nationally. Respondents were asked, "What do you think is the most important problem facing this country today?" Ten percent cited "peace, war, Cold War" in their response. Nine percent cited communism or "communist infiltration" as the most important problem, while 6 percent responded that Cuba was most important and 3 percent specified Russia. Only 2 percent said that Vietnam was America's most important problem, and fewer than 1 percent of respondents listed "Red China" as the most important problem facing the country. When asked specifically if they had "given any attention to developments in South Vietnam," only 37 percent answered "yes." Moreover, of those who had been paying attention to Vietnam, 51 percent said the United States was "handling affairs there . . . badly."[59]

Yet Americans had no clear prescriptions for the administration on how to solve the problem in Vietnam. Nearly exactly the same number of respondents (11 percent) favored "[getting] out of Vietnam," "definite military action to stop further aggression," or "[going] all the way or [pulling] out." Respondents making each of these recommendations were outnumbered over two to one (30 percent) by those respondents who simply did not know what to do next in Vietnam.[60]

A great deal has been written about the administration's deliberations on Vietnam in spring 1964. As instability in the South Vietnamese government grew, the administration began to contemplate direct U.S. military intervention in the conflict. From the very beginning, the administration concluded that this action should be accompanied by a congressional resolution of support. In fact, the administration produced a number of draft resolutions and even planned a "D-Day" sequence by which this resolution would be passed and direct U.S. military intervention would begin (with D-Day being the day the United States would begin bombing North Vietnam). However, through a series of internal meetings and conferences, culminating in the Honolulu conference in early June 1964, the administration concluded that there was insufficient support among three key constituencies—the American public, the U.S. Congress, and allies abroad—for escalation or passage of a congressional resolution. The administration embarked on a concerted public information, legislative lobbying, and diplomatic campaign. During this campaign, key members of the administration gradually concluded that a pretext— in the form of a North Vietnamese provocation—would be required to convince the American people to support escalation or the Congress to pass a resolution of support for direct U.S. military action in Vietnam.[61]

As the administration contemplated how to convince Congress and the American people to support direct U.S. military intervention in Vietnam, they immediately turned to the arguments based on the ideology of containment that they had been using since Johnson took office. The various versions of the draft resolutions written by National Security Advisor McGeorge Bundy were replete with these arguments. A draft version of this resolution written in May declared that the "Communist regime in North Viet Nam, with the aid and support of the Communist regime in China, has systematically flouted its obligations under [the Geneva Accords of 1954 ending the First Indochina War] and has engaged in aggression against the independence and territorial integrity of South Viet Nam" through subversion and terror. The draft resolution also accused North Vietnam of similar aggression against Laos. The draft made a claim, which would be frequently repeated by the administration throughout the remainder of 1964, that "the United States has no territorial, military or political ambitions in Southeast Asia." The draft resolution concluded that, because "the United States regards the preservation of the independence and integrity of the nations of South Viet Nam and Laos as vital to its national interest and to world peace."[62]

The administration also began to consider how the president would present such a resolution. Special Assistant to the President S. Douglas Cater identified four questions the White House would have to answer when presenting the proposed resolution:

1. Why is Congress being asked to adopt a resolution at this time?
2. Why do we have a national commitment to the faraway countries of Laos and South Viet Nam?
3. What is the present situation there?
4. What are our specific objectives in increasing our assistance?[63]

His answers to these questions were also firmly based in the arguments the administration had been making since Johnson took office, based on the containment of communism. The United States had to demonstrate that it was not "irresolute." The administration was acting on precedents set by Johnson's predecessors, who had "acted to preserve the free world's strategic interests in Asia." Cater suggested that the president should place this proposed resolution firmly in the tradition "starting with the Truman Doctrine to support Greece and Turkey, extending over four Administrations." He suggested that the president conclude by reminding his audience of President Eisenhower's words from 1959: "The loss of South Viet Nam would set in motion a crumbling process that could, as it progressed, have grave consequences for us and for freedom."[64]

Cater also suggested that the president reaffirm that the United States sought "no military base, no territory, no special position in this area of the world." Moreover, Cater would have had the president place the blame for the resolution firmly on the "willful aggression" of communists who were attempting the "further extension of Communist empire in South Asia." Cater also suggested that the president threaten North Vietnam for its aggression. "If such aggression from North Viet Nam continues," Cater recommended the President flatly state, "it may well be necessary to make [North Vietnam] . . . share in the destruction and the suffering."[65]

Cater also suggested a new argument that would become a mainstay in the administration's arsenal after the "Americanization" of the Vietnam War—that "Congress has repeatedly declared support for this commitment [to Southeast Asia], both by treaty of the Senate and joint resolution of both Houses."[66]

By May 23, 1964, a congressional resolution and a U.S. air strike began to coalesce into a single strategy. Officials in the administration began to describe a thirty-day process through which both air strikes and the congressional resolution would increase pressure on North Vietnam to cease subversion of South Vietnam.[67] The administration saw the ideology of containment as key to convincing Congress and the American public to support this move. McGeorge Bundy proposed that the president introduce the resolution in a speech on "D-30" (thirty days before the initiation of military strikes). In this speech, Bundy wrote, the president should tell the American people that the United States' only interest was protecting South Vietnam, not destroying North Vietnam. McGeorge Bundy also envisioned a D-13 revelation reminiscent of the disclosure of Soviet missiles in Cuba during the Cuban missile crisis. Bundy suggested that this revelation could be an "expanded 'Jorden Report.'"[68] The Jorden Report, written by William J. Jorden of the State Department's Policy Planning Council in December 1961, detailed North Vietnamese support to the Viet Cong.[69] Actual military strikes, Bundy suggested, would be preceded by a demand by Khanh "that North Vietnam stop aggression" on D-10, a demand that would be seconded by President Johnson in a speech to the American people on D-3. Military would prompt American diplomats to plead America's case to the UN: that America does not wish "to overthrow the North Vietnam regime nor to destroy the country, but to stop DRV-directed Viet Cong terrorism and resistance to pacification efforts in the South."[70]

This memorandum was the subject of a high-level meeting of members of the administration on May 24, 1964.[71] The focus of this meeting quickly turned to concerns over the current state of American public opinion on Vietnam, what escalations public sentiment could bear, and how to increase public support for escalation.[72] Out of these meetings came plans for a coordinate public information, legislative lobbying, and diplomatic campaign. It was this proposed course of action that was carried into the Honolulu conference on Vietnam in June 1964.[73]

By the end of the Honolulu conference, the Johnson administration had concluded that it needed to directly intervene militarily in South Vietnam if the government there was to survive. The administration also concluded that it needed a congressional resolution in support of this intervention. However, the administration also acknowledged that, despite over six months of using the ideology of containment of communism to justify intervention, the American public and Congress were not convinced that intervention was necessary or that the fate of South Vietnam was vital to U.S. security.[74] Over the course of the following two months, the administration would conclude that it needed a pretext in the form of a North Vietnamese provocation before it could begin direct military intervention in Vietnam or gain passage of a congressional resolution.

Within the administration, there was clearly an understanding that, despite over half a year of using arguments based on the ideology of military containment of communism to justify U.S. military intervention in Vietnam, the public was not ready to support an escalation. In a June 3, 1964, memorandum to Secretary of State Rusk, William Bundy, Assistant Secretary of State for East Asian and Pacific Affairs, wrote that the administration had failed to convince the American public of the seriousness of the stakes in Southeast Asia.[75] A separate June 3, 1964, State Department memorandum outlined Americans' unanswered questions. James Greenfield, the author of the memorandum, noted that the Jorden Report on the war was about to be released publicly for the first time. While many in the State Department believed that the report conclusively showed North Vietnamese complicity in the war, Greenfield wrote that this fact was already accepted by most Americans. Greenfield believed that Americans had "deeper questions" about the war. Among the questions that he believed Americans wanted answered was why the Viet Cong's morale seemed to be higher than the South Vietnamese government's, why the administration claimed that the United States was only providing advisors when it was clear that American troops were taking active part in the fighting, how America could win with self-imposed restrictions (including not entering North Vietnam), whether the Khanh government had sufficient public support to survive, why neutralization was not a viable alternative, and why the United Nations was not involved. Greenfield wrote that Americans were concerned that Vietnam was "going to turn into another Korean War, which will simply end in a stalemate after heavy American casualties" and that many Americans would be perfectly happy with Vietnam becoming communist, but as "a Titoist regime" in the mold of Yugoslavia. Greenfield believed that these questions had to be answered if the administration wanted public support for more aggressive action, or even continued support for actions already underway. Greenfield concluded by recommending an aggressive public information program addressed toward these questions.[76]

Perhaps in answer to this memorandum, Special Assistant for National Security Affairs Walt W. Rostow spent June 1964 writing proposed presidential speeches justifying direct U.S. action in Vietnam. On June 6, Rostow wrote a draft presidential speech listing justifications for U.S. involvement in Vietnam. As he described the speech later in an oral history, the intent of the speech was "producing a rationale for hitting the North." The speech was a virtual catalogue of the arguments based on the containment of communism that the administration had been making since the beginning of the year. In fact, many elements of the draft speech of June 6 would appear in President Johnson's speech at Syracuse University immediately after the Gulf of Tonkin incident, justifying U.S. air strikes against North Vietnam.[77]

The administration did not even believe that it had sufficient public support for the president to call for a congressional resolution of support for the defense of South Vietnam.[78] In a June 10 memorandum, McGeorge Bundy suggested that there were five "disagreeable questions" the administration had to answer to the satisfaction of the American public before such a dramatic escalation in the commitment of American prestige to Southeast Asia could be made. First, did the congressional resolution constitute a blank check? Bundy believed that, because large-scale escalation (which he defined as any escalation requiring a call-up of the Army Reserves) was not envisioned, this was not a blank check. Second, what types of force would this resolution authorize? Bundy suggested that no force would be used if it could be avoided. If aggression continued, Bundy wrote, force would be "carefully aimed at installations and activities which directly support covert aggression against the free people of Laos and South Vietnam." The national security advisor was adamant that the administration would not use force to "enlarge the action beyond what is absolutely required" or to "overthrow existing governments in North Vietnam or in Red China." Third, what change in June 1964 required an immediate resolution? In response, McGeorge Bundy wrote that a detailed, "candid account of the existing situation and hazard" must be provided to the American public. Next, would no other means besides U.S. military force achieve America's goals in Southeast Asia? Bundy believed that a primary goal of this resolution would be to help "allies" already fighting in Vietnam. Finally, and perhaps most importantly, was Southeast Asia important enough to U.S. national interests to warrant the commitment of American forces? Bundy believed such a commitment was warranted "because of the rights of the people there, because of our own commitment, because of the far-reaching effect of a failure, and because we can win if we stay with it."[79]

The idea of waiting for a pretext in the form of a North Vietnamese provocation before escalating the conflict or seeking a resolution formed gradually—almost imperceptibly—within the administration over late spring and early summer 1964. As early as May 15, 1964, U.S. Ambassador to South Vietnam Henry Cabot Lodge suggested that a "terroristic act of the proper magnitude" might trigger an attack on "a specific target in North Viet Nam." William Bundy, after lamenting in a memorandum in June that public sentiment had not yet been prepared for a congressional resolution, suggested that, if there were an "acute emergency" or "if the situation changes drastically," the administration might be able to "respond by emergency session" and gain passage of a resolution.[81]

The decision to wait for a pretext before seeking a congressional resolution was finally made during a National Security Council meeting on June 10, 1964.[82] Secretary Rusk suggested that "it would be disastrous if Congress refuses to vote a resolution proposed by the Administration or if the resolution was basically weakened during the course of the congressional debate."[83] He then raised the possibility that a crisis might be required before the congressional resolution could be sought.[84]

> We should ask for a resolution . . . only when the circumstances are such as to require action, and thereby, force Congressional action. There will be rallying around the President the moment it is clear to reasonable people that U.S. action is necessary.[85]

Attorney General Nicholas Katzenbach agreed that a crisis situation was needed, "pushing us to prompt action." He continued: "It would [be] much simpler to obtain approval of a resolution [from Congress] if U.S. actions are forcing the pace." Secretary McNamara was the first to suggest explicitly that the North Vietnamese might provide a provocation that would create impetus for the resolution. He suggested that "a Congressional resolution before September was unlikely unless the enemy [acted] suddenly in the area." The Council concluded that the administration would embark on a public information campaign designed to stir public (rather than congressional) interest in Vietnam and only pursue a congressional resolution "in the event of a dramatic event in Southeast Asia."[86]

At the same time the administration was reaching the conclusion that it needed a North Vietnamese provocation to gain passage of a congressional resolution, the perceived need for this resolution was also growing. First and foremost, a resolution was a prerequisite for direct U.S. military intervention in Vietnam. All of the attendees at the June 10 National Security Council meeting agreed that a congressional resolution was required before the administration could take direct U.S. military action in South Vietnam. CIA Director McCone was adamant that attacks on North Vietnam or the introduction of "U.S. troops on the ground in Southeast Asia would require a Congressional resolution."[87]

However, the administration also believed that a congressional resolution would serve other purposes. In a June 10 memorandum, McGeorge Bundy wrote that a congressional resolution would restrain the Soviet Union and Communist China from aggression in Southeast Asia much as "the Formosa Resolution, the Middle East Resolution, and, in a sense, the Vandenberg Resolution [which preceded the formation of NATO]" had restrained the communists in other parts of the world.[88] A resolution would also encourage U.S. allies in Southeast Asia. William Bundy wrote in a memorandum on June 12, 1964, that a congressional resolution was required to bolster leaders in Southeast Asia—especially Souvanna Phouma, Prime Minister of Laos, and Nguyen Khanh, leader of the military junta in South Vietnam. Most importantly, while McGeorge Bundy had suggested telling the American people that a congressional resolution was not a "blank check,"[89] William Bundy argued that a congressional resolution would give the president the flexibility for further escalation, absent any North Vietnamese provocation.[90]

While the administration waited for a "crisis" that would provide the political impetus for the passage of a congressional resolution, the administration continued to try to convince the American public of the need for U.S. military intervention in Vietnam. In a press conference on June 2, 1964, President Johnson again painted the U.S.

commitment to South Vietnamese independence as a continuation of his predecessors' policies: "America keeps her word, we are steadfast in a policy which has been followed for 10 years in three administrations."[91] Johnson concluded that the United States must not "fail to do its full share to meet the challenge which is posed by those who disturb the peace of Southeast Asia."[92] Later in the month, in a National Security Action Memorandum, President Johnson appointed Robert J. Manning as a coordinator of the administration's effort to "disseminate facts on Southeast Asia." Johnson did so, he wrote, because he was "not satisfied with the performance of the several departments" in building "domestic understanding and support" of the administration's "policy and purpose in [Southeast Asia]."[93] In a June 30, 1964, *New York Times* interview as he left office as the U.S. ambassador to Vietnam, Henry Cabot Lodge also advanced the administration's case. He told the *Times* that "the stakes are perfectly enormous" in Southeast Asia and declared that it was "utterly unthinkable" to "get out" and "turn it over to the Communists." And, while he recommended a range of options "short of war," he put the blame for the conflict on "Communist aggression" and the infiltration of supplies and men from the north. Lodge also alleged that "Red Chinese" were physically present in North Vietnam, assisting Hanoi in the war, furthering their plan for "Chinese Communist domination."[94]

The president also tried to convince members of Congress to support direct U.S. military intervention in Vietnam. In a phone conversation on June 11, 1964, President Johnson told Democratic Senator Richard B. Russell of Georgia, one of the most influential men in the Senate, that America's "national honor" was at stake and that the United States had to meet its treaty obligations to South Vietnam. He also argued that America was fighting for freedom in South Vietnam and that the United States needed some agreement to guarantee South Vietnamese independence before U.S. forces could withdraw.[95]

Russell remained skeptical, believing that the American people did not favor continued U.S. involvement in Vietnam. Russell advocated a United Nations settlement that would allow a U.S. withdrawal. Most importantly, Russell rejected the administration's claims that

U.S. military intervention was required to contain communism in Southeast Asia.[96]

> I do not agree with those "brain trusters" who say that this thing [South Vietnam] has got tremendous strategic and economic value and that we'll lose everything in Southeast . . . in Asia if we lose Vietnam. I don't think that's true.[97]

Still, Russell acknowledged that it was extremely difficult for the United States to leave precipitously, saying the results would "be disastrous."[98]

In addition to Senator Russell's private skepticism, some in the foreign policy establishment outside of government were beginning to openly question American policy in Vietnam. Hans Morgenthau, who had previously tentatively supported military containment arguments for U.S. involvement in Vietnam and advocated at least limited containment of China, began to question this objective. In a June 1964 article in the New Leader, Morgenthau accused the administration of making public statements aimed primarily at "deterring the enemy, hardening our friends, disarming the domestic opposition and preventing a catastrophe from occurring before November." Morgenthau argued that the situation had changed in Southeast Asia—the Sino-Soviet split meant that containment of communism did not necessarily require containment of China, and the erosion of anticommunist sentiment in South Vietnam made U.S. objectives suspect. "The government of Saigon is lucky," Morgenthau quipped, "when its troops just desert rather than join the Vietcong." Morgenthau now argued that the United States should only focus on containing communism where it hurt the Soviets or China; this was not the case, he claimed, in South Vietnam and Cambodia, both of which had deep cultural hostility toward China.[99]

Some in the media were equally skeptical of direct U.S. military intervention in Vietnam. Washington reporter Richard Starnes, in an editorial in the Evening News, reported from his recent work in Saigon that arguments claiming Vietnam to be a low-cost "laboratory" to refine antiguerilla warfare techniques misjudged the toll on American military officers committed to the conflict.[100] Pulitzer Prize–winning syndicated columnist Ralph McGill argued in his column that the presence of "hundreds of thousands" of Chinese—loyal to Peking—all across Southeast Asia, combined with the localism and unfamiliarity with Western democracy that pervaded Southeast Asia, made it impossible for the United States "conventionally to 'save' Southeast Asia."[101]

But these objections from the media were the exception rather than the rule. The vast majority of editorials on Vietnam either supported U.S. policy or urged more aggressive action in Southeast Asia. Most editors and journalists shared the administration's belief that it was important to contain the expansion of communism in Southeast Asia.[102]

Moreover, the press expected an escalation of the conflict in Vietnam. A *Time* article written days before the U.S. response to the Gulf of Tonkin attack (but published on August 7, 1964, just after the bombing) makes it clear that direct American action in Vietnam was a very real possibility. The article described U.S. plans, under certain conditions, to support "bombings inside North Viet Nam" in the form of "tit-for-tat reprisals," "general punishment of North Viet Nam from the air," or even the "blockading or mining Ho Chi Minh's ports."[103] This article was a remarkably accurate summary of the range of options that were actually being considered by the administration on the eve of the Gulf of Tonkin incident.

Yet two-thirds of Americans were still not even paying attention to Southeast Asia in summer 1964.[104] And the administration understood that the American public was not terribly concerned about Vietnam, did not approve of American policy in Vietnam, and yet did not wish to escalate the conflict there. In internal White House polling from Maryland between April and June 1964, compiled and reported to the administration in July, respondents in Maryland indicated that, despite heavy administration messaging on the topic of Vietnam, they were not terribly concerned about the conflict there. Forty-seven percent of respondents indicated that "racial problems," not Cold War issues, were the greatest "national issues of concern." Only 15 percent of Maryland respondents indicated that foreign relations was a concern, with only a third of those demanding the United States "take [a] firmer stand in Vietnam." More troubling for the administration, however, was that, although 63 percent of respondents approved of President Johnson's "handling [of] Khrushchev and the Russians," nearly as many (59 percent) disapproved of his "handling [of the] situation in Vietnam."[105]

This poll left the Johnson administration in a difficult predicament; Americans did not want the administration to escalate the conflict but did not approve of what the president was presently doing in Vietnam. Pollsters, in their analysis, referred to this phenomenon as "Cold War Frustrations." In hindsight, the suggestion provided by the authors of this report seems prescient—and reflected the administration's thinking that a pretext was needed. The pollsters assured the administration that, while voters were frustrated about Vietnam at the time, eventually the conflict would evolve to a "stage three" at which the situation would reach "a boiling point and become a severe crisis ([like] Suez, the Cuban missiles) at which time the country rallies to the support of an incumbent President."[106]

Since the administration took office, it had used containment to argue for U.S. military intervention in Vietnam. As summer 1964 wore on, the administration began to realize that it would need to take direct military action in Vietnam if the South Vietnamese government was going to survive. It also realized that it needed a congressional resolution to endorse such an escalation, to bolster flagging South Vietnamese morale, and to communicate to the United States' Cold War adversaries that it was serious about defending South Vietnamese sovereignty. But the Johnson administration also realized that there was insufficient public or congressional support for such escalations. The administration decided that it must have a pretext in the form of a North Vietnamese provocation to justify these escalations. In early August 1964, the administration believed the North Vietnamese provided this provocation.

Three months before the 1964 U.S. Presidential election, the USS *Maddox* was in the gulf the Gulf of Tonkin, off the coast of North Vietnam, supporting raids by South Vietnamese commandos (with American advisors in support). On August 2, 1964, three North Vietnamese patrol boats launched an attack on the *Maddox*. The attack was turned away, with one patrol boat sunk and the others damaged. On August 4, the *Maddox*, joined by the destroyer *Turner Joy*, reported that it had been attacked again. President Johnson responded by ordering the bombing of North Vietnam. A few days later, the Congress responded as well, with the so-called Tonkin Gulf Resolution, which gave President Johnson a free hand to answer any future communist aggression in Vietnam.[107]

A great deal has been written about the Gulf of Tonkin incident and the passage of the Tonkin Gulf Resolution. In fact, indicative of its prominence as a proxy argument for the "legitimacy" of the Vietnam War, it is among the war's most examined moments. While historians differ on the details, the historical consensus that has emerged over the past half-century is that the North Vietnamese attacks on the *Maddox* and *Turner Joy* on August 4, 1964, almost certainly did not happen and that the president used the supposed incident as a pretext to pass a resolution to widen American involvement in the Vietnam War while deceiving the public and the Congress as to his intention to do so. Historians have shown that the Johnson administration was misleading as to both the facts of the incident and the reason for the destroyer task force's presence in the Gulf of Tonkin that night. Finally, historians have shown that these deceptions were central to the passage of the Tonkin Gulf Resolution, which the president claimed as legal authority as he began a dramatic escalation of the war. Some historians go further, claiming the president was trying to provoke the North Vietnamese into giving him a pretext.[108]

In late summer 1964, the administration was eagerly awaiting a pretext for a congressional resolution and direct U.S. military intervention in Vietnam. Administration officials had emerged from the Honolulu conference in June 1964 convinced that the collapse of the government of South Vietnamese was imminent if the United States did not intervene. But they believed that there was insufficient congressional and U.S. public support for a resolution or direct U.S. military intervention; a "crisis" was needed to create the political impetus for escalation. However, when the North Vietnamese attacked the USS *Maddox* in the Gulf of Tonkin on August 2, 1964, the administration decided not to retaliate; they feared that the American people would not accept retaliation if the communists were not first warned. Instead, the president issued a stern warning to North Vietnam, sent additional forces—including another destroyer, the USS *Turner Joy*—to the gulf, and anxiously awaited a second attack. When it appeared that a second attack had occurred, the administration leapt at the opportunity to escalate U.S. military involvement in Vietnam, launching retaliatory air strikes against targets inside North Vietnam and asking Congress to pass a resolution endorsing the use of whatever military means the administration deemed necessary to defend the sovereignty of South Vietnam against what the administration claimed was communist aggression.[109]

However, in its haste to exploit what it believed was a blatant and irrefutable North Vietnamese provocation, the administration failed to thoroughly scrutinize the incident or investigate the many inconsistencies in the reports coming from the gulf on August 4, 1964.[110] Even as preparations were being made for retaliatory air strikes, follow-up reports from the Gulf of Tonkin were casting doubts that the North Vietnamese attack had occurred. Yet the administration went ahead with the retaliatory airstrike and hid their uncertainty about the North Vietnamese attack from Congress and the public.[111] The administration did believe the attacks had occurred when Johnson ordered the retaliation; they had been convinced by radio intercepts of the North Vietnamese talking about naval operations.[112]

The president and other administration members gave no hint of their uncertainty about the events of August 4, 1964, to Congress or to the American public, either before or after the retaliatory air strike.[113] Likewise, the administration continued to insist that the two destroyers were operating in uncontested international waters when they were, in fact, much closer to North Vietnam, well within the twelve-mile limit claimed by the North Vietnamese as their territorial waters. The administration also failed to mention—and occasionally denied—that the two ships were engaged in unmistakably provocative behavior. The destroyers were supporting raids inside North Vietnam being conducted by South Vietnamese special operations forces—an operation code-named OPLAN 34A—and gathering signals intelligence on the North Vietnamese—an operation code-named DESOTO.[114]

The administration's failure to tell Congress or the American people of its doubts about the incident—or the truth about the circumstances under which the supposed attack had occurred—had no immediate impact on the events of late summer 1964. However, these deceptions would return to haunt the administration in early 1968.

At a meeting in the president's office with congressional leaders on the evening of the supposed August 4 attack, President Johnson did not mention the OPLAN 34A raids to congressional leaders when he briefed them on the impending retaliatory air strike. In fact, in this meeting, Secretary of State Rusk, Secretary of Defense McNamara, and Chairman of the Joint Chiefs of Staff General Earle Wheeler emphasized that the North Vietnamese attack was unprovoked and that the United States had to respond.[116] Moreover, in an oral history, Republican Senator George D. Aiken of Vermont, a member of the Senate Foreign Relations Committee, recalled that none of the administration's representatives at this meeting, including the president, shared with the congressmen their uncertainty about whether the attacks had occurred.[117]

President Johnson first broached the topic of a resolution with congressional leaders at this August 4 meeting. There was virtually no dissent in this meeting. Senator Mansfield did read a paper expressing opposition to war in Vietnam, but the congressional leaders were otherwise supportive. Senator J. William Fulbright, chairman of the Senate Foreign Relations Committee, was convinced by Secretary McNamara's contention that the attacks would continue if the United States didn't respond. Republicans at the meeting were uniformly in favor of a resolution.[118] However, the congressmen knew that dissent would do little good; as Senator Aiken pointed out to the attendees, due to the probable groundswell of public support for military action, "by the time you send the resolution up here . . . there won't be anything for us to do but support you."[119] This was exactly the effect the administration had hoped for a month earlier, when it had decided to wait until after a North Vietnamese provocation to press for a congressional resolution.

While the Gulf of Tonkin incident served primarily as a pretext to gain passage of the administration's pre-drafted congressional resolution and escalate direct U.S. military involvement in Vietnam, the incident was also used as a proof of the argument the administration had been making since the beginning of the year: that the war in Vietnam was the result of communist aggression and that that aggression had to be confronted or it would continue to grow. The administration's statements after the August 2, 1964, attack against the *Maddox* were primarily intended to set the stage for a U.S. retaliation. In his public statement—his warning to the North Vietnamese—President Johnson said that he had ordered the destroyers to "attack any force which attacks them" and to do so "with the objective not only of driving off the force but of destroying it."[120] However, the president's comments also highlighted the aggressiveness of the North Vietnamese Communists. Johnson claimed that the attack had been unprovoked and had occurred in "international waters" (of course, neither was in fact the case).[121]

The retaliatory airstrikes after the supposed August 4, 1964, attack on the *Maddox* and *Turner Joy* were carefully timed to coincide with a public statement announcing the action.[122] This statement, too, highlighted North Vietnamese aggression. In this late-night address, President Johnson said that this second attack, on the *Maddox* and the *Turner Joy*, was also unprovoked and had likewise occurred in international waters (facts that the administration knew to be false).[123] Of course, cast in this deceptive light, the supposed attacks on the two U.S. destroyers seemed callous and provocative.

The press seemed convinced by these deceptions. After the retaliatory air strikes, newspapers across the country were filled with glowing editorials from reporters, syndicated journalists, and former presidents praising Johnson's response.[124] Moreover, no one in the press bothered to investigate the president's claims that the North Vietnamese had been guilty of provocations.[125] *Time* magazine reported that "Two torpedo-boat attacks against U.S. destroyers that had been steaming in international waters in the Gulf of Tonkin" had provoked the U.S. response. There was no hint of the administration's own doubts about the second attack.

The *New York Times* also seemed convinced by the administration's version of events. The August 5, 1964, issue of the *New York Times* faithfully reported the administration's version of the second attack on the *Maddox* and *Turner Joy*. The *Times* did note: "The North Vietnamese regime said Wednesday that the report of another attack on United States ships was a 'fabrication.'" But this denial was little more than a footnote in a story filled with the U.S. government's official version of the event.[126] As late as August 8, the AP was still reporting the official version of events, that two separate attacks had occurred against U.S. destroyers in the Gulf of Tonkin.[127]

The press did not miss the significance of the change in policy, from supporting the South Vietnamese to directly attacking the North with American air power, either. *Time* repeatedly emphasized the significance of the U.S. reprisal to the Cold War balance of power. Evoking the specter of the Cuban Missile Crisis, *Time* wrote, "In a sense, this nation had once more gone to the brink."[128]

Instead of investigating U.S. provocations which might have led to an attack on August 4, 1964, the press speculated as to why the North Vietnamese chose to attack the *Maddox* and the *Turner Joy*.[129] A few sources mentioned North Vietnamese accusations that the U.S. Navy had shelled their coast (the shelling had actually been by the South Vietnamese Navy, but with U.S.-supplied ships), but all accepted Robert McNamara's denials.[130] A *Time* article suggested the OPLAN 34A raids occurring in the area as a possible answer. "Some speculated," *Time* wrote, "that Hanoi had somehow connected the *Maddox* with recent South Vietnamese raids on Hon Me and the neighboring island of Hon Ngu." Ultimately, however, *Time* dismissed these raids as unconnected to the presence of the *Maddox* and *Turner Joy* in the Gulf of Tonkin.[131]

The press also seemed to understand that more U.S. military action was coming in Vietnam. The AP reported as early as August 5, the day after the air attack, that the attacks came "with this stern word from Secretary of Defense Robert S. McNamara: 'Whether this will be all that is necessary is up to the North Vietnamese.'"[132]

Given the president's deceptions and the press's unquestioning support, it is not surprising that the public reaction to the retaliatory strikes was overwhelmingly positive.[133] A Harris poll showed 85 percent approval for the president's handling of the crisis. A Gallup poll showed the exact same level of approval.[134] Moreover, public opinion of the president's handling of Vietnam in general had gone from 58 percent disapproving and 42 percent approving to 72 percent approving and 28 percent disapproving in a few brief days.[135]

After the incident and the retaliatory air strikes, the administration immediately returned to its use of containment to justify U.S. military intervention in Vietnam. The Gulf of Tonkin incident became an integral part of this framework of containment arguments. The incident was, the administration claimed, direct evidence of the North Vietnamese's aggressive intent in Southeast Asia. Likewise, the retaliatory air strikes were evidence of the administration's determination to stand up to this aggression, to contain communism in Southeast Asia.

Secretary of State Dean Rusk used the ideology of containment to justify this new U.S. military intervention in Vietnam in an interview with NBC News on August 5, 1964. In the process, Rusk perpetuated the administration's deceptive version of the Gulf of Tonkin incident. NBC diplomatic correspondent Elie Abel asked Rusk why it was necessary to conduct the retaliatory strikes so quickly, without first notifying U.S. allies. Rusk responded by reiterating the administration's official version of the event. The United States' ships had been attacked and "were dodging torpedoes" in "a vast expanse of international waters in which we have a perfect right to be."[136] Ignoring the fact that the ships were operating inside the twelve-mile limit claimed by North Vietnam as its territorial waters, Rusk added that U.S. ships could not be expected to "run a continuing gauntlet of torpedoes" or be "denied international waters in the Gulf of Tonkin." When asked by Abel if the North Vietnamese believed the United States was "a paper tiger," Rusk responded by reinforcing the idea that the United

States had a commitment to South Vietnam. "They could have made a basic miscalculation about what the commitment of the United States means in a situation of this sort."[137]

At a previously scheduled speech at Syracuse University, President Johnson also wove the Gulf of Tonkin incident into his use of containment to justify U.S. military intervention in Vietnam. The president said the Gulf of Tonkin incident was an act of North Vietnamese "aggression" against the United States, further evidence of North Vietnam's ongoing aggression against South Vietnam and Laos. President Johnson told his audience that the United States had a responsibility to stop this aggression. [138]

> So there can be no doubt about the responsibilities of men and the responsibilities of nations that are devoted to peace.
>
> Peace cannot be assured merely by assuring the safety of the United States destroyer MADDOX or the safety of other vessels of other flags.
>
> Peace requires that the existing agreements in the area be honored.[139]

"Peace," the president added, required that the United States stop North Vietnam's aggression.[140] The president concluded by reminding his audience in Syracuse of the lessons of Munich, a theme his administration had pressed unsuccessfully throughout the spring and summer 1964. "The world remembers, the world must never forget . . . that aggression unchallenged is aggression unleashed."[141] The president also returned to another theme from earlier in the summer 1964—that military containment of communism in Southeast Asia was a continuation of his predecessor's policies:

> For 10 years, three American Presidents—President Eisenhower, President Kennedy, and your present President—and the American people have been actively concerned with threats to the peace and security of the peoples of Southeast Asia from the communist government of North Vietnam.

> President Eisenhower sought—and President Kennedy sought—the same objectives that I still seek[142]

President Johnson also said that this "challenge" to peace and security in Southeast Asia was "the same challenge that we have faced with courage and that we have met with strength in Greece and Turkey, in Berlin and Korea, in Lebanon and in Cuba."[143] It was the challenge of communism to the Free World that the United States had already met with a strategy of military containment in other parts of the world.

At the same time that it launced air strikes against North Vietnam, the administration also pursued the other half of its escalation plan from early summer 1964: a congressional resolution endorsing any future U.S. military intervention the president chose to take to defend South Vietnam from communist aggression. To justify this resolution, President Johnson and his administration used the same arguments based on the ideology of containment that they had been using in their unsuccessful effort to convince the Congress and the American people to support U.S. military intervention in Vietnam since Johnson took office. However, with the addition of new evidence of North Vietnam's aggressive intent in Southeast Asia—the Gulf of Tonkin incident—(and with the omission of their doubts over whether the incident had occurred or the provocative nature of the U.S. destroyers' mission in the gulf) the administration succeeded in convincing the Congress and the American people to support a congressional resolution. However, the central deception during this period was that, despite the administration's private assurances to members of Congress that it did not intend to widen the war, the president fully intended to further escalate the war in Vietnam after he had his insurance policy against congressional dissent—the Tonkin Gulf Resolution.

While Senate leaders would, years later, claim that they had been deceived by the administration into passing the Tonkin Gulf Resolution, many of them were at least partly complicit in this deception. Senators Mike Mansfield, Richard B. Russell, and J. William Fulbright all had private misgivings about direct U.S. military intervention in Vietnam but did not share their reservations with their colleagues. Likewise,

each of these senators knew some details of the incident that contradicted administration testimony during hearings on the incident, but
said nothing.[144] And whatever the president's assurances to the contrary, the text of the resolution clearly endorsed U.S. military escalation in Vietnam and members of Congress clearly understood that the
resolution gave the president this power. In fact, this was the heart of
the power the Tonkin Gulf Resolution would later give the president
as an insurance policy against congressional dissent—the resolution
endorsed whatever means the president chose to use to stop communist aggression in Southeast Asia.

Right after the retaliatory air strikes, the president sent the
Congress a draft of the resolution that his administration had been
working on all summer, authorizing him to use force to protect the
sovereignty of South Vietnam.[145] This resolution was accompanied by
a strongly worded statement from President Johnson that wove his
deceptive account of the Gulf of Tonkin incident into his administration's older justifications for U.S. military intervention based on the
containment of communism. Johnson told Congress that U.S. naval
forces were "operating in international waters." It was in these supposedly undisputed waters that "the North Vietnamese regime had
conducted . . . deliberate attacks." The president told Congress that he
had, therefore, "directed air action against gun boats and supporting
facilities used in these hostile operations."[146] In this same statement,
he made the case that this reported aggression was part of a pattern
of North Vietnamese provocations. He cited attacks against U.S.
reconnaissance overflights in Laos—aircraft that were present at "the
request of the Government of Laos"—as further evidence of northern
aggression.[147] The president failed to mention that the United States
had retaliated with air strikes on this occasion as well.

The president indicated that a congressional resolution would
express "the unity and determination of the United States." He also
tied this resolution to the theme, from earlier in the summer, that
Vietnam was part of the United States' broader strategy of military
containment of communism. He told the Congress that this resolution would "state in the simplest terms the resolve and support of

the Congress for action to deal appropriately with attacks against our armed forces and to defend freedom and preserve peace in Southeast Asia." Further, this resolution was analogous to other resolutions that had also been intended to contain communism, including congressional resolutions passed "to meet the threats to Formosa in 1955, to meet the threat to the Middle East in 1957, and to meet the threat to Cuba in 1962."[148] Johnson added that Congress must pass a resolution of support for U.S. military intervention in Vietnam "to give convincing evidence to the aggressive Communist nations, and to the world as a whole," that "the United States is united in its determination to bring about the end of Communist subversion and aggression in [Southeast Asia]."[149] Just as he had in his speech at Syracuse University, President Johnson insisted that he was simply continuing the policy in Vietnam that he had inherited from his predecessors, "consistent and unchanged since 1954."[150]

The president also introduced a new argument for military intervention in South Vietnam in this message to Congress, one to which he returned frequently throughout the remainder of his presidency. He made the spurious claim that the Southeast Asia Collective Defense Treaty "obligates the United States and other members to act in accordance with their constitutional processes to meet communist aggression against any of the parties or protocol states."[151]

In this statement to Congress, the president elaborated on four reasons for U.S. military involvement in Southeast Asia that he had first proposed in a press conference on June 2, 1964. First, Johnson told Congress, "America keeps her word," honoring what he called the United States' "commitments." Second, harkening to the domino theory, Johnson told Congress, "The issue is the future of Southeast Asia as a whole." He added: "A threat to any nation in that region is a threat to all, and a threat to us." Once more, the president assured Congress and the world that the United States' motives for military intervention in Vietnam were pure. "Our purpose is peace," he assured the Congress. "We have no military, political, or territorial ambitions in the area." Finally, Johnson added that Vietnam was "not just a jungle war, but a struggle for freedom on every front of human activity." U.S. "military and economic assistance" was intended to help the "free nations" of Southeast Asia "repel aggression and strengthen their independence." Lest Congress be confused about the source of this aggression, Johnson stated explicitly that the "threat" to these nations was from the "communist regime" of North Vietnam, which had "constantly sought to take over South Vietnam and Laos" in violation of the 1954 Geneva Accords on Vietnam and the 1962 Geneva agreements on Laos.[152]

To usher his resolution through Congress, the president chose the Chairman of the Senate Foreign Relations Committee, J. William Fulbright.[153] The president assured the senator that the resolution would be used only to respond to the Gulf of Tonkin incident itself, an assurance that the senator passed on to his colleagues in the Senate.[154] Senator Fulbright had also been assured by National Security Advisor McGeorge Bundy and others that the OPLAN 34A raids were completely unrelated to the alleged attacks on August 4. Further, Fulbright knew nothing of the DESOTO signals intelligence mission in which the destroyers were also involved. Finally, Fulbright was kept in the dark as to other U.S. provocations over the summer and questions about the veracity of the August 4 attacks because Johnson considered him at risk to leak this information to the press.[155] Fulbright himself would say years later of the Gulf of Tonkin incident as he related it to the Senate during this debate, "It never occurred to me it didn't happen that way."[156]

The administration also actively and intentionally deceived the rest of Congress, as well. Secretary McNamara dominated the August 6 congressional hearings following the attacks, answering all but the most technical questions. In the process, he failed to mention anything about the OPLAN 34A raids that were taking place nearby the same night as the supposed Gulf of Tonkin attacks.[157] When confronted about the OPLAN 34A raids by Senator Wayne Morse (who had been tipped off by an unnamed Pentagon staffer), McNamara vehemently denied the raids were in any way related to the attack.[158] (While McNamara would maintain this denial through the remainder of his life, the evidence shows conclusively that members of the administration—including McNamara—in fact believed that North Vietnam might reasonably have connected the DESOTO patrols with the OPLAN 34A raids.)[159] With the administration denying any connection between the OPLAN 34A raids and the Gulf of Tonkin incident, it is not surprising that the OPLAN 34A raids played only a marginal role in the debate over the Tonkin Gulf Resolution. Senator J. William Fulbright echoed the administration's denials that the *Maddox* and *Turner Joy* had been involved in the 34A raids. There was no discussion at all of the raids in hearings or debate in the House of Representatives.[160]

McNamara also lied to Congress about a number of other matters. When asked for the ship logs, McNamara lied, saying they were still onboard when they were, in fact, already in Washington. McNamara told this lie either to cover the participation of the ships in the DESOTO radio intercept patrols or to hide the administration's doubts about the authenticity of the August 4 attacks.[161] Secretary of Defense McNamara also lied on the matter of whether the two ships were operating in international waters, saying that the *Maddox* and *Turner Joy* were thirty miles from shore when attacked, an assertion even contradicted soon after by Senator Fulbright, who told his colleagues, recalling private briefings on the patrols, that the ships were operating as close as three miles from shore.[162]

Fulbright and other senators would later claim that they were deceived into passing the Tonkin Gulf Resolution. But despite the catalogue of administration deceptions after the Gulf of Tonkin incident, Senate leaders were not blameless. Although they had misgivings about escalating the conflict in Vietnam, senior senators such as Armed Services Committee Chairman Richard B. Russell, Majority Leader Mike Mansfield, and Foreign Relations Committee Chairman J. William Fulbright kept those concerns to themselves while actively supporting the administration's effort to pass the resolution.[163] Senator Fulbright sat quietly during the hearings while Secretary Rusk portrayed the communist aggression in South Vietnam as a conspiracy directed from Moscow, a view from which Fulbright had publicly dissented in the past.[164] Both Senator Russell and Senator Fulbright had been fully briefed before the hearings about the OPLAN 34A raids and probably understood that the raids were provocative. Neither senator denied Senator Morse's charges to that effect during the perfunctory two-hour Senate hearings. Yet neither senator objected when Secretary McNamara denied that the raids were in any way connected to the incident.[165] Despite knowing that the destroyers had been involved in intelligence missions, Russell still rejected the notion that the United States had provoked the attack, noting that the U.S. Navy did not travel out into international waters to attack Russian ships off its own shore.[166] In fact, Senator Russell practically demanded that the United States respond to North Vietnamese aggression with U.S. military force. The United States wouldn't "be entitled to the respect of other nations," Russell insisted before his colleagues, "if it accepted the acts that have been committed . . . without undertaking to make some response."[167] Senate leaders also assisted the administration's effort by abbreviating the hearings and the debate. Even when Senator Wayne Morse implored his colleagues for more time to consider the measure, to bring in military leaders that opposed the resolution, Senator Fulbright insisted that it was an emergency situation and that deliberations had to be accelerated.[168] Senator Mansfield shares the blame for rushing through the resolution; as the Senate majority leader, it was his decision to limit debate on the floor.[169]

More importantly—as George Ball would later note in an oral history when asked whether Fulbright had been "fooled as to the intent of the resolution or its content"—the Tonkin Gulf Resolution *was* an endorsement of any future decision the President might make to use force to defend South Vietnam. As Ball noted, "The language was perfectly clear."[170] In fact, Fulbright conceded this point himself during the hearings on the resolution; in response to concerns from Senator Daniel Brewster of Maryland that "the resolution . . . would authorize or recommend or approve the landing of large American armies in Vietnam," Fulbright was forced to concede, "The language of the resolution would not prevent it. It would authorize whatever the Commander-in-Chief feels is necessary."[171]

The contemporary press also understood the resolution to be carte blanche. Both the *National Review* and the *New Republic* called the Tonkin Gulf Resolution a "blank check."[172] While the Congress may have believed the president did not wish to escalate the war, the floor debate had made it clear that the resolution gave him that power.[173]

There were a few in Congress who dissented; Senator Ernest Gruening of Alaska called the resolution a "predated declaration of war."[174] Senator Wayne Morse of Oregon insisted before his colleagues that "our actions in Asia today are the actions of warmaking [sic]" and "we have threatened war where no direct threat to American security is at stake."[175] As early as August 5, 1964, Senator Morse also challenged the president's version of the Gulf of Tonkin incident, claiming that U.S. ships had "acted as backups" for South Vietnamese vessels bombarding the North Vietnamese coast as part of the OPLAN 34A raids.[176] Other senators were less vocal but also voiced objections. Senator Gaylord Nelson objected to the sweeping scope of the resolution, while Senator George McGovern questioned tiny North Vietnam's motivations for attacking the United States.[177] Senator Fulbright quashed Senator Gaylord Nelson's attempt to amend the measure to limit its powers by assuring the Senate that President Johnson would not use the resolution to expand the war.[178] In response to Senator McGovern, Senator Fulbright noted that the resolution did not commit the United States to carry the war into the north as South Vietnamese leader Khanh wanted.[179]

The disparate and half-hearted objections of these senators, combined with the abbreviated floor debate, certainly hindered this tiny opposition bloc from coalescing into a unified resistance to the Tonkin Gulf Resolution.[180] Senator Morse's personality also alienated many senators.[181] However, the maneuvering by Fulbright, answering each objection and quelling congressional dissent, was probably decisive in the passage of the Tonkin Gulf Resolution.[182]

These few dissenters notwithstanding, why did most senators support the Tonkin Gulf Resolution if they had misgivings about escalating U.S. military intervention in Vietnam? Fulbright's unwavering support of President Johnson may have been a result of his personal relationship with the president.[183] When Lyndon Johnson was a senator, he referred to Senator Fulbright as his "Secretary of State."[185] Personal trust led Fulbright to believe Johnson's assurances that he would not use the resolution to widen the war in Vietnam. This trust would also lead to Fulbright's later sense of betrayal over the resolution, culminating in Fulbright's 1968 hearings on the Gulf of Tonkin incident.[185] Many senators may have also seen the Tonkin Gulf Resolution—much as the administration had seen it earlier in the summer—as an escalation in and of itself designed to deter Soviet and Chinese Communist aggression in Southeast Asia. When challenged during the hearings immediately after the Gulf of Tonkin incident that the resolution was unnecessarily broad, Russell pointed to "precedents for the resolution's extraordinary presidential powers in the Formosa Resolution (1954) and the Middle East Resolution (1957)," both of which he claimed had averted rather than led to war.[186] Moreover, with the exception of Senators Morse and Gruening, most in Congress did believe that the Gulf of Tonkin incident had happened as the administration described. Admittedly, the Congress chose to take only three days to unravel the incident and dedicated less than two hours of that time to hearings on the matter.[187] But Congress had little reason to investigate the incident since the president and the administration had already privately assured members of Congress that they did not intend to widen the war.[188] And, after all, it was an election year, a factor that weighed heavily on many senators' minds.[189]

However, beyond all of these reasons, in summer 1964 the Cold War consensus was still a very real, tangible phenomenon. To be sure, publicly questioning the tenets of the ideology of containment was still beyond the pale of domestic American politics; senators did not want to look "soft on Communism" in an election year.[190] However, the reasons the Senate supported the Tonkin Gulf Resolution ran deeper. The vast majority of senators, like the vast majority of Americans, believed that communists were aggressive and had to be contained—by military force if necessary—lest they consume the small nations on the periphery of the Free World that depended on American might for their survival. And for all of the senators' private misgivings about the utility of U.S. military forces in Vietnam, South Vietnam *was* a small U.S. ally on the periphery of the Free World that appeared to be suffering from aggressive subversion by its communist neighbor, North Vietnam. As unfavorable as the situation in Vietnam was, all of the facts seemed to fit with the ideology of containment.

Thus, Congress readily fell in behind the president. In the end, Gruening and Morse were the only two members of Congress to vote against the Tonkin Gulf Resolution, which gave the president a free hand to escalate U.S. military intervention in Southeast Asia.[191]

As written, the final resolution passed by the Congress was as much an endorsement of the administration's containment arguments for U.S. military intervention in Vietnam as it was an endorsement of potential future escalations. The final resolution began by reiterating the administration's version of the Gulf of Tonkin incident. North Vietnam had "deliberately and repeatedly attacked United States naval vessels lawfully present in international waters." The resolution then— as President Johnson had at his speech at Syracuse—tied this attack to the "deliberate and systematic campaign of aggression that the communist regime in North Vietnam" had perpetrated against Laos and South Vietnam, as well as the United States military forces operating in those countries.[192] The resolution next repeated two of the justifications based on military containment that the administration had been making since Johnson took office: that Southeast Asia was vital to U.S. security and that the United States had a commitment to South Vietnam. "The United States regards as vital to its national interest and to world peace the maintenance of international peace and security in southeast Asia," the resolution stated. Moreover, the United States had "obligations" to Southeast Asia under "the Charter of the United Nations" and "the Southeast Asia Collective Defense Treaty."[193]

For all of these reasons, the resolution declared:

> The Congress approves and supports the determination of the President, as Commander in Chief, to take all necessary

measures to repel any armed attack against the forces of the
United States and to prevent further aggression.[194]

There is no mistaking the language of the resolution. The Congress
had given its advance approval to the president "to take all necessary
measures"[195] to protect U.S. military forces *and* stop North Vietnamese
"aggression" in Southeast Asia. The president had his insurance policy
against future congressional dissent on Vietnam. Whatever their later
sentiments about the Vietnam War, all but two members of Congress
had endorsed U.S. military intervention to contain communism in
Southeast Asia.

However, if President Johnson believed that he had enlisted the
support of the Congress for a war in Vietnam, he was deceiving himself. In 1967, as congressional support for the war waned, Johnson

President Johnson signs the Tonkin Gulf Resolution, Washington, DC, August 10,
1964, Johnson Presidential Library.[196]
Source: Republic of Vietnam.

would say he had pursued the Tonkin Gulf Resolution because, "If we were going to ask them to stay the whole route . . . we ought to ask them to be there at the takeoff."[197] The president added that he wanted the Congress there "at the takeoff so they'll be with me on the landing."[198] President Johnson believed that President Truman had failed to enlist the support of Congress for the Korean War and did not wish to repeat his mistake.

But the Congress was *not* "there at the takeoff." The president had lied to the Congress about the circumstances under which he had asked for the resolution.[199] And, more importantly, the president had lied about what he intended to do with the authority embodied in the resolution.[200] During the Senate debate on the resolution, Senator J. William Fulbright explicitly dismissed the possibility that the president would use the resolution to go to war—based on assurances he had received from the White House.[201] Similarly, Congressman Thomas Morgan, chairman of the House Committee on Foreign Affairs, told the House of Representatives that the resolution was "definitely not an advance declaration of war. The Committee has been assured by the Secretary of State that the constitutional prerogative of the Congress in this respect will continue to be scrupulously observed."[202] Years later, Senator Nelson would call the assertion that the Congress had approved a dramatic escalation of the war in 1964 "political nonsense if not in fact pure hypocrisy."[203] When it approved the Tonkin Gulf Resolution, Congress was *not* voting for the massive escalation and full-scale war that would later develop in Vietnam.

This was, in fact, the central, most important deception surrounding the Gulf of Tonkin incident and the Tonkin Gulf Resolution. Despite private assurances to Senator Fulbright and others, President Lyndon Johnson and his administration absolutely intended to further escalate U.S. military involvement in Vietnam.

In fact, the administration was already looking for another opportunity to use U.S. military force in Vietnam. In a meeting of the administration on August 10, 1964, at which the president, Secretaries Rusk and McNamara, General Wheeler, and others were present, the president expressed his satisfaction with the congressional and public response to the retaliation. However, he warned that the administration could not fail "in the second challenge," a subsequent North Vietnamese provocation. He said that if the United States "should do nothing further," it would find itself "even worse off than before" the Gulf of Tonkin incident. "Instead of letting the other side have the ball," the president said, the administration "should be prepared to take it." Rusk suggested that the OPLAN 34A raids and DESOTO patrols should be suspended so that "responsibility for escalation" would remain "on the other side" (clearly demonstrating that, despite the administration's denials during the hearings, Rusk understood that the OPLAN 34A raids and DESOTO patrols were provocative). The president asked for "prompt study and recommendations" on further escalations that might be accomplished "with maximum results and minimum danger."[204]

The State Department provided these recommendations three days later. In a memorandum from August 13, 1964, William Bundy suggested continuing air strikes in Laos but suspending OPLAN 34A raids and DESOTO patrols in order to "avoid actions that would in any way take the onus off the Communist side for escalation." He wrote that, should the DESOTO patrols be resumed, "both for present purposes and to maintain the credibility of our account of the events of last week, they must be clearly dissociated from 34A operations both in fact and in physical appearance" (showing that Bundy, too, plainly understood that the North Vietnamese had associated the DESOTO patrols with the OPLAN 34A raids). Bundy suggested that, if DESOTO patrols resumed, they should be held at least twenty miles off shore and that they should "avoid penetrations of 11 miles or so." Ultimately, however, the resumption of DESOTO patrols *was* intended as a provocation. Bundy concluded: "the 20-mile distance would not appreciably change the chances of a North Vietnamese reaction, while it would deprive them of a propaganda argument (since a great many other countries also assert a 12-mile territorial waters limit)"[205] (clearly indicating that Bundy also knew that North Vietnam claimed a twelve-mile limit as its territorial waters and that the earlier DESOTO patrols had violated this limit).

The State Department also had ideas for retaliations, "tit-for-tat actions of opportunity" awaiting only "special VC or DRV activity." William P. Bundy suggested that, if the Viet Cong were to escalate with thus far "'unused dirty tricks' such as mining (or attacks) in the Saigon River, sabotage of major POL stocks, and terrorist attacks on U.S. dependents," the United States should respond with further escalations of attacks inside North Vietnam, "prompt and precise reprisal[s]" such as "mining the Haiphong channel and attacking the Haiphong POL"[206]

After the passage of the Tonkin Gulf Resolution, the administration resumed use of the ideology of containment of communism to build support for further U.S. military intervention in Vietnam. In this effort, the Gulf of Tonkin incident served as evidence of North Vietnamese aggression and the administration's retaliatory air strikes served as evidence of the administration's determination to contain this communist aggression. However, in the heat of a presidential race against Republican challenger Senator Barry Goldwater, the president also painted this retaliation as "measured" to contrast it with the statements Goldwater had made about his intent to stop communist aggression using more aggressive means. As the election approached and it became clear that Americans did not yet support further escalation, the president began to even give the American public assurances that he would not widen the war. This eleventh-hour ploy would return to haunt the president a few years later, when American public opinion began to sour on the war.

As early as the signing of the Tonkin Gulf Resolution, the president began laying the groundwork for future escalations. Reasserting the administration's version of the Gulf of Tonkin incident, the president claimed that the attack had been "deliberate and unprovoked acts of aggression." The president next asserted America's right to respond: "The cause of peace clearly required that we respond with a prompt and unmistakable reply." He also claimed that the Tonkin Gulf Resolution represented "unanimity"[207]—in Congress and with the American public— in support of a military response to North Vietnamese aggression, and that that endorsement had followed "in each House . . . [a] free and serious debate."[208] U.S. military intervention was not, the president claimed, in pursuit of American self-interest. Rather, the president reasserted the purity of the United States' aims in Southeast Asia, a claim that his administration had made throughout the summer. "In that region, there is nothing we covet," Johnson said, "nothing we seek—no territory, no military position, no political ambition."[209] However, the president concluded with an ominous pledge: "To any in Southeast Asia who ask our help in defending their freedom, we shall give it."[210]

As the State Department and the White House began to formulate recommendations for further escalations, the President continued to lay the foundations to justify future escalations. In a 12 August 1964 speech to the American Bar Association in New York City, the president said: "No one should think for a moment that we will be worn down, nor will we be driven out." But, at the same time, he emphasized that future escalations would be limited. "We will not be provoked into rashness," he told the audience. "We will continue to meet aggression with firmness and unprovoked attack with measured reply," just as the *Maddox* and *Turner Joy* had in the Gulf of Tonkin and the administration had with air strikes against torpedo boat installations in North Vietnam. President Johnson concluded by reminding his audience of his authority from Congress to continue to meet North Vietnamese provocations—and equated this congressional authorization with the approval of the American people. "That is the meaning of the resolution passed by your Congress with 502 votes in favor and only 2 opposed. That is the meaning of the national unity that we have shown to all the world last week."[211]

In arguing for U.S. military intervention in Southeast Asia, the president also drew once again on two ideas that his administration had used since he took office—that the U.S. military was protecting free people from communist aggression and that this policy was a continuation of his predecessors' policies. Johnson insisted that U.S. military presence in South Vietnam was absolutely necessary to contain communist expansion. Withdrawing that support, Johnson said, would be to "allow the freedom of brave people to be handed over to Communist tyranny." Such an act, Johnson concluded, was "strategically unwise" and "morally unthinkable."[212] This policy was, Johnson also insisted, the "one consistent aim" of his predecessors, "for ten years through the Eisenhower Administration, the Kennedy Administration, and this Administration." While he admitted that "the South Vietnamese have the basic responsibility" for their own defense, he also assured Americans that the United States would "engage our strength and our resources to whatever extent needed to help others repel aggression."[213]

While the president continued to make his case for military intervention in Vietnam with the American people, the White House planned its next escalation. The attendees at a strategy meeting held on September 7, 1964, after the return from Southeast Asia of newly confirmed U.S. ambassador to South Vietnam General Maxwell Taylor, decided that the original recommendations from McGeorge Bundy were the most prudent course. But the group also concluded that the United States should be postured to "respond to any future DRV attacks on U.S. units on a tit-for-tat basis."[214] On September 10, 1964, these recommendations became official U.S. policy. A National Security Action Memorandum directed the resumption of DESOTO patrols, followed by the resumption of OPLAN 34A raids. The president directed the administration to "be prepared to respond as appropriate against the DRV in the event of any attack on U.S. units or any special DRV/VC action against SVN."[215] The government was once more poised to retaliate against an anticipated North Vietnamese provocation.

Meanwhile, the president continued to use the ideology of military containment of communism to justify U.S. military involvement in Vietnam. At a Democratic Party fundraising dinner in New Orleans, President Johnson reminded his audience that "in the Truman doctrine and the Marshall plan of 1948 we made our commitment against the spread of communism." This commitment, Johnson claimed, had proved wrong those who argued "that communism would be irresistible" or "that war would be unavoidable." Johnson added that his was the first administration "since midcentury under which no Nation in the world has fallen to communism." Johnson cited his firm but restrained reply to repeated provocations from the communist world, including in the Gulf of Tonkin, where, Johnson said "we made a prompt reply, an appropriate reply. But we have never lost our heart and I hope we will never lose our head." Expanding on the lessons of Munich, Johnson warned any "would-be conqueror" not to mistake U.S. resolve as Kaiser Wilhelm had in World War I or Adolf Hitler had in World War II. Perhaps in a thinly veiled jab at the two senators who had voted against the Tonkin Gulf Resolution—Senators Morse and Gruening—Johnson added that Hitler had been "fooled" into his aggression "because a few Senators were preaching isolationism."[216]

The vast majority in the media embraced the president's use of containment to justify intervention in Vietnam with renewed enthusiasm after the Gulf of Tonkin incident. In fact, James "Scotty" Reston, then associate editor at the *New York Times*, was one of the few in the press to challenge the administration's use of the containment of communism. He wrote that both "President Johnson and Senator Goldwater are now following the domino theory about Vietnam." He asked three pointed questions about the administration's assertion that defending South Vietnam "is 'vital' to the security of the U.S."[217]

> Is this true? And if it is, can raising the stakes in the war be "controlled," as the Pentagon is so fond of saying? It would also be interesting to know whether President Johnson and Senator Goldwater propose to go on getting the United States involved in every tribal conflict in Africa and Asia.[218]

He concluded by criticizing the fact that the United States was increasing its "commitments there [in Vietnam] without agreeing within the Government about our objectives in that conflict."[219]

The Gulf of Tonkin incident and the administration's response had moved public opinion a bit, but not decisively, in favor of intervention in Vietnam. Internal White House polling in Kentucky from September and October 1964 showed that Kentuckians, like their

counterparts nationally, continued to see Vietnam as a less important issue than domestic concerns. In mid-October, only 10 percent
considered "handling the problem in Vietnam" as "most important" while 16 percent considered "providing jobs," 21 percent
considered "handling integration and segregation," and 26 percent
considered "the war on poverty" to be "most important." More
promising for the administration, however, by September, 58 percent
of Kentuckians expressed a favorable opinion of the president's handling of Vietnam (though that favorable rating would slip to 50 percent by mid-October).[220]

Perhaps most important for the Johnson administration on the
eve of the election, voters thought Johnson would be better than
Goldwater at dealing with international issues. Kentuckians favored
Johnson in both handling "Communist China" (63 percent to 17 percent) and "handling the Russians" (62 percent to 16 percent).[221] In
their analysis, the poll's authors suggested that the Johnson administration should exploit the president's strength on Cold War issues.
They wrote:

> We do advocate that he [President Johnson] start reminding
> the electorate of some of the specific irresponsible statements
> made by Goldwater on foreign policy . . . Barry Goldwater
> still scares people . . . speechwriters should make prolific use of
> Goldwater quotes on foreign policy.[222]

Johnson's campaign clearly took this advice to heart. A thirty-minute
television advertisement for President Johnson that aired on October
15, 1964, just weeks before the election, highlighted Goldwater's
more militant views on the United States' global competition with
the communist world. The ad began with a speech by President
Johnson that commemorated the one-year anniversary of the above-
ground nuclear test ban treaty. The president reminded his audience
that "a few lonely voices were raised in opposition." Lest someone
not understand that he was referring to Senator Barry Goldwater, the
president continued: "Among them was one who now seeks to lead

this nation." The president said that Goldwater's position on Cold War issues, "[opposing] efforts to reach peaceful agreements," was a prescription for the "continued . . . upward spiral of tension and danger."[223]

Johnson also used this advertisement to further his use of containment to justify U.S. military intervention in Vietnam. This advertisement repeatedly couched the conflict in Vietnam as yet another flashpoint in the Cold War competition between the free and communist worlds. Johnson painted his policies as a continuation of "the policy of every American president of both parties for the last 20 years."[224] Artfully, the President simultaneously reminded the audience of his response to the Gulf of Tonkin incident, tied that response to both the military containment of communism and his predecessor's policies, and posited that it was the United States obligation to continue those policies:

> We will stand firm in the defense of freedom, as President Kennedy did in Cuba, as we did when our destroyers were attacked around Vietnam. We will continue to serve notice to all the world: wherever liberty comes under fire, America will be there too, swiftly, decisively, and ready to make any sacrifice to make appropriate reply.[225]

Johnson returned to this idea at the end of his speech. The United States had been "the guardian at the gate of freedom" for twenty years, building U.S. military might so that America was the "greatest military power on earth." Moreover, the president recounted the ways he and his predecessors had used that military power in various Cold War flashpoints.[226]

> President Truman met Communist aggression in Greece and Turkey. President Eisenhower met Communist aggression in the Formosa Straits. President Kennedy met Communist aggression in Cuba. And when our destroyers were attacked, we met Communist aggression in the waters around Vietnam.[228]

The president had deftly placed Vietnam and the Gulf of Tonkin incident in the broader context of the Cold War.

Taking a cue from the pollsters about public fear of Barry Goldwater's Cold War policies, Johnson contrasted the policies of Barry Goldwater with those of the Cold War presidents. These presidents, President Johnson said, had "used our great power with restraint, never once taking a reckless risk which might plunge us into a large-scale war." Likewise, they had worked to settle disputes and "build bridges of understanding between people and between nations" including "working with the United Nations." Unnamed others, President Johnson claimed, attacked these policies: "We are told that we should consider using atomic weapons in Vietnam and even in Eastern Europe, should there be an uprising." President Johnson concluded that "this attack contradicts the entire course of America in the entire post-war period" and following this course would "discard the policies of the last 20 years. The peace of the world would be in grave danger."[228]

The president's speech was followed by a narrated film that also perpetuated the administration's dual themes—that the conflict in Vietnam was in fact a new front in the Cold War and that the president's measured approach was preferable to Goldwater's supposed rashness. In recalling the the Cuban missile crisis, for instance,[229] the narrator praised Kennedy's measured firmness:

> The country is closer to nuclear war than ever before. Use of United States strength might cause global holocaust. Retreating from the Soviet challenge would invite more aggression and endanger freedom around the world.[230]

The similarities to the Johnson administration's arguments for military involvement in Vietnam are inescapable. This segment was echoing the Johnson administration's arguments, based on the so-called lessons of Munich, that appeasement in Vietnam would invite further communist aggression and the fall of all of Southeast Asia.

While this campaign ad praised the president's "measured" prosecution of the Cold War in Vietnam, the ad stopped short of endorsing further U.S. military escalation in Southeast Asia. The ad showed footage of President Kennedy shaking the hands of U.S. soldiers in Vietnam, footage of then Vice President Johnson shaking hands with members of the South Vietnamese government during his visit to Vietnam, and finally footage of South Vietnamese soldiers storming off of U.S. helicopters and into battle.[231] Over this footage, the narrator repeated the theme of measured firmness:

> The struggle for Vietnamese independence must be carried on by the people of Vietnam. But we are helping them to fight their battle without taking rash action which might plunge millions of Americans into war.[232]

The Johnson campaign seemed to feel that the administration had not yet persuaded the American people to support increased direct U.S. military intervention in Vietnam.

As the administration had since August 4, 1964, this ad portrayed the Gulf of Tonkin incident as proof of communist aggression in Southeast Asia—and the retaliatory air strikes as evidence of the president's determination to contain that aggression. As footage rolled of U.S. naval ships in action, the narrator told the audience that it was in pursuit of the policy of military containment of communism that the United States "demonstrated that it would meet aggression with firmness" in the Gulf of Tonkin. The narrator stated flatly that, "on August 3, 1964, American naval forces were attacked for the second time with gunboats from North Vietnam" and that, after Johnson had consulted with his advisors, "American air power was ordered to attack the bases from which the gunboats had come." The narrator continued: "The communists could not doubt that force would be met with force." But, again evoking the specter of Goldwater, the narrator added: "But neither would we take rash and impulsive action which might plunge us into large-scale war." Quoting the president, the narrator concluded: "That firmness will always be measured."[233]

This ad concluded by reinforcing not just the theme that U.S. military intervention in Vietnam was part of the Cold War strategy of containment of communism, but arguing for the ideology of containment itself. The narrator began by conceding that "the Communists show signs of weakening," describing the growing Sino-Soviet split in the communist world. But, the narrator contended, as footage rolled of an angry-looking Soviet Premier Khrushchev giving a speech, "Its leaders are still dedicated to the destruction of freedom." Again echoing the supposed lessons of Munich, the narrator reminded the audience: "The world of 1964 is a world of danger, where weakness can bring an end to freedom." As footage rolled of Lyndon Johnson and his advisors in the White House, the narrator then reminded the audience of the dangers of electing Barry Goldwater as president: " . . . recklessness can bring an end to civilization." The ad then cut to footage of America's military land and sea arsenal, of nuclear missiles and fighter aircraft. As the footage rolled, a voiceover of a speech by Lyndon Johnson played, saying, "We have built this staggering strength that I have talked about not to destroy but to save. Not to put an end to civilization but to try to put an end to conflict."[234]

This full-throated defense of the Cold War consensus and the ideology of military containment as a means to prevent another world war was perfectly calibrated to appeal to the real sentiments of Americans in October 1964. Gallup polls from the period showed that Americans were afraid of a confrontation with the communist world. "War" and "nuclear war" together were Americans' biggest fears, while "peace" was the biggest hope. By October, "peace . . . [and] freedom from fear of war or devastation" were the greatest hope of 54 percent of Americans. When Americans were asked to look ten years into the future, their biggest fears remained "war" and "nuclear war." Their second biggest fear was "communism." By October, "war" or "nuclear war" was the greatest fear of over 51 percent of Americans.[235]

Americans' prescription for these fears was continued investment in national security. Admittedly, Americans consistently opposed foreign aid programs, with 44 percent believing that they should be "reduced" and 15 percent believing they should be "ended." However, when asked in September if the "American defense effort is proceeding at about the right rate," 58 percent of Americans believed it was, while 30 percent believed the rate should be "increased." These numbers remained virtually unchanged in October.[236]

Americans were also convinced that internationalism was important. Almost 74 percent of Americans believed that "the U.S. should cooperate fully with the United Nations." Likewise, 83 percent of Americans believed that "the U.S. should take into account the views of its allies in order to keep our alliances strong." Seventy-one percent of Americans rejected the proposition that the United States should "go [its] own way in international matters." Similarly, 70 percent rejected the notion that "the U.S. should mind its own business internationally and let other countries get along as best they can on their own." And most Americans wished to maintain U.S. dominance in world affairs. Nearly 60 percent agreed that "the U.S. should maintain its dominant position as the world's most powerful nation at all costs, even going to the very brink of war if necessary."[237]

Sentiments were less strong when respondents were asked about President Johnson. When asked in September, 55 percent did disagree that President Johnson's policies in the Cold War represented "a defeatist 'no win' policy on the international front by appeasing the Communists." However, 61 percent believed that "the U.S. should take a firmer stand against the Soviet Union than it has in recent years." Still, Americans agreed by 84 percent that "the U.S. should continue to negotiate with the Soviet Union on a broad front," a cornerstone of the Johnson administration's foreign policy.[238] And when asked in October, "How much trust and confidence do you have in what Lyndon Johnson stands for on international problems," 65 percent responded that they had a "very great deal" of or "considerable" trust in Johnson. When asked how much trust they had in Barry Goldwater on international issues, nearly the same proportion, 59 percent, had "not very much" trust or "none at all." These same proportions were seen between Johnson and Goldwater on Americans' trust in their respective ability to deal with the specific international issues of "preventing World War III," "handling Khruschchev [sic] and relations with Russia," "handling the problem of Communist China," and "controlling the use of nuclear weapons."[239]

Perhaps most encouraging for the president's aims in Southeast Asia, a Gallup poll in early October found that 89 percent of Americans had a "great deal" of or "considerable . . . concern" about "combatting world Communism." Americans were also now almost as concerned about communist expansion in Southeast Asia as they were about communist expansion in Europe. While 81 percent of Americans had a "great deal" of or "considerable . . . concern" about "relations with Russia," 76 percent now had a "great deal" of or "considerable . . . concern" about "the problem of Communist China." When asked which country "will turn out to be the greater threat to the U.S.—Soviet Russia or Communist China," 55 percent of Americans chose China as a greater threat. Moreover, 69 percent were now concerned "a great deal" or considerably by "the problem of Vietnam."[240]

However, the administration did not seem to believe that they had convinced Americans to support further U.S. military escalation in Vietnam. Consequently, even though the administration had already decided to resume the DESOTO patrols and OPLAN 34A raids in hopes of provoking a North Vietnamese response against which they could retaliate, they felt it necessary to reassure the American public that they did not intend to widen the war in Vietnam. Thus, on October 21, 1964, only a few weeks before the election, President Johnson made his famous pledge to an audience at Akron University: "We are not about to send American boys nine or ten thousand miles away from home to do what Asian boys ought to be doing for themselves." Johnson claimed that this was continuation of his predecessors' policies and contrasted this policy with reckless suggestions by those who "rattle their rockets some, and . . . bluff about their bombs," referring to his Republican opponent.[241]

President Johnson may have simply intended this comment as another assertion that his actions were "measured and fitting" in contrast to Goldwater's more aggressive suggestions for action in Vietnam. This comment was only slightly more forceful than other comments Johnson had made since the Gulf of Tonkin incident. Just before the Democratic National Convention in late August, Johnson had said that "others [presumably Goldwater] are eager to enlarge the conflict" by "sending American boys to do the job that Asian boys should do." In Texas, just after his nomination, he claimed that Goldwater's policies would "result in our committing a good many American boys to fighting a war that . . . ought to be fought by the boys of Asia." At a meeting with newspaper editors in New Hampshire in late September, President Johnson warned that Goldwater's suggestion that the United States begin heavy bombing of the north was "likely to involve American boys in a war in Asia with 700 million Chinese." He preferred, he said, that "the boys in Vietnam . . . do their own fighting."[242]

But, whatever he told himself, President Johnson had crossed a line; this *was* a pledge not to send ground troops to Vietnam. This pledge barely registered in the print media at the time, but this comment would return to haunt Johnson as support for the war began to wane.

Still, the president's effort to paint himself as the moderate alternative to Barry Goldwater helped convinced Americans to return President Johnson to the White House. In November; over 61 percent of Americans voted to reelect President Johnson, a victory that was due, at least in part, to the Gulf of Tonkin incident.[243]

During the first nine months of his presidency, President Johnson and his administration made a concerted effort to convince the American people of the need for U.S. military intervention in Vietnam. The administration used arguments firmly founded in the ideology of military containment of communism to make this case. These arguments appealed to the very real Cold War consensus; the American public, members of the press, and members of Congress readily accepted the basic precepts of containment ideology. However, despite a vigorous public information campaign by the administration using these arguments, in mid-summer 1964 the public and Congress did not support increased American military intervention in Vietnam.

The supposed attacks against the *U.S.S. Maddox* and *Turner Joy* on August 4, 1964, finally provided the political impetus for escalation of U.S. military involvement in Vietnam that nine months of administration rhetoric had failed to generate. President Lyndon Johnson used this incident as justification for a retaliatory air strike and a congressional endorsement—the Tonkin Gulf Resolution—to use military force to protect the sovereignty of South Vietnam from what his administration described as northern aggression. As soon as the president had this resolution in hand, he and his administration returned to the rhetoric of military containment of communism to justify the further U.S. military interventions it was planning in Vietnam.

President Johnson treated this congressional resolution as an endorsement of U.S. military intervention in Vietnam. Johnson believed he needed this endorsement in case military intervention later became unpopular with Congress—a lesson he believed he had learned from Truman's experience with Congress during the Korean War. In this context, the Tonkin Gulf Resolution was a sort of insurance policy against congressional dissent. And, to be fair, the language of the resolution *was* an endorsement—not just of the use of U.S. military force to contain communism in Southeast Asia, but of the administration's use of the containment of communism to justify that intervention.

For the American people, the Gulf of Tonkin incident was dramatic evidence of what the administration had been saying consistently since President Johnson took office: the war in South Vietnam was a war of aggression by North Vietnam and if the United States did not answer that aggression, North Vietnam's aggression would only grow. In this context, to the degree that Americans were paying attention to Vietnam at all in 1964, the retaliatory air strikes against North Vietnam and the Tonkin Gulf Resolution were evidence that the United States government had learned the lessons of Munich and was standing up to communist aggression.

For Congress, the Gulf of Tonkin incident was evidence that the United States' measures to that point—advisors, material aid, and air support to ARVN forces—had failed to deter northern aggression. In this context, the Tonkin Gulf Resolution was another escalation in and of itself. Much in the vein of the Formosa Resolution or the Middle East Resolution, the Tonkin Gulf Resolution was an expression of American intent to protect South Vietnamese sovereignty intended to discourage North Vietnam, Communist China, and the Soviet Union from persisting in their aggression. Congress intended this resolution to prevent a war, not to start one.

The administration had deceived the public and the Congress in its portrayal of the Gulf of Tonkin incident. And while during the congressional hearings and floor debate over the Tonkin Gulf Resolution, senators and congressmen were assured that the president did not intend to escalate the war in Vietnam, members of the administration and the president himself were privately planning to increase U.S. military involvement in Vietnam on a tit-for-tat basis in response to North Vietnamese provocations. However, because there was little congressional or press scrutiny of the facts of the incident, the administration's version of the events of August 4 was readily accepted by Congress and the public. And while Congress may have been deceived as to the facts of the Gulf of Tonkin incident and the president's intent for the resolution, the language of the Tonkin Gulf Resolution clearly expressed congressional approval for further U.S. military escalation in Southeast Asia.

While the administration had achieved its two short-term goals for Vietnam—a direct U.S. military intervention to bolster sagging spirits in the South Vietnamese government and a congressional resolution to inoculate the administration against later congressional dissent—it had sown the seeds for its own destruction. The administration lied to the Congress and the American people about the circumstances under which the Gulf of Tonkin incident supposedly occurred and, in its haste to retaliate, failed to properly scrutinize the incident before it acted. In 1968, full-scale press and congressional scrutiny of the events of August 4, 1964, would finally force President Lyndon Johnson to pay a terrible political price for his deception.

President Johnson bears some personal responsibility for his own demise. Admittedly, it was his administration that had assured members of Congress that they did not intend to widen the war in Vietnam at the same time they secretly planned future escalations. But—inadvertently or not—it was the president himself who promised voters that he would not introduce ground troops into direct combat in Vietnam. After the administration's lies surrounding the Gulf of Tonkin incident were revealed to the American people, this pledge would be used as a bludgeon to further crush Johnson's credibility with the American people.

But in the immediate aftermath of the Gulf of Tonkin incident, the administration's "measured and fitting" response played a large role in the president's victory over Senator Barry Goldwater in the presidential election. After the election, the Johnson administration would resume use of the ideology of containment—and occasionally use the precedent of this initial retaliatory air strike and the Tonkin Gulf Resolution itself—to justify "Americanizing" the Vietnam War through a series of escalations that culminated in the direct involvement of U.S. ground forces in the war. Throughout this period, a rapidly expanding list of opponents of the president's Vietnam policy would focus on these justifications based on containment to attack the growing U.S. military commitment in Vietnam.

Chapter 2

THE "AMERICANIZATION" OF THE VIETNAM WAR

B etween the 1964 presidential election and mid-summer 1965, the Johnson administration embarked on a series of escalations that would culminate in the direct involvement of U.S. ground forces in combat operations in Vietnam. Throughout this "Americanization" of the war, the Johnson administration continued to use of the ideology of military containment of communism to justify increasing U.S. military intervention in Vietnam.

Throughout this same period, a growing list of opponents of the U.S. military escalation tried to attack the president's Vietnam policy by arguing against the suitability of the strategy of military containment of communism to Vietnam and Southeast Asia. Some opponents also attacked the entire idea of military containment of communism, not just in Vietnam, but anywhere. This represented a dramatic broadening of the public debate on U.S. foreign policy; previously, questioning the tenets of the Cold War consensus had been beyond the pale of mainstream political discourse on foreign policy. Still, their attacks failed to persuade Congress or the American public to oppose the administration's policies in Vietnam.

Initially, the administration also relied on the tit-for-tat precedent of the retaliatory air strikes during the Gulf of Tonkin incident and the Tonkin Gulf Resolution itself as additional justifications for escalation. However, over the Americanization of the war, these arguments gradually receded from use until, finally, they had completely disappeared from the administration's rhetoric. Tit-for-tat justifications became unnecessary to the administration as it finally decided on its course of Americanizing the war—the justification for each escalation beyond this point was simply that the application of more U.S. military force was needed to contain communist expansion. Use of the Tonkin Gulf Resolution—the administration's insurance policy against congressional dissent—became unnecessary as a justification as it became clear that Congress would not make any public objections to the escalation or to the President's legal authority to escalate U.S. involvement in the conflict.

Only days before the U.S. presidential election of 1964, the Viet Cong shelled an airbase at Bien Hoa, killing several Americans and destroying a number of American B-57 bombers.[1] In December 1964, flush with victory by the largest popular margin as yet in history,[2] a newly elected President Johnson ordered the bombing of North Vietnamese supply routes through Laos. Yet Viet Cong escalation continued; the Viet Cong bombed a U.S. officer's billet in Saigon on Christmas Eve. This attack was followed, on February 7, 1965, by a Viet Cong attack on the American barracks at Pleiku, killing eight and wounding over a hundred. President Johnson responded later the same day with a bombing raid of over 132 bombers against three barracks in North Vietnam, an operation called "Flaming Dart." He also ordered the evacuation of American dependents from South Vietnam.[3]

After the election, the administration resumed its use of containment to justify increased U.S. military intervention in Vietnam. Most in the media remained supportive of these arguments, though a few figures in the media and academia did begin to attack the administration's use of containment to justify the war or the ideology of containment itself. There was no public congressional dissent immediately following the election, but there was private dissent from some key members of Congress. President Johnson seemed unconcerned with this dissent, probably because he felt secured by his insurance policy against congressional dissent, the Tonkin Gulf Resolution. The administration did occasionally harken to this insurance policy as a justification for further U.S. military intervention. It also invoked the tit-for-tat precedent set by the retaliatory air strikes after the Gulf of Tonkin incident. But these additional justifications were not really necessary; the American public largely accepted and agreed with the administration's use of containment to justify intervention in Vietnam.

Americans overwhelmingly (by 88 percent) wanted the United States to seek a negotiated settlement to the war in Vietnam in late 1964.[4] However, most Americans also indicated that they would support a further escalation of U.S. military involvement in Vietnam. The American public was not yet committed to the idea of sending ground troops to Vietnam; nearly 58 percent of Americans did say that they would "like to see" the United States "send more [troops] in," but only if the United States had "to make a choice between taking our men out of South Vietnam, or sending more men in." But the American public strongly believed (by a margin of 64 percent) that the United States "should . . . [be] involved with [its] military forces in Southeast Asia."[5] While the wording of this survey was ambiguous, the responses did indicate that a majority of Americans would rather escalate U.S. military involvement in the conflict than "lose" the war in Vietnam.

Just as before Johnson's election, there was little media dissent on Vietnam before the beginning of the Americanization of the war. In fact, many media figures repeated the administration's justifications for military intervention in Vietnam based on the containment of communism. For instance, columnist William R. Frye wrote that, while some wanted the U.S. military to pull out of Vietnam, "to pull out of Viet Nam would be to test the validity of the 'domino theory'—the theory that loss of Indochina would lead to loss of Thailand, Malaysia, the Philippines and much more." Frye quipped, "This theory may or may not be valid, but few in Washington are eager to risk a test."[6]

A few media figures did dissent. Syndicated columnist Drew Pearson took a mild swipe at presidential credibility on Vietnam, saying, "The American people have been getting only fragmentary information regarding the burden, the bungling in Vietnam." More importantly, however, Pearson was among the few media critics who had begun to attack one of President Johnson's primary justifications for intervention in Vietnam based on the ideology of containment—the domino theory. Pearson noted that similar claims about a domino theory were made about Cuba, but that "the trend in Latin America is toward the right."[7]

Washington Post columnist Joseph Alsop, a strong supporter of U.S. military intervention in Vietnam, counterattacked against the growing use of the domino theory as a pejorative term connoting an overly simplistic conception of the international situation in Southeast Asia. Alsop wrote that the White House was now frequently fielding the question: "Do you still believe in the domino theory?" Alsop added, "It is asked in a tone so scornful and accusing that little doubt remains about the current unpopularity of the 'domino theory' in White House circles." Alsop then proceeded to recount "a mass of evidence to sustain the 'domino theory,'" including purported communist gains in Thailand, the Philippines, and Formosa. "All this and other evidence indicates that the Chinese Communists are not merely hoping for an American defeat," Alsop wrote, "they are already preparing to take advantage of it through their rather considerable agent-net."[8]

There were signs that Congress had reservations about the administration's intent to escalate U.S. involvement in the war in Vietnam. In December 1964, the president received a concerned, private letter from Senate Majority Leader Mike Mansfield about Vietnam. Mansfield wrote that the administration remained on "a course in Viet Nam which takes us further and further out on the sagging limb." Mansfield warned that the recent attack at Bien Hoa might signal "a growing boldness in the Viet Cong." He also warned that, if the current weakness of the rotating South Vietnamese regimes continued, the United States would find that "preponderant responsibility for what transpires in South Viet Nam really rests with us even as it once had with the French." This, Mansfield wrote, was a recipe for a perpetual U.S. military presence in South Vietnam, and perhaps an extension of the conflict into Cambodia or resurgence of the conflict in Laos.[9]

Mansfield's prescription for the administration's impasse in Southeast Asia was for America to abandon its hope of containing Chinese influence in the region, "which is, in any event, culturally impossible and, in the long run, economically improbable." The feasible alternative, Mansfield suggested, was to "forestall Chinese political and military domination of the area" and foster the "development of native institutions of national independence, regional cooperation and popularly responsible government." This more limited goal fit with the "limited national interests" the United States had in Vietnam and, more importantly, the goal of eventual withdrawal of U.S. forces. Mansfield also had a number of specific policy recommendations designed to move the United States toward this broader goal—ending air strikes outside South Vietnam, fostering rapprochement between South Vietnam and Cambodia, bolstering Souvanna Phouma's efforts to stabilize Laos, allowing U.S. allies to normalize economic ties with North Vietnam, focusing on building an inclusive and legitimate government in South Vietnam and forcing it to negotiate with the Viet Cong, and starting direct negotiations with China.[10] But Mansfield stopped short of suggesting a pull-out of American forces from Vietnam. If these means were not successful, Mansfield concluded:

> . . . we had better begin now to face up to the likelihood of years and years of involvement and a vast increase in the commitment, and this should be spelled out in no uncertain terms to the people of the nation.[11]

Lyndon Johnson's response to Mansfield's concerns seemed to miss the point. Johnson claimed to agree with nearly all of Mansfield's assertions, yet he took "direct issue with" Mansfield's suggestion that the United States was "overcommitted" in Vietnam. "Given the size of the stake," Johnson continued, "it seems to me that we are doing only what we have to do."[12] Johnson did not seem to understand Mansfield's basic premise that the stakes in Vietnam were not worth the massive investment of money and military might that the president seemed about to commit.

Nor did the president seem alarmed that Senator Mansfield, influential majority leader of the Senate, had reservations about the President's course in Vietnam. If the president and the administration had seen the Tonkin Gulf Resolution as a "sense of the Senate" about U.S. military intervention as of August 1964, then Mansfield objections would have been a cause for alarm—and certainly would have prompted key members of the administration to meet with senators in an attempt to allay their concerns. Instead, the president sent the senator a short letter and then went forward with his plans to escalate the conflict. This is at least strong circumstantial evidence that the president saw the Tonkin Gulf Resolution as an insurance policy against congressional dissent rather than as a transitory sense of the Senate.

Despite the concern from some in the media and in Congress about the administration's use of containment to justify intervention in Vietnam, the administration continued to rely on these arguments in its effort to convince the American people. In an NBC news program called "A Conversation with Dean Rusk," Rusk rejected the term *domino theory* while embracing its precepts. Since the formation of North Vietnam, Rusk said, "Laos, and its neighbor, South Viet-Nam, came under direct pressure from North Viet-Nam." The source of this aggression was "the appetite proclaimed from Peiping."[13] He quickly added, citing the lessons of Munich:

> One doesn't require a "domino" theory to get at this. Peiping has announced the doctrine. It is there in the primitive notion of a militant world revolution which has been promoted by these veterans of the long march who now control mainland China. So we believe that you simply postpone temporarily an even greater crisis if you allow an announced course of aggression to succeed a step at a time on the road to a major catastrophe.[14]

Rusk also inaugurated a new theme in this interview, one that the administration would echo repeatedly over subsequent years: failing to honor the U.S. commitment to South Vietnam would cause other countries to doubt the United States' commitments to them. "If we were to abandon Southeast Asia," Rusk said, "this would cause them [other allies] to wonder what our commitments under such arrangements as NATO would mean."[15]

On January 4, 1965, the day after Rusk's appearance on NBC, the president gave his annual State of the Union Address. He, too, painted the conflict in Vietnam as only one flashpoint in the Cold War contest with "World Communism." He did concede the multipolarity of the communist threat, saying that each differs "in intensity and in danger" and that each requires "different attitudes and different answers." The president would seek comity with the Soviet Union and trade with Eastern Europe. However, the president warned that, "In Asia, communism wears a more aggressive face," a face that could be seen in Vietnam. Peace in Vietnam would come, Johnson said, "only when aggressors leave their neighbors in peace." But the United States would not "be found wanting" in defending the cause of freedom in South Vietnam.[16] This was an argument that the administration would frequently repeat through the remainder of Johnson's presidency: the United States must "hold out" until the Chinese become more moderate as the Soviets had.

In answer to his own question, "Why are we there," the president offered two answers. First, Johnson said, "Ten years ago our president pledged our help" in defeating "communist aggression." Johnson added, "Three presidents have supported that pledge. We will not break it now." Second, Johnson insisted, "Our own security is tied to the peace of Asia." Once more invoking the lessons of Munich, Johnson added, "Twice in one generation we have had to fight against aggression in the Far East. To ignore aggression now would only increase the danger of a much larger war."[17]

In early 1965, the administration also for the first time invoked the Tonkin Gulf Resolution as a justification for U.S. military intervention. In a speech on February 7, 1965, William P. Bundy said that the United States reasons for being in Vietnam were . . .

> . . . pretty well stated by Congress last August when it passed a resolution, following the Gulf of Tonkin affair, in which it stated that the United States "regards as vital to its national interest and world peace the maintenance of international peace and security in southeast Asia."[18]

Here, Bundy was using the resolution's endorsement of the administration's use of containment as a justification for intervention in Vietnam as a proof of the validity of those arguments. However, Bundy also repeated these arguments himself. While he insisted that he was not "using what's sometimes called 'the domino theory,' that anything happens automatically or quickly," Bundy still said that "if South Viet-Nam were to fall under Communist control it would become very much more difficult . . . to maintain the independence and freedom of Thailand, Cambodia, of Malaysia, and so on." Bundy also claimed that if "wars of national liberation" succeeded in South Vietnam, it would "be used elsewhere in the world."[19]

On February 8, 1965, when the president briefed congressional leaders, including Senators Fulbright and Mansfield, on his intent to again bomb the north—Operation "Flaming Dart"—the president told the congressional leaders that the air strikes were being launched in response to the attack on the American Barracks in Pleiku.[20] The president was invoking the tit-for-tat precedent set by the retaliatory air strikes after the Gulf of Tonkin resolution as a justification for further escalation.

However, the president also used the Tonkin Gulf Resolution to justify U.S. military intervention in Vietnam; speaking with these leaders, Johnson cited the resolution as his authority to respond to the bombing of the barracks at Pleiku. To head off congressional dissent before it began, the president was reminding members of Congress that they had endorsed his use of force to protect U.S. forces and to stop North Vietnamese aggression. Fulbright did voice concern about the presence of Chairman of the Soviet Council of Ministers Kosygin in North Vietnam during the air strikes. Mansfield pledged to support the president's decision, but still presented a memorandum to the president objecting to the quality of the South Vietnamese government.[21] Still, none of the congressional leaders questioned the validity of the Tonkin Gulf Resolution as a justification to escalate U.S. military involvement in the conflict. This muted response probably only served to reinforce the president's understanding of the Tonkin Gulf Resolution not as a transitory sense of the Congress but as a sort of insurance policy against congressional dissent.

Only days before the Flaming Dart air strikes, former U.S. ambassador to India John Kenneth Galbraith launched a concerted attack on the administration's policies in Vietnam. However, rather than attack the administration's recent use of the Tonkin Gulf Resolution as a justification for escalation, Galbraith attacked the administration's use of the ideology of military containment of communism. In fact, this was perhaps the broadest attack yet voiced in mainstream political discourse against the ideology of military containment itself. In an article in the *Atlantic Monthly* and in a speech in Pennsylvania at the annual Roosevelt Day dinner of the Americans for Democratic Action, Galbraith assailed America's dogmatic adherence to an "obsolete" postwar anticommunist foreign policy framework. Galbraith spoke of three generations of thought on foreign policy since World War II. The first was a hope of comity with the Soviet Union that was dashed by Stalinism. The second generation was a Cold War order assembled "against the monolithic power of communism." The third and contemporary generation was one in which détente with the Soviet Union was possible—if hardliners in the State Department and elsewhere abandoned the assumptions of the second generation and stopped "clinging, sometimes rather righteously, to the recent past." Embedded in Galbraith's analysis was a critique of the rigidity—"the litany"—of the Cold War consensus.[22] Galbraith also implicitly attacked President Johnson's contention that his Vietnam policy was a continuation of twenty years of U.S. policy:

> On domestic matters liberals invariably want and support and expect action. They do not praise continuity in our past approach. . . . But in foreign policy the mood is less urgent. Here both the liberal and the official instinct is to accept present policies. This is true whether they are right, wrong, or potentially disastrous. . . . We accept continuity in policies toward southeast Asia, China, the arms race, which are not working at all or which are certain to be a source of further deep trouble. We accept the view [in the State Department] . . . that improvement is the sort of annoying thing that restless outsiders and liberal Senators are always proposing.[23]

Galbraith concluded: "No man can afford to be thought soft on communism, Castro or the Panama Canal." Rejecting "sermons from those who say we must stand firm, must never underestimate the Chinese menace," Galbraith argued that rather than a "second generation policy . . . to be firmly immobile on China," the United States needed a "third-generation policy . . . that accepts reality—and avoids positions which are the prelude to failure."[24]

While China figured prominently in his critique of the Cold War consensus, Galbraith was assailing the consensus on a much broader front. From Panama to Pakistan to India to "the poor countries," Galbraith assailed U.S. policy as trapped in "second generation thinking."[25] Galbraith concluded:

> We will not be defiled or defeated or destroyed if we do business with governments very different from our own. And certainly we won't be hurt by bringing the defense of our policy abreast of the course we actually follow.[26]

The media, on the other hand, was largely supportive of the administration's use of containment to justify escalation in Vietnam, and frequently echoed these arguments. The day of the Flaming Dart reprisals, *Washington Post* writer Donald S. Sagoria asked, "Is the domino theory valid?" His answer was firmly founded in the arguments the administration had been making since early 1964 for U.S. military intervention in Vietnam. "Defeat for the United States in Vietnam," Sagoria wrote, " . . . would almost certainly encourage the Chinese and other communist parties in under-developed areas to believe that the Chinese model of 'liberation war' is neither so risky nor pointless, as the Russians have contended." Furthermore, a loss in South Vietnam would advance "China's major goal . . . to remove U.S. influence from Asia" by showing the United States to be a "paper tiger." The loss of South Vietnam, Sagoria wrote, would also result in "increased pressure on other pro-Western countries in Asia such as Thailand and Malaysia." A loss would likewise force the Soviets to "give increased moral support to such wars [of liberation]" to compete with the Chinese for favor in the Communist World.[27] Sagoria concluded by providing a more concise statement of the need for containment of communism in Southeast Asia than even the administration had to date been able to provide:

> The problem of how to contain Communism in Vietnam emerges inescapably as part of the much larger problem of how to contain Chinese power in Asia. While still in the minor leagues as a global power, China is now close to being the dominant regional power in Asia. The U.S. must either reconcile itself to this development, or be prepared for a long and costly effort.[28]

Even the editors of the *Eugene Register-Guard*, the newspaper of perennial dissenter Senator Wayne Morse's adopted hometown of Eugene, Oregon, were forced to admit the compelling logic of the domino theory. A February 11, 1965, editorial pilloried the "'moral commitment' argument" for U.S. military intervention in Vietnam and warned of "a full-scale war with the Chinese" if escalation continued. Yet, the *Register-Guard* still acknowledged the need for intervention in Vietnam: "The easy answer is to get out of there," the editorial said, "except for the 'domino theory.'" While the theory was "vigorously disputed," the editor noted that the domino theory "also has its knowledgeable and cautious champions." The editor also noted the growing communist threat in Cambodia, Thailand, Indonesia, and the Philippines.[29] The editorial then made a prediction every bit as dire as those made by Secretary of Defense Robert McNamara the previous year:

> If the domino theory is valid, leading to a bridging of the territory between China and Indonesia, the world would have a new and horrible iron curtain, stretched almost the length of the far Pacific. About half the people of the world live along this route, from Siberia to somewhere south of the equator. . . .
> If the domino theory is valid, America, in pulling out of that part of the world, would be taking the first step toward

the complete isolation of the Atlantic community from the Pacific community. Then the world would, indeed, be two armed camps.[30]

After the Flaming Dart attacks were executed, most in the press remained supportive of the administration and its arguments for intervention. Perhaps the only negative reaction came from James Reston of the *New York Times*. Still, Reston did not challenge the administration's use of the ideology of containment to justify increased U.S. military intervention in Vietnam. Instead Reston criticized the administration's lack of frankness on the nature of the escalation. Reston's February editorial insisted that the president "call a spade a bloody shovel" and admit that the United States "is in an undeclared and unexplained war" in Vietnam.[31]

By almost two to one, Americans supported the president's retaliatory air strikes,[32] and a February Harris Poll found that 60 percent of Americans had a positive opinion of how the president was "handling the situation in Vietnam."[33] More importantly, for the first time in a February Gallup poll, a plurality of Americans accepted Vietnam as "the most important problem facing [the United States] today."[34] And perhaps most importantly for the administration, the public accepted the president's justifications for U.S. military intervention based on containment of communism. The same Harris poll cited above showed that the American public agreed with the president that either the "Chinese Communists" (53 percent) or "North Vietnam[ese]" (26 percent) were "behind the attacks by the Viet Cong." Likewise, Americans, by 82 percent, accepted President Johnson's explanation that bombing was being executed to "punish communists" and about the same percentage believed that he was "right" to do so. Fifty-six percent believed it was "very important" to "win victory over aggression," 63 percent believed that intervening in Vietnam was "very important" to "defend the security of the United States," 66 percent believed it was "very important" to "help a non-communist nation resist communism," and 71 percent believed it was "very important" to "stop communist infiltration."

Seventy-nine percent of Americans also embraced the tenets of the domino theory, saying it was "very important" to "try to keep the communists from taking over all of Southeast Asia." The same percentage believed that if the United States withdrew "from Vietnam the Communists would take over all of Southeast Asia."[35] The same February Gallup poll cited above showed that 54 percent of Americans believed that if the United States withdrew forces from Vietnam, "Communists would go into Thailand and other countries [and] China [would] take over all of South East Asia."[36]

The American public's prescription for the war in Vietnam was bombing the North until it agreed to a settlement. Fully 75 percent of Americans favored "the United States asking for negotiations to settle the war in Vietnam," while 69 percent favored the continued bombing of North Vietnam "if [it was] the only way to save South Vietnam." Fifty-three percent believed that "stepped-up bombing in North Vietnam could lead to a negotiated settlement." Americans remained divided on the need for more U.S. ground troops. Only 48 percent supported "sending a large number of American troops to help save South Vietnam." Only 12 percent favored carrying "the war into North Vietnam at the risk of bringing Red China in."[37]

Only three days after the Pleiku attacks and the Flaming Dart reprisals, the Viet Cong attacked a hotel in Qui Nhon that was being used as a U.S. enlisted men's barracks. The attack caused the building to collapse, killing twenty-three soldiers and wounding twenty-one more, the largest number of American casualties in a single attack to date in the war. In response, Johnson approved a sustained bombing campaign dubbed Operation "Rolling Thunder" by the Pentagon. However, due to a series of technical and political delays, bombing did not actually begin until March 2, 1965.[38]

Soon after the beginning of Operation Rolling Thunder, the administration introduced not just advisors but American ground forces into South Vietnam. First, Johnson ordered the deployment of two Marine battalions to protect the massive American airbase at Danang in South Vietnam. About a month after the beginning of Rolling Thunder, on April 3, 1965, after a dramatic Viet Cong bombing of the U.S. embassy in Saigon, Johnson sent more Marines, this time to the region around Hue, with the expanded mission to conduct independent offensive operations.[39] The administration made no official announcement of this change of mission, a tacit escalation of the American military effort in Vietnam.

Instead, throughout the Rolling Thunder escalation and the first deployment of U.S. Marines to Vietnam, the administration continued to use the containment of communism to justify increasing U.S. military intervention. Most in the media embraced and frequently echoed these justifications. However, this period saw two significant changes in the texture of the debate over the growing Vietnam War. First, while they continued to occasionally cite the Tonkin Gulf Resolution as a legal justification for escalation, during this period the administration gradually made a decision to move away from tit-for-tat reprisals in response to North Vietnamese and Viet Cong provocations and toward a more regular program of escalation. As a result, tit-for-tat justifications for escalation began to recede from administration rhetoric. Second, some in the media, as well as a few radical dissenters, began to make their opposition to escalation heard, focusing their attacks on the administration's use of containment to justify escalation in Vietnam or the ideology of containment itself.

Throughout this period, the president continued to use the ideology of containment to justify increasing U.S. military intervention in Vietnam. In a speech to the National Industrial Conference in mid-February—after the attack at Qui Nhon but before the start of Rolling Thunder—the president emphasized the continuing communist aggression against South Vietnam. America, the president said, had joined "in the defense and protection of freedom of a brave people who are under attack that is controlled and that is directed from outside their country." The president also reiterated a theme he had last used in mid-1964, that "we have no ambition there for ourselves. We seek no dominion. We seek no conquest. We seek no wider war."

The president may have been saying publicly that he wanted "no wider war," but inside the administration, a consensus was forming to move beyond tit-for-tat retaliation in response to North Vietnamese provocations and toward a more regular program of escalation. George Ball, at the time perhaps the only opponent of escalation within the White House, opposed the stepwise, tit-for-tat escalation of U.S. military intervention in Vietnam on the grounds that it created a cycle of provocation and retaliation until "finally, you're going to find the war is running you, and we're not running the war."[40] Benjamin H. Read, in an oral interview from 1970, claims that Rolling Thunder was the beginning of a transition from tit-for-tat reprisals to a deliberate escalation of the war independent of North Vietnamese actions.[41] He said:

> Retaliation is not an attractive premise to base major action on, and you're comparing apples and oranges in the most classic sense if you're trying to judge whether to strike X target because of a barracks' dynamiting or the blowing up of a bus. And as I recall it, in two or three weeks after the Pleiku bombing, everyone wanted to get away from trying to rationalize it on the ground of retaliating for a specific incident. The incidents were coming thick and fast, and the bombing program began to be looked at as a regular course of action.[42]

However, the administration had not yet broken completely from tit-for-tat escalation. In an April 1965 National Security Action Memorandum, McGeorge Bundy explained that the intensity and tempo of the Rolling Thunder bombing would be driven by the rate of Viet Cong operations. The government, Bundy wrote, should even be prepared to "slow the pace [of the bombing] in the unlikely event VC slacked off sharply for what appeared to be more than a temporary operational lull."[43]

The president also continued to used the the tit-for-tat precedent set by the Gulf of Tonkin incident to justify the Rolling Thunder escalation. He insisted that U.S. military actions would continue as long as they were "justified and . . . made necessary by the continuing aggression of others." Yet like the retaliatory air strikes after the Gulf of Tonkin incident, the president added, "These actions will be measured and fitting and adequate."[44]

However, the administration also used containment to justify this escalation. The day after the president's speech, Secretary McNamara testified behind closed doors before the House Armed Services Committee. According to the Associated Press,[45] the secretary said:

> The stakes in South Viet Nam are far greater than the loss of one small country to communism. . . . We may be certain that as soon as they had established their control over South Viet Nam, the Communists would press their subversive operations in Laos and then in Thailand. . . . We would have to face this same problem all over again in another place or permit them to have all of Southeast Asia by default.[46]

The AP story added that McNamara insisted that South Vietnam was the place to stop the "Chinese Communist position favoring violent revolution," lest it spread to other regions. The Associated Press concluded, "McNamara appeared to embrace the 'domino theory' which holds that a stand must be made against communism lest one vulnerable Asian nation after another fall into the Red orbit."[47]

Some in the media began to challenge the administration's arguments for escalation based on containment. A front-page *New York Times* article from February 28, 1965, criticized the administration's evidence for northern complicity in the war in South Vietnam. The article recalled a recent State Department white paper describing increased North Vietnamese support of the Viet Cong. The *Times* was skeptical of the "major new evidence" that the State Department had provided about "the sinking . . . of a . . . ship loaded with Communist made small arms and ammunition," since the ship was "not much above the Oriental junk class." The article warned that "American policy has plunged dangerously beyond the one enunciated . . . by the President and Secretary McNamara of limiting ourselves to retaliatory action and shunning a wider war." The *Times* concluded by wondering what "massive air strikes would accomplish . . . except large-scale civilian casualties in industrial centers and ports," especially in the light of "the absence of any stable government in Saigon to fight or even to speak in the name of the South Vietnamese people."[48]

Otherwise, the press generally supported the administration's use of containment to justify the Rolling Thunder escalation. The Spartanburg, South Carolina, *Herald-Journal* recounted statements made by President Kennedy—highlighting their congruity with Johnson's later statements—to reinforce President Johnson's argument that he was simply continuing the policies of his predecessors. The article quoted Kennedy in September 1963, just before his death, saying that it "would be a great mistake" to withdraw from South Vietnam. With no hint of derogation, the *Herald-Journal* wrote that Kennedy subscribed to "the 'domino theory' in Southeast Asia"; the claimed Kennedy believed that the loss of South Vietnam would not only give China "an improved geographic position for a guerrilla assault on Malaya but would also give the impression that the wave of the future in Southeast Asia was China and the Communists." The editors then favorably compared these statements with statements by Johnson from January 1964 that "neutralization of South Viet Nam would only be another name for a Communist takeover" and with Johnson's February 17, 1965, statement that continuing U.S. military intervention in South Vietnam was "made necessary by the continuing aggression of others."[49]

On the eve of the initiation of Operation Rolling Thunder, the American public remained firmly behind the president. By late February, according to a Gallup poll, 85 percent of Americans said that they had "heard or read about the recent developments in Vietnam." Nearly two-thirds of Americans believed that "the U.S. is handling affairs in South Vietnam as well as could be expected." Moreover, 78 percent believed that the United States should "continue its present efforts in Vietnam" rather than "pull out." And despite the administration's assurances that it wanted no wider war in Vietnam, a narrow majority of Americans also expected that "the situation in Vietnam is likely to lead to a bigger war."[50]

Like tit-for-tat justifications, the use of the Tonkin Gulf Resolution as a justification for escalation was beginning to recede from the administration's rhetoric. State Department spokesman Robert McCloskey used the ideology of military containment as a justification in his announcement of the beginning of Operation Rolling Thunder. McCloskey explained, "What we have in Viet-Nam is armed aggression from the North against the Republic of Viet-Nam." The United States was "engaged" with South Vietnam "in collective defense against that armed aggression." McCloskey did also cite the Tonkin Gulf Resolution as a justification for Rolling Thunder—the only reference the administration made to this congressional endorsement of U.S. military intervention during the Rolling Thunder escalation. McCloskey said that the administration's legal basis for its intervention in Vietnam was the UN Charter, "the constitutional powers of the President and . . . the congressional resolution of August 1964 [the Tonkin Gulf Resolution]."[51]

That same day, Secretary of State Rusk made a much more impassioned defense of U.S. military intervention in South Vietnam using only the ideology of containment. While he insisted that he was not talking about "something up in the clouds called the domino theory," Rusk once more reiterated this theory's precepts. "Defeat of these aggressions is not only essential if Laos and South Viet-Nam are to remain independent," Rusk insisted, "it is important to the security of Southeast Asia as a whole." He reminded his audience that "Thailand has already been proclaimed as the next target by Peiping," as part of its "proclamation of militant, world revolution."[52]

The deployment of Marines to Vietnam after the beginning of Rolling Thunder generated some additional media opposition. Like other opposition during this period, opposition from the media was focused on the administration's use of containment to justify increasing U.S. military intervention in Vietnam. Just as the Spartanburg, South Carolina, *Herald-Journal* had previously used quotes from

Kennedy and Johnson to praise the administration's handling of the conflict in Vietnam, the paper now indicted members of the administration with their own pronouncements. The article recalled that McNamara, in a joint statement with then Chairman of the Joint Chiefs of Staff Taylor, had promised in October 1963, "The major part of the U.S. military task can be completed by the end of 1965."[53] The article also reminded readers that, in February 1964, McNamara said:

> I don't believe that we as a nation should assume the primary responsibility. . . . Our responsibility is not to substitute for the Vietnamese but to train them.[54]

Likewise, the article quoted Ambassador Lodge in June 1964 as saying that he didn't "see the need for more troops in Viet Nam." The article concluded by quoting the most extreme version of the domino theory asserted by the administration.[55] In September 1964, Ambassador Taylor said:

> It would be a major disaster for the United States to withdraw from Viet Nam. We could be pushed out of the western Pacific back to Honolulu.[56]

In response to the introduction of Marines in Vietnam, the *Eugene Register-Guard* also made an about-face from tepid support to outright hostility to the domino theory in its March 21, 1965, editorial. The editorial assailed the "so-called dominos theory, much and loosely thrown about by American pundits and politicians." The *Eugene Register-Guard* now pilloried this theory as positing that "the fall of South Viet Nam would, like one domino toppling all the others in a line, lead to the communization of Asia" pushing "America's line of defense . . . back to Pearl Harbor." The editorial claimed that the theory was doubted by many and that it was "a more pessimistic view than the facts warrant." The editorial claimed that the theory had captured the "minds of the U.S. strategists who are responsible for the

recent series of bombing raids against North Viet Nam." In direct contradiction to their editorial earlier in the year, the editors of the *Eugene
Register-Guard* now rejected this thinking, writing, "South Viet Nam
is not now and never was a strategic link in the chain the United States
built to contain Communist China."[57]

Yet, the editors of the *Eugene Register-Guard* still could not bring
themselves to say that South Vietnam should be abandoned. The editors wrote: "American prestige has been laid so on the line that defeat
has become virtually an unacceptable alternative to more and bigger
war." America, the editors continued, was faced with a "dilemma." On
the one hand, the communists were winning the guerilla war in the
field and had "shown no indication they intend to lose over the conference table a battle they are winning in the field." On the other hand,
"The United States . . . must demonstrate graphically to the Chinese
Communists, as it did to the Russians [during the Cuban missile cri-
sis], that they can be beaten."[58] The United States, the editors concluded, had no choice but to fight and win in Vietnam.

The Rolling Thunder escalation and the deployment of Marines
also generated the first significant opposition from radical dissenters.
Like opposition from the media, this opposition focused on President
Johnson's use of military containment to justify U.S. military intervention in Vietnam. However, radical dissenters also attacked the
broader ideology of military containment itself. In a March edition
of his newsletter *William Winter Comments*, California-based activist
William Winter attacked what he called a history of "self-defeating"
policies in U.S. relations with Communist China—from backing
"the Kuomintang of Chiang Kai-shek" simply "because it was 'anti-
Communist'" to denying China a seat in the United Nations. [59] But
his main attack was on the ideology of military containment itself.
Winter wrote: "After World War II it was accepted in Washington
that unless there were a display of American war power the Soviet
Union would expand its hegemony through military force." However,
Winter wrote, "since Stalin died, and the nuclear age became real-
ity," two things had become evident which undermined this idea.
First, Winter wrote, "The Soviet Union is no longer bent on military

aggression . . . because . . . there can be no success in nuclear conflict." Second, the United States had since discovered "that giving guns to little countries around Eurasia will not frighten the Russians or thwart their plans for military attack." Echoing Hans Morgenthau's objections to the application of the strategy of containment to Southeast Asia from the previous year, Winter added: "If the Russians are impressed by American military power it is not because of our bases but because of our nuclear arsenal." Winter added that even George Kennan, supposed architect of the strategy of containment, had since rejected the policy. Winter wrote that containment had forced the United States to support undemocratic regimes like those in Thailand and Saigon and regimes that openly defied Washington, such as that in Pakistan. "The 'containment' policy," Winter concluded, "is unrealistic and does not serve America's best interests. It should be reexamined. In fact, it should be scrapped."[60]

Despite this new opposition from the media and radical dissenters, the White House seemed to believe that the American public was firmly behind them as they introduced U.S. troops into the conflict in Vietnam. In a memorandum summarizing the results of a March 1965 Harris poll, White House staffer Hayes Redmond noted that 77 percent of Americans favored "continuing air raids on [North Vietnam]." Redmond noted that the "dominant view" from the poll was still to "hold the line." Redmond concluded that there was "support for air raids and [a] clear, overwhelming mandate to send as many U.S. troops there as necessary to withstand the Viet Cong attacks during Monsoon season."[61] This conclusion was at least partially contradicted by a Gallup Poll two weeks later. Sixty-eight percent of Americans did believe that the United States was "handling affairs in Vietnam as well as could be expected." However, when asked what the United States should do next in Vietnam, only 38 percent of those who expressed an opinion believed the United States should "send in more troops" or wage "all-out war." By contrast, 22 percent believed that the United States should withdraw and 20 percent believed that the United States should "continue [its] present policy" and "hold [its] ground."[62] While more Americans wanted escalation rather than withdrawal or a continuation of the status quo, this was by no means a "clear, overwhelming mandate" to send in ground troops.

While the American public may have been divided on whether it wanted to commit ground troops in Vietnam, a contemporary Gallup poll in April still showed that two thirds of Americans supported Johnson's policies in Vietnam after the deployment of U.S. Marines.[63] In early April, public approval of the president's handling of Vietnam had slipped slightly. Immediately after Rolling Thunder began, the president had a 60 percent favorable rating for his handling of Vietnam, but by the beginning of April had slipped to 57 percent. By a margin of 60 percent, Americans did believe that U.S. troops would be required to stop "Communist infiltration of South Vietnam," but opinions remained mixed on whether the United States should take that step. Forty percent favored "sending large numbers of U.S. troops to Vietnam," while nearly the same percentage opposed such a move with the remainder not sure.[64] In his analysis of these poll results, Lou Harris summarized the sentiment of Americans at the beginning of April:

> When asked what course we should follow in Vietnam today, 20 percent said the war should be carried into North Vietnam [with ground troops] . . . as well as air raids. Thirty-one percent thought we should negotiate with a view toward getting out, but the largest single group–46 percent–say we should hold the line doing what we need to do in order to maintain strength for the democratic position in South Vietnam.[65]

The administration had not yet created a consensus behind the use of U.S. ground troops in Vietnam.

On April 7, at the urging of his staff and in order to stem the early rumblings of dissent, President Johnson gave a primetime, televised address from Johns Hopkins University about the war.[66] The address offered "unconditional discussions" and massive aid for economic development of the Mekong River area, but also promised continued American resolve to support South Vietnam.[67]

In his Johns Hopkins speech, the president once more used the ideology of military containment to justify U.S. military intervention in Vietnam. This speech did silence some of the criticism in the media of escalation. However, after this speech, Senator J. William Fulbright became the first member of Congress (besides Senators Morse and Gruening) to speak out publicly against escalation and suggest a bombing pause—a measure the administration was finally reluctantly forced to take. In his public opposition to escalation, Fulbright attacked the administration's use of containment to justify the war. This opposition was soon joined by dissent from the media and radicals. That dissent, too, was focused on applicability of the ideology of containment to Vietnam.

President Johnson's Johns Hopkins speech is most frequently remembered for its offer of negotiations and aid to North Vietnam. But, examining the speech, it was at its heart a restatement of the arguments based on containment that the administration had been making for over a year to try to convince Americans to support U.S. military intervention in Vietnam. The president blamed North Vietnam for the conflict. "The first reality," Johnson said, "is that North Viet-Nam has attacked the independent nation of South Viet-Nam. Its object is total conquest." While the president conceded that "some of the people of South Viet-Nam are participating in attacks on their own government," the president quickly added, "Trained men and supplies, orders and arms, flow in a constant stream from north to south."[68] The president said the escalation of U.S. military intervention was required "to slow down aggression."[69] Invoking the lessons of Munich, the president said:

> Let no one think for a moment that retreat from Viet-Nam would bring an end to conflict. The battle would be renewed in one country, then another. The central lesson of our time is that the appetite of aggression is never satisfied. To withdraw from one battlefield means only to prepare for the next one.[70]

In this speech, the president did return to a tit-for-tat justification for the American escalation. The president said, "In recent months attacks on South Viet-Nam were stepped up. Thus it became necessary for us to increase our response and to make attacks by air."[71] Yet this justification was now steeped in the rhetoric of military containment. Johnson said that behind North Vietnam's increased aggression was "the deepening shadow of Communist China." He continued: "The rulers in Hanoi are urged on by Peiping. . . . The contest in Viet-Nam is part of a wider pattern of aggressive purposes."[72] Johnson also answered the objections of those, like Hans Morgenthau, who the president claimed said "all our effort there will be futile—that China's power is such that it is bound to dominate all southeast Asia." Johnson responded to this reasoning by saying, "There is no end to that argument until all of the nations of Asia are swallowed up."[73]

President Johnson also once more invoked the commitments made to South Vietnam by his predecessors. "Since 1954 every American President has offered support to the people of South Viet-Nam," Johnson said, "and I intend to keep that promise."[74] But the president also painted this commitment as part of the broader commitment of the United States to contain communism across the globe. Echoing Rusk's recent arguments about Vietnam being a test of the U.S. commitments, Johnson said:

> Around the globe, from Berlin to Thailand, are people whose well-being rests in part on the belief that they can count on us if they are attacked. To leave Viet-Nam to its fate would shake the confidence of all these people in the value of an American commitment and in the value of America's word. The result would be increased unrest and instability, and even wider war.[75]

The telegrams and letters the White House received in response to the speech were very positive.[76] As a result of the speech, the White House received half as many letters and telegrams per week as it had before the speech, and those that did arrive went from five to one against the president's policies in Vietnam to four to one in favor.[77] The response to the speech from the press—including the usually critical *New York Times*—was also positive.[78] James "Scotty" Reston of the *New York Times* frequently questioned the administration's justifications for U.S.

military intervention based on the containment of communism. But after the Johns Hopkins speech, he seemed to agree with these arguments. In an article in late April, Reston embraced a major administration argument: if communists succeed in using "wars of national liberation" in Vietnam, they will use this technique in other countries as well. Likewise, Reston joined the administration in placing the blame on Communist China. "What the Soviets attempted by political pressure on Western Europe, by threats of war over Berlin, by nuclear blackmail in Cuba and by their adventure in Korea," Reston wrote, "the Chinese communists are now trying to achieve by subversion and guerrilla warfare in Viet Nam." Reston also echoed the administration's assertions that the Soviets had embraced peaceful coexistence while the Chinese had not. And while Reston insisted that "one does not have to believe in the domino theory," he provided a warning as dire as any the administration had offered about the dangers of U.S. failure in Vietnam. If China could "triumph by limited war in Viet Nam," Reston wrote, "the problem of countering limited wars from the Sea of Japan to the Persian Gulf will be even more serious than it is today." After recounting alternative proposals on how to deal with the Chinese Communist threat in Vietnam—from abandoning Southeast Asia to using nuclear weapons to abandoning all of Asia—Reston endorsed the Johnson administration's approach of "hold[ing] the populous areas of South Viet Nam with . . . [U.S.] troops if necessary and meanwhile [using] . . . [U.S.] air and naval power to demonstrate that a continuation of the aggression in South Viet Nam will cost the communists in North Viet Nam more than they will gain in the South."[79]

In the following days, members of the administration gave several more speeches reinforcing the president's arguments from his Johns Hopkins speech. In a speech to the Detroit Economic Club, Leonard Unger, former U.S. ambassador to Laos, used nearly the exact same military containment rhetoric as the president. Unger repeated the administration's warnings about wars of national liberation. Unger insisted that, while this strategy "was defeated in Malaya and the Philippines," if it was not defeated in South Vietnam, it would emerge in "Africa and Latin America."[80] Secretary of State Rusk repeated the claims of northern aggression before the American Society of International Law only a few days later.[81]

Not all of the responses to the president's Johns Hopkins speech were positive. Perhaps the first public congressional dissent (outside of the consistent dissent of Senators Morse and Gruening) came from Senator J. William Fulbright about a week after the president's Johns Hopkins speech. And the target of Fulbright's dissent was the application of the ideology of military containment to the growing war in Vietnam. In a congressional hearing a little over a week after the president's speech, Secretary Rusk's insisted that a halt in the bombing "would only encourage the aggressor and dishearten our friends who bear the brunt of battle." Fulbright disagreed with the secretary in this hearing, saying that bombing might be counterproductive by causing the North Vietnamese to "dig in" and discouraging the Soviets from negotiating. Fulbright added that the United States should stop the bombing, noting, "We could resume bombing at any time if there is no response."[82]

In an interview after this hearing, Fulbright stepped back slightly from his dissent. He claimed that he still supported the administration's policies in Vietnam (though he equated these policies with the offer of negotiations and aid to North Vietnam from President Johnson's Johns Hopkins speech rather than the administration's escalation of U.S. military intervention). However, Fulbright questioned whether the North Vietnamese had absolute control over the Viet Cong. Fulbright added, "Before the escalation goes too far, a temporary cease-fire might be advisable."[83]

Fulbright's objection drew an angry response from the administration. Secretary of Defense McNamara both rejected Fulbright's suggestion and reiterated the argument that North Vietnamese aggression drove the war in Vietnam. "We have no indications," McNamara insisted, "that a cessation of the bombing would move the North Vietnamese to discussions leading to termination of their aggression in the South."[84] Of course, McNamara was mischaracterizing Fulbright's policy suggestion; Fulbright had not suggested a "cessation" of the bombing, but rather a pause in an effort to jumpstart negotiations.

Won't This Be Rather Difficult?

Source: Charles A. Wells, *Wells Newsletter*, Newtown PA, May 1, 1965, 1.[87]

Former ambassador to India John Kenneth Galbraith publicly supported Fulbright's call for a bombing pause and, while stopping just short of accusing the president of duplicity, claimed that the bombing made the president's promise of peace negotiations from the Johns Hopkins speech harder to deliver. In a letter to the *New York Times*, Galbraith wrote that bombing "hardened the morale of those under attack" and that the "raids undercut the offer of negotiations by the President." More than counterproductive, however, Galbraith claimed the raids were ineffectual since "they are not directed at cities, something that the President has scrupulously resisted." Presaging later attacks on the effect of the escalation in Vietnam on U.S. allies, Galbraith concluded, "Most importantly, the attacks are alienating our friends in Asia, Europe, and Africa and quite possibly strengthening and consolidating our opposition."[85]

The administration's refusal to implement a temporary bombing halt to give peace negotiations a chance also drew attacks from radical dissenters—attacks centered on the applicability of the ideology of containment to the growing war in Vietnam. Charles A. Wells published a political cartoon in his *Wells Newsletter* entitled "Won't This Be Rather Difficult?" depicting Lyndon Johnson running alongside Vietnamese villagers fleeing from American bombers. In a jab at President Johnson's Johns Hopkins speech, Johnson held a document in his hand labeled "[South] East Asia Aid Program."[86]

The extended caption beneath this cartoon claimed that "the whole world has been offended by our bombing of North Vietnam—the greatest, richest and most powerful nation on earth pouncing with the most ultra-modern weapons on a tiny impoverished illiterate Communist dictatorship." The caption also attacked the administration's dishonesty about the prosecution of the war. Wells warned, "Don't let our own propaganda brainwash you—civilians are being slaughtered."[88]

Fulbright's relatively narrow attack on the bombing of North Vietnam was also joined by much broader criticism from the press of the administration's use of the containment of communism to justify U.S. military intervention in Vietnam. An April 22, 1965, editorial from Fulbright's home state in the *Arkansas Gazette* began by reprinting a line from a May 9, 1954, editorial that criticized the French government in power during the French defeat at Dienbienphu for "the vacillating, unrealistic policies of their own ramshackle government which brought these magnificent soldiers to their terrible defeat." This new editorial then claimed that Westerners did not "understand Southeast Asia better now than they did 11 years ago." And while the editorial claimed that Americans were fond of mocking the French, who "were stupid to have attempted to cling to empire when the days of empire had passed," this stupidity was born of the common "Western delusion that Western arms could contain Asian aspirations."[89] The editorial followed by asking a tough question:

> How does one save from what we Americans view as a foreign invasion a country which cannot maintain the security of its own capital or of any other sizable piece of real estate[?][90]

The editorial warned: "If we intend to win it we had better get ready to run, and to man, the whole shooting match ourselves." The *Gazette* believed this was the making of "another Korea." This editorial also questioned whether air attacks could achieve "stabilization of the military situation in South Vietnam," prophetically adding, "If they fail to achieve [stability] soon, are we simply to extend them indefinitely?" The *Gazette* concluded by warning that bombing would eventually provoke a Chinese military response.[91]

Venerable dean of the Washington press corps Walter Lippmann challenged the administration's dogmatic adherence to "the so-called domino theory." He noted that, despite applying "this theory ever more vigorously," the United States was "not only isolated but increasingly opposed by every major power in Asia." Noting the objections of the major powers in Asia, from Pakistan to the Soviet Union, he wrote that "the dominoes are indeed falling, and they are falling away from us," because Asians perceived the U.S. war in Vietnam as "a war by white men from the west against nonwhite men in Asia." Lippmann's prescription was that the United States reject its instinctive adherence to "the white man's burden" and show the same enlightenment it was showing in its "illumination, which has come so recently here at home, that the American Negro must become a full, not a second class, citizen."[92]

Lippmann's critique of the application of the "white man's burden" to South Vietnam and the resultant reverse domino theory[93] echoed throughout the media. For instance, a *St. Petersburg Times* editorial claimed that the chief handicap to American troops' efforts was "the color of their skin." Explicitly dismissing the administration's arguments for U.S. military intervention in Vietnam based on military containment—particularly the administration's claims that it had no "interest in Asian territory" and that the current policy in Vietnam was part of a "long history of U.S. support of Asia for the Asians"—the editor claimed that Asians saw the growing war in Vietnam as "white men shooting Asians." Without explicitly citing Lippmann, the editorial also echoed the theme that the result of this policy was that the United States was experiencing a "reverse domino theory" of diminishing influence in Asia.[94]

Yet while the editors of the *St. Petersburg Times* agreed with Lippmann's analysis that the United States was critically handicapped in its war in South Vietnam because of the skincolor of its troops, the editors still believed that the Vietnam War must be fought. The editors quoted "Malaysian Prime Minister Tunku Abdul Rahman, his own country under guerrilla attack by Indonesia with Red China's blessing,"[95] as saying:

> I feel that the American action to help South Viet Nam is a proper one because unless America supports South Viet Nam there is no chance for this Republic [of Malaysia] to survive.[96]

This comment was an implicit proof of the domino theory; a Southeast Asian leader believed that, if South Vietnam fell to communism, his country would fall as well. As a result, the *St. Petersburg Times* endorsed "the core of U.S. objectives in Viet Nam," to force North Vietnam to respect the "national borders" of South Vietnam and not "interfere" in its affairs.[97]

Still, the power of the Lippmann's "reverse domino theory" argument finally forced the White House to respond. In a news conference the president was asked if "the United States is losing, rather than making, friends around the world, with its policy in Viet-Nam—sort of a falling domino theory in reverse?" The president responded that, following his Johns Hopkins speech, he had received "almost a universal approval" from U.S. allies (a deceptive statement since many of these leaders approved of the president's offer of negotiations rather than his continuing U.S. military escalation). The president said that, despite the fact that "our enemies would have you believe that we are following policies that are ill-advised," the United States was "following the same policies in Asia that we followed in Europe, that we followed in Turkey and Greece and Iran." The United States was "resisting aggression" in Vietnam and would continue "whether we make friends or lose friends."[98]

While tit-for-tat justifications for U.S. military intervention in Vietnam were rapidly receding from the administration's rhetoric, in this 28 April 1965 news conference, President Johnson once more used the tit-for-tat precedent set by the Gulf of Tonkin incident to justify his escalation. As with the air strikes after the Gulf of Tonkin incident, the president said, the United States had used its "great power with the utmost restraint . . . in the face of the most outrageous and brutal provocation against Vietnamese and against Americans alike." The president also reminded reporters that the United States had made no further escalations for six months after the Gulf of Tonkin airstrikes.[99] Johnson claimed that the North Vietnamese' a answer to this extraordinary restraint had been:

> . . . attack, and explosions, and indiscriminate murder. So it soon became clear that our restraint was viewed as weakness; our desire to limit conflict was viewed as a prelude to our surrender.[100]

Johnson concluded that the United States had to strike because it "could no longer stand by while attacks mounted and while the bases of the attackers were immune from reply."[101] Johnson later added:

> As long as they bomb in South Viet-Nam, as long as they bomb our sports arenas, and our theaters, and our embassies, and kill our women and our children and the Vietnamese soldiers, several thousand of whom have been killed since the first of the year, we think that we are justified in trying to slow down that operation and make them realize that it is very costly, and that their aggression should cease.[102]

The president also continued to use containment to justify escalation. In this same news conference, President Johnson explicitly invoked Munich in warning about the dangers of ignoring aggression:

> This is the clearest lesson of our time. From Munich until today we have learned that to yield to aggression brings only greater threats—and more destructive war. To stand firm is the only guarantee of lasting peace.[103]

North Vietnam was guilty of aggression, by the "covert infiltration of a regular combat unit of the North Vietnamese Army into South Viet-Nam." Likewise, Johnson said, "The great bulk of the weapons [which] the Viet Cong are using and with which they are supplied come from external sources."[104] In the final analysis, the president said:

> Independent South Vietnam has been attacked by North Vietnam. The object of that attack is total conquest. Defeat in South Vietnam would deliver a friendly nation to terror and repression.
>
> It would encourage and spur on those who seek to conquer all free nations that are within their reach. Our own welfare, our own freedom, would be in great danger.[105]

Still, the president insisted, America's "purpose is peaceful settlement. That purpose is to resist aggression. That purpose is to avoid a wider war." The president insisted, "Aggression [had] been halted . . . under President Truman, under President Eisenhower, under President Kennedy, and it will be true again in southeast Asia."[106]

The president also responded directly to Senator Fulbright's suggestion of a bombing pause in this news conference. The president was reminded by a reporter, "A number of critics of your Viet-Nam policy say they support our presence in South Viet-Nam, but do not support the bombing raids to the North." The president responded by wondering aloud "how some people can be so concerned with our bombing a cold bridge of steel and concrete in North Viet-Nam, but never open their mouths about a bomb being placed in our embassy in South Viet-Nam." He added, "There are not many civilians involved in a radar station, but we do try to make it ineffective so that they cannot plot our planes and shoot our boys out of the skies."[107] These arguments may have been persuasive to the American people, but they were also deceptive. There would, inevitably, be civilian casualties as a result of the U.S. bombing of North Vietnam. In late 1967, when Americans were confronted with indisputable evidence of civilian casualties, these comments would return to haunt the president and damage his credibility with the American people.

While dissent in the media was growing, most in the Washington press corps remained supportive of the president's use of the containment of communism to justify U.S. military intervention in Vietnam. During this same press conference, one journalist asked, "Do you think any of the participants in the national discussion on Viet-Nam could appropriately be likened to the appeasers of twenty-five or thirty years ago?" The question echoed statements the president had himself made about the lessons of Munich and those who had refused to acknowledge the threat of prewar Germany. Another journalist asked the president to "evaluate . . . the threat that has been posed by Red China to send volunteers into Viet-Nam if we escalate the war further?"[108] The question reinforced the administration argument that China was behind North Vietnamese aggression against South Vietnam. While the president demurred, not answering either question directly, the questions themselves supported the administration's arguments.

The Memphis, Tennessee, *Commercial Appeal* both supported the administration's arguments for U.S. military intervention in Vietnam and attacked Senator Fulbright's suggestion of a bombing halt. The editorial echoed five key elements of the administration's arguments for U.S. military intervention in Vietnam: "the infiltration of arms and troops from North Vietnam continues," "the Hanoi government maintains its close control over Viet Cong strategy," Peking and Moscow were also complicit in the war in Vietnam, "Red China and North Vietnam are embarked on an attempt to prove the efficacy of so-called wars of liberation," and "if they [China and North Vietnam] can gain control of South Vietnam there will be more such wars." The *Commercial Appeal* added that "the [Operation Rolling Thunder] air strikes have contributed significantly to an improvement in South Vietnamese morale." The editors wrote that Senator Fulbright knew all of these facts and, further, knew that "there has been no . . . attempt by any of the Communist powers to indicate an interest in Vietnam negotiation." Yet, the editorial charged, Fulbright was "unseemly" in creating "the impression among Americans that some solution might be possible if only we relaxed the pressure on North Vietnam." The *Commercial Appeal* added that Senator Fulbright's call for a bombing pause discouraged "the international support which the United States is seeking for the Saigon government."[109]

Other supporters of the president's policies in Vietnam also echoed his use of containment. In early May, Arthur H. Dean, chief negotiator during the Korean War, joined the debate on a bombing pausing firmly on the side of the administration. In a letter to the editor of the *New York Times*, Dean unequivocally echoed the administration's claim that "the Chinese Communists under Mao Tse-tung have aided and abetted Ho Chi Minh of North Vietnam in arming and building up the guerrilla forces infiltrating and operating in South Vietnam and Laos." Dean conceded that the North Vietnamese Communists "may or may not be able to control" the National Liberation Front, but still called the Viet Cong "guerrilla insurgents who are not only Communists but agents of North Vietnam."[110] Likewise, Dean repeated the administration's connection of the domino theory to the credibility of the United States' worldwide commitments.

> A defeat for us in Southeast Asia would have disastrous consequences for Thailand, Burma, Malaysia and Indonesia. The fall of Southeast Asia to the Communists—with resultant control of sea and air power—would certainly render much more difficult our ability to carry out our treaty obligations to parties in the SEATO, Australia and New Zealand. Minority parties in the Philippines to the East, and Formosa, Japan and Korea to the North might then demand that we get rid of mutual security treaties and of our bases in those countries so that they would be free to negotiate with Communist China. [111]

It was in the midst of this debate over a bombing pause that Secretary McNamara held a news conference and was famously asked whether he was "annoyed" that the growing war in South Vietnam had begun to be referred to as "McNamara's war." What is frequently missed was that McNamara's response to this question was yet another invocation of the ideology of containment to justify the war in Vietnam. McNamara said that he was happy to be associated with "a war that is being fought to preserve the freedom of a very brave people, an independent nation." McNamara also used this opportunity to claim that not just the Communist Chinese but also the Soviets endorsed wars of liberation "to subvert independent nations." McNamara concluded: "It is a strategy I feel we should oppose, and, while it is not my war, I don't object to my name being associated with it."[112]

Most Americans rejected the idea of a bombing pause in late April 1965. When asked whether the United States "should continue to bomb North Vietnam," 74 percent believed that the bombing "should continue." Likewise, two-thirds of Americans still believed that the United States "should . . . [be] involved with our military forces in Southeast Asia." However, there was still no clear consensus behind introducing large numbers of U.S. ground troops into the conflict in Vietnam. Only 35 percent of Americans supported sending in "more troops" or "all-out war" in Vietnam. By contrast, 20 percent wanted to "continue [the] present policy" in Vietnam and the same number wanted to "withdraw" (down 2 percent from the beginning of the month).[113]

Despite its disdain for the idea—and public opinion which opposed the a bombing halt—the administration would, only a few days later, bow to media pressure and implement the bombing pause Fulbright had suggested. Pulitzer Prize–winning journalist Arthur Krock criticized the administration not for its reversal but for its assault on the suggestion in the first place. In the article, Krock reported that the highest officials engaged in a "round of shooting-from-the-hip with Fulbright's suggestion as their target" before the administration actually embraced the suggestion and temporarily halted bombing. Krock described these attacks as an "instant hostility" that the sober idea of a temporary bombing halt did not merit. Krock cited Rusk as dismissing the idea on the grounds that "it would only encourage an aggressor and discourage our friends." Krock wrote that McNamara misrepresented Fulbright's suggestion as a "termination of the strikes," when Fulbright had in fact only recommended "a temporary ceasefire." Both

McNamara and Rusk, Krock added, had warned that a halt "would dishearten a brave people." Krock concluded by mocking the administration, noting that their deep philosophical objections to a bombing halt expired exactly twenty days after they began.[114]

Throughout the controversy over a bombing halt, radical dissenters continued to attack the administration's use of military containment to justify intervention in Vietnam. Charles A. Wells, in his *Wells Newsletter*, argued that it was Western opposition to the Vietnamese revolution that made the insurgents in Vietnam turn to communism. The United States' error in backing South Vietnam, Wells wrote, was adhering to "the unsound thesis that anybody who's against communism would make a good ally." The United States compounded its error by using tactics that matched "the insidious Red terror with napalm bombs and shrapnel, wiping out whole villages to get at a few Vietcong Communists—whom we usually missed." More importantly, Wells criticized the application of the military containment model to what he called "Asia's revolution" and attacked the "dangerous fable that a revolution can be subdued by force of arms." Comparing the indigenous war in Vietnam to the American, French, and Russian revolutions, Wells claimed that the Western motivation for stopping Asian revolutions was "so that the profitable exploitation of Asia's people and resources might continue."[115] This new, anti-imperialist critique of the Vietnam War presaged the arguments the Students for a Democratic Society and other radical dissenters would only begin to make later in the year.

Wells's prescription was threefold. "First," Wells wrote, "the U.S. air attacks on North Vietnam should cease. . . . Certainly if our intentions are to help people, we should stop killing them." Wells' second suggestion answered Walter Lippmann's argument that white men could not quell Asian conflicts. Wells wrote that "Asian allies" should be sent into South Vietnam "under the auspices of the United Nations to replace our white U.S. military units whose presence to most illiterate Vietnamese peasants is indistinguishable from that of the French." Only then, Wells wrote, could "the Mekong Delta project and all of its numerous subsidiaries . . . go into full action" and only then could "President Johnson's dramatic call for "unconditional negotiations" swing the weight of moral force at last to our side." Wells concluded: "Let the Communists attempt to block these efforts in Southeast Asia—if they dare."[116] Thus, in the final analysis, Wells was not rejecting the goal of blocking communist expansion in Vietnam, only the contemporary U.S. tactics for achieving that goal.

With the initiation of Rolling Thunder, a small but noticeable wave of anti-war sentiment began to move through the United States. In Congress, Senator J. William Fulbright began to speak openly against the administration's policy in Vietnam. The editorial pages of a number of newspapers, led by the *New York Times*, began to protest against the escalating conflict. And the University of Michigan held its first twelve-hour marathon "teach-in" against the war.[117] The primary target of these critics was the administration's use of the ideology of military containment of communism to justify U.S. military escalation in Vietnam.

The teach-in in Michigan was just one of a number of public academic events aimed at changing U.S. policy in Vietnam. Similar teach-ins and academic protest events occurred across the country. These events were probably most significant in that they represented a dramatic broadening of the scope of public debate over foreign policy. These academic dissenters were questioning Cold War precepts that had seldom been publicly challenged before. This was, in fact, a broad assault on the Cold War consensus and, while these scholars probably did not realize it at the time, they were firing the first volley in a foreign policy revolution. These academics had launched a frontal assault on the prevailing foreign policy paradigm and its application to the most important foreign policy challenge of the day. However, despite extensive media coverage of many of these events, this dissent had little effect on the American public opinion about the administration's policies in Vietnam.

Dissent in academia had been steadily growing even before the teach-ins, throughout early 1965. Hans Morgenthau, in an article for the *New Republic*, challenged the exclusive right of "liberty" over "communism" to the hearts of Asians. He wrote that liberty had won "the battle for the minds of men in Central and Western Europe" where "in popular aspiration political liberty has taken precedence over all other needs." But, he added, communism was bound to win in Asia, where "its tenets of social, economic and political equality have appealed to people for whom the removal of unequality [sic] has been the most urgent aspiration." This problem was compounded, Morgenthau wrote, by geography. Morgenthau concluded: "The restored power of China . . . makes an unanswerable case for Chinese influence in Asia."[118]

In an April article in *New York Times* magazine, Morgenthau challenged the notion that the United States could contain China in the conventional sense. He wrote: "While China is obviously no match for the United States in over-all power, China is largely immune to the specific types of power in which the superiority of the United States consists." He added, "To be defeated, China has to be conquered."[119] Morgenthau concluded:

> Physical conquest would require the deployment of millions of American soldiers on the mainland of Asia. No American military leader has ever advocated a course of action so fraught with incalculable risks, so uncertain of outcome, requiring sacrifices so out of proportion to the interests at stake and the benefits to be expected.[120]

Morgenthau was hardly the only academic to dissent against the growing escalation. A gathering of Asian studies scholars in San Francisco on April 2, 1965, produced a petition to the president signed by dozens of academics from across the United States. The petition was a direct attack on the application of the ideology of containment to the conflict in Southeast Asia; it expressed the scholars' concern that the United States had "taken a dangerous step forward through our policy of increasing escalation of the war, one which puts us on a direct collision course with China," a war from which "Communist China, like the Soviet Union in the wake of World War II, would emerge stronger than before."[121] The scholars believed that the U.S. policy in Southeast Asia rested on "three questionable assumptions":

> First . . . that the Soviet Union will, in a showdown, not support Communist China, and that therefore American power

can punish China with impunity. . . . Second . . . that China and North Vietnam, when confronted with punishing destruction, will surrender to force. The history of these two nations indicates just the opposite. . . . Third . . . that the existence of the war will create conditions for stability in South Vietnam, strengthen the South Vietnam army and create better conditions for winning the war in the South. The Viet Cong are powerful because of broad support from the Vietnamese peasantry, and because the latter have been alienated from the government by cruelty, impotence, and selfishness.[122]

These scholars insisted that U.S. policy in Southeast Asia was ultimately self-defeating because, while there were "'doves' and 'hawks' in Hanoi, Peking, and Moscow, just as in our own country," the communist doves' arguments were weakened by "America's implacable hostility" toward the communist world.[123]

This latter argument was echoed by Hans Morgenthau in a *New Republic* article published on May 1, 1965, only days before his appearance at a Washington teach-in. Morgenthau wrote that the U.S. intervention in Vietnam was making it harder for "those who have been identified with Khrushchev's policy of peaceful coexistence" to resist the calls for intervention from the Soviet "faction that favors the hard line of the Chinese."[124] Morgenthau concluded:

> The bombing of North Vietnam, a complete failure as an inducement to bring Hanoi to the negotiating table, is likely to succeed in bringing the Soviet Union to the battlefields of Southeast Asia.[125]

The Soviets wanted peaceful coexistence with the United States, Morgenthau wrote, but not at the cost of abdicating their position as leader of the world communist movement to the Chinese.[126]

Perhaps the most visible teach-in was the National Teach-In in Washington, DC, on May 15, 1965, organized by the Inter-University Committee for a Public Hearing on Viet Nam in Ann Arbor, Michigan. This teach-in drew some of the biggest names in academia to speak against the growing war in Vietnam and significant excerpts from this event were reprinted in the *New York Times*. The letter of invitation to the National Teach-In billed it as the largest teach-in yet, "a confrontation between scholars and scientists on the one hand, and on the other, members of the government." The letter promised that McGeorge Bundy would attend to "defend official policy" and that this "confrontation" between Bundy and a "reactor panel" would be telecast via telephone to universities across the country.[127]

From the start, the National Teach-In was intended as an attack on the use of the ideology of containment to justify the growing war in Vietnam. In a detailed draft of the itinerary for this teach-in, each panel was given a "keynote quotation," an argument based on the ideology of military containment of communism that the administration or the president had used to justify U.S. military intervention in Vietnam. Each quotation was then followed by a list of discussion topics, counter-contentions designed to discredit the initial quotation. For instance, the keynote quotation for the first panel was: "The first reality is that North Viet-Nam has attacked the independent nation of South Viet-Nam. Its object is total conquest." Suggested topics of discussion for this panel included questioning "the relation of the Hanoi government to the Viet Cong and National Liberation Front." In the second panel, the quotation was: "Over this war . . . is another reality: the deepening shadow of Communist China." Pointed questions suggested as subject matter included "What is the case against China?" and "What does it mean to 'contain' China?" In response to the administration's invocation of the domino theory, a panel would ask questions such as "What impact would political settlement in Viet-Nam have on Laos, Cambodia, Thailand, Indonesia, Malaysia, the Philippines, Burma?" Another panel would question the administration's assertion that the United States was supporting the self-determination of South Vietnam by questioning "the effect of our military involvement, strategy and tactics on the goal of self-determination for the Vietnamese of the South" and "the treatment of South Vietnamese who oppose the war or who want negotiations." A panel would examine whether the war in Vietnam was actually a "civil war" and what really was the "relation of the communist party to the National Liberation Front." A separate panel would ask: "What are the risks of war with China or the commitment of U.S. ground troops in either South or North Viet-Nam? At what point do nuclear weapons become necessary?" Another panel would scrutinize the ideology of containment itself, questioning the perception of "communism as a monolithic aggressor." One panel would question the United States' claim that it fought in defense of freedom.[128] Not surprisingly, soon after this revised agenda was published, McGeorge Bundy decided not to attend the National Teach-In, instead sending a written statement to be read to the attendees.

The teach-in itself was, as it had been billed, an organized attack on the administration's use of containment to justify U.S. military intervention in Vietnam. China scholar Mary Wright used her appearance at the National Teach-In to attack the administration's use of the lessons of Munich. Wright called comparisons of Communist China "to the position of Hitler's Germany or Imperial Japan . . . very dangerous intellectual exercises." Instead, she insisted that the United States had "to accept the fact of the existence of Communist China" and "extricate ourselves where we are clearly not wanted militarily." She concluded: "It's almost the last moment to retreat in Vietnam and salvage something."[129]

Professor George Kahin first embarked on what was, in mid-1965, still a rare line of attack on the war: he attacked the administration's credibility. Kahin charged: "Essential information has been withheld from the American public and crucial policy decisions concerning Southeast Asia have been made before the public has even been aware that a problem exists." Moreover, Kahin said that "the American press in Vietnam faces stronger restrictions than it ever has in wartime and . . . we are getting contradictions, double-talk and half-truths from the Government concerning the situation in Vietnam."[130] Citing a *New York Times* editorial, he added:

> High-ranking representatives of government in Washington and in Saigon have so obscured, confused or distorted the news from Vietnam or have made such fatuously erroneous

evaluations about the course of the war that the credibility of
the United States Government has been sacrificed.[131]

However, like his colleagues, Kahin's main target was the administration's application of the ideology of military containment to the
conflict in Vietnam. He said, "[The administration's] most consistent failure has been an inability both to appreciate the importance of
Asian nationalism and to work with rather than against this powerful
force." Attacking the administration's claim that it was continuing the
policies of its predecessors over the previous ten years, Kahin cited
all of the ways in which Johnson's policies differed with those of his
predecessors. "Secretary Acheson in 1950," Kahin noted, "stated that
America could not by itself create politically stable states in Asia."[132]
Kahin quoted President Kennedy as saying:

> In the final analysis it's [their] war—they're the ones who have
> to win it or lose it. We can help them, give them equipment.
> We can send our men out there as advisers, but they have to
> win it.[133]

Kahin added that the "trend towards a rapprochement with Russia
started by President Eisenhower and continued by President Kennedy"
had "been seriously affected by our policy in Vietnam and it will be
further undermined if we continue on our present course." Moreover,
Kahin said, "The possibility of cooperation between the United
States and Russia to contain China's power . . . is becoming ever
more remote." Kahin also derided those who adhered to "the simplistic domino theory," saying that the other regimes of Southeast Asia
would not "succumb to Communism" so long as they were "in har-
mony with their nation's nationalism [and] so long as they are wise
enough to meet the most pressing economic and social demands of
their people."[134]

Hans Morgenthau spoke in the National Teach-In in Washington
of the "basic inner contradictions" in American policy toward
Southeast Asia: that the United States had set "goals" in Asia "which

cannot be achieved with the means we are willing to employ." To achieve its stated goals in Asia, Morgenthau said, the administration "must be ready to go to war with China, with all that that implies." While Morgenthau conceded that the administration wanted a negotiated settlement to the conflict in Vietnam, he said that the administration had imposed "unspoken conditions" that made "a negotiated settlement at the moment impossible." These conditions included the administration's refusal "to negotiate with the Vietcong" and its "implicit condition" that U.S. forces "remain—at least for the time being—in South Vietnam." This self-defeating policy, Morgenthau concluded, played into Communist China's hands. "From the point of view of Peking," Morgenthau said, "nothing better could happen than the United States waging a war in Vietnam which it is not able to win and which it cannot afford to lose." Morgenthau quipped: "Peking . . . hasn't lost a single man in that conflict and has only lost, as far as we can tell, one gun, which Mr. McNamara showed the other day in a press conference."[135]

Academic support for the teach-in movement was by no means universal; many scholars supported the administration's policies in Vietnam and some even echoed the administration's use of containment to justify U.S. military intervention there. Eminent China scholar and Harvard professor John K. Fairbank originally agreed to defend U.S. policy in Vietnam at the National Teach-In. However, he ultimately did not appear and instead wrote a letter to the editors of the *Washington Post*. Fairbank did admit that the United States' "China-containment policy was . . . an out-of-date article." Still, he did not question the necessity to contain Chinese expansionism, only the present U.S. strategy to do so. He argued that, in addition to military means, the "problem . . . requires long-term action on the socio-political and diplomatic levels as well." Fairbank argued that the United States should permit Peking to enter the United Nations "to manipulate Chinese pride in our own interest under the slogan 'China should have her place in the world.'" Yet he stated unequivocally, "We still have to pursue military containment in some form or other."[136]

University of California-Berkeley professor and East-Asia expert Robert Scalapino did appear at the National Teach-In to defend the administration's use of containment to justify its policies in Vietnam. Scalapino answered his own question, "Is the Vietcong a truly indigenous force in South Vietnam and has it achieved its strength . . . through promoting socio-economic reform?" with a qualified "no." Scalapino said: "[The] Vietcong is a carbon copy of the Vietminh which preceded it." He added: "The real leaders of the Vietcong are, and have always been, those in small hard-core elements that are also members of the Communist party—and that party has Hanoi as its headquarters." To those who pointed out that "the Vietminh . . . until it came to power claimed to be a multiclass, multifront organization dedicated to national liberation of Vietnam," Scalapino answered: "It ended up as you well know under the domination of the Communist party and opponents were either liquidated, silenced or reformed."[137]

Scalapino defended the Johnson administration's ongoing escalation in Vietnam. The only alternatives were, he said, "withdrawal, negotiation, or escalation." To those who suggested withdrawal, Scalapino answered, "It is not merely that withdrawal would reduce American credibility with her allies and neutrals round the world, but it is also that it would be a green light to the new national liberation movements which are even now getting under way. . . . Peking has broadcast repeatedly its intent to support the Thai national liberation movement." Likewise, Scalapino argued, withdrawal would give China the upper hand in its argument with the Soviet Union over peaceful coexistence. "Withdrawal would prove that Peking was right," Scalapino said, "and make it virtually impossible for moderation to prevail inside the world Communist movement." Scalapino also argued that negotiation was an unrealistic option, saying that, while "we are still hoping that . . . Hanoi will come forward and break its tie, now more than two years old, with Peking and move into a new orbit of independence," the Chinese had to date rebuffed offers of negotiation.[138]

Answering a challenge from Professor Kahin that the United States was suppressing nationalism in South Vietnam, Scalapino argued: "The pressures which Communist China is putting upon the small neutralist countries today—unless they are counteracted by some balance of power in this region—will be antinationalist and increasingly satellite in character." Scalapino added: "Unless we can establish some balance of power in Asia, nationalism is going to go under in societies like Cambodia, it's going to go under in societies like Burma." Scalapino concluded, "The inexorable pressure of the big states that are just emerging now, of which China is one but not the only one, is going to submerge indigenous Asian nationalism in . . . its own self-interest."[139]

Scalapino used the lessons of Munich to answer a challenge from Professor Morgenthau that Scalapino's logic led inexorably to war with China or withdrawal. Scalapino responded, "I would say that withdrawal at this point will mean war . . . because I think it will inevitably settle . . . the issue of how to meet American imperialism as the Communists put it." This would, Scalapino concluded, "inevitably cause the launching not of a thousand ships, but a thousand revolts not just in Asia, but wherever this movement can get under way. And I think that that means war."[140]

Dr. Zbigniew Brzezinski, political science professor at Columbia University and future national security advisor to President Carter, also used the ideology of military containment to defend the Johnson administration's policy on Vietnam at the National Teach-In. Brzezinski echoed the administration's claims that its motives were altruistic in Southeast Asia. "We are not trying to overthrow the North Vietnamese government," Brzezinski said, "We are not trying to change an existing political situation." To those who argued that China should have hegemony in Asia because "China is the predominant power in the region,"[141] Brzezinski offered a variation on the lessons of Munich:

So was Japan in 1940. Does that mean we should not have taken the course we did? So was Germany in Europe in 1940. So was the Soviet Union in Europe in 1945-46. Yet this did not justify the conclusion that one should therefore disengage and in a self-fulfilling prophecy make right the assertion . . . that China is the predominant power and prove it by disengaging.[142]

Brzezinski concluded by answering those who said the president was ignoring offers of negotiation on Vietnam. "None of these proposals have been accepted," Brzezinski said, "because at the present time the other side makes a demand which involves a qualitative change in the political status quo."[143]

In his written statement to be read to attendees at the National Teach-In, McGeorge Bundy derided dissenters as a noisy minority. Bundy wrote that the Chinese claim and perhaps believe "that American policy is weaker because 700 faculty members have made a protest against our policy in Vietnam." However, he wrote, "The American people . . . know that those who are protesting are only a minority, indeed a small minority, of the American teachers and students." And further, "within that minority the great majority accept and respect the rights and duty of the American Administration to meet its constitutional responsibilities for the conduct of our foreign affairs."[144] Bundy also suggested that some present at the National Teach-In were "more interested in pressure upon the Administration than in fair discussion with its representatives."[145]

However, the remainder of Bundy's statement was a lengthy justification of U.S. military intervention in Vietnam based on the ideology of military containment of communism. "Our purpose there," Bundy wrote, "is peace for the people of Vietnam, the people of Southeast Asia, and the people of the United States."[146] Bundy claimed that his differences with the attendees were over "the nature of the politics of Asia . . . the legitimacy of force in the face of armed attack and . . . the true prospects and purposes of the people of Vietnam themselves."[147] Bundy also tried to construct some common ground between the dissenters and the administration: "None of us wants the war to be enlarged. All of us want a decent settlement." But from this point he departed into territory where many of the academics at the National Teach-In would not follow: "All of us seek a solution in which American troops can be honorably withdrawn. . . . All of us, I trust, are prepared to be steadfast in the pursuit of our purposes."[148]

The administration was very concerned—perhaps more concerned than the actual threat warranted—about the growing dissent in the academic community. In response, the administration launched a number of programs to counter the growing dissent on college campuses. The Public Affairs Bureau of the State Department spearheaded the most successful of these programs, which enlisted the aid of the American Friends of Vietnam (AFV).[149] When presented to the president, the AFV initiative was described as a "counter-offensive moving on college campuses to combat the 'get out of Viet Nam' beatniks," an effort led by a White House "counter-force, American Friends of Viet Nam, run by 'good' college professors."[150] The State Department hoped to help the AFV organize "perhaps a dozen community/university seminars throughout the country, under joint sponsorship with local World Affairs Councils."[151]

After the National Teach-In, the effort to stage a pro-administration event at Michigan State University moved into high gear. The final event that resulted from this effort occurred on June 1, 1965, with USIA director Carl Rowan and Vice President Hubert Humphrey present as the administration's representatives to reiterate the administration's use of containment to justify intervention in Vietnam.[152] Chester Cooper wrote to Jack Valenti after the event, "The large student audience was friendly and receptive to the Vice President's vigorous exposition of our Vietnam policy and to Rowan's exhortation for students to involve themselves constructively in the great causes of our time, specifically our effort to preserve Vietnamese independence."[153] However, the event garnered little news coverage compared to the National Teach-In.

In fact, while the teach-in movement represented a dramatic expansion of the previous boundaries of public debate over foreign policy in the Cold War, neither the teach-ins nor the AFV's counter-efforts had a significant impact on American public opinion. Moreover, Professor Kahin's attack on the administration's credibility had failed to gain traction in the broader media. It is true that, a few days after the national teach-in, David Wise wrote the first newspaper article using the phrase "credibility gap" to attack the administration's policies in Vietnam.[154] And, as historian Robert Dallek notes, by June 1965 a joke began to make the rounds that you could tell the president was telling the truth "when he pulls his ear lobe, scratches his chin," and you could tell he was lying "when he begins to move his lips."[155] But it would be another year before sustained attacks on the president's credibility began to resonate in the media. And throughout the period when the teach-ins were taking place, 66 percent of Americans consistently wanted the United States to stay on its present course in Vietnam.[156]

The escalation of air attacks and increases in the deployment of U.S. ground forces accelerated dramatically after Johnson's April 7, 1965, John Hopkins speech. May brought a renewed summer offensive from the Viet Cong. As the offensive intensified, the stability of the government of South Vietnam came increasingly into question. To halt the Viet Cong's progress, the president authorized the deployment of U.S. Army ground forces. Public attention temporarily turned to the Dominican Republic after a crisis there necessitated the deployment of Marines. Yet escalation in Vietnam continued unabated throughout the Dominican crisis. In June, as the Dominican crisis faded from the headlines, the president authorized the first B-52 strikes against Viet Cong positions inside South Vietnam and the deployment of the U.S. Army's airmobile division. Finally, after a highly publicized visit by Robert McNamara to South Vietnam and consultation with congressional leaders, the president announced in a noontime press conference in late July his decision to raise the number of troops in Vietnam to 125,000, with an additional 100,000 possible in the future.[157]

Throughout this period, the administration continued to use containment to justify its escalation of U.S. military intervention in Vietnam. These arguments were also frequently echoed by the administration's supporters in the media. On the other hand, tit-for-tat justifications and invocations of the Tonkin Gulf Resolution as a legal justification for escalation had virtually disappeared from the administration's rhetoric. The administration abandoned tit-for-tat justifications because it had finally decided to commit U.S. forces to contain communism in Vietnam; further escalations after this decision was made would be justified by military necessity rather than by specific actions by the North Vietnamese or Viet Cong. Likewise, once it became clear that most in Congress would not speak out against the escalation, it was no longer necessary for the administration to remind the public or Congress of the Tonkin Gulf Resolution, its insurance policy against congressional dissent.

Dissent against the escalation in Vietnam continued to grow throughout this period, and this dissent was squarely focused on the administration's use of containment to justify U.S. military intervention. The foreign policy revolution begun by academic dissenters was joined by radical protesters, who became much more active during this period, attacking both the ideology of containment and its application to Vietnam. Some in the media also attacked the administration's use of containment to justify the escalation. While Senator J. William Fulbright was the only member of Congress to mount significant public dissent against the escalation during this period, a number of congressional leaders shared their private doubts about escalation with the president. Both public and private congressional dissent was also focused on the president's use of containment to justify the growing U.S. military intervention in Vietnam. The administration's dismissive reaction to congressional dissent is at least strong circumstantial evidence that the president believed that the Tonkin Gulf Resolution gave him an ironclad insurance policy against these objections.

While the American public continued to strongly support the administration's use of containment to justify U.S. military intervention in Vietnam, the president's handling of the war in Vietnam, and the use of bombing to assist South Vietnam, the administration never successfully built a consensus among the American people behind the introduction of large numbers of ground troops in Vietnam before they took this final move.

In May 1965, the administration launched a major campaign to convince Americans that containment required U.S. military intervention in Vietnam. On May 4, 1965, the president addressed members of Congress at the White House during the signing of a supplemental appropriations bill for the war in Vietnam. Answering those who still wondered why the defense of South Vietnam was an American responsibility, the president answered: "There is no one else who can do the job. Our power alone, in the final test, can stand between expanding communism and independent Asian nations." The president argued that the United States must honor its commitment, especially since the communists were deliberately trying "to show that American commitment is worthless . . . and once they succeed in doing that, the gates are down and the road is open to expansion and to endless conquest." The president concluded by claiming that the "1954 . . . Southeast Asia Collective Defense Treaty . . . committed us to act to meet aggression against South Viet-Nam."[158]

Members of the administration also participated in this public information campaign. A few days after the president's speech, Secretary of State Dean Rusk spoke to the American Society of International Law and provided many of the same justifications.[159] George Ball reminded ministers of the lessons of Munich at the opening session of a meeting of the SEATO council ministers in London on May 3, 1965, that received heavy coverage in the American media.[160] On May 13, 1965, the first day of the bombing pause, the president spoke to the American Association of Editorial Cartoonists and again placed the blame for the continued conflict on China.[161] On the same day, in a speech to the Dallas Council on World Affairs, William P. Bundy blamed both the Soviet Union and Communist China for prolonging the conflict.[162] Nearly all of these speeches also warned of the new communist strategy of "wars of liberation."

Many media commentators echoed the administration's use of containment to justify escalation. Associated Press columnist James Marlow wrote in early May that the United States was "trying to prevent a Communist victory [in South Vietnam] in the belief it would lead eventually to Chinese domination of all Southeast Asia." Marlow went on to write that this fear was not unfounded since "China will have the H-bomb in two or three years" and could be expected to behave as the United States had "in the Western Hemisphere [with the Monroe doctrine]" and "Soviet Russia [does] with its satellites now." Echoing another of the administration's themes, Marlow wrote: "When some of the old and original leaders of Chinese Communism, like Mao Tze-tung, pass out of the picture and the Chinese society becomes more affluent, the Communist missionary fervor may lose some steam, as it seems to have done in Russia." However, Marlow warned, "The national interests of Red China will not diminish under a new leadership or under less ideological zeal."[163]

In the midst of the bombing pause and the distraction of the Dominican crisis, Americans lost some interest in Vietnam. A Gallup poll from mid-May found that more Americans continued to see Vietnam as "the most important problem facing this country today" than any other issue. But fewer Americans (22 percent) saw it as the most important issue compared to February (a drop of six percentage points). Two thirds of that slip had come at the expense of the "Dominican Republic," which four percent of Americans now believed was the "most important issue."[164]

The president and the administration had also lost ground in convincing Americans that ground troops were needed in Vietnam. A Gallup poll from mid-May showed that only 30 percent of Americans wanted to "send in more troops" or wage "all-out war" in Vietnam, down five percentage points from late April. The number of Americans who wanted to "continue [the] present policy" in Vietnam had increased by 7 percentage points to 29 percent during the same period. Perhaps the only good news for the administration was that the number of Americans who wanted to "withdraw troops" from Vietnam was down by 3 percentage points to 17 percent.[165]

Radical activist protests against U.S. policy in Vietnam grew dramatically during the late spring 1965. And the scope of the dissent by these radicals was even broader than that of academic dissenters; radicals objected not just to the application of the ideology of containment to the war in Vietnam but to the ideology of containment itself. Paul Potter, president of the Students for a Democratic Society (SDS), attacked both the growing Vietnam War and the broader ideology of containment in a speech to demonstrators at the Washington

Monument during a march on Washington on April 17, 1965. Potter claimed that Vietnam had "finally severed the last vestiges of illusion that morality and democracy are the guiding principles of American foreign policy." America had revealed its imperialism, Potter said, through "saccharine, self-righteous moralism that promises the Vietnamese a billion dollars of economic aid at the very moment we are delivering billions for economic and social destruction and political repression." Paraphrasing Senator Wayne Morse, Potter added, "The U.S. may well be the greatest threat to peace in the world today." Potter condemned the United States for repressing "the demand of ordinary people to have some opportunity to make their own lives," while insisting "that that struggle can be legitimately suppressed since it might lead to the development of a Communist system." The United States' effort to suppress the aspirations of the South Vietnamese people, Potter said, was ultimately self-defeating. "The war that we are creating and escalating in Southeast Asia is rapidly eroding the base of independence of North Vietnam as it is forced to turn to China and the Soviet Union."[166] Potter concluded by striking at the ideology of military containment itself. Potter insisted: "This country must come to understand that the creation of a Communist country in the world today is not an ultimate defeat."[167]

Despite this new dissent, the administration continued to use containment to justify the escalation of U.S. military intervention in Vietnam. Perhaps in response to growing dissent in academia, William Bundy appeared at the end of May before the faculty of the University of California at Berkeley to explain the administration's reasons for escalating the conflict. Bundy admitted that Eisenhower and Kennedy had not used U.S. forces in direct combat in Vietnam, but he still painted Johnson's escalation of U.S. participation in the conflict as a continuation of their policies. Further, he claimed that this escalation was necessitated by the aggression of North Vietnam.[168]

Bundy also repeated other themes that the administration had been using since early 1964. Bundy blamed the conflict in Vietnam on China, "a Communist regime still at the peak of its ideological fervor," which sought "domination and the denial of national self-determination and independence." Bundy did concede, "The other Communist nations of Asia, North Viet-Nam and North Korea . . . are not true satellites—indeed deep down, they too fear Chinese domination." However, he still called them "willing partners . . . working together with Communist China toward . . . subjugation of the true national independence of smaller countries." Likewise, while admitting that the Communist regime in North Vietnam "was a genuine nationalist movement," Bundy also insisted that the "dividing line between the two Viet-Nams" was every bit as valid a "political division as in Germany and Korea." Moreover, Bundy said, the North Vietnamese regime was "the heartbeat of the Viet Cong." Comparing the Viet Cong insurgency to the insurgency in Greece, Bundy added: "The Viet Cong have won control of major areas of the country, playing in part on propaganda and the undoubted weaknesses of Diem and his successors, but relying basically on massive intimidation of civilians."[169]

At an appearance in Chicago in June 1965, the president returned to the lessons of Munich. "In the 1930s," Johnson said, "we made our fate not by what we did but what we Americans failed to do." American "vacillation . . . hesitancy and irresolution" had "propelled . . . all mankind toward tragedy." Johnson concluded: "The failure of free men in the 1930s was not of the sword but of the soul." He insisted: "There just must be no such failure in the 1960s."[170]

On June 8, 1965, Assistant Secretary of State Robert McCloskey told reporters in a routine press conference that the new U.S. forces being deployed to Vietnam would be used for offensive operations.[171] This botched announcement of the deployment of U.S. Army soldiers to Vietnam caused some in the press to criticize the administration's transparency in escalating the war. In fact, while the administration had never publicly acknowledged it, Marines had been engaged in offensive operations in South Vietnam for over a month. The *New York Times* editorial page exploded over the revelation, with one stunned editor writing, "The American people were told by a minor State Department official yesterday, that, in effect, they were in a land war on the continent of Asia."[172] I. F. Stone immediately began calling the growing war in Vietnam "McCloskey's war." However, most of the media's criticism was focused not on the administration's transparency but on its containment arguments for military intervention in Vietnam. Stone called it "folly" to "tie down a major portion of U.S. military power in a minor theater of conflict."[173] Recalling Walter Lippmann's arguments about a misguided "white man's burden" in South Vietnam from April,[174] Stone wrote, "White men will be fighting colored men in an effort to put down a rebellion so deeply rooted that it has gone on for two decades." Stone added that this rebellion had already "extended its power steadily during the four years in which we trained, directed and supplied a satellite native army."[175]

Even through the dramatic news of U.S. troop movements in Vietnam[176]—and despite growing criticism from academics, activists, and the media—Americans continued to support the president's policies in Vietnam. A White House poll of likely voters in Minnesota—home state of both Vice President Hubert Humphrey and future antiwar presidential candidate Senator Eugene McCarthy—found that, while Minnesotans did not consider Vietnam the "most important" issue (it came in second behind "help for old people"), 52 percent had a favorable opinion of the president's "handling [of] the problem in Vietnam." Almost as many, 51 percent, had a favorable opinion of his "handling [of] Communist China," while 60 percent had a favorable opinion of his "handling [of] Russia and her leaders." Moreover, Minnesotans believed that the president should either continue his present course or further escalate the war in Vietnam. When asked what America should do next in Vietnam, the greatest number of respondents, 78 percent, agreed that America should "do as [it is], keep military pressure on but seek negotiation," while 56 percent agreed with the statement that America "should step up [its] military even more and win the war." By contrast, only 25 percent agreed that America should "stop U.S. bombing attacks" and only 10 percent agreed that America should "forget the whole thing and clear out." Seventy percent of Minnesotans agreed that the United States should "ask for negotiation right now," but this was probably received by the White House much as it was by the pollsters in their comments; their response was, "We have." Given these results, pollsters concluded,

"The people of Minnesota are solidly behind the President."[177] Polling in New York from the same period found nearly identical results.[178]

Not only did Americans agree with the present course in Vietnam, they accepted the president's use of the ideology of military containment of communism to justify U.S. military intervention in Vietnam. A National Gallup Poll from this same period asked those who believed the United States should continue its present course in Vietnam (63 percent of respondents) why they believed the United States should stay the course. Over half of respondents accepted some variation on the administration's argument that the United States had to win in Vietnam to maintain the credibility of its worldwide commitments. Another 40 percent explicitly accepted the contention that the United States had to stand firm in Vietnam to "contain communism." By contrast, none of those respondents who believed that America should "pull out" of Vietnam (23 percent) cited reasons that had been posited by dissident academics and other vocal opponents of the administration's policies in Vietnam. Thirty-one percent of those respondents who wanted Americans out of Vietnam cited high U.S. casualties. Just as many believed that Vietnam was "none of our business," while half as many (17 percent) believed that Vietnam was "a losing cause" or that the United States was "not getting anywhere" in winning the war.[179]

A Harris Poll a week later showed that the majority of Americans (69 percent) supported the president and his course in Vietnam. Yet support for introducing more U.S. ground troop in Vietnam was not nearly as strong. Only 47 percent of Americans believed the president should "send more troops," while nearly a quarter of Americans were still "not sure" whether the United States should send more troops. Lou Harris's conclusion was that this represented "a clear mandate for the President's course of action."[180] In reality, these results only indicated support for the state of the escalation at that moment; they did not necessarily indicate that the American public would continue to support the president's policy if he introduced large numbers of U.S. ground troops into the conflict. The administration had more work to do to convince the American public that U.S. military involvement in Vietnam should be further escalated.

This conclusion is supported by a National Opinion Research Center poll from June 1965. This poll found that 68 percent of Americans were following the situation in Vietnam "very" or "fairly closely." According to this poll, only 20 percent of Americans wanted the president to further escalate the conflict, less than half as many as were "completely satisfied" with the president's actions thus far. When asked specifically about the bombing of North Vietnam, 77 percent of Americans supported the bombing. Of those Americans who supported the bombing, slightly fewer believed the bombing should be escalated than believed the current level of bombing was about correct.[181]

The conclusion that Americans were not convinced that more U.S. ground troops were needed in Vietnam is even more dramatically illustrated by a Gallup poll from the beginning of June. The administration had made progress; over a third of respondents now believed that the United States should either "send in more troops" or wage "all-out war" in Vietnam, an increase of five percentage points from mid-May. However, this was simply a return to the levels of late April, before the Dominican crisis. This gain came at the cost of those Americans who wanted to "continue [the] present policy" in Vietnam, now 24 percent of Americans, a decrease of five percentage points from mid-May. More worrisome for the administration, 20 percent of Americans now wanted to "withdraw troops" from Vietnam, an increase of 3 percentage points from mid-May. The administration was no closer to convincing Americans that large numbers of U.S. ground troops were needed in Vietnam than it had been in mid-April.[182]

As part of the administration's continuing effort to mute academic dissent—and presumably to build a consensus among Americans for further escalation—McGeorge Bundy agreed to a nationally televised debate with foreign policy luminary Hans Morgenthau on June 21, 1965.[183] Despite Chester Cooper's best efforts to tailor the format of the debate to be more favorable to the administration,[184] the president was incensed with the results,[185] probably due to Bundy's poor showing in the face of Morgenthau's challenge to the administration's policies.

Late June brought more troubles for the administration. In April, Senator J. William Fulbright had angered the administration by calling for a bombing pause to jump start negotiations with North Vietnam. In late June, at the persistent urging of Harry Sions, former war correspondent and editor at Little, Brown, and Company,[186] Senator J. William Fulbright finally explicitly challenged the president's policies in Vietnam in an appearance on the *Today* show. While he did not denounce the president, Fulbright told Americans it was time to halt the escalation of the U.S. military commitment in Vietnam before it could no longer be stopped. Fulbright's office received 178 letters supporting Fulbright's position in the few days after the appearance, and only twenty-four letters opposed (though the two letters from Fulbright's home state of Arkansas were split evenly between support and opposition).[187] The administration did not publicly respond to this challenge, and the escalation continued unabated.

Moreover, while it generated a number of letters to Fulbright's office, this modest dissent against escalation had little effect on public opinion. A Gallup poll from late June showed almost no change in American public approval of President Johnson's "dealing with the situation in Vietnam" (63 percent). The answers from these Americans as to why they approved of the president's handling of the war revealed a deep faith in the wisdom of the government and reluctance to question authority. Nearly 40 percent simply answered that the president "knows best" or "knows more about" the problem in Vietnam than the public. Another 25 percent had fully embraced the president's containment justifications for U.S. military intervention, responding, "We must contain communism." Sixteen percent echoed the administration's argument that the United States must succeed in Vietnam in order to protect the credibility of its commitments across the globe. Of those 36 percent who disapproved of the president's handling of Vietnam, nearly a quarter disapproved because they thought the president was not being aggressive enough. None of the respondents who disapproved of the administration's policies in Vietnam echoed arguments made by academic or radical dissenters.[188]

While the conventional wisdom today is that the American public eventually abandoned the president on the issue of Vietnam because they expected a quick victory, this same poll shows that most Americans expected the United States to be no closer to victory in June 1966 than it was in June 1965. In fact, many Americans expected the war to be going much worse than it actually would be going in mid-1966. When asked in late June 1965 what they expected the war to look like in a year, only 35 percent of respondents expected "a military victory" or "a compromise peace . . . and fighting will have ended." Twenty-nine percent expected that there would be "little or no change in the Vietnam situation." Nearly as many (26 percent) believed that "the Red Chinese will have entered the war in Vietnam on a full scale basis," while 9 percent believed that "the war in Vietnam will have developed into a world war involving most of the major nations of the world."[189]

This same Gallup poll did show that the president and the administration were making progress in convincing Americans of the need for U.S. ground troops in Vietnam. When asked in late June, "What would you like to see the U.S. do next about Vietnam?" 40 percent of Americans now wanted the United States to either "send in more troops" or wage "all-out war" in Vietnam, an increase of five percentage points from the beginning of the month. This increase again came at the expense of those Americans who wanted to "continue [the] present policy" in Vietnam, now down to only 13 percent, a little more than half as many Americans as had held the same view at the beginning of June. Only 19 percent of Americans now wanted to "withdraw troops" from Vietnam (down one percentage point from early June).[190] Moreover, when Americans were asked whether "American efforts in Vietnam [should] be limited to only air and sea strikes" or whether "troops should . . . be committed to combat on the ground," 57 percent of Americans believed ground troops should be used.[191] While this does not demonstrate that a majority of Americans yet supported a massive increase in the number of U.S. ground troops in Vietnam, a majority did support the use of some U.S. ground troops in the conflict.

The dominant historical narrative that the American public did not realize that the president was taking the country into a ground war in Vietnam is also directly contradicted by this same Gallup poll from late June. When given a choice only between escalation, deescalation, or complete withdrawal, 74 percent of Americans chose escalation. Moreover— and in direct contradiction to those who would later say the president hid the escalation from the American people—when asked which of these options President Johnson was pursuing, 91 percent of Americans correctly identified that President Johnson was escalating the conflict.[192]

In light of these poll results, it is not surprising that the administration continued its effort to convince the American public that the United States needed to intervene militarily in Vietnam in order to contain communist expansion. In a radio interview on ABC radio in early July 1965, Secretary of State Rusk reiterated his theme from earlier in the year that Vietnam was a test of U.S. resolve to honor its commitments worldwide. When asked by journalist John Scali if Vietnam was a test of "the credibility of American pledges," Rusk said that, if America lost in South Vietnam, its "42 allies . . . should find themselves questioning the validity of the assurances of the United States with respect to their security." Thais and West Berliners, Rusk said, would conclude that U.S. promises "did not amount to very much." Rusk also reiterated the domino theory, saying that "South Viet-Nam is important in itself," and, if the United States was not successful in South Vietnam, "this begins to roll things up all over the world." Rusk also introduced a new argument that would be used repeatedly throughout the remainder of the Johnson presidency. Rusk claimed that the war in Vietnam was a holding action until China matured. "There has been a big argument between Moscow and Peiping," Rusk said, and "Peiping must also begin to work its way back toward the idea of mutual coexistence," the position of the Soviet Union.[193] The United States had to hold out in Southeast Asia until China embraced peaceful coexistence as the Soviet Union had.

As the announcement of the decision to deploy large numbers of U.S. Army Soldiers to Vietnam to participate in direct combat drew nearer, the *New York Times* took on one of President Johnson's primary containment justifications for military intervention in Vietnam. Attacking the president's "almost daily" assertions "that 'three Presidents have made the pledge for this nation' to defend South Vietnam against the Communists and that 'our national honor is at stake, our word is at stake,'"[194] the *Times* reminded its readers of President Kennedy's words on Vietnam from two years earlier:

> In the final analysis, it is their war. They are the ones who have to win it or lose it. We can help them, we can give them equipment, we can send our men out there as advisers, but they have to win it—the people of Vietnam against the Communists.[195]

But this dissent from the *New York Times* was the exception. The press remained largely supportive of the administration's use of the ideology of containment of communism to justify U.S. military intervention in Vietnam. For instance, NBC News planned a national broadcast for September 7, 1965, called "American White Paper" in which prominent academic, press, and administration figures would debate not just the merits of U.S. participation in the Vietnam War, but also the shape of U.S. foreign policy. A flier from July 1965 announcing this television event made it clear that the network had internalized the administration's containment justifications for intervention in Vietnam. This flier described an entire segment as being dedicated to "the Rise of Red China,"[196] adding:

> China has become a power to be reckoned with not only because of her internal achievements, but her external aspirations in Asia, Africa and Latin America—"The Third World." In Korea, China and the U.S. confronted each other for the first time as super powers. In India, French Indo-China, in the Formosa Straits, in the explosion of her atomic bomb, in Vietnam. China has made clear her intentions.[197]

This flier also echoed the administration's claims that the SEATO treaty was a "military [alliance]" designed to respond "to Red Chinese pressures" and that "United States involvement in Vietnam" was aimed at "Red China" and "China's challenge." The flier proposed for this segment the question of which policy would allow the United States to slow "the advance of China in the third world" just as "the policy of containment . . . slowed the advance of the U.S.S.R. in Europe."[198]

The American people had also deeply internalized the precepts of the Cold War consensus on the eve of the final Americanization of the Vietnam War. A National Opinion Research Center Poll from mid-June demonstrated that the American public strongly supported internationalism; when asked if "it will be best for the future of this country if we take an active part in world affairs," 79 percent of Americans agreed. Likewise, 85 percent of Americans believed the United States "should continue to belong to the United Nations." When asked, "During the last year or so, would you say that most other countries in the world have become more friendly to the United States, or less friendly," 55 percent of respondents did believe that other countries had become "less friendly." But when those Americans were asked why other countries were less friendly, only 35 percent said that it was a result of negative behaviors by the United States, such as "meddling in their affairs, trying to dominate their countries, impos[ing] our own ideas, [or] telling them what to do," or because the United States was "too warlike [or] aggressive." Rather, most of these Americans believed that the cause was related to over-generous foreign aid (28 percent), jealousy of American success (18 percent), or a result of "communist propaganda" or "communist infiltration" (18 percent). This poll also revealed that Americans continued to support the core tenet of the Cold War consensus, the utility of military intervention to contain communism. Americans were asked, "Suppose there is a revolution in one of the countries of South America, and it looks as though a communist government will take over. Do you think the United States should or should not send in American troops to prevent this?" Nearly 73 percent of Americans responded that the United States "should send American troops."[199]

Just before the announcement of the decision to deploy large numbers of U.S. Army soldiers to Vietnam to participate in direct combat, scholar and former U.S. ambassador to India John Kenneth Galbraith sent a private letter to President Johnson outlining a scheme to deescalate the conflict in Vietnam. In view of Galbraith's vocal opposition earlier in the year to the administration's use of containment to justify intervention in Vietnam, this letter was clearly a last-ditch effort to deter the president from going to war in Vietnam. Galbraith's memorandum, entitled "How to Take Ninety Percent of the Political Heat out of Vietnam," seemed calibrated to appeal to the president's political practicality, and was written in a gritty tone that was a caricature of President Johnson's plain-spoken public persona. Yet the thrust of Galbraith's arguments was to challenge the president's contention that Vietnam was part of the Cold War. Galbraith first posited five foundational assumptions he believed the president should embrace. First, "Vietnam is of no great intrinsic importance. Had it gone Communist after World War II we would be just as strong as now." Second, "no question of high principle is involved. It is their rascals or ours." Third, he conceded Johnson's concern that "we must show that we can't be thrown out—that we don't give up under fire." Next, Galbraith wrote, appealing to Johnson's political concerns, "It is right to consider the politics of the problem. A great many people who make policy do not have to take the political heat." But, finally, allaying the president's political concerns, Galbraith wrote, "Political questions are partly what we make them. Despite all of their efforts the Republicans could not make mileage last autumn out of Cuba."[200]

Given these assumptions, Galbraith suggested that the president take six concrete steps. First, he suggested, "Instruct officials and spokesmen to stop saying the future of mankind, the United States and human liberty is being decided in Vietnam. It isn't." Next, he suggested, "Stop saying that we are going to reconquer the whole country. . . . The easiest way to have a failure is to set one up for ourselves by promising to do what can't be done." Galbraith next suggested that the United States concentrate on holding a few areas and waiting for a political settlement. "Let us apply a policy of political patience in the area," Galbraith wrote. As a result, he wrote, "The Viet Cong will not attack these areas frontally. Casualties will be low."[201] Galbraith also called for an end to the bombing:

> Stop or gradually suspend the bombing north and south. This has slight military value, alarms our people and other countries and, above all, keeps the place at the top of the news with maximum attention there and minimum attention where it belongs. (I think it may harden resistance to negotiation also—but on this no one can be sure and I am confining myself here to facts.)[202]

This final parenthetical note was a refutation of the argument Galbraith had made in a letter published in the *New York Times* only a few months earlier, a concession no doubt designed to appease the president and his advisors. Finally, Galbraith suggested, "Keep open the offer of negotiations . . . someday they will come."[203]

Galbraith's predicted results for this policy were clearly designed to appeal to Johnson's political sensibilities:

1. Unless they attack head on, which we can rule out, we will prove our staying power. We won't be playing their game by sending our forces out into the jungle where ambush works.
2. The whole place will go on the back burner. Public attention will come back to areas of sound achievement of the Administration where it belongs.
3. The Republicans will bleat as Keating did about Cuba. That will hurt them more than us.
4. It will take the Russians off the hook and enable us to make progress there.[204]

Lest these prospects not be enough to entice the president, Galbraith added a few more enticements. First, this course of action would allow the administration to avoid the significant move of "calling up [the] reserve," which Galbraith wrote would add "to the publicity and wrong emphasis on Vietnam." Second, this course of action would extricate the president from the momentum of his "own eager beavers who do not consider the mood of our own people come the next election, and whose political teat is not in the wringer."[205]

Congress was equally skeptical about the wisdom of further escalation of the conflict in Vietnam on the eve of the president's announcement of the deployment of large numbers of U.S. ground troops. A few days before this announcement, the *New York Times*' E.W. Kenworthy surveyed the views in Congress on Johnson's escalation in Vietnam. His conclusion was that members of Congress privately disputed the President's use of containment to justify U.S. military intervention. Senators Morse and Gruening, Kenworthy wrote, opposed escalation on the grounds that it is "taking the nation down a road that may lead to nuclear war." Senators Mike Mansfield, J.W. Fulbright, Robert F. Kennedy, Jacob K. Javits, and George Aiken, Kenworthy wrote, believed it was "dangerously unrealistic to believe that the bombing of North Vietnam would force the Communists to the conference tables." Kenworthy wrote that most others in Congress were equally skeptical of the United States' policy in Vietnam but would not speak out publicly. In fact, Kenworthy wrote, virtually the only Congressmen who supported the president's policy were "those Republicans who ardently supported Barry Goldwater last year, such as Senator John G. [Tower] of Texas." Most in Congress, Kenworthy added, objected to the growing war on four grounds: bombing had been ineffective, the South Vietnamese government was weak, the war would eventually grow until the United States was doing all of the fighting, and the war was "'a hopeless venture' which can not be finally won."[206] Above all, Kenworthy concluded, Congress rejected the administration's military containment arguments for intervention:

[EXT] Many of these Senators question the "domino" theory first advanced by Secretary Dulles. They seriously doubt that South Vietnam is essential to American security.[207]

Kenworthy also provided four reasons why Congress was not more vocal in opposition: they did not want to dissent while troops were in harm's way, they realized the president had inherited the Vietnam problem, they had no alternatives to offer, and "they fear the cry of 'appeasement of Communism' will be raised against them." Kenworthy concluded that many were reluctant to publicly dissent because "they have noted the attacks made in some sections of the press on Senators Morse and Gruening."[208]

While most in Congress—except Senators Fulbright, Morse, and Gruening—did not speak out publicly against the escalation, some members of Congress privately confronted the president over his use of containment to justify the growing U.S. military intervention in Vietnam. The administration's reaction to this eleventh hour effort to stop the final Americanization of the Vietnam War provides further evidence that the president and the administration believed that the Tonkin Gulf Resolution had inoculated them against congressional dissent—a sort of "insurance policy" that remained in effect regardless of Congress' present sentiments about the war. This also explains why invocations of the resolution had disappeared from administration rhetoric. Since virtually the entire Congress was remaining silent on the issue of Vietnam, there was no need to remind the public that the Congress had passed the Tonkin Gulf Resolution expressing its support for the U.S. military intervention in the conflict.

This confrontation with members of Congress before the final Americanization of the war began the day before the president would finally announce the dramatic escalation of the number of U.S. ground forces in Vietnam. In a private meeting, the president discussed the potential deployment of 100,000 soldiers with Senate Majority Leader Mike Mansfield and other Senate leaders. The president told this assembly that the escalation was a temporary move to hold the line on North Vietnamese aggression until January and to give Secretary Rusk and Arthur Goldberg, the incoming U.S. ambassador to the UN, diplomatic room to extricate the United States from the conflict.[209]

In turn, Mansfield discussed the content of this meeting privately with Senators Russell, Fulbright, Sparkman, Aiken, and Cooper and penned a note for the president detailing the sentiments of these leaders on the idea of further escalating the conflict. These senators, first, believed that the required number of soldiers would be closer to 150,000. These senators also believed that the window for Russia to help in forging a peace settlement was rapidly closing and that "bridges to Eastern Europe" needed to be kept open to improve the chances of a peace settlement. Senators also suggested that the President explore direct contacts with China and France as a means to end the conflict. Senators believed that public support for the war was tentative at best, primarily because, like the senators, Americans were not convinced that Vietnam was "a 'vital' area of U.S. concern." Senators were also concerned that, if the "Goldberg-Rusk effort" failed, a substantially larger commitment would be required. The Senators also suggested some combination of an "enclave-strategy, a cessation of aerial bombardment and the use of all possible contacts to get negotiations underway." Mansfield's letter also highlighted the contradictory sentiments among Senate leaders: leaders believed, "The President was ill-advised to begin the bombing of North Viet Nam in the first place," but also believed, "The error was then compounded by the limited character of the bombing."[210] Mansfield concluded:

> There was obviously not a unanimity among the Members present on all of the points listed. But there was a very substantial agreement on many of them. Moreover, there was full agreement that insofar as Viet Nam is concerned we are deeply enmeshed in a place where we ought not to be; that the situation is rapidly going out of control; and that every effort should be made to extricate ourselves.[211]

President Johnson clearly no longer enjoyed the support of the Senate for escalation. In fact, Johnson *never* had gained the support of the Senate for escalation; Congress had intended the Tonkin Gulf Resolution as an instrument of containment to deter Soviet and Chinese Communist aggression—much like the Formosa Resolution or the Middle East Resolution which they believed had prevented war—rather than as an endorsement of the Americanization of the Vietnam War. Moreover, they had been privately assured by the administration before its passage that the resolution would not be used to escalate the war.

More than any other piece of evidence, the actions the president took after receiving this letter from Mansfield indicate that the president saw the Tonkin Gulf Resolution not as a "sense of the Congress" in August 1964 but as an insurance policy against congressional dissent that endured regardless of the present sentiments in Congress. Rather than going to Congress and trying to convince dissenting senators to support the administration's policies, Secretary of Defense McNamara prepared for the president a point-by-point refutation of the congressmen's views. McNamara rebutted Mansfield's objections to the administration's abandonment of "peaceful coexistence" by claiming that the Soviets abandoned it first in supporting "wars of liberation." In response to Mansfield's very real concern that Americans were "backing the president on Vietnam primarily because he is president, not necessarily out of any understanding or sympathy with policies on Vietnam," McNamara suggested "setting up a Task Force to explain our policies to the American people." Likewise, to counter Mansfield's concerns about growing racial tensions, McNamara suggested "the racial leaders throughout the country should be talked with, to make sure that they understand the danger of mixing Civil Rights and South Vietnam." Instead of talking directly to the senators about their concern that Vietnam was "by no means a vital area of U.S. concern," Secretary McNamara recounted for the president all of the administration's justifications for U.S. military intervention in Vietnam based on the ideology of military containment of communism.[212]

Mansfield's letter had been a last-ditch effort by the Senate to communicate to the president that they disapproved of his present course in Vietnam. Had the president believed that he required the continuing support of the Congress, his reaction to this letter would have been alarm and a massive effort to enlist congressional support. Instead, the president ignored their warning, confident that the Tonkin Gulf Resolution would prevent members of Congress from disagreeing publicly with his policies in Vietnam, regardless of their sentiments on the war. Instead of trying to persuade the Congress to support the administration's policies in Vietnam, the Johnson and McNamara reminded each other of how right they were and how wrong these members of Congress were. As if to underline this fact, the president sent McNamara's point-by-point refutation of the senator's concerns back to Mansfield, along with a cover letter praising Secretary McNamara as "the best Secretary of Defense in the history of this country."[213]

Perhaps the most prescient concern Senator Mansfield raised to the president was his observation that the American public was supporting Johnson simply because he was the president, rather than because they agreed with or understood his policies in Vietnam. This fact is confirmed by polling data from the eve of the president's announcement of a troop increase. The American public was clearly now paying attention to the war in Vietnam; the number of Americans who called Vietnam the "most important problem facing this country today" was up fifteen percentage points from its low in May.[214] Sixty-seven percent of Americans now approved of the president's handling of the war. Yet, confirming Senator Mansfield's fears that Americans were simply supporting the president because he was president, over half of those who supported Johnson's policies in Vietnam simply expressed unqualified faith that the president "knows best" or "knows more about" the situation in Vietnam. Most of the remainder explicitly endorsed the president's justifications for intervention either based on the containment of communism in Southeast Asia (17 percent) or maintaining the credibility of the United States' worldwide commitments (12 percent).[215]

At the insistence of his staff, the president made a televised announcement of his decision to send large numbers of American soldiers to Vietnam at midday on July 28, 1965. Historians frequently focus on the fact that this announcement was scheduled when the television audience would be smallest, strategically given between newsmagazine deadlines and obscured by the announcement at the same press conference of a nominee to the Supreme Court and a nominee to be director of Voice of America.[216] However, this news conference is equally notable as perhaps the president's most extensive use yet of the ideology of containment to justify U.S. military intervention in Vietnam.

President Johnson announcing troop deployments, July 28, 1965.

Source: U.S. Army, "Why Vietnam," Washington, D.C., 1965, National Archives.[217]

The president explained that he was raising the final troop strength in Vietnam to 125,000 men with the deployment of 100,000 more troops possible in the future. Johnson announced he would also more than double the draft but would not call up the Reserves. The president would also ask Congress for more money to prosecute the war early in 1966. His justifications for these actions were firmly founded in the ideology of military containment of communism. The president said that this action was required to contain communist expansion; it was necessary in order "to bring an end to aggression" by the communist north.[218] In a reference to the lessons of Munich, President Johnson said that three times in his lifetime, "in two world wars and in Korea, Americans have gone to far lands to fight for freedom." They had done so, Johnson claimed, because "we have learned at a terrible and brutal cost that retreat does not bring safety and weakness does not bring peace." Johnson also tied the lessons of Munich to the domino theory. "Surrender in Viet-Nam," Johnson claimed, would not bring peace.[219] Instead, Johnson continued:

> We learned from Hitler at Munich that success only feeds the appetite of aggression. The battle would be renewed in one country and then another country, bringing with it perhaps even larger and crueler conflict, as we have learned from the lessons of history.[220]

President Johnson, as had other administration officials, conceded that "some citizens of South Viet-Nam, at times with understandable grievances, have joined in the attack on their own government." But Johnson said he would not "let this mask the central fact that this is really war," that the insurgency was "guided by North Viet-Nam, and . . . spurred by Communist China." These forces intended "to conquer the South, to defeat American power, and to extend the Asiatic dominion of Communism."[221]

Johnson also repeated the administration's newer claim that Vietnam was a test of U.S. commitment to honor its promises. "If we are driven from the field in Viet-Nam," Johnson said, "then no nation can ever again have the same confidence in American protection." The president tied this newer argument to the much older argument, from early 1964, that his policies were a continuation of those of his predecessors. "Three presidents," he said, "President Eisenhower, President Kennedy, and your present president—over 11 years have committed themselves and have promised to help defend this small and valiant nation." The president also made the new argument that, if the United States left Vietnam, there would be a bloodbath of reprisal against those who had fought alongside the Americans. "We just cannot now dishonor our word," Johnson told the American public, "or abandon our commitment, or leave those who believed us and who trusted us to the terror and repression and murder that would follow."[222]

The president also restated his claim of altruistic intentions: "We do not seek the destruction of any government, nor do we covet a foot of any territory." But this time he added, "The people of South Vietnam shall have the right of choice, the right to shape their own destiny in free elections in the south . . . and they shall not have any government imposed upon them by force and terror."[223]

President Johnson concluded by echoing a promise that he had made weeks earlier in a speech in San Francisco. Johnson pledged "America's willingness to begin unconditional discussions with any government at any place at any time."[224] This promise would be recalled repeatedly over the following years by those who sought to impugn the [resident's credibility on the war; those critics would claim that the president was not, in fact, willing to negotiate.

This speech was also significant in that it was the last time the president or the administration would invoke the precedent of tit-for-tat reprisals for over a year.[225] The president explained:

> In recent months they [the North Vietnamese] have greatly increased their fighting forces and their attacks and the number of incidents. I have asked the Commanding General, General [William C.] Westmoreland, what more he needs to meet this mounting aggression. He has told me. We will meet his needs.[226]

Returning to his rhetoric from after the Gulf of Tonkin airstrikes, the president said that the deployment of troops was "carefully measured."[227]

In fact, despite this last invocation of a tit-for-tat justification for retaliation, by the time of this announcement the administration had completely abandoned tit-for-tat retaliation as a basis for escalation. In an internal memorandum for the president in June 1965, Secretary McNamara acknowledged that the primary purpose for the bombing of North Vietnam had been "first, to give us a better bargaining counter across the table from the North Vietnamese and, second, to interdict the flow of men and supplies from the North to the South." He added that the purpose of "reprisal" had been abandoned ever since the "Pleiku bombing" (Operation Flaming Dart).[228] The administration had decided to use U.S. military forces to contain communism in Vietnam; once this decision was made the justification for each escalation became its military necessity rather than the actions of the North Vietnamese or the Viet Cong.

The national press reported the president's July 28 message matter-of-factly, without alarm.[229] This tone was also tinged with a sense of relief, since both the public and the press had expected a larger escalation.[230] But these reports on the announcement also showed that the press accepted the administration's use of containment to justify this escalation. The editors of the *Lewiston Morning Tribune* from Lewiston, Idaho, wrote that the president's speech "served . . . to demonstrate conclusively and dramatically that the U.S. means every word when it says it will accept nothing short of total military victory or the opportunity to negotiate." Moreover, the *Tribune* echoed the administration's repeated claim that the Viet Cong was a puppet of North Vietnam and that the North Vietnamese were participating in the war in South Vietnam. The editors of the *Tribune* also echoed the administration's arguments based on the lessons of Munich: "The President does not believe in the so-called domino theory, [but] he certainly believes the Munich theory and intends to demonstrate conclusively that this nation will not back down to buy a few more months of peace." The *Tribune* called the "question of whether the United States should have gone into Viet Nam in the first place . . . almost a dead issue." Rather, the editors agreed with the president that "the only responsible way out is through victory or negotiated settlement."[231]

Columnist Joseph Alsop was relieved that the Johnson administration finally "[meant] business" about winning the war in Vietnam. Answering those critics who claimed "bombing the North is useless," Alsop responded, "The North has not really been bombed as yet." Alsop described the United States' efforts before 28 July 1965, primarily air strikes against North Vietnamese targets, as comparable to bombing "West Virginia's bridges, railroads and roads." Alsop wrote: "We should be indignant, humiliated . . . But in the end we would certainly not be alarmed." Alsop added: "We might even begin to laugh in our sleeves . . . if a powerful enemy made all sorts of statements about his bloody boldness and iron resolution and then just went on bombing West Virginia." Alsop was happy that the president had indicated in his July 28 announcement that he was finally committing sufficient U.S. force to convince the communists that the United States would not back down.[232]

Just as before the Gulf of Tonkin incident, the administration—and its media, academic, and activist supporters—used the ideology of military containment of communism as justification to "Americanize" the Vietnam War. Beyond these containment arguments for U.S. military intervention in Vietnam, the administration also occasionally relied on the precedents set by the Gulf of Tonkin incident. The reprisal airstrikes in response to the Gulf of Tonkin incident established the precedent of retaliation against North Vietnam for the actions of the Viet Cong. The Tonkin Gulf Resolution, the constitutional powers of the president, and prior congressional expressions of support for South Vietnamese independence such as the ratification of the SEATO treaty became the administration's legal justifications for U.S. military intervention in Vietnam.

However, by the time of the deployment of large numbers of U.S. Army soldiers to Vietnam, both tit-for-tat justifications and the Tonkin Gulf Resolution had virtually disappeared from administration rhetoric justifying U.S. military intervention in Vietnam. There is clear documentary evidence that tit-for-tat justifications for escalation were abandoned because the administration made the decision to stop escalating the war on a tit-for-tat basis and instead introduce forces on a more deliberate basis to contain communist expansion. While there is less direct evidence to explain the disappearance of the Tonkin Gulf Resolution from administration rhetoric, the most likely explanation—based on the lack of public congressional opposition to the escalation and the president's interactions with congressional leaders during this period—is that the president did not believe he needed the actual support of Congress, since he had the Tonkin Gulf Resolution, which he believed inoculated him—like a sort of "insurance policy"—against their dissent. However, during this period, congressional opposition to the administration's policy in Vietnam was muted. Evidence of this attitude would become much more apparent in 1967, as public congressional dissent grew and the president and the administration began to invoke the Tonkin Gulf Resolution as a weapon against the Congress.

A growing list of opponents of the U.S. military escalation—activists, academics, and media commentators chief among them—tried to change the president's policies in Vietnam by arguing against the suitability of the strategy of military containment of communism to Vietnam and Southeast Asia. Opponents also sometimes attacked the entire idea of military containment of communism, not just in Vietnam, but anywhere. These critiques represented a dramatic broadening of the public debate on U.S. foreign policy; previously, questioning the tenets of the Cold War consensus had been beyond the pale of mainstream political discourse. In fact, within academia and among radical dissenters, a new foreign policy movement—in fact, a foreign policy revolution—was stirring within this embryonic antiwar movement. The aim of these revolutionaries was not just to end the Vietnam War, but to reshape American foreign policy. As the war continued, this foreign policy revolution, fueled by dissent over the war, would gain traction among some members of Congress and grow into a political force in its own right.

Notably, few opponents of the escalation questioned the president's credibility on the escalation of the war. Virtually no one questioned the use of tit-for tat retaliation as a justification for escalation. And attacks on the facts of the Gulf of Tonkin incident or the legality of the Tonkin Gulf Resolution were virtually absent from opposition rhetoric. Opponents making these rare arguments were vastly outnumbered by the large number of opponents making arguments against the application of the ideology of military containment of communism to Southeast Asia.

All of these attacks on the administration's policies in Vietnam failed to persuade the American public to oppose the administration. In fact, the American public remained firmly behind the president throughout the Americanization of the Vietnam War, supporting bombing and embracing the administration's arguments for U.S.

military intervention based on the containment of communism. It is true that the administration never succeeded in building a public consensus behind the introduction of large numbers of U.S. ground troops in Vietnam, but as the administration introduced more and more ground troops to the conflict, the public continued to support the president and his policies in Vietnam.

The framework of public debate over the war in Vietnam established in late 1964 and the first half of 1965—between supporters using arguments based on the containment of communism and opponents arguing against the ideology of containment of communism or its applicability to the war in Vietnam—would remain the framework for debate until 1968. Public dissent in the Congress—especially in the Senate Foreign Relations Committee—grew during the period between mid-1965 and 1968. And that congressional criticism was firmly focused on the administration's use of containment to justify the war in Vietnam. As congressional dissent grew, the administration and its supporters began to reemphasize the Tonkin Gulf Resolution and use it as a weapon against Congress, claiming that it proved that the Congress had endorsed the escalation of U.S. military intervention in Vietnam. Yet, despite this explosion of dissent, the American public remained largely behind the president and his policies in Vietnam throughout this period. It was not until late 1966, when opponents of the administration's policies began to increasingly attack presidential credibility on Vietnam, that the tide of public opinion would begin to turn against the president.

Chapter 3

POLITICAL STALEMATE

The framework for public debate over the war in Vietnam established in the first half of 1965—between supporters using arguments based on the containment of communism and opponents arguing against the ideology of containment of communism or its applicability to the war in Vietnam—would remain largely unchanged until mid-1967. However, throughout this political stalemate, a new line of attack slowly took shape: attacks on the president's credibility over the war.

Public dissent in the Congress grew during this period—most dramatically in the Senate Foreign Relations Committee during hearings in 1966. And congressional opposition to the president's policies in Vietnam, like dissent from opponents in the media, focused on the suitability of military containment to the Vietnam War. Dissent also grew dramatically among radical protesters during this period, resulting most visibly in massive demonstrations in October and November 1965 and April 1967. Radical protesters opposed not just the application of the ideology of containment to Vietnam but the ideology of containment itself—and its impact on domestic and foreign policy.

While many of the administration's critics on Vietnam simply wanted to end the war, there was a small core of dissenters within this larger antiwar movement who wanted to move the United States beyond a foreign policy based on the ideology of military containment of communism. Within the Congress and academia, dissenters decried military containment as outmoded and argued that it had eroded the role of the Senate in advice and consent on foreign policy. Radical protesters decried the corrupting effect that the ideology of containment had on America's domestic and foreign policy. Together, these more fundamental critiques of U.S. foreign policy from Congress, academia, and the New Left constituted a foreign policy revolution bent on moving the United States beyond containment to a new foreign policy paradigm.

As early as late 1965, a new line of attack against the administration's policies in Vietnam began to take shape. Some opponents began to question the credibility of the president and his administration on the Vietnam War. Initially, these attacks on the president's credibility were sporadic and isolated. They did not begin to gain momentum until late 1966, when opponents first attacked the administration's credibility on civilian casualties. This was followed by an equally effective attack on the president's credibility on his willingness to negotiate.

Despite growing dissent, the American public continued to support the war in Vietnam and seemed to accept the president's justifications for military intervention in Vietnam based on the ideology of military containment. In fact, where Americans did disapprove of the president's policies in Vietnam, it was frequently because they did not believe these policies were aggressive enough.

As dissent in Congress grew, the administration occasionally reminded Congress and the American public of its insurance policy against congressional dissent—the Tonkin Gulf Resolution. Otherwise, the administration's stubborn response to growing dissent was to incessantly insist that the containment of communism demanded U.S. military intervention in Vietnam. The administration never explained to the majority of Americans who wanted a more aggressive approach to the war why it thought it could not adopt this policy. Likewise, the administration never developed an effective strategy for dealing with attacks on its credibility. Instead, the administration doggedly continued to justify the war using the ideology of military containment. As a result, while most Americans continued to support the war and the administration's justifications based on the containment of communism, in 1966 and 1967, Americans increasingly disapproved of the president's handling of the war and increasingly doubted his credibility.

In the weeks after the July 28, 1965, announcement of a dramatic increase in the number of U.S. ground troops in Vietnam, most Americans were intensely concerned about the growing war in Vietnam but continued to support the president. A White House poll of Pennsylvania voters found that a plurality of Pennsylvanians (40 percent) saw the Vietnam War as the most important issue facing the nation. And 53 percent of Pennsylvanians approved of the president's handling of the situation. Moreover, pollsters noted that many of those who did not approve of the president's policies in Vietnam disapproved because they wanted even greater escalation of the conflict.[1] A nationwide Gallup poll found almost identical concern over the issue of Vietnam nationally.[2]

After the announcement of troop deployments to Vietnam on July 28, 1965, the administration immediately returned to the use of the ideology of containment of communism to justify U.S. military intervention. In August 1965, the White House released a pamphlet (and similarly titled film) called "Why Vietnam?" This was a collection of statements and letters from presidents and administration officials since the Eisenhower administration. It was also a catalogue of the arguments based on the ideology of military containment that the Johnson administration had been using to justify U.S. military intervention in Vietnam since early 1964. First and foremost, the pamphlet supported the argument that President Johnson was continuing the policy of his predecessors over the previous eleven years. The pamphlet provided "historic documents" proving that "two American Presidents [had] define[d] and affirm[ed] the commitment of the United States to the people of South Vietnam." The pamphlet included letters from Eisenhower to Prime Minister Winston Churchill and President Diem and from Kennedy to President Diem that "describe[d] the issues at stake and pledge[d] United States assistance in South Vietnam's resistance to subversion and aggression." In at least one letter, Eisenhower recounted the lessons of Munich, telling Churchill: "We failed to halt Hirohito, Mussolini and Hitler by not acting in unity and in time. . . . May it not be that our nations have learned something from that lesson?" In another letter, to Diem, Eisenhower restated the Johnson administration's claim that the war was a result of communist aggression. He wrote that he wished to help South Vietnam build a state that could "discourage any who might wish to impose foreign ideology on your free people."[3]

The pamphlet also quoted members of the Johnson administration using containment to justify U.S. military intervention in Vietnam. Secretary of State Dean Rusk was quoted from a statement on August 3, 1965, citing specific numbers of men and types of equipment that had crossed the border from North to South Vietnam since 1959. In this statement, Rusk also claimed that the war was guided by "Communist North Vietnam, with the backing of Peiping and Moscow." Rusk also repeated the administration's promise that it did not "seek to destroy or overturn the communist regimes in Hanoi and Peiping," but rather to force North Vietnam to "cease their aggressions." Likewise, Rusk claimed that the Johnson administration wanted "no permanent bases and no special position" in Southeast Asia. In this statement Rusk also argued that Southeast Asia must be defended until Communist China matured and, like the Soviet Union, embraced peaceful coexistence. Rusk also placed the war in Vietnam in the context of other Cold War flashpoints, listing such confrontations against "aggressive appetites" in other places such as Iran, Turkey, Greece, West Berlin, Korea, Cuba, and the Congo. In restating the precepts of the domino theory, Rusk said that the loss of Southeast Asia "could drastically alter the strategic situation in Asia and the Pacific to the grave detriment of our own security and that of our Allies." This pamphlet cited Rusk as noting the recent deployment of a division from South Korea to Vietnam as evidence that other Asian countries believed the domino theory as well. Rusk also claimed that "the Chinese Communists have chosen to make South Vietnam the test case for their . . . so-called 'wars of national liberation,'" a technique Rusk claimed had also been embraced by Khrushchev. Rusk also claimed that the Vietnam War was a contest between the Soviet Union and Communist China for "prestige" within the Communist World and among "the non-aligned nations."[4]

In arguing for sustaining the credibility of U.S. commitments, Rusk listed Congress's explicit commitments to South Vietnam. Rusk noted that the Senate had ratified the SEATO treaty and numerous aid packages for South Vietnam which, Rusk claimed, committed the United States to act militarily in Vietnam. Rusk also cited the Tonkin Gulf Resolution as a commitment to South Vietnam. First, he stated the administration's version of the events of August 4, 1964—the Gulf of Tonkin incident.[5] Rusk then added:

> Congress, by a combined vote of 504 to 2, passed a resolution expressing its support for actions by the Executive "including the use of armed force" to meet aggression in Southeast Asia, including specifically aggression against South Vietnam. The resolution and the Congressional debate specifically envisaged that . . . the armed forces of the United States might be committed in the defense of South Vietnam in any way that seemed necessary, including employment in combat.[6]

Rusk was claiming that the Tonkin Gulf Resolution itself committed the United States to defend South Vietnam, an idea found nowhere in the text of the document. But, more importantly, he was also claiming that the resolution was an explicit endorsement of U.S. military intervention in Vietnam.[7] This passage omitted the important fact that the president had assured senators that he would not use the Tonkin Gulf Resolution to prosecute a war in Vietnam.

But such invocations by the administration of the Tonkin Gulf Resolution were rare, since congressional dissent in mid-1965 was likewise relatively rare. In late August 1965, Senator Ernest Gruening did threaten to attach an amendment to the defense appropriations bill that would have prohibited the Defense Department from sending draftees to Vietnam against their will. The core of Gruening's dissent was that the president had "sought no declaration of war from the only part of the Federal Government authorized by the constitution to declare war—the Congress." Gruening told his colleagues: "A vote against the amendment or a vote to table this amendment [would] be a vote to use the peacetime conscription laws to send draftees to fight and perchance to die" in Vietnam.[8] This attack on the president's policies in Vietnam was particularly significant in that it was not an attack on the administration's containment justifications for the war but an implicit attack on the validity of the Tonkin Gulf Resolution as a legal basis to prosecute the war—the only attack of its kind mounted by anyone in the Senate before the Tet Offensive.

Gruening only abandoned this effort after a personal call from the president in which Johnson promised that no draftees inducted before the end of the year would go to Vietnam before January 1966. In the letter certifying this agreement and thanking Gruening for relenting, the president avoided defending the Tonkin Gulf Resolution, instead defending U.S. military intervention using the ideology of containment of communism. He wrote that North Vietnam could not "evade its responsibility for aggression against South Vietnam." The bombing of North Vietnam was "a response in the North to Hanoi's expanded aggression in the South" intended to "persuade the aggressors to desist."[9]

Attacks on the president's credibility in 1965 were also rare. The Republican governor of Rhode Island, John Chafee (who would later serve as secretary of the Navy and U.S. senator), was one of the few government officials who did attack presidential credibility. In August 1965, Chafee argued that the president was disingenuous in telling the American people they could fight the Vietnam War without paying for it. "Never mind," Chafee quipped, "we'll put it off on future generations." Chafee also criticized the administration's claims of success in its bombing program. He called estimates of enemy losses to bombing "the closest thing to fiction writing we've seen in a long time."[10] Neither of these attacks was repeated by other critics of the administration and this attack on the administration's credibility quickly faded from the headlines.

These rare attacks on the Tonkin Gulf Resolution and the president's credibility aside, the vast majority of war opponents focused their attacks on the administration's arguments for military intervention based on the containment of communism. Edward J. Meeman, editor of the *Memphis Press-Scimitar*, objected that the United States, with its intervention in South Vietnam, was opening itself to charges of "colonial[ism]" or, worse, setting the stage for "World War III with nuclear destruction." Meeman believed it was "not the time for a final confrontation with world communism," since the Communist World was in the midst of a movement toward fragmentation and moderation. Meeman was prepared to give the president the benefit of the doubt, writing, "No man desires peace in Vietnam more than President Johnson." But Meeman added that the president was trying to achieve this peace by escalating "in order that our side will obtain a better military position." While he did concede that the United States must offer asylum "to the leaders and ringleaders of the Vietnamese patriots who would be liquidated by the Communists if they stayed," Meeman still advocated immediate withdrawal. This editorial also attacked the very core of the ideology of military containment: "The relative strength of Communism and Freedom is not determined by the number of square miles occupied by communists and governments labeled free." Meeman concluded, "Freedom's strength is in the unity of the peoples and the success of the free governments."[11]

Radical dissenters also focused their attacks on the administration's justifications based on the containment of communism. The Students for a Democratic Society (SDS) published a pamphlet, the *Vietnam Study Guide*, that was designed to assist activists in arguing against the Vietnam War. Among the suggestions was advice on how to show "how little proof the other side has been able to come up with" to prove North Vietnamese assistance to the Viet Cong. The pamphlet also provided instructions on how to disprove "the 'menace' of Communist Chinese expansionism which many people believe to be lurking behind the Communist thrust in Vietnam." The core of the SDS's antiwar argument was that a communist takeover of Vietnam was the inevitable result of anticolonial nationalism; this pamphlet claimed that, by intervening in Vietnam, the United States had in fact "reverse[d] a successful revolution in the South . . . by installing an anti-communist regime." The pamphlet concluded: "Do not try to paint communism as a picnic for the peasant masses; insist only that it is a better alternative than any which the United States is prepared to sponsor."[12]

In early August 1965, Secretaries Rusk and McNamara appeared in an interview on CBS News to reassert the ideology of containment as justification for the growing war in Vietnam. Journalist Harry Reasoner asked the secretaries how American "honor" and "security" were involved in the conflict in Vietnam. Rusk responded by arguing that the conflict was a result of communist aggression and that the United States had to honor its commitments. McNamara repeated his argument that the Vietnam War was "the model of the national liberation movement" and warned that it would be seen in Latin America and across Asia if it succeeded in Vietnam. Rusk insisted that the conflict was "about the life and death of the Nation." Rusk explained that "the essential fact" of the conflict was "that North Viet-Nam has sent tens of thousands of men and large quantities of arms into South Viet-Nam to take over that country by force." Rusk added that the United States was committed to stop this aggression in accordance with "the Southeast Asia Treaty," "the bilateral arrangements that President Eisenhower made with the Government of South Viet-Nam," and "the most formal declarations of three Presidents of both political parties."[13]

In this same interview, Rusk once more claimed that the Tonkin Gulf Resolution itself committed the United States to act to defend South Vietnam. Rusk explained that the United States was committed to the defense of South Vietnam by "regular authorizations and appropriations of the Congress in giving aid to South Viet-Nam." But he added that the United States was also bound by "the resolution of the Congress of last August."[14] Here again the Tonkin Gulf Resolution was being used not just an insurance policy against congressional dissent but as a supposed binding commitment to defend South Vietnam that could not be broken. No doubt because of its tenuous basis in fact— such a commitment is found nowhere in the text of the resolution— this was the last time anyone in the administration would make this claim. In fact, this is the last time the administration would invoke the resolution for nearly a year.

In this CBS interview, Kalischer, Kendrick, and Reasoner seemed skeptical of the administration's justifications for the war based on the ideology of the containment of communism. For instance, in obvious reference to Morley Safer's television news story about Marines burning the village of Cam Ne that had aired on August 5, only four days earlier,[15] Kendrick asked in a follow up to a question about national honor: "What about dishonor? What about the world image that we now present? We are burning villages, we are killing civilians." Attacking the contention that the United States was assisting the people of South Vietnam in preserving their freedom, Kalischer asked: "Are we reasonably assured that this government represents the people of South Viet-Nam or even a large number of the people in South Viet-Nam?" Evoking the specter of the Korean War, Kendrick asked if the United States was "still fighting the same war with Communist China that we were fighting in Korea." Reasoner questioned the application of the lessons of Munich to the Vietnam War; he said that Americans "have trouble understanding just what we mean when we speak in the pattern of having to defend it here or we will have to fight in some less suitable place." When Secretary Rusk claimed that the United States had to prove the value of its commitments to other countries outside of Vietnam, Kendrick immediately rebutted, "Is it possible that it is an [overcommitment]?"[16]

The pointed questions in this CBS interview aside, most in the media supported the administration's justifications for U.S. military intervention based on the containment of communism. In October 1965, columnist Alice Widener put the blame for the conflict squarely on Hanoi. "The openly avowed purpose of the Hanoi regime," she wrote, "is to overthrow the Saigon government and communize South Vietnam." In fact, Weidner wanted the administration to be even more aggressive in fighting the war. Widener criticized the president's "willingness to negotiate for a peaceful settlement of the issues in the war." She added: "The only message the Reds will 'get' is a knock-out blow that would blast Ho Chi Minh and his clique out of power in North Vietnam."[17]

The White House had evidence in late summer 1965 that much of the American public also felt the president was not being aggressive enough in Vietnam. Internal White House polling of voters in New Haven, Connecticut, showed that the president's favorable ratings on handling the conflict had slipped from 53 percent to 48 percent favorable between July and September. Moreover, 55 percent of New Haven voters wanted the president to "step up our military even more and win the war." It wasn't clear from this poll how these voters wanted the war "step[ed] up"; only 13 percent wanted to "bomb Red China" and only 24 percent wanted to "bomb Hanoi."[18]

A Gallup poll from late August and early September provided a clearer prescription. Most Americans were unequivocal in their support of the president's decision to defend the sovereignty of South Vietnam; when asked, "in view of the developments since we entered the fighting in Vietnam, do you think the U.S. made a mistake sending troops to fight in Vietnam," 71 percent of Americans who responded answered with an unqualified "no." However, Americans were nearly evenly split over the effectiveness of the U.S. efforts there. Slightly more of those Americans who had an opinion believed that the United States was doing "very well" in Vietnam, while slightly fewer believed that the United States was "not doing so well" in that conflict. However, of those who believed the United States was "not doing so well," nineteen percent believed that the United States needed "to go all the way" and wage "all out war." Another 10 percent believed the United States had placed "too many limitations" on the fighting forces already present in Vietnam for them to be successful. Six percent suggested that the United States needed "more troops [and] equipment" in Vietnam.[19] The administration was not doing anything to explain to these Americans why it was not being more aggressive in Vietnam.

Fall 1965 brought a marked increase in public opposition to the war. Two separate protestors, emulating Buddhist monks who had committed suicide by self-immolation years earlier in Vietnam, set themselves on fire in protest against the war—one in front of the Pentagon (just below Secretary McNamara's office window) and one in front of the United Nations. On October 16, 1965, radical protesters held antiwar demonstrations in forty American cities and several capitals in Europe. In November, protesters mounted a twenty thousand–man march on Washington.[20] Radical protesters objected not just to the application of containment to U.S. military intervention in Vietnam, but to the ideology of containment itself. During this same period, Senator J. William Fulbright's dissent against the war in Vietnam was joined by other members of Congress objecting to the administration's use of containment to justify the war. Most in the media and the American public rejected both radical protesters and more modest congressional dissent. The media even began to attack radical protesters as aiding communists. In fact, the excesses of radical protesters may have actually increased support for the president's handling of the war in Vietnam.

While radical protesters and the slightly increased dissent from Congress did little to shake public confidence in the president's policies in Vietnam, the administration was privately coming to the realization that it had two bigger problems with which to contend. First, many Americans objected to the president's policies in Vietnam because they were not aggressive enough. Others were beginning to doubt the administration's credibility. However, rather than address these problems, the administration stubbornly continued to use the ideology of military containment of communism to justify the war.

The fall 1965 protests staged by radical dissenters seemed almost designed to alienate middle-class Americans. Along with perennial dissenters like Dr. Benjamin Spock, the November protest also featured the National Coordinating Committee to End the War in Vietnam, whose president proudly announced he had received a letter from Nguyen Huu Tho, chairman of the Central Committee of the National Liberation Front, wishing him luck in advance of the march. Another group participating in the march, the Committee to Aid the National Liberation Front of Vietnam, used the protest as an opportunity to raise money to buy medical supplies for the Viet Cong, fly the National Liberation Front flag, and distribute North Vietnamese propaganda pamphlets.[21]

The Students for a Democratic Society (SDS), key organizers of the November march on Washington, sought more than an end to the war in Vietnam. The core of their dissent was their objection to the Cold War order, both in foreign and domestic policy. The SDS offered an alternative conception of post–World War II history that contrasted sharply with the administration's:

> Seemingly irreconcilable conflict between the two blocs created a world in which virtually every human value was distorted, all moral standards seemed weirdly irrelevant, all hopes and aspirations appeared Utopian. For the Cold War resulted in an arms race in which enormous resources and human energy were squandered and preparation for the murder of innocent millions became basic policy, while the elemental needs of these millions remained unsatisfied. It produced societies in which the requirements of huge military, industrial and political bureaucracies took precedence over all other social or individual priorities. It poisoned and corroded all aspects of intellectual activity. To it were sacrificed the essential ingredients of democratic process—free debate, the right to dissent, political engagement and controversy. And its final outcome was a balance of terror so precarious and so infinitely dangerous that, in the end, all interests and all security were in jeopardy.[22]

For the SDS, the Vietnam War was caused not by "communist aggression, but by the basic inability of the U.S. government to offer political and economic alternatives to people in revolutionary upsurge." Unless stopped, the administration's "resolve to meet revolution with force" would mean "the sure devastation of country after country in the Third World."[23] The SDS was doing more than dissenting on the war; it was joining the foreign policy revolution begun by academics earlier in the year.

The press was unsympathetic toward the protesters. An October 1965 political cartoon from the *Philadelphia Enquirer* captured the view of most in the media (and in the American public) toward the protesters.

This cartoon showed two young protesters, one carrying a sign that read, "Burn your draft card." The other, with longer hair and a beard, carried a partially obscured placard that appeared to say "Get

A cartoon portraying protestors as communists.

Source: Pierre Bellocq, *Philadelphia Inquirer*, October 21, 1965, p. 10. Reprinted with the permission of the artist.[24]

out of Vietnam." The two men also carried a bucket of glue and a ladder, and appeared to be leaving the place where they had just glued a poster to a brick wall. The poster contained a caricature of Mao Zedong pointing a finger as Uncle Sam did in older, World War II recruiting posters. The caption on the poster read, "I need you." The caption on the cartoon read, "Recruitment," implying that radical protesters were encouraging others to aid Communist China by opposing the war.[25]

As the season of protests continued, there were other indications that the vast majority of Americans rejected the arguments and tactics of these radical protesters. In a Gallup poll from early November, Americans were asked, "To what extent, if any, have the Communists been involved in the demonstrations over Viet Nam." Nearly 65 percent of Americans who expressed an opinion responded that the communists had "a lot" of involvement in the demonstrations, with another 23 percent believing that communists had "some" involvement in the protests.[26]

As the fall 1965 protests wore on, there were also indications that antiwar activism was actually increasing American public support for the president's policies in Vietnam. In a Gallup poll after the October protests across forty American cities, fully three quarters of Americans who expressed an opinion believed it was the right decision to intervene militarily in the conflict in Vietnam—an increase of over five percentage points from before the protests. Moreover, the prognosis for the war in Vietnam had improved markedly. Forty percent of Americans who expressed an opinion now believed the United States would "win" the Vietnam War, though slightly more Americans believed the war would end in "another Korea" or a less-than-optimal compromise peace. More conclusively, however, 69 percent of Americans who expressed an opinion now believed that the United States was doing "very well" in Vietnam—an increase of nearly twenty percentage points from before the fall protests.[27]

Interestingly, opinions also hardened in favor of politicians who advocated a stronger response in Vietnam after the fall protests. In early September 1965, a slight majority (53 percent) of Americans who had an opinion on the question would be "less inclined" to vote for "a candidate for Congress in your district [who] advocated sending a great many more men to Vietnam."[28] By early November, opinion had shifted dramatically on this question; nearly 60 percent of those expressing an opinion would be "more likely" to support such a candidate.[29]

During this season of antiwar protests, there was also increased congressional dissent, focused squarely on the administration's use of containment to justify the war. Just before the November protests, Senator J. William Fulbright decried what he called a "drift toward the role of global policeman." He added that there was something "fishy, something unhealthy about a nation which tries to tell the rest of the world how to run its business, when our own home-front is in such an untidy mess."[30] This speech made no more impact on the American public than radical activists' protests. But it was still significant in that it was more than just a dissent on U.S. military intervention in Vietnam; it was an attack on the Cold War consensus—the ideology of military containment itself. Fulbright had joined the foreign policy revolution.

In November 1965, a delegation of congressmen led by Senator Mike Mansfield travelled to South Vietnam on a fact-finding mission.[31] Upon his return from this trip, Democratic Senator Stephen M. Young of Ohio joined those few members of Congress publicly opposing the war. And Young's opposition was directed at the administration's contention that containment of communism required military intervention in Vietnam. Young said he was convinced that "South Viet Nam is of no strategic importance to the defense of the United States," that the bulk of Viet Cong guerillas were South Vietnamese, and that the United States had inadvertently intervened in a civil war. Young told reporters that while the domino theory may have been valid in the "Stalin era," it was no longer valid with "Moscow and Peking in bitter conflict." His prescription was a bombing halt. He implored the president to resist the "militarists" in the Pentagon who wanted an escalation of the bombing to include Haiphong and Hanoi. He also believed that the United States should include the Viet Cong and Hanoi in peace negotiations.[32]

Soon after, Pennsylvania Democratic Senator Joseph S. Clark joined the growing bloc of congressional dissenters by attacking the utility of military containment to the problem of Vietnam. In a speech in December 1965, Clark opposed further escalation of the war on the grounds that there was "very little hope of a military solution." He added: "For every acre of ground you take, you sent a coffin back." Clark proposed holing up in coastal enclaves to "make it clear we will never be driven out." Without explicitly mentioning the Tonkin Gulf Resolution, Clark also echoed Senator Ernest Gruening's earlier objection to the administration's legal basis for the war, saying that it was "completely illegal and unconstitutional." Yet Clark was not ready to endorse immediate withdrawal; he said that, now that the United States was in the war, it could not simply cut and run.[33]

Just as they had radical dissent, most in the media also rejected this congressional dissent. And they did so by echoing the administration's use of the ideology of military containment. The *Pine Bluff Commercial* from Senator J. William Fulbright's home state of Arkansas compared the aggression against South Vietnam to Hitler's

aggression against Czechoslovakia and those who opposed intervention in South Vietnam to those—like Neville Chamberlain—who the
Commercial claimed had failed to stand up to Hitler's aggression and
thus created the calamity of the Second World War. The *Commercial*
mocked those congressmen who wanted to abandon Vietnam: "People
will think. . . . Put it off, wait till they get to Thailand, make our stand
across the Mekong or in Malaya, or make Australia an invulnerable fortress continent." The editors wrote that Chamberlain may have wanted
noble goals, but in the end "Neville Chamberlain went to Munich.
And the war he had bargained away Czechoslovakia to prevent came
even before he left office." The editorial warned those who wanted
to leave Vietnam against believing "that peace can be purchased at
the price of a small country, that this is the aggressor's last territorial
demand."[34]

Even *New York Times* editor James "Scotty" Reston, erstwhile
critic of the administration's policies in Vietnam, was forced to admit
the compelling logic of the domino theory. In a December 1965 article, Reston wrote that, while India and Japan "do not believe in the
domino theory . . . they agree that an American defeat there would
gradually lead to the expansion of Peking's power all over South and
East Asia." Reston concluded: "American defense of Asia is unsatisfac-
tory, and increasingly costly, but it is the only policy there is and the
only one in prospect."[35]

While most in the media and the American public supported the
administration's use of containment to justify the war in Vietnam,
there were growing concerns within the administration that Americans
might begin to demand more forceful action. An internal administration memorandum written by Chester L. Cooper shows the way the
administration saw its public relations challenges in late 1965, after
the march on Washington. Cooper described four distinct groups that
must be engaged and the strategies to engage each. The first audience, pro-war activists, had generated a "great surge of goodwill which
could play a vital role in our efforts," but Cooper thought that this
group should be encouraged and assisted, lest it "die down as dramatically as it has grown." The second group, the "70 percent," were those

Americans who supported the president's policies, though Cooper worried that "many people probably do not even understand what it is that they are supporting."[36] Cooper believed the task with this group should be

> . . . to sustain and nourish this support through hostilities with its high casualties, negotiations with its frustrations, settlement with its inevitable compromises, and reconstruction with its high costs.[37]

The next group, "the Hawks," fell within the "70 percent" and, Cooper predicted, would become increasingly vocal in their demands for more violent means as the November 1966 midterm elections approached. Cooper wrote: "The basic task of surrounding and containing the Hawks will have to be done by the Administration, itself." The final group Cooper identified was the "Disaffected Left." Cooper wrote that "the main task here is to separate the confused or worried liberals from the hard-core left-cum-kooks." The former were "of particular importance, not only in terms of the prestige and respectability they give to the organized protestors of the left, but because they can play a useful role in the President's domestic programs." Cooper believed that the administration could "bring them around" by direct engagement.[38]

The administration's approach to deal with the "70 percent"[39] was to continue to argue for U.S. military intervention in Vietnam using the ideology of containment, and by December 1965 this approach seemed to be working. According to a December Gallup poll, 56 percent of Americans approved the president's handling of Vietnam.[40] However, the administration's approach—preaching to the converted about why military intervention was needed in Vietnam using the ideology of military containment—failed to deal with the problem of the "the Hawks,"[41] whom the same Gallup poll showed were a very large percentage of the "70 percent."[42] In December 1965, 59 percent of Americans who expressed an opinion believed that the president should "go all out in bombing North Vietnam until the

Communists are ready to negotiate."[43] When asked for specifics, 61 percent of Americans who had an opinion did oppose bombing North Vietnamese "big cities," but an even bigger percentage, 71 percent, favored "bombing industrial plants and factories in North Vietnam."[44] The administration was not effectively communicating to the majority of Americans—who wanted the administration to use more force in Vietnam—why it did not adopt that policy. In fact, only weeks after this poll, congressional pressure would force the president to further antagonize "hawks" by implementing a bombing pause.

Some in the administration were deeply concerned about this problem. In a letter in January 1966, Walt Rostow implored the president to level with the American people. The president needed to explain why the United States didn't "go all-out" in Vietnam. Rostow believed that this would be accepted by the majority of Americans "because 60% of the people are with you—and are always for the right thing when the President takes his stand." Rostow also believed that this same 60 percent of Americans "needs to feel we are doing our very best—in a good cause—without holding back." Rostow concluded by telling the president "that 60% doesn't have to be promised a quick or happy ending." These Americans, Rostow said, just needed to believe that all that could be done was being done.[45]

As 1965 came to a close, the administration also was receiving signals that it might have a growing problem with its credibility. In November 1965, I. F. Stone initiated a new line of criticism concerning government credibility on the war: that the president was deceptive in his claims that he sought negotiations. Reporting on a recent press conference, Stone wrote that reporters "tried to elicit what standards the government imposes in determining whether peace feelers are 'serious' or 'sincere.'" Stone wrote that the "spokesman retreated behind a smoke-screen of double-talk." Stone concluded: "The truth . . . is that we wait for a signal that the other side is ready, not to negotiate, but to surrender."[46]

Of course, I. F. Stone was a marginal voice in the debate over the war. Moreover, this was virtually the only attack on the administration's credibility during this period. However, the administration also received other warnings that its credibility on the issue of Vietnam might come into question. After a visit to Vietnam, author, movie producer, and friend of the administration John Secondari warned the administration that it might have a deep credibility problem with the Saigon press corps. In discussing the daily press briefings by Military Assistance Command–Vietnam—which the press had already taken to calling the "five o'clock follies"—Secondari said, "The Army has no friends among the press." Secondari blamed the military's overly optimistic reports on the war for the erosion of credibility.[47]

General Maxwell Taylor, former U.S. ambassador to South Vietnam, provided even more ominous warnings about threats to the administration's credibility in a letter to the president at the end of 1965. From numerous television and public appearances since returning to the United States, Taylor had drawn the conclusion that "there is . . . some suspicion that this government is holding back and perhaps concealing some of the facts." Taylor's suggestion to address this credibility problem was "many more high-level explanations to our people of the basic issues in South Viet-Nam to give them the feeling of being taken more into the confidence of their government."[48]

Rather than responding to these warnings about the erosion of his administration's credibility—or responding to the American public's demands for more aggressive means in prosecuting the war—the president stubbornly continued to use the ideology of military containment to justify U.S. military intervention in Vietnam. In his 1966 State of the Union Address, the president painted his policies in Vietnam as, "not an isolated episode, but another great event in the policy that we have followed with strong consistency since World War II." Vietnam was analogous to the "rebuild[ing of] Western Europe" or U.S. "aid to Greece and Turkey" or the defense of "the freedom of Berlin." Invoking his predecessors and their Cold War foreign policy achievements, he said, "In this pursuit we have defended against communist aggression—in Korea under President Truman—in the Formosa Straits under President Eisenhower—in Cuba under President Kennedy—and again in Vietnam." This current aggression, he added, came from "the ambitions of mainland China." But war had also come to Vietnam because, "little more than 6 years ago, North Vietnam decided on conquest" and began moving "soldiers and supplies . . . from North to South in a swelling stream."[49] Johnson also argued that the U.S. must honor its commitments to reassure all of its allies, not just South Vietnam. America, Johnson said, had made a "solemn pledge—a pledge which has grown through the commitments of three American Presidents." Moreover, Johnson added, "in Asia—and around the world—are countries whose independence rests, in large measure, on confidence in America's word and in America's protection."[50] If the United States failed in South Vietnam, the president concluded, it

> . . . would weaken that confidence, would undermine the independence of many lands, and would whet the appetite of aggression. We would have to fight in one land, and then we would have to fight in another—or abandon much of Asia to the domination of communists.[51]

On February 4, 1966, Senator J. William Fulbright's Committee began hearings to consider the president's request for an additional $415 million to fund the war. These hearings were an all-out assault on the administration's justifications for U.S. military intervention in Vietnam based on the containment of communism. They represented the first time that the Senate Foreign Relations Committee had publicly dissented on a U.S. military intervention since the beginning of the Cold War.[52] These hearings also marked the first consistent airing of criticism of the war by the national television networks since it had started.[53]

The president's response to this threat to his policies in Vietnam was twofold. First, he tried to overshadow the hearings with a series of publicity events. But the administration also responded to the hearings by reasserting that the containment of communism in Southeast Asia required U.S. military intervention in Vietnam and by attacking opponents of the war as aiding communists. This response was echoed by many of the administration's supporters in the media.

The administration and its supporters in the media also occasionally reminded the Congress and the American public of the Tonkin Gulf Resolution—both as its legal justification for prosecuting the war and as its insurance policy against congressional dissent.

These hearings generated very little new congressional dissent. The hearings also failed to convince the American people to abandon support for the war. Senator J. William Fulbright and his staff emerged from the hearings convinced that they had to weaken the power of the Tonkin Gulf Resolution as a weapon against congressional dissent before they could convince a majority in Congress to oppose the war. However, despite these sentiments, subsequent hearings in spring 1965 continued to focus on the applicability of containment to the war in Vietnam.

In early 1966, most Americans were still intensely concerned about the war and still largely accepted the administration's argument that the war was necessary in order to contain communism. A poll conducted by the Inter-University Consortium for Political Research found that 60 percent of Americans were worried "a great deal" by the war in Vietnam. This same poll found that, of those Americans who expressed an opinion, 68 percent would reject an American withdrawal from Vietnam if it "meant eventual control of south Viet Nam by the Viet Cong." Fully 85 percent of these Americans would reject an American withdrawal from Vietnam if it "meant the eventual loss of independence of other nations like Laos and Thailand."[54] While this does not necessarily prove that Americans believed the domino theory, it does show that they feared the consequences that that theory predicted. Another question showed that Americans had accepted the administration's claim that the Viet Cong was supported by, or even a proxy force, for the North Vietnamese. When asked "Who are the Viet Cong," slightly over 50 percent of those Americans who correctly identified them as the United States' adversaries in South Vietnam said that they were, in fact, "North Vietnamese" with another 36 percent identifying them as "South Vietnamese Communists."[55]

While the president enjoyed the support of the American people, he feared the impact the Fulbright hearings might have on that support. To blunt the impact of the hearings, the president attempted to preempt the event with several moves of his own. First, the president implemented a bombing pause on Christmas Eve 1965. Then, in January 1966, the president sent Vice President Hubert Humphrey, W. Averell Harriman, William Bundy, and Arthur Goldberg to foreign capitals in a very public "peace offensive" to find a negotiated settlement to the war.[56] The peace offensive had a dramatic impact in the American press. The cover of *Time* magazine featured the headline, "The U.S. Peace Offensive And The Communist Response."[57] In their syndicated column, Rowland Evans and Robert Novak were hopeful of the prospects for peace. However, even these sympathetic commentators admitted that the offensive was also aimed at "muffling the peaceniks."[58]

The American people clearly took notice of the peace offensive. According to internal White House polling conducted by Research Council, Inc., fully 60 percent of Americans were aware of the peace offensive only a week after it began. More importantly for the president, once told that it was occurring, 63 percent of Americans approved of the peace offensive. The same percentage believed that the president was doing an "excellent" or "pretty good" job in handling the war in Vietnam.[59]

However, this same poll revealed more troubling signals that Americans were beginning to question the administration's credibility on Vietnam. This polling did show that confidence in the authenticity of the president's desire for peace had increased markedly. In a poll conducted by CBS a few weeks before the offensive, only 44 percent of Americans said that "the Johnson administration is doing as much as it should" to negotiate a peaceful settlement in Vietnam. A week after the offensive began, that percentage had risen to 57 percent. However, when Americans were asked if they believed "that important information the public should have is being held back," only 38 percent of Americans answered that they were being told "all they ought to know." Forty-eight percent suspected "information [was] being held back." The pollsters concluded that the American public had "some reservations when it comes to the Administration's credibility."[60]

The administration's second effort to mute the effect of the Fulbright hearings was a conference in Honolulu with the leaders of South Vietnam.[61] The highly publicized conference included General William Westmoreland, Secretary of State Dean Rusk, Secretary of Defense Robert McNamara, and large White House and State Department public affairs teams. The event itself was political theater designed to prove the administration's arguments that the war was needed to contain communism. In a press conference, General Westmoreland told reporters that as many as one third of the regiments that American ground forces faced in South Vietnam were from North Vietnam. President Thieu thanked the United States for the casualties it had suffered to protect South Vietnamese "freedom."[62] In a speech during the conference, the president harkened to the lessons of Munich. "We cannot accept [dissenters'] logic that tyranny 10,000 miles away is not tyranny to concern us," Johnson said, "or that subjugation by an armed minority in Asia is different from subjugation by an armed minority in Europe." The president added: "In the forties and fifties we took our stand in Europe to protect the freedom of those threatened by aggression." The president asked: "If we had not then acted, what kind of Europe might there be today?" Johnson concluded: "If we allow the Communists to win in Viet-Nam, it will become easier and more appetizing for them to take over other countries in other parts of the world. We will have to fight again someplace else—at what cost no one knows."[63]

During a late night event upon the president's return to Washington, the president announced that he was sending Vice President Humphrey to Saigon and other Asian capitals to secure additional support for the U.S. effort in Vietnam—another move designed to blunt the impact of the Fulbright hearings. In the brief speech, the president implicitly derided the hearings as sowing disunity: "The road ahead may be long and may be difficult. It will require the unfailing unity of our people in support of the courageous young Americans who . . . are tonight fighting and suffering for us."[64] The message was clear: Americans—including protesters and dissenters in the Senate—needed to get behind the war effort and support the troops.

Unlike the peace offensive, the press was generally skeptical of the Honolulu conference, especially the promise to emerge from the conference to refocus the war effort on pacification. The *New York Post* wrote that while the conference sought to change the focus from defeating North Vietnam to pacifying South Vietnam, "the session inadvertently underscored the lack of interest of the junta in Saigon in anything but military conquest of the Viet Cong, to be carried out by stepped up U.S. armed efforts."[65] The Honolulu Conference may, in fact, have hurt rather than helped the administration in building public support for its policies in Vietnam. Before the conference, 57 percent of Americans approved of the president's handling of Vietnam.[66] A week after the Honolulu conference that percentage had slipped to just over 50 percent.[67]

The final act of preemptive sabotage against the Fulbright hearings came not from Washington but from Saigon. Barry Zorthian, chief public affairs coordinator in the U.S. embassy in Saigon, was instrumental in getting a story run in the *Washington Post* in the first days of the Fulbright hearings that accused the Congress of destroying U.S. and South Vietnamese morale and bolstering morale in North Vietnam and the broader Communist World.[68] Ward Just, the article's author, specifically cited Senator Robert F. Kennedy's proposal to "give the Vietcong . . . a share in a post war Vietnamese government." (Kennedy's actual proposal was simply to give the National Liberation Front a seat at negotiations in order to get negotiations started.) Just quoted South Vietnamese Prime Minister Nguyen Cao Ky as accusing Kennedy "of using 'the destiny of 20 million people' as an issue in the 1968 presidential campaign." Just quoted a U.S. official as saying of the Kennedy proposal, "To legitimize the Vietcong is to legitimize terrorism, and we do not see how, if this is done, the government here can last." Likewise, Just wrote that the "reaction to the Senate Foreign Relations Committee hearings" was "almost total dismay." He quoted a U.S. Army cavalry officer as saying: "[Troops] can understand draft card burners. . . . What they can't understand is U.S. Senators criticizing what we're doing here." U.S. officials believed that the time for debate had passed, Just wrote, and "that now we need some closing of ranks."[69]

Not all media criticism of dissenters was instigated by the administration. *U.S. News & World Report* reprinted an editorial by Alan McIntosh, publisher of the *Rock County Herald* in Luverne, Minnesota. The editorial, titled "I am a tired American," decried the incessant criticism of the United States at home and abroad by congressional, academic, and radical dissenters.[70] However, McIntosh also had criticism for the administration:

> I am a tired American—who gets more than a little bit weary of the clique in our State Department which chooses to regard a policy of timidity as prudent—the same group which subscribes to a "no win" policy in Vietnam.[71]

The administration had still done nothing to address its problem with "the hawks" who supported the war in Vietnam but wanted more forceful action.

Senator J. William Fulbright's hearings on the administration's supplemental request to prosecute the war in Vietnam, which began on February 4, 1966, were a televised assault on the administration's arguments that the war was necessary to contain communism.[72] One of the committee's first witnesses, former ambassador to France Lt. Gen. (ret.) James Gavin, warned that the American effort in Vietnam was likely to draw Communist China into the war. Gavin also warned that the U.S. commitment in Vietnam was "alarmingly out of balance" with U.S. interests in the region. Gavin also predicted that the administration was "slowly creeping" toward "the bombing of Hanoi or Peking," which he said would "achieve little" except further souring world opinion.[73]

Former ambassador to the Soviet Union—and key author of America's ideology of containment—George F. Kennan attacked the administration's use of containment to justify the war as well. Kennan was adamant that "deliberate expansion" of the conflict in vain pursuit of "something called 'victory'" was futile. Kennan also took aim at the Honolulu Conference under way at the time; while he stopped short of questioning the president's credibility, he did say it was "something

The 1966 Fulbright hearings.

Source: U.S. Senate Historical Office, 1966 Senate Foreign Relations Committee, hearings on the war in Vietnam, Washington, DC, February 1966.[74]

less than consistent" to hold the conference just as the peace offensive was collapsing. Kennan concluded by attacking the administration's argument that it was protecting the credibility of its worldwide commitments; Kennan argued that the world would respect the United States more if it succeeded in a "resolute and courageous liquidation of unsound positions" instead of continuing its "stubborn pursuit of extravagant or unpromising objectives."[75]

Secretary of State Dean Rusk's opening statement before the Senate Foreign Relations Committee served as the administration's rebuttal to these criticisms; Rusk claimed that three presidents, beginning with President Eisenhower, saw the Vietnam War as "deeply intertwined" with U.S. national security. Rusk also recounted the many commitments the United States had made to South Vietnam, including the "fundamental SEATO obligation," assurances given by President Eisenhower to assist South Vietnam in "resisting attempted subversion or aggression through military means," and declarations by President Kennedy that "the Republic of Viet-Nam shall not be lost to the Communists for lack of any support which the United States can render." Rusk also warned that "the loss of South Viet-Nam would set in motion a crumbling process that could, as it progressed, have grave consequences for us and for freedom," as "the remaining countries of Southeast Asia would be menaced" by communist expansion. Rusk acknowledged that "this view has often been referred to as the 'domino theory,'" but insisted that "I personally do not believe in such a theory if it means belief in a law of nature which requires the collapse of each neighboring state in an inevitable sequence." But Rusk still claimed that he was "deeply impressed with the probable effects worldwide . . . if the 'war of liberation' scores a significant victory there." He claimed that President Kennedy harbored this same concern.[76]

During the 1966 Fulbright hearings, Republican former Vice President Richard M. Nixon reentered the political fray, firmly supporting containment as a justification for intervention in Vietnam. In a pep talk to congressional Republican administrative assistants, Nixon said that the purpose of the war was "denying the Communists any reward for their aggression." Nixon then listed the dangers of not seeing the war to a successful conclusion; this list was a catalogue of the administration's arguments for the war. Nixon argued that abandoning Vietnam would be a death sentence for South Vietnamese "anti-communists," condemn Laos and Thailand to communist domination, and put Malaysia, the Philippines, and Indonesia at mortal risk. However, Nixon most feared that abandoning Vietnam would destroy the credibility of the United States' worldwide commitments. If the United States gave the communists a "reward for aggression," Nixon concluded, "the U.S. would be forced to fight other wars . . . [which] would begin to loom down the road."[77]

In the midst of the Fulbright hearings, Vice President Hubert Humphrey returned from his tour of Asian capitals ostensibly to enlist additional support for the war in Vietnam. Upon his return, the vice president summarized his findings in a press release that both used the containment to justify U.S. military intervention in Vietnam and attacked Congress for aiding communists by disheartening America's allies. The release said the war was "a broad effort to restrain the attempt by Asian communists to expand by force—as we assisted our European allies in resisting communist expansion in Europe after World War II." In an implicit proof of the domino theory, Humphrey also argued that "most Asian leaders are concerned about the belligerence and militancy of Communist China's attitudes." Humphrey concluded by making a thinly veiled attack on Senator J. William Fulbright and his hearings; the press release claimed that Asian leaders were concerned about "whether our American purpose, tenacity and will were strong enough to persevere in Southeast Asia." The release noted that Humphrey reassured these leaders of the "firmness of [America's] resolve but also our dedication to the rights of free discussion and dissent.[78] In other words, senatorial dissent was disheartening the United States' Asian allies. A few days later, Humphrey launched a similar attack on congressional dissenters at a speech to the National Press Club, suggesting the Senate Foreign Relations Committee was aiding communists with its dissent.[79]

The media was generally unsupportive of the hearings on Vietnam in the Senate Foreign Relations Committee. *New York Times* foreign correspondent C. L. Sulzberger echoed the administration's use of containment to justify U.S. military intervention in Vietnam, writing that Vietnam was an obligation that the United States was "forced to assume" as a result of World War II and the collapse of imperialism. Sulzberger wrote that "President Eisenhower resolved to prevent collapse of Southeast Asia and the rush of a new imperial dynamism down to Australia's border," a policy that was as "unpopular" as "the Truman Doctrine" when it was originally asserted in Greece. Sulzberger went on to argue that the administration's policies in Vietnam were, like those in Korea, Greece, and Iran before them, intended to contain communism. Sulzberger wrote: "The present showdown in Vietnam . . . seeks to prevent a hostile, dynamic tide from running across Thailand and Malaya to Singapore." Sulzberger also initiated a new argument that would eventually become a staple of the administration's case for the war.[80] Sulzberger argued that there were positive consequences of the domino theory; as the United States held the line in Vietnam, the other countries in Southeast Asia grew stronger and more resistant to communism.

> Since 1954 when we first became involved in Vietnam, significant changes have occurred in the Far Eastern position. Russia and China have split. Indonesia has reversed its pro-Chinese line. The British finally crushed the Malayan Communist rebellion and set up independent Malaysia. . . . It would be silly to consider all these events unrelated to Vietnam.[81]

Sulzberger insisted: "It is wrong to simplify the issue by such phrases as 'domino theory.'" But this did not stop Sulzberger from restating the theory's precepts: "if we crawl out of Vietnam now it is obvious that Southeast Asia right down to Australia will join our adversaries and that India will be outflanked." Sulzberger also warned that "Western Europe, which often voices doubts about our resolve, would have such doubts multiplied."[82]

Syndicated columnist Holmes Alexander likewise endorsed the administration's use of the ideology of containment to justify the war. In a column about the contrasting testimonies of Prof. Robert Scalapino, a supporter of the administration's Vietnam policy, and Prof. Hans Morgenthau, who had dissented on the administration's Vietnam policy since mid-1964, Alexander wrote, "The hawkishness of Scalapino is not jingoism, but the dovishness of Morgenthau is very close to defeatism." Scalapino, Alexander wrote, "bids us hold our ground. . . . That firmness will avert the awesome either/or choice of World War III or surrender." Morgenthau, Alexander wrote, "bids us to give way slowly. . . . Says there is wisdom in weakness and that our determination to fight it out in Asia 'ought to be gradually liquidated.'" Holmes also wrote that the two men differed on how to respond to the rise of China as a world power. Holmes characterized Scalapino's policy prescription as "military containment" and Morgenthau's preferred policy as "appeasement." Morgenthau, Holmes added, believed that the domino theory was a "myth" and that, "if we do not change our policy, we must be ready to go to war" with China.[83]

Not all in the press supported the administration's justifications for intervention in Vietnam. Only days before the Fulbright hearings, the *New York Times*' Drew Middleton attacked the administration's justification of the war as a means of containing communism. Middleton claimed, "The 'falling domino' theory . . . is rejected by all but a few diplomats" (though he did admit that those "few" included diplomats for countries in Southeast Asia). Middleton also attacked the administration's use of the lessons of Munich: "Few critics are impressed by the parallel . . . between Southeast Asia now and Europe in the nineteen-thirties, when Hitler was on the move." Middleton added: "Communist spokesmen tell [Asian and African countries] at every opportunity that it is the Americans, not the Chinese, who are following Hitler's course."[84]

One of the more electrifying moments of the 1966 Fulbright hearings was Senator Fulbright's apology to the American people for his role in the passage of the Tonkin Gulf Resolution. But even this *mea culpa* drew fire from the press. The Memphis, Tennessee, newspaper, the *Commercial Appeal*, attacked Senator J. William Fulbright for his change of heart about the war in Vietnam, "his tendency today to react to hindsight rather than foresight," as the *Commercial Appeal* put it. The editorial claimed, "Mr. Fulbright has cast himself in the role of the Johnson Administration's hair shirt."[85] The *Commercial Appeal* concluded:

> Senator Fulbright keeps picking at past mistakes. The longer he does, the longer we postpone an end to our troubles in the Far East. It's just too bad that the Arkansas senator couldn't have given us the benefit of his insights 10 or 12 years ago.[86]

The hearings themselves captivated the American public. A Mutual Broadcast survey from late February found that nearly three-quarters of American men and two-thirds of American women had heard about the hearings. And 60 percent of those Americans who had heard about the hearings had watched at least part of the hearings on television.[87] Fulbright was keen to capitalize on the attention his hearings had attracted. As early as February 28, 1966, before the hearings were even over, J. William Fulbright had secured an agreement with Random House to publish a transcript of the hearings.[88] In fact, as the power and reach of the committee hearings grew, Fulbright became bolder, even publicly inviting Vice President Hubert Humphrey to appear before the Committee in executive session to report on his recent trip to Asia.[89]

However, while the hearings made for dramatic televised political theater, they failed to generate much additional congressional dissent. In fact, Democratic Senator Richard B. Russell of Georgia was one of the only members of Congress to join Fulbright in public opposition to the war after the hearings. After the hearings, Russell suggested in a *U.S. News & World Report* interview that he favored a poll of the South Vietnamese people to determine if they wanted the United States military to remain in their country. "We can't possibly win," Russell said, "if we are fighting an enemy in front of us while the people we are supposed to be helping are against us and want us out of their country." Russell also explicitly rejected the domino theory. While he acknowledged that "Cambodia and Laos might go, along with South Vietnam," Russell said, "neither of them has any tremendous military value."[90] Russell said the United States made a mistake by committing its prestige "when our own interest is not directly involved."[91] Russell continued: "It's time we reexamine our entire position, however painful that re-examination might be." Russell concluded: "It wouldn't be easy for us to extricate ourselves, but we could do it." However, another key element of Russell's dissent was that the administration was not being aggressive enough in prosecuting the war. Russell insisted: "We should go in and win—or else get out,"[92] including the immediate blockade of the port of Haiphong and the bombing of Hanoi.[93] By failing to speak to those Americans who wanted more aggressive use of force in Vietnam, President Johnson had succeeded in alienating the most influential member of the Senate, a man whose support he very much needed.

The press clearly understood the significance of Russell's dissent. For instance, Max Frankel of the *New York Times* noted that Russell's dissent would be "influential in shaping the attitude of Congress toward the administration's conduct of the war" because "no member of Congress is held in higher respect for the integrity of his character and the care he expends in reaching conclusions."[94]

However, no other members of Congress spoke out against the war after Russell's comments. The reason for this absence of new congressional dissent may have been the president's insurance policy against congressional dissent—the Tonkin Gulf Resolution. Throughout the Fulbright hearings, the administration only made passing references to the resolution. However, Pulitzer Prize–winning journalist John M. Hightower explicitly wielded the Tonkin Gulf Resolution as a weapon against congressional dissenters. In an Associated Press article recapping how the United States became embroiled in the Vietnam War, Hightower explained that the president relied on his powers as commander in chief and the SEATO treaty. However, Hightower added, "Johnson relies much more on a resolution which Congress adopted in August 1964, shortly after the Gulf of Tonkin incidents." Hightower faithfully recounted the administration's version of the events of August 4, 1964,[95] and then added:

> The resolution stated that Congress "approves and supports" the determination of the President "as commander in chief" to take all necessary measures to repel attacks against U.S. forces "and to prevent further aggression."[96]

Hightower also reminded Americans that Senator J. William Fulbright "was strategist for the resolution in the Senate" and that the resolution's "purpose was to show congressional support for the President's course in Viet Nam."[97]

Whether or not it was in fact the case, Senator J. William Fulbright *believed* the reason more members of Congress had not joined his dissent was because of the Tonkin Gulf Resolution. As the hearings drew to a close with little additional congressional dissent, Fulbright and his staff concluded that they must weaken this resolution and that the avenue of that attack should be "the question of a declaration of war" and the legal basis for the war in Vietnam, which the committee staff believed was an issue on which the administration was vulnerable. Senate Foreign Relations Committee chief of staff Carl Marcy believed this presented the best prospects to limit the powers the president claimed he had been granted by the Tonkin Gulf Resolution.[98] Marcy suggested that the administration's supplemental spending bill be accompanied by a "sense of the Senate" rider that would amend the Tonkin Gulf Resolution in a way that tied the president's hands; it would insist that "the President . . . not expand the war without asking for a declaration of war."[99] In the end, however, despite much behind-the-scenes wrangling this amendment was never even formally introduced in the Senate Foreign Relations Committee. The hearings had focused on disputing the applicability of the ideology of containment of communism to the war in Vietnam; Fulbright had failed to build a case with his colleagues or the American public against the president's legal basis for prosecuting the war. Thus, after the 1966 Fulbright hearings, the administration's insurance policy against congressional dissent remained intact.

The conventional wisdom, as historian Joseph A. Fry puts it, is that these hearings made "opposition to the war respectable."[100] However, on balance, the 1966 Fulbright hearings on the Vietnam War had little impact on public opinion about the war. Fulbright did succeed in getting Americans to talk about the war. A Gallup poll after the hearings found that a plurality of Americans said that the Vietnam War was the main topic of conversation with family and friends during the week after the hearings. And public support for the president's handling of the war dropped two percentage points to 48 percent after the hearings. But the 42 percent of Americans who disapproved of the president's handling of Vietnam did not necessarily agree with Senator Fulbright. Of those who disapproved, 18 percent believed the United States "should be more aggressive" and "go all out" in Vietnam.

Another 5 percent believed the United States "should either go all out or get out" of Vietnam, and another 2 percent believed "more men and more material [were] needed."[101] In other words, over a quarter of those who disapproved of the president's handling of the war disapproved because they wanted him to further escalate the war.

It also appears that the administration and its supporters had succeeded in convincing many Americans that Fulbright was aiding the enemy. When Americans were specifically asked in early May about Senator Fulbright, only 36 percent of respondents claimed to know Fulbright's position on the war. When those 36 percent were asked what his position was, over half said they disagreed with his position. Also, of those who did know anything about Fulbright's position, 7 percent provided other derogatory descriptions of his position, 8 percent said he gave "aid and comfort to our enemies," and almost 1 percent said he was a "communist." In other words, nearly two-thirds of Americans had no idea what Fulbright's position was on the war, while another sixth of Americans knew his position and disagreed with it.[102]

In April, the Senate Foreign Relations Committee resumed hearings, this time on a $3.4 billion foreign aid bill. The issue of Vietnam dominated these hearings as well. However, rather than challenging the legal basis for the war, as Fulbright and his staffers had concluded they must after the first round of hearings, the arguments in these hearings continued to be over the applicability of the ideology of containment to the war in Vietnam. In testimony in this hearing, former U.S. ambassador to India John Kenneth Galbraith said he "never believed in the simplicities of the 'domino theory,'" citing the resiliency of Indonesia and Thailand to communist influence as just two counter-examples. Galbraith called South Vietnam "the wrong place to make a stand" against communist expansion. Galbraith insisted that South Vietnam was not "vital to the security of the United States" and added, "If we were not in Vietnam, all that part of the world would be enjoying the obscurity it so richly deserves." Galbraith's policy prescription was the same he had suggested to the president in a private letter the previous year, just before the president's July 1965 announcement of the deployment of large numbers of U.S. Army soldiers. Galbraith suggested that the United States should withdraw its troops to easily defensible enclaves and sue for peace.[103]

Secretaries Rusk and McNamara testified several more times before the Senate Foreign Relations Committee in late spring 1966, after the formal hearings on Vietnam had ended. At each of these engagements, the Secretaries reiterated the administration's arguments for U.S. military intervention in Vietnam based on the ideology of containment of communism. Neither addressed the public's demands for more aggressive action in Vietnam or growing questions about administration credibility on the war. Secretary McNamara met a hostile audience when he appeared before the Senate Foreign Relations Committee in late April. He claimed that the war was a result of North Vietnamese aggression and that nearly 5,000 soldiers infiltrated each month, many of them North Vietnamese Army units. While not wanting to sound "optimistic," McNamara still claimed that Vietnamese prisoners of war "expect that U.S. and government forces will win with their superior equipment and supplies." Senator Morse argued that victory or negotiated settlement was no closer in Vietnam. McNamara responded that, had U.S. troops "not been introduced . . . the Vietcong and North Vietnam would have won." McNamara also revived the "bloodbath" argument, claiming that the North Vietnamese "would have slaughtered thousands and probably tens of thousands of South Vietnamese" had America not intervened. In response to McNamara's insistence that without U.S. intervention "all of Southeast Asia would be in turmoil," Senator Morse responded, "That's a repetition in another form of the old fallacious domino theory."[104]

In response to the Fulbright hearings, the administration contemplated seeking a second congressional resolution, similar to the Tonkin Gulf Resolution, to reassert congressional endorsement of the Vietnam War. In meetings on the matter in February 1966, Secretaries Rusk and McNamara and presidential advisor Clark Clifford all opposed such a measure. Deputy Director of the Central Intelligence Agency for Plans Richard Helms (who would become the Director of the CIA four months later) warned the White House that any significant congressional opposition to a new resolution would be interpreted by Hanoi as an erosion of support for the war. Helms added that this "would strengthen the North Vietnamese Government in its consistent belief that domestic pressure is going to force the president to stand down the war and bring about an outcome similar to that which occurred with France in 1954."[105] The administration knew that congressional opposition to the war was growing, and it did not wish to test the strength of that opposition, especially before an international audience.

Members of the administration—who had consistently viewed the Tonkin Gulf Resolution as an insurance policy against congressional dissent—also did not feel that an additional resolution was needed. State Department legal advisor Leonard Meeker wrote a detailed legal opinion listing the legal authorities under which the president was able to prosecute the war in Vietnam. Among those authorities were "the constitutional powers of the President" and "the SEATO treaty." But the president was also given authority by the Congress, Meeker added, "in the joint resolution of August 10, 1964, and in authorization and appropriations acts for support of the U.S. military effort in Viet-Nam." These authorities, Meeker concluded, obviated the necessity of a declaration of war or another resolution.[106]

The administration clearly understood that the Tonkin Gulf Resolution was a powerful weapon against growing dissent in Congress. And while the administration never fully invoked their insurance policy during the February hearings, Dean Rusk did remind Senator Fulbright and the other senators of the Senate Foreign Relations Committee about Tonkin Gulf Resolution during his testimony in May 1966. Rusk argued that the president's authority to fight the war "stems from the constitutional powers of the President as Commander in Chief." But, Rusk added, the president also received authority from "the SEATO treaty, which forms part of the law of the land" and from "the Congress, in a joint resolution of August 1964 and in authorization and appropriation acts in support of the military effort in Viet-Nam." Rusk insisted that these acts showed the Congress had "given its approval and support to the president's action." Rusk concluded that precedents such as "the undeclared war with France in 1798–1800 and . . . actions in Korea and Lebanon" had established that a declaration of war was not required to fight the Vietnam War.[107]

Rusk came closer to wielding the Tonkin Gulf Resolution as a weapon against congressional dissent later in May at a speech to the Council on Foreign Relations in New York. He insisted:

> The resolution of August 1964, which the House of Representatives adopted unanimously and the Senate with only two negative votes, said that "the United States regards as vital to its national interest and to world peace the maintenance of international peace and security in Southeast Asia." It also said that "the United States is, therefore, prepared, as the President determines, to take all necessary steps, including the use of armed force, to assist any member or protocol state of the Southeast Asia Collective Defense Treaty requesting assistance in defense of its freedom."[108]

Rusk did not mention Senator Fulbright by name or attack him for his change of heart, but the implication was clear. The resolution was an immutable fact, a congressional endorsement that had not been formally withdrawn despite the present sentiments of some members of Congress.

Late spring 1966 brought a series of setbacks for the administration's efforts in Vietnam. However, rather than abandoning support for the war itself, public reaction to these setbacks was to demand more aggressive action by the U.S. military in Vietnam. The administration initially ignored these demands, instead continuing to insist that the containment of communism required U.S. military intervention in Vietnam—a sentiment with which most Americans already agreed. When that failed to arrest the drop in approval of the president's handling of the war, the administration finally responded by bombing Hanoi and Haiphong for the first time—justifying its actions as a tit-for-tat response to North Vietnamese escalations. This escalation restored public approval of the president's policies in Vietnam but also generated additional congressional dissent. Still, this entire episode highlighted the fact that the administration had done nothing to explain to the majority of Americans who wanted more aggressive action in Vietnam why it could not escalate the conflict more rapidly.

On April 13, 1966, a dramatic Viet Cong mortar attack on the Tan Son Nhut airbase in Saigon killed eight, including seven Americans, and wounded 160 U.S. and South Vietnamese servicemen. The attack also destroyed twelve U.S. helicopters and nine other aircraft.[109] At the same time, South Vietnamese Prime Minister Ky launched a crackdown on rebellious Buddhist soldiers in Da Nang, followed by a second offensive against a force of similar Buddhist troops in Hue.[110] Buddhists responded with a round of self-immolations by Buddhist monks and nuns. The president himself was forced to respond to these dramatic protests, calling the immolations "tragic and unnecessary."[111]

These setbacks in South Vietnam correlated with a drop in public support for the administration's policies in Vietnam. Approval of the president's handling of Vietnam dipped seven points to 41 percent, with 38 percent disapproving and 22 percent having "no opinion."[112] A poll a few weeks later showed a further erosion of public support for the president's handling of the war. Approval of the president's policies in Vietnam had slipped another percentage point, down to 40 percent. More dangerous for the administration, for the first time more Americans (42 percent) disapproved than approved of the president's handling of the war.[113]

But this poll also revealed that the public was reacting to bad news in Vietnam rather than to actions by radical protesters in the United States or the growing antiwar bloc in the Senate. Most Americans still wanted to fight the war. When asked if they would vote to continue the war if they had the opportunity, 58 percent of those Americans who had an opinion said they would. When those Americans who disapproved of the president's handling of the war were asked why they disapproved of the president's policy, 17 percent believed the United States should be "more aggressive" and "go all out" in Vietnam. Another 6 percent said that America should "either go all out or get out." Another 2 percent were more specific saying that "more men and material [were] needed." None of those who disapproved of the president's policy echoed arguments made by congressional or radical dissenters. Thus, at least 51 percent of Americans either agreed with the president's course in Vietnam or believed the United States should be even more aggressive.[114] The president and the administration still had done nothing to address the concerns of those "Hawks" who wanted more aggressive action by explaining why it did not escalate the war further in Vietnam.

Inside the government, this crisis of confidence in the president's policies in Vietnam came close to triggering a basic reassessment of the war. But publicly the administration's response to this crisis was to assert once more that containment of communism justified U.S. military intervention in Vietnam. The administration launched a full-scale public relations offensive beginning with a speech by Secretary of State Dean Rusk at the Council on Foreign Relations in late May 1966.[115] President Johnson made an even more impassioned defense of the need to contain communist aggression in Southeast Asia at the Tomb of the Unknown Soldier during a televised speech at a Memorial Day observance. Johnson recalled the names of soldiers killed in Greece, Berlin, Korea, the Taiwan Straits, Cuba, and Vietnam "in the resistance to aggression" and "the peace-building efforts that America has made since 1945." Invoking the lessons of Munich, Johnson added that through World War II, "We have learned that the time to stop aggression is when it first begins. And that is one reason that we are in South Vietnam today." Johnson understood that Americans were confused by the conflict in South Vietnam because it did not take the form of "organized divisions marching brazenly and openly across frontiers" but instead of infiltration and "well-organized assassination, kidnapping, [and] intimidation of civilians in remote villages." Yet Johnson insisted, "That kind of aggression is just as real and just as dangerous for the safety and independence of the people of South Vietnam as was the attack on South Korea in June of 1950." To those who argued that the Vietnam War was a civil war, Johnson insisted that it was "insurgency mounted from outside a nation." To those who argued that South Vietnam was too unstable, Johnson answered,

"Seldom has a people been called upon to build a nation and wage war against externally supported aggression at the same time." Johnson also invoked the ghost of his slain predecessor at this solemn military cemetery. Johnson insisted that his own policy was consistent with that of President Kennedy, who had said just before his death, "We want the war to be won, the communists to be contained, and the Americans to go home."[116] Hubert Humphrey echoed these same themes in a fiery speech at the commencement of the United States Military Academy at West Point only a week later.[117]

Despite setbacks in Vietnam, the press continued to support the administration's arguments for U.S. military intervention in Vietnam based on the containment of communism. Many in the media reiterated C. L. Sulzberger's argument about the positive implications of the domino theory. For instance, citing the Indonesian Congress's recent decision to name Lieutenant General Suharto as Communist President Sukarno's successor, the *St. Louis Globe-Democrat* predicted, "Before long Sukarno will be completely divorced from power as Indonesia moves to reestablish its economy and friendly relations with its neighbors." The editorial concluded: "The United States' firm stand against Red aggression in Vietnam should be credited with making the emergence of free Asian nations possible."[118]

However, despite a concerted campaigning by the administration, reinforced by sympathetic reporting in the press, public approval of the administration's handling of Vietnam continued to slip in June 1966. Moreover, this deterioration resulted directly from the administration's refusal to address the concerns of "hawks" who wanted the war escalated further. In mid-June 1966, only 38 percent of Americans approved of the president's handling of Vietnam (a slip of two more percentage points from late May) with 44 percent disapproving (an increase of two percentage points). This increase in disapproval was a direct result of those Americans who wanted to further escalate the war. When asked what they wanted the administration to do next, of those who had an opinion, only 12 percent wanted to de-escalate the conflict and only 17 percent wanted complete withdrawal. Nine percent wanted to hold the present course. In contrast, nearly two-thirds of Americans wanted to escalate the war in some say. Twenty-three percent wanted to escalate bombing but not send more troops. The greatest percentage, 42 percent, wanted to "quickly build up our forces in Vietnam to as many as one million men and make an all-out effort to defeat North Vietnam."[119] The administration had still done nothing to explain to the two-thirds of Americans who wanted more aggressive action why it wasn't escalating the war in the face of recent setbacks.

Instead, during a visit to the Omaha, Nebraska Municipal Docks to inspect a barge full of grain bound for India, President Lyndon Johnson once more used the ideology of military containment of communism to justify U.S. military intervention in Vietnam. Johnson said, "The North Vietnamese at this hour are trying to deny the people of South Viet-Nam the right to build their own nation." Johnson claimed that the United States was in South Vietnam because "South Viet-Nam is important to the security of the rest of . . . Asia." Adopting Sulzberger's argument about the positive implications of the domino theory, Johnson claimed this was true because "the nations of free Asia" that had once "[lain] under the shadow of Communist China" could now grow socially and economically because they were "shielded by the courage of the South Vietnamese" and because they were "convinced that the Vietnamese people and their allies are going to stand firm against the conqueror, or against aggression." Johnson explained: "Our fighting in Viet-Nam, therefore, is buying time not only for South Viet Nam, but it is buying time for a new and a vital, growing Asia to emerge and develop additional strength." Johnson also reiterated the lessons of Munich, "What happens in South Viet-Nam will determine . . . whether might makes right." If the United States failed in South Vietnam, Johnson concluded, "It will be an invitation to the would-be conqueror to keep on marching."[120]

In July 1966, the administration finally responded to those who wanted the war escalated by initiating its first bombing raids on fuel depots in Hanoi and Haiphong in North Vietnam. This action was applauded by most Americans. When asked if they approved of the escalation in bombing, 70 percent of Americans answered with an unqualified "yes." And with increased bombing and political tur-moil in South Vietnam receding from the headlines, the American public's approval of the president's handling of the war in Vietnam once more turned in favor of the administration. Forty-nine percent now approved of the president's policies in Vietnam (a jump of eleven points from the previous month) with only 35 percent disapproving (a drop of nine percentage points). But the administration had not completely sated the public's appetite for escalation. When asked what America should do next in Vietnam, 26 percent of Americans said the United States should continue its present policy. By contrast, 31 percent of Americans still wanted the war further escalated in some way. In fact, 2 percent of Americans wanted the United States to use nuclear weapons in Vietnam.[121]

Despite overwhelming public support for this escalation, the administration's explanation of his decision to begin this new bombing was strangely defensive. Rusk addressed the bombing of Hanoi and Haiphong from the SEATO conference taking place in Australia. His comments were notable as they marked the first time the administration had used the tit-for-tat precedent set by retaliatory air strikes during the Gulf of Tonkin incident as a justification for escalation since the president's noonday press conference on July 28, 1965, nearly a year earlier. Rusk said that the bombing was executed as a response to escalation by North Vietnam—the widening of the Ho Chi Minh Trail and the introduction of new North Vietnamese troops in South Vietnam. "The pace of escalation was imposed by the other side," Rusk added. Rusk also reiterated the president's assurances from a year earlier that the United States was "not asking [North Vietnam] for an unconditional surrender, an acre of North Vietnamese land, or a change in their regime." Instead, Rusk said, "All we ask is that they stop shooting and coming across the border."[122] The administration seemed oddly apologetic about this escalation, given its popularity with the American public.

Most in the media supported the administration's escalation. The editors of the *St. Louis Globe-Democrat* responded to the Soviet Union's protests over the peril to its ships in Haiphong by writing,

"Mr. Johnson should tell Russia to get its ships out of Haiphong harbor." The editors wanted even further escalation: "To make sure USSR vessels won't be in danger, the president could extend the blockade all up the North Vietnam coast." In addition to a blockade of North Vietnam, the *Globe-Democrat* also suggested "more vital bombing of enemy supply centers, industry and staging theaters in North Vietnam, Laos and Cambodia." The editors concluded, "America will not welsh on its Vietnam commitment."[123]

While public disapproval of the president's handling of the war was receding, dissent in the Senate grew. Interestingly, this dissent was aimed not at the administration's use of containment but at the Tonkin Gulf Resolution. In June 1966, Senator Milward L. Simpson wrote a letter to Under Secretary of Defense John T. McNaughton asking the department to declassify transcripts of a May 1966 executive session of the Senate Foreign Relations Committee in which the subject of the Gulf of Tonkin incident was discussed so that they could be released to the public. In the letter, he wrote, "Serious doubt has been cast upon the credibility of the Administration." He added, "After reading the transcript of the hearings, that doubt has not been erased."[124] Not surprisingly, the Department of Defense refused to declassify the transcripts since they would only reinforce (rather than "erase") doubts about the administration's account of the Gulf of Tonkin incident. In a letter to Senator Simpson, Senator Fulbright wrote that, while he had "no evidence regarding the veracity of the Administration" on the matter of the Gulf of Tonkin incident, he did have "some question that the incident was 'unprovoked.'"[125] These questions were probably only aggravated by the fact that the Department of Defense ultimately refused Senator Simpson's request to release the transcripts of the hearing.[126] While Simpson would eventually talk to the press about this refusal,[127] the matter failed to pique media interest in the Gulf of Tonkin incident in 1966. This episode was still significant as it marked the first public questioning of the facts of the Gulf of Tonkin incident by a member of Congress other than perennial dissenters Morse and Gruening.

Senator J. William Fulbright also persisted in his own dissent against the war. And, as Fulbright and his staffers had concluded was needed after the February 1966 hearings, this dissent was focused on the administration's legal basis for the war. During the debate on the foreign aid bill on the floor of the Senate, Fulbright argued against giving the president more than a one-year authorization because of the administration's "astonishing assertion" that it had committed troops to Vietnam because of the history of commitments to the region, including past foreign aid packages. Fulbright characterized this as a "tendency to escalate our commitments" without congressional advice and consent.[128]

Despite this new congressional dissent, most Americans continued to approve of the president's handling of the war by a narrow margin. Moreover, almost a third of those who disapproved of Johnson's policies disapproved because they wanted the war escalated in some way. In fact, when asked explicitly what the United States should do next, only 20 percent of Americans who had an opinion believed the United States should continue the war at its present level. By contrast, 61 percent believed the war should be escalated in some way.[129] The bump in approval the president had received by initiating the bombing of Hanoi and Haiphong had nearly vanished; the public's appetite for escalation had not been sated and the administration had done nothing to explain why it did not escalate further.

Instead, the administration continued to focus on its justifications for the war based on the ideology of military containment in its counteroffensive against dissenters through late summer 1966. In a speech in August, President Johnson claimed Americans understood that the goal in Vietnam was "that communism must be halted . . . as it was halted in Western Europe and in Greece and Turkey and Korea and the Caribbean." The president also repeated the possible positive consequences of the domino theory: that the U.S. presence in South Vietnam provided "a shield for those on whom the Communists prey" in order to "give them time to build." The president concluded that it was important not to "back down on our commitment, if we expect our friends around the world to have faith in our word."[130]

By the end of summer 1966, over a year after the president first announced the deployment of large numbers of troops to Vietnam, after dramatic hearings in the chambers of the Senate Foreign Relations Committee and an equally dramatic counteroffensive by the administration, pro- and anti-war factions had fought to a stalemate. Americans continued to approve of the president's handling of Vietnam by a narrow margin (42 percent approval, 38 percent disapproval). And 27 percent of those who disapproved of the president's handling of Vietnam wanted him to take more forceful action in the conflict.[131] When asked by Gallup if they believed "the U.S. made a mistake sending troops to fight in Vietnam," 58 percent of those Americans who had an opinion on the question, still said "no."[132] A majority of Americans still believed their country should be fighting the Vietnam War. But they wanted it fought more aggressively. And the administration had not explained to these Americans why it didn't do so.

In October 1966, on the eve of the 1966 midterm elections, the president made a highly publicized tour of the South Pacific and Southeast Asia, culminating in a trip to South Vietnam—his first since 1961 as vice president. This trip was designed to reinforce the president's assertion that the war was required to contain communism in Southeast Asia. In the end, however, the president had been fighting the wrong battle; the American people handed the Democratic party a series of defeats not because they disagreed with the administration's justifications for the war but because they wanted more aggressive action in Vietnam. After this defeat, the president for the first time addressed the majority of Americans who wanted him to be more aggressive in prosecuting the war. The president also addressed the new Congress, reminding them of his insurance policy against their dissent—the Tonkin Gulf Resolution.

Johnson's trip to Asia—and the speeches and events along the way—were calibrated to reinforce the domino theory: if South Vietnam fell, all of Southeast Asia would be threatened by communist expansion. In a visit with New Zealand opposition parliamentarian (and later Prime Minister) Norman Kirk, President Johnson recalled that, when he had last been in New Zealand, twenty-five years earlier, the country was threatened by a "snowball of aggression" from Japan that the world had failed to stop before it gathered strength. Now, Johnson claimed, the country was threatened by Chinese aggression. The United States was in South Vietnam, he added, to "keep the momentum from gathering" until it swept across Southeast Asia. The president added that South Vietnam was also a test of the United States' commitment to other allies who rely on its promises for their security.[133]

Another important moment in the president's Asia trip was a conference in Manila on October 24 and 25, 1966, of the leaders of seven Asian and Pacific nations—Australia, South Korea, New Zealand, the Philippines, Thailand, South Vietnam, and the United States. The text of the Joint Communiqué from this conference was a virtual catalogue of the administration's justifications for U.S. military intervention in South Vietnam based on the containment of communism. The war in Vietnam was a battle for "the future of Asia and the Pacific" that "bitter past experience" had taught the world must be fought. If North Vietnam was successful, South Vietnam would be "conquered by aggressive force." The United States and its allies had no designs in Communist Asia beyond "peace in South Vietnam and in the rest of Asia and the Pacific." This communiqué also marked the first time the Johnson administration responded to the infrequent attacks on the president's true willingness to negotiate; the communiqué asserted that the allies were "prepared to pursue any avenue which could lead to a secure and just peace, whether through discussion and negotiation or through reciprocal actions by both sides."[134]

Johnson followed the Manila Conference with a surprise visit to Vietnam where he reinforced the theme that the war in Vietnam was a war against aggression. In a speech at the Saigon airport, President Johnson said the United States was part of an allied effort "standing up to terror." In another speech to troops at Cam Ranh Bay, the president said that the United States was fighting "to show here . . . in Vietnam that aggression doesn't pay and can't succeed."[136]

The president's trip to Asia and the South Pacific generated a number of news stories in the media that supported the administration's arguments for intervention in Vietnam based on the containment of communism. CBS's special coverage of the president's Asian tour ran excerpts of an interview with Dean Rusk while providing no

Manila Conference of SEATO nations on the Vietnam War: (left to right) Prime
Minister Nguyen Cao Ky (South Vietnam), Prime Minister Harold Holt (Australia),
President Park Chung Hee (Korea), President Ferdinand Marcos (Philippines),
Prime Minister Keith Holyoake (New Zealand), Lt. Gen. Nguyen Van Thieu (South
Vietnam), Prime Minister Thanom Kittikachorn (Thailand), President Lyndon B.
Johnson (United States), October 24, 1966.

Source: Frank Wolfe, Johnson Presidential Library.[135]

criticism of the Secretary's claim that the fate of peace in Vietnam
rested in the hands of "Hanoi and Peking." Likewise, a voiceover of
footage of South Vietnamese Foreign Minister Tran Van Do arriving
in Manila for the conference uncritically reported that both South
Vietnam and South Korea would "argue against any concessions to
the Viet Cong."[137]

Even the coverage of the president's encounter with antiwar protesters in Australia was generally supportive. The report showed footage of protesters lining the president's motorcade route in Sydney's
Hyde Park. One protester stood with a sign that read "I'm American.
I represent (excluding the South) most Americans who are opposed to
our Vietnam war." The footage also showed protesters storming the

motorcade route and laying down in front of the president's vehicle, images that must have reminded American viewers of protesters attacking Vice President Nixon's motorcade in Venezuela almost a decade earlier. However, the voiceover of the footage referred to protesters as "Vietniks" and claimed that "the anti-Vietnam demonstrators, both numerically and politically, are a tiny fraction in Australian life."[138]

However, this CBS report concluded with commentary by Eric Sevareid, who clearly opposed the administration's policies in Vietnam. Sevareid did concede that "Hanoi and Peking" held the key to peace in South Vietnam, supporting the administration's argument that the war was a result of their aggression. He predicted that, if the Asia trip did not start negotiations, "then that tragic war is bound to be intensified and escalated still further." However, Sevareid said that, with escalation, "the danger [would be] increased of big power involvement and a spreading catastrophe."[139] He added:

> Asian Lilliputians in Vietnam have tied down Gulliver [the United States] with a thousand tiny threads. He heaves and struggles and smashes back with his one free fist, his bombing power. He makes threats, offers deals, promises to turn their land into a garden with his skills and his money, if they will sheathe their tiny arrows and let him up.[140]

Sevareid concluded by attacking the domino theory. If Rusk's "far-reaching rhetoric about Vietnam" was correct, Sevareid said, all of the free nations of Asia would be helping the United States in Vietnam. However, he concluded, "they do not believe in this apocalyptic hypothesis [the domino theory] in the first place."[141]

If the president's intention in his trip to Asia was to generate public approval for his handling of the war, then the effort was inconsequential; the trip did little to alter his public support. After the president's trip, a Gallup poll revealed that 43 percent of Americans approved of the president's handling of Vietnam, a bump of only one percentage point from September. Disapproval of his handling of the war fell by the same margin, to 40 percent.[142]

If the president's intention in his trip to Asia was to aid his party in the 1966 midterm elections, then the trip must be judged a failure. As the polls closed on November 8, 1966, the Democratic party had lost forty-seven House seats and two Senate seats.[143] But there is no indication that this vote against the president's party was a vote against the Vietnam War. Even after this disappointing election, when asked by Gallup if they believed "the United States made a mistake sending troops to fight in Vietnam," 63 percent of those Americans who expressed an opinion still said "no."[144] To the extent that the election was a referendum on the war at all, it was probably a vote for more forceful action in Vietnam—a Republican position.

It appears that the president believed that the midterm elections had been a vote for more forceful action in Vietnam. In the aftermath of the president's trip to Asia and the midterm elections, in his 1967 State of the Union Address, the president finally, for the first time, addressed the majority of Americans who wanted him to be more aggressive in prosecuting the war:

> Whether we can fight a war of limited objectives over a period of time, and keep alive the hope of independence and stability for people other than ourselves; whether we can continue to act with restraint when the temptation to "get it over with" is inviting but dangerous . . . whether we can do these without arousing the hatreds and the passions that are ordinarily loosed in time of war—on all these questions so much turns.[145]

What the president failed to do in this speech was to explain to the American people *why* it was dangerous to arouse these "hatreds and passions." This was a statement of intent not to escalate without a statement of explanation as to why he would not escalate. Thus, it did nothing to placate the "Hawks," those Americans who wanted more aggressive action in Vietnam.

The president also returned to his arsenal of arguments based on the ideology of containment to justify U.S. military intervention in this speech. The president reminded Americans of the lessons of

Munich. But he did so on this occasion not by warning of the dangers of inaction but by touting the benefits of action. The United States had "stood in Western Europe 20 years ago" and "the course of freedom was . . . changed for the better because of the courage of that stand." The United States had "stopped another kind of aggression . . . in Korea" four years later. "Imagine how different Asia might be today," Johnson told the Congress and the American people, "if we had failed to act when the Communist army of North Korea marched south." Johnson promised similar results in the present war. The president also once more touted the positive implications of the domino theory. Johnson claimed: "The performance of our men in Vietnam—backed by the American people—has created a feeling of confidence and unity among the independent nations of Asia and the Pacific." Recalling his recent trip to Asia, Johnson added: "Fear of external Communist conquest in many Asian nations is already subsiding—and with this, the spirit of hope is rising." Johnson also revived the argument that the United States had to hold out in Vietnam until China matured and the United States could "welcome a China which [has] decided to respect her neighbors' rights" into the world community.[146]

The president also took the opportunity of the State of the Union Address to remind the new Congress of his insurance policy against their dissent—the Tonkin Gulf Resolution. In answering his own question, "Why are we in Vietnam?" the president cited the SEATO treaty, North Vietnamese aggression, the threat Asian communism presented to all of Southeast Asia and the right of the South Vietnamese people to self-determination. But Johnson also said, "We are there because the Congress has pledged by solemn vote to take all necessary measures to prevent further aggression."[147] While he did not name this congressional resolution, the president made it clear that he meant the Tonkin Gulf Resolution by recalling its exact language: "take all necessary measures . . . to prevent further aggression."[148]

In spring 1965, the academic dissent of the teach-in movement (in opposition to the application of the ideology of containment to Vietnam) spawned an academic foreign policy revolution in opposition to the ideology of containment itself. In the aftermath of the

1966 Fulbright hearings, this embryonic foreign policy revolution finally began to coalesce into two distinct wings: a congressional and a radical wing. While academic revolutionaries continued their dissent, they were increasingly overwhelmed by or subsumed into the more dramatic dissent of the congressional and radical foreign policy revolutionaries. The congressional wing of the foreign policy revolution was squarely focused on the distorting effect that the ideology of military containment of communism had had on foreign policy formulation; they wished to reassert the prerogatives of Congress in advice and consent on foreign policy by attacking the ideology of containment to dismantle the elite Cold War consensus. The radical wing of the foreign policy revolution condemned the Cold War consensus on a much broader basis, attacking its impact on both foreign and domestic policy. This dissent eventually coalesced into opposition to American imperialism. Radical revolutionaries sought to convince Americans to reject the ideology of containment, the foundation of the Cold War consensus, by revealing to Americans the brutality of this imperialism both at home and abroad.

Immediately after the 1966 Fulbright hearings, at the same time that Fulbright and his staffers concluded that they must attack the administration's legal basis for the war to generate additional congressional dissent, they also reached another, more far-reaching conclusion. Fulbright and his staffers saw the erosion of congressional prerogatives in foreign policymaking as a corrosive by-product of a bigger problem: the outmoded ideology of military containment. In summarizing the conclusions of staffers after the hearings, Committee chief of staff Carl Marcy wrote that the Committee's goal should not just be to end the Vietnam War but to reassert the power of the Senate in advice and consent on America's foreign policy.[149]

This realization did not immediately coalesce into a strategy of opposition to the administration. The State Department applied back-channel pressure to committee chief of staff Carl Marcy, who in turn convinced Fulbright that "the Committee ought to legislate for a while."[150] The committee spent the balance of 1966 holding hearings on foreign aid (hearings that were still dominated by discussion of Vietnam) and NATO.[151] While Fulbright and his staffers knew the direction they wanted to move, it would be nearly a half year before they returned to the subject of hearings on the ideology of containment.

After the 1966 midterm elections, Fulbright and Committee staffers finally began planning in earnest to launch their foreign policy revolt. Committee staffer Norvill Jones initiated this discussion by suggesting that, in light of "the Executive Branch's taking a 'Senate be damned' attitude," it was finally time for the Senate to use hearings to reassert its role in the making of foreign policy.[152] Carl Marcy refined this idea to focus it squarely on the ideology of containment, under the banner, "The United States as a great power."[153] The first hearings, Marcy suggested, would engage Secretaries Rusk and McNamara, and ask:

> What are the current extent and the limits, if any, of United States involvement in international affairs; is the United States a global fireman; does our military sales program provide the matches for the flames we must extinguish; are we engaging in a cold war with China comparable in nature and duration with the one in postwar Europe?[154]

This was not just an attack on the administration's policies in Vietnam; this was an assault on the ideology of containment itself.

Nor were these hearings intended to be an intellectual exercise. Rather, they were intended as a political instrument to force President Johnson to include Congress in foreign policymaking. Early in the planning, Carl Marcy wrote that the Committee's ability to influence policy "depend[ed] for fulfillment on catching and focusing popular attention." To capture television coverage, Marcy added, the Committee had to "schedule witnesses with strong personalities whose names for the most part are well-known to the information media."[155] "The 'education' which the Committee should be interested in," Marcy wrote to Fulbright, "is that which will have an immediate and, hopefully, a decisive impact" on the president's behavior. The hearings needed "enough sex appeal," Marcy wrote, "to attract the attention

of the press and the Committee, and with the potentiality of changing (reversing) policy within the next year or two." Marcy hoped that
these hearings might have enough impact to force the president to sue
for peace before the 1968 elections. Marcy was especially concerned
that the president might become "so convinced of the need for a 'victory' [in Vietnam] before 1968 that he inadvertently brings on the
holocaust."[156]

Academic dissenters—who had begun this foreign policy revolution a year and a half earlier—would be incorporated into these hearings along with a much broader array of foreign policy elites. Historians
Arthur Schlesinger Jr. and Henry Steele Commager would be invited
to discuss the role of ideology in American foreign policy. But they
would be joined by foreign policy elites like George F. Kennan covering the multi-polarity of the Communist World, former U.S. ambassador to Japan Edwin O. Reischauer discussing the perception in Asia
of America as an imperialist power, and Dean Acheson, John Kenneth
Galbraith, and others exploring a variety of other topics ranging from
the impact of American cultural imperialism on Southeast Asia to the
overextension of American commitments to the impact of foreign policy on domestic programs to fight poverty.[157]

Discussions about the war in Vietnam would be a component of
these hearings. Marcy recommended beginning the hearings with "a
repeat performance of [the 1966 Fulbright hearings]." The next session would challenge Secretary Rusk over the progress of pacification.
However, the purpose of these sessions would be to highlight the
Committee's broader concern: the erosion of the power of Congress
in foreign policymaking. The next session, Marcy suggested, should
attack the president for making commitments in Manila during his
Asian tour without consulting Congress. The hearings would then
broaden into an examination of the Senate's authorities in advice and
consent on other foreign policy issues.[158]

However, in the end, the Senate Foreign Relations Committee
was never able to generate the coherent series of hearings that it
had envisioned. Secretary of State Dean Rusk, wary after the 1966
Fulbright hearings, maneuvered to avoid testifying in anything but

closed, executive sessions.[159] Secretary of Defense Robert McNamara initially did not respond to the invitation to testify at all.[160] Once pressed, Secretary McNamara's office delayed his appearance by insisting that he appear before the Senate Armed Services Committee before appearing before the Senate Foreign Relations Committee.[161] While some of the individual sessions the committee had planned still took place, these hearings were sporadic, occurring throughout 1967. Moreover, they failed to generate the dramatic media impact created by the 1966 Fulbright hearings. But the seeds of this new congressional foreign policy revolution to reassert the prerogatives of Congress in foreign policymaking had been planted. They would blossom in 1969 and increasingly constrain the Executive Branch's freedom of action, not just in Southeast Asia but around the world.

In early 1966, at the same time the congressional wing of the foreign policy revolution was beginning to take shape in opposition to the corrosive effect containment had had on Congress' role in foreign policymaking, the radical wing of the foreign policy revolution was nearing a year of opposition to the effect the Cold War consensus on both domestic and foreign policy. The Radical Education Project, in its statement of purpose, wrote that the United States suffered from a moral decay driven by "a deadening ideology of national chauvinism, celebrating the American Way of Life, the American Dream, the American Century." The mechanism of that decay was "anti-communism" an "ideological manipulation of belief, of what is true, what is good, what is possible, what is necessary." This ideology permitted a "cover to 'rationalize' the most brutal applications of military and economic power" in both international and domestic affairs—"the war in Vietnam or the oppression of the American underclass." The Project "reject[ed] the rhetoric of anti-communism and the myth of human affairs as a morality play between the forces of good and evil, capitalist freedom and communist slavery."[162]

Similarly, Students for a Democratic Society (SDS) national secretary Paul Booth and Chicago SDS leader Lee Webb proclaimed that "Negroes for an end to racism and economic discrimination [and] students and faculty for control over their own universities" would be the "political force . . . that will build a movement against war." More importantly, the two leaders continued, "their demands will rock the very foundations of the domestic concensus [sic] on which our foreign policy rests."[163]

Radical protesters saw the Vietnam War as a symptom of a broader ill that plagued America: the ideology of containment of communism. But in early 1966, no common theme had emerged in radical critique of the Cold War consensus. The SDS's Carl Oglesby was among the few in this period whose critiques were expressly anti-imperialist. Oglesby wrote that the Viet Cong insurgency was, in fact a "revolution." He added that the administration's aim was "to safeguard what they take to be American interests around the world against revolution or revolutionary change, which they always [call] Communism."[164] Oglesby continued:

> For all our official feeling for the millions who are enslaved to what we so self-righteously call the yoke of Communist tyranny, we make no real effort at all to crack through the much more vicious right-wing tyrannies that our businessmen traffic with or our nation profits from every day.[165]

Moreover, Oglesby wrote, while the administration decried the "international Red conspiracy to take over the world, we take only pride in our 6,000 military bases on foreign soil." Oglesby concluded that this false anticommunism "depicts our presence in other lands not as a coercion, but a protection. It allows us even to say that the napalm in Viet-Nam is only another aspect of our humanitarian love."[166]

Through 1966, anti-imperialism began to emerge as the primary radical critique of the Cold War consensus, nearly to the total exclusion of all others. By early 1967, radical protesters saw America's blatant imperialism as an opportunity.[167] National secretary of the SDS Gregory Calvert wrote:

> The importance of American aggressive imperialism for the development of a domestic movement, the importance of

Vietnam and the Vietnams to come, is that it reveals America to America, that the liberal facade is shattered and the American expansionist system reveals its brutality and aggressiveness and its dehumanizing horror in all its nakedness.[168]

It was this new *raison d'être*—showing the America the brutality of its anti-communist imperialism—that animated radical demonstrators as they embarked on their most ambitious protests yet in spring 1967.

Spring 1967 brought a dramatic wave of radical protests directed at the ideology of military containment of communism—the core of the Cold War consensus. Like earlier radical protests, the public and the press roundly rejected these protesters, with many accusing protesters of prolonging the war or aiding communists. Former vice president and 1968 presidential contender Richard Nixon also used the opportunity of these protests to conflate radical protesters with academic and congressional dissenters. Moreover, rather than cause Americans to reject the ideology of containment as protesters hoped, there is evidence that these protests actually bolstered public support for the administration and its policies in Vietnam.

The Spring Mobilization spilled onto the streets of New York and San Francisco on 15 April 1967. The Reverend Dr. Martin Luther King Jr. was among the chief organizers of a protest in New York that drew between 100,000 and 200,000 demonstrators to the United Nations.[169] The ostensible purpose of this protest was stated in a letter presented by the protest leaders to the United Nations Secretariat, reading:

We rally at the United Nations in order to affirm support of the [principles] of peace, universality, equal rights and self-determination of peoples embodied in the Charter and acclaimed by mankind, but violated by the United States.[170]

This Spring Mobilization also included a similar protest that drew about 50,000 demonstrators to San Francisco. At this protest, Mrs. Coretta King gave a speech calling on the president to "stop the bombing."[171] But despite the relatively subdued rhetoric of the protest leaders, radicals constituted the vast majority of the rank-and-file of these demonstrations. And they were demonstrating in opposition to American imperialism and its brutality at home and abroad.

This dissent seemed to alienate New Yorkers before the protests even began. An article about the impending protest from the *New York Times* warned that "the demonstration is expected to bring out several groups that have carried the blue and orange flag of the National Liberation Front in previous protests." The story also warned that "a group of draft-age youths were expected to burn their [draft] cards at the outset of the demonstration." Writer Douglas Robinson also warned that "the Spring Mobilization was joined by leftwing and radical groups, including Trotskyites, anarchists, Communists and Maoists." The story also quoted King aide Rev. James Bevel as saying before the protest, "White Americans are not going to deal in the problems of colored people when they're exterminating a whole nation of colored people." The very last sentence of the story made it clear where the *New York Times* stood on the protest: "A spokesman for the Communist party said that for the first time since the 1940s 'there'll be a number of us marching under the banner of our party.'"[172]

In April 1967 former Vice President Richard M. Nixon began a tour of Asia that culminated in a trip to Vietnam. From Tokyo on April 7, Nixon derided the protesters in the United States: "I recognize the right of dissent, but . . . the divisions in the United States . . . [prolong] the war."[173] On April 14, 1967, Nixon travelled to Saigon. In advance of the impending Spring Mobilization, he called for unity, urging critics of the war inside the Democratic Party for "a moratorium on the kind of criticism that gives aid and comfort to the enemy." Nixon again said that these divisions were a "major factor" in prolonging the war.[174] Nixon was conflating radical protesters with congressional dissenters.

In his coverage of the protest itself, the *New York Times'* Douglas Robinson was even more negative than he had been before the protests. Robinson cast the protesters as non–New Yorkers who "poured into New York on chartered buses, trains and cars from cities as far away as Pittsburgh, Cleveland, and Chicago." He also noted that many young people chanted "Hey, Hey, L.B.J., How Many Kids Did You Kill Today?" Robinson described New Yorkers greeting the protesters with "eggs and red paint." Robinson also unabashedly portrayed the demonstrators as un-American; among those arrested, he wrote, were "three youths . . . taken into custody when they tried to rush a float that depicted the Statue of Liberty." Robinson also wrote, "200 [draft] cards were burned" in Central Park. Robinson's assault on the Spring Mobilization culminated with his description of a group of protesters that had built a forty-foot tower and "attached a number of Liberation Front (Vietcong) flags, of blue and red with a gold star in the center." Robinson added, "Unidentified demonstrators set fire to an American flag held up on a flagstaff in the park before the march began."[175]

Coverage of the corresponding rally in San Francisco was a bit less adversarial. However, the report still noted that, except for western director of the United Auto Workers Paul Schrade, all of the other speakers called for unconditional and unilateral withdrawal from Vietnam. The story also noted that a group of black nationalists marched behind a banner reading "The Vietnam N.L.F. Never Called Us Niggers." The story also noted that among the banners reading "Bring the GI's Home!" and "Stop the Bombing!" was "one sign [that] showed the United States flag with a Nazi swastika superimposed."[176]

Nixon's reaction to the protests, given from his tour of Vietnam, was probably closer to the national mood. He said, "The irony is that marchers for peace prolong the war." He added, "The enemy realizes they will never win the war here, but think they may win it in the United States."[177]

The next day, Nixon followed with more criticism of dissenters. He railed against those Democratic members of Congress who were by their dissent contributing to the enemy's "monstrous delusion" that they could win the war.[178] He specifically identified Senate Majority Leader Senator Mike Mansfield and Senator Robert F. Kennedy as "prolonging the war." While he said that they were "misinformed but well intentioned," he also accused them of "raising false hopes for peace in the United States."[179] He attacked dissenters from the academic community, saying that they had tricked many young people into joining the peace movement. Nixon also took aim once more at radical protesters, saying that there was "no question" that the American Communist party was involved in the peace movement.[180] Once more, dissenters were being dismissed in the media as aiding communists.

As the Spring Mobilization ended, the president gave his answer to the demonstrators. On April 20, 1967, he began bombing Haiphong Harbor for the first time. This move was accompanied by a noticable uptick in public approval of the president's handling of the conflict. In late March, disapproval of the president's handling of the war had settled at 44 percent, with 39 percent approving.[181] After the bombing began, these numbers essentially reversed, with 43 percent of Americans approving of the president's handling of the war (a jump of four points) and 42 percent disapproving (a drop of two points). And over a quarter of the Americans who disapproved of the president's policy, disapproved because they wanted him to be even more aggressive in fighting the war. In fact, when Americans were asked specifically what they wanted the United States to "do next about Vietnam," only 9 percent of Americans who had an opinion wanted to continue present policy, whereas 51 percent wanted to escalate the war in some way. After the escalation of the bombing, most Americans still felt that fighting the war was the right thing to do; 58 percent of those Americans who answered said that the United States did not make "a mistake sending troops to fight in Vietnam." Moreover, 69 percent believed that the United States' "part in the war in Vietnam [was] morally justified."[182]

There is evidence that this hardening of public opinion in support of the war was not just a reaction to the bombing of Haiphong Harbor but also a consequence of the protests in New York and San Francisco. When Americans were asked if they had "ever participated in a peace rally on Vietnam," 99 percent said "no." When these respondents were asked if they "would . . . like to participate in a rally if one were organized" in their area, 86 percent still responded "no."[183] The overwhelming majority of Americans disapproved of radical protesters.

In late 1966, most opponents of the war continued to attack the administration's use of containment to justify the war just as they had

198 CONTAINMENT AND CREDIBILITY

since early 1965. And, within this larger group of dissenters, a small cadre of academic, radical, and congressional foreign policy revolutionaries had emerged opposed to the ideology of containment itself.

However, beginning in late 1966, a new line of attack against the administration's policies in Vietnam began to build momentum: attacks on the president's credibility. A handful of dissenters first attacked the administration's credibility on civilian casualties incurred by bombing Hanoi. Next, these dissenters attacked the credibility of the president's claims that he wanted negotiations to end the war. The administration's response to both of these attacks was disjointed and ineffective; in the end it was the media, rather than the administration, that defeated them—by painting these critics as aiding communists. These attacks generated significant new congressional dissent and were particularly effective because they reinforced sentiments already held by most Americans that the administration was lying to them about the war. The devastating effectiveness of these attacks on the administration's credibility also presaged the final collapse of Johnson's credibility that would occur in 1968.

The first effective and sustained attack on the president's credibility was on the subject of the bombing of North Vietnam. After the North Vietnamese granted the *New York Times'* Harrison Salisbury a visa, he went to North Vietnam and wrote a series of damaging stories in late 1966 that contradicted the administration's assertions about the surgical nature of bombing in the north.[184] Salisbury's first dispatch from Hanoi—published in the *New York Times* on Christmas Day 1966—was about a residential area of Hanoi destroyed by bombing. "Christmas Eve found residents in several parts of Hanoi still picking over the wreckage of homes said to have been damaged in the United States raids of Dec. 13 and 14," Salisbury wrote.[185] The heart of Salisbury's critique was that facts on the ground contradicted the administration's claims:

> United States officials have contended that no attacks in built-up or residential Hanoi have been authorized or carried out. They have also suggested that Hanoi residential damage in the two raids could have been caused by defensive surface to air missiles that misfired or fell short.[186]

An inset from the *Times* did add: "The State Department said Thursday that 'the possibility of an accident' could not be ruled out."[187] But the article then continued with Salisbury writing:

> This correspondent is no ballistics specialist, but inspection of several damaged sites and talks with witnesses make it clear that Hanoi residents certainly believed they were bombed by United States planes, that they certainly observed United States planes overhead and that damage certainly occurred right in the center of town.[188]

Salisbury also reported "considerable civilian casualties" as a result of the bombing.[189] A summary of this article written by the Associated Press was published in many newspapers across the country the day after Christmas.[190]

The following day, another article by Harrison Salisbury claimed that the town of Namdinh had been reduced to rubble and most of its 90,000 residents had fled the bombing. Salisbury claimed that 89 civilians had been killed and 405 wounded and "13 percent of the city's housing, including the homes of 12,464 people, have been destroyed." This despite, Salisbury wrote, the fact that "no American communiqué has asserted that Namdinh contains some facility that the United States regards as a military objective." In a vain attempt to destroy a textile factory, Salisbury wrote, "Forty-nine people were killed, 135 were wounded on Hang Thao [street] and 240 houses collapsed." This was accomplished, Salisbury added, by "eight bombs—MK-84's . . . huge weapons weighing about 2,000 pounds." Salisbury repeatedly referred to this attack as an "unannounced assault." Salisbury added, "United States planes are dropping an enormous weight of explosives on purely civilian targets."[191] This contradicted, Salisbury wrote, the president's assurances two and a half years earlier:

> President Johnson's announced policy that American targets in North Vietnam are steel and concrete rather than human

lives seems to have little connection with the reality of attacks carried out by United States Planes.[192]

Salisbury concluded by claiming that the bombing had little impact on North Vietnam's military capacity since bomb damage is easily repaired. The bombing, Salisbury wrote, "is hardly felt" by the North Vietnamese military.[193] As with the previous dispatch by Salisbury, a summary of this dispatch was filed by the Associated Press and ran in newspapers across the country a few days later.[194]

The administration was forced to acknowledge that civilian casualties occurred while bombing North Vietnam. While the Pentagon added in its statement, "all possible care is taken to avoid civilian casualties," it also added "it is impossible to avoid all damage to civilian areas." Some in the press remained skeptical; writer Neil Sheehan noted, "A number of . . . small [oil] dumps, both within and on the outskirts of Namdinh, have repeatedly been struck." Implicating President Johnson directly for these attacks on civilians, Sheehan wrote: "Where important and sensitive targets are concerned, such as the oil depots near Hanoi and Haiphong, the White House itself must give the authorization."[195]

These stories succeeded in creating new congressional dissent. Republican Congressman Ogden R. Reid of New York requested hearings and demanded to see aerial photography of the bombing in North Vietnam to confirm Salisbury's claims. Reid added that his call for hearings was in direct response to the contrast between the dispatches by Salisbury and the administration's claims that it was attacking only military targets. Democratic Congressman John E. Moss of California, chairman of the Government Information Subcommittee of the House Committee on Government Operations, also indicated he would call hearings on the controversy. Democratic Senator William Proxmire of Wisconsin said that the dispatches were "a very serious statement by a highly respected reporter" and warranted investigation.[196] Senator J. William Fulbright promised hearings with Secretary of Defense Robert McNamara and Secretary of State Dean Rusk about the civilian casualties.[197] Senator Karl E. Mundt, a South

Dakota Republican and member of the Senate Foreign Relations Committee, said he believed Secretaries Rusk and McNamara would also be questioned on "the effectiveness of the bombing" when hearings resumed in 1967.[198]

Not every member of Congress was sympathetic to Salisbury or his claims. Republican Senator Bourke B. Hickenlooper of Iowa said, "It is strange to me that [North Vietnam] will let a *New York Times* reporter in but not objective reporters."[199]

On December 29, 1966, the White House began a disjointed and largely ineffective counteroffensive against Salisbury's charges. The acting White House press secretary, George Christian, addressed Salisbury's charge that the president had approved bombing of civilian areas in Hanoi. Christian insisted: "No civilian targets have ever been authorized." One incredulous reporter pressed as to whether the president believed that the military had disobeyed his orders by attacking civilians in Hanoi. Christian could only respond, "No."[200]

Assistant Secretary of Defense for Public Affairs Arthur Sylvester was even less effective in disputing Salisbury's claims. He tried to put the 89 civilian deaths in perspective by noting that these deaths had occurred in 64 separate raids. To Sylvester, this number showed "rather precise, careful bombing," since this death toll averaged to only "one and a half persons a raid." But Sylvester was immediately forced to backtrack when he was asked whether this meant the Department of Defense accepted the figure of 89 civilian deaths as accurate. He could only answer: "I don't know if 8 or 89 people have been killed there." Nor would Sylvester say whether bomb damage photographs of the type Congressman Reid had demanded actually existed or, if they did, whether they confirmed or disproved Salisbury's claims. *New York Times* reporter Neil Sheehan was incredulous at this refusal, writing, "It is known that the Pentagon is in possession of aerial photographs showing damage to civilian areas in Namdinh."[201] Sheehan concluded of this discussion:

> Although he repeatedly declined to say whether the Defense Department's evidence confirmed or denied Mr. Salisbury's

reports, Mr. Sylvester criticized his dispatches for alleged "misstatements of fact."[202]

The most effective government response to the crisis came from Cmdr. Robert C. Mandeville, recently returned from Vietnam where he had been the commander of a squadron of Navy Intruder bombers. Mandeville called Salisbury's story "unbelievable" and disputed his claim that 2,000-pound bombs were used against Hanoi. He also said that Salisbury's textile factory had never been a target. In fact, he disputed that Namdinh was a target, saying, "Nobody wanted to go into that place, it was ringed with fire." Mandeville concluded: "I have never known of a target being assigned in North Vietnam that wasn't of tactical military value."[203] There is no direct evidence that this statement was prompted by the Pentagon or the White House, but it certainly helped their case more than any statements by administration officials.

Supporters of the administration in the press attacked Salisbury's dispatches by claiming they propagated communist propaganda. On December 30, 1966, Hanson W. Baldwin, military editor for the *New York Times*, wrote an article in defense of the administration that was published in newspapers across the country through the *New York Times* News Service. The story cited Admiral David L. McDonald, Chief of Naval Operations, and other military and civilian leaders touting the effectiveness of bombing. McDonald was quoted as saying that the bombing had "saved the lives of a lot of soldiers and Marines on the ground in South Vietnam." The article did note that Pentagon sources privately admitted that civilians had been killed, but Baldwin added, conflating Salisbury's reports with those of North Vietnamese propagandists,: "[Pentagon sources] said that North Vietnam's estimates of the number of civilian casualties suffered in the bombing raids, as reported in dispatches . . . by Harrison E. Salisbury . . . appear to be 'grossly exaggerated.'" Baldwin also included a passage written by British journalist Norman Barrymaine who, after visiting North Vietnam, noted severe damage to the North Vietnamese transport system, damage Salisbury denied had occurred. Barrymaine added that the bombing had not crippled North Vietnam "because of the enormous material aid being poured through the port of Haiphong from Russia, Poland, Czechoslovakia, East Germany, Albania and Red China."[204]

But even sympathetic reporter Hanson Baldwin was frustrated by the administration's confused response to this crisis of credibility. He concluded:

> Distorted, confusing or contradictory statements in Washington, inflated claims and undue secrecy in the Pentagon have aided the enemy's propaganda. Many officers in Washington, in Hawaii and in Saigon have advocated policies of greater frankness and some urged the issuance months ago of public explanations about civilian casualties and residential damage caused by U.S. bombing. But they were overruled.[205]

United Press International also implied that Salisbury's work was communist propaganda. In a December 30 article, the news service noted that "the Soviet Communist party newspaper Pravda printed excerpts today from a series of New York Times dispatches." The article added sardonically that "Pravda made no editorial comment in a brief forward" to Salisbury's dispatches.[206]

On December 31, 1966, evidence emerged that critics alleged proved Salisbury had propagated communist propaganda. A *Washington Post* article revealed that the figures Salisbury had cited in his dispatches were identical to those published in a communist propaganda pamphlet published by the North Vietnamese and distributed to foreign correspondents in Moscow in November 1966. Even more damning, the pamphlet was titled "Report on United States War Crimes in Nam-Dinh City." Assistant Secretary of Defense Sylvester, initially rocked by the bombing controversy, was quick to tell reporters that he found the coincidence of these matching figures "very interesting."[207] Deputy Assistant Secretary of Defense for Public Affairs Phil G. Goulding said: "The *New York Times* simply did not take the time to research the matter themselves—or, indeed, to ask our assistance."[208] *New York Times* editors provided a tepid response, claiming that the similarity in the figures was "not surprising" since Salisbury had already written that the casualty figures came from the North Vietnamese.[209] But the damage was already done.[210] Harrison Salisbury had been dismissed by the media much as radical protesters from the 1965 march on Washington had been dismissed—with charges that he was aiding the communists. The bombing controversy quickly faded from the headlines.

However, no sooner had the crisis of credibility surrounding bombing abated than Salisbury initiated a new crisis of credibility for the administration. This crisis began when North Vietnamese Premier Pham Van Dong, in an interview with Salisbury, seemed to indicate a softening of his position on negotiations. In the past, Hanoi had insisted on four preconditions for negotiations: withdrawal of U.S. forces, adherence to the Geneva agreement until reunification was complete, National Liberation Front participation in South Vietnam's government, and eventual reunification of Vietnam. In his interview, Dong indicated that these four points were not "conditions" for peace talks, but "valid conclusions for discussions."[211]

The *New York Times* editorial page launched its attack the following day, claiming that the administration was disingenuous in its claims that it desired negotiations. The occasion was Secretary General of the United Nations U Thant's claim in a December 30, 1966, letter to Ambassador Goldberg that cessation of the bombing of the north was a prerequisite to peace. A January 5, 1967, *Times* editorial noted that the Johnson administration agreed that this was the necessary "first step toward peace" but that the administration refused to take this step until it got a guarantee of a "reciprocal response" from Hanoi. "This reply," the editors of the *Times* wrote, "clearly shunts aside Mr. Thant's initial proposal in the mediation mission the United States itself asked the Secretary General to undertake." Quoting the administration's request to U Thant for mediation, the editors added that the president had promised to "cooperate fully with [U Thant] in getting such discussions started promptly." The editors added: "It is a promise . . . that now is brought into doubt."[212] The core of this critique was that the president was dishonest when he claimed that he wanted negotiations to end the war.

Around the same time, the General Assembly of the National Council of Churches issued a statement of its position on the Vietnam War to its member churches that included a stark indictment of the credibility and "the candor of the U.S. Government and its public officials with the public concerning major aspects of the war." According to the Council, "Conflicting policy statements" had created " . . . a continuing crisis of credibility." Among its complaints, the Council asked for more candor from the administration on "[t]he efforts of the Government to negotiate and the replies to them . . . ; the willingness of the Government to negotiate with the National Liberation Front . . . ; willingness to arrange for a phased withdrawal of U.S. forces under international supervision."[213] The Council believed the administration was being dishonest about its willingness to negotiate to end the conflict.

The administration was equally ineffective in dealing with this new challenge to its credibility. It dismissed the seeming change of tone from Hanoi, with one unnamed administration official saying that it was "a distinction without a difference," a change of phrase but not substance. Dean Rusk still promised, "We stand ready—now and at any time in the future—to sit down with representatives of Hanoi."[214] This response did nothing to defuse the crisis.

Arthur Sylvester, recently resigned as Assistant Secretary of Defense for Public Affairs after his disastrous handing of the crisis of credibility on bombing, responded to these new accusations by again attacking Harrison Salisbury. In a speech to the Chicago Headline Club in mid-January, he called Salisbury a "Hanoi-picked correspondent" and said he was "appalled when the *Times* published propaganda statistics concerning alleged civilian casualties on its front page, without attribution of any kind."[215] This outburst also did little to defuse the crisis of credibility over negotiations.

The subject of presidential credibility in seeking a negotiated settlement gained traction and became a heated topic of debate in the media. On February 11, David Susskind launched a televised assault on presidential credibility on his talk show.[216] In a political cartoon a few days earlier, Don Hesse attacked those dissenters who attacked the president on his true desire to negotiate.

A cartoon defending the administration's credibility on peace negotiations.

Source: Don Hesse, McNaught Syndicate, *Springdale News*, February 7, 1967.[217]

The cartoon depicted Ho Chi Minh thumbing his nose, with what appeared to be a bespectacled, bow-tied academic pointing at him. Above this academic was the label "'Peace at Any Price' Group." The caption read "See—He's Making Peace Gestures."[218] The implication was that dissenters were themselves deceptive in suggesting that North Vietnam was giving genuine signals that it desired peace.

These crises of credibility did have an effect on public support for the president's policies in Vietnam. By mid-January 1967 Americans had once more begun to disapprove of the president's handling of Vietnam, with 43 percent disapproving and only 38 percent approving.[219] Two weeks later, disapproval of the president's handling of the conflict had risen to 44 percent, though when Americans were asked "Do you think the U.S. made a mistake sending troops to fight in Vietnam," 62 percent of those who expressed an opinion still said "no."[220] This drop in approval was not a repudiation of the president's intransigence on negotiations; the president and the administration were more in tune with the American people on the issue of negotiations and a bombing halt than the secretary general. When Americans were specifically asked about U Thant's peace proposal, including a unilateral cessation of the bombing, Americans who expressed an opinion narrowly rejected it.[221] When asked in February 1967, 73 percent of Americans who expressed an opinion said that the United States should "continue the bombing of North Vietnam." Seventy-three percent of Americans who had an opinion said that continued bombing would "help" rather than "hurt the chances for a settlement of the Vietnam War."[222] This drop in approval of the president's handling of the war was not a shift to U Thant's position on negotiations or a bombing halt but rather a reaction to questions about the president's credibility.

When UN Secretary General U Thant finally joined the public debate over negotiations, he argued, "There will be no move toward peace so long as the bombing of North Vietnam is going on." However, Thant also dissented on the administration's use of containment to justify the war. He disagreed with the administration's contention that the war prosecuted by the Viet Cong was directed from North

Vietnam[223] and contested the administration's contention that South Vietnam was "strategically vital to Western interests and Western security."[224] If Thant's aim was to force the administration into negotiations or a bombing halt, these latter statements were counterproductive; by questioning the administration's use of containment to justify the war rather than questioning its credibility on negotiations, U Thant had inadvertently shifted the conversation to the administration's strong suit.

As a result of Thant's misstep, on January 12, 1967, on the *Today* show with interviewer Joseph C. Harsch, Secretary Rusk was able to defend the administration's justifications for the war rather than its credibility on negotiations. Harsch asked the Secretary to respond to UN Secretary General U Thant's charge that he did not believe "that South Viet-Nam is strategically vital to Western interests and Western security." Rusk returned to the lessons of Munich. "If the momentum of aggression should begin to roll in that part of the world," Rusk insisted, " . . . then that seems to put us back on the trail that led us into World War II." Adding a warning about nuclear war, Rusk said: "We've got to hang on to those lessons, because if they lead us into World War III, there won't be much left from which we can draw lessons and start over again."[225]

The media also largely rejected U Thant's objections to the administration's containment justifications for its policies in Vietnam. The *New York Times* reported that ambassadors from seven Asian nations disputed the secretary general's assessment, implicitly proving the domino theory. The *Times* reported that these ambassadors met with Thant and told him that "they considered Vietnam important to their security and that of Southeast Asia and adjacent lands." Even after this meeting, according to the article, U Thant "again rejected the domino theory." The article concluded by noting that the Asian ambassadors also disputed U Thant's comparison of South Vietnam to Yugoslavia in making the case for neutralization of Vietnam because Yugoslavia did not border the Soviet Union, as Vietnam did China.[226]

Just as with radical protesters and Harrison Salisbury, the media also painted U Thant as complicit with communists. The Associated

Press reported that Soviet Communist Party Leader Leonid Brezhnev agreed with Secretary General U Thant. According to the AP, Brezhnev agreed with U Thant that "the United States bombing raids on targets in Hanoi had raised 'new obstacles' to a settlement of the Vietnam War." Brezhnev also agreed with the *Time*'s claim that the administration was deceptive when it said it sought peace. Brezhnev, the article claimed, expressed "skepticism of statements by the United States officials that they wished to end the war by negotiations." The AP quoted Brezhnev: "Who will believe the calls for peace if these calls are accompanied by provocative actions? . . . '"[227] Just as with the protesters from the 1965 march on Washington and critics of the administration's credibility on bombing, critics of the administration's true willingness to negotiate now were being attacked as complicit with communists.

Still these attacks on the administration's credibility continued to erode approval of the president's policies in Vietnam. A growing plurality of Americans disapproved of the president's handling of the conflict. However, this did not correspond to an erosion of support for the war; 61 percent of Americans who had an opinion continued to answer that "the U.S. did the right thing in sending troops to Vietnam to try to prevent Communist expansion."[228]

Rather, disapproval of the administration's policies in Vietnam was growing because these attacks on the president's credibility reinforced a growing perception among the American people that the administration was lying to them about Vietnam. In March 1967, Gallup asked a cross-section of Americans, "Do you think the Johnson administration is or is not telling the public all they should know about the Vietnam War?" Fully 65 percent responded that the administration "is not telling the truth," with 23 percent believing the administration was truthful and eleven percent not sure.[229] This was a dramatic reversal from early 1965, when Americans implicitly trusted their government and said that the administration knew better than the public when it came to U.S. policy in Vietnam. Like the concerns of "hawks," the administration had done nothing to address questions about its credibility.

By spring 1967, the administration had two growing problems with American public opinion of its handling of the war. First, "hawks"—the majority of Americans—wanted the administration to be more aggressive in prosecuting the war. Second, and more seriously, most Americans believed the administration was lying to them about the war. However, instead of dealing with these problems, the administration continued to stubbornly use the ideology of military containment of communism to justify U.S. military intervention in Vietnam—sentiments with which most Americans already agreed. This did have the effect of refocusing opposition to the war on attacks on the administration's use of containment. However, this did nothing to address the administration's problems with "hawks" or with those who doubted its credibility.

In mid-1967, the administration finally responded to sagging confidence in its credibility by enlisting General William C. Westmoreland—commander of Military Assistance Command-Vietnam (MAC-V)—and General Harold K. Johnson—Army Chief of Staff—in the public debate over the Vietnam War. General Westmoreland echoed the administration's use of containment to justify the war and attacked dissenters for hurting the war effort. Johnson attacked dissenters and offered optimistic predictions of future success in Vietnam.

However, just as General Johnson was raising public expectations to unreasonably high levels, two Associated Press reporters raised new questions about the administration's credibility surrounding the Gulf of Tonkin incident. These two seemingly unrelated developments would set in motion a chain reaction that would ultimately end the Johnson presidency and permanently transform the public debate over the Vietnam War.

In late April 1967, Lyndon Johnson recalled General William Westmoreland, Commander of MAC-V and the senior U.S. ground forces commander in South Vietnam, to confer on the war and speak before Congress.[230] The move was unprecedented; an American commander had never before been recalled from the warzone to speak to the American public about a war while it was still being fought.

During the trip, Westmoreland echoed the administration's use of the ideology of containment of communism to justify military intervention, telling a joint session of Congress that American troops were providing a "shield of security behind which the Republic of Vietnam can develop and prosper . . . for its own sake and for the future and freedom of all of Southeast Asia." Westmoreland also attacked dissent as sowing disunity and hurting the American war effort in Vietnam. Westmoreland told Congress that the communists believed America's "Achilles' heel is our resolve." In an obvious reference to congressional dissenters, he added, "Your continued strong support is vital to the success of our mission."[231]

The key to General Westmoreland's effectiveness as an advocate for the president's policies in Vietnam was his perceived credibility on the war. Nationally syndicated commentator James Marlow focused on Westmoreland's claim that, as Marlow put it, "the criticism here at home gives the Viet Cong and the North Vietnamese an impression of American disunity and encourages them to keep fighting." Marlow noted that Senator George McGovern claimed the president had "put [Westmoreland] up to saying" these things. In defense of Westmoreland, Marlow invoked former U.S. ambassador to South Vietnam Henry Cabot Lodge, writing that Lodge had earlier made the same accusations against dissenters in a *New York Times* interview. Marlow quoted Lodge as saying (in a veiled reference to the Salisbury dispatches) that the United States would be more successful in the war "if, in the United States, we were to give the appearance of unity and if it were no longer possible for Hanoi to toss in some kind of bone and we all start snarling at each other over it." Marlow wrote that Lodge's criticism was especially credible since Lodge was both a Republican and no longer a member of the government.[232] The unspoken idea that underpinned this article was that both men—Westmoreland and Lodge—were more credible than critics of the war because they had served in Vietnam.

Throughout this period, President Johnson and his administration continued to use the ideology of military containment to justify the war. In March 1967, President Johnson told the Tennessee legislature that there was "growing evidence that the defense of Viet-Nam held the key to the political and economic future of free Asia."[233] William P. Bundy told an audience in Indianapolis on May 3, 1967, that the United States was in Vietnam to "preserve South Viet-Nam's right to work out its own future without external interference." The United States was also acting, Bundy claimed, "to fulfill a commitment that evolved through the actions of Presidents Eisenhower, Kennedy, and Johnson." Bundy added that U.S. presence in South Vietnam proved that the United States would honor its commitments to all of the nations of Southeast Asia whose "security requires a continuing United States ability to act."[234]

The administration's focus on the ideology of containment—rather than on repairing its credibility or explaining to the "Hawks" why it did not take more aggressive action in Vietnam—was tragically unnecessary. The American people already understood and accepted the administration's containment justifications for the war. When Gallup asked Americans to explain why the United States was fighting in Vietnam in their "own words," fully 23 percent of Americans said the United States was fighting to "stop the spread of Communism." Six percent of Americans responded that the United States was fighting to protect "the right of the South Vietnamese to choose their own form of government." Another 6 percent of Americans responded with some variation on the domino theory. Four percent of respondents echoed the administration's argument that communism was an external threat that the United States had to "keep . . . out of . . . South Vietnam," while four percent said the United States was fighting to bring peace to Vietnam. Three percent of Americans argued that the United States was fighting in Vietnam to protect the credibility of its commitments worldwide or to "show we are willing to help." Two percent of Americans said that the United States was acting at the request of the South Vietnamese to stop "aggression" and the "spread of Communism."[235]

Not only was the administration preaching to the converted when it argued the need to contain communism in Southeast Asia, the administration and its supporters were also wasting time attacking dissenters. The American people had already roundly rejected dissenters and their attacks on the applicability of military containment to the war in Vietnam or the ideology of military containment itself. All told, only 6 percent of respondents provided any reason for the American military intervention in Vietnam other than those repeatedly provided by the president, the administration, and sympathetic media. And none of those 6 percent echoed reasons posited by radical dissenters, such as imperialism.[236]

The entry of General Westmoreland into the debate and the administration's stubborn persistence in using the ideology of containment to justify the war did have the effect of refocusing dissent on this unassailable front rather than on the administration's credibility. In June 1967, *Value Line Investment Survey* published a scathing indictment of the ideology of military containment. The *Survey* wrote, "The futility of the containment policy was highlighted a few years ago when a Communist state sprang up off our very shores [in Cuba]." "The Containment Policy is merely a negative military response," the *Survey* added, "to Communist initiative wherever and whenever the Communists choose to take it." While the *Survey* admitted that containment might have been effective immediately after World War II, it added, "Its establishment as a long term policy has cost this country thousands of lives, billions of dollars, and the distrust of nearly all nations." Even worse, the *Survey* wrote, "it has not stopped the spread of Communism, nor will it." While the *Survey* conceded that the United States did have interests in Southeast Asia and a legal basis to prosecute the war in Vietnam, the article said, "U.S. interests in that part of the world are peripheral, at most, its commitments nebulous, to say the least, and its identification with the will or the people or the area most doubtful." The *Survey* also made the novel argument that the turn of underdeveloped nations to communism might be good for world stability, since "people sweating their lives out to produce both food and capital" under an inefficient and exploitative communist regime "have little time or energy for military adventure." Moreover, the *Survey* claimed, "These underdeveloped nations . . . create a strain on the troubled economies of the

Soviet Union and Communist China, sapping their ability to expand further."[237]

The administration's obsessive use of the ideology of containment to justify its intervention in Vietnam also had the effect of refocusing the administration's supporters in the media on these arguments. For instance, the leaking of a Republican position paper on the war in Vietnam provided an opportunity for the Associated Press to defend the administration's argument that it had inherited its policies in Vietnam from previous administrations. According to the AP, "the report's main point is that the Democrats, under Presidents Johnson and John F. Kennedy, and not the Republicans under President Dwight D. Eisenhower," had started America's war in Vietnam. The article took issue with this contention, noting that "Truman began a policy of giving the French aid" during their war against the Viet Minh and "Eisenhower continued the Truman aid policy" because "he shared Truman's fears about the Communist intentions." The AP also noted that Eisenhower had espoused the domino theory and had contended that "Vietnam was the cork in the bottle," the key to containing communism in Southeast Asia. The article did admit that Eisenhower opposed the deployment of troops. However, the AP added that it was not until "South Vietnam seemed in danger of being engulfed by the Viet Cong and the North" that President Johnson sent troops to Vietnam. The AP concluded that "[b]oth Kennedy and Johnson shared the Truman-Eisenhower fear that communism was on the march and had to be stopped."[238]

While the public may have embraced the president's reasons for intervening militarily in Vietnam, by mid-May they once more disapproved of his handling of that intervention.[239] In late May 1967, the U.S. and South Vietnamese troops entered the demilitarized zone between North and South Vietnam to engage the North Vietnamese Army for the first time. This escalation—perhaps in combination with General Westmoreland's entry into the debate over the war—produced a slight rebound in approval of the president's handling of the war.[240] But this bump in approval was short-lived. By mid-July, 52 percent disapproved of the president's handling of the war, while approval had dropped to 34 percent.[241] Yet Americans had not abandoned support for the war itself. When asked, 54 percent of Americans who had an opinion believed the United States had not "made a mistake sending troops to fight in Vietnam." Moreover, only 12 percent of Americans who expressed an opinion believed the United States was losing the war in Vietnam. The remainder believed the United States was either at a standstill or "making progress."[242]

In August 1967—at least in part in response to an article by R. W. Apple in the *New York Times* in which he quoted an anonymous American general as saying that the effort in Vietnam was a "failure"— Army Chief of Staff General Harold K. Johnson was enlisted in the Vietnam War debate.[243] And his contribution to that debate was unbridled enthusiasm over the prospects for the war. On the heels of a request for an additional forty-five thousand troops for Vietnam, Army General Johnson went on an eleven-day tour of Vietnam.[244] In interviews with the press upon his return, General Johnson blasted those who claimed the Vietnam War had become a stalemate, instead claiming, "We're winning the war." General Johnson also promised that the forty-five thousand–troop increase would be the last, saying, "This [troop increase] should be, with circumstances substantially as they are now, adequate to provide a degree of momentum that will see us through to a solution in Vietnam." Under cross-examination, Johnson provided some caveats to this prediction: the new troop level of 525,000 would be enough as long as North Korea or Communist China did not send troops to South Vietnam and as long as the bombing of North Vietnam continued at its current rate. These caveats aside, Johnson claimed that there would be "very real evidence of progress and forward movement" in Vietnam by the end of the year. Johnson also maintained that, for the first time in this trip, he had seen "significant evidence of progress" in the quality of the Army of the Republic of Vietnam (ARVN). He predicted similar progress in the security of roads and the growth of the South Vietnamese economy by the end of the year.[245]

Just as General Johnson was preparing to provide these new, audaciously optimistic predictions for the war, Associated Press (AP) writers

Harry F. Rosenthal and Tom Stewart published a groundbreaking article about the Gulf of Tonkin incident. The article itself initially got very little attention; it was not even published in many AP outlets. But the article did appear in a few papers across the country—most importantly the *Arkansas Gazette*, from Senator Fulbright's home state of Arkansas.[246] While this article went largely unnoticed at the time, it would set in motion a chain of events that would end both the escalation of the Vietnam War and, ultimately, the Johnson presidency.

This AP article was extraordinary in that it was the first serious questioning of the facts of the Gulf of Tonkin incident in the national media:

> What happened that week in the Gulf of Tonkin? . . . Who fired the first shot, and why? Was it a warning, as officially announced, or was it a salvo to kill? Was the Maddox on a routine patrol—and if so, what about the mysterious "black box" so prominent between her stacks? What about that somewhat wraithlike second engagement—on a night that was "dark as the hubs of hell"—in which many of those involved had serious doubts that they were firing at a real enemy? Had the Maddox participated in, or provided cover for, a South Vietnamese attack on a North Vietnamese island in the same area a few days before, as Hanoi charged?[247]

These were questions that had seldom been expressed in a national new source, and certainly never together or in such an accusatory tone.

Rosenthal and Stewart's answers to these questions just as explosive. The article told of an electronic countermeasure suite brought aboard to monitor North Vietnamese communications—"nobody was allowed in there"—and its cryptic caretakers who "kept pretty much to themselves." Lt. Raymond Connell, officer of the deck on the *Maddox* on August 2, 1964, said that the first shots were fired by U.S. warships and were not warning shots: "It was shoot to kill." The situation on the night of August 4, 1964, Rosenthal and Stewart wrote, was confused with ships not tracking the same enemy targets. Lt. Connell said flatly, "We didn't have any targets." Aircraft scoured the area but could not find the enemy PT boats that the destroyers claimed they had detected. Though he insisted that he had seen a spotlight from a PT boat, even Captain Barnhart of the *Turner Joy* admitted, "Contacts could have been caused by the turbulence the ships created themselves; the radar contact might have been caused by the weather; the torpedo sightings may have been in error." Rosenthal and Stewart also noted, "The North Vietnamese regime branded the account of the night incident a fabrication." Most damning, however, Rosenthal and Stewart wrote, "The Congress was told nothing" of the administration's doubts about the incident.[248]

The administration, like much of the country, ignored this report. What little publicity these questions did raise was quickly overwhelmed by General Harold K. Johnson's rosy predictions for success in Vietnam. But these optimistic predictions could not have been more poorly timed. At the same time Johnson was making these statements, the North Vietnamese and Viet Cong were preparing to launch a massive, nationwide assault in South Vietnam—the Tet Offensive. All of these forces—the administration's increasingly optimistic predictions for the war, new questions about the administration's credibility, and the impending communist offensive—would collide in early 1968 and set the stage for a *coup de grâce* by the Senate Foreign Relations Committee that would destroy public faith in the administration's credibility, end both the escalation of the war and the Johnson presidency, and permanently alter the framework for debate of the Vietnam War.

In the two years following the president's announcement of massive troop deployments to Vietnam on July 28, 1965, the framework for public debate of the Vietnam War remained largely unchanged. The president and the administration and their supporters in the media argued for U.S. military intervention in Vietnam using the ideology of military containment. Opponents of U.S. military intervention—the Senate Foreign Relations Committee, radical protesters, academics, and media commentators chief among them—tried to change the president's policies in Vietnam by arguing against the suitability of the ideology of military containment of communism to Vietnam and Southeast Asia. Some opponents—especially radical protesters—also occasionally attacked the entire ideology of military containment of communism, not just in Vietnam, but anywhere. These radical critiques were most dramatically expressed during the march on Washington in November 1965 and the even larger Spring Mobilization in April 1967.

The scale and breadth of criticism of the ideology of containment—and even the volume of narrower attacks on the application of containment to the U.S. military intervention in Vietnam—is, in retrospect, truly breathtaking. This explosion of dissent against the Cold War consensus stood in stark contrast to the political climate in America from the end of World War II to late 1964, when attacks on the ideology of containment and U.S. military intervention abroad were rare, even in Congress. Before 1965, criticism of the ideology of containment or its application to any given foreign policy problem was simply beyond the pale of acceptable public discourse on foreign policy. The controversy sparked by the Vietnam War had suddenly and dramatically opened these topics to debate.

It was this broadening of the scope of public debate over foreign policy that created the space for a new political movement: a foreign policy revolution. Within the menagerie of opponents of the war, there was a core of dissenters in Congress, academia, and the New Left who did not just seek an end to the Vietnam War but an end to the stranglehold the ideology of containment had on American foreign policy. These foreign policy revolutionaries opposed the ideology of containment for different reasons. Congressional and academic revolutionaries saw the Vietnam War as the logical consequence of an outmoded foreign policy ideology and believed that containment had eroded the role of the Congress in advice and consent on foreign policy. Radical revolutionaries believed that rabid anticommunism had made America imperialistic abroad and repressive at home. All wanted to see the United States move beyond the ideology of military containment of communism to a new foreign policy paradigm.

However, while dissenters on the war questioned the Cold War consensus, the American public continued to believe in its precepts and the ideology of containment. Despite over two years of relentless attack by the opposition, most Americans continued to believe that the containment of communism in Southeast Asia was a necessary goal that justified the Vietnam War. Moreover, most Americans were "hawks," wanting the United States to be even more aggressive in defending the sovereignty of South Vietnam from what they saw as aggression from North Vietnam, supported by China and the Soviet Union.

Only a few times over this two-year period did the events of August 1964 in the Gulf of Tonkin impact public debate over the war. Officials in the administration and their supporters in the media occasionally reminded Congress that it had overwhelmingly approved the Tonkin Gulf Resolution—wielding the resolution like an "insurance policy" against congressional dissent. On at least one occasion—to justify new bombing in Hanoi—the administration relied on the tit-for-tat precedent established by the reprisal air strikes in response to the Gulf of Tonkin incident. The Tonkin Gulf Resolution, along with the Constitutional powers of the president, and prior congressional expressions of support for South Vietnamese independence such as the ratification of the SEATO treaty, was also occasionally invoked as the administration's legal basis for U.S. military intervention in Vietnam.

Prior to fall 1966, attacks on the president's credibility were rare, usually centered on claims that the administration was being dishonest about progress in the war. In late 1966, attacks on the administration's credibility began to gain momentum. Critics first questioned the administration's credibility concerning civilian casualties in the bombing of the north. Then they attacked the president's credibility about his willingness to negotiate with the north. These critiques resonated with the American people and by mid-1967 most Americans believed the administration was lying to them about aspects of the war.

The president and the administration never effectively addressed growing doubts about their credibility. Likewise, the president and the administration never explained to the "Hawks" why the United

States could not use more aggressive means in Vietnam. Instead, the administration doggedly continued to justify the war using the ideology of military containment. It is the failure to address these concerns, rather than the failure of the president to justify military intervention in Vietnam, that led to the continuing decline in public approval of the president's handling of the war in 1966 and 1967.

In late summer 1967, two Associated Press reporters questioned the administration's account of the Gulf of Tonkin incident. Despite these new questions about its credibility, the administration would continue to make ever more optimistic claims and ambitious predictions for success in Vietnam through fall 1967. At the same time, the Senate Foreign Relations Committee made the fateful decision to hold hearings in 1968 not on the administration's use of military containment to justify the Vietnam War but on the facts of the Gulf of Tonkin incident. These hearings would occur just as the Vietnamese Communists' 1968 Tet Offensive called into question the credibility of the administration's optimistic predictions from summer and fall 1967.

The convergence of these events would dramatically alter the course of the war. This collision ended the Johnson presidency and changed the framework of public debate over the war from arguments over the applicability of the ideology of containment to Vietnam to arguments over the credibility of the government on the issue of Vietnam. This change in the framework of debate would, in turn, ultimately end the Vietnam War.

Chapter 4

THE COLLAPSE OF CREDIBILITY

In late 1967, the administration began to make increasingly optimistic predictions for future success in the Vietnam War. At the same time, the administration began to ever more forcefully wield its insurance policy against congressional dissent—the Tonkin Gulf Resolution. In response, Senator J. William Fulbright and the staff of the Senate Foreign Relations Committee made the fateful decision to hold hearings in 1968 not on the administration's use of the containment of communism to justify the war but on the facts of the Gulf of Tonkin incident. Fulbright and his staff made this decision for two reasons. First, Fulbright and his staff had concluded as early as 1966 that they must undermine the Tonkin Gulf Resolution before most in Congress would publicly dissent against the war. More importantly, however, Fulbright and his staff concluded that attacking the Cold War consensus had failed to persuade the American public or the Congress to oppose the war and had, in fact, caused the American public to reject dissenters.

These hearings on the Gulf of Tonkin incident would occur just as North Vietnam and the Viet Cong launched a massive, nationwide, surprise attack in January 1968—the Tet Offensive—that called into question the credibility of the administration's optimistic predictions from summer and fall 1967. Some opponents had already begun, as early as late 1966, to attack the administration's credibility on issues such as civilian casualties caused by the bombing of the north and the administration's true willingness to negotiate. As a result, by February 1968, most Americans already believed the administration was lying to them. The 1968 Fulbright hearings were simply a dramatic and conclusive final proof of administration deception. With public confidence in his credibility in ruins, the president was forced to end the escalation of the Vietnam War and withdraw from the presidential race.

The convergence of these events would dramatically alter the public debate over the war. While supporters of the Vietnam War continued to use the ideology of containment to justify the war, opponents began to focus increasingly on a presidential "credibility gap" on Vietnam. Their first target was inconsistency in the administration's version of the events surrounding the Gulf of Tonkin incident. But attacks on the president's credibility rapidly expanded to virtually every facet of the administration's prosecution of the war.

While these attacks were effective in persuading many in Congress to oppose the war and did convince most Americans to reject President Johnson and his heir-apparent, Vice President Hubert Humphrey, these attacks did not convince most Americans to abandon support for the war. Americans rejected political candidates and radical dissenters who continued to attack the ideology of containment or suggest that the United States should abandon its effort to contain communism in Vietnam. Instead, by a narrow majority, Americans supported Richard Nixon and trusted his unspecified policies to bring the war to an honorable end.

By August 1967, most Americans were losing patience with the administration's refusal to "go all out" to win the war in Vietnam. And, as a result, the president saw a serious erosion of support for his handling of the war. At the beginning of August only 32 percent of Americans approved of his handling of the war, while 54 percent of Americans disapproved.[1] By the end of August, approval fell further, to 27 percent, with 60 percent disapproving. As had been the case earlier in the summer, much of this disapproval was a result of the American public's desire for more aggressive action in Vietnam. Of those who disapproved, 18 percent wanted the president to be "more aggressive" and "go all out." Another nine percent believed the United States "should either go all out or get out." (Admittedly, less than one percent, wanted to send "more men and material.") When asked how they "feel about the war in Vietnam" most Americans clearly wanted to continue the war. Only 35 percent of those who had an opinion believed "the U.S. should begin to withdraw its troops." By contrast, 11 percent thought that "the U.S. should carry on its present level of fighting" and the majority of Americans who had an opinion—54 percent—felt that "the U.S. should increase the strength of its attacks against North Vietnam." Americans also rejected dissenters' argument about the risk that the United States might draw the Communist Chinese into the war; most Americans who had an opinion (52 percent) accepted that "if the North Vietnamese show signs of giving in . . . Communist China will . . . send many troops to help North Vietnam."[2]

There are also indications that those Americans who wanted to escalate the war were beginning to look to the Republican Party. When asked who they thought "would be in a better position to bring an end to the war in Vietnam—a Democratic president or a Republican president," the largest percentage of Americans who had an opinion (40 percent) said it would make "no difference." However, of those Americans who felt it would make a difference, 59 percent chose Republicans.[3]

Despite the erosion of support for the president's handling of the war, most in the media continued to echo the administration's use of the containment to justify the war throughout late summer 1967. In an article in August 1967, Associated Press commentator James Marlow supported the president's claim that he was simply continuing his predecessor's policies. Marlow noted that President Truman "gave the French billions of dollars in aid, starting in 1950, to help them stop the Communists in Indochina." After partition, he added, President Eisenhower continued to support South Vietnam and "entered into an agreement—the Southeast Asia Treaty—with other nations in the area to help them . . . repel Communist aggression." Marlow wrote that Eisenhower supported the "'falling domino' theory," quoting Eisenhower as saying that the fall of South Vietnam would lead to a "crumbling process that could, as it progressed, have grave consequences for us and for freedom." Marlow also claimed that President Kennedy "agreed with Eisenhower's domino theory."[4]

While some in the media had begun attacking administration's credibility, most of the administration's opponents in the media continued to attack the administration's use of the containment of communism to justify the war. An editorial in the *Pittsburgh Post-Gazette* claimed, "President Johnson simply is not explaining our presence [in Vietnam] in generally acceptable terms" to the American people. The *Post-Gazette* mocked the administration's stubborn insistence on recounting its justification's for the war in Vietnam writing that, by now, Americans "should know his explanations by rote." Still, this editorial insisted, Americans "simply aren't buying them."[5] But the *Post-Gazette* was wrong. In fact, contemporary polling data showed that Americans were buying Johnson's explanations; most Americans, when asked, echoed the president's use of the ideology of containment to justify the war.[6]

While most Americans supported the administration's use of containment to justify the war, by late summer 1967, many in Congress were beginning to express serious doubts about the administration's policies in Southeast Asia. And like media dissenter, members of Congress attacked the administration's use of the ideology of military containment to justify military intervention in the region. In an interview with the *New York Times*' Don Oberdorfer, Senator Richard B. Russell said that he regretted having not publicly objected thirteen years earlier when Assistant Secretary of State Thruston B. Morton told him that the Eisenhower administration was sending military aid to Vietnam. Oberdorfer also noted that Morton himself, now a senator, had since changed his mind about Vietnam. Morton now argued, according to Oberdorfer, "Japan to an extent should take the lead in the Orient. We just cannot police this entire world."[7] Senator Milton R. Young, senior Republican on the Defense Appropriations Subcommittee, had also joined this dissent, arguing that Cuba was more important than Southeast Asia and Vietnam was not "worth the price."[8]

President Johnson responded to growing dissent in Congress by finally fully invoking his insurance policy against their dissent—the

Tonkin Gulf Resolution—in a speech before the National Legislative Conference in San Antonio on September 29, 1967. Johnson said that the United States had made commitments to defend South Vietnam. These commitments, he claimed, came from the SEATO treaty but were also reasserted by "Members of the United States Congress . . . in a resolution that it passed in 1964 by a vote of 504 to 2."[9] Johnson said this resolution gave him authority:

> . . . to take all necessary steps, including the use of armed force, to assist any member or protocol state of the Southeast Asia Collective Defense Treaty requesting assistance in defense of its freedom.[10]

Johnson also reiterated that containment of communism required U.S. military intervention in Vietnam. The president said, "Three Presidents and the elected representatives of our people have chosen to defend this Asian nation." Further, Johnson explained that communist "aggression was a threat not only to the immediate victim but to the United States of America and to the peace and security of the entire world of which we in America are a very vital part." Johnson invoked the lessons of Munich: "All that we have learned in this tragic century strongly suggest[s]" that a "Southeast Asia dominated by communist power would bring a third world war much closer to terrible reality." This warning was accompanied by a lengthy proof of the domino theory using the statements of leaders from the region. The president concluded, "By seeing this struggle through now we are greatly reducing the chances of a much larger war—perhaps a nuclear war."[11]

However, the main purpose of the president's speech was to outline his terms for peace. In the process, the president for the first time addressed attacks on his credibility—specifically claims that he did not truly desire peace. To those critics, Johnson again assured Americans that he was prepared to negotiate with anyone, any place, at any time. However, he conditioned any ceasefire on a commitment "that while discussions proceed, North Vietnam would not take advantage of the bombing cessation or limitation."[12]

The president's invocation of the Tonkin Gulf Resolution as a weapon against congressional dissent was echoed by his administration. Dean Rusk was combative, telling reporters in a news conference that Congress had called Asian security vital. Rusk added that it was "where two-thirds of the world's people live, no less vital to us as a nation than is peace in our own hemisphere or in the NATO area."[13] Rusk then even more explicitly invoked the Tonkin Gulf Resolution as a weapon against congressional dissent, insisting:

> Now what I don't understand is that Senators would declare in August, 1964, that the United States considers it a vital national interest of this country that there be international peace and security of Southeast Asia. And, then, two years later, some of them seem to brush that aside as having no validity.[14]

Rusk quipped: "On which occasion were they right?" Rusk added, "These are not matters that change with the wind."[15] Rusk repeated this point in an interview with USIA a few days later.[16] Two weeks after that, in an address in Columbus, Indiana, Rusk didn't name the Tonkin Gulf Resolution, but did quote it.[17] The administration had finally made the decision to use the resolution to silence congressional dissent.

Media supporters echoed the administration's confrontational tone in wielding the Tonkin Gulf Resolution against Congress—and reminding the public of Senator J. William Fulbright's role in passing the resolution. In an August 1967 article, commentator James Marlow recounted the administration's version of the Gulf of Tonkin incident and then recalled that, as a result, the president had "asked Congress to approve a resolution backing him up. Congress did on Aug. 7, 1964, in a joint resolution which the House okayed 416 to 0 and the Senate approved 88 to 2." Marlow then recalled that Senator Wayne Morse had later proposed repealing the resolution.[18] Marlow wrote:

> Before the senators voted, Johnson sent word that those who wanted to "reverse" the 1964 resolution because they had a

"change of heart" should go ahead and vote that way. But the Senate killed the Morse proposal 92 to 5 by tabling it. One of the five voting against tabling was Sen. J.W. Fulbright, chairman of the Senate's Foreign Relations Committee. He'd had a change of heart.[19]

Marlow reminded his readers that Fulbright "was the one who had steered the Tonkin resolution through the Senate in 1964." Marlow derided Fulbright for his supposed claim that "he didn't realize how much of a blank check the resolution had given Johnson."[20] This whole criticism of Fulbright, of course, ignores the very important fact that the administration had assured Congress that it did not intend to use the resolution to escalate the war. Fulbright had not had a "change of heart"; he had consistently opposed escalation of the war and was the first senator to publicly speak out against it. But this was a painfully effective attack that would be incessantly repeated until the resolution was finally repealed, years later.

While the president and the administration had finally unleashed the full power of their insurance policy against congressional dissent—the Tonkin Gulf Resolution—it had little effect on approval of Johnson's handling of the war. In September approval of his handling of Vietnam had risen slightly, by two points, to 29 percent, while disapproval had dropped by two points to 58 percent.[21] More importantly, the aggressive use of the Tonkin Gulf Resolution as a weapon against Fulbright personally was almost certainly a factor in Senator J. William Fulbright's decision to hold hearings on the Gulf of Tonkin incident in early 1968.

In October 1967, radical protesters mounted a two hundred thousand–man march on Washington that they called the Mobilization.[22] As with previous radical protests, the Mobilization was roundly rejected by both the media and the American people. And just as with previous protests, there is evidence that the Mobilization actually bolstered public support of the president's policies in Vietnam. Radical protesters emerged from the Mobilization even more radicalized and increasingly disillusioned with the stubborn resilience of the Cold War consensus among the American people. Many radicals began to see the American public not as the target of persuasion but as the obstacle to change.

The framework for debate of the war during this period remained largely unchanged from the previous two and half years—between the supporters of the president using containment to justify the war and opponents attacking the use of containment to justify the war. In the aftermath of the Mobilization, some members of Congress and some in the media reaffirmed their support for the administration's use of containment to justify the war. Others in Congress and the media attacked the administration's use of containment to justify the war. At least one Republican presidential hopeful also came out in opposition to the war; his dissent, too, focused on the administration's use of the ideology of containment to justify the war.

The public mood on the eve of the Mobilization was as favorable as it had been since the start of the Vietnam War to the aims of radical demonstrators. Two weeks before the march, when asked if they thought "the United States made a mistake sending troops to fight in Vietnam," for the first time ever, a majority Americans who had an opinion (52 percent) answered "yes." Likewise, Americans, by an overwhelming majority, believed the administration was lying to them; 77 percent of Americans who expressed an opinion believed, "The Johnson administration . . . is not telling the public all they should know about the Vietnam war." When Americans were asked if the United States should send troops "if a situation like Vietnam were to develop in another part of the world," two thirds of Americans who had an opinion answered "no."[23]

However, Americans were not yet ready to quit the war. When asked how they "feel about the war in Vietnam," only 33 percent of Americans who expressed a view wanted to withdraw. Eleven percent wanted to carry on the war at "its present level of fighting" and the greatest percentage (56 percent) believed the United States should "increase the strength of its attacks against North Vietnam." When asked specifically if they would support a bombing halt if it would "improve our chances in Vietnam for meaningful peace talks," 70 percent of Americans who had an opinion would "continue bombing" North Vietnam. When Americans were asked what they would do next in Vietnam, of those Americans who expressed a view, 73 percent opposed an extended bombing pause to promote negotiations, while 61 percent opposed the suggestion that the United States "should withdraw [its] troops now." The same percentage approved when asked if they would support the present plan: "continue to bomb selected targets in North Vietnam as at present and keep military pressures" until "the north agrees to negotiate." In fact, Americans only rejected the possible use of atomic weapons by a narrow margin (54 percent to 46 percent).[24]

There are some indications that Americans continued to support the war because they accepted the administration's contention that military intervention was necessary to contain of communism. When asked if the Vietnam War would start or prevent World War III, by a narrow margin (51 percent to 49 percent) those Americans who had an opinion agree with the administration's argument, based on the lessons of Munich, that the Vietnam War "may prevent" World War III.[25]

The Mobilization itself did little to effect American public support for the war in Vietnam. This was due in no small part to the tactics and rhetoric of the radical protesters, which alienated much of the American public. Demonstrators gave speeches and carried banners praising communist revolutionary Che Guevara and Chinese Communist Mao Zedong. Political firebrand Abbie Hoffman promised to stop the war by using meditation to levitate the Pentagon ten feet off the ground and exorcize its evil spirits.[26] Some of the protesters broke off from the main march, rushed the Pentagon, and were beaten by police and arrested.[27]

The media was as unsupportive of the October 1967 Mobilization as it had been of previous radical demonstrations. The Long Island *Newsday* said that "dissenters make up in noise [what they] lack in numbers" but that these protesters "do not impress the great mass of Americans who remain quietly confident about our role in Vietnam and are aware of what would happen if we gave up the struggle." *Newsday* derided the protesters as aiding the enemy: "antiwar

The 1967 mobilization protests.

Source: Frank Wolfe, Vietnam War protesters at the March on the Pentagon, October 21, 1967, Johnson Presidential Library.[28]

demonstrations . . . give Ho Chi Minh false encouragement and the propaganda he requires to keep his people fighting." The editorial lamented that Ho Chi Minh could not see the "silent center" of America, "the backbone of the nation" that was "naturally distressed [and] concerned but determined to see the war through to an honorable settlement that fortifies the sacrifices we have made to keep a tiny Asian nation free."[29]

The *Canton Repository* from Canton, Ohio, was even more vitriolic in lashing out at demonstrators. The editors wrote that there was much more at stake in Vietnam than "has been expressed in the shrill yelps of bearded youths, their girlfriends and dreamy-eyed hippie cultists." This editorial, too, spoke of a "great silent center" that was "fed up with the caterwauling of rioters and sensation-mongers threatening to turn a public issue into anarchy."[31]

Pete Hamill of the *Washington News* was one of the few media figures to support radical protesters. In a fiery speech before the

Emergency Civil Liberties Committee, Hamill echoed the radical protesters' discontent with the state of American society and their recurring theme that anticommunism had distorted American values.[31] Hamill said that radical demonstrators were "really lecturing us":

> They are telling us that they no longer believe the tired rhetoric of the 1940s. They are telling us that they do not care whether some foreign country chooses one economic system over another, at least not while the climate of bigotry and injustice in this country makes our credibility very slim indeed.[32]

The American public roundly rejected the rhetoric and tactics of radical protesters. In fact, these demonstrations may have actually increased support for the war. Pollster Lou Harris wrote in a *Washington Post* article in December that "the peace march to the Pentagon, the picketing of Administration officials, campus uprisings and clashes between draft protestors and police appear to have had an effect opposite to that intended by the organizers." He wrote that, as a result of the protests, more Americans supported the war in Vietnam. Specifically, he cited poll results showing that "the number of people doubtful about the Vietnamese war was thirteen points higher before the recent wave of demonstrations than it is today." He also wrote, "Americans reject the militant methods pursued by some opponents of U.S. involvement in Vietnam." Most Americans appeared to agree with the argument made by both former Vice President Richard Nixon and General William C. Westmoreland that protests and dissent prolonged the war. According to Harris, 76 percent of Americans believed that the demonstrations "encourage Communists to fight all the harder." He also wrote that 68 percent of Americans believed the antiwar demonstrations were "acts of disloyalty against the boys in Vietnam." Harris did write that Americans accepted the right to dissent and the right to peacefully demonstrate, though he noted that the percentage of people believing in these rights had dropped significantly since July 1967. Seventy percent of Americans, he added, believed that the antiwar protests displayed a "'lack of dignity,' 'lack of respect for law and order' and 'exhibitionist behavior.'"[33]

There is also evidence that the Mobilization increased approval president's handling of the war. After the Mobilization, a majority of Americans still disapproved of the president's handling of Vietnam, but the margin of that disapproval had narrowed. Only 52 percent of Americans disapproved of the president's handling of Vietnam (a drop of six percentage points). Thirty-seven percent of Americans now approved of the president's handling of the war (an increase of eight points).[34] By mid-November, public approval of the president's handling of the war increased further, with 40 percent approving (an increase of three points) and only 49 percent disapproving (a drop of three points).[35]

More troubling for the president, however, support for his party continued to erode. When asked "which political party—the Republican or the Democratic—do you think is better able to end the war in Vietnam," 29 percent of Americans who had an opinion said they would do the "same." However, the largest percentage (44 percent) now said the Republican party would do a better job,[36] a jump of nine percentage points since late August.

In response to America's reaction to the October 1967 Mobilization, radical activists emerged more radicalized and disconnected from the mainstream of American society. A narrative began to emerge among radicals after the Mobilization that American society was beyond saving. The radical magazine *The Movement* decried the American worker, who was "pushed unceasingly through the processing of school, military and job." *The Movement* wrote that, to succeed, radicals must break "the massive, unthinking, unchallenged racism and patriotism (anti-communism) which these communities [workers] share with the rest of white America."[37] *The Movement* wrote that the Cold War consensus was the heart of radicalism's problem: "Anti-communism is the strongest force holding a people alienated from their government in support of that government." *The Movement*'s prescription was to show the American worker "the way people live in Cuba and North Vietnam, in Eastern European countries and . . . all over the new revolutionary third world countries." Radicals had to show Americans "the particular way people live in the countries Americans have been taught to hate."[38]

The American public was no longer a group whose opinions must be changed but rather had become an obstacle to changing society. New Left radical and former Yale professor Staughton Lynd wrote after the Mobilization that the "movement" had "redefined itself as a movement against racist capitalist imperialism at home and abroad." He added: "The question is no longer that American society *has* a problem. What we think now is that American society *is* a problem"[39] (emphasis is Lynd's).

While radical protesters focused their dissent on the ideology of containment and its effect on society, other opponents of the war continued to attack the administration's use of the containment of communism to justify military intervention in Vietnam. In a lengthy *New York Times* article, former ambassador to India John Kenneth Galbraith called the Vietnam War a "massive miscalculation—perhaps the worst in history." He wrote that "proponents of the military solution" misjudged the North Vietnamese's capacity for "reasonable calculation." He added that supporters of the war were misguided in their belief that the United States had "only to raise sufficiently the cost of the war" to cause North Vietnam to capitulate. Instead, Galbraith wrote, this view "has turned out to be sharply in conflict with circumstances." Galbraith also disagreed that the war was "centrally guided" by a "conspiratorial aspect of Communism." Galbraith argued, "Since we took this decision, its whole foundation has collapsed." The heart of Galbraith's dissent was that it was nationalism, not communism, that drove the conflict. As a result, he wrote, "our presence in the conflict . . . further weakens the nationalist identification of the Government of Saigon." Galbraith claimed that the war was a civil struggle between competing governments. He added: "In much of the country the Vietcong has been the effective governing authority for 10 years or more." America's error, he argued, was that it was "quixotic to believe we had an obligation to eliminate Communist Power in all South Vietnam." This problem was compounded, he added, because "no force can be conscripted to oppose the nationalist instinct of its own people." Galbraith's prescription was to "abandon the objective of total reconquest" and accept that "in most of rural South Vietnam we must expect that such central authority as there is will henceforth be exercised by the Vietcong." Galbraith contended that the United States had been "brain washed" to believe the domino theory, "rather more by Asians than by our own people." The solution to the dilemma was to "correct [the] miscalculations" of U.S. policy in Vietnam by ending the war.[40]

Galbraith took a sympathetic tone in discussing the administration's credibility problems, arguing that they were the inevitable consequence of a disastrous policy. The problem, he wrote, was the "highly obdurate nature of facts." The administration was forced to argue that the government in Saigon had "stability" and "democratic instincts," that the South Vietnamese Army had sufficient capability, that military and pacification programs were successful, and that escalation held promise for better results. However, Galbraith wrote, "time and time again these claims have been denied by events." Galbraith quipped that Army Chief of Staff General Harold K. Johnson had just returned "from his eighth consecutive encouraging visit to Vietnam in three and a half years." The consequence of this official optimism, Galbraith wrote, was that "almost anything now said in defense of the war is suspect." Galbraith also joined those who accused the administration of lying about its willingness to negotiate: "If one does not wish to negotiate, he can always do so in a manner that insures [sic] failure." Rather than continue to insist that the fate of the world rested on the outcome of the war in Vietnam, Galbraith suggested, "both the White House and the State Department would show more respect for the taste and intelligence of the American people if they resorted on occasion to understatement."[41]

As the protests in Washington raged, some members of Congress spoke out in support of the administration's use of the containment of communism to justify continued U.S. military intervention in Vietnam. Republican Senator Wallace F. Bennett of Utah argued that the Vietnam War was actually a battle in a Third World War, waged by the Communist World through wars of liberation, with the goal of world conquest. Bennett cited the positive implications of the domino theory, that U.S. resolve had reversed the Communization of the rest of Southeast Asia. Withdrawal before the U.S. had secured South Vietnamese independence, Bennett argued, "would not only reward Communist aggression, and confirm the effectiveness of their so-called wars of liberation, but would inevitably encourage further Communist military adventures elsewhere."[42] Maryland Democratic Senator Daniel B. Brewster also agreed that U.S. intervention in Vietnam was required to contain communism, but insisted on the floor of the Senate that the administration needed to take even more aggressive action in Vietnam.[43]

Despite these expressions of support from some members, of Congress, congressional dissent continued to grow. And this dissent was focused on the administration's use of containment to justify the war. Senator J. William Fulbright took to the floor of the Senate to urge his colleagues to support a sense of the Senate resolution sponsored by Senate majority leader Mike Mansfield of Montana that would ask the United Nations to intervene to resolve what Fulbright called the "revolting and degrading" war in Vietnam. This resolution attracted fifty-nine cosponsors. Fulbright added: "In this open-ended and frustrating and divisive war the United States has no choice but to seek a settlement." But the heart of Fulbright's critique was an attack on the application of the ideology of containment to the conflict, which Fulbright said had "raised [the war] from a guerrilla war to an internationalized war." Democratic Senators Phillip A. Hart of Michigan and Stephen M. Young of Ohio supported Fulbright's call for the resolution.[44] Democratic Senator Joseph D. Tydings of Maryland objected to the "continuous escalation" of the conflict.[45]

As the Mobilization and its critics receded from the headlines at least one presidential hopeful came out against the war. His critique, too, was against the application of the ideology of containment to the conflict. In November 1967, Republican Governor George Romney of Michigan reversed his earlier support for the war, claiming that he had been "brainwashed" by military briefings on the war and that the war was in fact a "tragic mistake." His criticism was that, as the war and pacification efforts were "Americanized," the South Vietnamese did less to secure their own freedom. Further, he argued that the escalation had exacerbated the "conflict that now exists between Communism and freedom." Romney did accept that the war was being directed by North Vietnamese and Chinese Communists. However, Romney dissented on the domino theory, believing that the United States had, in fact, created the conditions under which the domino theory might play out when it "built this thing [Vietnam] up" into a major confrontation. Still, Romney believed it was "unthinkable that the United States should withdraw," though, confusingly, he also said that the war could not be won "by bombing and military action." It appears Governor Romney had taken his cue from a Republican strategy paper published earlier in the year. Democratic Presidents Kennedy and Johnson, Romney claimed, were responsible for the United States' "entrapment" in Vietnam. By contrast, Romney said, "We must acknowledge the wisdom of President Eisenhower's decision 13 years ago not to deploy ground troops in Vietnam."[46] Of course, this analysis ignored the fact that, since at least 1965, the consistent Republican position had been that the war should be escalated even more rapidly than the Johnson administration had chosen to escalate it.

Romney's policy prescription was to give the National Liberation Front a seat at negotiations in hope of splitting nationalists from the communists within their movement. Romney also indicated that he would accept neutralization of Southeast Asia. Romney likewise proposed the vague outlines of a broader foreign policy philosophy, a more restrained form of military containment. Romney claimed that the United States risked becoming exhausted "running around on a bucket brigade trying to put out every fire that comes along." His thresholds for intervention would be whether the prospective situation was a "genuine threat to the balance of world peace . . . and [had an] . . . absence of local resources to meet that threat."[47] In the end, this early Republican presidential hopeful would prove an ineffective campaigner and leave the race by February 1968.

In late 1967, Senator J. William Fulbright and the staffers of the Senate Foreign Relations Committee made the fateful decision to change their strategy for attacking the administration's policies in Vietnam. Since mid-1965, Fulbright had attacked the administration's use of containment to justify the war and the broader ideology of military containment of communism itself. Fulbright and his staff reached the conclusion in late 1967 that these attacks had not only failed to persuade Congress or the American public to oppose the war, but had actually alienated the American public. Instead, Fulbright and the Senate Foreign Relations Committee decided to attack the credibility of the administration's account of the Gulf of Tonkin incident in order to undermine the Tonkin Gulf Resolution—the administration's insurance policy against congressional dissent—in a more focused effort to force the president to end the war.

Throughout the second half of 1967, the administration continued to doggedly insist that containment of communism in Southeast Asia required U.S. military intervention in Vietnam. The administration did nothing to address the concerns of "hawks"—a majority of Americans—who wanted the president to be more aggressive in Vietnam. Likewise, the administration did nothing to address the concerns of the majority of Americans who doubted the president's credibility. Instead, in late 1967, the president doubled down on his strategy, once more recalling General Westmoreland to tout America's successes in Vietnam, raising public expectations to precariously high levels. This move could not have been more poorly timed, as the Tet Offensive in early 1968 would soon call into question all of the administration's rosy predictions from late 1967.

Senator J. William Fulbright's decision to hold hearings in 1968 was the result of the convergence of a number of factors, including the efforts by other members of Congress to end the war, the White House's increasing use of the Tonkin Gulf Resolution as a weapon against congressional dissent, and the failure of Fulbright's previous dissent—against the ideology of containment and its application to the war in Vietnam—to change Johnson's policies in Vietnam. Interestingly, Fulbright and his staffers were not just concerned that

Fulbright's dissent against the Cold War consensus had failed to change administration policy; they were also concerned that this dissent was causing Americans to associate congressional dissenters with radical dissenters, who they believed had alienated the American public with their tactics and rhetoric. And from the beginning, it is clear that the aim of the 1968 Fulbright hearings would be twofold: to undermine the Tonkin Gulf Resolution as a weapon against congressional dissent and to damage the president's credibility with the American people.

In August 1967, Republican Congressman Paul Findley, an opponent of the war, appeared on a television panel on KMOX in St. Louis to discuss the Vietnam War. He was joined on the panel by prominent St. Louis lawyer Kenneth Teasdale. Teasdale was the husband of the former Anna Fulbright, Senator J. William Fulbright's daughter.[48] After the filming concluded the two men discussed a resolution Findley was sponsoring in the House demanding an investigation of the Tonkin Gulf Resolution. As a result of this conversation, Findley sent this resolution to Fulbright.[49]

The resolution itself was co-sponsored by twenty-one other congressmen. It was introduced but never brought to a vote by the full House. The resolution began with a complaint about how the war was being executed, as "a war of gradualism which has not caused the communist forces in South Vietnam to respect the territorial integrity of that country." It charged that the United States had done nothing to stem the flow of North Vietnamese supplies, that the South Vietnamese Army was ineffectual, that the Marines were besieged at Khe Sanh, and that "there [was] no indication that the military and political activities of the United States since 1964 have in any way brought a settlement closer."[50] But its main charge was against the validity of the Tonkin Gulf Resolution as a legal basis for the war:

> Substantial doubt exists among Members of Congress and the American public as to whether the Gulf of Tonkin Resolution of August 1964 . . . provides adequate authority to the President to deal with the military situation in Southeast Asia.[51]

This resolution demanded that the House Committee on Foreign Affairs hold hearings on "the implementation of the Gulf of Tonkin Resolution . . . and . . . consider whether it empowers the president to carry forward military operations of the current scope and magnitude in Southeast Asia." This resolution also suggested that the Resolution might need "modification in light of changing political and military conditions."[52] This was substantially the same aim that Fulbright had sought but failed to achieve at the end of his hearings in 1966.

At the same time that Fulbright received a copy of this House resolution from Findley, the Senate Foreign Relations Committee was considering Senate Resolution 151, a resolution to reassert the role of the Congress in advice and consent on foreign policy.[53] This resolution was the culmination of a half year of sporadic hearings the Senate Foreign Relations Committee had held on the ideology of containment as part of a series staffers called, "The United States as a great power."[54] The chief complaint of this resolution was that the "accurate definition of the term 'national commitment' in recent years has become obscured." This resolution simply reasserted that national commitments could only be enacted jointly by the executive and legislative branch through "a treaty, convention, or other legislative instrumentality specifically intended to give effect to such a commitment."[55] Fulbright and his staffers hoped that this resolution could be used as a weapon in their foreign policy revolution to reestablish the role of Congress in foreign policymaking and, ultimately, the first step in moving beyond the Cold War foreign policy paradigm of containment. But this resolution was relatively tepid in comparison to the House's resolution on the Tonkin Gulf Resolution.

In September 1967, former judge and constitutional scholar Dr. Albert Levitt testified before the Senate Foreign Relations Committee about the National Commitments Resolution and insisted that the entire legal basis on which the president was waging the war in Vietnam—including the Tonkin Gulf Resolution—was invalid.[56] Unfortunately for the congressional wing of the foreign policy revolution, the limited scope of the National Commitments Resolution being considered in the Senate would do nothing to bind the president or amend or repeal the Tonkin Gulf Resolution. In fact, in August 1967, historian W. Stull Holt testified before the Committee that the resolution would have no effect on the president at all.[57] Under Secretary of State Nicholas Katzenbach only underlined the Senate's impotence in foregin policy making when he told the Senate Foreign Relations Committee during these hearings that the Tonkin Gulf Resolution was the "functional equivalent of a declaration of war."[58]

Fulbright persisted in trying to refine and tailor this resolution to tie the president's hands in making future commitments. However, as he tried to modify the resolution, he met with opposition from his colleagues—even inside the Foreign Relations Committee—and was forced to exempt both the Vietnam War and emergency situations from the effects of the resolution, effectively stripping the resolution of the dual powers he had initially intended it to wield—to weaken the Tonkin Gulf Resolution and to reassert the power of the Senate in advice and consent on foreign policy. Fulbright was then forced to delay further consideration of the resolution until 1968.[59] Fulbright succeeded in getting the findings of the hearings on the resolution published in the New York Times.[60] However, in the end this resolution was delayed again and not voted by the full Senate until 1969. Moreover, this effort did nothing tangible to call into question the president's authority to weaken the Tonkin Gulf Resolution or reassert the role of Congress in foreign policymaking.

Just as this effort was falling apart, the administration began to ever more forcefully invoke the Tonkin Gulf Resolution as a weapon against congressional dissent, beginning with the president's speech in San Antonio in September 1967. It was in this climate of increasing antagonism by the president and his administration that Fulbright and the staffers of the Senate Foreign Relations Committee gathered to regroup and consider their next move.

Discussions among Fulbright and his staffers at the time make it clear that the committee was searching for a way to inflict political damage on President Johnson in hopes of getting him to change course in Vietnam. In December, as the committee discussed how to move forward with hearings, discussions proceeded on two tracks.

The first possible hearing subject was on the "responsibilities of the United States" as a world power. This subject was essentially a continuation of the series, "The United States as a great power," conceived in late 1966, that had only produced a few isolated hearings and the failed National Commitments Resolution. Carl Marcy suggested that these hearings be retooled to be "frankly political (hopefully with educational side effects)." To achieve this goal, Marcy suggested inviting a list of 1968 presidential hopefuls—including former Vice President Richard Nixon, Senator Eugene McCarthy, and Governor George Romney—to testify. Marcy suggested that this be followed by the "broad educational (really political) act of hearings" with opponents of the administration's policies in Vietnam "such as [Prof. George] Kahin, [former Ambassador George] Kennan, [Gen. (ret.) David M.] Shoup, [Gen. (ret.) Matthew B. Ridgway], and returned veterans."[61] In a later conception of this series of hearings, the witness list was even more confrontational, including Governor Ronald Reagan and Johnson nemesis Senator Robert F. Kennedy.[62] Staffer Norvill Jones agreed with Carl Marcy's proposed hearings.[63]

However, staffers Don Henderson and Bill Bader disagreed with Carl Marcy. They wanted to hold hearings on the specific topic of the Gulf of Tonkin incident.[64] In late 1967, probably in response to the Associated Press's July 1967 article questioning the Gulf of Tonkin incident, Fulbright had ordered staffer Bill Bader to begin an investigation of the Gulf of Tonkin incident.[65] As a result of this investigation, Bader had amassed a large amount of evidence and witness testimony calling into question the administration's account of the incident. Henderson argued that the previous year's abortive attempt to hold hearings on America's role as a world power had had "mediocre results and minor impact precisely because their theme was so large and almost amorphous in the eyes of the general public." He suggested that the problem with these hearings was that "growing dissension in this country has gone beyond the point of encouraging dispassionate and impartial examination of alternative ways of viewing the world and the United States role." Henderson also suggested that, since 1968 was an election year, bringing presidential candidates to testify, as Marcy had suggested, might "split [the committee] beyond retrieval and damage its effectiveness as an alternate voice to that of the Administration" and also "damage rather than help presidential candidates." Instead, Henderson suggested, "Greater impact would be gained by less generalization and more concrete information" and, for that reason, "Tonkin Gulf hearings would be made to order." Referring to Bill Bader's preliminary staff study about the Gulf of Tonkin incident, Henderson added, "I think we already have the [ammunition] prepared for dramatic hearings early next session." Henderson concluded that the Committee's role was "to restrain the Administration and the military by demonstrating their deficiencies and by trying to examine concrete alternatives to what they are doing" and, while "it would be most desirable if these latter could be developed out of a broad alternative framework of policy thinking," Henderson didn't "believe the situation or the nation will stand still for the process."[66]

Perhaps the decisive factor in convincing Fulbright to abandon his attacks on the ideology of containment was the perception among staffers that these attacks were causing the American public to associate the committee with radical dissenters who they believed had alienated mainstream Americans with their tactics and rhetoric. Staffer Peter Riddleberger joined Don Henderson in rejecting the idea of hearings on the role of the United States as a world power. He wrote to Senator Fulbright, "These types of hearings are appealing to a narrowing group of Americans, namely the 'new left' and the academic community." Riddleberger observed that these groups had already alienated the American public and, in identifying itself with these dissenters, the committee might unintentionally help the president. To prove his point, Riddleberger attached the recent article from the *Washington Post* by pollster Louis Harris about the American public's growing animosity toward radical demonstrators who were attacking the Cold War consensus. Next, Riddleberger cited the growing volume of letters to the committee attacking the senator's critiques of the president's use of the ideology of containment.[67] Riddleberger recommended that the committee stop attacking the Cold War consensus and instead focus on the Gulf of Tonkin incident.

In light of these cautions from Riddleberger, the administration's increasingly aggressive invocation of the Tonkin Gulf Resolution as an insurance policy against congressional dissent, Fulbright's repeated failed attempts to weaken the Tonkin Gulf Resolution in the past, and Fulbright's recent correspondence with Congressman Paul Findley about his own Tonkin Gulf Resolution hearings, hearings on the Gulf of Tonkin incident must have seemed made to order. They were a straightforward way to weaken the administration's insurance policy against congressional dissent, the Tonkin Gulf Resolution, without further alienating Americans by attacking the Cold War consensus. There is no evidence that Fulbright understood that his decision would change the entire framework of debate over the Vietnam War. Rather, it appears that the decision to hold hearings on the Gulf of Tonkin incident was much more narrowly focused on undermining the Tonkin Gulf Resolution by attacking the president's credibility on this single event.

Within a week of Riddleberger's letter, Senator Fulbright and the Senate Foreign Relations Committee had decided to hold its hearings in early 1968 on the Gulf of Tonkin incident. And it was clear from the beginning that the Committee had two targets: the president's credibility and the Tonkin Gulf Resolution. On December 21, 1967, Senator Fulbright released previously classified testimony by Assistant Secretary of State William P. Bundy that confirmed that the administration had written a draft of the Tonkin Gulf Resolution before the Gulf of Tonkin incident ever occurred. In this testimony, Bundy stunned Senator Fulbright by saying, "We had contingent drafts . . . for some time prior to that." Fulbright responded incredulously, "What do you mean, prior to when?" Bundy answered, "Prior to August 1964." Bundy quickly tried to cover his mistake: "But this is a matter of normal contingency planning. No serious thought had been given to it, to the best of my knowledge, prior to the Gulf of Tonkin." But Fulbright pressed, asking what the purpose of the draft was "if it occurred before [the incident]?" Bundy only made matters worse with his response: "We had always anticipated . . . the possibility that things might take [a] more drastic turn at any time and that it would be wise to seek an affirmation of the desires of and intent of the Congress."[68] Fulbright had launched a direct assault on the Tonkin Gulf Resolution, and the Gulf of Tonkin incident was the weapon he would use to fight the president.

This press release generated a great deal of media attention, with many news sources drawing the entirely accurate conclusion that the Gulf of Tonkin incident had been a pretext for action the administration had wanted to take all along. Some media sources also, for the first time, echoed the accusations made by the Associated Press in July 1967 that the attack on the *Maddox* and *Turner Joy* on the night of August 4, 1964, had never happened. For instance, a United Press International story about the press release, carried in papers across the country, reported that "certain statements recently have indicated that torpedoes may not have been fired at the U.S. vessels."[69]

The committee followed this release with an official announcement that it would hold hearings on the Gulf of Tonkin incident. The committee received a flurry of letters supporting the decision. The committee also received a number of letters from people with information about the event that was indeed helpful in the hearings.[70]

As this new threat to the president was taking shape in the Senate Foreign Relations Committee, the president recalled General William C. Westmoreland to the United States to buoy sagging American spirits and shore up public approval of his policies in Vietnam. In a press conference on November 22, 1967, at the Pentagon, Westmoreland boasted that the Viet Cong was forced to buy Cambodian rice because U.S. military forces had blocked its supply routes from the north.[71] In a National Press Club speech, Westmoreland was optimistic about the future, telling the audience that the United States was entering a new phase in the war "when the end begins to come into view." He said that during this phase, the Viet Cong would be "cut up and near collapse" while the South Vietnamese Army would become more professional and more competent in facing Viet Cong forces.[72] He predicted that U.S. troop reductions in South Vietnam would begin within two years. Westmoreland also announced a new military strategy, saying that the United States would begin to "provide new military equipment to revitalize the Vietnamese army and prepare them to take on an ever-increasing share of the war."[73] Westmoreland promised that bases would progressively be handed over to South Vietnamese forces and that "the Vietnamese will take charge of the final mopping-up of the Vietcong, a task which will probably last several years."[74] Westmoreland also said that the stockpiling of logistics for the war in South Vietnam was complete—meaning more equipment would not be sent to Vietnam.[75]

Americans seemed preconditioned by similar statements by Westmoreland and General Harold K. Johnson earlier in the summer to believe this rosy assessment. By mid-November, for the first time in over a year, a clear majority of Americans (55 percent) who had an opinion believed that the "United States and its allies are . . . making progress" in Vietnam.[76] Moreover, while Americans were by December evenly split on whether the United States "made a mistake sending troops to fight in Vietnam,"[77] 60 percent of Americans who had an opinion identified themselves as "hawk[s]" when the term was defined as those who "want to step up our military effort in Vietnam."[78]

The administration clearly intended Westmoreland's speeches to bolster public approval of the president's policies in Vietnam. Westmoreland made a number of claims about the ineffectiveness of the Viet Cong. He said the Viet Cong was losing its grip on and credibility with the population. Westmoreland also claimed the Viet Cong was no longer able to extract taxes or recruits from the people of South Vietnam, forcing North Vietnam to "plug the gap." Westmoreland dismissed the massive North Vietnamese offensive against Marines at Khe Sanh as a failed attempt to overshadow the inauguration of the new South Vietnamese president.[79] Instead, Westmoreland's claims served only to compound the administration's error from late summer 1967, when General Johnson made similar optimistic projections about progress in Vietnam. This gratuitous optimism could not have been more poorly timed; in just two months, the Viet Cong would dramatically demonstrate that it had plenty of fight left in it.

The administration also probably intended to improve public approval of its policies in Vietnam with its next move. On November

29, 1967, the administration announced the resignation of Secretary of Defense Robert S. McNamara, with an effective date early in 1968.[80] In part, this move was made to counter the growing influence of Johnson's political rival presidential contender Robert F. Kennedy, over the secretary.[81] However, McNamara had recently expressed very serious private doubts about the American course in Vietnam, suggesting to the president that he stop the escalation of troop numbers in Vietnam and initiate a unilateral bombing halt (a course the president would actually adopt five months later).[82] Admittedly, McNamara had questioned the efficacy of bombing before—in hearings before the Senate Armed Services Committee.[83] But in an oral history from 1975, McNamara himself acknowledged that this latter dissent on bombing might have "advanced the time of my departure by a few months."[84]

Otherwise, the president's response to the deepening threat to his credibility was to—ever more acrimoniously—insist that U.S. military intervention in Vietnam was required to contain communism. Johnson also, for the first time, attacked dissenters as aiding communists. In an interview with Dan Rather and Frank Reynolds for CBS News, Johnson lashed out at those critics who demanded a bombing halt. Johnson began by reiterating his claim that the Vietnam War was a war against communist aggression. He said the United States had to continue to fight until it was "obvious to North Vietnam and all of those supporting North Vietnam that we are not going to cut and run, that South Vietnam is not going to be a prize for them to gain." Johnson added that the future of South Vietnam was "up to the people of South Vietnam. Not to North Vietnam or not to China or the Soviets or the United States." The president then attacked the idea of a unilateral bombing halt: "We're not going to be so soft-headed, so puddin'-headed as to say we'll stop our half of the war and hope and pray that they stop theirs." Johnson implied that opponents of the war were giving the communists a hope of victory—the first time the president himself had made this charge; "[The communists] think that if they are firm," Johnson said, " . . . they will develop enough sympathy and understanding in this country, and hatred for the war in this country that their will will outlast our will."[85]

Administration supporters also used the ideology of containment to justify the war. Echoing the positive consequences of the domino theory, Syndicated columnist Roscoe Drummond argued that, as a result of the United States stand in South Vietnam, "the whole arc in the Western Pacific from Japan, South Korea, and Taiwan to Australia and New Zealand is accomplishing an economic development of great promise." Drummond touted the ouster of Sukarno from Indonesia as a direct result of the United States' "checking Communist expansion-by-force at the Vietnamese gate." He called this phenomenon "the domino theory in reverse," adding, "As it becomes evident that we are staying in Vietnam, the 'dominoes,' which were teetering, are beginning to stand more firmly on their feet." While he wrote that the domino theory was "perhaps oversimplified as a phrase," he still echoed its precepts, writing that "nearly all the political leaders of Southeast Asia affirm that the security of their nation rests in large part on our success in defending South Vietnam." Drummond also echoed the administration's argument that it was continuing its predecessors' policies, writing, "President Eisenhower, President Kennedy and President Johnson all explicitly concluded that the safety and independence of all Southeast Asia were at stake in the U.S. defense of South Vietnam."[86]

This administration's fiery counteroffensive in anticipation of the Senate Foreign Relations Committee's impending hearings, along with the General Westmoreland's unbridled optimism, had a noticeable positive effect on public opinion. The gap between those who disapproved and those who approved of the president's handling of Vietnam narrowed noticeably, with 46 percent disapproving (a drop of 3 percentage points from November) and 40 percent approving. Where Americans disapproved of Johnson's policies, most disapproved because the president was not being aggressive enough; over two thirds of Americans now identified themselves as "hawk[s]," wanting "to step up our military effort in Vietnam."[87]

In addition to the administration's counteroffensive, the impending Fulbright hearings also produced a new wave of opposition attacks on the president's credibility. The Associated Press republished its report on the Gulf of Tonkin incident, which had been virtually ignored in

July 1967. This December 1967 follow-up article by Harry Rosenthal was largely the same report published in July. However, it did include new information, like testimony from former Navy Lieutenant John White that, on the night of August 4, the two destroyers were sending "confusing radio messages" to each other indicating that the crews themselves "were not certain they were being attacked." The article also quoted Ensign Richard Corsette, who said it was his "firm belief" that every contact he detected "was weather."[88]

The impending hearings on the credibility of the administration's account of the Gulf of Tonkin incident also reinvigorated older attacks on presidential credibility, namely accusations that the president did not truly want negotiations as he claimed.

A cartoon attacking the administration's credibility on negotiations.

Source: Paul Conrad, *Lewiston Morning Tribune*, January 11, 1968. Used by permission of the Conrad estate.[89]

In a political cartoon by Paul Conrad, Lyndon Johnson is shown at a podium, presumably saying he wants peace, while kicking behind a curtain signals such as a stop sign, an olive branch, and a phone call from Hanoi. The caption reads: "We are waiting for a signal from Hanoi."[90] The implication, of course, was that the president was intentionally ignoring signals from North Vietnam because he wanted to continue the war.

The approach of the Fulbright hearings, and the new questions about President Johnson's credibility caused some supporters of the administration in the media to begin equivocating. John Chamberlain had staunchly supported the administration's use of the containment of communism to justify military intervention in Vietnam for three years. In January 1968, he still tepidly supported the administration's argument that it was continuing "commitments that date back even to Eisenhower days" but he then launched into an assault on the administration's credibility on the war. Citing arguments from Eliot Janeway's book, *The Economics of Crisis*, Chamberlain attacked outgoing Secretary of Defense Robert McNamara, who, Janeway claimed, "failed in 1966 to keep the Treasury—and, presumably, the White House itself—continuously informed of the rate of increase in war spending." But this problem was also a result of what Chamberlain cited Janeway as calling a "secret plan of war escalation in Vietnam" and a "refusal to make timely and continuous disclosure of his war plans to Congress."[91]

Lester Markel, generally a supporter of the war, wrote an article for the *New York Times* that echoed the administration's use of ideology of military containment to justify the war. But Markel was critical, almost pitying, of Johnson's inability to be believed. Markel, after an interview with Johnson, wrote that the private President Johnson was very believable but "the public Johnson is the convivial but not quite convincing Texan." People didn't believe Johnson, Markel added, "because Mr. Johnson has achieved many of his ends by manipulation and, even though such maneuvers may be in the best causes, it is difficult for him to shed the habit."[92]

The president remained out of the debate over his credibility, instead continuing to use the ideology of containment to justify the war. In his 1968 State of the Union Address, the president joked about growing congressional dissent, saying that, as he walked into the House chamber, he remembered "what Sam Rayburn told me many years ago: The Congress always extends a very warm welcome to the president—as he comes in." The president then launched into a defense of the progress in Vietnam, citing recent elections. The president also revived his argument about the positive consequences of the domino theory, arguing that, "In Asia, the nations from Korea and Japan to Indonesia and Singapore worked behind America's shield to strengthen their economies and to broaden their political cooperation." Still, the president warned that "the enemy continues to pour men and material across frontiers and into battle." Attacking dissenters, the president said that the North Vietnamese "hope that America's will to persevere can be broken." The president insisted: "Aggression will never prevail."[93]

In NBC's coverage of the president's State of the Union Address, David Brinkley also lashed out at dissenters who he claimed were taking "a great partisan political pleasure in ridiculing his [the president's] failures." Brinkley attacked the "many half-grown protesters and many half-educated academics" who he said liked to "prance around jeering and ridiculing and making funny noises and carrying funny signs in neurotic displays that tell more about the protesters than about what they're protesting." Brinkley added that it was "no doubt . . . a lot of fun to pour scorn on the president and to wallow in a warm tub of self-righteousness, but no one has shown clearly how that helps." Brinkley concluded by warning: "It is fairly easy to destroy a President, but it is also possible to destroy the system along with him. And if the system goes, the right to dissent goes with it."[94]

While the administration did not defend its own credibility, some of its supporters did. Another NBC segment covering the 1968 State of the Union Address featured former Senator Paul Douglas in an interview with reporter Robert Goralski. Paul Douglas was the chairman of an organization called the Citizens' Committee for Peace with Freedom in Vietnam—which also included former President Eisenhower and Gen. (ret.) Omar Bradley among others. This organization had been actively defending the administration's use of containment to justify the Vietnam War since mid-1967. (In fact, while the fact was never publicly disclosed, Douglas was coordinating his message directly with the White House.)[95] In this interview, however, Douglas defended the president's credibility on the subject of negotiations. Douglas argued that North Vietnam demanded an end to the bombing of the north, but didn't "pledge themselves to anything." Douglas compared this nonoffer to what he claimed had been the duplicitous negotiating tactics of North Korea: "We called off our attacks when we had the Commies on the run to go into conference with them . . . they talked for two years. During that time, the communists continued to attack and caused many thousands of casualties." Douglas insisted that this was part of a communist strategy to outlast the United States: "The Communist world thinks that they can gradually force us to call off our military action."[96]

As the 1968 Fulbright hearings approached, supporters of the administration's policies in Vietnam also confronted Senator Fulbright directly. On *Meet the Press*, Peter Lisagor from the *Chicago Daily News* asked Fulbright whether the hearings were simply "an effort to discredit the administration." Fulbright deflected the question, saying many witnesses had "voluntarily written" or made "personal calls." Fulbright argued that the Senate Foreign Relations Committee would be "derelict in [its] duty" if it did not investigate. Lisagor pressed, asking why the Committee did not instead investigate the attack on Pleiku in 1965, since this event had actually initiated continuous bombing. Fulbright's response to this question again made it clear that the Committee's real aim was to undermine the president's insurance policy against congressional dissent—the Tonkin Gulf Resolution. Fulbright explained that the Committee had a "special responsibility" to investigate the circumstances surrounding the resolution since his Committee had "acted unanimously" to send it forward to the full Senate. He added that it was also important because, "in the words of the attorney general, now the Undersecretary of State, [the resolution] was the equivalent—the functional equivalent—of a declaration of war."[97]

But Fulbright also hoped to undermine the president's credibility. In a letter to historian Henry Steele Commager, Fulbright wrote, "It is quite clear that the affair of the *Maddox* was not as represented to the public but proving it is another matter." He added, "The credibility gap, has become so much a way of life that I am not sure the people of this country will care even if I prove that the affair of the *Maddox* was a fraud." But he promised to try.[98]

On January 23, 1968, North Koreans boarded and captured the USS *Pueblo* off of the coast of North Korea. The ship was conducting a surveillance mission and traveling well inside the fifteen-mile limit claimed by the North Koreans as their international waters— circumstances eerily similar to the circumstances of the Gulf of Tonkin incident.[99] The stage was nearly set for the Senate Foreign Relations Committee to deal a decisive blow to the administration's credibility.

In the early morning hours of January 31, 1968, just before the Fulbright Committee's attack on the Gulf of Tonkin incident came to fruition, the North Vietnamese and the Viet Cong called into question the administration's optimistic claims of progress from late 1967 by launching a dramatic nationwide offensive, the Tet Offensive, that dealt a serious blow to the president's credibility. North Vietnamese Army (NVA) and Viet Cong forces stunned the U.S. and South Vietnamese militaries by breaking the Tet cease-fire and striking over a hundred different locations simultaneously. Around 67,000 enemy troops would eventually be committed to the effort (against nearly 1.1 million U.S. and South Vietnamese troops).[100] The targets of the offensive stunned the American people as well. Three NVA divisions and around 3,000 Viet Cong "irregulars" penetrated Saigon, the heart of the American presence in Vietnam. Sappers even breached and, for a few minutes, threatened to overtake U.S. forces at the American embassy itself.[101]

The Tet Offensive was most important to the public debate over the Vietnam War because it called into question the credibility of the administration's overly optimistic claims of success and predictions for the future from summer and fall 1967. The Tet Offensive both damaged Johnson's credibility and increased the public demands for more aggressive action in Vietnam. Yet, rather than defend his credibility or explain to "hawks" why he could not escalate the conflict further, the president continued to stubbornly use containment to justify the war. Had the Tet Offensive been the final blow to President Johnson's credibility, his policies in Vietnam might have survived the Tet Offensive. However, coming as it did just before the 1968 Fulbright hearings, the Tet Offensive set the stage for the final collapse of Johnson's credibility and his presidency

The significant developments in the first hours of the offensive focused the attention of the American public on Vietnam. General Westmoreland used that focus, immediately following the attack on the embassy, to present an upbeat assessment of the way U.S. and Army of the Republic of Vietnam (ARVN) forces had met the challenge from the embassy grounds. This assessment initially dominated the headlines but generated public skepticism when contrasted with the pictures of the violence inside the embassy.[102]

Television coverage of the Tet Offensive, transmitted into millions of American households every night, had a powerful psychological impact on the American people.[103] Peter Arnett's coverage of the siege of the U.S. embassy in Saigon and his erroneous initial report that the communists had seized part of the embassy were repeated on news broadcasts and in newspapers across the United States.[104] This Associated Press story also included the notorious comment from a U.S. Army major stating of the town of Ben Tre, "It became necessary to destroy the town to save it."[15] Powerful images such as the picture and video of Brigadier General Nguyen Ngoc Loan shooting a prisoner in the head left an indelible mark on the American psyche.[106]

The Tet Offensive had an immediate, negative impact on approval of the president's handling of the war, with 54 percent disapproving (a jump of eight points) and only 37 percent approving (a drop of three points) of his handling of the war just a few days after the offensive began. However, the American public's immediate reaction to the offensive was not to abandon support for the war but rather to demand more aggressive action; immediately after the offensive began, 73 percent of Americans identified themselves as "hawks" (a jump of six percentage points). And Americans were in no mood for accommodations to the North Vietnamese to start negotiations; when asked if they supported a bombing halt to start peace talks, 82 percent of Americans who had an opinion said they wanted the United States to "continue bombing."[107]

The Tet Offensive was most damaging to the administration because it called into question the administration's glowing assessments and predictions from summer and fall 1967. NBC News special coverage in the first days of the Tet Offensive showed Americans on patrol with Vietnamese policemen. A voiceover by reporter Wilson Hall said: "These U.S. troops and the South Vietnamese policemen are on combat duty—half a block from the U.S. embassy." These pictures would have been jarring to most Americans, who were used to the city of Saigon being relatively peaceful, a place where U.S. soldiers could walk freely through the streets. After a scene of sniper fire near the embassy, Hall added that these troops now understood "how fanatical and resourceful the Viet Cong are." Likewise, Sydney Lizzard reported from the studio that the "ferocity of the fighting in Vietnam" was such that "more Americans were killed than in any previous week of the war."[108] These statements were a direct contradiction of Westmoreland's estimates of waning Viet Cong capability and rosy predictions for the future from November 1967.

The White House, the Pentagon, and Military Assistance Command–Vietnam (MAC-V) compounded this error by continuing to provide upbeat assessments even after the offensive began. And the media relentlessly attacked the credibility of these assessments as well. Television reporter Robert Guralski told audiences that the administration had reported that "nearly 15,000 Communists are believed to have lost their lives" compared to fewer than 1,500 U.S. and South Vietnamese casualties. Guralski said that this "gaping disparity between allied and communist losses has raised doubts on the authenticity of numbers of enemy killed." The report then cut to an exchange between Robert McNamara and a reporter on *Meet the Press* in which the reporter cornered the secretary into admitting that these casualty figures came from the South Vietnamese and were not reliable.[109]

Democratic Senator Albert Gore Sr. of Tennessee, a member of the Senate Foreign Relations Committee, wasted no time in reminding his colleagues and the American public of the administration's optimistic predictions for the war from only a few months earlier. Gore noted that "the optimism" of General Westmoreland's speech at the National Press Club "has now been rendered unreal." Gore also took aim at the Tonkin Gulf Resolution, saying that "the American people are baffled by the circumstances in which we find ourselves." He blamed this bafflement on the Congress's having "entered into a war by inadvertence," since the Senate had voted on the Tonkin Gulf Resolution with assurances from the White House that it would not be used to start a war in Vietnam. As a result, Gore claimed, the United States' "moral leadership has been seriously eroded," the country had a "balance-of-payments problem," and "dissent at home . . . has reached such proportions that the country is more seriously threatened with ruinous disruption than at any time since the Civil War."[110]

President Johnson's response to this deepening threat to his credibility was to attack dissenters as cowards while continuing to stubbornly insist the war was required to contain of communism. In a meeting with eleven young war dissenters in the oval office, Johnson told them he understood why they opposed the war: "None of us want to die" (implying their dissent was a result of their fear of going to war). Johnson then insisted—in a very colloquial restatement of the lessons of Munich—"If an aggressor comes on your front porch and runs you off tonight, he'll be back tomorrow and run you out of your bedroom." Johnson also restated the domino theory, claiming that if the United States lost in Vietnam, Thailand "and a good many other countries I won't name" would also be threatened by communist takeover.[111]

The pervading sense of crisis in America during the Tet Offensive cannot be overstated. The staff of the Senate Foreign Relations Committee received an anonymous but credible tip that experts on the use of nuclear weapons were being moved into Vietnam, and many of the staffers suspected the administration might be contemplating the use of nuclear weapons at Khe Sanh.[112] The American public had similar concerns; Fulbright's office received as many as 150 telegrams in the days before the hearings urging the senator to do something to prevent the use of nuclear weapons in Vietnam.[113] The president himself was asked in a press conference whether he had been asked for authority to use nuclear weapons. When Secretary of State Rusk was pressed on the topic in a letter from Senator Fulbright, he denied that the administration was considering using nuclear weapons but did admit that nuclear expert Professor Richard Garwin had been sent to Vietnam to "discuss technical matters of a non-nuclear nature."[114] Chairman of the Joint Chiefs of Staff Earle Wheeler made a televised statement that he did not believe these weapons would be needed in Khe Sanh, but he did not rule out their use.[115] It was in this atmosphere of deep crisis that the 1968 Fulbright hearings began.

In February 1968, only a few short weeks after the beginning of the Tet Offensive, Fulbright dealt another severe blow to the president's credibility by holding his hearings that showed that the president had lied about the Gulf of Tonkin incident. The subject of the 1968 Fulbright hearings was the administration's credibility about the Gulf of Tonkin incident. However, Fulbright's true aim was to undermine the president's insurance policy against congressional dissent—the Tonkin Gulf Resolution. Fulbright's Senate Foreign Relations Committee hearings were damaging to the president because they began in the early weeks of the Tet Offensive, at a time when the American public had grown impatient with the war.[116] However, the hearings were even more damaging because they reinforced a public perception that the administration was lying about the war and had been for some time. The immediate effect of the hearings was to raise questions in the media about the validity of the Tonkin Gulf Resolution as a legal basis for the war. The hearings also seriously undermined public support for the war and refocused antiwar rhetoric on attacks on the administration's credibility.

In his opening statement at the hearing, which was held in a closed, executive session on February 20, 1968, Secretary McNamara insisted that both attacks on U.S. vessels—the day attack by North Vietnamese torpedo boats on August 2, 1964, and the night attack on August 4—had in fact occurred. While he acknowledged that there was some question as to sonar readings and that radar readings "may be subject to interpretation and argument" he insisted that the administration had "incontrovertible evidence of these attacks" based on radio intercepts of North Vietnamese transmissions from the night of August 4. Likewise, McNamara also dismissed those who claimed that the signals intelligence equipment aboard the *Maddox* "changed the essential nature of the patrol" in some way. McNamara insisted that the Congress knew of this equipment at the time of the August 6, 1964, hearings. McNamara also insisted that "sufficient information was in the hands of [the] president . . . to establish beyond any doubt then or now that an attack had taken place" before the order to retaliate was given. McNamara was even more adamant in his denunciation of accusations that the United States had provoked the attack on August 4, 1964. He said, "I can only characterize such insinuations as monstrous."[117]

The provocative nature of the DESOTO patrols was a key issue of the hearings. Fulbright established that the *Maddox* was ordered to "penetrate the territorial waters of North Vietnam . . . assuming their territorial waters was twelve miles." McNamara admitted that the *Maddox* was ordered to go as close as eight miles to the coast and as close as four miles to coastal islands. Fulbright even got McNamara to acknowledge that the United States recognized Communist China's twelve-mile limit. However, McNamara would not admit that North Vietnam had declared its territorial waters to extend to twelve miles. Senator Morse returned to this issue later, noting that Assistant Secretary of Defense John McNaughton had testified in May 1966 that North Vietnam asserted a twelve-mile limit. McNamara first claimed that testimony was "ambiguous" and then simply said McNaughton "was wrong." Senator Pell later added more evidence, noting that, in an English language broadcast about the August 2, 1964, attacks, the North Vietnamese claimed that the *Maddox* was attacked in their "territorial waters." However, this was not quite a smoking gun; this broadcast had not occurred until August 5, 1964, the day after the supposed August 4 attacks. Still, Pell insisted that the heart of the matter was "not so much a question of recognizing or not recognizing. We do not willfully want to provoke more hostilities."[118]

Another element of the Committee's case that the DESOTO patrols had been provocative was their proximity to OPLAN 34A raids being conducted at the same time by South Vietnamese naval and special operations forces. Senators John Cooper, Wayne Morse, and J. William Fulbright established that, in his testimony on August 6, McNamara had said, "Our Navy played absolutely no part in it, was not associated with it, was not aware of any South Vietnamese actions, if there were any." McNamara repeatedly reaffirmed this statement in the 1968 hearing, saying that Captain Herrick had since confirmed this fact to be true. The Committee then showed that this testimony was directly contradicted by a cable sent to the *Maddox* days before the Gulf of Tonkin incident instructing Captain Herrick to assist the OPLAN 34A raids: "Draw NVN [North Vietnamese navy] PGMS [patrol boats] to northward away from the area of 34A operations." If the *Maddox* was instructed to draw North Vietnamese boats away from the OPLAN 34A raids, Morse argued, it was clearly participating in the operation and the North Vietnamese had the "right to attack them on the high seas." McNamara began denying that he had said the *Maddox* had no knowledge of the OPLAN 34A raids, but Senator Gore would not let McNamara escape: "That was not what you told the committee [on August 6, 1964] though, Mr. Secretary." McNamara tried to protest that captured North Vietnamese seamen had claimed that they believed the DESOTO patrol was not connected to the OPLAN 34A raids, but Morse dismissed this contention, saying that it in no way indicated "what the naval operators of North Vietnam not captured were thinking." Fulbright provided more evidence that the proximity of the patrol to the OPLAN 34A raids was provocative. He quoted a cable sent by the *Maddox* on August 3 that "DRV [Democratic Republic of Vietnam] considers patrol directly involved with 34-A operations . . . and have already indicated readiness to treat us in that category." McNamara claimed that Captain Herrick had since recanted this assessment, saying there was no basis for it. Fulbright objected that it had been a provocation to continue the patrol after this cable from Herrick, indicating "that the North Vietnamese regarded them as hostile." McNamara argued that they continued to patrol because they were "operating legally and entirely within [their] rights." Republican Senator John Williams of Delaware was incredulous, noting that the patrol would have been within its rights, based on its orders, to approach within four miles Hon Me island, target of the OPLAN 34A raid. Morse concluded that, since the United States had supplied the South Vietnamese ships and trained the sailors, "It would be a very reasonable conclusion if [the North Vietnamese] thought there was a connection" to the DESOTO patrol. He added: "I happen to think there was a very clear connection."[119]

The nature of the DESOTO patrol as a signals intelligence patrol was also an issue in the hearings. Senator Eugene McCarthy attacked the Secretary's assertion that the DESOTO patrols were in no way related to the OPLAN 34A raids by questioning whether intelligence gained from communication intercepts was used to identify targets for future raids. Senator Morse went further, insisting that "the *Maddox* was, on this occasion, a spy-ship." He added, "Quite a different body of international law applies to spy activities than applies to other activities" on the high seas.[120]

Senator Fulbright used the recent USS *Pueblo* incident as a tool to highlight the provocative nature of the DESOTO patrols on August 4, 1964. Fulbright noted that, in a recent *Meet the Press* interview, McNamara had said that "the *Pueblo* was not given air cover and an armed escort because this would have been provocative to the North Koreans." Fulbright wondered aloud, "Why would not the same term apply in the Gulf of Tonkin, particularly since the *Maddox* and the *Turner Joy* had orders that would take them within what the North Vietnamese considered to be territorial waters?" Fulbright asked if the *Pueblo* had been given similar orders to the *Maddox* and *Turner Joy*. McNamara refused to answer.[121]

The committee also attacked the specifics of the administration's account of the two patrols on August 2 and 4, 1964. Senator Fulbright questioned whether warning shots were fired on August 2, 1964, as McNamara had testified on August 6, 1964. Senator Fulbright cited Admiral (ret.) Arnold True's letter to him saying that warning shots were never fired in naval combat. Fulbright also cited a statement from "a gunnery officer aboard the *Maddox*" quoted in the July 16, 1967, Associated Press article as saying that no warning shots were fired.[122]

In fact, Fulbright questioned whether the second incident even occurred and condemned the administration for not sharing its doubts with Congress. Fulbright noted Captain Herrick's cable right after the supposed August 4 attack that "many recorded contacts and torpedoes fired appear doubtful. Freak weather effects and [an] over-eager sonarman may have accounted for many reports" and his recommendation that there be "a complete evaluation before any further action." Fulbright also noted that the *Turner Joy* reported that it had detected no radar throughout the attack. Fulbright then got General Wheeler, also present at the hearings, to admit that it would be nearly impossible for the boats to find the destroyers on so dark a night without radar. Later in the hearing, Senator Gore noted that "Admiral Moorer of CincPac cabled the *Maddox* and *Turner Joy* to report immediate confirmation of the earlier attack on them" even after the retaliatory air strikes had been ordered. Morse reminded the committee that he had asked for the logs based on tips from anonymous sources at the Pentagon and was denied them.[123]

The committee also directly challenged the evidence that the administration had claimed proved an attack had occurred. McNamara claimed that a review of the communications intelligence from the North Vietnamese had convinced the administration that an attack had occurred. Senator Fulbright and Senator Morse immediately countered, noting that the signals intelligence suggested only one PT boat and two machine gun boats would attack, yet as many as twenty-two torpedoes (requiring eleven PT boats) were reported. Senator Pell was dubious that the North Vietnamese would order two small boats armed only with machine guns to attack two U.S. destroyers. Fulbright also challenged the interrogations that McNamara cited as evidence that the North Vietnamese had not connected the DESOTO patrols with the OPLAN 34A raids. Fulbright showed that, in the navy's own report on its interrogation of the prisoners, two prisoners claimed that "no PT's could have been involved" while another prisoner "specifically and strongly denies that any attack took place."

Fulbright added that "the North Vietnamese boasted of their attack on the *Maddox* on August 2 and yet vehemently denied that there had been an incident on August 4."[124]

Once the committee had cornered Secretary McNamara, Senator Fulbright attempted to explicitly use doubts about the Gulf of Tonkin incident to nullify the president's insurance policy against congressional dissent—the Tonkin Gulf Resolution. Fulbright questioned whether the Gulf of Tonkin incident was a pretext for a military intervention that the administration had intended to take anyway. He reminded the committee of the statement the Secretary of Defense had made only two weeks before the 1968 hearings on *Meet the Press* that "three and a half years ago the South Vietnamese forces were on the verge of defeat," implying that action had been necessary in summer 1964. McNamara could only say that he had "misestimated the date" and meant summer 1965. Fulbright noted that in July 1964 General Kanh of South Vietnam had given a speech "calling for carrying the war to the north." Senator Fulbright suggested that Kanh may have demanded more forceful U.S. action. Senator Fulbright quoted a *New York Times* article from July 1964 that said that "the Pentagon at that time was arguing in favor of extending the war into North Vietnam." Fulbright also asked if "fighter bombers . . . moved into Vietnam and Thailand immediately after" the Gulf of Tonkin incident had been given the order before the incident. However, Senator Fulbright's most compelling evidence was William Bundy's admission in 1966 that a draft of the Resolution had existed before the Gulf of Tonkin incident. Fulbright asked McNamara if he had seen "the contingency draft of what became the Southeast Asia resolution before it was ready." Morse was more explicit, saying the administration had "in their pocket a resolution ready to spring on us." Senator Case was more concerned "about the use of this resolution subsequently in ways that were never intended by Congress." Both Morse and Fulbright disputed the idea that the Tonkin Gulf Resolution could serve as the "functional equivalent" of a declaration of war as Undersecretary of State Katzenbach had claimed. Morse called this assertion "of course pure nonsense legally."[125]

Fulbright's conclusion was aimed squarely at the Tonkin Gulf Resolution: "I think it was very unfair to ask us to vote upon a resolution when the state of the evidence was as uncertain as I think it now is."[126] This idea—that the Tonkin Gulf Resolution had no power if it was obtained under false pretenses—would, for the remainder of the war, be the foundation of congressional attacks on the Tonkin Gulf Resolution as a weapon against their dissent. In the 1966 Fulbright hearings, Senator Fulbright had apologized to the nation for his role in the passage of the Tonkin Gulf Resolution. At the conclusion of the 1968 Fulbright hearing, Fulbright could now amend that apology to place the blame back on the administration:

> We met . . . for 1 hour and 40 minutes . . . and we accepted your statement completely without doubt. . . . Of course all my statements were based upon your testimony. I had no independent evidence. . . . It never occurred to me that there was the slightest doubt. . . . I regret it more than anything I have ever done in my life, that I was the vehicle which took that resolution to the floor and defended it in complete reliance upon information which, to say the very least, is somewhat dubious at this time.[127]

Referring to Captain Herrick's cable urging no retaliation until facts were clearer, Fulbright added, "If I had known of that one telegram, if that had been put before me on the 6th of August, I certainly don't believe I would have rushed into action."[128]

Senator Gore was even angrier: "I feel that I have been misled, and that the American people have been misled." Senator Gore had reached a conclusion from the hearings that would echo well beyond the Vietnam War. Gore told McNamara: "I do not think, Mr. Secretary, the second attack has been established by your testimony today at all." When McNamara tried to protest, Gore added: "I think there is more question now than when you came." Gore insisted that the DESOTO patrol was too close to the OPLAN 34A raids. He insisted that the patrol was provocative because it was a spy mission, too close to the North Vietnamese coast, and supported by air cover.[129] Finally, Gore added:

> . . . the administration was hasty, acted precipitately, inadvisedly [sic], unwisely, out of proportion to the provocation in launching 64 bombing attacks on North Vietnam out of a confused, uncertain situation on a murky night, which one of the sailors described as one dark as the knob of hell; and, particularly, 5 hours after the task force commander had cabled that he doubted that there were any attacks, and recommended no further action be taken until it was thoroughly canvassed and reviewed.[130]

As the hearing concluded, the committee and McNamara agreed not to speak to the press about the contents of the hearing. However, as soon as the participants left the committee chambers, McNamara released the radio intercepts that supported his version of the events of August 4, 1964, and his opening statement from the hearing that accusations that the administration had provoked the incident to start a war were "monstrous." Fulbright responded with his own statement, saying that no one on the committee had said "there was a deliberate conspiracy to create the Gulf of Tonkin crisis" and that McNamara "suggests a straw man in order to knock it down." Fulbright charged that McNamara had released only that "highly classified information . . . which serves his purposes" while he had "*not* seen fit to declassify information relating to sonar on the *Maddox*; he has kept secret important communications from the task force that indicated doubt about the reported attack on August 4" (the emphasis is Fulbright's).[131] Fulbright concluded:

> Security classification is intended to protect the nation from an *enemy, not to* protect one branch of government against another or the public, not to protect the American people from knowledge of mistakes. [(emphasis is Fulbright's)][132]

Though there is no evidence of how he obtained a copy of the transcript from the hearing, soon after Fulbright's press release, the *New*

264 • CONTAINMENT AND CREDIBILITY

York Times' John W. Finney published a damningly accurate summary of the hearing.[133] Finney wrote that the *Maddox* and *Turner Joy* were "not instructed to break off their intelligence-gathering patrol off the coast of North Vietnam" even after the two destroyers "warned higher command that North Vietnam regarded them as enemy craft." Finney wondered whether "there [was] an element of provocation on the part of the destroyers that induced the North Vietnamese to attack" and if "the Administration [had] sufficient proof of the attack at the time to warrant" the passage of the Tonkin Gulf Resolution, which the *New York Times* reminded its readers "was later to be described by the State Department as 'a functional equivalent' of a declaration of war against North Vietnam." The *Times* noted that McNamara emphatically insisted that he had "conclusive proof," but added that the committee members "were unconvinced by the McNamara testimony." Finney wrote that Fulbright and Gore "went so far as to suggest that the administration had misled Congress about details of the incident when it sought approval of the Tonkin resolution in 1964." Finney detailed the questions about whether the August 4, 1964, attacks had happened and the conflicting reports coming out of the Gulf of Tonkin that night. Finney also wrote that Fulbright convincingly disproved McNamara's testimony from August 6, 1964, that Captain Herrick did not know about the OPLAN 34A raids.[134] These were charges that had never been leveled before by a national news agency.

The same day, E. W. Kenworthy published an even more confrontational article in the *New York Times* about the Senate Foreign Relations Committee's reaction to the McNamara testimony, writing that "at least nine of the committee's 19 members believe that the Administration over-reacted and that it also withheld some very important facts and was less than candid in presenting others." Kenworthy wrote that Senator Fulbright believed "Mr. McNamara had treaded close to deception on Aug. 6, 1964." Kenworthy also recounted "the messages to the Maddox seeking clarification of what had happened even after the retaliatory strike had been ordered." Kenworthy cited Senator Gore's conclusion that the administration had acted precipitously "out of a confused, uncertain situation on, a murky night."[135]

More importantly, E. W. Kenworthy echoed the committee's conclusions about the Tonkin Gulf Resolution. He quoted Fulbright's conclusion, "I think it was very unfair to ask us [Congress] to vote upon a resolution . . . when the state of evidence was as uncertain as I think it now is." This article added that Fulbright was angry that the Senate was asked to take up "'the functional equivalent' of a declaration of war upon evidence of this kind. . . . Even the commander [of the Maddox] . . . recommended that nothing be done until the evidence was further evaluated" (the inserts and omissions in the quotation are Kenworthy's). Kenworthy wrote that Senator Case objected to the use of the "resolution to escalate United States involvement" in South Vietnam while Senator Morse objected to the contingent drafts of the Resolution that existed before the Gulf of Tonkin incident ever occurred.[136] This article marked the first public use of questions about the Gulf of Tonkin incident to undermine the Tonkin Gulf Resolution—the president's insurance policy against congressional dissent.

The 1968 Fulbright hearing had an immediate negative impact on approval of the president's handling of the Vietnam War. As details of the hearing were reported in the media, disapproval of the president's handling of the war rose to 58 percent, with only 32 percent approving. Moreover, after the hearings 54 percent of Americans who had an opinion believed that the United States had "made a mistake sending troops to fight in Vietnam." Still, Americans were not ready to quit the war. When asked, 69 percent of Americans who had an opinion still identified themselves as "hawks," wanting the United States to "step up our military effort in Vietnam."[137]

The 1968 Fulbright hearing also generated new congressional dissent. Republican Senator Mark Hatfield of Oregon (a freshman senator elected in the 1966 midterm elections) introduced a resolution that would prevent the president from placing ground forces in Southeast Asian countries outside of South Vietnam without congressional consent.[138] This resolution was particularly significant in that its language explicitly stated that it was intended to prevent the president from "widening . . . the conflict beyond the intended authorization of the

Gulf of Tonkin Resolution"[139] (though this new resolution was silent on whether the president had already violated congressional intent, as some senators had claimed in the Fulbright hearing).

Another direct effect of the Fulbright hearing was to dramatically alter dissent against the Vietnam War. Almost immediately following the hearing, opponents of the war began to abandon attacks on the ideology of containment and its application to the war in Vietnam. Instead, opponents began to increasingly attack presidential credibility. In an article in *Parade* magazine, Lloyd Shearer accused the administration of dishonesty in its supposed persecution of dissenters. The cases in question were those of perennial dissenter Dr. Benjamin Spock and Rev. William Sloane Coffin Jr., who were charged with aiding draft resistors. Shearer portrayed this persecution as a betrayal, writing that Spock campaigned for Johnson and quoting Spock as saying he believed the president "when he promised not to send American boys to fight the war in Vietnam." Spock added that, after he won the election, Johnson phoned him and said: "'I hope, Dr. Spock, I will be worthy of your trust." Shearer concluded by quoting the Council of Bishops in South Vietnam which denounced the South Vietnamese government by asking, "How can there be peace . . . when those in responsible places mask their false promises behind rhetoric? How can peace prevail if laziness, hypocrisy, and corruption prevail everywhere in society?"[140] Shearer's implication, of course, was that one could say the same thing about the Johnson administration.

Even the administration's stubborn insistence on using the containment of communism to justify U.S. military intervention in Vietnam—which would have previously been attacked by disputing the arguments themselves—was now cast as a form of dishonesty. In a story about the president's campaign rhetoric in the New Hampshire primaries, syndicated columnist Drew Pearson wrote that the president "takes a vigorous public position against so-called communism in Asia while trying to improve relations with communist countries in Europe." He continued that, while Johnson's surrogates in New Hampshire were "warning voters that the 'communists in Vietnam were watching,' Johnson's ambassador in Geneva had signed the most far-reaching pact with the Soviet Union ever reached." Pearson then recounted the moderation of communism that was sweeping Eastern Europe and admitted, "President Johnson is all too aware of these shifting developments inside the onetime rigid communist world." Pearson even admitted, "LBJ has been more farsighted than any other President in shaping America[n] policy to meet the shifts." But this was just the preface to an attack on the president's credibility; the president was thinking one thing but saying something else. Pearson wrote, "[Johnson] hasn't told his speechwriters and his campaign strategists to revamp what they tell the American people, either in New Hampshire or elsewhere around the nation."[141]

In the March 16, 1968, issue of *Parade* magazine, Lloyd Shearer made a similar case, noting that Senator Lyndon Johnson had disputed Secretary of State John Foster Dulles's assertion of the domino theory and opposed Dulles' desire to invade Vietnam in 1954.[142] The implication, of course, was that the president was dishonest in espousing a domino theory he had once found unconvincing and embracing a policy of war that he had previously rejected.

Historians frequently cite Walter Cronkite's famous declaration on February 27, 1968, about the futility of the Vietnam War as a turning point in American public support for the president. But Cronkite's commentary at the end of a special report after his return from South Vietnam was particularly devastating to the president because it spoke directly to the belief most Americans already held that they were being lied to by their government. In the week before Walter Cronkite made these comments, Americans had become deeply skeptical of official optimism about the war. Only 32 percent of those polled believed America was making progress in Vietnam and the same small percentage approved of Johnson's handling of the war.[143] Cronkite simply gave voice to America's skepticism of official optimism:

> To say that we are closer to victory today is to believe, in the face of the evidence, the optimists that have been wrong in the past. . . . In the off chance that military and political analysts are right, in the next few months we must test the

enemy's intentions in case this is indeed his last big gasp before negotiations.[144]

This pronouncement did have a further negative impact on public opinion. Johnson's job approval dropped to 36 percent[145] and approval of Johnson's policies in Vietnam dropped to 26 percent.[146]

In the aftermath of Fulbright's hearings on the Gulf of Tonkin incident in 1968, the president's credibility was in shambles. Political maneuvering by the Pentagon further eroded the administration's credibility and provided an opening for Senator Fulbright to deliver a death blow to the Tonkin Gulf Resolution as the president's insurance policy against congressional dissent. Rather than shore up its credibility, the administration continued to stubbornly use the containment of communism to justify the war. However, as attacks on its credibility mounted daily and hopes for the Democratic primary race seemed ever more remote, the president finally decided to stop his escalation in Vietnam and withdraw from the presidential race. This did little to slow attacks on the president's credibility. In fact, only radical protesters and the antiwar presidential candidates continued to attack the ideology of containment in late spring 1968; other opponents of the war had almost exclusively begun to attack the administration's credibility. But the president's move did have an immediate negative effect on the American public's willingness to continue the war in Vietnam. In fact, in the aftermath of the president's dramatic moves to jumpstart the peace process, the American public began to abandon its support for the war in Vietnam.

In the midst of the administration's growing crisis of credibility, Chairman of the Joint Chiefs of Staff General Earle Wheeler maneuvered General Westmoreland into requesting 206,000 more troops as part of Wheeler's own bureaucratic quest to force President Johnson to mobilize the U.S. Army Reserves. The *New York Times*' Neil Sheehan and Hedrick Smith were the first to break the story.[147] Westmoreland was forced to turn down the troops, presumably in order to protect his optimistic assessment of the Tet Offensive. The president denied that the request had been made, also presumably in order to protect his optimistic assessments. These denials only deepened the president's crisis of credibility.[148]

These troop requests also provided the opening for which the Senate Foreign Relations Committee and its chairman, Senator Fulbright, had been waiting. On March 7, 1968, Fulbright called for congressional debate on this proposed expansion of the war. In his speech on the Senate floor, Fulbright made it clear that his real target was the president's insurance policy against congressional dissent, the Tonkin Gulf Resolution. He reminded his colleagues that the president had promised not to use the resolution to expand the war and had promised not to send American boys to fight a war in Asia. Fulbright concluded that this made the Tonkin Gulf Resolution, "like any contract based on misrepresentation[,] . . . null and void."[149]

Fulbright firmly placed the last nail in the coffin of the Tonkin Gulf Resolution as an insurance policy against congressional dissent on 12 March 1968, when Secretary of State Dean Rusk appeared before the Senate Foreign Relations Committee. After an angry exchange between the Secretary and Senator Fulbright, Rusk tried to invoke the administration's insurance policy against congressional dissent one last time. He reminded the Chairman that "Congress itself, with two dissenting votes," had agreed to the Tonkin Gulf Resolution. Fulbright replied that the administration had used the resolution as "a method of avoiding and preventing both consultation and discussion," noting that the secretary had testified for less than two hours before the resolution was passed. Rusk retorted that "there was time, if the Congress wanted to take more time."[150] Fulbright replied angrily,

> The Administration insisted that . . . its purpose [was to deter North Vietnam] and it was not to enlarge the war and so on. . . . What I am proposing is that we not follow this old system of just accepting anything the Administration sends down without question, which we have literally done and did in August '64. We had entirely too much confidence, in my opinion, in the wisdom of this or any Administration.[151]

Fulbright was no longer talking about deception surrounding the Gulf of Tonkin incident. Instead, he had arrived at the heart of the matter: the administration had lied to Congress about its intent for the resolution before its passage. It was *this* administration deception, Fulbright insisted, that invalidated the Tonkin Gulf Resolution.

With attacks on the administration's credibility mounting daily, the president also faced the New Hampshire primary against Senate Foreign Relations Committee member and war opponent Senator Eugene McCarthy. However, unlike most in the antiwar movement by spring 1968, McCarthy continued to oppose the application of the ideology of containment to Vietnam. Syndicated columnist Drew Pearson praised the candidacy of Eugene McCarthy for doing "two healthy things." First, Pearson wrote, his candidacy gave "the people of New Hampshire a choice to vote for or against war." However, McCarthy had also broken the taboo "which stymied American foreign policy in John Foster Dulles's day"—the taboo against opposing the Cold War consensus for fear of being called soft on communism. He wrote that the Johnson camp had resurrected "the old Joe McCarthy bugaboo" with radio ads warning, "The communists in Vietnam are watching the New Hampshire primary. . . . Don't vote for fuzzy thinking and surrender." Pearson concluded by echoing Eugene McCarthy's argument that "what motivates the Vietnamese is nationalism, not communism."[152]

On March 12, President Johnson narrowly defeated Senator Eugene McCarthy in the New Hampshire primary. This was widely seen as a *de facto* defeat for the president that boosted the profile of McCarthy as a viable candidate. The president's political troubles deepened further on March 19, 1968, when Senator Robert F. Kennedy entered the presidential race.

The president's response to these new threats to his presidency was to once more use the ideology of military containment to defend U.S. military intervention in Vietnam. In a March 19 foreign policy briefing, the president gave an impassioned defense of the centrality of the Vietnam War to America's future in the world. He said that America's foreign policy objective was "to build a world in which we and our children and our neighbors throughout the world may live in freedom," adding that "the heritage of 5,000 years of human civilization . . . hangs on our success." Johnson challenged the American people to persevere: "History has elected to probe the depth of our commitment to freedom. How strongly are we really devoted to resist the tide of aggression?" He added that the American people were participants in the Vietnam War: "Aggression fights not only on the battlefield of the village and hill and jungle and city. The enemy has reached out to fight in the hearts and minds of the American people." The president said, "He has mounted a heavy and a calculated attack on our character as a people—on our confidence and our will as a nation." Lyndon Johnson said the Tet Offensive was "aimed squarely at the citizens of America. It is an assault that is designed to crack America's will." Johnson added, "It is designed to make some men want to surrender; it is designed to make other men want to withdraw; it is designed to trouble and worry and confuse others." Johnson claimed the communists sought "more than the destruction of the Pacific dream where a new and prospering Asia sees its hopeful future." The president concluded that the American people were "the aggressor's real target because of what we represent. . . . What other nation in the world is going to stand up and protect the little man's freedom anywhere in the world?"[153]

In this speech, the president also made his most impassioned defense yet of the application of the lesson of Munich to the Vietnam War. He compared those dissenters who wanted to give up the fight in Vietnam to those "well-meaning, sincere, good people around this entire country" who, before World War II, "were pledging themselves never to bear arms" and "castigating our Government for any involvement beyond our own shores." Johnson said that President Roosevelt had "warned the world that . . . the shadow of aggression threatened not only the nations that were immediately in the aggressor's path, but it threatened the future of all free men and women." Because of the lack of foresight of these earlier dissenters, Johnson claimed, "It took some time and it took a world catastrophe to wake men up and for them to finally hear that message when we were attacked." Johnson implored the American people: "So, let this generation of ours learn from the mistakes of the past. Let us recognize that there is no resigning from world responsibility."[154]

Many supporters in the media of the administration, muted since the beginning of the Tet Offensive, followed suit. John Chamberlain had wavered in his support of the administration as the Fulbright hearings approached, but returned to full-throated support of the president after the hearings. Chamberlain argued that the debate was over: "The domino theory is less of a theory than it is a living present reality." The North Vietnamese, Chamberlain claimed, were "overrunning government outposts in northern and central Laos" while, in Cambodia, "Prince Norodom Sihanouk, no lover of Americans, has suddenly become vocal in his alarm about the domino theory as it may affect his country." In Thailand, Chamberlain added, "Thai troops had destroyed a secret Communist guerilla camp near the Laotian border" just as "Rusk was supplying the documentation of the workings of the domino theory in Cambodia for his senatorial inquisitors." Because the domino theory was playing out, Chamberlain added, "the latest tactic of those who think the U.S. has no business in Southeast Asia is to say that it hardly matters whether communism spreads or not." As evidence of this new opposition tactic, Chamberlain cited John Kenneth Galbraith as claiming "all Asian villages are alike no matter who runs them."[155]

Arguments from the administration and its supporters about the necessity of the Vietnam War to contain communism were not just unnecessary; they missed the heart of the American public's dissatisfaction with the Johnson administration. The majority of Americans already agreed with the president that the Vietnam War was necessary to contain communism. What most Americans doubted was the president's honesty and his willingness to apply sufficient means to win the war. Presumably in an effort to address at least the latter of these points, President Johnson announced on March 22, 1968, that General Westmoreland would be replaced as the commander of MAC-V by Westmoreland's deputy, General Creighton Abrams.[156] This move did nothing to stop the bleeding, as it failed to address Johnson's more serious problem, doubts about his credibility.

With the administration's crisis of credibility deepening daily, *Esquire* magazine published an article by David Wise about the Gulf of Tonkin incident that focused on the ways in which the Congress had been deceived called "Remember the *Maddox*!" (referencing the battle cry of the SpanishAmerican War, "Remember the *Maine*," about a similarly dubious supposed attack on a U.S. naval vessel).[157] This article was significant in that it was the first to explicitly echo Senator Fulbright's charge that the Tonkin Gulf Resolution had been obtained from Congress under false pretenses. The article began by unequivocally identifying the Tonkin Gulf Resolution as the president's insurance policy against congressional dissent:

> [After the incident] the President persuaded Congress to pass his Gulf of Tonkin Resolution authorizing the President to take "all necessary steps" to defend South Vietnam. He has since used this resolution as a blank check to escalate the conflict, and he has dared Congress to repeal it, knowing it will not. The resolution has been his single greatest trump card in prosecuting the war.[158]

Wise added, "Some Congressmen came to feel they may have been misled into passing the resolution." Wise also wrote, "The Pentagon's version of the incident is open to question. The evidence is sometimes conflicting, and many assertions of the Defense Department at the time have since turned out to be incorrect." Despite the fact that this incident was "murky [and] confused," Wise wrote, the incident was "used by the Administration as the Pearl Harbor of the Vietnam war." Wise' lengthy *Esquire* exposé then recounted all of the evidence that had been amassed by spring 1968 that called into question the administration's account of the events of August 4, 1964—the provocative nature of the patrols, the questions over whether the incident even happened, and the ways in which the administration hid its doubts from Congress.[159]

Wise returned at the end of the article to his main point: the Tonkin Gulf Resolution had been passed under false pretenses. He wrote, "Some members of the Senate Foreign Relations Committee felt that the resolution had been passed chiefly in order to back the president after U.S. ships had been attacked and to express approval of the retaliatory air raid." However, he added, "They were chagrined three years later to find Johnson using the resolution as a broad approval to fight a major land war." Wise also reminded readers that William Bundy admitted that there had been "contingent drafts" of the resolution before the incident. Wise wrote, "The feeling began to grow in Congress that Tonkin Gulf might have been an incident waiting to happen." Wise added that the issue came to a head when Nicholas Katzenbach told the Foreign Relations Committee that the president didn't need the resolution but, in Wise' words, "Congress had passed it and ought to have known what it was doing."[160] Wise concluded:

> The Johnson Administration, for a variety of domestic political and foreign policy reasons, seized eagerly upon fragmentary, confused reports from the Tonkin Gulf and presented them to Congress and the public as accomplished facts. The Administration had its contingency drafts ready for just such an incident. And when many of those "facts" turned out to be erroneous, it would not concede this.[161]

Wised concluded, "It was a classic example of how government, by shaping and controlling information about a military event, can whip up popular emotion and bend Congress and the public to its will."[162]

As its crisis of credibility deepened daily, internal White House polling revealed serious trouble for the president in the upcoming primaries. One poll showed that, while he enjoyed 67 percent approval with New York voters, Johnson had only 47 percent approval—compared to Robert Kennedy's 65 percent approval—among self-identified liberals.[163] And Johnson's numbers were even worse in the rest of the country.[164]

It was in this atmosphere of political vulnerability that president gave his televised speech on March 31, 1968. Johnson began by, once more, using the containment of communism to argue for continued U.S. military intervention in Vietnam. He reminded Americans of the positive implications of the domino theory, saying, "A number of [Southeast Asia's] nations have shown what can be accomplished under conditions of security." He added: "We can rightly judge—as responsible Southeast Asians themselves do—that the progress of the past 3 years would have been far less likely—if not completely impossible—if America's sons and others had not made their stand in Vietnam." The war in Vietnam was "vital not only to the security of Southeast Asia, but . . . to the security of every American."[165] The president also warned the negative consequences of the domino theory, saying, "Peace and self-determination in Vietnam is directly related to the future of all of Southeast Asia." The president claimed that this had been the aim of U.S. involvement in Vietnam "under three presidents, three separate Administrations."[166]

The president also recalled his broken insurance policy against congressional dissent. Among the commitments he said the United States still had to South Vietnam were the "Resolutions of the Congress [that] testify to the need to resist aggression in the world and in Southeast Asia."[167] It was almost as if the president could not believe that Congress had managed to slip from the noose he had prepared for them.

The president concluded his speech with a bombshell; he announced that he would institute an unconditional bombing halt everywhere in North Vietnam except the area just above the demilitarized zone (DMZ). He also said that he would not run for reelection to the presidency.[168] Johnson claimed that both moves were intended to bring the North Vietnamese to the table to reach a settlement that would allow the United States to leave and South Vietnam to survive as an independent country. This speech was followed by an announcement by the new secretary of defense, Clark Clifford, that the escalation of troops in Vietnam end after the deployment of the final fifty thousand troops that the president had announced in his speech.[169]

President Johnson announcing that he will not run for reelection, March 31, 1968.

Source: Yoichi Okamoto, President Lyndon B. Johnson addresses the Nation, announcing a bombing halt in Vietnam and his intention not to run for reelection, March 31, 1968, Johnson Presidential Library.[170]

The immediate reaction to the president's announcement that he would not run was shock. But many believed that the move would also end the president's crisis of credibility. Edwin Newman, in NBC coverage immediately following the speech, said the announcement would "stagger the entire world," calling it the "biggest bombshell of this year, and in fact of many years in politics." Newman did note, "The President took the diplomatic offensive tonight and, in doing so, somewhat disarmed his critics here at home." Newman added that the president's decision to stop the bombing "undercuts the critics here at home that say Mr. Johnson is not serious about negotiations." Newman concluded that those critics would be "on the spot if nothing comes of tonight's moves." In a later panel segment during this broadcast, Democratic Senator (and future vice president) Walter Mondale of Minnesota used the announcement to defend the president's credibility, saying, "The President was more committed to the objectives of peace than some rhetoric and style has permitted the public to accept."[171]

The reaction the day after the president's withdrawal from the presidential race was unbridled, if unwarranted, optimism that the president's gesture made the end of the war a foregone conclusion. But this optimism was eclipsed by renewed skepticism about the president's honesty. In NBC News coverage of Senator Robert F. Kennedy's news conference in reaction to the president's announcement, reporter Edward Newman seemed to think the war would no longer be a political issue, saying Kennedy "would continue his campaign" since "there were other issues in the campaign besides Vietnam." In his own comments, however, Kennedy seemed more concerned that Johnson might renege on his promise not to run for reelection. Kennedy repeatedly said that he took Johnson "at his word that he is not going to run and he is not going to submit to a draft," as if he hoped to increase the cost for the president should he break this promise.[172]

The initial reaction of staffers on the Senate Foreign Relations Committee to the president's withdrawal from the Democratic primary race likewise reflected their own deep suspicion of the president. In an internal memo from chief of staff Carl Marcy to Senator Fulbright, Marcy warned that, since the president had "no constituency to satisfy or hold him back," he had great power over the remainder of his presidency "for good or evil." He could "escalate in Vietnam over the protests of the 'doves'; or 'cut and run' over the protests of the 'hawks.'"[173] Marcy's suspicion of the president was so deep that the only possibility that Marcy did not suggest was that the president would do exactly what he had promised in his March 31, 1968, speech—halt almost all bombing in North Vietnam and start negotiations with Hanoi.

Many in the American public were just as suspicious of the administration. The *Lewiston Morning Tribune* printed a letter to the editor from a Jesse Merlan decrying new Secretary of Defense Clark Clifford's "promises we can 'return U.S. soldiers from Vietnam' even as we sent 50,000 more troops." Merlan quipped: "On paper and in windy speeches, we've been returning 'our boys' since 1963."[174]

Supporters of the war were incensed by the president's move and lashed out. Consistent administration supporter C. L. Sulzberger of the *New York Times* used the president's own words to attack the bombing halt as a surrender to communism. Sulzberger repeatedly reminded his readers that the president "insisted that no small nation anywhere would be safe if the U.S. 'got out of Vietnam.'" Using the president's argument that he was continuing the policies of his predecessors, Sulzberger wrote, "either the U.S. has been wrong in its Southeast Asian policy under the last three Presidents or it is wrong today." Using the president's arguments about South Vietnam being a test of U.S. commitments around the world, Sulzberger concluded that it was doubtful whether "nations will continue to rely on U.S. resolve . . . as the President himself warned, they will no longer feel safe anywhere."[175]

The public seemed to approve of the president's dramatic moves on March 31, 1968. Americans were much more positive about the president's policies in Vietnam after his decision not to run, with 48 percent disapproving of his handling of the war and 42 percent approving—essentially erasing the precipitous drop in approval the president had experienced since the start of the Tet Offensive. Also, while most Americans had disapproved of the idea of a bombing halt before it was instituted, after the president enacted the partial bombing halt, 72 percent of Americans who had an opinion approved of the move.[176]

However, the president's move also had an immediate negative impact on the American public's willingness to continue the war. After the president's dramatic moves for peace on March 31, 1968, 55 percent of Americans who had an opinion now said it was a mistake to send troops to Vietnam. Only 51 percent of Americans who expressed an opinion still identified themselves as "hawk[s]," while 49 percent now identified themselves as "Dove[s]."[177] The magnitude of this shift in public opinion cannot be overstated. As a result of the president's dramatic moves to jumpstart the peace process, nearly one-fifth of the American public abandoned their support for the war. It is not in any way an exaggeration to say that this is the moment when the American public began to give up on the Vietnam War.

While the administration and its supporters still continued to use the ideology of containment to argue for U.S. military intervention in Vietnam, opposition to the war had decisively shifted to attacks on the administration's credibility. Even Senator J. William Fulbright, who had spent the previous three years spearheading the foreign policy revolution to dismantle the Cold War consensus, now focused his attacks on the president's credibility. Fulbright still attacked the administration's use of containment to justify the war, calling the domino theory "nonsense." But this was little more than a refrain before he attacked the administration's reluctance to begin negotiations. Fulbright reminded the country that the president had said he would negotiate anywhere at any time but was now balking at the North Vietnamese's suggestions of sites for negotiations.[178] Fulbright was not just engaging in political rhetoric. Staffers on the Senate Foreign Relations Committee were deeply skeptical that the president truly wanted negotiations.[179]

While the mainstream opposition to the Vietnam War had decisively shifted to attacks on the administration's credibility on the war, radical dissenters continued to use anti-imperialist rhetoric to attack the ideology of containment itself. The Students for a Democratic Society (SDS) continued to argue that "US policy in Vietnam [was] part of a global strategy for containing revolutionary change in the 'Third World' nations of Asia, Africa, and Latin America." According to the SDS, "Rather than the result of an essentially good government's mistaken decisions, we see the world wide exploitation and oppression of those insurgent peoples as the logical conclusion of the giant US corporations' expanding and necessary search for higher profits and strategic resources."[180]

The California Peace and Freedom Movement also embraced this anti-imperialist critique of American foreign policy. The Movement argued that the Vietnam War was "the logical consequence of an American economic imperialism which requires the subordination of foreign resources, markets, and political structures to the needs of corporate property and profit." The Movement criticized this foreign policy paradigm as using the "pretense of protecting the world from Communism" to support "reactionary regimes throughout the world" and thwart "the aspirations of its peoples . . . maintaining them in a condition of bondage." The Movement concluded by calling the wars generated by this foreign policy paradigm "imperialistic interventions."[181]

These radical dissenters rejected the dissent of antiwar presidential candidates—who continued to attack the application of the ideology of containment to the war in Vietnam—on the grounds that their dissent was not radical enough. SDS President Carl Oglesby wrote an open letter to those radicals who might support antiwar candidate Eugene McCarthy, urging them to instead withdraw from the American political process. Oglesby wrote that McCarthy's "overriding objective is the defense of the same American Empire which we find flatly unsupportable." McCarthy's antiwar stance was not a rejection of the Cold War consensus but a "pre-condition of revamped containment/ imperialism." Oglesby added that this was also the objective of the military-industrial complex that had become concerned with the security of its economic hegemony in Europe and Latin America. Oglesby wrote: "McCarthy . . . among all the candidates, possibly understood this best, maybe even first. That may be commendable." However, Oglesby added, "McCarthy's 'practicality' amounts in the end to the adulteration of the necessary critique of the War, the obscuring of its sources in the system of American expansionism." Radicals should, in Oglesby's opinion, reject McCarthy's antiwar campaign because he wanted to end the war for the wrong reasons. McCarthy's ultimate objective, Oglesby wrote, was "the retention and even reinforcing of the Truman-to-Johnson containment line."[182]

As the presidential race took shape after the departure of President Johnson from the campaign, the Democratic Party was split on the issue of the Vietnam War. The antiwar wing represented by Eugene McCarthy and Robert Kennedy sought a rapid negotiated settlement that would include the National Liberation Front in the South Vietnamese government—thus sacrificing the goal of containment of communism in Southeast Asia in order to end the war. Vice President Hubert Humphrey was never specific about his particular desires for the war but was generally understood to embrace President Johnson's use of the containment of communism to justify holding out for a more favorable settlement of the war. However, Hubert Humphrey was soon saddled with the same credibility problems that had crippled President Johnson.

While the candidates debated over the ideology of containment and its applicability to the war in Vietnam, elsewhere the public debate over the war had moved beyond this framework. Instead, advocates of continuing the war to a successful conclusion continued to use the containment of communism to justify their position. On the other hand, with the exception of radical protesters and antiwar candidates, almost all other opponents of the war shifted their attacks to the administration's credibility.

Robert Kennedy entered the Democratic primary race as an antiwar candidate in mid-March 1968. The platform for his candidacy was compromising the objective of containing communism in Vietnam in order to end the war. In announcing his candidacy, he claimed that he was running because the "country is on a perilous course." He ran to enact new policies "to end the bloodshed in Vietnam." His critique of the war was that the ideology of containment was not achieving America's goals in Southeast Asia; rather, it held the "growing risk of world war" and "further destroys the country and the people it was meant to save." Kennedy also implicitly indicted the administration's credibility: "The reality of recent events in Vietnam has been glossed over with illusions." However, this critique was secondary to Kennedy's attack on the application of the ideology of containment to Vietnam. Kennedy favored "deescalating the struggle." He wanted the South Vietnamese to take more responsibility for their own defense (the strategy Westmoreland had announced before the Tet Offensive). Kennedy wanted the United States to stop bombing North Vietnam (a step Johnson would take less than two weeks later). In fact, the only true point of departure from Johnson's policies in Vietnam was that Kennedy accepted that "the National Liberation Front is going to play a role in the future political process of South Vietnam."[183]

The entry of Robert Kennedy into the Democratic Primary race created a media-ready conflict between Senator Eugene McCarthy and

Senator Kennedy; before the New Hampshire primary, Kennedy had supposedly encouraged McCarthy to run and assured him he would not enter the race. This conflict was repeatedly stoked by the media.[184]

However, despite their rivalry, the two men revealed that— their deep desire that the other man not be the Democratic nominee notwithstanding—their positions on both the Vietnam War and the broader ideology of containment were nearly identical. Eugene McCarthy's policy prescription was "de-escalating the war in Vietnam, drawing back from some of our advanced positions while still holding strength in Vietnam" and a recognition "that we have to have a new government in South Vietnam . . . and . . . that that new government would include the National Liberation Front." Kennedy favored an end to corruption in Saigon, an end to "the search and destroy missions by American troops and American Marines," a push to force South Vietnamese to draft its eighteen- and nineteen-year olds, and insisting that "the government [in] Saigon . . . begin their own negotiations with the National Liberation Front."[185]

The two men differed little on the broader ideology of containment, either. McCarthy emphasized that the United States should only be involved in places where it had "clear obligations" such as Formosa, the Middle East, and Western Europe. Kennedy believed that the line should be drawn "between external aggression and internal turmoil." But both still clearly supported the idea of using military containment to block communist aggression; both simply disagreed with the president that Vietnam was a case of communist aggression.[186] More than any other presidential candidate in 1968, Robert Kennedy sought to identify with radical dissenters, claiming that he had "listened to the young people of our nation and their anger about the war that they are sent to fight and about the world that they are about to inherit."[187] However, Kennedy's unqualified support of the ideology of containment almost certainly undercut his appeal to increasingly anti-imperialist radical protesters.

The most consistent critique of both McCarthy's and Kennedy's campaigns was that they aided communists. The first question Kennedy received at the announcement of his candidacy was from a reporter who noted, "At the Budapest conference Gus Hall, head of the Communist Party, said that he welcomes McCarthy's campaign to set up this new antiwar movement." The reporter asked Kennedy, "Are you going to accept his endorsement, too?" While this question was greeted with jeers from other journalists at the Kennedy news conference,[188] this charge would continue to plague McCarthy even after Robert Kennedy's assassination on June 6, 1968.

While presidential candidates debated the suitability of the ideology of containment to the Vietnam War, most opponents of the war had already shifted their attacks to the administration's credibility. With sales of his new book *Anything but the Truth* brisk, author Erwin Knoll made the rounds of the Washington talk shows to promote his book. Knoll appeared on Washington, DC. ABC affiliate WJLA on *Here's Barbara* and pilloried the administration for its deceptiveness. Knoll recalled that the president had given the Pentagon a smaller troop increase than it had asked for and then got the generals to agree on camera that the increase was adequate. "It was all a put up job. It was an artificial show of unanimity of the kind we've gotten so used to." Knoll questioned "some of the news that is coming out of Vietnam during these [peace] talks" as well as "incredibly cheerful assessments emanating from Vietnam . . . these highly dubious casualty counts." Knoll said it was a "disconcerting experience . . . being out in the field in the morning and seeing an action take place and then hearing it described at the military briefing in Saigon in the afternoon and finding it very difficult to reconcile." Knoll blamed the White House's tendency to believe "we're better off if we make it look better than it is because maybe we're just about to turn the corner. Maybe three weeks from now or six months from now everything really is going to be alright and then we'll look fine." He added that the "incredible catalogue of reassuring statements on Vietnam that goes back to the early 60s . . . look silly in retrospect. Preposterous in retrospect." However, he claimed, "the depressing thing is that the same kind of statement is still being made."[189]

The president's credibility problems extended to his heir-apparent, Vice President Hubert Humphrey, as well. Former White House communications director and *Newsweek* editor Bill Moyers appeared on *Late Night* with guest host David Frost in July and was forced into the uncomfortable position of defending the president's—and Hubert Humphrey's—credibility against attacks by former Kennedy and current McCarthy speechwriter Dick Goodwin. Moyers set the trap himself before Goodwin joined the set by saying that Humphrey would have to "to rebuild the image of Washington, which I think in the country right now is not a very exciting one." When questioned, Moyers added, "The war in Vietnam has turned majority of the people against Washington and against the administration." Frost cornered Moyers, noting that a few weeks earlier, Moyers had "suggested that [Humphrey] was just about to lay bare his private doubts about Vietnam," but that Humphrey had not done so and, in fact, "he doesn't seem to have any." Moyers demurred—and deepened the hole—by saying that Humphrey was "in a bit of a strait-jacket" and couldn't say what he really thought about Vietnam while he was part of the administration. When Richard Goodwin emerged after the commercial break, he savaged Moyers on Humphrey's credibility. He said, "It's extraordinary that the Vice President has so many supporters who seem to be for him on the basis that he hasn't meant anything he's said in the last five years." In response to nervous laughter from the audience, Goodwin recounted all of the recent statements of support Humphrey had made about the war. Goodwin added that Humphrey, who owed his political fortunes to the Johnson camp, "has an enormous handicap to overcome." Moyers only ended the assault by saying that the sooner "the next President can terminate the war in Vietnam, the sooner he will have 30 billion dollars a year" to fix America's domestic problems. The prospect of ending the war drew enthusiastic applause.[190]

Continued upheaval in the Democratic Party had a visible negative effect on public sentiments about the party. In late July 1968, a plurality of Americans (46 percent) believed Vietnam was "the most important problem" facing the United States in this election year. When asked which party would do a better job in dealing with this problem, a plurality (37 percent) of Americans who had an opinion believed the Republicans would do a better job (with 33 percent believing it would make no difference).[191] By August, nearly 42 percent of Americans who had an opinion believed the Republicans would do a better job.[192]

Americans were also clearly providing the next president with a policy prescription. When asked about an unnamed candidate who promised they would "turn over more of the fighting in Vietnam to the South Vietnamese and that as of next January 1 the U.S. should withdraw some of our troops," 78 percent of Americans who had an opinion said that they would vote for this candidate.[193]

Many supporters of the war in the media, who had been dispirited since the president's withdrawal from the presidential race, remained dejected. John Chamberlain decried the victory of peace candidate Paul O'Dwyer in the New York Democratic senatorial primary as yet another indication that "our Vietnamese engagement has been lost." Admonishing the American public he added, "As a people, we have declared not our inability to win the war but our unwillingness to pay the price that would be demanded of us to do it." Citing all of the candidates who had rejected the war, Chamberlain claimed that a sort of "domino theory" had swept the American political landscape. Chamberlain also joined the dwindling number of "hawks" in attacking Johnson for having failed to use the measures required to win the war. "The enemy was assured at all times of a steady flow of weapons and food from Soviet Russia and Red China," he claimed. Recounting the administration's argument that Vietnam was a test of U.S. commitment, Chamberlain warned that, in 1969, "Every other nation in the world, whether large or small, will be seeking new alliances, or new sources of internal cohesion and strength." Chamberlain suggested that the American public ask its presidential candidates, "Which one . . . will be able to give West Germany and Japan, Thailand and Israel, Venezuela and Brazil, Spain and India, the reassurance that we can reform our lines and keep at least some of the dominoes from falling."[194]

A Soviet crackdown in Czechoslovakia began to breathe new life into those in the media who supported the war. Joseph Alsop used the crackdown in Czechoslovakia to attack "those men of the left whose indignation waxes so hot when it is a question of Western or even American 'imperialism.'" Unlike dissenters in America, Alsop wrote, Soviets "do not parrot twaddle about the 'discredited domino theory.'" The Soviets, Alsop claimed, "knew that sooner or later the dominoes would begin tumbling in Eastern Europe if freedom was permitted to be reborn there." Moreover, Alsop claimed, this new Soviet boldness was born of "the kind of collapse of American resolve that Sens. Eugene McCarthy, Ted Kennedy and others now are seeking to promote."[195] Albert Parry of the *New York Times*[196] and nationally syndicated columnist Don Maclean[197] made similar arguments about the crackdown in Czechoslovakia.

The Tet Offensive and the dramatic political changes that followed in Washington in the first half of 1968 had substantially quieted radical demonstrators. The movement reemerged at the Democratic National Convention held in Chicago in August 1968. Just as in previous radical protests, the demonstrators in Chicago demonstrated in opposition to the ideology of containment and its distorting effect on foreign and domestic policy in the United States. While these demonstrations raged outside, Democratic Party leaders inside the convention debated the applicability of the ideology of containment to the Vietnam War and whether to compromise the goal of containment of communism in Southeast Asia to end the war.

While the Democratic Party was in disarray, the Republican Party quickly unified behind a platform supporting the use of the ideology of containment of communism to justify the war. It is in this context that Republican candidate Richard Nixon made vague promises about bringing the war to an "honorable end," which most in the media and the American public understood to mean continuing the war to a conclusion that contained communism in Southeast Asia. It was also in the context of support for the ideology of containment that Nixon attacked radical protesters who continued to attack the Cold War consensus—most dramatically at the violent protests at the Democratic National Convention.

It gradually became evident that Democratic nominee Hubert Humphrey would lose the election, in large part due to the same credibility issues that had ended the Johnson presidency. In response, Humphrey and the president made a series of eleventh-hour moves designed to bridge the divide between antiwar Democrats and those supporters of Humphrey who wanted to hold on in Vietnam for a more favorable settlement. In the end, while this closed the gap between Humphrey and Nixon, it was not enough to convince a majority of Americans to support Humphrey. By unmistakably identifying himself with the ideology of military containment of communism, Nixon was able to defeat Humphrey by a narrow margin to become president of the United States.

The protesters at the Democratic National Convention in Chicago, like those in earlier antiwar protests, were primarily young radicals, many waving Viet Cong and other communist flags.[198] The security forces that Mayor Daley assembled to meet the protests included over 7,000 U.S. Army National Guard soldiers. The violent clash between demonstrators and these security forces dominated coverage of the convention.[199] Several photographers and reporters were caught up in the violence, magnifying this effect.[200] These demonstrations were preceded by demonstrations at over 100 different colleges, including violent confrontations between police and students at Columbia University.[201]

Just as with previous radical protests, the tactics and rhetoric or radical dissenters in Chicago alienated most Americans. As McCarthy supporter Sam Brown later said, "The Chicago episode [was] a disaster that alienated many Americans sympathetic to the antiwar movement."[202] The violence of the demonstrations at the Chicago convention also hurt Hubert Humphrey's chances against Republican nominee Richard Nixon.[203] Nixon would repeatedly play on the American public's shock at the brutality of the images from the demonstrations by promising to restore the "rule of law."

Inside the convention, an equally tumultuous political struggle was taking place over the position the Democratic party platform would take on the Vietnam War. Antiwar Democrats argued that the party should abandon the goal of containing communism in Southeast Asia in order to end the war. Senator J. William Fulbright argued before the platform committee that the platform should acknowledge that

> . . . the war in Vietnam is essentially a civil war which involves no direct threat to the national security of the United States. That the war cannot be won without running unacceptable risks, including the risk of a world war. But that, nonetheless, a unilateral American withdrawal would leave a situation of confusion and disorder in South Vietnam. Accordingly, the Democratic Party [should commit] itself to a policy of seeking, through the Paris peace negotiations a peace settlement based on the principles of self-determination and neutralization.[204]

Senator George McGovern, representing supporters of slain candidate Robert Kennedy, argued that the platform should contain a pledge that the United States would "cease our opposition to participation by the NLF in the government of South Vietnam."[205] McGovern also proposed that the platform contain a "60-days-to-peace" plan that included the immediate withdrawal of 275,000 U.S. troops. Senator Eugene McCarthy's camp argued only that the platform should include support for communist participation in a coalition government in South Vietnam.[206]

While Vice President Hubert Humphrey was less specific about his own policy prescription, he rejected suggestions that would end the war without containing communist expansion into South Vietnam. Humphrey implied that such suggestions would alienate the American people and urged antiwar delegates to be practical by reminding them that none of the urgent domestic needs of the country would be addressed if Richard Nixon became president. Humphrey even suggested that he might make either McGovern or McCarthy his running-mate (in the end he chose Democratic Senator Edmund Muskie of Maine instead). Humphrey also promised he would "do all that is humanly possible without regard to my own political future to bring . . . peace as speedily and as honorably as I can." The emphasis on "honorably" separated him from the other two men, who had laid out terms for ending the war that he believed the American people would not accept.[207]

Johnson administration officials took the opportunity of the platform committee to once more use the ideology of containment to argue for continued U.S. military intervention in Vietnam. Secretary of State Dean Rusk took the extraordinary step of appearing before the Democratic party platform committee—presumably on behalf of the Humphrey camp—to argue against making any concessions to the North Vietnamese a part of the Democratic party platform. In a reference to the lessons of Munich, Rusk equated antiwar recommendations to saying, "Give the aggressor another bite—perhaps he'll be satisfied." Rusk also argued against saying, "It's too far away," "It's not our business," or "Security treaties should be ignored if they come to involve cost, pain and sacrifice." Rusk claimed that there was no need to debate the "domino theory" since the communists were already active across Southeast Asia. He added that events in Southeast Asia were directly tied to U.S. and world security. Like Humphrey, Rusk argued that the Democratic platform should affirm the party's desire for "an early but honorable peace that will enable the peoples of Asia to live together in freedom."[208]

In the end, the Democratic platform reflected President Johnson's and Vice President Humphrey's wishes. As House Majority Leader Carl Albert would recall in an oral history a year later, Johnson had "selected the temporary and permanent officers of the convention, and everything was run by the National Committee through him."[209]

In many regards, the 1968 Democratic National Convention was the high-water mark of opposition to the Cold War consensus that had begun in 1965. By August 1968, most other opponents of the war—including the congressional wing of the foreign policy revolution—had already stopped attacking the ideology of containment or its application to the war in Vietnam. Instead, they had begun to almost exclusively attack the administration's credibility. Only in Chicago, inside and outside the convention hall, did opposition to the ideology of containment continue. Inside the hall, peace candidates who attacked the application of containment to Vietnam were defeated and Hubert Humphrey—who advocated an "honorable peace" that would preserve the goal of containment in Vietnam—became the Democratic presidential nominee. Outside the convention, radical protesters were dispirited by their failure to persuade the American public to reject the Cold War consensus. While radical demonstrations would continue through the Moratorium in October 1969, radicals began to increasingly abandon the strategy of demonstrations against the ideology of containment after the Democratic National Convention. Some drifted toward explicit communism. A tiny fraction drifted toward militant insurgency. The remainder simply drifted away from the antiwar movement and toward other radical causes.[210] Most importantly, however, both the demonstrations outside the hall and the debate inside the hall alienated the American public, alienation on which the Republican party capitalized.

The Republican Party was united in its belief in the ideology of containment and its applicability to the war in Vietnam. At a news conference before his nomination at the Republican National Convention in Miami Beach, Florida, Richard Nixon made it clear he had no intentions of surrendering in Vietnam. Nixon insisted, "I do *not* think the war is unwinnable" (emphasis is the candidate's). He added that he did not want to be president "for the purpose of presiding over the destruction of the credibility of the American power throughout this world." Nixon intended to compel the North Vietnamese to negotiate through more forceful military action.[211]

In his acceptance speech after his nomination at the convention, Nixon reiterated the theme that Vietnam was a test of U.S. commitments worldwide. The election would decide "not only the future of America," Nixon insisted, "but the future of peace and freedom of the world for the last third of the Twentieth Century." Nixon also renewed his pledge to use more forceful action in Vietnam, saying that it was time for "new leadership in America" when "the strongest nation in the world can be tied down for four years by a war in Vietnam with no end in sight." Nixon promised both to "bring an honorable end to the war in Vietnam" and to create a foreign policy that would "prevent more Vietnams."[212]

The press clearly believed that Nixon would be the more aggressive candidate in Vietnam. Global News Service journalist Robert Lucas wrote that the Johnson administration believed Nixon's nomination would give the administration additional bargaining power in Vietnam. Lucas wrote that "Nixon is anathema to the Russians, a reaction resulting from Nixon's vaunted anti-Communist position over many years." Lucas added that Nixon's "anti-Communist stance has been his most consistent ideological commitment over the years." Lucas noted that the former vice president had advocated sending U.S. troops to assist the French during their rout in Indochina. Lucas also noted that Nixon had ever since criticized "U.S. war policy in Vietnam as vacillating and inadequate" and attacked the "'piecemeal' and tardy deployment of U.S. military forces in Vietnam." Lucas also noted that Nixon wanted "more intense employment of airpower in the war as an alternative to 'ground forces' in winning." Lucas concluded that these convictions were a result of Nixon's strong belief in the "'domino theory' of resistance to North Vietnamese aggression as necessary to prevent a Red engulfment of Asia."[213]

However, Nixon's campaign was not just a campaign to find an "honorable end" to the war that preserved the goals of containment of communism in Southeast Asia. It was also a campaign against radical demonstrators. Richard Nixon had repeatedly lashed out against demonstrators as prolonging the war in 1967. As a presidential candidate, Nixon campaigned against "lawlessness," which the media understood to mean radical and civil rights demonstrators. In a June 1968 article, syndicated columnist Andrew Tully wrote about the Republican Party's use of the phrase, "violence in the streets." Tully noted that the antiviolence plank in the Republican platform was simply "We will not tolerate violence!" with the underlining and exclamation point provided by the platform committee. Tully added that, while this plank wouldn't please academics, "it warms the [cockles] of Main Street's heart" to hear a candidate declare that the United States (quoting the text of the platform) "must reestablish the principle that men are accountable for what they do." Moreover, Tully clearly understood who Nixon was talking about; he wrote that it was "not the whole country that is sick, but only a noisy and vicious minority." Tully concluded that campaigning against radical demonstrators was a winning issue for Republicans.[214]

Tully was right that the American people were concerned about this issue. In September, a plurality of the American people—42 percent of Americans—continued to see Vietnam as the most important issue. However, 34 percent of Americans cited various other issues that were related to radical dissenters or demonstrators, including "crime," "juvenile delinquency [and] hippies," "unrest in this country," "college demonstrations," "draft card burning," "anti-war demonstrations," or "youth protests." Moreover, of those who thought either party would do better in handling this problem, 62 percent believed Republicans would "do a better job."[215] Further, while some in the media decried the police violence against protesters in Chicago at the Democratic National Convention, 65 percent of Americans who had an opinion approved of "the way the Chicago police dealt with the young people who were registering their protest against the Vietnam war at the time of the Democratic convention."[216]

Richard Nixon made direct appeals to the majority of the American electorate that decried radical demonstrators and their opposition to the Cold War consensus. In his acceptance speech at the Republican National Convention, Nixon said that he was running because "the greatest tradition of the rule of law is plagued by unprecedented lawlessness" and because "the President of the United States cannot travel . . . to any major city at home without fear of a hostile demonstration." He added: "A nation that can't keep the peace at home won't be trusted to keep the peace abroad." Nixon also directly confronted those who he said claimed "law and order is the code word for racism," saying that the Republican goal was "justice for every American." Nixon even stole an argument from radicals themselves; he said that black Americans "don't want to be a colony in a nation."[217]

After the nominating conventions, Richard Nixon had a commanding lead over Hubert Humphrey. Over two-thirds of Americans believed that Nixon could do "a better job of dealing with the Vietnam War" than Hubert Humphrey.[218] By September, Humphrey had narrowed that gap only slightly, with 64 percent still believing Nixon would do a better job with the war. Interestingly, while 62 percent of Americans who had an opinion saw Nixon as a "hawk" on the war,[219] they did not necessarily expect him to escalate the war. When asked what Nixon would do about the war if elected, only 16 percent of Americans who had an opinion expected him to escalate the war. The largest percentage, 44 percent, took the former vice president at his word, agreeing that he would "try to end the war." However, Americans also understood that Nixon's pledge to find an "honorable end" to the war was not a pledge to withdraw precipitously; only seven percent of respondents expected Nixon to deescalate the conflict. Nor did Nixon appeal to Americans only on the issue of the Vietnam War. When asked for whom they would vote if a negotiated settlement were reached in Paris, a plurality of Americans who had an opinion, 47 percent, still said they would vote for Nixon.[220]

Another factor contributing to Nixon's success was the administration's continued credibility problems. The *New York Times* accused the president of dishonesty in not truly supporting Vice President Humphrey's presidential bid and not truly wanting peace. The *Times* wrote that Johnson was sabotaging the campaign and trying to keep the war going with "an emotional defense of his old Vietnam policies." The *Times* wrote, "Johnson spoke out again this week on Vietnam [in] tough terms that can only diminish prospects for progress in the Paris peace talks and undermine whatever efforts Vice President Humphrey may be trying to make to advance a more moderate Vietnam position." Likewise, the *Times* wrote, Johnson "frustrated" Humphrey's effort to unify the party during the platform committee meetings with "a hard-line Presidential address before the Veterans of Foreign Wars." The *Times* was roundly critical of the president's continued use of containment to justify the war, including the "discredited domino theory," the "flimsy pretext of a SEATO obligation," the "highly dubious argument" that Vietnam was vital to U.S. security, and "his vow not to stop the bombing of North Vietnam without assurances of reciprocity." The *Times* added that the president contradicted "two Secretaries of Defense" by insisting that a bombing halt would "permit the enemy to increase its capacity severalfold [sic] in ten days" and increase U.S. casualties. However, these attacks on the president's use of the ideology of containment were now cast as evidence of the president's dishonesty. The *New York Times* primary critique was that the president did not truly want to end the war. The *Times* called this talk "intemperate rhetoric" and a "retreat from the President's own encouraging initiative of last March 31." The *Times* concluded that this talk was deliberately intended to frustrate the efforts of both "American negotiators in Paris [and] the Democratic nominee for the presidency,"[221] presumably because the president believed Nixon would be more likely to continue the war in Vietnam if elected.

As the presidential election approached, even some Democrats ran against the lack of presidential credibility. Jesse Unruh, speaker of the California Assembly and Hubert Humphrey's honorary campaign vice chairman in California, unleashed a broadside against the administration's dishonesty during a speech that was excerpted on the *CBS Evening News*. Unruh said that "many people have lost faith in this administration." He warned: "No government can survive if it is not built upon the sound basis of truth and credibility." While Unruh claimed that the administration had faltered by embarking "upon its mistaken path in Vietnam," he claimed its larger failure was that "it consistently and categorically misled the people about the progress of the war and its purposes." Unruh believed that the next president must hold to "a policy of utmost candor with the American people." He added, "Politicians have got to start leveling with the people. They've got to stop managing the news as if justifying their policies was their only mission in life."[222]

While many in the media and the American public had abandoned support of the president, they had not yet completely abandoned support for the war. When asked in late September if they thought "the United States made a mistake sending troops to fight in Vietnam, 59 percent of Americans who had an opinion answered "yes." However, when asked to describe their own position on the war, 53 percent of those who answered still called themselves "hawks" (an increase of 2 percentage points since the president's March 31 announcement).[223]

Moreover, when asked whether they would be "more likely to vote for" Nixon or Humphrey if each "were to take a stronger peace position on Vietnam," two thirds of respondents answered "no" regardless of which candidate they supported.[224]

On September 30, with Humphrey lagging badly in national polls behind Nixon, the vice president made a dramatic pledge designed to capture the votes of those former supporters of McCarthy and Kennedy who wanted a negotiated settlement in Vietnam—even if it meant compromising the goal of containing communism in Southeast Asia. The speech itself was the work of Johnson aide George Ball who had left the White House to help Humphrey's faltering campaign.[225] In a nationally televised speech taped in Salt Lake City, Utah, the vice president promised that, if elected, he would "stop the bombing of the north as an acceptable risk for peace because I believe it could lead to success in the negotiations and thereby shorten the war." He did, however, equivocate by saying he would look for some reciprocal action, such as North Vietnam restoring the demilitarized zone between North and South Vietnam, first. However, his aides described this caveat as "window-dressing," claiming Humphrey was committed to a bombing halt. Both aides and Humphrey himself hoped that the move would be interpreted by former McCarthy and Kennedy supporters in the Democratic Party as a break from President Johnson.[226]

While Humphrey painted this move as taking a risk for peace, it was not that risky—at least in terms of domestic politics. When Americans were asked only two weeks earlier if the United States should "stop all bombing of North Vietnam but with the understanding that if after one or two months the North Vietnamese [do not] begin to remove their soldiers from South Vietnam that the U.S. would then decide whether to bomb all of North Vietnam including the cities," 55 percent of Americans who had an opinion agreed with this course of action.[227]

However, the equivocation in Humphrey's pledge to stop the bombing opened him to attacks on his credibility. In a letter to the editor of the *New York Times*, reader John Fisher asked of this caveat to a bombing halt, "Does the Vice President attempt to fool the American people deliberately with such a declaration?" Harkening to earlier attacks on Johnson's true desire for negotiations, Fisher added, "The 'new' declaration by Mr. Humphrey is once again conditioned by the same Johnsonian hoax that peace depends on the doings of the North Vietnamese." Fisher also reminded his fellow readers, "Mr. Humphrey has been endorsing Johnson's and his own bombing policy for years and as recently as during the Chicago convention, in clear opposition to the McCarthy platform against the bombing." Fisher concluded by calling the pledge a "smoke screen" and "a late-hour maneuver to get the votes from peace-minded Americans."[228]

Still, this pledge did seem to help Humphrey with voters. In mid-October, when asked who would do "a better job of dealing with the Vietnam War," only 61 percent of those Americans who chose a candidate chose Nixon, a slip of three points from September.[229]

On November 1, 1968, in another last-minute attempt to buoy the vice president's campaign, President Johnson announced a bombing halt across all of North Vietnam.[230] In the end these two moves would cause a surge in the polls for Humphrey, but not be enough to put him past Nixon in the election. Hubert Humphrey lost the election by a half-million votes.[231]

While the election of Richard Nixon was a narrow rejection of President Johnson's chosen successor, Hubert Humphrey, it was not a national repudiation of the Cold War consensus or a vote to quit the war in Vietnam and abandon the goal of containment of communism in Southeast Asia. Candidates across the country who had run against the ideology of containment were soundly defeated. Moreover, Richard Nixon was understood by the media and the American people to be a Cold Warrior and a "hawk" on the war in Vietnam. Still, the American public gave Nixon a clear policy prescription as he prepared to take office: begin to hand the war over to the South Vietnamese and gradually bring U.S. troops home as the Army of the Republic of Vietnam was ready to take the fight.

As President-elect Richard Nixon prepared to take office, it is clear that he understood that the framework for the debate of the war had shifted, with supporters continuing to use containment to justify the war but opponents now attacking the president's credibility; in response Nixon's administration-in-waiting moved to shore up his credibility before he took office.

The 1968 election was a repudiation of those candidates who opposed the Cold War consensus. Of course, Eugene McCarthy—whose campaign advocated abandoning the objective of containing communism in Vietnam to end the war—was rejected by Democratic voters in favor of Hubert Humphrey. But in other races, voters also rejected those who attacked the Cold War consensus. For instance, Earl Faircloth, conservative Florida Attorney General, was defeated in the Democratic Primary for the U.S. Senate after running a campaign founded on moving beyond a foreign policy based on containment.[232] New York City Council President Paul O'Dwyer lost his bid for the U.S. Senate against Republican incumbent Jacob K. Javits. O'Dwyer's campaign was founded on an attack against Javits's use of containment to justify the war in Vietnam and, in the later days of the campaign, against the ideology of containment itself.[233] Even perennial congressional dissenter Wayne Morse lost his reelection bid in Oregon to relatively unknown Republican challenger Robert Packwood. Packwood ran directly against Wayne Morse's attacks on the application of the ideology of containment to the war in Vietnam. At one campaign stop, for instance, Packwood decried Morse's statement that "our aid in Vietnam is identical to the Russian invasion of Czechoslovakia." Even a tacit endorsement and highly favorable news segment on *ABC Evening News* by reporter Jim Burnes was not enough to save Morse's Senate seat.[234]

After the election, supporters of the war, flush with victory, reasserted that the containment of communism justified continued U.S. military intervention in Vietnam. A few days before the inauguration, syndicated columnist Ernest Cuneo claimed that the Philippines' drift away from the United States and toward Communist China was yet another proof of the domino theory. Philippine Foreign Secretary General Carlos P. Romulo, Cuneo wrote, had declared that "the American people will not consent to involving [their] troops in Asia" after Vietnam. As a result, Romulo suggested that the Philippines find "alternate fallback arrangements" with Communist China. Cuneo wrote that "this de facto recognition of Peking and simultaneous expression of hope of withdrawal of the naval and air power from U.S. bases amounts to a breathtaking reversal of the Philippines' basic strategy and policy." Cuneo wrote: "Clearly, the dominoes in Asia are beginning to wobble . . . the Philippines may have been lost by the Senate Foreign Relations Committee in Washington."[235]

The election was not a repudiation of the Vietnam War. A *U.S. News & World Report* article about a poll conducted by the magazine about expectations for the new president made it clear that Americans wanted the president to end the war in Vietnam, but they did not want "abject surrender." Rather, they wanted a peace that achieved the goal of containing communism in Southeast Asia. One respondent was quoted as saying: "I want Nixon to settle the war, but I want an honorable peace." Another respondent wanted an escalation of the war: "Nixon will be tougher in prosecuting the war, and will listen more to the advice of military leaders." Another said, "Nixon will go into Vietnam and win this war as quickly as possible with all the military force needed." A respondent from Houston said, "I hope the war gets top priority. I want to see it get headed toward a logical conclusion. People just want to see an end in sight." Another hoped, "Nixon might get tougher with Saigon."[236] According to *U.S. News & World Report*, America had voted for a more aggressive strategy to compel the north to end the war.

The Nixon administration-in-waiting understood that President Johnson's loss of credibility had been his undoing, and moved to shore up Nixon's credibility before he took office. From the very earliest interviews with reporters, members of the incoming administration emphasized that they would be transparent and honest with the American people. In an interview on the *NBC Evening News*, incoming press secretary Herb Klein claimed that he was part of a "major effort by the President-elect to present to the American people all of the facts possible." Klein added that this was part of the president-elect's pledge to bring "truth in government." He added (perhaps ironically, in retrospect), "Truth will become the hallmark of the

Nixon administration. . . . I'm charged directly by the President to emphasize to every department of government that more facts should be made available." Klein assured the American people, "We'll be able to eliminate any kind of possibility of a credibility gap in this administration."[237]

The American people had, by a narrow margin, elected Richard Nixon to bring an "honorable end" to the war, which they understood to mean ending U.S. military intervention in Vietnam in a way that preserved the goal of containing communism in Southeast Asia. Immediately after the election, the American people did not give the president-elect a clear policy prescription for how to achieve that goal.[238] However, as the inauguration approached, a popular consensus on the desired course for the war in Vietnam began to emerge. In a Gallup poll in December 1968, by a narrow margin, Americans agreed that the United States "should continue to supply military supplies to South Vietnam but that we should let them take over the fighting and make all the decisions about peace and dealings with the Vietcong."[239] A few weeks later, 64 percent of Americans who had an opinion agreed that "the time has come to begin to reduce month by month the number of U.S. soldiers in Vietnam."[240] This policy prescription—arming and incrementally handing the war over to the Army of the Republic of Vietnam while gradually reducing the number of U.S. troops in the country—would become the heart of Richard Nixon's policy in Vietnam after his inauguration. He would call it "Vietnamization."

On the eve of the inauguration of President-elect Richard Nixon, President Johnson delivered his final State of the Union Address. In addressing the future of the Cold War, the president once more in this final public address stubbornly justified his war in Vietnam using the ideology of military containment. At the end of the bloodiest year in the Vietnam War, he said that peace was closer than it had ever been since "North Vietnam began its invasion with its regular forces more than 4 years ago." He also said that the United States had proved "that America cares about [South Vietnam's] freedom, and it also cares about America's own vital interests in Asia and throughout the Pacific." Likewise, the North Vietnamese now knew "that they cannot achieve their aggressive purposes by force." As the president closed, he begrudgingly thanked Senate Majority Leader Mike Mansfield and Senator Richard B. Russell. He said he also appreciated "the most generous cooperation from the leaders of the Republican party in the Congress of the United States, Senator Dirksen and Congressman Gerald Ford, the Minority Leader."[241] He did not thank his own party or his once close friend Senator J. William Fulbright.

In late summer 1967, two Associated Press reporters questioned the administration's account of the Gulf of Tonkin incident just as administration officials were making their boldest predictions yet about success in Vietnam. Soon after, in an effort to weaken the administration's insurance policy against congressional dissent—the Tonkin Gulf Resolution—the Senate Foreign Relations Committee made the fateful decision to hold hearings in 1968 not on the administration's use of the containment of communism to justify the Vietnam War but on the facts of the Gulf of Tonkin incident. These hearings would occur just as the Vietnamese Communists' 1968 Tet Offensive called into question the credibility of the administration's optimistic predictions from summer and fall 1967.

As a result of these dramatic events, attacks on the administration's use of military containment of communism to justify the war, along with attacks on the broader ideology of containment, became much less frequent. Instead, opponents of the war increasingly attacked the president's and the administration's credibility. At first, these attacks centered on the facts of the Gulf of Tonkin incident and abuse of the Tonkin Gulf Resolution. However, criticism quickly spread to attacks on the administration's credibility about virtually every facet of the war. The president's credibility collapsed and he was forced to end the escalation of the war and withdraw from the presidential race.

In 1964, the administration had used the Gulf of Tonkin incident as political impetus to gain passage of its insurance policy against congressional dissent—the Tonkin Gulf Resolution. At the time, Congress saw the Gulf of Tonkin incident as evidence of the failure of the modest U.S. intervention in Vietnam to date to deter northern aggression; they saw the Tonkin Gulf Resolution—much like the

Formosa Resolution or the Middle East Resolution—as an escalation in and of itself, designed to deter further aggression by North Vietnam, Communist China, and the Soviet Union. The American people saw the Gulf of Tonkin incident as a proof of the lessons of Munich that aggression breeds more aggression; in that context, both retaliatory air strikes and the Tonkin Gulf Resolution were evidence that the Johnson administration had learned the lessons of Munich and was standing up to communist aggression.

By 1968, both the Gulf of Tonkin incident and the Tonkin Gulf Resolution had taken on a completely different character. For the president, the Tonkin Gulf Resolution remained the administration's insurance policy against congressional dissent. Whatever members of Congress might claim they had understood the resolution to mean or understood the president's intentions to be, the text of the Resolution was clear; it endorsed the president's decision to use whatever military means he desired to stop communist aggression in Southeast Asia. However, the Gulf of Tonkin incident was the chink in this otherwise impenetrable armor against congressional dissent. In its haste to gain passage of the Tonkin Gulf Resolution, the administration had overlooked many inconsistencies in the reports from the night of August 4, 1964. Moreover, the administration had deliberately deceived the Congress as to many important facts about that night. And, of course, the president and the administration had lied to Congress and the American people about their intent for the resolution, telling them that they had no intention of escalating the war.

For the Congress, the Gulf of Tonkin incident was incontrovertible evidence that the administration had lied to obtain the Tonkin Gulf Resolution, which had protected the president from congressional dissent for over three years. Congressional opponents of the war used the administration's deceptions surrounding the Gulf of Tonkin incident to undermine the power of this resolution over Congress. In the process, they devastated the president's credibility with the American people.

For the American public, revelations about the Gulf of Tonkin incident were just one more dramatic proof of the administration's deceptiveness. In late 1966, the media began to increasingly call into question the administration's credibility on a host of issues from civilian casualties caused by bombing the north to the administration's true willingness to negotiate with North Vietnam to end the war. Next, the Tet Offensive called into question all of the administration's optimistic claims from summer and fall 1967 about progress in the war. In this context, the revelations from the 1968 Fulbright hearings were simply the final straw. With his credibility in shambles, the president was ultimately forced to the end of the escalation of the war and withdraw from the presidential race.

For opponents of the war beyond the Senate Foreign Relations Committee, the aftermath of the 1968 Fulbright hearings was dramatic proof of the effectiveness of attacks on the administration's credibility. As a result, attacks on the administration's credibility rapidly expanded to virtually every facet of the war, quickly overwhelming the increasingly rare attacks on the administration's use of containment to justify the war—attacks that for three years had failed to turn Americans against the administration or its policies in Vietnam.

In fact, after the 1968 Fulbright hearings only two significant groups continued to attack the ideology of containment or its application to the Vietnam War. The first, most visible group was radical protesters. In demonstrations—most significantly the demonstrations outside the Democratic National Convention in Chicago—radicals decried America's imperialism and its corrosive effect on oppressed peoples abroad and at home. The second significant group was antiwar candidates in the 1968 elections, attacking the application of containment to the war in Vietnam. Most visibly, Senators Eugene McCarthy and Robert Kennedy both advocated abandoning the goal of containment in Southeast Asia in order to end the war.

Throughout this transformation of opposition to the war, the president, the administration, and other war supporters in Congress and the media continued to use the containment of communism to justify U.S. military intervention in Vietnam. The American public agreed with the goal of containment of communism and agreed that containment required continued U.S. military intervention in

Vietnam. Moreover, they roundly rejected those critics—primarily radical dissenters and antiwar political candidates—who continued to attack these justifications or the broader ideology of containment.

Former Vice President Richard Nixon won the presidential election by identifying himself with the Cold War consensus and the ideology of containment. He also won the election by joining the American people in rejecting radical protesters who attacked the ideology of containment. He succeeded in convincing a narrow majority of voters to trust him to bring the war to an "honorable end," which most in the public and the press understood as an end to the war that preserved the goal of containing communism in Southeast Asia.

The year 1968 marked the final death of the foreign policy revolution. This foreign policy revolution began in 1965 and had been led by a coterie of dissenters—including members of Congress, academics, and radical protesters—who not only opposed the war, but sought to move the United States beyond a foreign policy based on the ideology of military containment of communism. Senator J. William Fulbright had abandoned the goal of changing American foreign policy the previous year and instead decided to focus on the narrower objective of ending the war; he abandoned attacks on the ideology of containment and its application to Vietnam in favor of attacks on the president's credibility. Radical protesters did not give up their revolution until, in the aftermath of the 1968 Democratic National Convention, they realized that they had failed to convince the American public to abandon the ideology of containment. While congressional revolutionaries would continue to try to impose limits on presidential power in foreign policy and a tiny minority of radical protesters would drift toward militant opposition to America itself, attempts to turn the American public away from the Cold War consensus largely ceased after 1968.

The new framework for the debate over the Vietnam War established in 1968—between supporters using the ideology of containment to justify continued military intervention in Vietnam and opponents attacking administration credibility—would remain the framework for the debate through the end of the war. President

Richard Nixon used troop withdrawals to counter attacks on his credibility, but the invasion of Cambodia, the disastrous invasion of Laos, the results of the My Lai massacre trial, massive demonstrations led by Vietnam veterans, and the release of the Pentagon Papers would severely weaken Nixon's credibility and ultimately force him to end the Vietnam War.

Chapter 5

ENDING AMERICA'S VIETNAM WAR

From his inauguration until the end of the war, President Richard Nixon and his supporters used the containment of communism to justify continuing the war in Vietnam to what the president called an "honorable end." On the other hand, by the time President Nixon took office, attacks on the use of the ideology of military containment of communism to justify the Vietnam War and on the broader foreign policy paradigm of military containment had virtually disappeared. In fact, only a dwindling number of radical protesters used these arguments. Instead, antiwar arguments had largely narrowed to themes surrounding presidential deceptiveness in the initiation, conduct, and resolution of the war. Initially, opponents of the war were unable to undermine the president's credibility on the war. However, after the Cambodian Incursion in 1970 and a series of blows to the president's credibility in 1971—including the weak performance of South Vietnamese forces during the Laos Incursion, the My Lai trial verdict, protests by the Vietnam Veterans Against the War, and the release of the Pentagon Papers—attacks by opponents of the war on the president's credibility became increasingly effective.

To sustain his credibility with the majority of the American people through this period, the president used the announcements of troop withdrawals from Vietnam—which most Americans perceived as the president's making good on his promise to end the war—to bolster his credibility. These troop withdrawals bought the president the time he needed to try to negotiate a more favorable end to the war. However, Nixon could not employ this tactic indefinitely; there were a finite number of troops in Vietnam to be withdrawn. Ultimately, Nixon ran out of troops to withdraw and was forced to accept a humiliating compromise peace that left North Vietnamese troops in South Vietnam and set the stage for the ultimate destruction of that country.

As soon as President Nixon took office, the framework for public debate of the war established in 1968—between supporters using containment to justify continuing the war and opponents attacking the administration's credibility—immediately reasserted itself. Supporters of the war—including former President Johnson—argued that the war should continue until the goal of containing communism in Southeast Asia could be assured. Opponents of the war struggled to find ways to effectively attack the president's credibility, but their main charge was the president's failure to make good on his campaign pledge to end the war. To neutralize this attack, the Nixon administration began to withdraw U.S. troops from Vietnam. In essence, the president "bought" credibility with the American people by withdrawing troops—a tactic Nixon would use repeatedly through the remainder of the war.

When President Richard Nixon took office in January 1969, over a half-million Americans were fighting in Vietnam and dying at a rate of over a thousand per month.[1] Nixon was elected on the promise of "peace with honor." His new strategy to achieve this goal was "Vietnamization": gradually drawing down American forces while handing off the war to South Vietnamese forces.[2] For this strategy to work, however, Nixon had to keep both the North Vietnamese Army and the American people at bay long enough to arm and train the Army of the Republic of Vietnam (ARVN) to stand alone.

The American public in January 1969 was ambivalent about the war. Fifty-six percent of those Americans who had an opinion believed "the U.S. made a mistake sending troops to fight in Vietnam."[3] But most Americans were prepared to give the new president time to see his strategy through to completion in order to protect America's supposed gains in South Vietnam.

Just as during the Johnson presidency, after the inauguration supporters of the war used the containment of communism to justify continuing the war in Vietnam. A diagram from the Associated Press

The domino theory.

Source: Associated Press, *The Gettysburg Times*, January 25, 1969.[4]

from just after the inauguration provided an intuitive illustration of the domino theory.

The illustration was of a booted foot marked with the hammer and sickle of the Communist Party kicking over domino-shaped tiles marked with the names and outlines of the countries of Southeast Asia, beginning with Vietnam. The text in the diagram stated matter-of-factly, "If Communism triumphs in one Asian country, the others will fall one by one."[5]

The Associated Press story that accompanied this picture conceded that "the domino theory of a possible communist takeover in Asia may be dead in official Washington" but insisted that it was still alive and well in Southeast Asian capitals and among many western diplomats. The story quoted one British diplomat as saying, "The name of the game is still dominoes." The article also argued that SEATO had been founded by the United States "to prevent the dominoes from falling." The article added, "Diplomats from several Asian countries said they feared the eventual U.S. withdrawal from Vietnam would signal a general disengagement in the region." The AP article concluded by noting that diplomats believed the countries of Southeast Asia would fall if there was a lack of "American determination" and that this fall would include "Indonesia, the world's fifth most populous nation."[6]

Former President Lyndon Johnson remained in the debate over the Vietnam War after his departure from office, and likewise used containment to justify the war in Vietnam. In the February 1969 *Reader's Digest*, Johnson did belatedly defend himself against the attacks on his credibility that had driven him from office, writing that the credibility gap was caused not by his dishonesty but by "the gap between the intelligence information that a president deals with daily, and the public's grasp of foreign events as reported by the media." But his main purpose was to once more use containment to justify the war.[7] Recalling the lessons of Munich, Johnson wrote:

> Had [Winston Churchill] been heeded earlier, and had Britain . . . made a stand when Nazi troops moved on the Sudetenland, he would probably have been politically roasted for involvement in an obscure, faraway place—and for [putting] credence in a ridiculous "domino" theory that if the Sudetenland went, then Czechoslovakia, Poland, France—all of Europe—would not be far behind.[8]

Johnson added, "My profoundest hope is that America's resistance in Vietnam will discourage future aggressors."[9] Johnson concluded, "The penalty I paid for facing duty in Vietnam was a high one, but it was nothing compared to the penalties that would have been exacted had I not done so."[10]

Continuing the framework for debate of the war established the previous year, opponents of the war largely ignored these invocations of the ideology of containment to justify the war. Instead, opponents in the media began to look for ways to attack the new president's credibility. Eric Sevareid of CBS expected the new administration to "fall into the same trap of its own making as did the Johnson regime." He predicted that the administration would "lose its credibility with the people . . . on Vietnam . . . by evasions and misleading promises."[11]

Congressional dissenters, who had been so successful in undermining the Johnson administration by attacking its credibility in 1968, immediately began to look for similar ways to undermine the Nixon administration's credibility after Nixon took office. Their first target was the Pentagon's plan for anti–ballistic missile defense. In hearings on the Pentagon plan, the Senate Foreign Relations Committee raised the possibility of a Nixon credibility gap. Senator Fulbright claimed in these hearings that the administration had tried to "pull the wool over" the Committee's eyes over the cost of an ABM system. Reporter Marvin Kalb concluded that the Committee had been "turned on by suspicions of a new credibility gap" and was "now thinking of investigating Pentagon subsidizing of universities."[12]

Television reporter Eric Sevareid was waiting on the other side of the antiballistic missile debacle to claim prescience—and tie these attacks on the administration's credibility to the issue of Vietnam. Sevareid said the administration's supposedly growing credibility problems were a direct result of Vietnam: "On the matter of withdrawing some American troops from the Vietnam this year, the waters are . . . muddled." While Nixon would not commit to any withdrawals, Sevareid said, "It was his own people who had inspired the stories about a firm decision to make some withdrawals." Sevareid believed that this might have been "a ploy to quiet public opinion and thus buy time." If this was the case, Sevareid added, "It's a dangerous game." He warned, "If public hopes are built up and later events knock them down, from such small cracks in complete candor do credibility gaps develop."[13]

As the months of the Nixon presidency failed to produce discernible moves toward peace, Congress began to follow the press' lead and attack the president's credibility on ending the war. Republican Senator George D. Aiken of Vermont, senior Republican on the Senate Foreign Relations Committee, took to the floor of the Senate to demand that the administration begin the withdrawal of U.S. forces from Vietnam, saying, "We have now accomplished our purpose as far as South

Vietnam is concerned." Senator Aiken complained, "The hundred days are up" and it was time for the administration to declare its intentions. Senate majority leader Mike Mansfield and assistant Democratic leader Edward Kennedy endorsed this call, as did Republican Senators Jacob K. Javits of New York and Charles H. Percy of Illinois.[14]

War opponents in the media echoed these attacks on the administration's credibility on withdrawals. For instance, I.F. Stone compared the Nixon administration's failure to begin troop withdrawals to President Johnson's Johns Hopkins speech in April 1965. He said, "Johnson deluded many people into believing that he was moving toward peace at the very moment he was committing the first U.S. combat troops to the South." Nixon was doing the same, Stone contended, by promising negotiations and withdrawals while doing neither.[15]

It is through this formulation created by Congress and echoed by the media that troop withdrawals became inextricably linked with the president's credibility. And through this same formulation, troop withdrawals became the currency of credibility that President Nixon could use to purchase approval for his policies in Vietnam. But, while this formulation may have been a creation of opponents of the war, it had its foundations in the American public's impatience. In March 1969, for the first time, a majority of Americans were ready to end the war. Forty-two percent of Americans who had an opinion either wanted to continue the war or step up U.S. efforts—either with or without continued negotiations. By contrast, 57 percent of Americans either wanted to leave immediately, slowly draw down forces, or negotiate a settlement without regard to the "honorable peace" Nixon had promised.[16]

It is entirely possible that President Nixon had decided not to withdraw troops from Vietnam yet because he seemed to have an extraordinarily deep reservoir of credibility from the time he took office. In fact, at the end of May, before the president had made any discernible moves to end the war, approval of his handling of Vietnam was still on the rise. For the first time in his presidency, a majority of Americans (52 percent) approved of Nixon's handling of the war, while only 25 percent disapproved.[17] This was an uptick of eight percentage points in approval from April,[18] and it came despite the fact that in early May 1969, the *New York Times* broke the story that President Nixon had begun secret bombing of North Vietnamese logistics bases inside Cambodia—Operation MENU—without telling Congress or the American people.[19] However, Americans were giving Nixon a clear policy prescription. When asked if "the time has come to begin to reduce month by month the number of U.S. Soldiers in Vietnam," 70 percent of Americans who had an opinion said "yes."[20]

While supporters continued to use containment to justify the Vietnam War after the inauguration, President Nixon and his administration were initially reluctant to echo this rhetoric. And this reluctance drew some frustrated criticism from the war's supporters in the media. Conservative columnist William F. Buckley lamented:

> It has been a while since we heard from Mr. Nixon his views on the justification of the American effort in Vietnam. In the past he has stoutly maintained . . . that we are there necessarily, that the alternatives to fighting there are infinitely worse by any calculation. Now does Mr. Nixon still believe that?[21]

Buckley believed it was important for the president to declare his sentiments because, "if . . . Mr. Nixon no longer believes in the Domino Theory . . . then he is presumably prepared to make concessions which he would not otherwise be prepared to make." If, on the other hand, Buckley wrote, the president still believed that containment of Communism required continuing the war, "he should tell us that too." Buckley added, "Patience is easier to come by if we believe that the war is necessary and just." With U.S. troops dying "at the rate . . . 50 per day," Buckley wrote, "that is an appalling sum to pay unless the vital interests of the Republic are at stake." Buckley did acknowledge that president had asserted containment as a justification before the election, but concluded, "Wars require continual reaffirmation."[22]

One could argue that President Nixon had not yet endorsed the ideology of containment because his conception of containment differed from that of his predecessors. Historian John Lewis Gaddis, for instance, argues that Nixon saw containment not as a military strategy but as a diplomatic strategy and détente with the Soviet Union and China as an instrument to achieve the goals of that strategy.[23] But, throughout his presidency, Nixon never made any significant move (outside of Southeast Asia) to dismantle the bulwark of military containment. And he would repeatedly argue that Vietnam must be fought to an "honorable end" to protect the credibility of America's commitment to military containment around the world.

On June 8, 1969, after meeting with South Vietnamese President Thieu at Midway Island, the president finally appeased his supporters with a joint statement that made at least half-hearted use of the ideology of containment to defend the war in Vietnam. The statement said that the war was necessary to protect "self-determination for the people of South Vietnam." According to the statement, Nixon and Thieu agreed, "The form of government under which the people of South Vietnam will live should be decided by the people themselves." The two presidents rejected "any attempt to impose upon the Republic of Vietnam any system or program or any particular form of government." The war in Vietnam, according to this statement, was an effort to help South Vietnam "maintain its freedom."[24] Admittedly, this statement lacked many of the strident claims that other supporters of the war continued to make, including invocations of the domino theory or the lessons of Munich or charges of North Vietnamese, Communist Chinese, and Soviet complicity in the conflict.

Moreover, this statement was overshadowed by a speech the previous day in which the president finally announced the withdrawal of twenty-five thousand troops from Vietnam.[25] The president painted this move as a sign of the success of his strategy of Vietnamization. At least publicly, President Thieu supported this explanation. He told reporters at Midway that the move should not be called "withdrawal" but rather "replacement."[26]

However, this announcement of troop withdrawals was greeted with impatience by the American people. Forty-seven percent of Americans who had an opinion signaled that they wanted the withdrawal to proceed at a faster pace while 34 percent wanted the withdrawal to continue at its present pace (despite the fact that Nixon had made no promises about further withdrawals after the first twenty-five thousand troops departed). However, most Americans did not want a precipitous withdrawal from Vietnam. When asked if the United States "should withdraw all [its] troops from Vietnam immediately," 68 percent opposed such a move.[27]

This public reaction to troop withdrawals in mid-1969 illustrates the complexity of the formulation the press had created by tying the president's credibility to troop withdrawals. In September 1969, in a memorandum to the president, National Security Advisor Henry Kissinger would worry that troop withdrawals might rapidly become "like salted peanuts. . . . The more U.S. troops come home, the more will be demanded."[28] The president would repeatedly be challenged to withdraw a sufficient number of troops to bolster public confidence in his credibility without creating an inexorable momentum (by withdrawing too many troops) or irresistible demand (by withdrawing too few troops) for total withdrawal before he could achieve his desired concessions at the conference table to preserve the goal of containment in Southeast Asia.

On this occasion, it appears that Nixon may have withdrawn too few troops. The president's announcement had little impact on approval of Nixon's policies in Vietnam. After the announcement, 54 percent of Americans approved of the president's handling of Vietnam, while 30 percent disapproved. Yet after the withdrawal, Americans were much less eager to continue the war. When asked what the United States should do next in Vietnam, only 20 percent of Americans who had an opinion expressed that they wanted to continue the war to an "honorable end" either by maintaining the present level or escalating the use of force. The remaining 80 percent expressed that they wanted to end the war with no mention of an "honorable peace," with the largest percentage (40 percent) wanting to "stop fighting" and "get out as soon as we can."[29]

With the lackluster response to the president's announcement of troop withdrawals, congressional dissenters intensified their attacks on the president's credibility. Democratic Senator Stuart Symington of Missouri—a member of the Senate Foreign Relations Committee— spearheaded an effort to call attention to U.S. combat operations that had been ongoing for years in Laos. After a September 1969 *Time* magazine article revealed that the Senate Foreign Relations Committee and Senate Armed Services Committee would take up hearings "to determine whether American armed forces were already committed to combat in Laos," Stuart Symington took to the floor to remind his colleagues that a month earlier, in August 1969, he had said on the floor, "We have been at war in Laos for years and it is time the American people knew more of the facts." Symington said there would be hearings in the new Subcommittee on Security Agreements and Commitments Abroad that would "seek to put on the record as much detail as possible on our involvement in that country, along with the political/military agreements, understandings and commitments that have fanned the policy basis for that involvement." This effort was clearly an attack on the administration's credibility. Symington concluded, "For too long we have permitted our activities abroad to be carried on behind a cloak of secrecy." He added, "And often that secrecy veils such activities from the people in this country and their elected officials—not from the enemy."[30]

In September 1969, as these new attacks on his credibility were taking shape in the Congress, President Nixon announced that he would withdraw an additional thirty-five thousand soldiers from Vietnam before Christmas, presumably to shore up his credibility with the American people. In this same speech, Nixon also recapped his "major efforts" to bring an end to the war and said, "The time for meaningful negotiations has . . . arrived." He added that he was offering a withdrawal of all U.S. and allied forces over a twelve-month period in exchange for a mutual withdrawal of North Vietnamese troops.[31]

This announcement did not completely blunt the negative effect of the new congressional attacks on the president's credibility. Before the announcement of troop withdrawals, 54 percent of Americans approved of his policies in Vietnam, while 27 percent disapproved.[32]

After the announcement, only 53 percent approved of his handling of the war, while 31 percent disapproved.[33] There is some evidence that this slip may have also been a result of sentiments that Nixon was not withdrawing fast enough. When asked two weeks after the announcement about the pace of withdrawals, a narrow majority of Americans who had an opinion (51 percent) wanted the president to withdraw troops "faster," while 37 percent wanted him to continue the withdrawal at the present rate. When asked if the Senate should pass "legislation to require the withdrawal of all United States troops from Vietnam by the end of next year," nearly two thirds of Americans who had an opinion said the Senate should pass such a bill.[34] And, by the end of October, when asked whether they would describe themselves as a "'hawk' or as a 'dove'" when hawks were defined as those who "want to step up our military effort in Vietnam" and "Doves" were defined as those who "want to reduce our military effort in Vietnam," nearly two thirds of Americans who had an opinion described themselves as "doves."[35] Americans were ready to end the Vietnam War.

The antiwar movement responded to the president's announcement of more troop withdrawals less than two weeks later with a march it called the "Moratorium." The Moratorium, unlike previous radical protests, received significant support from establishment political figures. Still, like earlier demonstrations against the use of containment to justify the war, the Moratorium drew the ire of the press and the American public. President Nixon responded to these protests by finally giving his full-throated support to the application of the ideology of containment to the war in Vietnam in what has since become known as the "silent majority" speech. The Nixon administration's supporters responded to these protests by staging a week of prowar demonstrations over the Veterans Day holiday called "National Unity Week" that echoed the administration's use of containment to justify continuing the war. The American public responded to this entire episode with increased approval of the administration's policies in Vietnam. The radical protester movement emerged from this episode even more radicalized; many radicals abandoned the strategy of demonstrations against the ideology of containment, either embracing other causes or abandoning politics altogether, while a few turned to explicit support of communism and a tiny fraction of those embraced a new strategy of militant insurgency against America itself.

The Moratorium was, by any measure, a massive protest against the Vietnam War. Demonstrations were held across the United States, but the most visible protest was in Washington. On October 14, 1969, thousands of protesters marched by candlelight the four miles from Arlington National Cemetery to the National Mall. The same night, police clashed with smaller groups that tried to march on the South Vietnamese embassy. On October 15, the nation's capital saw the largest crowd of protesters it had ever drawn; by noon, 325,000 or more demonstrators filled over forty-one acres of the National Mall.[36]

The Moratorium itself, unlike previous radical protests, received significant support from establishment figures. In October 1969, over 108 congressional dissenters endorsed a resolution of support for both the October 15 Moratorium Against the War and increased troop withdrawals. Republican Representative Paul Findley of Illinois, speaking about this resolution, said, "President Nixon should be supported in the determination that he himself has expressed, under which all remaining ground combat forces will be withdrawn from Vietnam at the earliest practical date."[37] In another show of support for the Moratorium, congressional staffers staged a forty-five-minute silent protest on the East Front of the Capitol.[38]

Many political leaders supported the demonstrations by appearing at locations across the country. Senator George McGovern appeared at a demonstration at the Boston Common that reporter Morton Dean said was "the largest Vietnam peace demonstration ever seen in Massachusetts." At this protests, McGovern defended protesters against charges that they aided the enemy with their dissent by claiming (in Dean's words) that "the Moratorium demonstrates the highest patriotism."[39] Speaking at Moratorium demonstrations in New York, Mayor John Lindsay used the opportunity to attack the president's credibility, saying the protesters were "saying no to illusions and fantasies. They are saying yes to reality. And they are saying yes to peace."[40] At the demonstration in Washington, DC, former Senator Ernest

Gruening echoed the radical protesters' attacks on the use of containment to justify the war. He said that the war was "precisely the wrong course" to "stop Chinese expansion into Southeast Asia."[41] Instead, he said (in an excerpt shown on the *CBS Evening News*):

> We should, instead, have supported Ho Chi Minh, a Moscow trained Communist, but pre-eminently a nationalist, who embodied the Vietnamese' fear and dislike of the Chinese, and under who's leadership, the Vietnamese would have resisted Chinese expansion, had it been threatened, which is by no means certain.[42]

Despite this establishment support, press coverage of the protests was generally negative. CBS coverage of the Moratorium showed throngs of radical youth in New York screaming, "ONE, TWO, THREE, FOUR! I DON'T WANNA GO TO WAR!" This only served to reinforce perceptions created by President Johnson the previous year that radical demonstrators were protesting because of cowardice—perceptions that would have been anathema to older Americans, many of whom served in World War II.[43] The protests were also marred by agitators who vandalized military sites such as Fort Benning, Georgia. Inside Fort Benning, CBS showed an interview with a U.S. Army captain, an instructor at the Airborne School. The captain said, "Dissent and demonstration in a democratic society, if it's constructive and positive, is a good thing." However, he added, "I don't have any sympathy with professional agitators who are violence merchants." The story then cut to scenes of Savannah, Georgia, which, the reporter said, had "given up 71 of its sons in the Vietnam war." The streets were lined with American flags "in opposition to the Moratorium." In an interview, Savannah Mayor J. Curtis Lewis called the Moratorium "ill-advised and perhaps unpatriotic in many respects." When asked how the protests were unpatriotic, he added, "Our President is attempting to negotiate an honorable peace and I think it brings aid and comfort to the enemy." He added that participating in the protests was "tantamount to treason." In a separate segment, reporter Bill Stout said that Stanford students were "denounced as hippy freaks" when they tried to take "their Moratorium message aboard a morning commuter train." Another story showed a Chicago policemen confronting long-haired radical protesters saying, to the cheers of bystanders, "If you don't like the country, don't want to serve, move out of it!" The story also showed clean-cut young people in business attire protesting against the Moratorium in Indianapolis and Des Moines.[44]

President Nixon responded to the Moratorium on November 3, 1969, in a televised speech.[45] The speech was a broadside against radical dissenters. He noted that protesters in San Francisco had carried signs saying, "Lose in Vietnam, bring the boys home." He insisted that he, too, wanted to end the war. However, in Nixon's first invocation of the lessons of Munich since taking office, he told these radicals that he wanted to end the war in "a way which will increase the chance that their younger brothers and their sons will not have to fight in some future Vietnam someplace in the world." Nixon said he "would be untrue to [his] oath of office" if he allowed "the policy of this nation to be dictated by the minority . . . who attempt to impose" their views "on the nation by mounting demonstrations in the street." Instead of bowing to this "vocal minority" he appealed to "the great silent majority" of Americans for support.[46]

The "silent majority" speech was not just an attack on radical demonstrators. It was also a defense of Nixon's credibility. The president claimed:

> One of the reasons for the deep divisions in this nation about Vietnam is that many Americans have lost confidence in what their government has told them about our policy. The American people cannot and should not be asked to support a policy which involves the overriding issues of war and peace unless they know the truth about that policy.[47]

While the previous administration had lied to Americans, Nixon claimed, he would level with them. Nixon clearly understood that his credibility was tied to ending the war. Thus, Nixon reminded

Americans that bombing had been reduced 20 percent, the South Vietnamese were taking more responsibility for their own defense, U.S. casualties were down to their lowest point in three years, enemy infiltration was down 80 percent, and most importantly "by December 15, over 60,000 men will have been withdrawn from South Vietnam—including 20 percent of all of our combat troops."[48] In defending himself against the charge that he was not withdrawing troops fast enough—an attack on his credibility on ending the war—Nixon said that "the rate of withdrawal will depend on developments" in negotiations, enemy activity, and "the training program of the South Vietnamese forces." President Nixon also used the "silent majority" speech to tie his policy of Vietnamization to a broader strategy he called the "Nixon Doctrine" of helping nations defend themselves rather than using direct military intervention.[49]

This speech was also Nixon's most impassioned defense since taking office of the war in Vietnam as necessary to contain communism. Nixon said that, when he took office, "there were some who urged I end the war at once by ordering the immediate withdrawal of all American forces." He claimed that he had rejected what "would have been a popular and easy course to follow," instead, thinking "of the effect . . . on the next generation and the future of peace and freedom in America and the world." Nixon insisted that the "fundamental issue" of the war was that "North Vietnam, with the logistical support of Communist China and the Soviet Union, had launched a campaign to impose a Communist government on South Vietnam."[50]

Nixon provided an interesting variation on Lyndon Johnson's argument that he was continuing his predecessors' policies—beginning with President Eisenhower—in defending South Vietnam. Nixon cited the many statements by Kennedy and Eisenhower about the importance of South Vietnam and Southeast Asia to U.S. security. However, whereas Lyndon Johnson had completely embraced the policy of his predecessors, Nixon was subtly critical of Johnson. Nixon acknowledged that many said "President Johnson's decision to send American combat forces to South Vietnam was wrong." Nixon added that he himself had been "strongly critical of the way the war has been conducted." Yet

Nixon said that the question "facing us today is now that we are in the war, [what's] the best way to end it?"[51] This was an interesting rhetorical device that absolved Nixon of responsibility for a war that he had enthusiastically and repeatedly endorsed before he became president.

Regardless of his predecessor's policies, President Nixon argued that the war had to be continued until the goal of containing communism in Southeast Asia was assured. Nixon claimed that a "precipitate withdrawal from Vietnam would be a disaster not only for South Vietnam but for the United States and for the cause of peace" since tens of thousands of South Vietnamese anticommunists would be slaughtered and "this first defeat in our nation's history would result in a collapse of confidence in American leadership, not only in Asia but throughout the world" by calling into question the value of U.S. commitments to other allies. Nixon insisted that his pledge for an "honorable peace" had been a pledge "to end the war in a way that we could win the peace."[52] While opponents of the war might disagree with this assertion, this was how Nixon's pledge to continue the war to an "honorable peace" had been understood by the press and the American public before the 1968 presidential election.

The "silent majority" speech succeeded in sating the public's appetite for faster troop withdrawals. After the silent majority speech, nearly two thirds of Americans who had an opinion were "satisfied . . . with the rate at which the United States is withdrawing its troops from Vietnam," despite the absence of any new announcements of withdrawals. Moreover, when asked if they supported the call by "some United States senators" for the United States to "withdraw all our troops from Vietnam immediately," 76 percent of Americans who had an opinion opposed such a move.[53] Most Americans did still want President Nixon to end the war, but after the "silent majority" speech, they were willing to give him more time to obtain a settlement that preserved the goal of containing communism in Southeast Asia.

In the aftermath of Nixon's "silent majority" speech, the pro-war faction moved to exploit this success. In an effort called "National Unity Week," which ran from November 9 to 16, 1969, and strategically included Veterans Day, the president, the administration, and their supporters launched a coordinated attack on dissenters and defense of the necessity of the war to contain communism. In a televised visit with wounded veterans at a government hospital in Virginia on Veterans Day, President Nixon was greeted by a wounded major who said, "I'm definitely against all this Moratorium business. These people ought to be packed up and sent to Vietnam." The comment elicited a smile from the president. In a separate National Unity Week event at the Grand Ole Opry, Texas Republican Senator John Tower insisted, "We have a commitment in Southeast Asia." He claimed that radical dissenters wanted the United States to "unilaterally withdraw" and "accept a camouflaged surrender." Tower concluded that such a move would "destroy the credibility of the United States as the leader of the free world." Retired General Omar Bradley, at a separate speech in Los Angeles, told an audience, "We must leave Vietnam only with honor."[54]

As with previous protests, the Moratorium—and the pro-war response, the "silent majority" speech and National Unity Week—increased public support for the president's policies in Vietnam. Before this episode, 58 percent of Americans had approved of the president's handling of the Vietnam War, while 33 percent disapproved.[55] After the Moratorium and the "silent majority" speech (but during National Unity Week), 65 percent of Americans approved of the president's handling of the war while only 25 percent disapproved—a shift of over seven percentage points in favor of the president.[56]

However, this "bump" in public support was short lived. Immediately after the "silent majority" speech, Nixon's job approval rating jumped to 68 percent, a jump of five points from March 1969.[57] By December, however, that "bump" had evaporated. Nixon's approval rating at the end of 1969, 61 percent, was virtually unchanged from the beginning of the year.[58] Nixon and his antiwar opponents had fought each other to a stalemate.

While Americans' opinion of the president remained positive but largely unchanged over 1969, the majority of Americans disapproved of the Moratorium and radical protesters, despite the significant support from establishment politicians. After the Moratorium and the

President's National Unity Week response, 65 percent of Americans who had an opinion opposed the radical demonstrations. The reactions of these Americans ranged from those who believed the protests were "a waste of time" to those who believed Americans should "support our men, our country, [and] our President," to those who believed the protests were either "Communist-backed" or "encouraging the Communists" to keep fighting.[59] Admittedly, as bad as these reactions were, they were less negative than reactions to previous protests staged by radical demonstrators.

But this slight drop in disapproval of radical dissent was not enough to rescue the radical protest movement from demise. In scale, establishment support, and public acceptance, the Moratorium was the most successful radical demonstration yet launched against the war. But behind the scenes, the radical wing of the foreign policy revolution was actually in the midst of disintegration. Beginning with the October 1967 Mobilization and culminating in the protests at the Democratic National Convention in Chicago in August 1968, many radicals concluded that American society was beyond saving. Some of these radicals drifted toward explicit embrace of communism. A tiny minority concluded that America could only be changed through violent revolution. In the process, these new communist dissenters destroyed the organizational structure that had held the radical antiwar movement together.

The Students for a Democratic Society organization, once the flagship of student radicalism in America, was crippled by demoralization after the Democratic National Convention. In the aftermath of the demonstrations in Chicago, the organization was coopted in what was essentially a bloodless coup by the Progressive Labor Party. At first, the party was simply another faction within the SDS framework. But the Progressive Labor Party slowly moved into a leadership role, coopted the more moderate founding principles of the SDS and replaced them with hard-line Marxist ideology, and expelled those more moderate leftists who did not agree.[60] Those radicals who departed in this exodus suddenly found themselves without an organization to coordinate their dissent against the war; this disaffected majority or radicals rapidly splintered into dozens of subgroups, many dedicated to issues completely unrelated to the war.[61]

A tiny minority of radicals drifted not just toward communism, but toward violent revolution against the United States. The Weatherman movement emerged from the splintering SDS believing that violent means were necessary to change American society. In the Weatherman manifesto, "You Don't Need a Weatherman to Know Which Way the Wind Blows" (the Bob Dylan lyric from which the movement took its name), the members of this new, more militant movement declared that their goal was "the destruction of US imperialism and the achievement of a classless world: world communism." They believed the mechanism for this destruction would be "the military forces of the US overextending themselves around the world and being defeated piecemeal." In this context, "struggle within the US will be a vital part of this process, but when the revolution triumphs in the US it will have been made by the people of the whole world."[62] Radical journalist Andrew Kopkind wrote that the Weatherman movement believed "opposition to US imperialism is the major international struggle today, and the 'primary contradiction' of capitalism." The movement identified itself with Third World guerillas and, as Kopkind wrote, "those of the 'internal' black colony within the US." In this construction, Kopkind wrote, "the role of white radicals is primarily (although importantly) supportive and extensive."[63]

In some respect, the Moratorium was the debut of this new violent communist insurgency. Among the about three thousand protesters who tried to storm the South Vietnamese embassy on November 14 were two hundred to three hundred instigators, members of the Weatherman movement.[64]

Some in the New Left attacked this radical move toward communism. David Horowitz tried to warn the Weatherman movement that the New Left did not just grow out of disaffection with liberalism. It also grew out of the failure of the Old Left's "old-line Marxism." He concluded, "The failure of Marxist . . . vanguard parties to build revolutionary movements in the advanced capitalist countries is an historic fact that no revolutionary can afford to ignore."[65] Carl Oglesby warned that Marxism-Leninism's "*ideology* is wrong" (emphasis is Oglesby's). This new militant communist wave overtaking the SDS, the organization of which Oglesby had once been president, was "much less in response to experience than to the pressure of the tradition." Oglesby lamented that his organization now "employed a grossly simplified base-and-superstructure model to explain away the fact that labor does not appear to think what we think it ought to think."[66]

But these warnings went unheeded. By late winter and early spring 1970, the Weatherman movement had metastasized into the Weatherman Underground. Thug violence during street protests gave way to a bombing campaign against banks and government buildings—the infrastructure of "Pig Amerika."[67] For this tiny minority of radical protesters at least, the idealism and hope of the New Left for a reformed America had transformed into hate and a determination to tear America down.

From mid-1969 to early 1970, war supporters in the media, former Johnson administration officials, and former President Johnson himself began to once more invoke the Tonkin Gulf Resolution as a weapon against congressional dissent. In response, Congress began the effort that would finally repeal the Tonkin Gulf Resolution. At the outset, there was a great deal of confusion as to exactly what effect repeal would have on the Nixon administration. Some in Congress and the media believed that repeal would force the president to end the war. Those members of Congress who had once supported the failed foreign policy revolution believed repeal would at least be a symbolic reassertion of congressional authority in foreign policymaking. After initially opposing the effort, the Nixon administration came out in support of repeal in an effort to neutralize its power as a vote against the Vietnam War. While they supported repeal, members of the administration made it clear that repeal of the Tonkin Gulf Resolution would not prevent them from continuing the war in Vietnam to an "honorable end."

After the 1968 Fulbright hearings, the Tonkin Gulf Resolution was robbed of its power as an insurance policy against congressional dissent for the Johnson administration. The hearings conclusively proved that the resolution had been obtained under false pretenses, absolving Congress of guilt for voting for it. However, after the inauguration of President Nixon, some supporters of the war began to wield the Tonkin Gulf Resolution as a weapon against Fulbright himself. For instance, after Fulbright told an audience at the National War College that the war was "immoral and disastrous," ABC News reporter Howard K. Smith, in a commentary on the *ABC Evening News*, pilloried Fulbright by reminding Americans that the senator had "led [the resolution] to passage by a vote of 88 to two." Smith also noted that the resolution "specifically told the president to take . . . 'all necessary steps, including armed force' in Vietnam." Smith quipped, "Senator Fulbright says he's changed his mind." However, Smith added that that possibility was "foreseen in the resolution" and that Congress could "void and rescind support for the war by a simple, majority vote," but that Fulbright had failed to propose that step. Smith concluded, "There are doubtless words to describe a leader who, in a time of trial, faces responsibility by looking the other way. And, no doubt, history will find those words."[68]

Perhaps in response to such attacks, the Senate Foreign Relations Committee renewed its effort to pass the National Commitments Resolution. This resolution, initially proposed in 1967 by the congressional wing of the foreign policy revolution, asserted that, per the U.S. Constitution, the president could only institute foreign policy commitments with the advice and consent of Congress. As this new resolution neared passage, ABC Reporter Howard K. Smith retooled his use of the Tonkin Gulf Resolution to attack not just Fulbright but also the National Commitments Resolution and the entire Congress. Smith claimed that the National Commitments Resolution had "a lot of anger over Vietnam pushing it." However, Smith added, "in 1964, President Johnson *did* consult Congress, and it passed the Tonkin Resolution which says bluntly, 'the United States will, as the President directs, take all steps, including armed force,' in Vietnam'" (emphasis is Smith's). Smith also noted that the Tonkin Gulf Resolution included a clause allowing the Congress to repeal it with "a simple, majority vote without Presidential veto." Smith chided the Congress that he said "clamor[ed] for a right they already have but won't use." Smith also attacked congressional dissenters directly, adding, "Their clamor undoubtedly encourages the Communists not to negotiate, and the casualties go on rising."[69]

Another factor that no doubt drove Congress to contemplate repeal of the Tonkin Gulf Resolution was an effort by some members of the former Johnson administration to rewrite history. In July 1969, Clark Clifford told historian Paige Mulhollan that Congress had been fully supportive of the administration's military intervention in Vietnam in 1964. He said that the Congress later tried to "prove to the public that they had been misled in the facts regarding the attack on some of our naval vessels in the Gulf of Tonkin and that having been misled they passed the Tonkin Resolution." However, he added, at the time the Tonkin Gulf Resolution was passed, "the support for our involvement in Viet Nam in the Executive Branch was solid and the support in the Legislative Branch was solid." Further, Clifford claimed, "It was rare to find a voice that counselled caution or advised that we not do it. The support for our involvement there was really overwhelming." It was only later, Clifford claimed, that the Congress "backtracked" on the issue.[70] Clifford made a similar claim the same month in *Foreign Affairs* magazine. He noted that as "our involvement became greater . . . so did most public and private assessments of the correctness of our course." He said that this approval of U.S. intervention in Vietnam was the reason "the Tonkin Gulf resolution was adopted by the Congress in 1964 by a vote of 504 to 2." He even cited the language of the resolution as proving the Congress approved of the president's "use of armed force . . . in defense of . . . freedom."[71]

These claims were, of course, a complete misrepresentation of the facts. It is true that members of Congress did not publicly dissent on U.S. military intervention in Vietnam before the Gulf of Tonkin incident. However, Democratic Senator Richard B. Russell of Georgia, at the time perhaps the most influential legislator in America, shared his private misgivings with President Johnson almost a month before the Gulf of Tonkin incident.[72]

Dean Rusk joined Clifford's effort to rewrite history in his own oral history in September 1969. He noted that "Paragraph II of [the Tonkin Gulf Resolution] . . . was not about the Gulf of Tonkin, but was about Southeast Asia." When asked by Mulhollan specifically about Senator Fulbright's claim that "he didn't understand it to mean what it was later said to mean,"[73] Rusk was incredulous. He said:

> I recall one Senator asked Senator Fulbright whether this resolution would encompass the dispatch of large numbers of forces to South Viet Nam. Senator Fulbright said, "Yes, the resolution would cover that."[74]

Rusk added, "Some of them later changed their minds, and . . . tried to throw some cloud upon the resolution itself. But there was no doubt about it at the time the resolution was passed." Rusk added that the Resolution had "very simple language" and said that "Senator Fulbright told me at the close of Secretary McNamara's and my testimony that this was the best resolution of this sort that he had ever seen presented to the Senate." Rusk concluded, "Perhaps we made a mistake in not calling it the Fulbright Resolution."[75]

This account of the passage of the Tonkin Gulf Resolution, too, was a lie. Rusk clearly overlooked the fact that members of Congress had been assured privately by the Johnson administration that it would not use the resolution to escalate U.S. military intervention in Vietnam.

In late 1969, in response to this resurgent—and ahistorical—use of the Tonkin Gulf Resolution to attack the Congress and Senator Fulbright in particular, the repeal effort began. The first proposal to repeal the Tonkin Gulf Resolution was drafted in October 1969, just before the Moratorium. Republican Senator Jacob Javits of New York and Democratic Senator Claiborne Pell of Rhode Island suggested that the Tonkin Gulf Resolution be repealed with an effective date at the end of 1970.[76]

From the beginning of this effort, there was a great deal of confusion in the press as to what effect repeal would actually have on the president's ability to wage the war in Vietnam. David Brinkley concluded of the Javits-Pell Resolution, "The President would no longer have any power to keep any American armed forces in Vietnam."[77] ABC Reporter Bob Clark believed the repeal would "stop all combat operations at the end of next year."[78]

In reality repeal of the Tonkin Gulf Resolution, in and of itself, would not end the war. Thus, the Javits-Pell Resolution also demanded that "all American combat troops" be withdrawn "by the end of 1970." Yet, the resolution also allowed that some forces would remain until the United States had "provide[d] asylum for those in South Vietnam whose lives would be endangered by such action," an answer to the "bloodbath" argument for continuing the war.[79]

Likewise, from the beginning, repeal was inextricably linked to doubts about the facts of the Gulf of Tonkin incident. During debate on repeal, many senators said that they doubted that the attacks of August 4, 1964, had taken place at all. Others doubted the Johnson administration's claim that the attacks had been unprovoked. Yet other senators doubted that the Tonkin Gulf Resolution gave the president authority for the war that had been waged since its passage.[80] The press also connected repeal of the Tonkin Gulf Resolution to the Johnson administration's dishonesty about the Gulf of Tonkin incident. For instance, NBC anchor David Brinkley, in a story about Senator Javits's motion to repeal the Tonkin Gulf Resolution, said that, since August 1964, "many doubts have been raised about what happened in the Tonkin Gulf that night and, in fact, doubts that anything happened at all."[81]

The Javits-Pell Resolution was not the only measure to repeal the Tonkin Gulf Resolution that Congress was considering. New York Democratic Senator Charles Goodell proposed a resolution called the "Vietnam Disengagement Act of 1969." In addition to repeal, this resolution demanded that all U.S. troops—not just "combat troops"—be withdrawn from South Vietnam by December 1, 1970.[82] The most moderate measure for repeal of the Tonkin Gulf Resolution to be proposed in 1969 came from Senator Young of Ohio. His resolution would simply repeal the Tonkin Gulf Resolution without placing any other restrictions on the administration.[83] In the end, none of these resolutions would see a vote in the Senate.

Instead, it was a repeal measure from Republican Senator Charles Mathias of Maryland, intended to neutralize attacks on President Nixon's power to continue the war, that would reach a vote by the full Senate. Mathias suggested in his news conference in December 1969 announcing his resolution that Congress repeal the Tonkin Gulf Resolution and, at the same time, explicitly "endorse President Nixon's plan for an accelerated gradual withdrawal of troops." Mathias added that this would "deliberately replace the Johnson plan with the Nixon plan."[84]

This resolution was also precisely calibrated to appeal to the former members of the congressional wing of the failed foreign policy revolution—who still sought to reassert the role of Congress in foreign policymaking. When questioned by ABC News reporter Bob Clark, Senator Mathias said that his "resolution would clearly imply that there should be no new escalation of the Vietnam war without some congressional acquiescence in that policy."[85] Mathias's resolution was also a measure to, as he put it, "clear away the accumulated debris of cold war authorizations which were enacted as long as 15 years ago . . . which collectively grant the President broad and unreviewed [sic] powers to intervene militarily around the world." These authorizations included resolutions on "Quemoy-Matsu [in the Taiwan Straits], Lebanon, Cuba, and the Tonkin Gulf."[86] The Mathias Resolution was later expanded to also repeal the State of Emergency declared by President Truman, giving him wartime powers in peacetime, which technically remained in effect.[87] Mathias told former foreign policy revolutionaries that, while his resolution would not end the war, the "fundamental question" the resolution addressed was, "Is the Senate . . . either obsolete or optional in the making of American foreign and defense policies?"[88]

By a narrow margin, the Mathias Resolution seemed to be closer than alternate repeal measures to the sentiments of the American public. Only 44 percent of Americans who had an opinion wanted to withdraw troops "immediately" or "by the end of 1970" (which was the thrust of the Javits-Pell Resolution). In contrast, slightly more Americans who had an opinion wanted to withdraw troops "but take as many years to do this as are needed to turn the war over to the South Vietnamese" (the administration's policy and the course endorsed by the Mathias Resolution). When combined with the 12 percent of Americans who still wanted to "send more troops to Vietnam and step up fighting," it seems that a majority in the American public were prepared to give the President a freehand to bring the Vietnam War to an "honorable end."[89]

While the fight to repeal the Tonkin Gulf Resolution began to take shape, the broader framework for debate of the war—between supporters using containment to justify the war and opponents attacking the administration's credibility—continued to play out in the media. Senator Stuart Symington resumed his attacks on the administration's credibility on the issue of Laos. In a speech on the floor of the Senate, Symington recounted recent media reports that claimed "400 United States planes yesterday attacked in Laos" and that "the primary targets of these attacks were far away from the Ho Chi Minh trail." Symington said, "The secret war in Laos and our role in it are growing." Symington added that the administration was concealing "American activities in Laos behind an official cloak of secrecy, while permitting unofficial leaks to the news media." He added that this behavior would lead to "problems comparable to those which developed during the past Administration": the development of a new credibility gap. Symington reminded his colleagues that Nixon himself, in his November 3, 1969, "silent majority" speech, had admitted that a lack of credibility in the previous administration had caused "the deep divisions in this nation" and that Americans deserved to "know the truth about [Vietnam] policy."[90]

Symington's renewed attacks on the administration's credibility over Laos might have had no more effect than his attacks the previous year, but for administration's bungled response. In early March 1970, President Nixon claimed that "no American stationed in Laos has ever been killed in ground combat operations." However, this was quickly followed by a statement from the administraton that no more than three Americans had been killed, all in the air war over Laos. This, in turn was followed by the admission that four hundred had been killed, fifty of them CIA or civilians. This, too, turned out to be wrong. The administration was forced to admit its error, first saying twenty-six but later saying fewer than fifty had been killed in "ground hostile actions." Dan Rather mused that, "despite all of this, the White House insists that the President *is* correct when he says no American ever has been killed in ground combat operations" (emphasis is Rather's). Rather added: "This is the kind of confusing, contradictory jungle of semantics reporters and the president's public relations men have been battling over on the question of Laos." Rather concluded by noting: "Reporters say that whatever misleading impressions may have been created, the President and his men have only themselves to blame."[91]

In late March 1970, Senator Stuart Symington again took to the floor of the Senate, this time to attack the administration's failure to disclose top secret testimony about U.S. involvement in Laos. He then detailed all of the stories that had appeared in the press about U.S. military intervention in Laos, including "an American-directed secret army" fighting throughout Southeast Asia. Symington concluded by urging "the State Department to agree to telling the American people the facts" about Laos, "a legitimate matter of public concern for the citizens of the United States."[92]

Reporter Stanley Karnow stopped short of charging outright administration dishonesty over Laos. Still, he wrote in March 1970, because of the rising tensions in Laos, Cambodia, and Thailand, "President Nixon may feel compelled to escalate the American commitment to the region despite his repeated pledges to reduce the U.S. posture in the area"[93] (an implicit attack on Nixon's true willingness to end the war).

As the flap over Laos receded from the headlines, the administration returned to its strong suit: using the ideology of military containment of communism to justify continuing the war in Vietnam. In an interview in April 1970 with reporter George Watson of the *ABC Evening News*, U.S. ambassador to South Vietnam Ellsworth Bunker argued that continued U.S. military intervention in Vietnam was "important in maintaining credibility of our commitments that we've made in SEATO and the United Nations to resist aggression."

He added that the Communists were testing the "patience and the will of the American people."[94]

In February 1970, the Nixon administration got help from an unexpected source: former President Lyndon Johnson returned to the Vietnam War debate. Not surprisingly, as he had throughout his presidency, Johnson used containment to defend the war. Invoking the lessons of Munich, Johnson told interviewer Walter Cronkite that he had prosecuted the war because "Hitler's aggression almost destroyed the world and we believe that Communist aggression will destroy it if somebody doesn't stand up to it."[95]

Johnson also joined members of his former administration in using the Tonkin Gulf Resolution as a weapon against his nemesis, Senator Fulbright. The former president told Cronkite that he had sought the Tonkin Gulf Resolution rather than a declaration of war because he was afraid that either the Communist Chinese or the Soviets might have a secret treaty with North Vietnam that compelled them to enter the war[96] (implying that the resolution was the "functional equivalent of a declaration of war," as Undersecretary of State Katzenbach had once claimed). Johnson added that the resolution should have been called the "Fulbright Resolution . . . because Senator Fulbright introduced it, with his knowledge, with his approval, with his consent. He passed it, he voted for it, 82 to [two]."[97] It was only when the "going got rough," Johnson added, that Fulbright disavowed the Resolution.[98] Johnson added:

> Don't tell me a Rhodes Scholar didn't understand everything in that Resolution, because we said to him at the White House and every other member of that committee, that the President of the United States is not about to commit forces and undertake actions to deter aggression in South Vietnam to prevent this Communist conspiracy, unless and until the American People, through their Congress, sign on to go in.[99]

He repeated the charge later: "It never occurred to me that Senator Fulbright—this Rhodes Scholar—didn't understand what was in that language. I called him to the White House and said this is the reason I want it."[100] Again, this was clearly a lie. The Johnson administration had explicitly told members of Congress that they did not intend to use the resolution to expand the war.

Senator J. William Fulbright responded with a fiery counterattack. His first target was the Johnson administration's credibility on the Gulf of Tonkin incident. Fulbright told CBS reporter Marvin Kalb that Johnson had failed to mention "that the basis for considering this resolution and passing . . . it was utterly false." Fulbright added that Secretary McNamara "had a very good idea" that the information he provided to the Congress about the Gulf of Tonkin incident was "untrue." Fulbright cited the cable from Captain Herrick on August 4, 1964, that warned of doubts that the attack had occurred. Fulbright told Kalb that if that one piece of information "had been made available to the Committee at that time . . . I don't believe they'd pass the resolution." Fulbright added, "The events, as [the administration] related them, of August 4, 1964, were not true. . . . It was not an unprovoked and deliberate attack. In fact . . . there was no attack at all." Fulbright later told reporters, "It just never occurred to me that the President of the United States would lie to the . . . Members of the Senate." He added, "I was completely taken in, as was the whole Senate." Fulbright concluded that the resolution was "justified" by "an absolute misrepresentation of the facts."[101]

Fulbright also told reporters that Johnson and his administration had lied to him and other senators about their intent to use the resolution to escalate the war. Fulbright did concede that the resolution "speaks for itself. . . . I grant that I can read."[102] However, he added, "He [the President] represented it, and so did his spokesmen, the secretaries, not as . . . an authority to widen the war and attack North Vietnam . . . but as a way to prevent the widening of the war."[103] Fulbright also reminded Americans:

> The President, Johnson, was running on the basis of no wider war. He made speeches against widening the war. He made speeches in which he said, "I'm not about to send American boys to Asia to do the fighting of Asian boys."[104]

(While Fulbright was correct that the administration had assured Congress that it would not use the resolution to expand the war, this last claim was deceptive; the president did not start making his claims about "American boys" not fighting wars for "Asian boys" until late August, after the resolution was already passed.) Fulbright concluded, "The rationale for the Resolution was . . . it will be a warning to the North Vietnamese and they will no longer infiltrate—they'll quit!"[105]

The press seemed to almost take both sides of the debate over repeal of the Tonkin Gulf Resolution. In describing the Tonkin Gulf Resolution, television reporters and anchors frequently supported the Johnson administration's claim that the resolution was the "functional equivalent of a declaration of war." In the process, they implicitly rejected Fulbright's claim that the administration had misrepresented its intentions for the resolution. ABC's Frank Reynolds said that the resolution "authorized the President to take all measures to repel armed attacks against the forces of the United States and to prevent further aggression" and claimed that congressional leaders later "had second thoughts about the resolution."[106] CBS's Walter Cronkite said that the Tonkin Gulf Resolution "has served as a substitute for a declaration of war in Vietnam."[107] NBC's David Brinkley said that the Tonkin Gulf Resolution "gave President Johnson power to do whatever he wanted to do in Vietnam."[108] Howard K. Smith claimed that the Tonkin Gulf Resolution "became President Johnson's mandate for escalation."[109]

However, television reporters also repeatedly echoed Senator Fulbright's claim that the Tonkin Gulf Resolution was obtained under false pretenses. For instance, David Brinkley said in March 1970, "Ever since [the Gulf of Tonkin incident], there have been disputes about what actually happened, if anything did."[110] Likewise, Chet Huntley repeatedly referred to the Gulf of Tonkin incident as the "alleged enemy attacks."[111]

At first, the Nixon administration resisted congressional effort to repeal the Tonkin Gulf Resolution. However, the administration quickly realized the significance a repeal of the Tonkin Gulf Resolution could have for the antiwar bloc and moved to end the debate. The administration's first move was to change its position to support of repeal. In March 1970, the administration began to claim that the administration did not need the Tonkin Gulf Resolution to prosecute the war. Instead, they insisted that the president's authority to continue the war derived from his powers as commander in chief of the armed forces.[112]

Initially, Fulbright did not seem to understand the significance of the administration's change of position. He called the move "most enlightened and conciliatory."[113] However, as this administration strategy developed, Fulbright realized he had been outflanked. By early April 1970, Fulbright was forced to admit that repeal of the Tonkin Gulf Resolution would have no effect on the war in Vietnam, though he continued to insist that repeal might restrain the administration from using military intervention in Cambodia or Laos.[114]

The press seemed to agree. After the motion to repeal the Tonkin Gulf Resolution was approved unanimously by the Senate Foreign Relations Committee on 10 April 1970,[115] David Brinkley said that repeal "would be more a symbolic gesture than anything else and would have no effect on the war."[116] The administration had settled the debate over what effect repeal of the Tonkin Gulf Resolution would have on the president; it would have none at all.

The fight over repeal of the Tonkin Gulf Resolution in the Congress did have a negative effect on approval of the president's handling of the war. In mid-January 1970, the president was still enjoying the after-effects of the Moratorium and National Unity Week, with 65 percent approval of his policies in Vietnam compared to 24 percent disapproval.[117] By early March, approval of President Nixon's handling of the war had slipped to 53 percent, while 33 percent disapproved.[118]

As a result of the president's solid anti-communist credentials, "Hawks" had been reduced to only a tiny fraction of those who disapproved of President Nixon's handling of the war since he took office. His tough-on-communism reputation also gave Nixon a flexibility in dealing with the military that President Johnson had never enjoyed. Thus, in early 1970, when General Creighton Abrams asked President Richard Nixon to pause troop withdrawals to give Vietnamization time to take hold, Nixon was able to ignore Abrams' advice. On April 20,

1970, despite the misgivings of "hawks" like perennial war supporter and columnist Joseph Alsop,[119] the president announced the phased withdrawal of 150,000 troops over the next year. Nixon told his advisors at the time that the move was intended to "drop a bombshell on the gathering spring storm of antiwar protest."[120] The president was also no doubt trying to repair the damage done to his credibility by the repeal fight and revelations over U.S. bombing in Laos. Most likely, however, this move was a preemptive investment in his credibility before his move a few weeks later: the invasion of Cambodia.

In late April 1970, in response to political upheaval in Cambodia, the president decided to use U.S. forces to invade Cambodia to destabilize North Vietnamese forces fighting there and assist the new government of Lon Nol. The president's decision to invade Cambodia was initially popular with the American people. However, the move sparked a convulsive wave of radical protests against the war that left six students dead and culminated in over a hundred thousand protesters demonstrating on the National Mall in Washington. The Cambodian Incursion sparked an equally passionate wave of dissent in Congress. The heart of congressional criticism was an attack on the president's credibility: the Cambodian Incursion was an expansion of the war, proof that the president was breaking his promise to end the war. By contrast, radical protesters primarily attacked the ideology of military containment of communism, just as they had in previous radical demonstrations. And, just as with previous radical demonstrations, these attacks on the Cold War consensus alienated most in the media and the American public.

The reasons for the Cambodian Incursion were deeply rooted in President Nixon's strategy for exit from Vietnam: Vietnamization. Since the beginning of his tenure as the commander of Military Assistance Command–Vietnam, General Creighton Abrams's strategy for the Vietnam War had been to interdict enemy supplies. The success of this strategy had forced North Vietnam to build massive supply bases in Cambodia, just out of reach of American ground forces.[121] As long as these bases remained intact, less than fifty miles from Saigon, U.S. troops could not fully withdraw from South Vietnam with any prospect that the country would survive after their departure.[122] Political upheaval inside Cambodia provided an opportunity for President Nixon to deal with this threat. Cambodian Prince Sihanouk, who had long tolerated the presence of North Vietnamese forces in his country, was deposed by Defense Minister Lon Nol, who demanded the removal of North Vietnamese forces from his territory within forty-eight hours. North Vietnam responded by marching for Phnom Penh alongside Cambodian Communists, the Khmer Rouge.[123] President Nixon responded with a combined invasion of U.S. and South Vietnamese forces into Cambodia.

On the eve of the Cambodian Incursion, the administration was already facing the first substantial challenge to its credibility on ending the war, a crisis of its own making. The administration had already damaged its credibility with its conflicting statements on U.S. casualties in Laos. Then on April 28, 1970, in response to Senator Stuart Symington's relentless attacks on the administration's credibility on Laos, the administration finally released excerpts of the top secret transcripts on Laos that the senator had been demanding for months. Rather than silencing Symington, this move prompted the senator to escalate his attacks on the president's credibility. In a letter to the editor of the *Washington Post*, Symington attacked the administration's contention that "United States military forces can be sent by the President into combat for five years, in a country such as Laos, without a treaty or any other congressional authorization, solely under the 'authority of the President to conduct foreign policy.'" Symington also took issue with the administration's "policy of official secrecy toward United States activity in Laos," comparing it to the administration's lack of candor about the growing war in Cambodia. Symington also implied that the administration was about to undertake a "secret expansion of the ground war."[124] These charges proved prescient.

The Cambodian Incursion delivered severe blow to President Nixon's credibility on bringing the war to an "honorable end." And the severity of this blow was once more magnified by the administration's own conflicting statements. On April 26, 1970, Nixon authorized U.S. air support to an ARVN offensive inside Cambodia.

On Wednesday, April 29, reports of the ARVN offensive hit the Associated Press wires.[125] Echoing assurances from the administration, television news reports led Americans to believe that the incursion into Cambodia would be solely a South Vietnamese operation. For instance, in an April 30, 1970, *NBC Evening News* broadcast, Robert Goralski reported that U.S. helicopter gunships would be involved in the incursion. However, he and other television news reporters repeatedly emphasized that U.S. forces were only minor actors in the operation.[126] Yet on the evening of April 30, on President Nixon's order, U.S. forces invaded Cambodia at a point called the Fishhook, about fifty miles from Saigon. About ninety minutes after the operation began, Nixon went on television and told America it was engaged in a ground war in Cambodia.[127]

The operation caught the North Vietnamese completely by surprise and inflicted serious losses on the North Vietnamese in terms of casualties and lost equipment and facilities. The impressive ARVN performance during the campaign also gave that military force a much-needed boost in morale.[128] In short, the Cambodian Incursion was a tactical success. But it came at a high domestic political cost.

The president used the ideology of containment to justify his move into Cambodia. Nixon insisted that the incursion was a response to communist aggression: "Intransigence at the conference table, belligerence in Hanoi, massive military aggression in Laos and Cambodia, and stepped-up attacks in South Vietnam." Nixon said America had to respond to this aggression or "the credibility of the United States would be destroyed in every area of the world where only the power of the United States deters aggression."[129]

The president also struck preemptively at radical protesters in anticipation of their outrage. He told Americans that they lived "in an age of anarchy, both abroad and at home." He tied communist aggression abroad to what he called the radicals' "mindless attacks on all the great institutions which have been created by free civilizations in the last 500 years." Lest anyone not understand that he was talking about radical protesters, particularly those on American campuses, he added, "Even here in the United States, great universities are being systematically destroyed." Explicitly tying his incursion in Cambodia to this domestic radicalism, he said that if America "acts like a pitiful, helpless giant, the forces of totalitarianism and anarchy will threaten free nations and free institutions throughout the world."[130] America had to respond to the threat of communism both abroad and at home.

But the president clearly understood that the Cambodian incursion threatened his credibility on ending the war. Thus, he also worked hard to mitigate the damage to his credibility. In his speech announcing the incursion, before he even announced the move, he reminded Americans that he had already approved the withdrawal of 150,000 U.S. troops. After he broke the news about the incursion, he insisted that the move was "indispensable for the continuing success of that withdrawal program." Nixon reminded Americans that he had "promised to end this war," but also that he had "promised to win a just peace." He explained that the Cambodian incursion was needed to keep both promises.[131] Throughout the incursion, Nixon would repeatedly assure the American people that his objectives were limited and that U.S. troops would withdraw as soon as the Viet Cong's headquarters inside Cambodia was destroyed and North Vietnamese troops were driven off.[132] But the damage was done. Rather than bringing the war to an "honorable end," Nixon seemed to be expanding the war in Southeast Asia.

As Nixon had expected, the response of radical protesters to the Cambodian Incursion was explosive, with increasingly violent clashes erupting on American campuses and in the capital itself. In impromptu remarks to Pentagon employees on April 30, 1970, Nixon again lashed out at these protesters, contrasting the courage of America's fighting men with "these bums . . . blowing up the campuses."[133] These remarks resonated with most Americans, who had consistently dismissed radical protesters. However, these comments by the president also sparked more protests. And in one of these protest at Kent State University in Ohio, National Guardsmen killed four students and wounded many more. This tragedy ignited yet more student protests across the nation, including a protest at Jackson State where two more students were killed. Many other universities were closed due to the protests.[134] On May 9, antiwar protesters staged a rally in Washington that drew as many as a hundred thousand people.[135]

Ohio National Guard troops at Kent State University, May 4, 1970.

Source: Department of Justice, "Ohio National Guard Troops on the Kent State University Campus," May 4, 1970, National Archives at Chicago.[136]

As with previous radical demonstrations, protesters attacked the ideology of containment. For instance, organizers of a student strike at the University of Washington hoped that their strike would serve to educate students and the broader public in Seattle about topics such as "How Imperialism Works" and "Third World Colonies in the US."[137] After the killing of students at Kent State, strike organizers at the University of North Carolina—echoing the radical theme that the ideology of containment had created oppressed "colonies" within the United States—wrote that "the reality of oppression" suffered by black Americans had "finally come home to white Americans."[138]

The radical demonstrations over the Cambodian Incursion were, in many respects, the last gasp of radical dissent over the war based on opposition to the ideology of containment. Most other opponents of the war—especially in the media and in Congress—had already decisively shifted their opposition from attacks on the ideology of containment to attacks on the president's credibility. While many radicals continued to oppose the ideology of containment after these demonstrations, in subsequent protests—especially protests the following year by the Vietnam Veterans Against the War—their opposition would be subsumed by the much greater volume of attacks on the president's credibility.

And as with previous radical demonstrations, the media was dismissive of these protesters. For a little less than two weeks, the protests dominated television news coverage, with the Kent State shooting marking the peak of that coverage and also drawing perhaps the only press sympathy during the protest over the Cambodian Incursion. However, as unrest spilled into Washington, coverage began not only to wane but also became increasingly critical. For example, beginning a report on the departure of protesters from Washington, NBC anchor David Brinkley quipped, "There were so many Volkswagens getting out of Washington, it looked like a traffic jam in Berlin." Reporter Charles Quinn then followed with a report on students who stayed behind to lobby Congress. In the report, a "Yale student" told a Congressman that "the belief that an American life is worth more than a North Vietnamese or South Vietnamese life is somewhat of a distortion of priorities upon people's lives."[139] This student's assertion almost certainly clashed with the sensibilities of average Americans; in a Gallup poll conducted a few months later, when asked "why the United States has not yet been able to find an honorable way out of the Vietnam War," 26 percent of Americans said the United States still had not gone "all out [in prosecuting the war]," while nearly as many blamed the protesters for prolonging the conflict.[140]

Also as with previous radical demonstrations, Americans rejected those who dissented against the Cold War consensus. When asked a month after the Cambodian Incursion concluded what they believed was "the most important problem facing this country," 24 percent of Americans responded that "Vietnam" was the most important problem. However, 34 percent responded with problems related to radical protesters or the counterculture, including answers such as "youth protests, unrest on campus, demonstrations, [and] hippies," "law and order," "crime and juvenile delinquency," or "drug problems"[141] (while hippies, radical protesters, and members of the counterculture were distinctly different groups, mainstream Americans—and war supporters attacking radicals—frequently conflated them). Moreover, when asked why the United States hadn't ended the war yet, 29 percent of Americans who had an opinion said that the United States hadn't "gone all out," while nearly as many Americans (27 percent) said, "Protests have hurt our ability to deal with the Communists."[142]

Moreover, while radical protesters were outraged by the move of U.S. troops into Cambodia, the Cambodian Incursion was initially popular with the American public. Before the incursion (just after the news that charges had been proffered against Captain Medina over the My Lai massacre) approval of Nixon's handling of the war was at its lowest point since he took office. For the first time, less than a majority of Americans, 46 percent, approved of his policies in Vietnam, while 41 percent disapproved.[143] Before the invasion of Cambodia began, the introduction of ground troops into the country was unpopular, with 59 percent of Americans polled by Gallup opposed.[144] However, after the beginning of the Cambodian Incursion (and, of course, the president's preemptive announcement of the withdrawal of 150,000 troops), 53 percent of Americans again approved of his handling of the war, while 37 percent disapproved. Moreover, fully 93 percent of Americans had heard about the Cambodian Incursion and 59 percent who had an opinion approved of how President Nixon was "handling the Cambodian situation."[145]

While radical demonstrators continued to attack the ideology of containment, opponents of the incursion in the media focused their attacks on the president's credibility. I. F. Stone was unequivocal in claiming that the Cambodian Incursion proved President Nixon's dishonesty. Stone wrote, "As usual the country is not being told the truth about why we went into Cambodia." Stone noted, "Nixon pictured the attack across the border as a preemptive exercise to hit an 'enemy building up to launch massive attacks on our forces and those of South Vietnam.'" However, citing reports from Republican Congressmen Hamilton Fish of New York, Stone wrote that the administration had a different justification in private White House briefings. Stone reported that Fish said, "The present military thrust into Cambodia hinged largely on the reportedly surprise overthrow of Prince Sihanouk." Fish added, "U.S. intelligence had known for years of those enclaves from which attacks on South Vietnam have been launched." It was only when Sihanouk was overthrown that the administration decided to attack, to "counter any invasion . . . allowing NVA [North Vietnamese Army] forces to enlarge their occupied areas."[146]

Congressional dissenters were also outraged by the Cambodian Incursion. And their attacks on the president over the incursion were also directed at the president's credibility. In an *NBC Evening News* report the first evening of the incursion, Paul Duke reported on a number of Democratic senators making dire predictions of an impending constitutional crisis, followed by Republican senators predicting disaster at the mid-term elections.[147] Senator Mike Mansfield called the incursion an "ill-advised adventure" and observed that invading Cambodia was unlikely to reduce casualties as Nixon had promised. Even former Vice President Hubert Humphrey joined the chorus of critics using the Cambodian Incursion to attack the president's credibility. He called the incursion both an "expansion" and an "escalation" of the war. But it was Senator Fulbright who led the charge against Nixon's credibility, noting that instead of bringing the war to an end, the incursion was "a very substantial expansion of the war in Indochina." Fulbright also noted that Nixon's move was a violation of the National Commitments Resolution passed the previous year and reminded Americans of the congressional effort already in progress to repeal the Tonkin Gulf Resolution.[148]

In August 1964, the Gulf of Tonkin incident had given President Johnson the political impetus to gain passage of the Tonkin Gulf Resolution, his insurance policy against congressional dissent. In April 1970, the Cambodian Incursion finally gave Congress the political impetus to repeal it. Moreover, after the Cambodian

Incursion, the fight to repeal the Tonkin Gulf Resolution took on a new character; for former members of the congressional wing of the failed foreign policy revolution, repeal became symbolic of their effort to reassert congressional power in advice and consent on foreign policy. At the same time Congress moved to repeal the Tonkin Gulf Resolution, it also moved to pass the Cooper-Church amendment to explicitly prevent the president from using U.S. military force to intervene on behalf of South Vietnamese forces in Cambodia. The president was able to weaken the impact of the Cooper-Church amendment by having caveats inserted into the final measure. He was also able to rob the repeal of the Tonkin Gulf Resolution of some of its symbolic power by having a congressional ally actually make the motion to repeal it. However, these dramatic reassertions of congressional power in foreign policymaking—the first of their kind since the beginning of the Cold War—were still seen by the media as a repudiation of the war by the Congress. And, most importantly, the entire episode—the incursion and repeal—significantly damaged the president's credibility. However, after this episode, the debate over the war rapidly settled back into its pattern from the previous two years, with opponents of the war attacking the president's credibility and supporters using containment to justify continuing the war.

After the Cambodian incursion, the Senate Foreign Relations Committee clearly saw the vote to repeal the Tonkin Gulf Resolution as a reassertion of congressional authority in foreign policy. Likewise, they saw repeal as necessary to give force to the National Commitments Resolution passed the previous year. In a report on repeal, the Committee contended:

> Commitment without the consent or knowledge of Congress of at least 8,000 American soldiers to fight in Cambodia . . . evidences a conviction by the Executive that it is at liberty to ignore the national commitments resolution and to take over both the war and treaty powers of Congress when congressional authority in these areas becomes inconvenient.[149]

In justifying the Cambodian Incursion, the Committee added, the president referred only "to his powers as Commander in Chief of the Armed Forces."[150] This was not just an attack on the president's credibility. This was a declaration by the former congressional wing of the failed foreign policy revolution that ended in 1968 that, even if they could not move the United States beyond a foreign policy founded on the ideology of military containment of communism, they would still demand their congressional prerogative of advice and consent on foreign policy.

At the same time repeal was being considered by Congress, a more explicit prohibition on the use of U.S. military force in Southeast Asia was also being considered. Because there was still significant confusion over what effect repeal of the Tonkin Gulf Resolution would actually have on the president's power to prosecute the war in Southeast Asia, Republican Senator John Sherman Cooper of Kentucky and Democratic Senator Frank Church of Idaho introduced the Cooper-Church amendment, which would prohibit the administration from supporting South Vietnamese troops in Cambodia, forbid bombing in support of their operations in Cambodia, and make it illegal for the president to spend funds to support U.S. troops in Cambodia after the end of June 1970.

The administration clearly understood this amendment as a threat to its ability to continue the war. Thus, the administration worked through supporters in the Senate to revise the Cooper-Church amendment to emphasize the power of the president as commander-in-chief to protect U.S. troops anywhere in the world. Dissenters in Congress immediately counterattacked; Fulbright told reporters in a news conference that the administration could use this altered amendment to "say to the Senate and the House in the future, well you've already given the president approval of anything he chooses to do in defense of the lives of his troops." Democratic Senator Robert Byrd of West Virginia, author of this pro-administration change to the Cooper-Church Amendment, defended his change, saying, "The President . . . clearly has an obligation to consult Congress before entering into any new commitment or entering any new war." Byrd added, "The Byrd amendment, as passed by the Senate today, does not relieve him of that obligation."[151]

The media saw the Byrd amendment as a serious weakening of the original intent of the Cooper-Church amendment. CBS reporter Bruce Morton rightly noted that the Byrd Amendment would "allow the president to send U.S. troops back into Cambodia, if he thought it would protect U.S. forces in Vietnam or hasten their withdrawal." Many in Congress agreed; Senate Majority Leader Mike Mansfield called the Byrd Amendment "another Gulf of Tonkin Resolution."[152]

However, the president's bolder move was to co-opt the repeal of the Tonkin Gulf Resolution by having Republican Senator Bob Dole of Kansas introduce a separate amendment which would repeal the Tonkin Gulf Resolution, stealing victory from the antiwar bloc.[153] The administration claimed, according to Chet Huntley on the *NBC Evening News*, that the Resolution had "outlived its usefulness" and was "obsolete."[154] Congressional Republican leaders echoed these sentiments. Republican Senator Hugh Scott of Pennsylvania said in a press conference, "The Tonkin Gulf Resolution is not relevant to the foreign policy of this administration. It was deemed relevant to another administration which was in the process of escalating the war. This administration is in the process of de-escalating." Scott spoke of the repeal like an administrative action: "I personally intend to vote for the repeal of the Tonkin Resolution. I think it's a good time to clean the decks of a lot of these things that are coming up."[155] The goal Senator J. William Fulbright had sought at least since early 1966, after his first hearings on the war, had been reduced to a matter of housekeeping. President Nixon was attempting to rob repeal of the Tonkin Gulf Resolution of its symbolic value for opponents of the war.

The irony of the administration's support for repeal of the Tonkin Gulf Resolution was not lost on the media. Bruce Morton noted, "Administration hardliners like John Tower voted *for* repeal. Repeal's leading advocate, J. William Fulbright, voted *against* it" (emphasis is Morton's).[156] Frank Reynolds noted that, while "Mr. Nixon has been very busy fighting restraints on his authority . . . he is enthusiastically *for* repeal of Tonkin Gulf" (emphasis is Reynolds's).[157] Reynolds smirked at the notion that "both sides claim to have won a victory," though it was not clear "how everybody can win without somebody losing." Reynolds joked, "No wonder the ballparks are crowded."[158]

Fulbright was incensed at the White House's move. As Frank Reynolds put it, "Fulbright has practically made it his life's work to have the Gulf of Tonkin Resolution repealed" and "he was outraged yesterday when another Senator stood up and allowed that it might be time to repeal it."[159] Bruce Morton added that Fulbright said, "Stealing a man's bill is a little like stealing his cow."[160] Reporter Bob Clark said, "For Senator Fulbright and other long-time war critics, it was sort of like having the winning touchdown in the big game scored by an imposter in a borrowed uniform."[161] After the passage of the Dole amendment, Fulbright forced a second vote, on an identical motion to repeal the Tonkin Gulf Resolution. This only had the effect of making the Arkansas senator the butt of a round of jokes on the network evening news broadcasts since, as David Brinkley noted on the *NBC Evening News*, "President Nixon . . . keeps saying that he doesn't need the resolution and that he can carry on the war without it."[162]

Despite having been outflanked by the administration, Senator J. William Fulbright continued to claim that repeal of the Tonkin Gulf Resolution removed the administration's constitutional authority to prosecute the war. Dole and other congressional supporters of the president claimed that his authority as commander-in-chief of the armed forces allowed him to continue the war. Fulbright called these assertions "very radical and unprecedented,"[163] Fulbright told a news conference, "I think [repeal] removes any constitutional authority for the continuation of the war." He added, "It would certainly remove any authority, I think, to expand the war into China, into Thailand, or elsewhere."[164]

Yet most media outlets agreed with the administration and its supporters that repeal did not limit the president's ability to continue the war.[165] Fulbright's argument was severely weakened by the fact that it was at odds with the arguments that dissenters in the Senate had been making about the Tonkin Gulf Resolution for the previous six years: that President Johnson had misrepresented his intent for the

Tonkin Gulf Resolution and that Congress had never intended it as a blank check to prosecute the war. Fulbright could not simultaneously disagree with former Attorney General Katzenbach's assertion that the Tonkin Gulf Resolution was the "functional equivalent" of a declaration of war and at the same time claim that repeal of that resolution robbed the president of authority to continue the war. In fact, as if to underline this point, before repeal was passed by the House, former Attorney General Nicholas Katzenbach was actually brought back to Congress to repeat his assertion that the Tonkin Gulf Resolution was the "functional equivalent" of a declaration of war.[166] In the end, the repeal had no immediate effect on Nixon and the war continued.

In fact, for most members of Congress, the effort to repeal the Tonkin Gulf Resolution had not been about ending the war. Rather, it was a move by those former members of the failed foreign policy revolution to reassert the role of Congress in foreign policymaking. Still, the media saw the vote to repeal the Resolution as a repudiation of the war. In a report on the vote to repeal the resolution, Charles Quinn noted, "Six years ago, the Senate voted overwhelmingly to give its authority to expand the war in South Vietnam. And now, today, six years later, it voted almost as overwhelmingly, to take that authority away."[167] Former Senator Ernest Gruening told reporter Tony Sargent, "I hope that the obvious deduction from this action is that we should get out!"[168]

In many respects, this entire episode—the Cambodian Incursion, passage of the Cooper-Church amendment, and the repeal of the Tonkin Gulf Resolution—marked the resurrection of the foreign policy revolution in Congress. To be certain, dissenters in Congress had abandoned their public opposition to the Cold War consensus and their efforts to move America beyond a foreign policy based on the ideology of containment. However, the passage of the Copper-Church amendment and the repeal of the Tonkin Gulf Resolution marked a dramatic reassertion of the power of the Senate in advice and consent on foreign policymaking, the instrument these former revolutionaries had always sought to break the Cold War consensus. These votes were only the first in a series of victories, including the Case-Church amendment that prohibited further U.S. military operations in Vietnam after the signing of the Paris Peace Accords and the 1973 War Powers Act that limited the president's ability to use military force abroad without the consent of Congress. Moreover, for the remainder of the Cold War, these former foreign policy revolutionaries would form the bulwark of opposition to each administration's attempts to use military force to contain communism abroad.

Many opponents of the war also used the repeal of the Tonkin Gulf Resolution as an opportunity to attack the president's credibility, tying deceptions by the Johnson administration in obtaining the Tonkin Gulf Resolution to those of the Nixon administration in continuing the war. Former Senator Ernest Gruening, as one of only two members of Congress to vote against the Resolution, was interviewed by NBC reporter Cal Thomas on his reaction to repeal. Gruening used the opportunity to attack both President Johnson's and President Nixon's credibility. He said flatly that the Senate was "tricked into this war. They were lied into this war." He claimed that his former colleagues in Congress had been "hornswoggled" and "bamboozled" and that the United States had not, as the Johnson administration claimed, "been wantonly attacked and . . . had to retaliate with these measures."[169] He added that the American public was still being lied to by Nixon. He said:

> There is constant deception as to what's being done and will be done. There isn't a word of . . . credibility that's been given to Mr. Nixon's promise to end the war. It was very obvious to me, from the time he made his declaration on December Third a year and a half ago, that he was not gonna end the war but he was merely perpetuating it.[170]

Gruening hoped that the Senate would "go the rest of the way and stop voting for the military appropriations to continue this obscene slaughter, this wholly needless slaughter."[171]

Some in the media also used repeal as an opportunity to attack Nixon's credibility. After this episode, ABC reporter Frank Reynolds, generally a Nixon supporter, turned on the president and began attacking his credibility. Reynolds noted that the administration had repeatedly said it would "use American airpower to interdict enemy supply lines and prevent troop concentrations that could eventually threaten the safety of American forces in Vietnam." While Reynolds generally agreed with this policy, he attacked Secretary Laird's claim that "U.S. airstrikes are not to be carried out merely to support Cambodian troops fighting the Communists." Reynolds said, "Since Sunday, American correspondents have seen American planes doing exactly that." Reynolds noted there was "a gap if not a conflict between policy as stated in Washington and as carried out in the field." Reynolds warned the administration, "One of the factors that contributed to opposition to the war was the suspicion that the government was not telling the whole story." He suggested with a smirk that the administration "say in Washington what men with good eyesight have seen us doing in Cambodia."[172]

Despite these blows to the president's credibility, most Americans still approved of the president's policies in Vietnam. Even after the Cambodian Incursion, the death of six students on college campuses during protests, and the repeal of the Tonkin Gulf Resolution, a majority of Americans (55 percent) approved of the president's handling of the war, while 32 percent disapproved. However, a majority of Americans (53 percent) who had an opinion now either favored immediate withdrawal of U.S. troops or a withdrawal within twelve months.[173] Americans were losing patience with Vietnamization of the war.

While opponents of the war used the opportunity of repeal of the Tonkin Gulf Resolution to attack the administration's credibility, supporters of the war used the continued fighting in Cambodia as evidence that containing communism required that the United States continue the Vietnam War. In August 1970, ABC News reported statements by new Cambodian Premier Lon Nol, in an interview with Western reporters, that "the Cambodian people [are] the aggressed people" and that that aggression was from North Vietnam. In a voiceover, reporter George Watson said that General Lon Nol "obviously believes in the domino theory of communist expansion. If Cambodia falls, he said, the next target will be Thailand." Watson added that Lon Nol said that "withdrawal from Vietnam should be slowed down and even delayed." From this story, the *ABC Evening News* cut to a story about Senator J. William Fulbright blocking aid for Cambodia,[174] implying that congressional dissenters were aiding the communists.

Howard K. Smith of ABC News—who had once chided Congress for not trying to repeal the Tonkin Gulf Resolution—also used the ideology of containment to justify the war and attack the antiwar bloc in Congress. Smith said, "Those who can, take no action to stop" the war in Vietnam. He added that it would be easy for Congress to turn off money for the war and that the communists would probably let U.S. forces leave unmolested, as they had the French years earlier. He then asked, "Why doesn't Congress put its vote where its mouth is, and do that?" Smith answered, "Deep down, Congress believes the men who have sat where all bucks stop have been right." He added, "Once that last stretch of Pacific coastline is closed by an aggressive force, the rest of South Asia, India too, might soon unravel perhaps all the way to the Middle East, as John Kennedy predicted." Congress did not act, Smith concluded, because "it believes the American people would, soon after the surrender, exact political penalties" for the loss of Southeast Asia. Smith added, "In its bosom, Congress believes the domino theory might prove right now, as it so terribly did when the Japanese closed that same coastal stretch in 1941."[175]

With the media attacking the congressional antiwar bloc, it is not surprising that the midterm congressional elections in November 1970 gave the president some relief from congressional dissenters. Republican Senator Charles E. Goodell of New York—author in 1969 of the most extreme proposal for repeal of the Tonkin Gulf Resolution—was defeated by a conservative challenger with White House backing. Democratic Senator Albert Gore Sr. of Tennessee—a vocal critic of the president in the Senate Foreign Relations Committee—was defeated by a Republican challenger. While, of course, numerous other factors besides public sentiment about the war also played a role in the outcome of these elections, President Nixon still portrayed it as a defeat of his antiwar critics. In a ninety-minute interview with Washington reporters after the election, President Nixon said that the defeat of these two dissenters was evidence that the country supported his policies in Vietnam.[176]

Despite this victory, attacks on the president's credibility only increased after the elections. After a failed raid by U.S. forces on the North Vietnamese camp at Son Tay in an attempt to rescue U.S. prisoners of war, ABC reporter Edward P. Morgan said, "Laughter echoed through the Senate Foreign Relations Committee room, when Defense Secretary Laird insisted to Senator Fulbright that the intelligence on the abortive effort to rescue prisoners in North Vietnam was excellent." Morgan asked incredulously, "The brave men returned downcast and empty handed because the prisoners had been moved possibly more than a month before. This reflects *excellent* intelligence?" The heart of Morgan's critique, however, was not government incompetence but the administration's deceptiveness. Morgan asked, "Can't the President be candid with the country? Is it possible that his administration can't level with itself?" Morgan concluded, "We seem to be back at credibility gap."[177]

ABC's Bill Lawrence joined the attack on the president's credibility on the Son Tay raids a few days later. He began, "Credibility gulch, that wide separation between known facts and official announcements, now seems to be just as huge, just as forbidding in the Nixon administration as it was when Lyndon Johnson was President." Lawrence warned, "The gulch ultimately claimed the LBJ presidency and its principal characters, wiping out their earlier and better accomplishments, leaving barely a trace." Lawrence recalled, "Defense Secretary Laird first claimed that [the Son Tay raid] had been the only operation that took place that day north of the 19th parallel." However, Lawrence added, "Every day, including today, we learn that it included something more including diversionary flights by carrier aircraft and intensive bombing of military and civilian targets near the camp and near Hanoi." Lawrence added, "Fulbright, who fought LBJ as hard or harder than he does Nixon, stopped just short of calling Laird a liar. But Fulbright came so close to doing so he might just as well have gone all the way." Lawrence warned the president, "When an administration loses credibility on Vietnam, it loses credibility on all things."[178]

The year 1971 brought a series of setbacks for the administration that struck at the core of the president's credibility. In early 1971, the South Vietnamese attacked into Laos to cut North Vietnamese supply routes. They ran headlong into a force of 36,000 North Vietnamese and were badly mauled, calling into question the credibility of the administration's claims about the success of Vietnamization. Soon after, a verdict was returned in the My Lai massacre trial of Lieutenant Calley. While this event, in and of itself, had little impact on the administration's credibility, it once more reminded the public of the atrocity at My Lai just as the Vietnam Veterans Against the War (VVAW) launched a massive protest in Washington against what they claimed were the administration's lies about the brutal conduct of the war. No sooner had this crisis abated than the Pentagon Papers were released, providing the administration's opponents with an opportunity to attack the credibility of both past and present administrations. In response to this crisis of credibility, the president turned once more to his only defense against attacks on his credibility: troop withdrawals. In April 1971, in the midst of this crisis, the administration announced an acceleration of already-announced troop withdrawals.

Even before these setbacks, attacks on the administration's credibility on the Vietnam War had already increased dramatically at the beginning of 1971. In a story on January 6, 1971, David Brinkley reported that Secretary of Defense Melvin Laird had announced that the "American combat role in Vietnam would be over by next summer." However, Brinkley noted, the Secretary was contradicted later by a Pentagon statement that said, "Laird did not mean that Americans would not shoot or be shot at . . . what he meant was that Americans would no longer launch any major offensives." Brinkley quipped, "It was not clear how the Pentagon knew what Laird meant better than Laird knew what he meant."[179]

Moreover, these mounting attacks on the administration's credibility took place in an atmosphere of daily bad news about the war. The media provided heavy coverage of the trials stemming from the

My Lai massacre, constantly reminding the American public of this atrocity from 1968. *NBC Evening News* also aired a three-part series with a number of follow-ups in early 1971 on drug use and deteriorating morale among U.S. soldiers in Vietnam.[180]

The administration did still have supporters in the media, and some of these supporters took up the defense of the president's credibility. ABC's Howard K. Smith admitted, "President Nixon, due to events in Asia, now has acquired a credibility gap." However, Smith added, this was to be expected since, "like Air Force One and a lease on Camp David, a credibility gap comes with the job." He added that Johnson and Kennedy "had one too," as did Presidents Wilson and Roosevelt with respect to the First and Second World Wars, respectively. Smith dismissed the credibility gap as a result of "foreign affairs resist[ing] our control." Smith concluded, "A skeptical press is a virtue, but so is a mite of understanding." He added, "Mr. Nixon's central pledge is to wind down the war. And, undeniably, he's so far done that."[181]

Still, Americans were losing patience with Vietnamization and were hungry for the withdrawal of all U.S. troops from Vietnam. When asked if "you would like to have your Congressman vote for or against" a proposal to "require the United States government to bring home all United States Troops from Vietnam before the end of this year 1971," 77 percent of Americans who expressed an opinion wanted their Congressman to "vote for" such a proposal.[182]

President Nixon clearly sensed this impatience. In a televised interview from the White House, Nixon still used the ideology of containment to defend continuing the war; he said that the United States would "bring a just peace" to Vietnam, implying that he would only withdraw U.S. troops when the goal of containing communism was secured. However, the president also called the war "one of the nightmares we inherited" and promised, "We are ending that war." The president promised that he would not resume full-scale bombing of North Vietnam (but did not rule out retaliatory airstrikes). And he repeatedly reemphasized that the United States was "on the way out" of Vietnam and that the "end of . . . America's combat role in

Vietnam is in sight."[183] The president did not even talk about the war in Vietnam in his 1971 State of the Union Address.[184]

In was against this backdrop of waning American patience that the administration's credibility was dealt a severe blow by circumstances in Southeast Asia in early 1971. By 1971, Vietnamization had dramatically increased ARVN capability. Seemingly overnight, the South Vietnamese military had become among the largest and best-equipped militaries in the world and, when properly led, was surprisingly effective.[185] This capability was put to the test when, Over General Creghton Abrams' objection, ARVN forces invaded Laos in February 1971. Two ARVN divisions crossed the border with U.S. air support, only to be mauled by over 36,000 North Vietnamese Army regulars supported by the newest Russian armor. After six weeks of the most savage fighting of the war, the decimated South Vietnamese divisions retreated back across the border.[186] This episode was particularly damaging to the administration's credibility because it called into question the administration's claims about the success of Vietnamization and, more importantly, President Nixon's claim from only weeks earlier that "the end . . . is in sight." The failure of Vietnamization implied more fighting for U.S. troops. This debacle also sparked a new congressional effort to further limit presidential power and a flurry of new attacks on the administration's credibility—including a detailed *60 Minutes* story on the Gulf of Tonkin incident.

The Nixon administration magnified the damage the Laos Incursion dealt to its credibility with its own statements before and during the operation. Before the incursion, the administration insisted, as reporter Marvin Kalb reported, "There will be no major South Vietnamese move into Laos." Senators were immediately skeptical, and Kalb noted that, despite these denials, the South Vietnamese were conducting "probe[s]" into Laos."[187] After the operation began, the Nixon administration made matters worse by setting unreasonably high expectations for the incursion. On February 8, 1971, Herbert Kaplow reported on the *NBC Evening News*, "The President said that the Laotian operation, if it goes well, will make it impossible for the enemy to conduct a major offensive in South Vietnam for at least another year."[188] As the situation deteriorated, the media began to focus on the difference between the situation on the ground and the Pentagon's rhetoric. For instance, on the February 24, 1971, *NBC Evening News*, reporter John Chancellor said:

> The 16,000-man force of South Vietnamese on the ground in Laos remains stalled at the limit of American artillery protection but far short of its original objectives. Nevertheless, at a big Pentagon press briefing today, officials said things were not going badly.[189]

The news story then cut to a confrontation between Secretary of Defense Laird and a reporter. Laird said, "I believe that this operation, even if it was to terminate . . . now has been successful in disrupting logistics supplies." An unnamed reporter then asked, "Are you saying, in effect, that the field reports . . . about an operation that is bogged down 16 to 17 miles inside of Laos . . . are incorrect?" A stone-faced Laird replied, "No, the operation is going according to plan." The report then immediately cut to the evacuation of a South Vietnamese soldier wounded in the fight in Laos, identified only as a member of "a crack unit that crossed into Laos and was badly mauled and broken."[190]

The South Vietnamese evacuation from Laos provided more fuel for media attacks on the administration's credibility on Vietnamization. As reporter Tom Streithorst reported, "The generals of the ARVN high command insist that the withdrawal is going according to plan," footage showed "panicked ARVN soldiers" hanging from the skids of departing US helicopters, "desperate" to escape the advancing North Vietnamese. As if to punctuate the point that the failure of the South Vietnamese meant more fighting for U.S. troops, the report then cut to American soldiers, fighting at the Laotian border to protect the withdrawal and blunt the North Vietnamese counterattack. The report concluded with an interview with angry and dispirited American soldiers who told the story of an American artillery unit that was forced to destroy its guns and flee the North Vietnamese advance.[191]

Democratic presidential hopeful Senator Edmund Muskie was among the many politicians to use the failure of South Vietnamese forces in Laos to attack the administration's credibility on its policy of Vietnamization of the war. In a speech excerpted on the *CBS Evening News*, Muskie said, "The credibility of Vietnamization has been diluted and cast into doubt by the performance of the South Vietnamese forces [in Laos], which can mean nothing more than a prolongation of the war and our involvement in it."[192]

The Laos Incursion was a serious blow both to approval of the president's handling of the war in Vietnam and to the American public's patience with Vietnamization. In late February, 86 percent of Americans had heard about events in Laos. And they were not happy about them; for the first time in the Nixon presidency, more Americans disapproved (45 percent) than approved (43 percent) of the president's policies in Vietnam. The majority of Americans (55 percent) who had an opinion believed that the setback in Laos would lengthen the war. And Americans were ready to end the war; 72 percent of Americans who had an opinion said they were "for" a proposal "to require the U.S. government to bring home all U.S. troops from Vietnam before the end of this year 1971." Of those who supported such a proposal, 62 percent were for withdraw "regardless of what happens there after U.S. troops leave."[193] The majority of Americans no longer cared if the war came to an "honorable end."

Most importantly, however, Laos was a severe blow to President Nixon's credibility. In the midst of the operation, Americans were asked, "Do you think the Nixon administration is or is not telling the public all they should know about the Vietnam war?" Over two thirds of Americans (69 percent) said they were not.[194]

Perhaps as a response to this crisis and the possible use of U.S. ground forces in the Laos Incursion, dissenters in Congress began an effort to limit presidential power which would ultimately become the 1973 War Powers Act. As with the Cooper-Church amendment and the repeal of the Tonkin Gulf Resolution, this was not just an attack on the president's credibility; it was another move by the former congressional wing of the failed foreign policy revolution to reassert the power of the Congress in advice and consent on foreign policymaking. The bill would only permit the president to commit U.S. forces to meet an attack on the United States or its troops abroad, protect American lives or property, or fulfill a U.S. commitment to an ally. However, the president could only continue such a military action for 30 days without congressional approval. In many ways, this effort was the final break of the elite Cold War consensus among the framers of American foreign policy. While many members of Congress continued to embrace some or all of the precepts of the ideology of military containment, most of the senators behind this bill did not.

Just as the furor over the Laos Incursion was abating, the media revived earlier attacks on administration. In a March 1971 episode of the CBS News program *60 Minutes*, reporter Morley Safer recounted the catalog of questions about the Gulf of Tonkin incident—including whether it had happened at all—and attacked the Johnson administration's deception in obtaining the Tonkin Gulf Resolution. While this was not a direct attack on the Nixon administration's credibility, this attack was still significant for two reasons. First, it presaged the accusations contained in the soon-to-be-released Pentagon Papers that the war was started under false pretenses. Second, it popularized the idea that the Vietnam War was begun under false pretenses for those Americans who did not read newspapers or news magazines and got most of their news from television—a significant majority of Americans by 1971.[195]

Safer began the story by saying that the Gulf of Tonkin incident had "become as controversial as the war itself." His central question was, "The U.S. destroyers *Maddox* and *Turner Joy* were attacked by communist torpedo boats. Or, were they?"[196] Safer concluded that the first attack, on August 2, 1964, had definitely happened. However, Safer was unforgiving on questions about the second attack on August 4, 1964. He said, "Senate investigators now believe there never was any battle that night." Safer highlighted nearly every discrepancy identified during the 1968 Fulbright hearings. Safer included an interview with main gun director Patrick Park, now a civilian. Safer asked, "Do you think, that night, August 4th, in the pitch black, in a heavy swell, rainstorms, was there anything to shoot at out there?" Park responded, "No, I don't . . . I'm certain that there was not anything to shoot at." Safer interspersed clips of his cross-examination of Captain Herrick with interviews of Park and other crew members who contradicted his account of the incident.[197]

Safer also recounted the provocative nature of the patrols, including the mysterious "black box" that Safer said Secretary McNamara had testified was used to "*stimulate* North Vietnamese and Communist Chinese radar" (emphasis is Safer's). Safer then immediately cut to former Senator Wayne Morse who said, "The *Maddox* was a spy ship." Safer also called into question the location of the DESOTO patrols. He showed Morse saying that the *Maddox* "went into the national waters of North Vietnam." Morse concluded, "We weren't looking for a peaceful out, for we intended to make war." Safer also highlighted the OPLAN 34A raids that McNamara had "left out or didn't know or touched on too lightly" during hearings on 6 August 1964. Safer highlighted that McNamara had testified there was no connection between the DESOTO patrols and the OPLAN 34A raids, even though cables from the navy at the time contradicted this claim.[198]

Morley Safer was sympathetic in describing Senator Fulbright's role in the passage of the Tonkin Gulf Resolution. Safer did say that Fulbright was "President Johnson's principal ally in steering the Tonkin Gulf Resolution through the Senate." However, he added, Fulbright "spent many of the next six years trying to repeal the resolution." Fulbright said in an interview in the story, "I personally am convinced in my own mind that no attack took place on the 4th." Safer added, in a voiceover of McNamara's briefing to reporters in August 1964, "But on the night of August 4, 1964, hardly anyone doubted Secretary of Defense Robert McNamara's official version." Safer said that McNamara's version of the attack was that the ships "had been illegally and deliberately attacked while on normal, routine patrol somewhere near the middle of Tonkin Gulf." However, Safer added, "Senator Fulbright disagrees." In the story, Fulbright once more claimed that, if he had been given the infamous telegram from Captain Herrick about his doubts over the Gulf of Tonkin incident, the Tonkin

Gulf Resolution would have never been passed. Safer then showed and read the text of Herrick's message, which concluded, "Suggest complete evaluation before any further action."[199]

Safer also accused Johnson of misleading the Congress as to what he intended to do with the resolution.[200] After showing the president explaining to Walter Cronkite the previous year that he had not sought a declaration of war because he feared that the Soviet Union or Communist China had a secret treaty with North Vietnam, Safer cut to Fulbright saying, "He used to say in his speeches, 'I'm not about to send American boys to Asia to fight the battles that Asian boys should fight,' and similar statements."[201]

Safer also claimed that the U.S. military had been complicit in the deception. He said that the U.S. Navy interviewed all of the participants on the two destroyers but that "testimony only of those who thought they had seen enemy action was later presented to the Fulbright Committee." Wayne Morse concluded, grinning, "If you rely upon the American military for credibility then you're easy prey."[202]

Safer concluded by arguing that the Gulf of Tonkin incident was a pretext for action the Johnson administration wanted to take anyway. Safer asked former Assistant Secretary of Defense Paul Wonkey, "Were we waiting for an incident at the time?"[203] Wonkey responded:

> . . . Probably we were on the alert for the kind of provocation that would lead us to react, yes. And the Tonkin Gulf incident just provided the trigger for an American response that would have occurred in any event at some point in history.[204]

Safer noted that Congress had finally repealed the Tonkin Gulf Resolution. He added, "Senator Fulbright's argument was the resolution, like any other contract based on misrepresentation, was null and void."[205]

Just as the disastrous Laos Incursion began to fade from the headlines, a verdict was returned in the My Lai massacre trial of Lieutenant William Calley. While this event, in and of itself, had little impact on the administration's credibility, it reminded the public of the atrocity at My Lai just as the Vietnam Veterans Against the War (VVAW) launched a massive protest in Washington. This demonstration was markedly different from the radical demonstrations that had descended on Washington, DC, since the beginning of the war. While the VVAW did occasionally attack the administration's use of containment to justify continuing the war and did defend radical protesters, the heart of the VVAW's critique of the war—as explained by VVAW leader John Kerry in testimony before the Senate Foreign Relations Committee during the demonstrations—was that the United States was engaged in war crimes in Vietnam and that the administration was hiding this fact from the American people. The media took these and other veteran protesters much more seriously than they ever had radical protesters, forcing the administration to respond both with troop withdrawals. While this measure failed to restore Nixon's credibility with the American people to its highs from before the Cambodian Incursion, the announcement did prevent a further erosion of his credibility after the VVAW protests. It also restored some of the approval of Nixon's policies in Vietnam that had been lost during the Laos Incursion.

The American public first heard reports of the massacre at My Lai in late 1969. Stories of the incident captivated the public, with 95 percent of Americans saying they had heard about the incident in December 1969. However, from the very beginning, most Americans were sympathetic to the perpetrators, with 65 percent of Americans who had an opinion believing that "soldiers who took part in the shooting" should not "be punished."[206] On March 29, 1971, in the aftermath of the disastrous Laos Incursion, a verdict was handed down for Lieutenant William Calley in his long, highly publicized trial over the My Lai massacre. Public uproar erupted over the verdict and the severity of the sentence (life at hard labor). Nixon, after a review, reduced the sentence to twenty years in prison (of which Calley ultimately only served three and a half years). Nixon also ordered Calley released pending his appeal.[207]

This episode, in and of itself, had little impact on the president's credibility. However, at the same time the final chapter of the My Lai tragedy was being written, a new threat to the administration's credibility on Vietnam was taking shape. In January, the VVAW conducted their "winter soldier" U.S. war crimes investigation at a Howard Johnson's Motor Lodge in Detroit.[208] This event was all the more dramatic because it echoed perceptions of the war already created by reports of the My Lai massacre. Moreover, both the My Lai massacre and the "winter soldier" investigation provided ammunition for the VVAW's true purpose—to attack the administration's credibility on its conduct of the war. The VVAW's contention was that the United States was committing war crimes in Vietnam and that the administration was hiding this fact from the American people—lying by omission of important facts that the VVAW contended Americans had the right to know.

In April, the group marched on Washington. Their demonstration included a number of highly publicized events, including laying wreaths at Arlington National Cemetery and throwing their medals over a fence at the Capitol. On April 22, VVAW member and future U.S. Senator and Secretary of State John Kerry testified before the Fulbright Committee and famously asked, "How do you ask a man to be the last man to die for a mistake?" The demonstration culminated on April 24 with between 200,000 and 500,000 protesters gathering in Washington, and another 150,000 gathering in San Francisco. Some protesters stayed for a week, camping on the National Mall before being dispersed by Capitol police.[209] While only a fraction of the large number of demonstrators on April 24 were actually veterans, the former service members drew the vast majority of media coverage, creating the impression that hundreds of thousands of veterans were protesting the war.

A key element of the success of the VVAW demonstrations when compared to earlier, radical demonstrations was that veterans were seen as more credible on the topic of the war. The television news media clearly took these protesters more seriously. At the end of journalist Ron Nessen's report on the demonstrations, he said, "At least these antiwar demonstrators have been to Vietnam and know firsthand what they are demonstrating against."[210] In another report, David Brinkley stoically explained that a group of veterans was arrested for demonstrating at the Supreme Court. "Among them were two veterans who lost both their legs in the war and were in wheelchairs. They demanded to be arrested too. The police refused." Brinkley's report featured none of his former dismissive sarcasm about protesters. Footage then cut, in rapid succession, to hundreds of veterans chanting and singing on the steps of the Supreme Court, hundreds of police marching toward them with clubs, and the veterans being marched solemnly away, their hands cuffed behind their heads.[211]

Veteran protesters played to this perception of greater credibility. CBS reporter Bruce Morton interviewed members of the "Concerned Officers' Movement," which included active duty officers protesting the war. These officers explicitly stated that they more responsible and could better communicate with what they called "middle America" than radical protesters. Navy Lieutenant Junior Grade Robert Brown said that most Americans "have just been completely turned off by a lot of radical talk and rhetoric and we felt that the most effective [way] to effect change was to be responsible."[212]

The VVAW used this greater appeal to "middle America" to get greater coverage of its charges of U.S. war crimes and its attacks on administration credibility. VVAW leader (and future senator, presidential candidate, and Secretary of State) John Kerry was a central figure in the protests. Kerry is most frequently remembered for his testimony before the Senate Foreign Relations Committee that every day "someone has to die so that President Nixon won't be . . . the first President to lose a war."[213] However, Kerry primarily argued that veterans were more credible than any other group on the war. And his main critique of the war was that the administration was lying to the American people about its brutality. In an interview on the *CBS Evening News*, Kerry claimed that veterans could provide "the truth about this war more than any other group in this country." He added, "Men who fought the war . . . know what it's like . . . know what we're fighting . . . know what they've been made to do." Kerry concluded, "We can tell people with more credibility the dangers of our present course than anybody else."[214]

The Senate Foreign Relations Committee had been attacking the president's credibility since he took office. Thus, it is not surprising that they asked Kerry to testify before the Committee while his group was in Washington. Fulbright made it clear in his opening statement for the hearing with John Kerry that he was asking Kerry to testify about the administration's lack of credibility on the war. He said, "As you know, there has grown up in this town a feeling that it is extremely difficult to get accurate information about the war and I don't know a better source than you and your associates."[215]

The VVAW's attack on the administration's credibility centered on the accusation that it was hiding war crimes in Vietnam. Kerry clearly understood the power that the recent My Lai massacre trial verdict held over the public imagination and reminded Americans of that incident during his testimony. In the hearings, John Kerry purported to tell America the facts of "what this country, in a sense, made [veterans] do" in Vietnam. Kerry famously told the Committee that the U.S. military was using tactics "reminiscent of Genghis Khan" in Vietnam. Kerry claimed that the United States was violating the Geneva Conventions that it claimed to embrace with its "use of free fire zones, harassment interdiction fire, search and destroy missions, the bombings, the torture of prisoners, the killing of prisoners, accepted policy by many units in South Vietnam." Kerry claimed that veterans had been compelled to commit "crimes" in Vietnam and that those crimes threatened the country more than communist expansion ever could. But Kerry was not just attacking the U.S. military; he was also attacking the Nixon administration's credibility. Kerry indicted the administration for "rationaliz[ing] destroying villages in order to save them."[216] Of course, this was a conflation of the Johnson and Nixon administrations; this statement about destroying a village to save it was made by a U.S. military officer during the Tet Offensive, before Nixon ever took office. Still, there was, in this rhetorical construction, an embedded, if implicit, attack on the administration's credibility: if the administration was responsible for this brutality in Vietnam, and the American people were not aware of it, then the administration was lying to Americans by hiding the true nature of the war from them.

But Kerry also attacked the Nixon administration's credibility more explicitly by recalling other lies he claimed the president had told about Vietnam. Kerry railed against the administration for claiming that "no ground troops are in Laos, so it is all right to kill Laotians by remote control." Kerry insisted, "There is absolutely no difference between ground troops and a helicopter, and yet people have accepted a differentiation fed them by the administration." He added, "Believe me the helicopter crews fill the same body bags and they wreak the same kind of damage on the Vietnamese and Laotian countryside as anybody else."[217] Kerry decried the administration's "falsification of body counts, in fact the glorification of body counts" and its repeated claims that "the back of the enemy was about to break." When directly questioned by Senator Symington as to whether it was "possible . . . to get accurate and undistorted information through official military channels," Kerry claimed that reports he himself had sent to his superiors were later reported in *Stars and Stripes*, and "the very mission we had been on had been doubled in figures and tripled in figures."[218]

John Kerry's defense of radical demonstrators during the hearing was probably less well received by the American public. Kerry railed against Vice President Agnew's claim in 1970 that the media "glamorize[d] the criminal misfits of society while our best men die in Asian rice paddies to preserve the freedom which most of those misfits abuse." Kerry said that it was "those [Agnew] calls misfits [who] were standing up for us in a way that nobody else in this country dared to." Likewise Kerry believed that veterans could not "consider ourselves America's best men when we are ashamed of and hated what we were called on to do in Southeast Asia."[219]

John Kerry probably further alienated the majority of Americans— who still embraced the Cold War consensus—with his attacks on the administration's continued use of containment to justify the war. He argued that the Vietnam War was "a civil war, an effort by a people who had for years been seeking their liberation from any colonial influence whatsoever." He also said that most Vietnamese "didn't even know the difference between communism and democracy. They only wanted to work in rice paddies without helicopters strafing them and bombs with napalm burning their villages and tearing their country apart." Kerry and his associates rejected the very premise that Southeast Asia was vital to the "preservation of freedom" and called such assertions "criminal hypocrisy." He insisted America could not "fight communism all over the world" and could not "right every wrong." Kerry believed that the United States was still behaving as if it was opposed by a "communist monolith" and using "cold war precepts which are no longer applicable."[220]

Congressional dissenters had largely abandoned attacks on the ideology of containment since 1968. However, these comments from Kerry succeeded in eliciting similar comments from some members of the Committee. Senator Claiborne Pell said, "This war was really just as wrong, immoral, and unrelated to our national interests five years ago as it is today." Senator Fulbright lamented that the United States' policy of military containment since the Second World War had cost $1.5 trillion, robbing the Congress of the ability to deal with many pressing social problems. Fulbright also restated the chief complaint of former congressional members of the failed foreign policy revolution: the Cold War had also "eroded the role of the Congress" in foreign policymaking.[221]

President Nixon clearly understood the impact the demonstrations would have even before they occurred. Thus, presumably to blunt the effect of the VVAW protest, Nixon used the only weapon he had in his arsenal to protect his credibility: troop withdrawals. The president announced on April 7, 1971, that he was accelerating the withdrawal of troops from Vietnam; he would withdraw an additional 100,000 troops between May 1 and December 1, 1971.[222]

This preemptive strike against the VVAW protests appears to have at least prevented the American public's opinion of the president's credibility from slipping further. Immediately following the April protests and John Kerry's testimony, a Gallup poll showed that trust in President Nixon's credibility was virtually unchanged from February. When asked if the administration was "telling the public all they should know about the Vietnam war," two thirds of Americans still said it was not.[223]

However, otherwise the protests seemed to have helped the president. In the aftermath of the Laos Incursion, the verdict in the Calley trial, and the protests, more Americans (50 percent) once more approved of the president's handling of the war than disapproved (39 percent).[224] This was a rebound of more than 7 percentage points from March, when more people had disapproved than approved of Nixon's policies in Vietnam. This may have been a secondary effect of the announcement of accelerated troop withdrawals or a result of John Kerry's and the Congress' ill-advised attacks on the ideology of military containment of communism.

Just as news surrounding the VVAW protests was abating, the *New York Times* announced in June 1971 that it would publish the Pentagon Papers, a collection of secret documents leaked to the paper by former Rand Corporation analyst, Daniel Ellsberg. Despite the fact that the papers only implicated the Kennedy and Johnson administrations in possible deception, President Nixon took the extraordinary step of filing an injunction to prevent publication. The publication went forward only after this injunction was overturned by the U.S. Supreme Court.[225]

While these papers were primarily a threat to the credibility of the Eisenhower, Kennedy, and Johnson administrations, the papers still had an impact on the Nixon administration and its credibility. First, the papers reinforced the impression—first created by the revelations of the Johnson administration's deception in getting the Tonkin Gulf Resolution—that the war was somehow illegitimate because it was initiated under false pretenses. Second, publicity, news stories, and interviews surrounding the release of the papers afforded opponents of the war numerous opportunities to attack the credibility not just of previous administrations, but also of the Nixon administration. Supporters of the war were forced, once more, to defend the credibility of past and present administrations.

While the papers were a threat to the credibility of past and present administrations, they also supported the Johnson administration's claim that Eisenhower, Kennedy, and Johnson had all favored intervention in Vietnam to contain communist aggression. Thus, the

Pentagon Papers provided supporters of the war with an opportunity to reassert that the war in Vietnam was required to contain communism in Southeast Asia. This was especially important since, over the months of crisis since the Laos Incursion, supporters of the war had seldom had the opportunity to make these arguments, having been preoccupied with defending the Nixon administration's credibility.

Many in the media focused on the revelations in the papers about the Gulf of Tonkin incident and the Tonkin Gulf Resolution, reinforcing perception that the war was illegitimate as it had been initiated under false pretenses. CBS News aired a special on the Pentagon Papers that featured an extensive segment on the revelations in the papers about the Tonkin Gulf Resolution. In the introduction to this segment, Bernard Kalb noted that, during the 1964 presidential campaign, President Johnson repeatedly insisted that he "would not send American boys to fight Asian boys' wars" while the "the United States was stage managing South Vietnamese commando raids against the North, patrolling the Gulf of Tonkin with destroyers, flying U2s over North Vietnam. Altogether . . . named operation 34A." While this report did not question whether the August 4, 1964, attack against U.S. destroyers in the Gulf of Tonkin occurred, it did note that this "elaborate program of covert military operations against North Vietnam" was referred to by the Joint Chiefs of Staff as "a provocation strategy." This story also noted, "Congress passed a resolution prepared months before by a high State Department official authorizing the President to take whatever military action [was] required to repel communist aggression."[226]

This segment also featured a panel discussion with reporter Bernard Kalb, Senator J. William Fulbright, and former National Security Advisor Walt Rostow. In this segment, both Kalb and Fulbright reinforced the idea that the war was somehow illegitimate because it had been initiated under false pretenses. Senator Fulbright claimed that he had supported the Tonkin Gulf Resolution because he had "accepted the story given to us by the President and Mr. [McNamara] and Mr. Rusk. I believed General Wheeler." Later he added, "We were not told the truth about even the incident on the

Fourth of August. I doubt it occurred at all." Fulbright claimed that OPLAN 34A was kept secret and despite "three different hearings about this matter they concealed this and . . . misrepresented these preliminary activities." Fulbright added, "I thought Barry Goldwater was the man who represented [a war] policy and the President was genuinely interested in preventing a war." He also said, "The resolution was presented to us as a resolution to prevent a war. . . . If you do this . . . the North Vietnamese would see the futility of pursuing this matter and there would not be any wider war." Rostow disputed that the president had hidden his provocations from Americans. He claimed that the president had told Americans and the Congress that "he was not going to give up on the treaty commitment." He did admit that the president had said that he "was not going to use American power carelessly" but refused to concede that President Johnson had promised before his election that he would not deploy troops to Vietnam.[227] The truth, of course, lay somewhere in between. President Johnson did not make his public promises about not sending "American boys" to Vietnam until *after* the Tonkin Gulf Resolution was passed. But he did make those promises before he was elected. And, more importantly, the administration had given these assurances to Congress privately *before* the Tonkin Gulf Resolution was passed.

This same special report also tied the Pentagon Papers to other presidential deceptions by both Presidents Johnson and Nixon. Bernard Kalb set the tone for this discussion: "The war in Vietnam has often been camouflaged by misleading statistics of body counts, weapons captured, hamlets pacified." Kalb claimed, "The Pentagon Papers have touched off the deepest controversies centering on whether the Presidents and their men deceived the people."[228] This latter segment included a panel discussion with Republican Senator John Tower of Texas, Senator J. William Fulbright, historian Arthur Schlesinger Jr., Walt Rostow, Max Frankel of the *New York Times*, and Crosby Noyes of the *Washington Evening Star*. During most of this panel discussion, opponents of the war attacked not only President Johnson's but also President Nixon's credibility. Fulbright claimed that not only had

Presidents Johnson and Nixon ignored Congress, they had also lied to Congress:

> The lack of candor, the withholding of knowledge of events, the absence of any genuine consultation with elected representatives of the people is compelling evidence of an attitude on the part of the small coterie of decision makers which is antidemocratic and contrary to the fundamental principles of our constitution.[229]

Arthur Schlesinger noted that Kennedy used to say, "in the final analysis, it is [the South Vietnamese'] war . . . they are the ones who have to win it or lose it." Fulbright immediately retorted, "Johnson said exactly the same thing, too." Fulbright said that Johnson never chose to "consult [Congress] in the sense of telling them the truth and seeking their . . . advice. There was a complete contempt for the Congress." Instead, he added, "there was only an effort to manipulate and deceive them. . . . I don't think Congress was ever told the truth in any sense." Rostow tried to corner the senator: "Senator, isn't . . . it true that until 1965 at least that you were in complete agreement with our policies and the assumptions on which they were based?" Fulbright quipped, "Well, until I discovered what they *were*" (emphasis is Fulbright's).[230]

　While the Pentagon Papers highlighted presidential deception, they also supported the argument—based on the ideology of containment—repeatedly made by the Johnson administration: Eisenhower and Kennedy agreed that U.S. intervention was required in Vietnam to contain communist aggression. In this same segment, moderator Bernard Kalb admitted that the Pentagon Papers revealed that Johnson and his predecessors were genuine in their repeated declarations that the Vietnam War was required to contain communism. Kalb acknowledged that the Kennedy administration "recognize[d] that commitment. They agree[d] to a boost in the advisors; they approve[d] of covert actions against North Vietnam." Walt Rostow argued explicitly that President Johnson's predecessors had supported the defense of South Vietnam: "The critical thing that happened in that period was the SEATO treaty. . . . The President of the United States quite openly decided that the protection of that area from takeover, the maintenance of its independence against communism was in the highest national interest." Rostow also noted that Senators Mansfield and Humphrey had supported this commitment. John Tower echoed these sentiments. Even erstwhile critic of the war Arthur Schlesinger was forced to admit that "President Kennedy repeatedly in public statements expressed . . . [that] we had an interest of some sort in preventing South Vietnam from being taken over by the communists." Later, he added that Kennedy believed in the domino theory and believed that the independence of Southeast Asia "was vital to the American interest including . . . its relationship to the Indian subcontinent through Burma."[231]

Rostow also argued that the war in Vietnam was a result of communist aggression: "After the November 1957 conference in Moscow . . . the North Vietnamese came away with the conviction that they had the backing of both Peking and Moscow in moving to restart the war." Walt Rostow added that the decision to begin bombing North Vietnam did not come until February 1965, when "the weight of the North Vietnamese regular units began to be felt very seriously" and "Sukarno had joined Peking. . . . Peking was announcing Thailand was next."[232] (This final claim is simply not true; the administration decided on further bombing of North Vietnam on a tit-for-tat basis as early as late summer 1964, immediately after the passage of the Tonkin Gulf Resolution.)

As had been the pattern since 1968, opponents of the war did not attack these invocations of the ideology of containment directly. Rather, they attacked administration credibility. Faced with the evidence provided by the Pentagon Papers that previous administrations *had* believed that the containment of communism required intervention in Vietnam, Arthur Schlesinger made a tortured attempt to portray this belief itself as a form of deception. He said that the Pentagon Papers "accentuate the basic mystery that is why anyone ever supported that Vietnam so involved the American national interest or so threatened the security of the United States." He added, "There is far too much deception here, but there is also a terrifying amount of self-deception." He concluded, "the great lesson . . . to be drawn from [the papers] is don't trust your leaders until they earn and justify that trust by telling the truth to the people."[233]

The release of the Pentagon Papers, coming after all of the other blows the president had suffered in the first half of 1971, hurt approval of the president's policies in Vietnam. After the release of the Pentagon Papers, more Americans (41 percent) once more disapproved than approved (36 percent) of the president's handling of the war in Vietnam.[234] This represented a drop of 14 percentage points in approval of the president's handling of the war since the VVAW protests.

A complex combination of factors was responsible for this drop in approval of President Nixon's handling of the war. Increased doubts about the president's credibility no doubt contributed to this drop in approval. But this drop was also caused in part by the general perception that the war was illegitimate because it was begun under false pretenses—a perception reinforced by the release of the Pentagon Papers. The cumulative effect of the release of the Papers, along with perceptions about the brutality of the war created by the My Lai massacre trial and the VVAW protests, had by June 1971 convinced 58 percent of Americans that the war was "immoral."[235] This drop in approval of Nixon's policies in Vietnam was also a result of growing impatience with the president's efforts to find an "honorable end" to the war. When asked if they were satisfied with the rate of withdrawal of troops, 53 percent of Americans who had an opinion believed the pace was "too slow."[236]

This crisis of credibility might have spelled an end to the Nixon presidency but for an interesting phenomenon that was emerging in American sentiments on the president and the war. After the president's spring 1971 announcement that he was accelerating troop withdrawals—a preemptive strike on the VVAW protests—the president and his administration became virtually silent on the war, seldom speaking about its progress or their reasons for continuing it. The administration was distancing itself from the Vietnam War.

This effect is reflected in polls on the president's personal favorability. Nixon began 1971 with a 57 percent approval rating,[237] but by May the cumulative effect of the Laos Incursion, the Calley Trial, and the VVAW protests had taken their toll; Nixon's approval had dropped to 48 percent.[238] Approval of the president remained unchanged after the publication of the Pentagon Papers.[239] Then Nixon and his administration stopped talking about the war. Soon after, president Nixon announced that he would go to China in 1972 and Captain Medina was acquitted in his My Lai massacre trial—without comment from the administration. By October 1971, while Americans were still fed up with the war, Nixon's personal approval ratings had rebounded from their lows earlier in the year. When asked if they were supporters or critics of president Nixon, a majority of Americans who had an opinion (51 percent) said they were "strong" or "moderate supporter[s]" of the president. More importantly for the president, however, his credibility also improved markedly. When asked if they approved or disapproved of the president's "degree of frankness and openness in dealing with the American public," a narrow majority of Americans (51 percent) approved, a jump of nearly twenty percentage points from spring 1971.[240]

Sometime in late 1971, the Vietnam War became a political orphan. Not only had the war disappeared from the administration's rhetoric, it was also fading from the headlines. Troop levels had dropped significantly from their high of 543,000 in April 1969 to 191,000 in November 1971. Moreover, casualties in Vietnam had also dropped significantly; only sixty-six American service members died in Vietnam in November 1971, the lowest casualty figure since May 1967.[241] Perhaps most Americans simply believed that the war was essentially over and had begun to judge President Nixon on other factors. Still, President Nixon had to fulfill his campaign pledge and end the Vietnam War or else his fate would once more be tied to this unpopular war.

At the beginning of 1972, Richard Nixon could still hope to deliver on his promise from the 1968 presidential campaign to bring "peace with honor" in Vietnam. However, in order to continue to frustrate the North Vietnamese's ambitions in Southeast Asia, President Nixon had to win the 1972 presidential election. Nixon's strategy to defeat the field of challengers was to walk a fine line between justifying the continuation of the war to an "honorable end" and denying responsibility for it. On the one hand, he would announce progress in negotiations and escalate bombing to "punish" the North for not negotiating to demonstrate progress to the American public in moving the war toward an "honorable end." Nixon would also re-enter the Vietnam War debate, resuming the use of the containment of communism to justify continuing the war to an "honorable end." Meanwhile, Nixon's supporters warned of the danger to American prisoners of war if Nixon was not reelected to bring the war to an "honorable end." On the other hand, to prevent his personal popularity from become once more entangled with the war, Nixon's supporters frequently reminded voters that it was Democrats who had started the war. In the process, despite four years of mounting evidence that it had been obtained under false pretenses, the Tonkin Gulf Resolution once more became a weapon against dissent. In this deceptive political shorthand, those members of Congress who had voted for the resolution had voted for the war that had cost America tens of thousands of lives over the subsequent eight years.

The strategy of the field of presidential hopefuls in 1972 was dramatically different from the strategy of antiwar presidential candidates in 1968. In 1968, opponents of the war in the presidential race attacked the Johnson administration's use of the ideology of military containment of communism to justify the war. By 1972, in the aftermath of the failed foreign policy revolution, opponents of the war had largely abandoned this strategy. A few of the president's Democratic challengers still occasionally attacked the administration's use of containment to justify continuing the Vietnam War, their attacks were primarily focused on the administration's credibility.

CBS News commentator Eric Severed was perhaps President Nixon's most vocal critic in on television in 1972, and his barbs were aimed squarely at Nixon's credibility. In one editorial, Eric Sevareid claimed, "The credibility gap in this capital is beginning to take on the proportions of the San Andreas Fault." The occasion of this hyperbole was the president's statement in a CBS interview that he had renewed bombing of Hanoi because North Vietnam broke its implicit understanding from 1968 that it would not reescalate the war and because the North had rejected a proposal to return U.S. prisoners of war in exchange for a date certain for withdrawal of U.S. troops. Sevareid said, "Senators and former government officials are now severely challenging both statements."[242] Sevareid added:

> The public has a right to the truth. The government often withholds truth for acceptable reasons, but when it deliberately distorts the truth in public that is another matter. The Pentagon Papers demonstrated that this is what happened repeatedly on Vietnam.[243]

Sevareid concluded, "Admitting mistakes, said Mr. Nixon Sunday night, destroys one's credibility. . . . Surely the operating truth is that what destroys credibility . . . is concealing mistakes and being found out."[244]

Many congressional dissenters also continued to attack the president's credibility on the war. In his 1972 State of the Union Address, President Nixon's only comment on the Vietnam War was to say that it was "com[ing] to an end."[245] In the Democratic Party's response to the president's 1972 State of the Union Address, Democratic Senator Frank Church of Idaho attacked the president's continued use of containment to justify the war as deceptive (despite the fact that Nixon and his administration had not actually provided such justifications since early 1971).[246] Church said:

> President Nixon tells us that we can't give up the war until we ensure the future of South Vietnam. Common sense tells us that there's no way to ensure Vietnam's future. One day, we will have to leave. And when we do, the future of Vietnam will revert to the people who live there, the Vietnamese themselves, in whose hands it should have been left from the beginning.[247]

Church concluded, "Until we elect a Democratic President pledged to withdraw all of our remaining forces from Vietnam, we'll remain chained to this senseless, endless war."[248] This was an implicit attack on the credibility of President Nixon, who had promised four years earlier that *he* would end the war.

Democratic presidential hopefuls also attacked the credibility of the Nixon administration. For instance, in a speech in January 1972, Senator Edmund Muskie claimed he was running because "the next president . . . [must] have the capacity to reach out to every American whoever he or she is, and be *believed*! And be believed!" (emphasis is Muskie's). In his summation, reporter Frank Reynolds said that Muskie believed that positions on individual issues were less important "if the candidate is able to make people trust him."[249]

In fact, even some Republican presidential hopefuls were attacking the Nixon administration's credibility. Republican Representative Pete McCloskey Jr. of California told CBS reporter Morton Dean, "I think that this issue of truth in government is perhaps more important even than Vietnam. The main issue of my campaign today is forcing this government to tell the truth." When asked if the issue was "going to be the credibility gap," McCloskey quipped, "There isn't just a gap in credibility these days. There is no credibility in the Nixon administration."[250]

To silence Democratic challengers—and to distance the president from the war—Republican supporters of the president frequently reminded Americans that it was the Democrats who had started the war in Vietnam. For instance, Republican Senator Bob Dole of Kansas told television viewers on the *ABC Evening News*:

> Self-righteous denunciations are not going to make anyone forget that McGovern and Humphrey and Muskie and Kennedy . . . backed the effort to put this nation into Vietnam right up to the hilt. And all of these men who aspire to the Presidency who are now in the Senate voted for the Gulf of Tonkin Resolution which was tantamount to a declaration of war. . . . I think those who wrongly sent American boys to Southeast Asia are under an obligation to support the President as he rightly brings them home.[251]

Dole's analysis, of course, implicitly supported both the idea that the Tonkin Gulf Resolution *did* give Johnson authority to fight the war and the idea that senators believed they were voting to authorize a full-scale war when they voted for the Tonkin Gulf Resolution (clearly erroneous, given the Johnson administration's private assurances to the contrary). It also ignores the fact that, unlike Democratic members of Congress, Republican members of Congress voted unanimously for the Tonkin Gulf Resolution and were among the fiercest "hawks" throughout the Johnson presidency.

The president had to balance his desire to distance himself from the war with his desire to end the war in a way that preserved the goal of containing communism in Southeast Asia. Thus, he had to demonstrate progress in bringing the war to an "honorable end." It was probably toward this end that the Nixon administration revealed in early 1972 that Henry Kissinger had been involved in secret peace talks with North Vietnam for months and that the administration had proposed a plan for peace. The American public responded very favorably to the revelation of secret peace talks. For most of 1971, more Americans had disapproved than approved of the president's policies in Vietnam. After President Nixon's revelation of Kissinger's secret talks, 53 percent of Americans approved of the president's handling of the war, while only 39 percent disapproved, a dramatic reversal of public opinion.[252] While the president had, throughout his presidency, used troop withdrawals to purchase credibility with the American people, as troop numbers in Vietnam dwindled (by 1972, 158,000 and dropping fast),[253] these withdrawals also began to positively impact approval of his policies in Vietnam. Of the majority of Americans who approved of his policies, 45 percent specifically cited troop withdrawals—not negotiations—as the reason for their approval. Moreover, after the announcement of negotiations, the president's critics quickly began losing ground in convincing Americans that the president was dishonest; of the minority of Americans who did disapprove of the president's handling of the war, only 30 percent cited the president's dishonesty as the reason for their disapproval.[254]

Still, the announcement of progress in negotiations did little to neutralize Vietnam as a political issue. In an election-year special, Walter Cronkite claimed that the president had "virtually nullified Vietnam as an issue in campaign '72" and inoculated himself against attacks on his credibility with "troop withdrawals and his latest peace offer." McGovern rejected this notion outright, saying that he would still campaign on a date certain for withdrawal from Vietnam and would also, as reporter Michele Clark put it, "lean more heavily on the credibility gap between the Nixon administration and the American people." Likewise, Clark said McGovern would highlight that the American people had "been misled so many times that [McGovern] has serious doubts that the president has told the whole truth." She also said that McGovern would "increase his attacks on the secrecy of this administration" while emphasizing the "image of honesty and straight-forwardness that McGovern has tried to build."[255]

Other presidential hopefuls also insisted that the war was still a campaign issue. Democratic Senator Eugene McCarthy denied that the peace plan would neutralize the war as an issue. He continued his calls from the 1968 campaign for the Viet Cong to be included in a South Vietnamese coalition government.[256] Republican Representative Pete McCloskey was probably the candidate most hurt by the announcement of negotiations. McCloskey had run on the president's credibility on negotiations, claiming that he was not truly trying to end the war. As reporter Ike Pappas put it, "The revelation that the administration has been working secretly for months to end the war has thus weakened McCloskey's argument." Pappas continued, "[McCloskey] now admits that the conscious impression amongst most voters is that the war is almost over and that it is no longer a political issue." Still, McCloskey claimed that the war remained an issue until the prisoners of war were returned and the bombs stopped falling.[257]

In late March 1972, the North Vietnamese launched a Spring Offensive that would eventually involve six North Vietnamese Army divisions. This massive conventional assault against South Vietnam offered another opportunity for the administration to show progress in bringing the war to an end by "getting tough" with North Vietnam with dramatically escalated bombing. The offensive also offered the administration's supporters an opportunity to return to the use of the ideology of containment to justify continuing the war. In April 1972, in a report about the Spring Offensive, ABC News reminded Americans that the North Vietnamese received their war supplies from the Soviet Union. This report claimed that "80 percent of the military aid given the North Vietnamese comes from the Soviet Union." In a voiceover of ships in Haiphong Harbor, reporter Roger Peterson added that this aid included "tanks, planes, guns, and ammunition." Over a picture of antiaircraft guns, Peterson added, "Other weapons include hundreds of antiaircraft guns such as these installed around the outskirts of Hanoi." Peterson concluded, "The Soviets supplied the equipment to give Hanoi the potential to switch from guerilla warfare to the full scale attacks currently underway."[258] According to Peterson, the war in Vietnam was a war of communist aggression backed by Moscow.

ABC News' Howard K. Smith also used containment to defend the president's continuing the war to an "honorable end." In fact, Smith complained about President Nixon's absence from the Vietnam War debate since early 1971, saying that the president should remind Americans of the importance of South Vietnam to American security. Smith said that the Nixon administration "has never fully explained why keeping South Vietnam non-Communist is a vital U.S. interest." (This is probably an unfair charge; while Nixon had been largely silent on Vietnam for most of 1971, he had repeatedly used containment to justify the war earlier in his presidency.) Smith reminded his audience that "Johnson and Kennedy explained it with the domino theory which I believe had validity." Smith added, "If the Communists seized Vietnam, it would so whet their ambitions and intimidate their neighbors that all South Asia would fall in time." Smith claimed this would lead to "a bigger war to stop a bigger aggressive coalition." Smith did admit that China had lost some of its revolutionary zeal and that Indonesia was much less prone to communist takeover than it had been at the beginning of the Vietnam War. Smith also reckoned that Nixon "did not want to defend the arguments of past administrations that got us *in*. It seemed easier to defend its own policy of getting us *out*" (emphasis is Smith's). However, Smith concluded that, since "we are clearly doing *more* than getting out" (emphasis is again Smith's), Nixon owed America an explanation as to why he was "fighting, just as Johnson did, to keep South Vietnam non-Communist." He needed to explain, Smith said, "exactly why it is worth the sacrifice."[259]

In response to these calls for his return to the debate over the Vietnam War, President Nixon did finally reassert that the containment of communism required continuing the war. Recalling the bloodbath arguments of the previous administration,[260] he said:

> If the United States betrays the millions of people who have relied on us in Vietnam, the President of the United States, whoever he is, will not deserve or receive the respect which is essential if the United States is to continue to play the great role we are destined to play, of helping to build a new structure of peace in the world.[261]

Nixon also argued, "If the Communists win militarily in Vietnam, the risk of war in other parts of the world would be enormously increased."[262]

Nixon's opponents in the media responded to his return to the Vietnam War debate with renewed attacks on his credibility. Walter Cronkite attacked the administration's claim that it was withdrawing troops from Vietnam as misleading. He noted that "6,000 GIs were withdrawn from Vietnam last week, but 1,000 Marines were sent there, so the net drop was 5,000." However, he added, "16,000 additional naval personnel were dispatched for off-shore duty," but "the Pentagon doesn't count the men on ships or in Thailand among the 85,000 they say are left in Vietnam." Still, Cronkite quipped, "simple arithmetic shows that 11,000 more GIs went to the war last week than came home."[263]

In May, the president decided to mine Haiphong Harbor. The announced reason was to prevent the resupply of North Vietnam by the Soviet Union. However, the Soviet Union had been supplying arms to North Vietnam for years. Admittedly, a renewed North Vietnamese offensive was making gains in the south. The mining of Haiphong was at least partially intended to blunt that offensive and put more pressure on the North Vietnamese to accept a negotiated settlement. However, another major reason for this move, like the announcement of negotiations and the president's reentry into the Vietnam War debate, was to demonstrate progress to the American people in bringing the war to an "honorable end."

Former Vice President Hubert Humphrey used this move to attack the president's credibility. Humphrey did say, "The course [Nixon] has chosen is filled with unpredictable danger." But this was only the prelude to an attack on the president's credibility on ending the war. Humphrey added, "It offers no real hope of ending the war, nor of protecting American forces. It does not speed up the date of the withdrawal of American forces."[264] Mining of Haiphong Harbor was an escalation, a violation of the president's promise to end the war.

In response to Democratic objections to the mining of Haiphong, conservative Democratic presidential candidate and Alabama Governor George Wallace joined President Nixon's supporters in attacking liberal Democrats by reminding Americans that they had started the war. Wallace said, "These liberal Senators . . . all of 'em voted for the Gulf of Tonkin Resolution that got us into the war, but once we got into it, then they ran around and said don't get it over with, don't win it." He added that this vacillation was "the cause of the . . . predicament that we are in now."[265] Despite four years of mounting evidence that the Tonkin Gulf Resolution had been obtained under false pretenses, it was still being used as a weapon against dissent.

As McGovern pulled into the lead in the Democratic primary, a weapon that Nixon's supporters frequently wielded against him was the fate of prisoners of war in North Vietnam. Not only did this line of attack target McGovern's proposal for a date certain to withdraw from Vietnam, it also served as yet another justification for continuing the war to an "honorable end." Veteran John O'Neill, leader of Concerned Vietnam Veterans for Nixon, was among the speakers at a sparsely attended rally in Washington, DC, covered by ABC News. He said, "Senator McGovern promises peace through massive defense cuts and through a unilateral withdrawal in Vietnam that would leave our brothers rotting in North Vietnamese jails." In the *ABC Evening News* story about the rally, attendee Elizabeth Hill (identified in a caption as a "P.O.W. wife") added, "We must not let Senator McGovern's naïve and unrealistic thinking render futile the efforts to bring our prisoners home. It's not going to be as simple as just pulling out our troops and begging." A man identified as Dwight Reeves added that McGovern had helped send these prisoners of war to Vietnam "in 1964 when he voted for the Tonkin Resolution."[266] This, of course, once more suggested that the Tonkin Gulf Resolution had given Johnson authority to prosecute the war and ignored the fact that the Johnson administration had assured Congress that it would not use the resolution to escalate the conflict.

Reporter Frank Tomlinson did question the credibility of the group—and implicitly the president's credibility—in his summation of the story. He said, "This group denied any connection with the White House or the Committee to Re-elect the President, saying that most of the veterans supporting Nixon are Democrats."[267] What Tomlinson did not know was that, in fact, John O'Neill had stood in the Oval Office a year earlier and received marching orders directly from President Nixon on how to attack the antiwar movement.[268]

Senator McGovern also contributed to his own failure in the presidential campaign. After McGovern sent supporter Pierre Salinger to Paris to talk to North Vietnamese negotiators, White House Press Secretary Ron Ziegler said that this would make negotiations tougher, adding, "We are concerned." Republican Senator Robert Griffin of Michigan was more direct in a speech at a press conference from the Republican National Convention in Miami Beach: "Senator McGovern doesn't stand a chance in November unless the Vietnam War continues until after Election Day." Griffin claimed that this was the only explanation for why "an amateur diplomat from Senator McGovern's entourage would meddle and inject himself into the official negotiations which are going on to end the war and release the prisoners of war." (This is a particularly interesting charge given that the Nixon campaign actually did meddle in negotiations four years earlier for much the same reason.) McGovern's initial denials that he had sent Salinger to Paris only made matters worse, providing a rare opportunity for Nixon supporters to turn the tables on McGovern; Griffin said, "Senator McGovern's credibility, which was something less than a thousand percent, that . . . credibility *gap* . . . has now widened until it is as wide as the Atlantic Ocean" (emphasis is Griffin's). After McGovern admitted that he had sent Salinger to Paris, even NBC reporter John Chancellor acknowledged, "The Salinger affair has given McGovern something of a credibility problem."[269]

McGovern counterattacked against Nixon's credibility, saying, "The Nixon administration has had three and a half years to bring the war to an end and bring our prisoners of war home, and it has failed to accomplish that objective." He added that Henry Kissinger was presently "on a highly publicized global junket on the eve of the Republican National Convention. And *that* is what is interfering with quiet, serious professional negotiating far more than anyone else possibly could" (emphasis is McGovern's). He concluded, "Mr. Nixon has manipulated Mr. Kissinger and he has manipulated American public opinion to appear to be negotiating seriously, when actually he has been stalling to prop up General Thieu's government in Saigon."[270] This counterattack did little to mitigate McGovern's self-inflicted credibility problems.

As the election approached, the Watergate scandal that would ultimately end the Nixon presidency began to become an additional target for those wanting to attack the president's credibility. In fact, the president's critics were frustrated that the public was not more outraged by the growing scandal. In October 1972, Eric Sevareid claimed, "One reason for apparent public apathy about the Watergate scandal is widespread suspicion of press honesty and fairness." Sevareid blamed this suspicion of the press on "prolonged attacks by the president's chosen instrument, Vice President Agnew," which began in 1969.[271] Sevareid claimed that this was part of a calculated strategy:

Mr. Nixon had carefully studied the Johnson credibility gap. And what better way to avoid or postpone your own credibility gap as the inevitable troubles arise than to impugn in advance the credibility of those trying to report and explain your actions. . . . Professional political propagandists managed to persuade a fair part of the public that practicing journalists were the propagandists.[272]

In Sevareid's conception, the public's failure to be outraged by the president's deception was, itself, evidence of the president's deception.

On the eve of the presidential election, it was clear that Richard Nixon would win by a landslide. Yet, despite the seeming inevitability of his defeat, George McGovern continued to attack President Nixon's credibility right up to Election Day. In an interview with CBS's Bruce Morton and Bob Schieffer just before the election, Senator George McGovern claimed that the president's credibility gap on Vietnam was a symptom of a deeper immorality in the Nixon administration, also evidenced by the growing Watergate scandal. McGovern said, "The moral standards of the government have deteriorated very rapidly under the present administration." For the Nixon administration, he added, "it's politics as usual, for one political committee to wiretap the headquarters of another. And to maintain a fund that we believe to be at least $700 thousand that is used for no other purpose except political sabotage." McGovern said the continuing of the war was also immoral: "The continuance of this war, the tragic level of bombardment that has continued. I really regard it as evil." Yet, confusingly, McGovern also claimed that the *absence* of U.S. troops in Vietnam was immoral: "I regard it as immoral that for the first time in our history, we're involved in an enterprise that we're not willing anymore to die for ourselves but we're stilling willing to kill for . . . even when innocent people's lives are involved." McGovern also hinted that the looming prospect of a peace settlement was a lie: "There was simply the hope of a settlement which was escalated into a virtual promise of peace." In response to Morton's question about whether there was "a public feeling of having been conned about the war by the administration," McGovern added, "There has been too much deception both here at home and now even in the issue of war and peace itself." He summarized the president's claim: "He said to the American people, well we're not going to have peace before the election, but if you trust me for another four years, we will have peace after the election." McGovern reminded Americans, "That's the same thing he told us four years ago and I think it's going to be widely rejected at the polls on Tuesday."[273]

Signing the Vietnam peace agreement.

Source: Robert L. Knudsen, "Paris peace talks Vietnam peace agreement signing," January 27, 1973, Nixon Presidential Library.[274]

It wasn't rejected. Nixon was reelected in 1972 by a wide margin. Moreover, his postelection bombing of the North (the so-called "Christmas bombing") convinced the South Vietnamese to agree to the accord reached with North Vietnam in Paris. However, because of troop withdrawals, the Nixon administration had long since ran out of sufficient forces in South Vietnam to threaten North Vietnamese ambitions and force better terms at the negotiating table. Rather than an "honorable end" to the war that preserved the goal of containment of communism in Southeast Asia, Nixon was forced to accept the continuing presence of North Vietnamese forces in the south, a humiliating compromise that set the stage for the eventual destruction of South Vietnam.[275]

The framework for debate of the war established in 1968—between supporters using containment to justify continuing the war to an "honorable end" and opponents attacking the president's credibility—remained the framework for debate of the war until the end of U.S. military involvement in Vietnam in 1973. Throughout his presidency, Nixon, his administration, and supporters of the war from the former administration and the media used the ideology of military containment of communism to justify continuing the war in Vietnam to an "honorable end." In contrast, by the time of the inauguration of President Richard Nixon, attacks on the use of the ideology of military containment of communism to justify the Vietnam War or the broader foreign policy paradigm of military containment had virtually ceased. Instead, most opponents of the war attacked administration credibility on the initiation, conduct, and resolution of the war.

President Nixon's best, most effective weapon against attacks on his credibility was troop withdrawals, which most in the American public equated with the administration making good on its pledge to end the war. This formula—using troop withdrawals to buy credibility with the American people—was actually established by opponents of the war. Early in the Nixon presidency, dissenters struggled to find effective ways to attack the president's credibility until they began to attack him for failing to take sufficient steps to fulfill his pledge to end the war. Nixon responded with troop withdrawals. Through this process, troop withdrawals became the currency for the administration to "purchase" credibility with the American people. The president would return to this tactic repeatedly to sustain his credibility through the end of the war.

In 1970 and 1971, a number of events threatened to destroy Nixon's credibility and bring the war to an earlier end. Nixon's decision to use U.S. troops to invade Cambodia in 1970—an expansion of the conflict by any measure—called into question the administration's true willingness to end the war. The abysmal performance of the Army of the Republic of Vietnam during its invasion of Laos in early 1971 called into question the credibility of the president's claims about the success of his policy of Vietnamization of the war. The publicity surrounding the end of the My Lai massacre trials put U.S. war crimes at the forefront of Americans' minds just as the Vietnam Veterans Against the War led massive demonstrations in Washington against an administration that they claimed was lying to the American people about the true brutality of the war. Finally, the release of the Pentagon Papers both contributed to the already pervasive public perception that the war was illegitimate because it had been initiated under false pretenses and provided an opportunity for Nixon's opponents to redouble their attacks on his credibility. Nixon tried to mitigate the impact of these blows to his credibility with the announcement that he would accelerate troop withdrawals. While this announcement halted the precipitous drop in confidence in the president's credibility, after this crisis of credibility, most Americans no longer believed the president or supported his policies in Vietnam.

In fact, this crisis might have ended the Nixon presidency, but for an interesting phenomenon that began to take shape in American public opinion in the second half of 1971. The president and his administration stopped talking about the Vietnam War and, slowly, Americans began to separate their perceptions of the war from their perceptions of the Nixon administration; President Nixon's personal approval began to climb and perceptions of his credibility began to recover from their lows after the release of the Pentagon Papers. At the same time, American patience with the Vietnam War was rapidly running out. The Vietnam War had become a political orphan.

Yet these two tactics—using troop withdrawals to sustain his credibility and distancing himself from the war to improve his personal approval—presented problems for President Nixon in 1972, in the midst of the presidential race. At the beginning of 1972, Nixon could still hope to end the war on terms that might preserve his goal of containing communism in Southeast Asia—if he could compel the North and South Vietnamese to accept a negotiated settlement, keep the American people from forcing an earlier end to the war, and, of course, win the election. However, the mechanism Nixon had used to sustain his credibility for the previous three years—exchanging troop withdrawals for credibility with the American people—threatened this goal; if he was going to compel them to accept a settlement, Nixon needed to sustain sufficient ground forces in Vietnam to present a credible obstacle to North Vietnamese ambitions and reassure the South Vietnamese of continued U.S. support. Likewise, Nixon could not convince Americans to continue to support the war if he never talked about it; ultimately he was forced to re-enter the debate over the war, which only invited more attacks on his credibility on ending it. The president was able to use the announcement of progress in negotiations, the escalation of bombing, and the mining of Haiphong Harbor as alternate means to sustain his credibility on ending the war, but troop withdrawals remained his primary tool. Moreover, the field of presidential hopefuls were relentlessly in their attacks on Nixon's credibility. Eventually, the president ran out of troops to withdraw and was forced to accept a humiliating compromise peace that set the stage for the final destruction of South Vietnam.

The former members of the failed foreign policy revolution—that small subset of the broader antiwar movement that had sought not just to end the war but also to move the United States beyond a foreign policy founded in the ideology of military containment of communism—remained in the public debate over the war after their revolution collapsed in 1968. While revolutionaries in Congress were not able to move the United States beyond a foreign policy of containment as they had once hoped, they were successful in progressively limiting presidential power in foreign policy. Their first modest victory came in the passage of the National Commitments Resolution in 1969. However, this first victory was followed by others. The Cambodian Incursion created the political impetus for congressional foreign policy revolutionaries to pass the Cooper-Church amendment to prevent the administration from supporting South Vietnamese troops in Cambodia. The invasion of Cambodia also provided these congressional revolutionaries with the momentum to repeal the Tonkin Gulf Resolution. More victories would come after the end of U.S. military intervention in Vietnam, including the Case-Church amendment to block further U.S. military intervention in Vietnam, Laos, or Cambodia and, finally, the 1973 War Powers Act that reasserted congressional power in war-making.

The radical revolutionaries of the foreign policy revolution were less successful after 1968 in achieving progress toward their goal of turning American society away from the ideology of containment. While there would be a number of large radical protests during the Nixon administration, including the Moratorium and the protests after the Cambodian Incursion, radical dissent was increasingly subsumed by the Vietnam veteran protest movement, which was seen as much more credible by the media and focused its dissent on the administration's credibility on its conduct of the war. As radical demonstrations receded from the Vietnam War debate, many radical protesters moved to other causes or fading into the counterculture. A few moved from relatively benign anti-imperialist rhetoric to hardliner Marxism, further separating themselves from the mainstream of American society. And a tiny minority, the most militant of these radicals, actually turned to anti-imperialist insurgency against their own country.

The framework for public debate of foreign policy issues established in the latter half of the Vietnam War—between supporters of military intervention using justifications based on the ideology of containment and dissenters attacking the administration's credibility—would have a lasting impact on American foreign policy far beyond the Vietnam War. First, because opponents of intervention attacked the administration's credibility rather than its use of containment to justify intervention or the ideology of containment itself, the American public continued to embrace the Cold War consensus after the Vietnam War. Second, this framework for debate of foreign policy would frequently recur in the debate of other military interventions throughout the remainder of the Cold War. Nearly every time a military intervention was contemplated by the administration, this pattern of public debate reassert itself.

Chapter 6

REFIGHTING THE VIETNAM WAR .

The change in the opposition's strategy for public debate of the Vietnam War in 1968—from attacking the administration's use of containment to justify the war to attacking the administration's credibility—had two significant consequences that reverberated beyond the Vietnam War, to the end of the Cold War. First, because opponents of U.S. military intervention in Vietnam stopped attacking the ideology of military containment of communism—the core of the Cold War consensus—this ideology remained largely unchallenged from 1968 through the end of the war. As a result, not surprisingly, after the war most in the American public continued to embrace the Cold War consensus, even if a significant portion of the foreign policymaking elite in and out of government had abandoned part or all of it.

Second, the framework for debate established during the latter half of the Vietnam War—between those using the ideology of military containment of communism to justify military intervention and those opposing military intervention by attacking the administration's credibility—frequently reemerged when interventions were contemplated throughout the remainder of the Cold War. When North Vietnam launched a massive offensive in South Vietnam in 1975, the new Ford administration contemplated military intervention to contain this communist aggression. The framework for public debate of foreign policy established during the latter half of the Vietnam War immediately reasserted itself. When Ronald Reagan took office, he advocated a series of military interventions to block or roll back communist expansion in Central America—and used the ideology of containment to justify these interventions. The framework of foreign policy debate established during the Vietnam War once more reasserted itself, with opponents attacking the Reagan administration's credibility to slow or block these interventions.

Because opponents of the war largely stopped attacking the ideology of military containment of communism and its application to the war in Vietnam in 1968 and instead began attacking the administration's credibility, the American public continued to embrace the ideology of military containment of communism—the core of the Cold War consensus—after the end of the Vietnam War. In fact, three years after the departure of U.S. military forces from Vietnam—a year after the fall of Saigon to North Vietnamese Communists and in the midst of an economic downturn—the American public was even more supportive of the Cold War consensus than it had been immediately following the war. Even young college students, today frequently conflated with radical dissenters, still embraced many of the tenets of military containment. On the other hand, the Cold War consensus among foreign policy leaders in and out of government—the foreign policy elite—was broken. Some members of this elite continued to embrace some or all of the precepts of containment after the war while others rejected them. Yet even among these foreign policy elites, the majority still embraced many tenets of military containment.

A number of scholars have argued that the Cold War consensus collapsed during or after the Vietnam War.[1] Yet polling data from after the end of the Vietnam War clearly shows that the American public continued to hold to the Cold War consensus—a belief in military containment of communism—after the Vietnam War. The response of most Americans to a number of questions, ranging from their belief in continued United States military strength to where that strength should be postured to when that strength should be used in direct military intervention to block communist expansion indicates that they still accepted the precepts of military containment.

A year after the end of America's participation in the Vietnam War, most in the American public clearly still believed in maintaining the tools of military containment and were still worried about the threat of communist expansion. For instance, when asked about the goal of "maintaining respect for the United States in other countries," a majority of Americans who had an opinion (51 percent) said the country had "lost some" or "lost much ground." However, most Americans' prescription for restoring the United States' position in the world was renewed military strength. When asked their opinion about "spending for defense and military purposes," a majority of Americans who had an opinion (60 percent) believed spending should be "increased" or "kept at [its] present level." Moreover, when asked how concerned they were about a series of problems, Americans indicated that they still believed in the aims of military containment. A majority of Americans who had an opinion were concerned "a great deal" or "a fair amount" about "maintaining respect for the U.S. in other countries" (78 percent), "maintaining close relations with our allies" (78 percent), "the problem of Communist China" (65 percent), "the problem of the Soviet Union" (70 percent), and "the threat of Communism" (68 percent).[2]

Most Americans also explicitly endorsed maintaining a large military presence, forward-deployed on the periphery of the Communist World to discourage communist expansion in Europe and Asia. When asked what the United States should do "over the next few" years with its total military power, even when reminded of "the high cost of more defense and military forces," 44 percent of Americans who had an opinion believed America's military power should be "kept at [its] present level" while 43 percent believed it should be "increased." And Americans believed that these forces should be used to contain communism; when asked about America's "substantial military forces stationed in Western Europe for defense purposes," 56 percent of Americans who had an opinion believed this force should be "kept at [its] present level." Even more Americans (58 percent) believed that "military forces stationed in Asia for defense purposes, including in Japan, South Korea, and Thailand," should be "kept at [their] present level."[3]

Admittedly, the polling data is more ambiguous on the question of whether the American people were still willing to use military force to actually fight against communist expansion and where they were willing to do so. By a narrow margin most Americans who had an opinion (51 percent) were no longer willing to "take all necessary steps, including the use of armed force, to prevent the spread of communism to any other parts of the free world." But the operative word here was "any" and this particular poll was silent on the question of specific areas Americans *would* be willing to "use armed force" to block communist expansion. Moreover, by an even greater margin most Americans (52 percent) were willing to, "at all costs, even going to the very brink of war if necessary," do anything required to ensure the United States "maintain[ed] its dominant position as the world's most powerful nation."[4]

Polling data was not ambiguous at all in showing that Americans believed they had sacrificed enough blood and treasure for Vietnam. When asked if they believed the United States had "under the circumstances made the best deal it could to settle the conflict" in Vietnam, the majority of Americans (77 percent) who had an opinion, agreed that it had. Moreover, most Americans had no appetite for providing *any* support to South Vietnam. When asked if the "United States should continue to provide military equipment and supplies to the government of South Vietnam to help it combat the Communist forces," a majority of Americans who expressed an opinion (56 percent) said the United States "should not."[5] These sentiments were almost certainly on the minds of members of Congress as they considered President Ford's request to renew U.S. military intervention to rescue South Vietnam from a North Vietnamese offensive a year later.

Counterintuitively, in 1976, a year after the fall of Saigon that marked the final loss of America's Vietnam War and during a severe economic downturn in the United States, it appears that even more Americans embraced the Cold War consensus than had done so in 1974. While the polling data is less complete, when asked about many elements of the ideology of military containment of communism—the core of the Cold War consensus—more Americans agreed with these precepts than had in 1974. In June 1976, despite the fact that a majority of Americans (55 percent) identified economic fears, such as "deterioration in or [an] inadequate standard of living," "unemployment," or "economic instability" as their greatest fears, Americans were still willing to spend money to maintain the tools of military containment around the world. When asked about the "amount the United States is now spending for defense and military purposes" over two-thirds of Americans believed that spending should either be "increased" or kept at its "present level." Even when told "the U.S. is now spending a good deal abroad" to maintain "military bases in many parts of the world and the military forces stationed there," a majority of Americans (53 percent) still wanted spending on the stationing of forces abroad "increased" or kept at its "present level." Moreover, two thirds of Americans who had an opinion believed that, if they were attacked by the Soviet Union, the United States should "come to the defense of its major European allies with military force." A majority of Americans (53 percent) believed America should also "come to the defense of Japan with military force if it is attacked by Soviet Russia or Communist China." A majority of Americans who had an opinion (55 percent) believed that "the U.S. should maintain its dominant position as the world's most powerful nation at all costs, even going to the very brink of war if necessary." Most importantly, a narrow majority of Americans who had an opinion (just over 50 percent) now believed that "the U.S. should take all necessary steps, including the use of armed force, to prevent the spread of communism to any other party of the free world." Again, the operative word in this question was "any," and this was a reversal from 1974 when a narrow majority would *not* use armed force to protect "any" part of the free world. Americans were also more concerned than they had been in 1974 about the threats with which military containment was meant to contend. Fifty-eight percent of Americans were concerned "a great deal" or "a fair amount" about "the problem of Communist China," while 68 percent were concerned "a great deal" or "a fair amount" about "the problem of the Soviet Union," and 73 percent were concerned "a great deal" or "a fair amount" about "the threat of Communism."[6]

There was a clear divide between young and old—especially among young college students—on the Cold War consensus. Younger Americans both were less passionate about maintaining the tools of military containment and were less apt to believe in the altruism of American foreign policy than their older counterparts. In spring 1973, young college students, by a margin of 79 percent, favored "cutting back defense spending and using the money for domestic needs." Eighty-nine percent of college students "strongly" or "partially" agreed with the statement that "our foreign policy is based on our own narrow economic and power interests."[7]

However, despite nearly a decade of radical protests against the ideology of containment, most college students had not been radicalized. Sixty-seven percent of students partially or strongly agreed that they were "sick and tired of hearing people attack patriotism, morality, and other American values." Only 18 percent of college students believed "radical change" or "an entirely new" "American society" and "American life" was needed. Most American college students did not see themselves as radicals or identify with radical politics. When asked in spring 1973, only 8 percent of college students felt "a sense of identification" with "the New Left," only seven percent identified with "the counterculture," only six percent identified with "The Movement," and only four percent identified with "the Old Left." Admittedly, college students were not much more amenable to mainstream politics than they were to radical politics; only 21 percent identified with "conservatives" and only 34 percent identified with "liberals."[8]

Moreover, while young college students were less supportive than older Americans of spending money to retain the tools of military containment, most still accepted containment's goals. When asked what values were worth fighting for, more college students did say "containing communism" and "maintaining our position in the world" were "not worth fighting for." However by a larger margin, most college students said "protecting our allies," "counteracting aggression," and "protecting our national interests" *were* "worth fighting for."[9] These goals, based on the ideology of containment, were among those that both the Johnson and the Nixon administration had used to justify the Vietnam War.

Young people who were not college students were asked these same questions by pollsters. Their answers show that nonstudent youth held more of the precepts of the Cold War consensus than their counter-parts in college. By a huge margin, most non-student youth believed "containing communism" and "maintaining our position in the world" *were* "worth fighting for." The majority of nonstudent youth even believed "fighting for our honor" was "worth fighting for." Still, neither a majority of college students nor a majority of nonstudent youth believed "keeping a commitment" was "worth fighting for."[10]

Many scholars have argued that the Cold War consensus was both a popular consensus held by the broader American public and a pol-icy consensus amongst elites.[11] Many of these scholars argue that the Vietnam War broke the consensus among elites but that the consensus among the American public survived the war.[12] To a certain extent, an examination of polling data from the years after the Vietnam War supports this contention. However, the Cold War consensus among foreign policy elites was not completely shattered; some of the precepts of military containment continued to enjoy nearly universal support among foreign policy leaders.

The Cold War consensus held by the elite coterie of foreign pol-icy formulators was significantly weaker than the consensus held by the broader American public. The Council on Foreign Relations con-ducted a poll of foreign policy "leaders" that shows that these elites did not believe as strongly in retaining the tools of military containment as did the broader American populace. The Council on Foreign Relations found that a majority of these leaders (56 percent) wanted "defense spending" "cut back," while only 33 percent wanted spending "kept [the] same." Still, of those leaders who would cut spending, 56 percent would not cut back spending "if it meant that our military strength would fall behind that of the Soviet Union." The majority of these lead-ers (73 percent) wanted "military aid to other nations . . . cut back." Nearly two thirds of these leaders wanted "secret political operations of the CIA . . . cut back." These leaders were also more reluctant to use military force to assist "friendly countries" if they were "attacked." Only 32 percent said they would, "if necessary, send American troops and manpower" along with "military aid [and] economic aid" to assist friendly countries. In contrast, 44 percent would send "some military aid as well as economic aid, but . . . not involve any American troops or manpower."[13]

Yet, when asked about specific countries, there were situations where even foreign policy leaders would use military force to contain the expansion of communism. When asked which specific situations would justify "U.S. military involvement, including the use of U.S. troops," a majority said that they would deploy troops if "Western Europe were invaded" (75 percent) or "the Russians took over West Berlin" (53 percent).[14]

Moreover, these leaders continued to support providing military aid and forces to Europe and were still concerned about the threat of communist expansion in a number of other regions around the world. Sixty-one percent of these leaders would "keep [our] commitment what it is" to NATO and a majority of leaders surveyed by the Council of Foreign Relations believed that it "would be [a] threat to the United States" if countries in many regions turned communist— including "Western European Countries" (65 percent), "Japan" (63 percent), and "Latin American countries" (52 percent).[15]

These foreign policy leaders also still believed in internationalism and embraced at least some of the tools, tactics, and goals of containment. The vast majority of these leaders (98 percent) wanted the United States to continue to "take an active part in world affairs." Likewise, a majority of these foreign policy elites (83 percent) still believed that the "willingness" of the United States "to make military commitments to other countries and to keep them" was either "very" or "somewhat important." Even more telling, a majority of these leaders (81 percent) still believed that the goal of "containing communism" was "very" or "somewhat important." An overwhelming majority (95 percent) believed "defending our allies' security" was "very" or "somewhat important" and nearly as many (90 percent) accepted the lessons of Munich that it was "very" or "somewhat important" to protect "weaker nations against foreign aggression." Likewise, a majority of these leaders (76 percent) agreed "strongly" or "somewhat" that "the only way peace can exist in this world is when a country like the United States who wants peace is strong enough to back up warnings to possible aggressor nations that they can't get away with aggression." The majority of foreign policy leaders (90 percent) even believed it was "justified" "to back governments which believe in our free enterprise system but not in democracy" if "there is some advantage to the United States in it" (a consequence of the ideology of containment that drew deep criticism from foreign policy revolutionaries in the first half of the Vietnam War).[16]

In 1968, opponents of the war largely stopped attacking the administration's use of the ideology of military containment of communism to justify U.S. military intervention in Vietnam. Instead, they began to increasingly focus their attacks on the administration's credibility. This framework for debate of the Vietnam War established in 1968—between supporters using the ideology of military containment of communism to justify continuing the war and opponents attacking the administration's credibility—would remain the framework throughout the remainder of the war.

One enduring consequence of this change in opposition strategy was that, even after U.S. military involvement in Vietnam was over, this framework for debate would frequently reassert itself. Nearly every time that an administration contemplated a military intervention to combat what it perceived as communist expansion, it would use the ideology of military containment of communism to justify that intervention. And each time an administration used containment to argue for military intervention, opponents would begin to attack the administration's credibility.

After the Vietnam War, President Nixon used the containment of communism to justify continued air strikes to support America's Southeast Asian allies. Congressional opponents attacked Nixon's credibility to end this intervention. When North Vietnam began its final spring offensive against South Vietnam in 1975, the new Ford administration contemplated military intervention to its South Vietnamese ally from communist aggression. The framework of public debate of foreign policy established during the latter half of the Vietnam War—between the use of the ideology of military containment of communism to justify intervention and attacks on the administration's credibility to block intervention—once more reasserted itself. In the end, opponents of this intervention won the day-and President Ford was unable to intervene.

After the departure of U.S. ground forces from South Vietnam, the Nixon administration continued to use American air power to support friendly forces fighting communists across Southeast Asia. In June 1973, congressional opponents of this continued military intervention tried to limit the president's ability to use airpower in Cambodia and Laos. The president vetoed this measure—a veto upheld by the House—and used containment to justify his move. However, ultimately, the Congress—led by the former members of the failed foreign policy revolution—passed the Case-Church amendment, which prohibited the administration from intervening militarily in Southeast Asia.[17]

Some opponents of further U.S. military intervention in Southeast Asia did attack the Nixon administration's use of containment to justify continued intervention. For instance, Senator Edward Kennedy wondered if the United States was really prepared to "rush back in as soon as the next domino starts to fall."[18]

However, most opponents of continued intervention attacked President Nixon's credibility. Reporter Tom Jarriel reminded Americans that the president had once described Cambodia as "the purest form of the Nixon Doctrine" of providing only aid and not military forces to help countries help themselves before he began demanding the power to intervene militarily with U.S. forces.[19]

As the final North Vietnamese offensive in South Vietnam loomed, the Ford administration used the ideology of containment to justify renewed aid to South Vietnam. Assistant Secretary of State Phillip Habib claimed that the United States had a responsibility to those South Vietnamese who had supported the United States during the war—a variation on the "bloodbath" argument. Habib added, "This country should not abandon people who are prepared to defend themselves and should supply the resources adequate to the task."[20] The Ford administration also used other containment arguments to justify continued assistance to South Vietnam. Habib cited the domino theory, adding that if aid was not provided, "the situation in South Vietnam will erode, and the situation in Cambodia will become increasingly dangerous." Secretary of State Henry Kissinger cited the credibility of U.S. commitments, saying that failure to help South Vietnam would hurt the administration's ability to engage in negotiations in the Middle East.[21]

As South Vietnamese forces fell back before the North Vietnamese onslaught, some opponents of renewed military intervention in South Vietnam attacked the administration's use of containment to justify the war. Republican Senator John Tower of Texas, once a strong supporter of the war, said that statements by the Thai government that "suggested that Americans should depart" were indications "that they feel that the American presence is no longer valuable in Southeast Asia." Democratic Senator Franck Church of Idaho said that U.S. "security never has been at stake in that part of the world."[22]

But attacks on administration credibility were much more prevalent. Frank Church said of repeated calls for aid to Southeast Asia, "New arguments have to be thought up every year to keep us there. And there comes a time when a grown up people should say 'enough.'" Reporter Catherin Mackin of NBC News claimed that the administration's calls for support to South Vietnam were a political ploy. She cited "some Democrats" when she claimed, "President Ford is engaged [in] a word-war with Congress so that he will have someone to blame if Cambodia falls." She added, "These Democrats say that if President Ford really believed United States' security is involved in Cambodia, then he would ask Congress for troops and a lot more money."[23]

As the North Vietnamese invasion intensified, others in Congress also used charges of the administration's dishonesty to block efforts to support South Vietnam. Senator Henry Jackson charged that the administration had made "secret agreements" with Saigon. White House spokesman Ron Nessen was forced to concede that South Vietnam had been given assurances of a "vigorous reaction" from the United States in the event of "massive" North Vietnamese aggression. In response, Jackson launched a Senate investigation into the matter to expose "secret maneuvering" by the administration that he claimed might damage American "credibility" abroad.[24]

President Ford and his advisors discuss the evacuation of Saigon.

Source: White House Photographic Office, Secretary of State Henry Kissinger interrupting a meeting between President Gerald R. Ford and senior advisers to relay the latest information on the U.S. evacuation of Saigon, April 29, 1975, Gerald R. Ford Library.[25]

After the fall of Saigon on April 30, 1975, some former supporters of intervention began to claim that the loss of South Vietnam had already resulted in the dire consequences predicted by the ideology of containment. In a report the day after the fall of Saigon, reporter John Chancellor said the domino theory was "much on the minds of leaders in the Philippines now." Jack Perkins added that Philippine leaders were telling their people, "The United States, whatever it may promise, is not to be depended upon in this part of the world anymore." Perkins added that "Philippine officials [had begun] asking the next question: Then why should they allow the Americans to keep military bases here?" Perkins warned, "President Ceausescu of Rumania [visited] the Philippines, the first time a communist chief of state had ever been allowed to come here." Perkins also noted that both Philippine President Marcos and his wife were visiting China to establish diplomatic ties. The story included an interview with Philippine journalist Teodoro Valencia who said, "Events have proven that America's word cannot be trusted. . . . Especially if the American President makes the commitment, we don't believe it." As if to underscore that this was a proof of the domino theory, Perkins asked Valencia, "The United States today doesn't have the influence that it did before the fall of South Vietnam and Cambodia?" Valencia answered flatly: "No." John Chancellor added after the story that the United States was about to lose bases in Thailand as well.[26]

The fall of Cambodia and Laos to communists was also used by former advocates of U.S. military intervention in Southeast Asia as a proof of the domino theory. In a story about the impending withdrawal of troops from Thailand, Harry Reasoner said that, after the fall of South Vietnam, Cambodia, and Laos, "Thailand is now the only country of the area friendly to the United States." In a voiceover of Thai soldiers patrolling the jungle using U.S. equipment, Reasoner said, "There are those that feel that Thailand not only looks like Vietnam but may end that way, too." Reasoner noted, "North Vietnam, now without a war to worry about, has increased its supply of weapons and some say even manpower to the Thai guerilla movement." Reasoner added in a voiceover of captured U.S. equipment emblazoned with the flag of North Vietnam, "North Vietnam is the dominating power in Southeast Asia now. With an arsenal of captured American planes, weapons, and supplies, Hanoi's potential influence is awesome." Reasoner continued, "That power, coupled with a nearly completed withdrawal of American forces from Thailand, is keeping the old domino theory alive." Reasoner added that the Thai Prime Minister was "trying to reach a political understanding with his Communist neighbors." Reasoner concluded, "Whether this domino indeed falls years after that seems, at this point, to depend on whether Hanoi wants it to."[27]

CBS News launched a very effective counterattack to this contention by ABC News that the domino theory might play out in Thailand by attacking the domino theory itself as an example of administration dishonesty. A CBS news story about the shifting alignment of Thailand included Thai Prime Minister Kukrit Pramoj saying, "The domino theory is [a] purely American invention because, 10 years ago, [the] United States wanted very much, for reasons of its own, to be involved in the affairs of this part of the world."[28]

One of the most dramatic episodes in the Reagan presidency was the scandal surrounding his illegal arming of Contra rebels in Nicaragua with funds from arms sales to Iran. But this devastating blow to Reagan's credibility was actually the culmination of nearly six years of sustained attacks to block his efforts to intervene in Central America. From the time Ronald Reagan took office, he used the ideology of military containment of communism to justify a series of interventions to block or roll back communist expansion in Central America. Opponents of these interventions—almost reflexively—used the strategy of opposition to U.S. military intervention established in the latter half of the Vietnam War: they attacked the administration's credibility. The Iran-Contra scandal was only the final, most dramatic offensive of this campaign.

Candidate Ronald Reagan made it clear, even before he was elected to the presidency, that he was running to reassert the ideology of military containment in American foreign policy.[29] Reagan told Americans:

> When we . . . cast our eyes abroad, we see . . . [a] sorry chapter on the record of the present administration.
>
> As [a] Soviet combat brigade trains in Cuba, just 90 miles from our shores.
>
> A Soviet army of invasion occupies Afghanistan, further threatening our vital interests in the Middle East.
>
> America's defense strength is at its lowest ebb in a generation, while the Soviet Union is vastly outspending us in both strategic and conventional arms.
>
> Our European allies, looking nervously at the growing menace from the East, turn to us for leadership and fail to find it. . . .

Adversaries large and small test our will and seek to confound our resolve, but we are given weakness when we need strength; vacillation when the times demand firmness.[30]

Almost immediately upon taking office, President Ronald Reagan began to use the ideology of containment to justify U.S. intervention abroad. Reagan's first goal was ending the communist insurgency in El Salvador. He promised to be aggressive in the use of diplomacy and military aid because the United States would "not just sit passively by and let this hemisphere be invaded by outside forces." Senator Howard Baker, a supporter of the Reagan administration's aggressive policies in Central America, used the same arguments, saying, "This administration is making a clear, unambiguous, straightforward statement that Castro's not going to have a free hand."[31]

Some in the media also used the ideology of military containment to justify intervention. ABC's Frank Reynolds said that El Salvador "has become, in fact, an East-West confrontation by proxy." Barrie Dunsmore added, "Captured documents released last week pointed to direct Cuban and indirect Soviet involvement in the arming of El Salvador's leftist insurgents." This news story then showed an animated map that would become a staple of the debate over intervention, reproduced and reshown by every network over the following five years: a map of Central America being consumed by a red wave moving outward from Cuba to cover the region all the way to Mexico and Panama. In a voiceover of this animation, Dunsmore said, "The modern-day domino theory is that Cuba currently has strong influence in Nicaragua. If El Salvador is subverted, Honduras and Guatemala will be next, making Mexico very vulnerable." Dunsmore did add a note of caution on the administration's decision to make a stand in El Salvador. He said, "Vietnam may not be an accurate comparison, but having made a stand, it's hard to see where you stop, if the other side doesn't."[32]

Some in the media and Congress attacked the administration's use of containment to justify intervention in El Salvador. Charles Gibson said, "To some members of Congress, what the administration is considering in El Salvador has a familiar ring." He added that El Salvador was "Vietnam in the making." Gibson's news story also showed testimony from former Ambassador to El Salvador Robert White saying that El Salvador faced more danger from security forces of the Right than Leftists. White also insisted that communists couldn't take over the country even if the United States didn't "send one piece of equipment." Gibson concluded that the administration's claim that "if El Salvador falls to the Communists, other countries may fall . . . sounded like a new domino theory."[33]

The media also used leaders from the region to attack the administration's use of containment to justify military intervention in Central America. Reporter Charles Kraus travelled to Mexico City to interview Mexican Foreign Secretary Jorge Castaneda. Kraus began the story with yet another animated depiction of the domino theory in Central America, with Nicaragua, El Salvador, Guatemala, and the remainder of Central America through Mexico progressively turning red. The story then cut to Castaneda, who said, "We don't have [to] fear for our security because our society we think is a strong society." Castaneda concluded, "We're not sure that the domino effect will take place in Central America." Kraus concluded this story by saying that Mexico "has excellent relations with Cuba and Nicaragua's new revolutionary government" and "does not share the Reagan administration's view of other Leftist regimes coming to power in Latin America." He added that Mexico did not "subscribe to the domino theory which now has some currency in Washington."[34]

However, the immediate response from Congress to President Reagan's reassertion of the ideology of containment to justify intervention in Central America—conditioned by the framework of debate established in the latter half of the Vietnam War—was to attack the administration's credibility. And the Congress' first target was CIA Director William Casey. At first, members of Congress attacked Casey personally, blasting him in a press conference over a *New York Times* story that revealed that a New Orleans judge had ruled that he had misled business investors in 1968. The Congress also attacked the credibility of Covert Operations Director Max Hugel after he resigned over personal financial issues. But attacks rapidly spread to questions over three covert operations the CIA was undertaking around the world: increased arms smuggling to mujahedeen in Afghanistan, a secret CIA monitoring station on the Chinese border with the Soviet Union built to track Soviet missile tests, and a secret force of U.S.-backed Cambodians searching for American prisoners of war in that country. Senators claimed that they had learned about all of these operations from press reports rather than from the CIA itself.[35]

Despite these attacks on its credibility, the administration continued to use containment to justify intervention in Central America. Assistant Secretary of State Thomas Enders told Congress in his testimony in February 1982:

> The decisive battle for Central America is now underway in El Salvador. For if, after Nicaragua, El Salvador is captured by a violent minority, who in Central America will not live in fear? How long will it be before major U.S. strategic interests, the canal, the sea lanes, or oil supplies would be at risk?[36]

When Congressman Clarence Long suggested that this was the same logic that had plunged the United States into the Vietnam War, Enders responded, "This is very close to us. This is happening right next to us. This is not Vietnam on the other side of the world. This is right next door to us."[37]

Some in the media continued to attack the administration's use of containment to justify intervention. In one story, Dan Rather repeatedly and incredulously warned the American people that "the domino theory in Central America was [being] resurrected." In a voiceover of a map of Central America, Rather added, "Secretary of State Haig warned that a crisis . . . similar to that in El Salvador is now threatening neighboring Guatemala. And that, Haig said, could pose a very fundamental threat to Mexico." Rather also quoted Haig as saying this process was "a clear, self-influencing sequence of events which could sweep all of Central America into a Cuba-dominated region." But the heart of Rather's critique was the implication that the Reagan administration was being dishonest in cloaking the conflict in Central America in Cold War garb; Rather's skepticism was palpable as he told his viewers, "Haig and other administration members have argued repeatedly that rebels in El Salvador are being directed by outsiders."[38]

Despite these criticisms, the Reagan administration was making a compelling case that the Soviet Union, through Cuba, was supporting communists in Central America. Haig revealed that a Nicaraguan captured fighting with the El Salvador guerillas admitted that they were directed by Cubans and the USSR. Haig also provided Congress with evidence that Soviet-built tanks, artillery, and anti-aircraft guns were being supplied to the rebels. Haig told a congressional committee, "Two thousand Cuban military advisors are in Nicaragua. *Two thousand*. That's almost one for every twenty soldiers" (emphasis is Haig's). As a senator tried to interrupt, Haig continued, "Four to five thousand Cuban technicians and teachers. Seventy Soviet military advisors. Thirty from North Korea, Bulgaria, GDR, and also the PLO."[39]

By 1983, the Reagan administration was calling for the deployment of trainers to Central America to help the forces of friendly governments combat the growing communist insurgency. And, again, the administration turned to the ideology of containment to justify this military intervention. Reagan told Americans in a news conference, "It isn't nutmeg that's at stake in the Caribbean and Central America; it is the United States' national security." He added that the Soviets wanted to Communize the region to cause U.S. forces to concentrate on America's southern border, giving the Soviet Union a freer hand in the rest of the world. He concluded, "That is the reason the guerillas must be stopped in El Salvador."[40]

Members of the administration went even further. Caspar Weinberger claimed the Soviets were trying to "attack" the United States in an "incremental way, from the south." Weinberger echoed Reagan's claim that this would "pressure" the United States to "pull ourselves out of Europe and out of Japan and Korea and establish some kind of a fortress America concept, which would serve the Soviet purposes very well globally."[41]

Senator John Tower, who had disputed the application of the ideology of containment to the Ford administration's proposal for renewed intervention in South Vietnam a decade earlier, supported the containment of communism in Central America. And, interestingly (given that he had disputed the validity of the domino theory after the Vietnam War), he used the precedent of Southeast Asia to warn that the domino theory presented real danger in Central America. He said, "The domino theory could very well work in Central America." He added, "After all, it did work in Southeast Asia. When South Vietnam fell, there went [Cambodia] and Laos."[42] Senator John Warner similarly supported the administration's use of containment: "Unless we support the President, in all likelihood, we'll see a further spread of communism in this very important part of the world."[43]

While they initially attacked the administration's use of containment to justify intervention in Central America, the media gradually began to follow the lead of congressional opponents of intervention by attacking the administration's credibility. For instance, after Reagan claimed that some El Salvadoran soldiers were going into battle with only one magazine of ammunition, Anne Garrels went to El Salvador and interviewed El Salvadoran soldiers to show that this was a lie or, at least, an exaggeration.[44]

Meanwhile, Congress continued to attack the administration's credibility on El Salvador. In February 1983, two U.S. Army Special Forces soldiers were wounded while accompanying El Salvadoran government forces on a military operation—an activity the administration had said U.S. military trainers would not undertake. The administration compounded the problem when it first said the soldiers were injured in a training flight before admitting it had been a "combat situation." Three Green Berets were expelled from the country over the matter, but the damage was done. Representative Michael Barnes, chairman of the House Subcommittee on Latin America said, "Once again we have a situation where the administration puts out one line, which just wasn't credible from the beginning." He added, "You didn't have to be a military expert to know you don't train people 15 kilometers from where the war is going on." Barnes concluded, "Two days later [the administration] has to say, 'Well sorry about that, that wasn't true, now here's the facts.'" Representative Jim Leach added that the Green Berets expelled from the country were just "scapegoats" for the administration's deception.[45]

The following year, covert operations in Central America provided another opportunity for Congress to attack the administration's credibility. In an act of obvious political theater, Vice Chairman of the Senate Intelligence Committee Democratic Senator Pat Moynihan resigned from his position in protest over the Reagan administration's mining of Nicaraguan harbors to block the supply of Soviet arms to that country from Cuba. Moynihan insisted angrily, "They did not brief us." Senator Patrick Leahy described this as part of an historical pattern of substituting covert activity for foreign policy. Former Secretary of State Henry Kissinger unintentionally magnified the scale of this event when—in order to support the administration's calls for funds to support El Salvador—he said that U.S. troops would eventually have to be sent to the region if Congress didn't approve funds. He said on *This Week*, "In two years or less, we're going to arrive at precisely this point where we will have to decide whether the only way . . . we can save this [is] by American forces." Congressional opponents of intervention immediately responded by claiming that the Reagan administration had secret plans to expand the war in Central America. The administration could only respond by saying it was no longer mining the harbors.[46]

This attack on the administration's credibility was quickly followed by another attack on CIA Director William Casey's credibility over more covert operations against Nicaragua that were not disclosed to Congress; in essence, Casey was accused of lying by omission of important facts (that he was legally required to provide). In addition to not revealing the mining of Nicaraguan harbors, the CIA also attacked Nicaragua's oil storage facilities—allegedly without first telling Congress. Reporter Robert Schakne said that, in violation of a 1980 law, the CIA had provided "no advance notification of either the oil storage raids or the mining and no detailed briefing about the mining for the Senate until this month." Schakne added,

"Not since the mid-1970s has relations between the CIA and the Congress been so poisonous." Schakne noted that one Republican senator on the Intelligence Committee gave Casey a "two on a scale of ten in matters of trust," while a Democratic Senate staffer said that "Casey's attitude toward Congress adds up to criminal casualness." Representative Norman Mineta said in an interview in this story that another Republican senator described Casey "as a person who, if your coat was on fire, wouldn't tell you unless you ask him." Senator David Durenberger added, "You have to be able to say. . . . We trust that you've told us everything there is to know on which we can base our judgment. [If] we don't have that trust, then the whole system collapses."[47]

President Reagan responded to these growing threats to his administration's credibility with even more explicit warnings of the dangers of inaction in Central America. He told a news conference that, if Congress failed to act, "We face the risk that a hundred million people from Panama to our open southern border could come under the control of pro-Soviet regimes." He added that such an outcome would "threaten the United States with violence, economic chaos, and a human tidal wave of refugees."[48]

The following year, the debate over Central America shifted to support for Contra rebels fighting inside Nicaragua against the communist regime. Reagan warned Congress that defeat of the measure to provide aid to the Contras could "deliver Nicaragua permanently to the communist bloc. Defeat for the Contras would mean a second Cuba on the mainland of North America." Secretary of State George Shultz added that, without help to the "democratic opposition" in Nicaragua, "hope for democracy in Nicaragua is doomed and progress elsewhere in Central America could be undone."[49]

In a variation on the lessons of Munich a few days later, Defense Secretary Caspar Weinberger said in Senate testimony that funds to support the Contras was required "to prevent a war."[50] Reagan made a similar claim a few days later, saying that those opposing aid were "courting disaster and history will hold them accountable." He added, "If we don't want to see the map of Central America covered in a sea of red, eventually lapping at our own borders, we must act, now."[51] In a radio address a few days later, Reagan warned of the "growing danger from the Soviets, East Germans, Bulgarians, North Koreans, Cubans, and PLO camped on our doorstep."[52] In a press conference a few days after this address, Reagan appeared with a table full of Soviet arms he claimed were captured from El Salvadoran guerillas and supplied by Nicaragua. He said that, if the United States didn't act, "Americans will in the not-too-distant future, look to the South and see a string of anti-American communist dictatorships. It will be an irreparable disaster."[53]

In March 1986, CBS News launched a coordinated attack against the president's credibility on Central America. In a *CBS Evening News* story by Phil Jones, a series of Congressmen and experts attacked the president. House Speaker Tip O'Neill accused the president of dishonesty, saying that, while he claimed he did not, Reagan actually wanted to send U.S. troops to Nicaragua. The story then cut to video of the president warning of a "sea of red, eventually lapping at our own borders." Reporter Phil Jones responded by calling this warning an "alleged crisis." The story then cut to William Schneider of the American Enterprise Institute who claimed that the president was trying to scare Americans by saying "that if we don't stop the Sandinistas in Nicaragua, they'll end up in San Diego or Texas," implying that the president's use of containment to justify intervention was itself dishonest. Senator Mark Hatfield claimed that the president was hiding the true cost of his intervention, saying, "It's a hundred million this year. What's going to be the figure next year?" Hatfield asked, "Where is the light at the end of the tunnel?"[54]

In the end, the Reagan administration won this fight for funding to support limited intervention in Central America. CBS News attributed this victory not to the strength of the administration's arguments—its use of containment to justify intervention in Central America—but to arm-twisting and backdoor political wrangling. CBS reporter Bob Schieffer said, "When the president described what might happen in Nicaragua this week if Congress turned down the aid, he did it in the harshest terms." Reagan was shown giving a speech from the Oval Office in which he said, "We will have to confront the reality of a Soviet military beachhead within our defense perimeters about 500 miles from Mexico." However, the rest of the story was about how the president had won the victory not through the strength of this argument, but because of "heavy lobbying" of Congress behind closed doors. A series of experts, including Norman Ornstein from the American Enterprise Institute, House Speaker Tip O'Neill, and Representative Jim Leach described the lobbying effort by the White House as bullying of the Congress into submission.[55] This political victory was, in this construction, itself proof of the administration's deceptiveness.

And ultimately this victory would be a hollow one; a few short months later the story of the Iran-Contra scandal would break and the Reagan administration would be plunged into a crisis of credibility from which it would never fully recover.

The questions that have for decades preoccupied historians about the events that began America's direct military intervention in the Vietnam War—the Gulf of Tonkin incident and the passage of the Tonkin Gulf Resolution—are compelling. Did the attacks on August 4, 1964, against the USS *Maddox* and *Turner Joy* actually happen? No, though at the time the administration almost certainly believed that they had.[56] Were these destroyers involved in clearly provocative activities in what North Vietnam considered its territorial waters and in close proximity to offensive operations conducted by the South Vietnamese Navy with U.S. assistance? Absolutely, yes. Did the president and the administration fully anticipate that there would be further escalations at the same time that they were assuring members of Congress that they would not use the Tonkin Gulf Resolution to escalate the war? Yes. Historians are correct to point out the pivotal importance of the Gulf of Tonkin incident and the Tonkin Gulf Resolution to the domestic political debate over the Vietnam War, but the questions they have asked, in many ways, missed the larger point.

A much more important question is why did the president need the Tonkin Gulf Resolution so badly that he was willing to do anything to get it? Lyndon Johnson's historical frame of reference as he embarked on the Vietnam War was the Korean War, a war that Johnson believed unraveled because President Truman had failed to obtain congressional endorsement.[57] From the way President Johnson used the Tonkin Gulf Resolution after he got it, it seems clear that he sought the resolution as an insurance policy against congressional dissent. In this context, the resolution was an end in and of itself.[58] It didn't matter to the president how he got the resolution, as long as he got it.

If there was, in fact, a Cold War consensus, why did the president have to engage in deception to obtain passage of the Tonkin Gulf Resolution? For Johnson, the obstacles to passage of this resolution were several key leaders in Congress who were privately skeptical of Johnson's contention that military intervention in Southeast Asia was required to prevent a communist takeover of Southeast Asia. For Johnson, the Gulf of Tonkin incident served as a pretext, providing the political impetus to overcome congressional reluctance and gain passage of this resolution. However, to get this vital piece of paper, Johnson had to deceive Congress as to the facts of the Gulf of Tonkin incident and as to his true intentions for the resolution. The administration's lies about the Gulf of Tonkin incident and the circumstances under which it supposedly occurred were necessary to conceal the questionable elements of the incident that these skeptical legislators might use to thwart the president's will. The administration's lies about its true intentions for the resolution were necessary because key leaders in Congress had already made it abundantly clear that they believed the situation in Vietnam was neither important enough to warrant direct U.S. military intervention nor salvageable in a conventional military sense.

Another important question is why, if they did not want the United States to intervene militarily in Vietnam, did members of Congress nearly unanimously pass such a broad-reaching resolution? Of course, the president had assured them that he wanted no wider war and would not use the Tonkin Gulf Resolution to escalate the war. But why give the president an expression of support for something he claimed he wasn't going to do anyway? For Congress, the Tonkin Gulf Resolution was itself an escalation, designed to communicate to the Soviet Union, China, and North Vietnam that the United States was willing to intervene militarily to prevent the spread of communism in Southeast Asia. To Congress, this resolution was very much in the vein of the Formosa Resolution or the Middle East Resolution that had preceded it—resolutions that warned the United States' Cold War adversaries that America would intervene militarily to protect the sovereignty of specific countries and regions around the world. Most members of Congress believed that such resolutions had actually prevented wars.[59] Congress saw the Tonkin Gulf Resolution as an instrument of containment, in and of itself, rather than a congressional endorsement of escalation. In this context, the Gulf of Tonkin incident (as it was portrayed to Congress by the administration) was simply further evidence of North Vietnamese aggression, evidence that the United States' measures to that point had been insufficient to restrain North Vietnamese ambitions and that a sterner measure—the Tonkin Gulf Resolution—was needed to communicate to the communists that America would stand by South Vietnam.

How did the American people perceive the Gulf of Tonkin incident and the Tonkin Gulf Resolution? By August 1964, President Johnson and his administration had been telling the American people for over half a year that Southeast Asia was threatened by communist aggression much as the world had been threatened by aggression from the Axis powers before World War II. In this context, the Gulf of Tonkin incident was probably perceived as proof of the lessons of Munich, that aggression unanswered breeds more aggression. To the extent that any American was paying attention to Vietnam in late summer 1964, the United States' retaliatory air strikes and the passage of the Tonkin Gulf Resolution were proof that the United States—under the leadership of Lyndon Johnson—would stand up to aggression rather than bow to it as British Prime Minister Neville Chamberlain supposedly had at Munich over two decades earlier. And this response was also proof that Johnson's answer to aggression would be "measured and fitting" rather than excessive and extreme, as Johnson claimed Senator Barry Goldwater's policies would be.

As the president began to commit more and more U.S. military forces to direct action in the Vietnam War, the Gulf of Tonkin incident and the Tonkin Gulf Resolution receded from the public debate. Instead, the Johnson administration incessantly repeated that the containment of communism in Southeast Asia required U.S. military intervention in South Vietnam. Opponents of the growing war in Vietnam attacked the application of the ideology of containment to the war, pointing out the myriad of ways in which the conflict did not fit the Cold War model of containment. Some opponents of the war, especially radicals, academics, and a few members of Congress— foreign policy revolutionaries who sought to dismantle the Cold War consensus—even attacked the ideology of containment itself.

Just what was the ideology of military containment? The rhetoric of the Johnson and Nixon administrations and their supporters— highlighted throughout this book—sheds considerable light on this question. Central to this ideology were the lessons of Munich that aggression must be deterred or met early, or it would only grow in danger. This larger principle was the foundation of a subordinate principle—the domino theory—which posited that once one country falls to aggression, adjacent countries will follow (since the appetite of aggression only "grows with feeding," as members of the Johnson administration were fond of saying). The next component of this ideology was the zero-sum game; the fall of any country or region of the free world to communism would damage U.S. national security. Not only would the fall of one small country "whet the appetite" of the communist aggressors for more conquest, but advocates of intervention also frequently cited the tens of millions of people who would be condemned to live under communist oppression with the fall of each small country. In essence, the Cold War was a battle for the "hearts and minds" of every person on earth; each person lost by the Free World was gained by the Communist World and vice versa. The final element of this ideology was the central importance of the United States in the latticework of security agreements—such as NATO and SEATO—to the security of the Free World; if the United States failed to honor its commitment to one ally, other allies would begin to doubt

America's commitment to them as well, possibly causing these security agreements to disintegrate and all of America's allies to slip one by one into the orbit of the Communist World.

These tenets of the ideology of military containment of communism—the core of the Cold War consensus[60]—rested on a more foundational set of meta-principles that were held by the vast majority of Americans but were seldom stated explicitly. At the center of the lessons of Munich was the meta-principle that communists were aggressive, bent on world conquest, and had to be deterred; with the rise of Communist China, the threat of this aggression to the third world—through "wars of liberation"—became a particular concern. The second, and perhaps more fundamental meta-principle that undergirded the ideology of military containment was the necessity of military strength—one could not deter or stop aggression as the lessons of Munich demanded if one did not have a military force to either serve as a deterrent or with which to actually prosecute a military intervention. An important corollary to this meta-principle was the idea of forward deployment of America's military forces along the periphery of the Communist World; a military force could only serve as a deterrent if it was placed in a position to "block" communist expansion. This unstated requirement of containment was carefully interlaced with another meta-principle, the myth of American altruism; U.S. bases abroad were not U.S. territories but a form of military assistance to protect the freedom of America's allies from communist aggression.

Senator J. William Fulbright and his staff were right in their analysis in late 1967; despite the debacle of the Vietnam War, the American public continued to embrace the Cold War consensus—an unquestioning acceptance of the ideology of military containment of communism. The way the public repeatedly rejected radical protesters who attacked the ideology of containment, the way the public rejected presidential and congressional peace candidates in 1968 who attacked the application of containment to the war in Vietnam, and the way the public responded in poll questions on their sentiments about continuing the war to an "honorable end" (which was almost universally understood as an end that preserved the goal of containing communism in Southeast Asia) all testify to Americans' unwavering faith in the ideology of containment throughout the Vietnam War.

Why did Americans continue to embrace the Cold War consensus even in the midst of its most disastrous consequences—an interminable war on the other side of the world that was devouring America's blood and treasure? First, most Americans agreed with the administration's contention that the Vietnam War was a war of communist aggression against South Vietnam. The Vietnam War certainly *looked* like a war of communist aggression. North Vietnam *was* getting material aid from Communist China and the Soviet Union. The North Vietnamese *were* sending material aid to the South Vietnamese Communists. And North Vietnamese troops *were* fighting in South Vietnam against U.S. and South Vietnamese government troops. Second and even more fundamentally, however, the use of containment to justify military intervention in Vietnam spoke to meta-principles held by the vast majority of Americans: communists were aggressive and could only be stopped by military force, forward deployed in defense of America's allies. Most Americans had, to varying degrees, internalized these basic precepts of containment—the bulwark of the Cold War consensus—and consistently rejected all those who argued against them.

In fact, the case for the containment of communism in Vietnam was so compelling that, in late 1967 and early 1968, opponent of the war quit challenging it. Once it was clear that their attacks on the Cold War consensus were only alienating the American people, most opponents of the war changed their strategy and began attacking the administration's credibility on the war. It was then that the Gulf of Tonkin incident and the Tonkin Gulf Resolution suddenly reemerged as a central issue to the debate over Vietnam.

For the Johnson administration, the Tonkin Gulf Resolution remained their insurance policy against congressional dissent. Whatever members of Congress might say, all but two of them had voted for the resolution. And whatever congressional dissenters might claim the president told them before its passage, the text of the resolution clearly endorsed the president's decision to take whatever measures he chose to stop communist aggression against South Vietnam. However, there was one chink in what might otherwise be an impenetrable armor against Congress: the Gulf of Tonkin incident—the supposed attacks on the USS *Maddox* and *Turner Joy* on August 4, 1964—had not happened. And the administration had told a number of lies about the circumstances under which the incident supposedly *had* occurred. While Johnson would repeatedly say after he left office that the Tonkin Gulf Resolution should have been called the Fulbright Resolution (because Fulbright was so instrumental in its passage), it was not. It was called the Tonkin Gulf Resolution and questions about the Gulf of Tonkin incident would hang from the resolution like a millstone.

For congressional dissenters, the Gulf of Tonkin incident was compelling evidence that President Johnson had lied to get the United States into a war in Vietnam. When considered objectively, this logic seems tortured. Whether or not the Gulf of Tonkin incident occurred should be easily separable from whether the Tonkin Gulf Resolution was really a congressional endorsement of the war. The most important deception wrought by President Johnson was not his administration's lies about the Gulf of Tonkin incident but their private assurances to members of Congress that the president would not use the resolution to escalate the war. But in the circus of American mass politics, things are seldom so simple. While Fulbright would repeatedly remind Americans of the president's public pronouncements during the 1964 presidential campaign that he would not send "American boys" to fight in a war for "Asian boys" (assurances that were not actually given until after the Tonkin Gulf Resolution was passed), he never convinced the majority of Americans that this deception had taken place.

But the deceptions surrounding the Gulf of Tonkin incident were easily proven. And it was easy to convince Americans that the incident and the passage of the resolution were a single event. The incident had happened just before the Tonkin Gulf Resolution was passed. Moreover, the only hearings held before the passage of Tonkin Gulf Resolution were about the Gulf of Tonkin incident. The resolution—at least colloquially—even bore the incident's name. And perhaps most importantly, the Gulf of Tonkin incident had been the administration's pretext to gain passage of the Tonkin Gulf Resolution. In this context, members of the administration were actually the architects of the logic that connected the incident to the resolution.

Thus, proof of the administration's deceptions surrounding the Gulf of Tonkin incident became a sort of political shorthand for the real, more complicated deception in which the president had engaged. And it served this role admirably. By the beginning of 1968, most Americans had already reached the conclusion that the president had been lying to them since the beginning of the war. In early 1967, a small cadre of opponents of the war had already begun a steady drumbeat of attacks on the administration's credibility—including questions about the administration's credibility on civilian casualties caused by bombing North Vietnam and whether the president truly wanted negotiations to end the war. Then, on the eve of hearings on the Gulf of Tonkin incident, the Tet Offensive began and called into question the credibility of the administration's rosy predictions for the war from the second half of 1967. Revelations that the Gulf of Tonkin incident, the incident that had presumably initiated the Americanization of the war, probably hadn't happened were simply the final straw. By the end of spring 1968, after Fulbright's hearings on the Gulf of Tonkin incident had taken full effect with the American public, the president's credibility with the American people was in shambles. In the face of what promised to be a bitter and desperate primary battle, Johnson withdrew from the presidential race.

In retrospect, 1967 was perhaps the most important year in the Cold War. Historians usually identify 1968 as the pivotal year of the Vietnam War. They focus on the assassinations of Senator Robert F. Kennedy and the Reverend Dr. Martin Luther King Jr. or the tumultuous Democratic National Convention. A few historians rightly identify the role that the Tet Offensive played in ending the escalation of the Vietnam War or ending the Johnson presidency. However, while the year 1968 had a huge impact on the Vietnam War, 1967 altered the course—or perhaps, more appropriately, preserved the course—of the entire Cold War. It was in 1967 that attacks on presidential credibility finally began to gain momentum. These attacks critically weakened the president's credibility with the American people, setting the stage for the final collapse of Johnson's credibility in 1968. It was in mid-1967 that the administration began to make ever more optimistic predictions for the future of Vietnam; both General Harold K. Johnson and General William C. Westmoreland set the American public's expectations unreasonably high at the end of 1967. Those expectations would be crushed in 1968 when the Tet Offensive began, dealing another serious blow to the president's credibility. It was in 1967 that the press first asked real questions about the Gulf of Tonkin incident; an obscure Associated Press article exposed glaring inconsistencies in the administration's version of the events of August 4, 1964. While these charges would go largely unnoticed by the American public in 1967, they provided the ammunition for the Senate Foreign Relations Committee to attack the administration's credibility in the 1968 Fulbright hearings. And, most importantly, it was in 1967 that Fulbright made the crucial decision to hold hearings in 1968 on the Gulf of Tonkin incident. Fulbright and his staffers had already concluded in 1966 that they must undermine the Tonkin Gulf Resolution—the administration's insurance policy against congressional dissent—before they could convince significant numbers in Congress to join them in public opposition to the war. In 1967, they reached the much more important realization that attacking the ideology of containment—the core of the Cold War consensus—was alienating the American public; they needed to switch tactics and attack the administration's credibility if they were going to end the war.

This decision in 1967 to attack presidential credibility rather than the ideology of containment had long-term consequences that Fulbright and his staffers could not possibly have predicted. Of course, this change in tactics encouraged most in the opposition to follow suit beginning in 1968, permanently altering the framework for debate over the war. Before the 1968 Fulbright hearings, the framework for debate had been between supporters using the ideology of containment to justify the war and opponents attacking the ideology of containment or its applicability to Vietnam. After 1968, the framework for debate of the war was irrevocably altered, with supporters continuing to use the ideology of containment to justify the war but opponents now attacking the administration's credibility instead of the ideology of containment. This change in tactics ultimately ended the war. To sustain his credibility against relentless attack, President Nixon was repeatedly forced to withdraw troops to prove he was making good on his promise to bring the war to an "honorable end." Eventually, the president ran out of troops to withdraw and was forced to accept a humiliating compromise peace that set the stage for the final destruction of South Vietnam.

Fulbright's fateful decision in 1967 to hold hearings on the Gulf of Tonkin incident rather than on the ideology of containment also had other far-reaching effects that would last well beyond the Vietnam War. First, the framework for public debate of military interventions created by Fulbright's decision—between supporters using the ideology of containment and opponents attacking the administration's credibility—would remain the framework for debate of military interventions through the end of the Cold War. However, much more importantly, because the framework for debate of the war changed in 1968, opponents of the war stopped challenging the ideology of containment and the American public continued to embrace the Cold War consensus and the ideology of containment until the end of the Cold War.

And it is in this sense that 1967 was the year that saved the Cold War. In 1967, the Cold War consensus—and the resiliency of the ideology of containment with the American people—triumphed over the foreign policy revolution that had tried to overturn it. Academic, congressional, radical, and media dissenters had been attacking the application of ideology of containment to Vietnam since early 1965. And within this broader opposition, foreign policy revolutionaries had been attacking the ideology of containment itself, trying to dismantle the Cold War consensus. In 1967, Senator J. William Fulbright, nominal leader of the congressional wing of the foreign policy revolution, conceded defeat. He accepted that two and a half years of attacking the Cold War consensus had only succeeded in alienating the American public. He abandoned the effort and instead laid plans to launch a devastating attack on the administration's credibility with the narrower objective of ending the Vietnam War. Over the following year, nearly the entire antiwar movement followed suit, and the foreign policy revolution came to an end.

Many scholars—including Michael H. Hunt, Fredrick Merk, Walter McDougall,[61] and numerous others—have written about the power of ideology in American foreign policy. The ideology of containment was no less powerful than the foreign policy ideologies that had preceded it. This ideology was forged from the fire of World War II, the bloodiest conflict in the history of mankind. It blossomed in American politics in the shadow of the very real threat of atomic annihilation and was nurtured by a paranoid fear of communist infiltration in the 1950s. By 1964, an entire generation had grown up knowing no other framework for public debate over foreign policy; there were ideas that were inside the bounds of acceptable public discourse on foreign policy and ideas that were beyond the pale.

This book has shown the mechanism by which a widely held foreign policy ideology resists change, even in the midst of its most unacceptable consequences. The American public *believed* that communist expansion must be contained, using military force if necessary. The Johnson administration had convinced Americans that communists were trying to conquer Southeast Asia beginning with South Vietnam. Opponents of U.S. military intervention in Vietnam—and the foreign policy revolutionaries within this opposition who opposed the ideology of containment itself—posited a myriad of logical arguments for why the war in Vietnam was not a case of communist aggression or why the ideology of containment was outmoded and obsolete. But these opposition arguments consistently fell beyond the pale of what most Americans considered acceptable public discourse on foreign policy, and they were roundly rejected. Opponents of the war eventually abandoned this strategy and instead focused their attacks on administration credibility to bring the war to an end.

As this work is being written, the United States is in the grips of a new foreign policy ideology—the War on Terror. This ideology posits that Islamic extremists must be defeated abroad before they can perpetrate terrorist attacks inside the United States. This ideology was forged in the fires of the World Trade Center and the Pentagon on September 11, 2001. This ideology blossomed in the days after 9/11, as anthrax-laden letters arrived in congressional buildings and newsrooms and as shoe bombers and underwear bombers boarded planes to conduct further attacks. It has reshaped what infringements the American people are willing to accept on their liberties as they board planes, talk on their cell phones, or use the Internet. This ideology has spawned two wars, the war in Iraq and the war in Afghanistan, that have cost the United States trillions of dollars and over six thousand American lives. And, as this work is being written, the ideology of the War on Terror has embroiled the United States in yet another war, this time against the heirs to al Qaida in Iraq—the Islamic State in Iraq and Syria (ISIS).

The Cold War consensus was not ended by the power of opposition arguments against the ideology of containment. This consensus was not ended by a disastrous war in Southeast Asia—the logical consequence of the ideology of military containment of communism. The Cold War consensus was ended by the collapse of the Soviet Union, the seeming democratization of Eastern Europe, and the rise of market economies in East and Southeast Asia. In other words, the Cold War consensus ended because the United States ostensibly won the Cold War.

How does America end the War on Terror? How does the United States "win" that war? Must the United States kill or convert every Muslim who holds to one of the many Salafist schools of Islam that we deem "extremist"? Does the United States have to defeat all of the literally dozens of Islamic terrorist organizations around the world bent on attacking America? Is simply the destruction of ISIS enough (no small task, given both America's inability to defeat al Qaida in Iraq after eight years of war and ISIS's considerably more plentiful resources)? With this new foreign policy ideology, the United States may have inadvertently condemned itself to a century of costly and fruitless warfare across the globe.

BIBLIOGRAPHY

Archives

The American Presidency Project. University of California San Bernardino, http://www.presidency.ucsb.edu/.

Fulbright Papers. University of Arkansas Library, Fayetteville, AR.

Harry Bridges Center for Labor History. University of Washington, Seattle, WA.

Lyndon B. Johnson Presidential Library. University of Texas, Austin, TX.

Miller Center. University of Virginia, http://millercenter.org/.

Pentagon Papers. National Archives, Washington, D.C., http://www.archives.gov/research/pentagon-papers/.

Records of the Office of the Chancellor. Wilson Library, University of North Carolina at Chapel Hill.

Roper Public Opinion Research Center. University of Connecticut, http://www.ropercenter.uconn.edu/.

Vanderbilt Television News Archive. Vanderbilt University, Nashville, TN.

Books

Beggs, A. Dwayne. *The Vietnam War Dissent of Ernest Gruening And Wayne Morse. 1964–1968.* Dissertation, Bowling Green, 2010.

Brands, H. W. *The Strange Death of American Liberalism.* New Haven, CT: Yale University, 2001.

_____, Darren Pierson, and Reynolds S. Kiefer. *The Use of Force after the Cold War.* College Station, TX: Texas A&M University, 2000.

Brinkley, Douglas, and Luke Nichter, eds. *The Nixon Tapes.* New York: Houghton Mifflin Harcourt, 2014.

Brody, Richard A., Paul Ekman, Edwin B. Parker, Nelson W. Polsby, Peter H. Rossi, Paul B. Sheatsley, and Sidney Verba. *Public Opinion and the War in Vietnam.* Inter-University Consortium for Political Research, Winter 1966.

Brown, Eugene. *J. William Fulbright: Advice and Dissent.* Iowa City: University of Iowa, 1985.

Craig, Campbell, and Fredrik Logevall. *America's Cold War: The Politics of Insecurity.* Cambridge, MA: Harvard University, 2009.

Dallek, Robert. *Flawed Giant: Lyndon Johnson and His Times, 1961–1973.* New York: Oxford University, 1998.

_____. *Lyndon B. Johnson: Portrait of a President.* New York: Oxford University, 2004.

Ford, Ronnie E. *Tet 1968: Understanding the Surprise.* New York: Frank Cass, 1995.

Fordham, Benjamin O. *Building the Cold War Consensus: The Political Economy of U.S. National Security Policy, 1949–51.* Ann Arbor, MI: University of Michigan, 2001.

Fry, Joseph A. *Debating Vietnam: Fulbright, Stennis, and Their Senate Hearings.* Lanham, MD: Rowman & Littlefield, 2006.

Gaddis, John Lewis. *Strategies of Containment: A Critical Appraisal of Postwar American National Security Policy.* New York: Oxford University, 1982.

Gibbons, William Conrad. *The U. S. Government and the Vietnam War: Executive and Legislative Roles and Relationships: July 1965–January 1968*. Princeton, NJ: Princeton University, 1995.

_____. *The U.S. Government and the Vietnam War: Executive and Legislative Roles and Relationships, Part I*. Princeton, NJ: Princeton University, 1986.

Grow, Michael. *U.S. Presidents and Latin American Interventions: Pursuing Regime Change in the Cold War*. Lawerence: University Press of Kansas, 2008.

Hammond, William M. *Public Affairs: The Military and the Media, 1962–1968*. Washington, DC: Center for Military History, U.S. Army, 1988.

Helsing, Jeffrey W. *Johnson's War/Johnson's Great Society: The Guns and Butter Trap*. Westport, CT: Praeger, 2000.

Herring, George C. *America's Longest War: The United States and Vietnam, 1950–1975*. Boston: McGraw-Hill, 2002.

Hess, Gary. *Presidential Decisions for War: Korea, Vietnam, the Persian Gulf, and Iraq*. Baltimore, MD: Johns Hopkins University, 2009.

Hunt, Michael H. *Ideology and US Foreign Policy*. New Haven, CT: Yale University, 1987.

_____. *Lyndon Johnson's War: America's Cold War Crusade in Vietnam 1945–1968*. New York: Hill and Wang, 1996.

Johnson, Robert David. *Congress and the Cold War*. New York: Cambridge University, 2006.

Kaiser, David E. *American Tragedy: Kennedy, Johnson, and the Origins of the Vietnam War*. Cambridge, MA: Harvard University, 2000.

Karnow, Stanley. *Vietnam: A History*. New York: Penguin, 1997.

Kimball, Jeffrey P. *To Reason Why: The Debate about the Causes of U.S. Involvement in the Vietnam War*. Eugene, OR: Resource, 1990.

Langguth, A.J. *Our Vietnam: The War 1954–1975*. New York: Simon & Schuster, 2000.

Lee, J. Edward, and H. C. "Toby" Haynsworth. *Nixon, Ford and the Abandonment of South Vietnam*. Jefferson, NC: McFarland, 2002.

Lewy, Guenter. *America in Vietnam*. New York: Oxford University Press, 1980.

Liebovich, Louis. *The Press and the Modern Presidency: Myths and Mindsets from Kennedy to Election 2000*. Westport, CT: Praeger, 2001.

Logevall, Fredrik. *Choosing War: The Lost Chance for Peace and the Escalation of War in Vietnam*. Berkeley: University of California, 1999.

McGirr, Lisa. *Suburban Warriors: The Origins of the New American Right*. Princeton, NJ: Princeton University, 2001.

McMaster, H. R. *Dereliction of Duty: Lyndon Johnson, Robert McNamara, the Joint Chiefs of Staff, and the Lies that Led to Vietnam*. New York: HarperCollins, 1997.

Melanson, Richard A. *American Foreign Policy Since the Vietnam War: The Search for Consensus from Nixon to Clinton*. Armonk, NY: M. E. Sharpe, 2000.

Moïse, Edwin E. *Tonkin Gulf and the Escalation of the Vietnam War*. Chapel Hill, NC: University of North Carolina, 1996.

Moser, Richard R. *The New Winter Soldiers: GI and Veteran Dissent During the Vietnam Era*. New Brunswick, NJ: Rutgers University, 1996.

Oberdorfer, Don. *Tet!* New York: Avon Books, 1971.

Pisor, Robert. *The End of the Line: The Siege of Khe Sanh*. New York: W. W. Norton and Company, 1982.

Prados, John, and Margaret Pratt Porter, eds. *Inside the Pentagon Papers*. Lawrence: University Press of Kansas, 2004.

Record, Jeffrey. *The Wrong War: Why We Lost in Vietnam*. Annapolis, MD: Naval Institute Press, 1998.

Roselle, Laura. *Media and the Politics of Failure: Great Powers, Communication Strategies, and Military Defeats*. New York: Palgrave Macmillan, 2006.

Rossinow, Doug. *The Politics of Authenticity: Liberalism, Christianity, and the New Left in America*. New York: Columbia, 1998.

Rudenstine, David. *The Day the Presses Stopped: A History of the Pentagon Papers Case*. Berkeley and Los Angeles: University of California, 1996.

Sanders, Jerry Wayne. *Peddlers of Crisis: The Committee on the Present Danger and the Politics of Containment*. Cambridge, MA: South End, 1983.

Shaw, John M. *The Cambodian Campaign: The 1970 Offensive and America's Vietnam War*. Lawrence: University Press of Kansas, 2005.

Siff, Ezra Y. *Why the Senate Slept: The Gulf of Tonkin Resolution and the Beginning of America's Vietnam War*. Westport, CT: Praeger, 1999.

Small, Melvin. *Johnson, Nixon, and the Doves*. New Brunswick, NJ: Rutgers University, 1988.

Spencer, Graham. *The Media and Peace: From Vietnam to the "War on Terror."* New York: Palgrave Macmillan, 2005.

Starry, Donn A. *Mounted Combat in Vietnam*. Washington, DC: Department of the Army, 1989.

Towle, Michael J. *Out of Touch: The Presidency and Public Opinion*. College Station: Texas A&M University, 2004.

Turner, Kathleen J. *Lyndon Johnson's Dual War: Vietnam and the Press*. Chicago: University of Chicago, 1985.

VanDeMark, Brian. *Into the Quagmire: Lyndon Johnson and the Escalation of the Vietnam War*. New York: Oxford University Press, 1991.

Wells, Tom. *The War Within: America's Battle over Vietnam*. Oakland: University of California, 1994.

———. *Wild Man: The Life and Times of Daniel Ellsberg*. New York: Palgrave, 2001.

Westad, Odd Arne. *The Global Cold War: Third World Interventions and the Making of Our Times*. Cambridge, UK: Cambridge University, 2005.

Wittkopf, Eugene R. *Faces of Internationalism: Public Opinion and American Foreign Policy*. Durham, NC: Duke University, 1990.

Woods, Randall Bennett. *J. William Fulbright, Vietnam, and the Search for a Cold War Foreign Policy*. Cambridge: Cambridge University, 1998.

Articles from Books

Asbley, Karin, Bill Ayers, Bernardine Dohrn, John Jacobs, Jeff Jones, Gerry Long, Home Machtinger, Jim Mellen, Terry Robbins, Mark Rudd and Steve Tappis. "You Don't Need a Weatherman to Know Which Way the Wind Blows." *New Left Notes*. June 18, 1969. In *Weatherman*, edited by Harold Jacobs, 34. San Francisco: Ramparts, 1970.

California Peace and Freedom Movement. "California Peace and Freedom Movement Program." Founding Convention, Richmond, CA, March 1968. In *The New Left: A Documentary History*, edited by Massimo Teodori, 408. Indianapolis, IN: Bobbs-Merrill, 1969.

Calvert, Gregory. "In White America: Radical Consciousness And Social Change." Princeton Conference Speech, February 1967. In *The National Guardian*. March 25, 1967. In *The New Left: A Documentary History*, edited by Massimo Teodori, 380. Indianapolis, IN: Bobbs-Merrill, 1969.

Horowitz, David. "Hand-Me-Down Marxism In The New Left." *Ramparts*. September 1969. In *Weatherman*, edited by Harold Jacobs, 60. San Francisco: Ramparts, 1970.

Kahin, George McT. "Bureaucracy's Call for U.S. Ground Troops." In *To Reason Why: The Debate about the Causes of U.S. Involvement in the Vietnam War*, edited by Jeffrey P. Kimball, 240. Eugene, OR: Resource, 1990.

Kopkind, Andrew. "The Real SDS Stands Up." *Hard Times.* June 30, 1969. In *Weatherman,* edited by Harold Jacobs, 22. San Francisco: Ramparts, 1970.

Hayden, Tom. "Justice in the Streets." in *Trial* by Holt, Rinehart, Winston, Tom Hayden, 1970. In *Weatherman,* edited by Harold Jacobs, 173–174. San Francisco: Ramparts, 1970.

LaFeber, Walter. "The Tension between Democracy and Capitalism during the American Century." In *The Ambiguous Legacy: U.S. Foreign Relations in the "American Century,"* edited by Michael J. Hogan, 152–182. New York: Cambridge University, 1999.

Lynd, Staughton. "Resistance; From Mood To Strategy." *Liberation.* December 1967. In *The New Left: A Documentary History,* edited by Massimo Teodori, 287. Indianapolis, IN: Bobbs-Merrill, 1969.

Movement. "We've Got to Reach Our Own People." *The Movement.* November 1967. In *The New Left: A Documentary History,* edited by Massimo Teodori, 280. Indianapolis, IN: Bobbs-Merrill, 1969.

Oglesby, Carl. "1969." in "Notes on a Decade Ready for the Dustbin." *Liberation.* August-September 1969. In *Weatherman,* edited by Harold Jacobs, 74. San Francisco: Ramparts, 1970.

_____. "An Open Letter to McCarthy Supporters." 1968, In *The New Left: A Documentary History* by Massimo Teodori, 412. Indianapolis, IN: Bobbs-Merrill, 1969.

Porter, Gareth. "Explaining the Vietnam War: Dominant and Contending Paradigms." In *Making Sense of the Vietnam Wars: Local, National, and Transnational Perspectives,* edited by Mark Philip Bradley and Marilyn B. Young, 67–90. New York: Oxford University Press, 2008.

Students for a Democratic Society. "America and New Era." October 1965, In *The New Left: A Documentary History,* edited by Massimo Teodori, 159. Indianapolis, IN: Bobbs-Merrill, 1969.

Weinstein, James. "Weatherman: A Lot of Thunder but a Short Reign." *Socialist Revolution.* January–February 1970. In *Weatherman,* edited by Harold Jacobs, 223. San Francisco: Ramparts, 1970.

Williams, Kevin. "Vietnam: The First Living Room War." In *The Fog of War: The Media on the Battlefield,* edited by Derrik Mercer, Geoff Mungham, Kevin Williams, and Sir Tom Hopkinson, 213–260. London: Heinemann, 1987.

Woods, Randall Bennett. "The Rhetoric of Dissent: J. William Fulbright, Vietnam, and the Crisis of International Liberalism." In *Critical Reflections on the Cold War: Linking Rhetoric and History,* edited by Martin J. Medhurst and H. W. Brands, 187. College Station: Texas A&M University, 2000.

Journal Articles

Aldrich, George H. "Questions of International Law Raised by the Seizure of the U.S.S. *Pueblo.*" *Proceedings of the American Society of International Law at Its Annual Meeting (1921–1969),* American Society of International Law 63, Perspectives for International Legal Development (April 24–26, 1969): 2–6.

Barton, Allen H. "Fault Lines in American Elite Consensus." *Daedalus* 109, No. 3 (Summer 1980): 1–24.

Brzezinski, Zbigniew. "How the Cold War Was Played." *Foreign Affairs* 51, No. 1 (October 1972): 181–209.

Clifford, Clark M. "A Viet Nam Reappraisal: The Personal History of One Man's View and How It Evolved." *Foreign Affairs,* Council on Foreign Relations 47, No. 4 (July 1969): 601–622.

Cowans, Jon. "A Deepening Disbelief: The American Movie Hero in Vietnam, 1958–1968." *The Journal of American–East Asian Relations* 17, No. 4 (2010): 324.

Fordham, Benjamin O. "The Evolution of Republican and Democratic Positions on Cold War Military Spending: A Historical Puzzle." *Social Science History*, Volume 31, Number 4 (Winter 2007): 603–636.

Friedberg, Aaron L. "Why Didn't the United States Become a Garrison State?" *International Security* 16 (Spring 1992): 109–142.

Goldbloom, Maurice J. "Johnson So Far III: Foreign Policy." *Commentary*, American Jewish Committee 39, No. 6 (June 1965): 47–55.

Graebner, Norman A. "The President as Commander in Chief: A Study in Power." *Journal of Military History* 57, No. 1 (January 1993), 111–132.

Hall, Simon. "The Response of the Moderate Wing of the Civil Rights Movement to the War in Vietnam." *The Historical Journal* 46, No. 3 (September 2003): 669–701.

Hershberg, James G. "Peace Probes and the Bombing Pause: Hungarian and Polish Diplomacy During the Vietnam War, December 1965–January 1966." *Journal of Cold War Studies* 5, No. 2 (Spring 2003): 32–67.

Huebner, Andrew J. "Rethinking American Press Coverage of the Vietnam War, 1965–68." *Journalism History* 31, No. 3 (Fall 2005): 150–161.

Hunt, Andrew. "'When Did the Sixties Happen?' Searching for New Directions." *Journal of Social History* 33, No. 1 (Autumn, 1999): 147–161.

Johnson, Robert David. "The Origins of Dissent: Senate Liberals and Vietnam, 1959–1964." *Pacific Historical Review* 65, No. 2 (May 1996): 249–275.

Kane, John. "American Values or Human Rights? U.S. Foreign Policy and the Fractured Myth of Virtuous Power." *Presidential Studies Quarterly* 33, No. 4 (December 2003): 772–800.

Kauffman, Christopher J. "Politics, Programs, and Protests: Catholic Relief Services in Vietnam, 1954–1975." *Catholic Historical Review* 91, No. 2 (April 2005), 223–250.

Kerber, Linda K. "The Meanings of Citizenship." *Journal of American History* 84, No. 3 (December 1997), 833–854.

Lockard, Craig A. "Meeting Yesterday Head-on: The Vietnam War in Vietnamese, American, and World History." *Journal of World History* 5, No. 2 (Fall 1994): 227–270.

Miller, Linda B. "Morality in Foreign Policy: A Failed Consensus." *Daedalus* 109, No. 3, (Summer 1980): 143–158.

Meernik, James. "Presidential Support in Congress: Conflict and Consensus on Foreign and Defense Policy." *Journal of Politics* 55, No. 3 (Aug. 1993): 569–587.

Roberts, Priscilla. "'All the Right People': The Historiography of the American Foreign Policy Establishment." *Journal of American Studies* 26, No. 3 (December 1992): 409–434.

———. "'The Council Has Been Your Creation': Hamilton Fish Armstrong, Paradigm of the American Foreign Policy Establishment." *Journal of American Studies* 35, No. 1 (April 2001): 65–94.

Schmitz, David F. and Natalie Fousekis. "Frank Church, the Senate, and the Emergence of Dissent on the Vietnam War." *Pacific Historical Review* 63, No. 4 (November 1994): 561–581.

Seo, Jungkun. "The Party Politics of 'Guns versus Butter' in Post-Vietnam America." *Journal of American Studies*, 45, No. 2 (2011): 317–336.

Thorne, Christopher. "American Political Culture and the End of the Cold War." *Journal of American Studies* 26, No. 3 (December 1992): 303–330.

Ziemke, Caroline F. "Senator Richard B. Russell and the 'Lost Cause' in Vietnam, 1954–1968." *Georgia Historical Quarterly* 72, No. 1 (Spring 1988), 30–71.

Magazine Articles

Rosenberg, Milton J. "The Decline and Rise of the Cold War Consensus." *Bulletin of the Atomic Scientists*, March 1981.

Shearer, Lloyd. "The Baby Doctor and the Chaplain." *Parade*, March 3, 1968.

Time. "A Measured & Fitting Response." *Time*, August 14, 1964. Accessed November 3, 2008. http://www.time.com/time/magazine/article/0,9171,897224,00.html.

Time. "Action in Tonkin Gulf." *Time*, August 1964. Accessed September 3, 2008. http://www.time.com/ time/magazine/article/0,9171,897225,00.html.

Time. "The Airmobile Division." *Time*, June 25, 1965. Accessed October 26, 2008. http://www.time.com/time/ magazine/article/0,9171,833759,00.html.

Time. "Toward the Showdown?" *Time*, August 7, 1964. Accessed November 3, 2008. http://www.time.com/time/ magazine/article/0,9171,871317,00.html.

Time. "U.S. Peace Offensive." *Time*, January 14, 1966.

US News & World Report. "'What's Expected of a New President: Nationwide Survey.'" *US News & World Report*, December 16, 1968.

Wise, David. "Remember the *Maddox!*" *Esquire*, April 1968.

Unpublished Manuscript

Hamilton, Joseph Bruce. "Faux Casus Belli: The Role of Unsubstantiated Attacks in the Initiation of Military Action for Domestic Political Purposes." PhD diss., Fletcher School of Law and Diplomacy, 2000.

NOTES

Introduction

1. Ronnie E. Ford, *Tet 1968: Understanding the Surprise*, (New York: Frank Cass, 1995), 1–4.

Chapter 1

1. Stanley Karnow, *Vietnam: A History* (New York: Penguin, 1997), 264.
2. Dean Rusk, transcript of news conference, May 4, 1961, excerpted in memorandum by William J. Jorden, for Chester L. Cooper, June 21, 1965, Files of McGeorge Bundy, box 18, McGeorge Bundy May–June 1965 Teach-In, National Security File, Lyndon B. Johnson Presidential Library (Austin, TX).
3. Lyndon B. Johnson, Joint Communique issues at Saigon by Vice President Johnson and President Diem of Viet Nam, 13 May 1961, excerpted in memorandum by William J. Jorden, for Chester L. Cooper, June 21, 1965, Files of McGeorge Bundy, box 18, McGeorge Bundy May–June 1965 Teach-In, National Security File, Lyndon B. Johnson Presidential Library (Austin, TX).
4. Karnow, *Vietnam*, 267; A. J. Langguth, *Our Vietnam: The War 1954–1975* (New York: Simon & Schuster, 2000), 131–132.
5. Dean Rusk, news conference, transcript, November 17, 1961, excerpted in memorandum by William J. Jorden, for Chester L. Cooper, June 21, 1965, Files of McGeorge Bundy, box 18, McGeorge Bundy May–June 1965 Teach-In, National Security File, Lyndon B. Johnson Presidential Library (Austin, TX).
6. Republic of Vietnam, Photo, Vice President Johnson's Farewell Breakfast with President Diem in South Vietnam, Saigon, May 13, 1961, Photo Archive, Lyndon B. Johnson Presidential Library (Austin, TX), accessed July 26, 2015, http://www.lbjlibrary.net/collections/photo-archive.html.
7. Langguth, *Our Vietnam*, 144.
8. Hans J. Morgenthau, "The Political and Military Strategy of the United States," *Bulletin of the Atomic Scientists*, October 1954, excerpted in memorandum by William J. Jorden, for Chester L. Cooper, "SUBJECT: Views of Hans Morgenthau on U.S. Policy in Vietnam," May 14, 1965, Files of McGeorge Bundy, box 18, McGeorge Bundy May–June 1965 Teach-In, National Security File, Lyndon B. Johnson Presidential Library (Austin, TX).
9. Hans J. Morgenthau, "New Pattern of World Politics," *New Republic*, January 1957, excerpted in memorandum by William J. Jorden, for Chester L. Cooper, "SUBJECT: Views of Hans Morgenthau on U.S. Policy in Vietnam," May 14, 1965, Files of McGeorge Bundy, box 18, McGeorge Bundy May–June 1965 Teach-In, National Security File, Lyndon B. Johnson Presidential Library (Austin, TX).
10. Hans J. Morgenthau, "Asia: The American Algeria," *Commentary*, July 1961, excerpted in memorandum by William J. Jorden, for Chester L. Cooper, "SUBJECT: Views of Hans Morgenthau on U.S. Policy in Vietnam," May 14, 1965, Files of McGeorge Bundy, box 18, McGeorge Bundy May–June 1965 Teach-In, National Security File, Lyndon B. Johnson Presidential Library (Austin, TX).

11. Hans J. Morgenthau, "The Perils of Political Empiricism," *Commentary*, July 1962, excerpted in memorandum by William J. Jorden, for Chester L. Cooper, "SUBJECT: Views of Hans Morgenthau on U.S. Policy in Vietnam," May 14, 1965, Files of McGeorge Bundy, box 18, McGeorge Bundy May–June 1965 Teach-In, National Security File, Lyndon B. Johnson Presidential Library (Austin, TX).

12. Hans J. Morgenthau, "Foreign Policy Objectives," *Overseas*, September 1962, 13, Files of McGeorge Bundy, box 18, McGeorge Bundy May–June 1965 Teach-In, National Security File, Lyndon B. Johnson Presidential Library (Austin, TX).

13. Hans J. Morgenthau, "The Impotence of American Power," *Commentary*, November 1963, 13, Files of McGeorge Bundy, box 18, McGeorge Bundy May–June 1965 Teach-In, National Security File, Lyndon B. Johnson Presidential Library (Austin, TX).

14. Langguth, *Our Vietnam*, 185–186.

15. Louis Liebovich, *The Press and the Modern Presidency: Myths And Mindsets from Kennedy to Election 2000* (Westport, CT: Praeger, 2001), 57.

16. Liebovich, *The Press and the Modern Presidency*, 57; Jeffrey Record, *The Wrong War: Why We Lost in Vietnam* (Annapolis, MD: Naval Institute Press, 1998), xvii–viii; Karnow, *Vietnam*, 272.

17. Karnow, *Vietnam*, 275–276.

18. Andrew J. Huebner, "Rethinking American Press Coverage of the Vietnam War, 1965–68," *Journalism History*, Vol. 31, No. 3 (Fall 2005): 150–161.

19. Langguth, *Our Vietnam*, 149.

20. William M. Hammond, *Public Affairs: The Military and the Media, 1962–1968* (Washington, DC: Center for Military History, U.S. Army, 1988), 23.

21. Liebovich, *The Press and the Modern Presidency*, 56.

22. Wayne Morse, statement on the floor of the Senate, "Vietnam—Another Korea?" *Congressional Record*, Washington, DC, June 12, 1962, 9171, Files of McGeorge Bundy, box 18, McGeorge Bundy May–June 1965 Teach-In, National Security File, Lyndon B. Johnson Presidential Library (Austin, TX).

23. Hans J. Morgenthau, "Vietnam—Another Korea?" article from *Foreign Policy*, reprinted in *Congressional Record*, Washington, DC, June 12, 1962, 9171, Files of McGeorge Bundy, box 18, McGeorge Bundy May–June 1965 Teach-In, National Security File, Lyndon B. Johnson Presidential Library (Austin, TX).

24. Record, *The Wrong War*, xviii; Hammond, *Public Affairs, 1962–1968*, 31, 34, 37; Langguth, *Our Vietnam*, 196–198, 201–204, 206; Karnow, *Vietnam*, 279.

25. Hammond, *Public Affairs, 1962–1968*, 39; Karnow, *Vietnam*, 297, 301; Langguth, *Our Vietnam*, 215–216; Liebovich, *The Press and the Modern Presidency*, 29.

26. Langguth, *Our Vietnam*, 218–219.

27. Jeffrey P. Kimball, *To Reason Why: The Debate about the Causes of U.S. Involvement in the Vietnam War* (Eugene, OR: Resource, 1990), 36.

28. Langguth, *Our Vietnam*, 284.

29. Langguth, *Our Vietnam*, 284.

30. McGeorge Bundy, *A Study of Attitudes toward Cold War Issues*, produced in cooperation with Benton & Bowles Research Services (Washington, DC: The White House, May 16, 1963), John F. Kennedy Presidential Library (Boston, MA), accessed January 24, 2014, http://www.jfklibrary.org/Asset-Viewer/Archives/JFKPOF-062-020.aspx.

31. Bundy, *A Study of Attitudes toward Cold War Issues*.

32. Bundy, *A Study of Attitudes toward Cold War Issues*.

33. The Gallup Organization, *Gallup Poll #682* (Williamstown, MA: The Roper Public Opinion Research Center, December 12–17, 1963), 9–10.

34. McGeorge Bundy, "National Security Action Memoranda 273: South Vietnam," (Washington, DC: The White House, 26 November 1963), Lyndon B. Johnson Presidential Library (Austin, TX), accessed January 9, 2013, http://www.lbjlib.utexas.edu/johnson/archives.hom/NSAMs/nsam273.asp.

35. Recording of telephone conversation between Lyndon B. Johnson and Robert McNamara, February 25, 1964, 11:45 a.m., Citation #2191, Tape WH6402.21, Recordings and Transcripts of Conversations and Meetings, Lyndon B. Johnson Presidential Library (Austin, TX).

36. Lyndon B. Johnson, speech at St. Louis Bicentennial Dinner, transcript, St. Louis, MO, February 14, 1964, excerpted in memorandum by William J. Jorden, for Chester L. Cooper, June 21, 1965, Files of McGeorge Bundy, box 18, McGeorge Bundy May–June 1965 Teach-In, National Security File, Lyndon B. Johnson Presidential Library (Austin, TX).

37. Lyndon B. Johnson, speech in Los Angeles, transcript, Los Angeles, CA, February 21, 1964, excerpted in memorandum by William J. Jorden, for Chester L. Cooper, June 21, 1965, Files of McGeorge Bundy, box 18, McGeorge Bundy May–June 1965 Teach-In, National Security File, Lyndon B. Johnson Presidential Library (Austin, TX).

38. Recording of telephone conversation between Lyndon B. Johnson and Robert S. McNamara, February 25, 1964, 11:45 a.m.

39. Johnson, speech in Los Angeles, transcript, Los Angeles, CA, February 21, 1964.

40. Video of television interview of Lyndon B. Johnson by William Lawrence (ABC), David Brinkley (NBC), Eric Savareid (CBS), March 15, 1964, "A Conversation with the President: The First Hundred Days," Video #MP518, Audiovisual Materials, Motion Pictures, Lyndon B. Johnson Presidential Library (Austin, TX).

41. Video of television interview of Lyndon B. Johnson by William Lawrence (ABC) . . .

42. Video of television interview of Lyndon B. Johnson by William Lawrence (ABC) . . .

43. Video of television interview of Lyndon B. Johnson by William Lawrence (ABC) . . .

44. Video of television interview of Lyndon B. Johnson by William Lawrence (ABC) . . .

45. United Press International, "Johnson Stresses Viet Nam Backing," UPI, *Palm Beach Daily News*, March 16, 1964, 1.

46. Robert S. McNamara, "United States Policy in Vietnam,' by Robert S. McNamara, Secretary of Defense, 26 March 1964, Department of State Bulletin, 13 April 1964, p. 562," Vietnam Task Force, Office of the Secretary of Defense, [Part V. A.] Justification of the War. Public Statements. Volume II: D—The Johnson Administration, D-5-7, National Archives, Washington, DC, accessed October 11, 2012, http://www.archives.gov/research/pentagon-papers/.

47. McNamara, "'United States Policy in Vietnam.'"

48. McNamara, "'United States Policy in Vietnam.'"

49. Robert S. McNamara, "'The Defense of the Free World,' Robert S. McNamara, Secretary of Defense, before the national Ind Conf Bd, 21 May 1964, Department of State Bulletin, 8 June 1964, p. 895," Vietnam Task Force, Office of the Secretary of Defense, [Part V. A.] Justification of the War. Public Statements. Volume II: D—The Johnson Administration, D-10, National Archives, Washington, DC, accessed October 11, 2012, http://www.archives.gov/research/pentagon-papers/.

50. Adlai Stevenson, "'U.S. Calls for Frontier Patrol to Help Prevent Border Incidents Between Cambodia and Vietnam,' Statement by Adlai Stevenson to Security Council, 21 May 1964, Department of State Bulletin, 8 June 1964, p. 908," Vietnam Task Force, Office of the

Secretary of Defense, [Part V. A.] Justification of the War. Public Statements. Volume II: D—The Johnson Administration, D-9, National Archives, Washington, DC, accessed October 11, 2012, http://www.archives.gov/research/pentagon-papers/.

51. McNamara, "'United States Policy in Vietnam.'"

52. Dean Rusk, "'Laos and Viet-Nam—A Prescription for Peace,' Address by Secretary Rusk before the American Law Institute, Washington, D.C., 22 May 1964, Department of State Bulletin, 8 June 1964, p. 890," Vietnam Task Force, Office of the Secretary of Defense, [Part V. A.] Justification of the War. Public Statements. Volume II: D—The Johnson Administration, D-11, National Archives, Washington, D.C., accessed October 11, 2012, http://www.archives.gov/research/pentagon-papers/.

53. J. William Fulbright, "Excerpts from a Statement on Foreign Policy by Senator J. W. Fulbright, March 25, 1964," transcript, March 25, 1964, Series 96 Audiovisual Material, 96.4 Film and Slides (Transcriptions), Box 12. Folder 32, Fulbright, Foreign Policy, March 25, 1964, Fulbright Papers, University of Arkansas (Fayetteville, AR).

54. Fulbright, "Excerpts from a Statement on Foreign Policy by Senator J. W. Fulbright."

55. A. Robert Smith, "U.S. 'Totally Rejects' Viet Nam Pull-Out," *Eugene Register-Guard*, Eugene, Oregon, April 10, 1964, 16A.

56. Smith, "U.S. 'Totally Rejects' Viet Nam Pull-Out."

57. Benton & Bowles, "A Study of Attitudes toward Cold War Issues," Information Management Department, Benton & Bowles, March 1964, box 80 [1 of 2], folder PR16 PUBLIC OPINION POLLS (April 1964–June 1965) [4 of 4], Central File, Lyndon B. Johnson Presidential Library (Austin, TX).

58. Oliver Quayle and Company, "Surveys of Public Opinion in New York, California, Oklahoma, Ohio, Indiana and Maryland, Study #154," Oliver Quayle and Company, Bronxville, NY, April 1964, box 80 [1 of 2], folder PR16 PUBLIC OPINION POLLS (April 1964–June 1965) [4 of 4], Central File, Lyndon B. Johnson Presidential Library (Austin, TX).

59. Gallup Organization, *Gallup Poll #689* (Williamstown, MA: The Roper Public Opinion Research Center, April 24–29, 1964), 5–7.

60. Gallup, *Gallup Poll #689*.

61. Fredrik Logevall, *Choosing War: The Lost Chance for Peace and the Escalation of War in Vietnam* (Berkeley, CA: University of California, 1999), 134–192; H. R. McMaster, *Dereliction of Duty: Lyndon Johnson, Robert McNamara, the Joint Chiefs of Staff, and the Lies that Led to Vietnam* (New York: HarperCollins, 1997), 85–106.

62. George Ball, Draft Resolution on Southeast Asia, May 1964, Files of McGeorge Bundy, box 18, folder Meetings on Southeast Asia, Vol. 1, National Security File, Lyndon B. Johnson Presidential Library (Austin, TX).

63. Douglass Cater, memorandum for McGeorge Bundy describing presidential statement to accompany a proposed Southeast Asia resolution, May 23, 1964, Files of McGeorge Bundy, box 18, folder Meetings on Southeast Asia, Vol. 1, National Security File, Lyndon B. Johnson Presidential Library (Austin, TX).

64. Cater, memorandum for McGeorge Bundy describing presidential statement . . .

65. Cater, memorandum for McGeorge Bundy describing presidential statement . . .

66. Cater, memorandum for McGeorge Bundy describing presidential statement . . .

67. Vietnam Task Force, "Chronology," Vietnam Task Force, Office of the Secretary of Defense, [Part IV. C.] Evolution of the War, Direct Action: The Johnson Commitments, 1964–1968. Volume II: A, Military Pressures Against NVN, February–June 1964, xx–xxvii, National Archives, Washington, D.C., accessed October 11, 2012, http://www.archives.gov/research/pentagon-papers/.

68. McGeorge Bundy, draft memorandum for president describing options for action in Southeast Asia, "SUBJECT: Scenario for Strikes on North Viet Nam," May 23, 1964, Files of McGeorge Bundy, box 18, folder Meetings on Southeast Asia, Vol. 1, National Security File, Lyndon B. Johnson Presidential Library (Austin, TX).

69. Guenter Lewy, *America in Vietnam* (New York: Oxford University Press, 1980), 23.

70. Bundy, "SUBJECT: Scenario for Strikes on North Viet Nam."

71. Bromley Smith, "Summary Record of the Meeting on Southeast Asia, Situation Room, May 24, 1964, 11:00 AM," May 24, 1964, Files of McGeorge Bundy, box 18, folder Meetings on Southeast Asia, Vol. 1, National Security File, Lyndon B. Johnson Presidential Library (Austin, TX).

72. Smith, "Summary Record of the Meeting on Southeast Asia."

73. Vietnam Task Force, "Chronology," Vietnam Task Force, Office of the Secretary of Defense, [Part IV. C.] *Evolution of the War*, Direct Action: The Johnson Commitments, 1964–1968. Volume II: A, Military Pressures Against NVN, February–June 1964, xx–xxvii, National Archives, Washington, DC, accessed October 11, 2012, http://www.archives.gov/research/pentagon-papers/.

74. Vietnam Task Force, "Chronology." Vietnam Task Force, Office of the Secretary of Defense, [Part IV. C.].

75. Vietnam Task Force, "Chronology," Vietnam Task Force, Office of the Secretary of Defense, [Part IV. C.].

76. James L. Greenfield, memorandum for Mr. Paul Southwick, State Department, "SUBJECT: Domestic U.S. Public Affairs Aspects of South East Asia Situation," June 3, 1964, box 71 [1 of 2], folder ND 19-CO 312 VIETNAM (Situation In) (1964–1965) [4 OF 4], Central File, Lyndon B. Johnson Presidential Library (Austin, TX).

77. Transcript, Walt W. Rostow Oral History Interview I, March 21, 1969, by Paige E. Mulhollan, Internet Copy, Lyndon B. Johnson Presidential Library (Austin, TX), 11–13.

78. William Bundy, Memo for record, "Tuesday Afternoon Session in Honolulu, June 2, 1964," June 3, 1964 (In State Dept Material, Vol 1.), pp. 4–7, from Vietnam Task Force, Office of the Secretary of Defense, [Part IV. C.] Evolution of the War, Direct Action: The Johnson Commitments, 1964–1968. Volume II: A, Military Pressures Against NVN, February–June 1964, 33, National Archives, Washington, DC, accessed October 11, 2012, http://www.archives.gov/research/pentagon-papers/.

79. McGeorge Bundy, "SUBJECT: Alternative public positions for U. S. on Southeast Asia for the period July 1–November 15," June 10, 1964, Files of McGeorge Bundy, box 18, folder Meetings on Southeast Asia, Vol. 1, National Security File, Lyndon B. Johnson Presidential Library (Austin, TX).

80. Henry Cabot Lodge, "For the President from Lodge," American Embassy in Saigon, May 15, 1964, from Vietnam Task Force, Office of the Secretary of Defense [Part VI. C.], Settlement of the Conflict. Histories of Contacts Volume I—Negotiations, 1965–1966, 14–15, National Archives, Washington, DC, accessed October 11, 2012, http://www.archives.gov/research/pentagon-papers/.

81. Bundy, "SUBJECT: Alternative public positions for U. S. on Southeast Asia . . . "

82. Unknown, "AGENDA FOR 5:30 MEETING, June 10," June 10, 1964, Files of McGeorge Bundy, box 18, folder Meetings on Southeast Asia, Vol. 1, National Security File, Lyndon B. Johnson Presidential Library (Austin, TX).

83. Bromely Smith, "Summary Record of the Meeting on Southeast Asia. Cabinet Room, June 10, 1964, 5:30 PM. Southeast Asia (without the President)," June 10, 1964, Files of

McGeorge Bundy, box 18, folder Meetings on Southeast Asia, Vol. 1, National Security File, Lyndon B. Johnson Presidential Library (Austin, TX).

84. Smith, "Summary Record of the Meeting on Southeast Asia. Cabinet Room, June 10, 1964, 5:30 PM."

85. Smith, "Summary Record of the Meeting on Southeast Asia. Cabinet Room, June 10, 1964, 5:30 PM."

86. Smith, "Summary Record of the Meeting on Southeast Asia. Cabinet Room, June 10, 1964, 5:30 PM."

87. Smith, "Summary Record of the Meeting on Southeast Asia. Cabinet Room, June 10, 1964, 5:30 PM."

88. Bundy, "SUBJECT: Alternative public positions for U. S. on Southeast Asia for the period July 1 . . . "

89. Bundy, "SUBJECT: Alternative public positions for U. S. on Southeast Asia for the period July 1 . . . ".

90. Vietnam Task Force, "Chronology," Vietnam Task Force, Office of the Secretary of Defense, [Part IV. C.].

91. Lyndon B. Johnson, "'President Outlines Basic Themes of U.S. policy in Southeast Asia,' Statement by President Johnson at his News Conference on June 2, 1964, Department of State Bulletin, 22 June 1964, p. 953," Vietnam Task Force, Office of the Secretary of Defense, [Part V. A.], Justification of the War. Public Statements. Volume II: D—The Johnson Administration, D-11-12, National Archives, Washington, DC, accessed October 11, 2012, http://www.archives.gov/research/pentagon-papers/.

92. Lyndon B. Johnson, press conference, transcript, Washington, DC, June 2, 1964, excerpted in memorandum by William J. Jorden, for Chester L. Cooper, June 21, 1965, Files of McGeorge Bundy, box 18, McGeorge Bundy May–June 1965 Teach-In, National Security File, Lyndon B. Johnson Presidential Library (Austin, TX).

93. Lyndon B. Johnson, "National Security Action Memoranda 308: Designation of Robert J. Manning to Disseminate Facts on Southeast Asia," (Washington, DC: The White House, June 22, 1964), Lyndon B. Johnson Presidential Library (Austin, TX), accessed January 9, 2013, http://www.lbjlib.utexas.edu/johnson/archives.hom/NSAMs/nsam308.asp.

94. Special to the New York Times, "Transcript of Interview with Ex-Ambassador Lodge on His Return from Vietnam," New York Times, June 30, 1964, 14, ProQuest Historical Newspapers: The New York Times (1851–2009).

95. Recording of telephone conversation between Lyndon B. Johnson and Richard Russell, June 11, 1964, 12:26 p.m., Citation #3681, Recordings of Telephone Conversations—White House Series, Recordings and Transcripts of Conversations and Meetings, Lyndon B. Johnson Presidential Library (Austin, TX).

96. Recording of telephone conversation between Lyndon B. Johnson and Richard Russell, June 11, 1964, 12:26 p.m.

97. Recording of telephone conversation between Lyndon B. Johnson and Richard Russell, June 11, 1964, 12:26 p.m.

98. Recording of telephone conversation between Lyndon B. Johnson and Richard Russell, June 11, 1964, 12:26 p.m.

99. Hans J. Morgenthau, "The Realities of Containment," New Leader, June 8, 1964, 13, Files of McGeorge Bundy, box 18, McGeorge Bundy May–June 1965 Teach-In, National Security File, Lyndon B. Johnson Presidential Library (Austin, TX).

100. Richard Starnes, "Whole Truth Untold in South Viet Nam," *The Evening News*, Newburgh, New York, May 21, 1964, 6A.

101. Ralph McGill, "Agony without Ecstasy," *Miami News*, June 8, 1964, 6A.

102. Michael H. Hunt, *Lyndon Johnson's War: America's Cold War Crusade in Vietnam 1945–1968* (New York: Hill and Wang, 1996), 100.

103. "Toward the Showdown?" *Time*, August 7, 1964, accessed November 3, 2008, http://www.time.com/time/ magazine/article/0,9171,871317,00.html.

104. McMaster, *Dereliction of Duty*, 125.

105. Oliver Quayle and Company, "A SURVEY OF THE PRESIDENTIAL RACE IN MARYLAND, Study #167," Bronxville, NY, July 1964, box 80 [1 of 2], folder PR16 PUBLIC OPINION POLLS (April 1964–June 1965) [3 of 4], Central File, Lyndon B. Johnson Presidential Library (Austin, TX).

106. Oliver Quayle and Company, "A SURVEY OF THE PRESIDENTIAL RACE IN MARYLAND, Study #167."

107. Karnow, *Vietnam*, 375–392.

108. Christopher J. Kauffman, "Politics, Programs, and Protests: Catholic Relief Services in Vietnam, 1954–1975," *Catholic Historical Review*, Vol. 91, No. 2 (April 2005), 223–250; Joseph Bruce Hamilton, Faux Casus Belli: The Role of Unsubstantiated Attacks in the Initiation of Military Action for Domestic Political Purposes (Dissertation in International Relations, Fletcher School of Law and Diplomacy, March 2000), 136-7, 128–130; Logevall, *Choosing War*, 194.

109. Langguth, *Our Vietnam* . . . , 279; Jeffrey W. Helsing, *Johnson's War/Johnson's Great Society: The Guns and Butter Trap* (Westport, CT: Praeger, 2000) . . . , 4; Hunt, *Lyndon Johnson's War* . . . , 82–83; Kauffman, "Politics, Programs, and Protests . . . "; Hamilton, Faux Casus Belli . . . , 136-7, 128–130; Logevall, *Choosing War*, 197, 199–201, 202; Edwin E. Moïse, *Tonkin Gulf and the Escalation of the Vietnam War* (Chapel Hill, NC: University of North Carolina, 1996), xi–xii, xiv, 203, 240, 225; Randall Bennett Woods, *J. William Fulbright, Vietnam, and the Search for a Cold War Foreign Policy* (Cambridge: Cambridge University, 1998), 72.

110. Langguth, *Our Vietnam* . . . , 279; Helsing, *Johnson's War/Johnson's Great Society* . . . , 4; Hunt, *Lyndon Johnson's War* . . . , 82–83; Kauffman, "Politics, Programs, and Protests . . . "; Hamilton, Faux Casus Belli . . . , 136-7, 128–130; Logevall, *Choosing War*, 197, 199–201, 202; Moïse, *Tonkin Gulf and the Escalation of the Vietnam War*, xi–xii, xiv, 203, 240, 225; Woods, *J. William Fulbright* . . . , 72.

111. Kathleen J. Turner, *Lyndon Johnson's Dual War: Vietnam and the Press* (Chicago: University of Chicago, 1985), 82; Liebovich, *The Press and the Modern Presidency*, 37; Logevall, *Choosing War*, 198; Randall Bennett Woods, *J. William Fulbright, Vietnam, and the Search for a Cold War Foreign Policy* (Cambridge: Cambridge University, 1998), 75.

112. Moïse, *Tonkin Gulf and the Escalation of the Vietnam War*, xi–xii, 203, 240; Woods, *J. William Fulbright* . . . , 74.

113. Moïse, *Tonkin Gulf and the Escalation of the Vietnam War*, xi–xii, 203, 240.

114. Moïse, *Tonkin Gulf and the Escalation of the Vietnam War*, xi–xii, 203, 240; Kauffman, "Politics, Programs, and Protests"; Logevall, *Choosing War*, 197, 199–201.

115. Helsing, *Johnson's War/Johnson's Great Society*, 31–33, 35.

116. Logevall, *Choosing War*, 198.

117. Transcript, George D. Aiken Oral History Interview, October 10, 1968, by Paige E. Mulhollan, Internet Copy, Lyndon B. Johnson Presidential Library (Austin, TX), 4.

118. Woods, *J. William Fulbright . . .* , 73.

119. Logevall, *Choosing War*, 198.

120. White House, Office of the White House Press Secretary, *Statement by the President* (Washington, DC: Office of the white House Press Secretary, August 3, 1964), 1.

121. White House, Office of the White House Press Secretary, *Statement by the President* (Washington, DC: Office of the white House Press Secretary, August 3, 1964), 1.

122. McMaster, *Dereliction of Duty*, 126–127, 135–136; Langguth, *Our Vietnam*, 304; Kathleen J. Turner, *Lyndon Johnson's Dual War: Vietnam and the Press* (Chicago: University of Chicago, 1985), 83.

123. McMaster, *Dereliction of Duty*, 134.

124. Turner, *Lyndon Johnson's Dual War*, 85; Langguth, *Our Vietnam*, 304; Karnow, *Vietnam*, 390.

125. Turner, *Lyndon Johnson's Dual War*, 85.

126. Arnold H. Lubasch, "Reds Driven Off," *New York Times*, August 5, 1964, 1.

127. Associated Press, "U.S. Patrols in the Gulf of Tonkin Will Be Halted Temporarily," *Milwaukee Journal*, August 8, 1964, 12.

128. "A Measured & Fitting Response," *Time*, August 14, 1964, accessed November 3, 2008, http://www.time.com/time/magazine/article/0,9171,897224,00.html.

129. Moïse, *Tonkin Gulf and the Escalation of the Vietnam War*, 228–234, 238–239.

130. Moïse, *Tonkin Gulf and the Escalation of the Vietnam War*, 228–234, 238–239.

131. "Action in Tonkin Gulf," *Time*, August 14, 1964, accessed September 3, 2008, http://www.time.com/ time/magazine/article/0,9171,897225,00.html.

132. Associated Press, "Damage Heavy; Two Aircraft Reported Lost," *Free-Lance Star*, Fredericksburg, VA, August 5, 1964, 1.

133. Karnow, *Vietnam*, 390; Turner, *Lyndon Johnson's Dual War*, 85; Helsing, *Johnson's War/Johnson's Great Society*, 4; Hunt, *Lyndon Johnson's War*, 100; Hammond, *Public Affairs, 1962–1968*, 101.

134. Karnow, *Vietnam*, 390.

135. Moïse, *Tonkin Gulf and the Escalation of the Vietnam War*, 225.

136. Dean Rusk, "'Secretary Rusk Discusses Asian Situation on NBC Program," 5 August 1964, Department of State Bulletin, 24 August 1964, p. 268," Vietnam Task Force, Office of the Secretary of Defense, [Part V. A.] Justification of the War. Public Statements. Volume II: D—The Johnson Administration, D-16, National Archives, Washington, DC, accessed October 11, 2012, http://www.archives.gov/research/pentagon-papers/.

137. Lyndon B. Johnson, "'Address by the President,' Syracuse University, 5 August 1964, Department of State Bulletin, 24 August 1964, p. 260," Vietnam Task Force, Office of the Secretary of Defense, [Part V. A.], Justification of the War. Public Statements. Volume II: D—The Johnson Administration, D-13-14, National Archives, Washington, DC, accessed October 11, 2012, http://www.archives.gov/research/pentagon-papers/.

138. Lyndon B. Johnson, "'Address by the President,' Syracuse University, 5 August 1964, Department of State Bulletin, 24 August 1964, p. 260," Vietnam Task Force, Office of the Secretary of Defense, [Part V. A.], Justification of the War. Public Statements. Volume II: D—The Johnson Administration, D-13-14, National Archives, Washington, D.C., accessed October 11, 11, 2012, http://www.archives.gov/research/pentagon-papers/.

139. Lyndon B. Johnson, "'Address by the President,' Syracuse University, 5 August 1964, Department of State Bulletin, 24 August 1964, p. 260," Vietnam Task Force, Office of the Secretary of Defense, [Part V. A.], Justification of the War. Public Statements. Volume II:

D—The Johnson Administration, D-13-14, National Archives, Washington, DC, accessed October 11, 2012, http://www.archives.gov/research/pentagon-papers/.

140. Lyndon B. Johnson, "'Address by the President,' Syracuse University, 5 August 1964, Department of State Bulletin, 24 August 1964, p. 260," Vietnam Task Force, Office of the Secretary of Defense, [Part V. A.], Justification of the War. Public Statements. Volume II: D—The Johnson Administration, D-13-14, National Archives, Washington, DC, accessed October 11, 2012, http://www.archives.gov/research/pentagon-papers/.

141. I. F. Stone, "What Few Know About the Tonkin Bay Incidents," *I. F. Stone's Weekly*, Vol. 12, No. 28 (August 24, 1964), 1.

142. Lyndon B. Johnson, "'Address by the President,' Syracuse University, 5 August 1964, Department of State Bulletin, 24 August 1964, p. 260," Vietnam Task Force, Office of the Secretary of Defense, [Part V. A.], Justification of the War. Public Statements. Volume II: D—The Johnson Administration, D-13-14, National Archives, Washington, DC, accessed October 11, 2012, http://www.archives.gov/research/pentagon-papers/.

143. Lyndon B. Johnson, "'Address by the President,' Syracuse University, 5 August 1964, Department of State Bulletin, 24 August 1964, p. 260," Vietnam Task Force, Office of the Secretary of Defense, [Part V. A.], Justification of the War. Public Statements. Volume II: D—The Johnson Administration, D-13-14, National Archives, Washington, DC, accessed October 11, 2012, http://www.archives.gov/research/pentagon-papers/.

144. Eugene Brown, *J. William Fulbright: Advice and Dissent* (Iowa City, IA: University of Iowa, 1985), 63; Karnow, *Vietnam*, 390; Moïse, *Tonkin Gulf and the Escalation of the Vietnam War*, 266–267; Linda K. Kerber, "The Meanings of Citizenship," *Journal of American History*, Vol. 84, No. 3 (December 1997), 833–854; Logevall, *Choosing War*, xxii–xxiii.

145. Brown, *J. William Fulbright*, 63.

146. White House, Office of the White House Press Secretary, *Message to U.S. Congress Regarding Tonkin Gulf incidents* (Washington, DC: Office of the White House Press Secretary, August 5, 1964), 1.

147. White House, Office of the White House Press Secretary, *Message to U.S. Congress Regarding Tonkin Gulf incidents* (Washington, DC: Office of the White House Press Secretary, August 5, 1964), 1, 2 .

148. White House, Office of the White House Press Secretary, *Message to U.S. Congress Regarding Tonkin Gulf incidents* (Washington, DC: Office of the White House Press Secretary, August 5, 1964), 1.

149. White House, Office of the White House Press Secretary, *Message to U.S. Congress Regarding Tonkin Gulf incidents* (Washington, DC: Office of the White House Press Secretary, August 5, 1964), 2.

150. Lyndon B. Johnson, "'President's Message to Congress,' 5 August 1964, Department of State Bulletin, 24 August 1964, p. 261," Vietnam Task Force, Office of the Secretary of Defense, [Part V. A.], Justification of the War. Public Statements. Volume II: D— The Johnson Administration, D-14-15, National Archives, Washington, D.C., accessed October 11, 2012, http://www.archives.gov/research/pentagon-papers/.

151. White House, Office of the White House Press Secretary, *Message to U.S. Congress Regarding Tonkin Gulf Incidents* (Washington, DC: Office of the White House Press Secretary, August 5, 1964), 1.

152. Lyndon B. Johnson, "'President's Message to Congress,' 5 August 1964, Department of State Bulletin, 24 August 1964, p. 261," Vietnam Task Force, Office of the Secretary of Defense, [Part V. A.], Justification of the War. Public Statements. Volume II: D—The

Johnson Administration, D-14-15, National Archives, Washington, D.C., accessed October 11, 2012, http://www.archives.gov/research/pentagon-papers/.

153. Karnow, *Vietnam*, 390; Moïse, *Tonkin Gulf and the Escalation of the Vietnam War*, 266–267; Logevall, *Choosing War*, 203.

154. Kerber, "The Meanings of Citizenship."

155. Woods, *J. William Fulbright . . .* , 75–76.

156. Brown, *J. William Fulbright*, 64.

157. Helsing, *Johnson's War/Johnson's Great Society*, 32–33; McMaster, *Dereliction of Duty*, 134; Woods, *J. William Fulbright . . .* , 76–77.

158. Woods, *J. William Fulbright . . .* , 77; Logevall, *Choosing War*, 203; Ezra Y. Siff, *Why the Senate Slept: The Gulf of Tonkin Resolution and the Beginning of America's Vietnam War* (Westport, CT: Praeger, 1999), 21.

159. Woods, *J. William Fulbright . . .* , 75; Transcript, George Ball Oral History Interview I, July 8, 1971, by Paige E. Mulhollan, Internet Copy, Lyndon B. Johnson Presidential Library (Austin, TX), 13–15; Moïse, *Tonkin Gulf and the Escalation of the Vietnam War*, 228.

160. Moïse, *Tonkin Gulf and the Escalation of the Vietnam War*, 226–227.

161. Woods, *J. William Fulbright . . .* , 165–166.

162. Siff, *Why the Senate Slept*, 30.

163. Logevall, *Choosing War*, xxii–xxiii.

164. Brown, *J. William Fulbright*, 64.

165. Caroline F. Ziemke, "Senator Richard B. Russell and the 'Lost Cause' in Vietnam, 1954–1968," *Georgia Historical Quarterly*, Vol. 72, No. 1 (Spring, 1988), 30–71.

166. Ziemke, "Senator Richard B. Russell . . . ," 30–71.

167. Ziemke, "Senator Richard B. Russell . . . ," 30–71.

168. Siff, *Why the Senate Slept*, xv.

169. Siff, *Why the Senate Slept*, xv.

170. Transcript, George Ball Oral History Interview I, July 8, 1971, by Paige E. Mulhollan, Internet Copy, Lyndon B. Johnson Presidential Library (Austin, TX), 13–15.

171. Brown, *J. William Fulbright*, 65.

172. Siff, *Why the Senate Slept*, 33.

173. Siff, *Why the Senate Slept*, 33; Logevall, *Choosing War*, 204.

174. Woods, *J. William Fulbright . . .* , 77; Logevall, *Choosing War*, 204; Robert David Johnson, "The Origins of Dissent: Senate Liberals and Vietnam, 1959–1964," *Pacific Historical Review*, Vol. 65, No. 2 (May 1996), 249–275.

175. Brown, *J. William Fulbright*, 64.

176. Siff, *Why the Senate Slept*, 20–21.

177. Siff, *Why the Senate Slept*, xvi; Woods, *J. William Fulbright . . .* , 77.

178. Logevall, *Choosing War*, 203; Brown, *J. William Fulbright*, 66; Siff, *Why the Senate Slept*, 36–38.

179. Brown, *J. William Fulbright*, 65.

180. Johnson, "The Origins of Dissent," 249–275.

181. Logevall, *Choosing War*, 204.

182. Woods, *J. William Fulbright . . .* , 77–78.

183. Woods, *J. William Fulbright . . .* , 76.

184. Siff, *Why the Senate Slept*, xvi.

185. Woods, *J. William Fulbright . . .* , 76.

186. Ziemke, "Senator Richard B. Russell . . . ," 30–71.

187. Siff, *Why the Senate Slept*, 13–14.

188. Siff, *Why the Senate Slept*, 15–16.

189. Brown, *J. William Fulbright*, 63.

190. Logevall, *Choosing War*, 204; Woods, *J. William Fulbright . . .*, 77–78.

191. Hunt, *Lyndon Johnson's War*, 100.

192. Congress of the United States, "Text of Joint Resolution, August 7, Department of State Bulletin, 24 August 1964, p. 268," Vietnam Task Force, Office of the Secretary of Defense, [Part V. A.] Justification of the War. Public Statements. Volume II: D—The Johnson Administration, D-16-17, National Archives, Washington, DC, accessed October 11, 2012, http://www.archives.gov/research/pentagon-papers/.

193. Congress of the United States, "Text of Public Law 88-408 [H.J. Res. 1145], 78 Stat. 384, approved Aug. 10, 1964," Vietnam Task Force, Office of the Secretary of Defense, [Part IV. C.] Evolution of the War, Direct Action: The Johnson Commitments, 1964–1968. Volume II: b—July–October 1964, Tab C, National Archives, Washington, DC, accessed October 11, 2012, http://www.archives.gov/research/pentagon-papers/.

194. Congress of the United States, "Text of Joint Resolution, August 7, Department of State Bulletin, 24 August 1964, p. 268," Vietnam Task Force, Office of the Secretary of Defense, [Part V. A.] Justification of the War. Public Statements. Volume II: D—The Johnson Administration, D-16-17, National Archives, Washington, DC, accessed October 11, 2012, http://www.archives.gov/research/pentagon-papers/.

195. Congress of the United States, "Text of Joint Resolution, August 7, Department of State Bulletin, 24 August 1964, p. 268," Vietnam Task Force, Office of the Secretary of Defense, [Part V. A.] Justification of the War. Public Statements. Volume II: D--The Johnson Administration, D-16-17, National Archives, Washington, DC, accessed October 11, 2012, http://www.archives.gov/research/pentagon-papers/.

196. Cecil Stoughton, Photo, President Johnson signs the Tonkin Gulf Resolution, Washington, DC, August 10, 1964, Photo Archive, Lyndon B. Johnson Presidential Library (Austin, TX), accessed July 26, 2015, http://www.lbjlibrary.net/collections/photo-archive.html.

197. Norman A. Graebner, "The President as Commander in Chief: A Study in Power," *Journal of Military History*, Vol. 57, No. 1 (January 1993), 111–132.

198. Moïse, *Tonkin Gulf and the Escalation of the Vietnam War*, 226.

199. Moïse, *Tonkin Gulf and the Escalation of the Vietnam War*, 226–227.

200. Moïse, *Tonkin Gulf and the Escalation of the Vietnam War*, 226–227.

201. Moïse, *Tonkin Gulf and the Escalation of the Vietnam War*, 226–227.

202. Moïse, *Tonkin Gulf and the Escalation of the Vietnam War*, 226–227.

203. Siff, *Why the Senate Slept*, 108.

204. McGeorge Bundy, memorandum for record, "August 10, 1964, 12:35 PM -Meeting in Cabinet Room," 10 August 1964, Files of McGeorge Bundy, box 18, folder Meetings on Southeast Asia, Vol. 1, National Security File, Lyndon B. Johnson Presidential Library (Austin, TX).

205. William P. Bundy, Third Draft, "NEXT COURSES OF ACTION IN SOUTHEAST ASIA," August 13, 1964, Files of McGeorge Bundy, box 18, folder Meetings on Southeast Asia, Vol. 1, National Security File, Lyndon B. Johnson Presidential Library (Austin, TX).

206. William P. Bundy, Third Draft, "NEXT COURSES OF ACTION IN SOUTHEAST ASIA," August 13, 1964, Files of McGeorge Bundy, box 18, folder Meetings on Southeast Asia, Vol. 1, National Security File, Lyndon B. Johnson Presidential Library (Austin, TX).

207. Lyndon B. Johnson, statement at the signing of H.J. 1145, transcript, Washington, DC, August 10, 1964, excerpted in memorandum by William J. Jorden, for Chester L. Cooper, June 21, 1965, Files of McGeorge Bundy, box 18, McGeorge Bundy May–June 1965 Teach-In, National Security File, Lyndon B. Johnson Presidential Library (Austin, TX).

208. White House, Office of the White House Press Secretary, *Remarks of the President upon the Signing of H.J. 1145 Joint Resolution to Promote the Maintenance of International Peace and Security in Southeast Asia in the East Room* (Washington, DC: Office of the White House Press Secretary, August 10, 1964), 1.

209. Lyndon B. Johnson, statement at the signing of H.J. 1145, transcript, Washington, DC, August 10, 1964, excerpted in memorandum by William J. Jorden, for Chester L. Cooper, June 21, 1965, Files of McGeorge Bundy, box 18, McGeorge Bundy May–June 1965 Teach-In, National Security File, Lyndon B. Johnson Presidential Library (Austin, TX).

210. White House, Office of the White House Press Secretary, *Remarks of the President upon the Signing of H.J. 1145 Joint Resolution to Promote the Maintenance of International Peace and Security in Southeast Asia in the East Room* (Washington, DC: Office of the White House Press Secretary, August 10, 1964), 1.

211. Lyndon Baines Johnson, President's Remarks at the American Bar Association, New York City, August 12, 1964, National Security File: Speech File, Box 1, Lyndon Banes Johnson Library, Austin, TX.

212. Lyndon Baines Johnson, President's Remarks at the American Bar Association, New York City, August 12, 1964, National Security File: Speech File, Box 1, Lyndon Banes Johnson Library, Austin, TX.

213. Lyndon B. Johnson, speech to Convention of the American Bar Association, transcript, New York, August 12, 1964, excerpted in memorandum by William J. Jorden, for Chester L. Cooper, June 21, 1965, Files of McGeorge Bundy, box 18, McGeorge Bundy May-June 1965 Teach-In, National Security File, Lyndon B. Johnson Presidential Library (Austin, TX).

214. Vietnam Task Force, "Chronology," Vietnam Task Force, Office of the Secretary of Defense, [Part IV. C.], Evolution of the War, Direct Action: The Johnson Commitments, 1964–1968. Volume II: B, Military Pressures Against NVN, July–October 1964, 7–8, National Archives, Washington, DC, accessed October 11, 2012, http://www.archives.gov/research/pentagon-papers/.

215. McGeorge Bundy, "National Security Action Memorandum 314: Resumption of Operations in SEA," (Washington, DC: The White House, September 10, 1964), Lyndon B. Johnson Presidential Library (Austin, TX), accessed January 9, 2013, http://www.lbjlib.utexas.edu/johnson/archives.hom/NSAMs/nsam314.asp.

216. Lyndon B. Johnson, "Remarks at a Fundraising Dinner in New Orleans, October 9, 1964," in *Public Papers of the Presidents of the United States: Lyndon B. Johnson, 1963–64.* Volume II, entry 648 (Washington, DC: Government Printing Office, 1965), 1281–1288, accessed January 3, 2013, http://www.lbjlibrary.net/collections/selected-speeches/november-1963-1964/10-09-1964.html.

217. James "Scotty" Reston, "Washington: The Unresolved Questions of the Campaign," *New York Times,* October 4, 1964, E10, *New York Times* (1923–Current file), ProQuest Historical Newspapers: *The New York Times* (1851–2009).

218. James "Scotty" Reston, "Washington: The Unresolved Questions of the Campaign," *New York Times,* October 4, 1964, E10, *New York Times* (1923–Current file), ProQuest Historical Newspapers: *New York Times* (1851–2009).

219. James "Scotty" Reston, "Washington: The Unresolved Questions of the Campaign," *New York Times*, October 4, 1964, E10, *New York Times* (1923–Current file), ProQuest Historical Newspapers: *New York Times* (1851–2009).

220. Oliver Quayle and Company, "A Survey of the Presidential Race in Kentucky, Wave III, Study #213," Bronxville, NY, October 1964, box 80 [1 of 2], folder PR16 Public Opinion Polls (April 1964–June 1965) [2 of 4], Central File, Lyndon B. Johnson Presidential Library (Austin, TX).

221. Oliver Quayle and Company, "A Survey of the Presidential Race in Kentucky, Wave III, Study #213," Bronxville, NY, October 1964, box 80 [1 of 2], folder PR16 Public Opinion Polls (April 1964–June 1965) [2 of 4], Central File, Lyndon B. Johnson Presidential Library (Austin, TX).

222. Oliver Quayle and Company, "A Survey of the Presidential Race in Kentucky, Wave III, Study #213," Bronxville, NY, October 1964, box 80 [1 of 2], folder PR16 Public Opinion Polls (April 1964–June 1965) [2 of 4], Central File, Lyndon B. Johnson Presidential Library (Austin, TX).

223. Lyndon B. Johnson, "DNC-64-38-T: Quest for Peace w/ Pres. Johnson Speech," Democratic National Committee, black and white with sound, October 15, 1964, Video #MP649, "Quest for Peace," Audiovisual Material, Motion Pictures, Lyndon B. Johnson Presidential Library (Austin, TX).

224. Lyndon B. Johnson, "DNC-64-38-T: Quest for Peace w/ Pres. Johnson Speech," Democratic National Committee, black and white with sound, October 15, 1964, Video #MP649, "Quest for Peace," Audiovisual Material, Motion Pictures, Lyndon B. Johnson Presidential Library (Austin, TX).

225. Lyndon B. Johnson, "DNC-64-38-T: Quest for Peace w/ Pres. Johnson Speech," Democratic National Committee, black and white with sound, October 15, 1964, Video #MP649, "Quest for Peace," Audiovisual Material, Motion Pictures, Lyndon B. Johnson Presidential Library (Austin, TX).

226. Lyndon B. Johnson, "LBJ Speech & Promotional Campaign video," *Campaign 1964*, black and white with sound, 27 minutes, August–November 1964, Video #MP648, "Johnson Half Hour Speech, Campaign '64," Audiovisual Material, Motion Pictures, Lyndon B. Johnson Presidential Library (Austin, TX).

227. Lyndon B. Johnson, "LBJ Speech & Promotional Campaign video," *Campaign 1964*, black and white with sound, 27 minutes, August–November 1964, Video #MP648, "Johnson Half Hour Speech, Campaign '64," Audiovisual Material, Motion Pictures, Lyndon B. Johnson Presidential Library (Austin, TX).

228. Lyndon B. Johnson, "LBJ Speech & Promotional Campaign video," *Campaign 1964*, black and white with sound, 27 minutes, August–November 1964, Video #MP648, "Johnson Half Hour Speech, Campaign '64," Audiovisual Material, Motion Pictures, Lyndon B. Johnson Presidential Library (Austin, TX).

229. Lyndon B. Johnson, "DNC-64-38-T: Quest for Peace w/ Pres. Johnson Speech", Democratic National Committee, black and white with sound, October 15, 1964, Video #MP649, "Quest for Peace," Audiovisual Material, Motion Pictures, Lyndon B. Johnson Presidential Library (Austin, TX).

230. Lyndon B. Johnson, "DNC-64-38-T: Quest for Peace w/ Pres. Johnson Speech", Democratic National Committee, black and white with sound, October 15, 1964, Video #MP649, "Quest for Peace," Audiovisual Material, Motion Pictures, Lyndon B. Johnson Presidential Library (Austin, TX).

231. Lyndon B. Johnson, "DNC-64-38-T: Quest for Peace w/ Pres. Johnson Speech", Democratic National Committee, black and white with sound, October 15, 1964, Video #MP649, "Quest for Peace," Audiovisual Material, Motion Pictures, Lyndon B. Johnson Presidential Library (Austin, TX).

232. Lyndon B. Johnson, "DNC-64-38-T: Quest for Peace w/ Pres. Johnson Speech", Democratic National Committee, black and white with sound, October 15, 1964, Video #MP649, "Quest for Peace," Audiovisual Material, Motion Pictures, Lyndon B. Johnson Presidential Library (Austin, TX).

233. Lyndon B. Johnson, "DNC-64-38-T: Quest for Peace w/ Pres. Johnson Speech", Democratic National Committee, black and white with sound, October 15, 1964, Video #MP649, "Quest for Peace," Audiovisual Material, Motion Pictures, Lyndon B. Johnson Presidential Library (Austin, TX).

234. Lyndon B. Johnson, "DNC-64-38-T: Quest for Peace w/ Pres. Johnson Speech", Democratic National Committee, black and white with sound, October 15, 1964, Video #MP649, "Quest for Peace," Audiovisual Material, Motion Pictures, Lyndon B. Johnson Presidential Library (Austin, TX).

235. The Gallup Organization, *Gallup/Potomac Poll #1964-633POS: National Survey of Attitudes, Hopes, and Fears* (Williamstown, MA: The Roper Public Opinion Research Center, September 1964), 11–12, 39–48; The Gallup Organization, *Gallup/Potomac Poll #1964-637POS: National Survey of Attitudes, Hopes, and Fears* (Williamstown, MA: The Roper Public Opinion Research Center, October 1964), 7–29, 31.

236. The Gallup Organization, *Gallup/Potomac Poll #1964-633POS: National Survey of Attitudes, Hopes, and Fears* (Williamstown, MA: The Roper Public Opinion Research Center, September 1964), 11–12, 39–48; The Gallup Organization, *Gallup/Potomac Poll #1964-637POS: National Survey of Attitudes, Hopes, and Fears* (Williamstown, MA: The Roper Public Opinion Research Center, October 1964), 7–29, 31.

237. The Gallup Organization, *Gallup/Potomac Poll #1964-633POS: National Survey of Attitudes, Hopes, and Fears* (Williamstown, MA: The Roper Public Opinion Research Center, September 1964), 73–77.

238. The Gallup Organization, *Gallup/Potomac Poll #1964-633POS: National Survey of Attitudes, Hopes, and Fears* (Williamstown, MA: The Roper Public Opinion Research Center, September 1964), 73–77.

239. The Gallup Organization, *Gallup/Potomac Poll #1964-633POS: National Survey of Attitudes, Hopes, and Fears* (Williamstown, MA: The Roper Public Opinion Research Center, September 1964), 73–77.

240. The Gallup Organization, *Gallup/Potomac Poll #1964-637POS: National Survey of Attitudes, Hopes, and Fears* (Williamstown, MA: The Roper Public Opinion Research Center, October 1964), 36–42, 43–53.

241. Lyndon Johnson, "693 -Remarks in Memorial Hall, Akron University," October 21, 1964, accessed January 36, 2015, American Presidency Project, http://www.presidency.ucsb.edu/ws/?pid=26635.

242. Brian VanDeMark, *Into the Quagmire: Lyndon Johnson and the Escalation of the Vietnam War,* (New York: Oxford University, 1991), 18–19.

243. Liebovich, *The Press and the Modern Presidency*, 38; Hunt, *Lyndon Johnson's War*, 90.

Chapter 2

1. Stanley Karnow, *Vietnam: A History* (New York: Penguin, 1997), 417–429.

2. Robert Dallek, *Lyndon B. Johnson: Portrait of a President* (New York: Oxford University, 2004), 191.

3. Karnow, *Vietnam*, 417–429.
4. The Gallup Organization, *Gallup Poll #704* (Williamstown, MA: The Roper Public Opinion Research Center, January 7–12, 1965), 10.
5. The Gallup Organization, *Gallup Poll #704* (Williamstown, MA: The Roper Public Opinion Research Center, January 7–12, 1965), 10.
6. William R. Frye, "The U.S. May Try Brass Knuckles," United Nations, New York, *The Sunday Sun*, Vancouver, BC, January 2, 1965, 4.
7. Drew Pearson, "Washington Merry Go Round: No Progress in 18 Years," Washington, DC, *Prescott Evening Courier*, Prescott, AZ, December 3, 1964, 4.
8. Joseph Alsop, "Deep Trouble Brewing," Washington, *Saskatoon Star-Phoenix*, Saskatoon, Saskatchewan, February 3, 1965, 1.
9. Mike Mansfield, letter for President Johnson, "Subject: Developments in Viet Nam," December 9, 1964, box 12, folder CO 312 Vietnam (1964–1965), Central File, Lyndon B. Johnson Presidential Library (Austin, TX).
10. Mike Mansfield, letter for President Johnson, "Subject: Developments in Viet Nam," December 9, 1964, box 12, folder CO 312 Vietnam (1964–1965), Central File, Lyndon B. Johnson Presidential Library (Austin, TX).
11. Mike Mansfield, letter for President Johnson, "Subject: Developments in Viet Nam," December 9, 1964, box 12, folder CO 312 Vietnam (1964–1965), Central File, Lyndon B. Johnson Presidential Library (Austin, TX).
12. Lyndon B. Johnson, letter to Senator Mike Mansfield, December 17, 1964, box 12, folder CO 312 VIETNAM (1964-1965), Central File, Lyndon B. Johnson Presidential Library (Austin, TX).
13. Dean Rusk, "A Conversation with Dean Rusk, NBC News Program, on January 3, 1965," Department of State Bulletin, 18 January 1965, p. 64," Vietnam Task Force, Office of the Secretary of Defense, [Part V. A.] Justification of the War. Public Statements. Volume II: D—The Johnson Administration, D-25, National Archives, Washington, DC, accessed October 11, 2012, http://www.archives.gov/research/pentagon-papers/.
14. Dean Rusk, "A Conversation with Dean Rusk, NBC News Program, on January 3, 1965, Department of State Bulletin, 18 January 1965, p. 64," Vietnam Task Force, Office of the Secretary of Defense, [Part V. A.] Justification of the War. Public Statements. Volume II: D—The Johnson Administration, D-25, National Archives, Washington, DC, accessed October 11, 2012, http://www.archives.gov/research/pentagon-papers/.
15. Dean Rusk, "A Conversation with Dean Rusk, NBC News Program, on January 3, 1965, Department of State Bulletin, 18 January 1965, p. 64," Vietnam Task Force, Office of the Secretary of Defense, [Part V. A.] Justification of the War. Public Statements. Volume II: D—The Johnson Administration, D-25, National Archives, Washington, DC, accessed October 11, 2012, http://www.archives.gov/research/pentagon-papers/.
16. Lyndon B. Johnson, "Annual Message to the Congress on the State of the Union, January 4, 1965," in *Public Papers of the Presidents of the United States: Lyndon B. Johnson, 1965*. Volume I, entry 2, (Washington, DC: Government Printing Office, 1966), 1–9, accessed January 6, 2013, http://www.lbjlibrary.net/collections/selected-speeches/1965/01-04-1965.html.
17. Lyndon B. Johnson, "The State of the Union Address of the President to the Congress, January 4, 1965, Public Papers of the Presidents, Johnson, 1965, p. 3," Vietnam Task Force, Office of the Secretary of Defense, [Part V. A.] Justification of the War. Public Statements. Volume II: D—The Johnson Administration, D-25, National Archives, Washington, DC, accessed October 11, 2012, http://www.archives.gov/research/pentagon-papers/.
18. William P. Bundy, "William Bundy Discusses Vietnam Situation, February 7, 1965, Department of State Bulletin, March 8, 1965, p. 292," Vietnam Task Force, Office of

the Secretary of Defense, [Part V. A.] Justification of the War. Public Statements. Volume II: D--The Johnson Administration, D-27, National Archives, Washington, DC, accessed October 11, 2012, http://www.archives.gov/research/pentagon-papers/.

19. William P. Bundy, "William Bundy Discusses Vietnam Situation, February 7, 1965, Department of State Bulletin, March 8, 1965, p. 292," Vietnam Task Force, Office of the Secretary of Defense, [Part V. A.] Justification of the War. Public Statements. Volume II: D—The Johnson Administration, D-27, National Archives, Washington, D.C., accessed October 11, 2012, http://www.archives.gov/research/pentagon-papers/.

20. Transcript, George Ball Oral History Interview I, July 8, 1971, by Paige E. Mulhollan, Internet Copy, Lyndon B. Johnson Presidential Library (Austin, TX), 18–20.

21. Karnow, *Vietnam*, 417–429; Fredrik Logevall, *Choosing War: The Lost Chance for Peace and the Escalation of War in Vietnam* (Berkeley, CA: University of California, 1999), 330; Randall Bennett Woods, *J. William Fulbright, Vietnam, and the Search for a Cold War Foreign Policy* (Cambridge: Cambridge University, 1998), 85.

22. John Kenneth Galbraith, "Foreign Policy and Passing Generations," speech by John Kenneth Galbraith at the southeastern Pennsylvania Roosevelt Day dinner of the Americans for Democratic Action, Philadelphia, PA, January 30, 1965, reprinted in *Congressional Record*, February 2, 1965, 1806–1807, Series 48 Foreign Relations Committee, 48-1 General 1965, Box 7, Folder 1, University of Arkansas Library (Fayetteville, AR).

23. John Kenneth Galbraith, "Foreign Policy and Passing Generations," speech by John Kenneth Galbraith at the southeastern Pennsylvania Roosevelt Day dinner of the Americans for Democratic Action, Philadelphia, PA, January 30, 1965, reprinted in *Congressional Record*, February 2, 1965, 1806–1807, Series 48 Foreign Relations Committee, 48-1 General 1965, Box 7, Folder 1, University of Arkansas Library (Fayetteville, AR).

24. John Kenneth Galbraith, "Foreign Policy and Passing Generations," speech by John Kenneth Galbraith at the southeastern Pennsylvania Roosevelt Day dinner of the Americans for Democratic Action, Philadelphia, PA, January 30, 1965, reprinted in *Congressional Record*, February 2, 1965, 1806–1807, Series 48 Foreign Relations Committee, 48-1 General 1965, Box 7, Folder 1, University of Arkansas Library (Fayetteville, AR).

25. John Kenneth Galbraith, "Foreign Policy and Passing Generations," speech by John Kenneth Galbraith at the southeastern Pennsylvania Roosevelt Day dinner of the Americans for Democratic Action, Philadelphia, PA, January 30, 1965, reprinted in *Congressional Record*, February 2, 1965, 1806–1807, Series 48 Foreign Relations Committee, 48-1 General 1965, Box 7, Folder 1, University of Arkansas Library (Fayetteville, AR).

26. John Kenneth Galbraith, "Foreign Policy and Passing Generations," speech by John Kenneth Galbraith at the southeastern Pennsylvania Roosevelt Day dinner of the Americans for Democratic Action, Philadelphia, PA, January 30, 1965, reprinted in *Congressional Record*, February 2, 1965, 1806–1807, Series 48 Foreign Relations Committee, 48-1 General 1965, Box 7, Folder 1, University of Arkansas Library (Fayetteville, AR).

27. Donald S. Sagoria, "The 'Domino' Theory in Vietnam," New York, *Calgary Herald*, Calgary, Alberta, Canada, February 8, 1965, 5.

28. Donald S. Sagoria, "The 'Domino' Theory in Vietnam," New York, *Calgary Herald*, Calgary, Alberta, Canada, February 8, 1965, 5.

29. Eugene Register-Guard, "The Key Is the 'Domino Theory,'" *Eugene Register-Guard*, Eugene Oregon, February 11, 1965, 10A.

30. Eugene Register-Guard, "The Key Is the 'Domino Theory,'" *Eugene Register-Guard*, Eugene Oregon, February 11, 1965, 10A.

31. Karnow, *Vietnam*, 429; Jeffrey W. Helsing, *Johnson's War/Johnson's Great Society: The Guns and Butter Trap* (Westport, CT: Praeger, 2000), 81–82.

32. Karnow, *Vietnam*, 430; Laura Roselle, *Media and the Politics of Failure: Great Powers, Communication Strategies, and Military Defeats* (New York: Palgrave Macmillan, 2006), 34–35.
33. Lou Harris, document covering public opinion polling on Vietnam and China, [February 15, 1965], box 71 [1 of 2], folder ND 19-CO 312 VIETNAM (Situation In) (1964-1965) [4 OF 4], Central File, Lyndon B. Johnson Presidential Library (Austin, TX).
34. The Gallup Organization, *Gallup Poll #706* (Williamstown, MA: The Roper Public Opinion Research Center, February 19–24, 1965), 6–8.
35. Lou Harris, document covering public opinion polling on Vietnam and China, [February 15, 1965], box 71 [1 of 2], folder ND 19-CO 312 VIETNAM (Situation In) (1964-1965) [4 OF 4], Central File, Lyndon B. Johnson Presidential Library (Austin, TX).
36. The Gallup Organization, *Gallup Poll #706* (Williamstown, MA: The Roper Public Opinion Research Center, February 19–24, 1965), 19–20.
37. Lou Harris, document covering public opinion polling on Vietnam and China, [February 15, 1965], box 71 [1 of 2], folder ND 19-CO 312 Vietnam (Situation In) (1964-1965) [4 OF 4], Central File, Lyndon B. Johnson Presidential Library (Austin, TX).
38. H. R. McMaster, *Dereliction of Duty: Lyndon Johnson, Robert McNamara, the Joint Chiefs of Staff, and the Lies That Led to Vietnam* (New York: HarperCollins, 1997), 226–260.
39. McMaster, *Dereliction of Duty*, 220, 239, 244, 254, 260–261; A. J. Langguth, *Our Vietnam: The War 1954–1975* (New York: Simon & Schuster, 2000), 341, 352; Roselle, *Media and the Politics of Failure*, 30, 31; Helsing, *Johnson's War:/Johnson's Great Society*, 81; David E. Kaiser, *American Tragedy: Kennedy, Johnson, and the Origins of the Vietnam War* (Cambridge, MA: Harvard University, 2000), 413.
40. Transcript, George Ball Oral History Interview I, 8 July 1971, by Paige E. Mulhollan, Internet Copy, Lyndon B. Johnson Presidential Library (Austin, TX), 18–20.
41. Transcript, Benjamin H. Read Oral History Interview II, March 1970, by Paige E. Mulhollan, Internet Copy, Lyndon B. Johnson Presidential Library (Austin, TX), 4–6.
42. Transcript, Benjamin H. Read Oral History Interview II, March 1970, by Paige E. Mulhollan, Internet Copy, Lyndon B. Johnson Presidential Library (Austin, TX), 4–6.
43. McGeorge Bundy, "National Security Action Memoranda 328: Presidential Decisions with Respect to Vietnam," (Washington, DC: The White House, April 6, 1965), Lyndon B. Johnson Presidential Library (Austin, TX), accessed January 9, 2013, http://www.lbjlib.utexas.edu/johnson/archives.hom/NSAMs/nsam328.asp.
44. Lyndon B. Johnson, speech to National Industrial Conference Board, Sheraton-Park Hotel, transcript, 17 February 1965, excerpted in memorandum by William J. Jorden, for Chester L. Cooper, June 21, 1965, Files of McGeorge Bundy, box 18, McGeorge Bundy May–June 1965 Teach-In, National Security File, Lyndon B. Johnson Presidential Library (Austin, TX).
45. Associated Press, "Situation in Viet Nam Not Hopeless, Says McNamara," Associated Press, Washington, *Evening News*, Newburgh, NY, February 18, 1965, 1.
46. Associated Press, "Situation in Viet Nam Not Hopeless, Says McNamara," Associated Press, Washington, *Evening News*, Newburgh, NY, February 18, 1965, 1.
47. Associated Press, "Situation in Viet Nam Not Hopeless, Says McNamara," Associated Press, Washington, *Evening News*, Newburgh, NY, February 18, 1965, 1.
48. New York Times, "Storm Signals Over Asia," *New York Times*, February 28, 1965, reprinted in *William Winter Comments*, Sausalito, CA, March 8, 1965, 1, Series 48 Foreign Relations Committee, 48-1 General 1965, Box 7, Folder 1, Fulbright Papers, University of Arkansas Library (Fayetteville, AR).
49. Herald-Journal, "Viet Nam Policy: What Our Leaders Have Said," *Herald-Journal*, Spartanburg, S.C., February 23, 1965, 3.

50. The Gallup Organization, *Gallup Poll #706* (Williamstown, MA: The Roper Public Opinion Research Center, February 19–24, 1965), 18–19.

51. Robert J. McCLoskey, "'Viet-Nam Action Called 'Collective Defense Against Armed Aggression','/ Department Statement read to news correspondents on March 4, 1965 by Robert J. McCloskey, Director, Office of News, Department of State Bulletin, March 22, 1965, p. 403," Vietnam Task Force, Office of the Secretary of Defense, [Part V. A.] Justification of the War. Public Statements. Volume II: D—The Johnson Administration, D-30-31, National Archives, Washington, DC, accessed October 11, 2012, http://www.archives.gov/research/pentagon-papers/.

52. Dean Rusk, "'Some Fundamentals of American Policy,' Address by Secretary Rusk Before the U.S. Council of the International Chamber of Commerce at New York, March 4, 1965, Department of State Bulletin, March 22, 1965, p. 401," Vietnam Task Force, Office of the Secretary of Defense, [Part V. A.] Justification of the War. Public Statements. Volume II: D—The Johnson Administration, D-30, National Archives, Washington, DC, accessed October 11, 2012, http://www.archives.gov/research/pentagon-papers/.

53. Herald-Journal, "Viet Nam Policy: What Our Leaders Have Said," *Herald-Journal*, Spartanburg, SC, February 23, 1965, 3.

54. Herald-Journal, "Viet Nam Policy: What Our Leaders Have Said," *Herald-Journal*, Spartanburg, SC, February 23, 1965, 3.

55. Herald-Journal, "Viet Nam Policy: What Our Leaders Have Said," *Herald-Journal*, Spartanburg, SC, February 23, 1965, 3.

56. Herald-Journal, "Viet Nam Policy: What Our Leaders Have Said," *Herald-Journal*, Spartanburg, SC, February 23, 1965, 3.

57. Eugene Register-Guard, "U.S. Still Unable to Find Keys to Success," *Eugene Register-Guard*, Eugene, OR, March 21, 1965, 8A.

58. Eugene Register-Guard, "U.S. Still Unable to Find Keys to Success," *Eugene Register-Guard*, Eugene, OR, March 21, 1965, 8A.

59. William Winter Comments, "United States and China," *William Winter Comments*, Sausalito, CA, March 8, 1965, 4, Series 48 Foreign Relations Committee, 48-1 General 1965, Box 7, Folder 1, Fulbright Papers, University of Arkansas Library (Fayetteville, AR).

60. William Winter Comments, "United States and 'Containment,'" *William Winter Comments*, Sausalito, CA, March 8, 1965, 3, Series 48 Foreign Relations Committee, 48-1 General 1965, Box 7, Folder 1, Fulbright Papers, University of Arkansas Library (Fayetteville, AR).

61. Hayes Redmond, note on Harris Poll numbers, [March 9, 1965], box 80 [2 of 2], folder PR16 Public Opinion Polls (August–December 1965) [2 of 2], Central File, Lyndon B. Johnson Presidential Library (Austin, TX).

62. The Gallup Organization, *Gallup Poll #706* (Williamstown, MA: The Roper Public Opinion Research Center, April 2–7, 1965), 6–8.

63. Michael H. Hunt, *Lyndon Johnson's War: America's Cold War Crusade in Vietnam 1945–1968* (New York: Hill and Wang, 1996), 92–100.

64. Lou Harris, document covering public opinion polling on Vietnam and China, [April 6, 1965], box 71 [1 of 2], folder ND 19-CO 312 Vietnam (Situation In) (1964–1965) [4 OF 4], Central File, Lyndon B. Johnson Presidential Library (Austin, TX).

65. Lou Harris, document covering public opinion polling on Vietnam and China, [April 6, 1965], box 71 [1 of 2], folder ND 19-CO 312 Vietnam (Situation In) (1964–1965) [4 OF 4], Central File, Lyndon B. Johnson Presidential Library (Austin, TX).

66. Kaiser, *American Tragedy*, 412; McMaster, *Dereliction of Duty*, 259; Langguth, *Our Vietnam*, 352-353; Kathleen J. Turner, *Lyndon Johnson's Dual War: Vietnam and the Press*

(Chicago: University of Chicago, 1985), 119, 122–123; Roselle, *Media and the Politics of Failure*, 31; Hunt, *Lyndon Johnson's War*, 93.

67. Hunt, *Lyndon Johnson's War*, 92–93; Turner, *Lyndon Johnson's Dual War*, 119–120, 127; McMaster, *Dereliction of Duty*, 259–260; Langguth, *Our Vietnam*, 354; Karnow, *Vietnam*, 429–433; Jeffrey P. Kimball, *To Reason Why: The Debate about the Causes of U.S. Involvement in the Vietnam War* (Eugene, OR: Resource, 1990), 38; Roselle, *Media and the Politics of Failure*, 32.

68. Lyndon B. Johnson, "Address at Johns Hopkins University: 'Peace Without Conquest,' April 7, 1965," in *Public Papers of the Presidents of the United States: Lyndon B. Johnson, 1965*. Volume I, entry 172 (Washington, D. C.: Government Printing Office, 1966), 394–399, accessed January 6, 2013, http://www.lbjlibrary.net/collections/selected-speeches/1965/04-07-1965.html.

69. Lyndon B. Johnson, "'Pattern for Peace in Southeast Asia,' Address by President Johnson at John Hopkins University, Baltimore Maryland on April 7, 1965, Department of State Bulletin, April 26, 1965, p. 607," Vietnam Task Force, Office of the Secretary of Defense, [Part V. A.] Justification of the War. Public Statements. Volume II: D—The Johnson Administration, D-31-32, National Archives, Washington, DC, accessed October 11, 2012, http://www.archives.gov/research/pentagon-papers/.

70. Johnson, "'Pattern for Peace in Southeast Asia.'"

71. Johnson, "'Pattern for Peace in Southeast Asia.'"

72. Johnson, "'Pattern for Peace in Southeast Asia.'"

73. Johnson, "Address at Johns Hopkins University."

74. Johnson, "'Pattern for Peace in Southeast Asia.'"

75. Johnson, "'Pattern for Peace in Southeast Asia.'"

76. McMaster, *Dereliction of Duty*, 259–260; Langguth, *Our Vietnam*, 356.

77. Turner, *Lyndon Johnson's Dual War*, 130.

78. Turner, *Lyndon Johnson's Dual War*, 129.

79. James "Scotty" Reston, "Lack of strategy in limited war poses warning of future trouble," Washington, *Press-Courier*, Oxnard, CA, April 27, 1965, 12.

80. Leonard Unger, "Address by Leonard Unger, Deputy Assistant Secretary for Far Eastern Affairs, Before the Detroit Economic Club, 'Present Objectives and Future Possibilities in Southeast Asia,' April 19, 1965, Department of State Bulletin, May 10, 1965, p. 712," Vietnam Task Force, Office of the Secretary of Defense, [Part V. A.] Justification of the War. Public Statements. Volume II: D—The Johnson Administration, D-33-35, National Archives, Washington, DC, accessed October 11, 2012, http://www.archives.gov/research/pentagon-papers/.

81. Dean Rusk, "Address by Secretary Rusk, Made Before the American Society of International Law on April 23, 1965, Department of State Bulletin, May 10, 1965, p. 697," Vietnam Task Force, Office of the Secretary of Defense, [Part V. A.] Justification of the War. Public Statements. Volume II: D—The Johnson Administration, D-37, National Archives, Washington, DC, accessed October 11, 2012, http://www.archives.gov/research/pentagon-papers/.

82. Associated Press, "U.S. Navy Warplanes Edge Closer to Hanoi As Rainy Season Nears: Fulbright Urges Raid Halt; Sennis Sees War Step-Up," Associated Press, Washington, *Commercial Appeal*, Memphis, TN, 19 April 1965, 1, Series 48 Foreign Relations Committee, 48-1 General 1965, Box 7, Folder 1, Fulbright Papers, University of Arkansas Library (Fayetteville, AR).

83. Associated Press, "U.S. Navy Warplanes Edge Closer to Hanoi As Rainy Season Nears."

84. Associated Press, "U.S. Navy Warplanes Edge Closer to Hanoi As Rainy Season Nears."

85. John Kenneth Galbraith, letter to the editor, *New York Times*, April 27, 1965, reprinted in "Johnson So Far III: Foreign Policy" by Maurice J. Goldbloom, American Jewish Committee, *Commentary*, Vol. 39, No. 6 (June 1965): 47–55, in Series 48 Foreign Relations Committee, 48-1 General 1965, Box 7, Folder 2, Fulbright Papers, University of Arkansas Library (Fayetteville, AR).

86. Charles A. Wells, "Won't this be rather difficult," political cartoon and text, *Wells Newsletter*, Newtown PA, May 1, 1965, 1, Series 48 Foreign Relations Committee, 48-1 General 1965, Box 7, Folder 2, Fulbright Papers, University of Arkansas Library (Fayetteville, AR).

87. Wells, "Won't this be rather difficult."

88. Wells, "Won't this be rather difficult."

89. Arkansas Gazette, "Dien Bien Phu: Lesson Learned and Forgotten," editorial, *Arkansas Gazette*, Little Rock, AR, 22 April 1965, 6A, Series 48 Foreign Relations Committee, 48-1 General 1965, Box 7, Folder 2, Fulbright Papers, University of Arkansas Library (Fayetteville, AR).

90. Arkansas Gazette, "Dien Bien Phu: Lesson Learned and Forgotten."

91. Arkansas Gazette, "Dien Bien Phu: Lesson Learned and Forgotten."

92. Walter Lippmann, "Asians Resent White Man's Intrusion in Viet War," *Milwaukee Sentinel*, April 23, 1965, 14.

93. Lippmann, "Asians Resent White Man's Intrusion in Viet War."

94. St. Petersburg Times, "Awakening the East," *St. Petersburg Times*, St. Petersburg, FL, May 1, 1965, 10-A.

95. St. Petersburg Times, "Awakening the East."

96. St. Petersburg Times, "Awakening the East."

97. St. Petersburg Times, "Awakening the East."

98. Lyndon B. Johnson, "Transcript of the President's News Conference on Foreign and Domestic Matters," *New York Times,* April 28, 1965, 16, ProQuest Historical Newspapers: *The New York Times* (1851–2009).

99. Johnson, "Transcript of the President's News Conference on Foreign and Domestic Matters."

100. Johnson, "Transcript of the President's News Conference on Foreign and Domestic Matters."

101. Johnson, "Transcript of the President's News Conference on Foreign and Domestic Matters."

102. Johnson, "Transcript of the President's News Conference on Foreign and Domestic Matters."

103. Lyndon B. Johnson, "Statement by President Johnson at a News Conference at the White House on April 27, 1965 and Transcript of Secretary of Defense Robert S. McNamara's New [sic] Conference of April 26, 1965 on the Situation in Viet-Nam, Department of State Bulletin, May 17, 1965, p. 748," Vietnam Task Force, Office of the Secretary of Defense, [Part V. A.] Justification of the War. Public Statements. Volume II: D—The Johnson Administration, D-39-40, National Archives, Washington, DC, accessed October 11, 2012, http://www.archives.gov/research/pentagon-papers/

104. Johnson, "Statement by President Johnson at a News Conference at the White House on April 27, 1965."

105. Johnson, "Transcript of the President's News Conference on Foreign and Domestic Matters."

106. Johnson, "Transcript of the President's News Conference on Foreign and Domestic Matters."

107. Johnson, "Transcript of the President's News Conference on Foreign and Domestic Matters."

108. Johnson, "Transcript of the President's News Conference on Foreign and Domestic Matters."

109. Commercial Appeal, "No Time to Pause," editorial, *Commercial Appeal*, Memphis, TN, April 30, 1965, Series 48 Foreign Relations Committee, 48-1 General 1965, Box 7, Folder 2, Fulbright Papers, University of Arkansas Library (Fayetteville, AR).

110. Arthur H. Dean, letter to the editor of the *New York Times* in support of Vietnam policy, May 7, 1965, Files of McGeorge Bundy, box 18, McGeorge Bundy May–June 1965 Teach-In, National Security File, Lyndon B. Johnson Presidential Library (Austin, TX).

111. Dean, letter to the editor of the *New York Times* in support of Vietnam policy, 7 May 1965.

112. Robert S. McNamara, "Statement by President Johnson at a News Conference at the White House on April 27, 1965 and Transcript of Secretary of Defense Robert S. McNamara's New [sic] Conference of April 26, 1965 on the Situation in Viet-Nam, Department of State Bulletin, May 17, 1965, p. 748," Vietnam Task Force, Office of the Secretary of Defense, [Part V. A.] Justification of the War. Public Statements. Volume II: D—The Johnson Administration, D-39-41, National Archives, Washington, DC, accessed October 11, 2012, http://www.archives.gov/research/pentagon-papers/.

113. Gallup Organization, *Gallup Poll #706* (Williamstown, MA: The Roper Public Opinion Research Center, April 23–28, 1965), 7–10.

114. Arthur Krock, "Fulbright's Refused Stone Now at the Headstone," Washington, DC, *New York Times* News Service, May 18, 1965, Series 48 Foreign Relations Committee, 48-1 General 1965, Box 7, Folder 2, Fulbright Papers, University of Arkansas Library (Fayetteville, AR).

115. Charles A. Wells, "X-Ray and Forecast: Out of History—From Revolution to Reconciliation," *Wells Newsletter*, Newtown PA, May 1, 1965, 1, Series 48 Foreign Relations Committee, 48-1 General 1965, Box 7, Folder 2, Fulbright Papers, University of Arkansas Library (Fayetteville, AR).

116. Wells, "X-Ray and Forecast."

117. McMaster, *Dereliction of Duty*, 226–260.

118. Hans J. Morgenthau, "The Immaturity of Our Asian Policy: Ideological Windmills," *New Republic*, March 12, 1965, excerpted in memorandum by William J. Jorden, for Chester L. Cooper, "SUBJECT: Views of Hans Morgenthau on U.S. Policy in Vietnam," May 14, 1965, Files of McGeorge Bundy, box 18, McGeorge Bundy May–June 1965 Teach-In, National Security File, Lyndon B. Johnson Presidential Library (Austin, TX).

119. Hans J. Morgenthau, "We Are Deluding Ourselves in Vietnam," *New York Times Magazine*, April 18, 1965, excerpted in memorandum by William J. Jorden, for Chester L. Cooper, "SUBJECT: Views of Hans Morgenthau on U.S. Policy in Vietnam," May 14, 1965, Files of McGeorge Bundy, box 18, McGeorge Bundy May–June 1965 Teach-In, National Security File, Lyndon B. Johnson Presidential Library (Austin, TX).

120. Morgenthau, "We Are Deluding Ourselves in Vietnam."

121. Conference of Asian Scholars, Petition to President Johnson on Vietnam policy dated April 2, 1965 with cover letter by Stanley Sheinbaum dated April 13, 1965, Files of McGeorge Bundy, box 18, McGeorge Bundy May–June 1965 Teach-In, National Security File, Lyndon B. Johnson Presidential Library (Austin, TX).

122. Conference of Asian Scholars, Petition to President Johnson on Vietnam policy dated April 2, 1965.

123. Conference of Asian Scholars, Petition to President Johnson on Vietnam policy dated April 2, 1965.

124. Hans J. Morgenthau, "Russia, the U.S. and Vietnam," *New Republic*, May 1, 1965, 12, Files of McGeorge Bundy, box 18, McGeorge Bundy May–June 1965 Teach-In, National Security File, Lyndon B. Johnson Presidential Library (Austin, TX).

125. Morgenthau, "Russia, the U.S. and Vietnam."

126. Morgenthau, "Russia, the U.S. and Vietnam."

127. The Inter-University Committee for a Public Hearing on Viet Nam, letter soliciting donations or participation in National Teach-in, Ann Arbor, MI, [May 1965], Files of McGeorge Bundy, box 18, McGeorge Bundy May–June 1965 Teach-In, National Security File, Lyndon B. Johnson Presidential Library (Austin, TX).

128. Inter-University Committee for a Public Hearing on Viet Nam, "National 'Teach-In' on Viet-Nam," list of of attendees and itinerary panel discussions, May 1965, Files of McGeorge Bundy, box 18, McGeorge Bundy May–June 1965 Teach-In, National Security File, Lyndon B. Johnson Presidential Library (Austin, TX).

129. Mary Wright, "Excerpts From National Teach-In on Vietnam Policy and Text of Bundy Statement," *New York Times*, May 17, 1965, 30, ProQuest Historical Newspapers: *The New York Times* (1851–2009).

130. George M. Kahin, "Excerpts From National Teach-In on Vietnam Policy and Text of Bundy Statement," *New York Times*, May 17, 1965, 30, ProQuest Historical Newspapers: *The New York Times* (1851–2009).

131. Kahin, "Excerpts from National Teach-In on Vietnam Policy and Text of Bundy Statement."

132. Kahin, "Excerpts from National Teach-In on Vietnam Policy and Text of Bundy Statement."

133. Kahin, "Excerpts from National Teach-In on Vietnam Policy and Text of Bundy Statement."

134. Kahin, "Excerpts from National Teach-In on Vietnam Policy and Text of Bundy Statement."

135. Hans Morgenthau, "Excerpts from National Teach-In on Vietnam Policy and Text of Bundy Statement," *New York Times*, May 17, 1965, 30, ProQuest Historical Newspapers: *New York Times* (1851–2009).

136. John K. Fairbank, letter to the editor of the *Washington Post* in support of Vietnam policy, May 11, 1965, Files of McGeorge Bundy, box 18, McGeorge Bundy May–June 1965 Teach-In, National Security File, Lyndon B. Johnson Presidential Library (Austin, TX).

137. Robert Scalapino, "Excerpts From National Teach-In on Vietnam Policy and Text of Bundy Statement," *New York Times*, May 17, 1965, 30, ProQuest Historical Newspapers: *New York Times* (1851–2009).

138. Scalapino, "Excerpts from National Teach-In on Vietnam Policy and Text of Bundy Statement."

139. Scalapino, "Excerpts from National Teach-In on Vietnam Policy and Text of Bundy Statement."

140. Scalapino, "Excerpts from National Teach-In on Vietnam Policy and Text of Bundy Statement."

141. Morgenthau, "Excerpts from National Teach-In on Vietnam Policy and Text of Bundy Statement."

142. Morgenthau, "Excerpts From National Teach-In on Vietnam Policy and Text of Bundy Statement."

143. Morgenthau, "Excerpts from National Teach-In on Vietnam Policy and Text of Bundy Statement."

144. McGeorge Bundy, "Excerpts from National Teach-In on Vietnam Policy and Text of Bundy Statement," *New York Times*, May 17, 1965, 30, ProQuest Historical Newspapers: *New York Times* (1851–2009).

145. McGeorge Bundy, written statement to Teach-In, "Text of Statement by McGeorge Bundy," May 15, 1965, Files of McGeorge Bundy, box 18, McGeorge Bundy May–June 1965 Teach-In, National Security File, Lyndon B. Johnson Presidential Library (Austin, TX).

146. Bundy, "Excerpts from National Teach-In on Vietnam Policy and Text of Bundy Statement."

147. Bundy, written statement to Teach-In, "Text of Statement by McGeorge Bundy."

148. Bundy, "Excerpts from National Teach-In on Vietnam Policy and Text of Bundy Statement."

149. Chester L. Cooper, memorandum for Jack Valenti, "SUBJECT: The American Friends of Vietnam Program," May 5, 1965, box 12, folder CO 312 VIETNAM (1964–1965), Central File, Lyndon B. Johnson Presidential Library (Austin, TX).

150. Jack Valenti, memorandum for President Johnson on AFV college campus campaign, May 7, 1965, box 12, folder CO 312 Vietnam (1964–1965), Central File, Lyndon B. Johnson Presidential Library (Austin, TX).

151. Cooper, memorandum for Jack Valenti, "SUBJECT: The American Friends of Vietnam Program."

152. Tom Wells, *The War Within: America's Battle over Vietnam* (Oakland, CA: University of California, 1994), 34.

153. Cooper, memorandum for Jack Valenti, "SUBJECT: The American Friends of Vietnam Program."

154. David Wise, "Dilemma in 'Credibility,'" *Mason City Globe Gazette*, Mason City, IA, *New York Herald Tribune* News Service, Washington, DC, May 31, 1965, 4.

155. Dallek, *Lyndon B. Johnson*, 253–271.

156. Turner, *Lyndon Johnson's Dual War*, 114–116; Hunt, *Lyndon Johnson's War*, 100.

157. Karnow, *Vietnam*, 432–450.

158. Lyndon B. Johnson, "Remarks by President Johnson at White house Before House and Senate Committees on May 4, 1965, 'Congress Approves Supplemental Appropriation for Vietnam,' Department of State Bulletin, May 24, 1965, p. 817," Vietnam Task Force, Office of the Secretary of Defense, [Part V. A.] Justification of the War. Public Statements. Volume II: D—The Johnson Administration, D-41-42, National Archives, Washington, DC, accessed October 11, 2012, http://www.archives.gov/research/pentagon-papers/.

159. Dean Rusk, "Address by Secretary Rusk, Made Before the American Society of International Law on April 23, 1965, Department of State Bulletin, May 10, 1965, p. 697," Vietnam Task Force, Office of the Secretary of Defense, [Part V. A.] Justification of the War. Public Statements. Volume II: D—The Johnson Administration, D-38-39, National Archives, Washington, DC, accessed October 11, 2012, http://www.archives.gov/research/pentagon-papers/.

160. George Ball, "Statement by Secretary Ball on May 3, 1965 at the Opening Session of the SEATO Council Ministers' 10th Meeting at London, Department of State Bulletin, June 7, 1965, p. 922," Vietnam Task Force, Office of the Secretary of Defense, [Part V. A.] Justification of the War. Public Statements. Volume II: D—The Johnson Administration, D-41, National Archives, Washington, D.C., accessed October 11, 2012, http://www.archives.gov/research/pentagon-papers/.

161. Lyndon B. Johnson, "Viet-Nam: The Third Face of War," Address made to Association of American Editorial Cartoonists at the White House, May 13, 1965, from Vietnam Task Force, Office of the Secretary of Defense, [Part VI. C.] Settlement of the Conflict. Histories of Contacts. Volume I—Negotiations, 1965–1966, 116, National Archives, Washington, DC, accessed October 11, 2012, http://www.archives.gov/research/pentagon-papers/.

162. William P. Bundy, "Address by William P. Bundy Before Dallas Council on World Affairs on May 13, 1965, 'Reality and Myth Concerning South Vietnam,' Department of State Bulletin, June 7, 1965, p. 893," Vietnam Task Force, Office of the Secretary of Defense, [Part V. A.] Justification of the War. Public Statements. Volume II: D--The Johnson Administration, D-44-45, National Archives, Washington, D.C., accessed October 11, 2012, http://www.archives.gov/research/pentagon-papers/

163. James Marlow, "Viet Nam Conflict May Prove Only Minor Prelude to Big Act," Associated Press, *Fort Scott Tribune*, Fort Scott, KS, May 21, 1965, 2.

164. Gallup Organization, *Gallup Poll #1965-0711: Johnson/Vietnam/Dominican Republican/ Labor Unions/Political Parties* (Williamstown, MA: The Roper Public Opinion Research Center, May 13–18, 1965), 6–8.

165. Gallup, *Gallup Poll #1965-0711: Johnson/Vietnam/Dominican Republican* . . . , 9–11.

166. Paul Potter, "The Incredible War," excerpts from April 17, 1965 speech, published in *National Guardian*, April 29, 1965, reprinted in *The New Left: A Documentary History* by Massimo Teodori (Indianapolis, IN: Bobbs-Merrill, 1969), 228–230.

167. Paul Potter, "The Incredible War," excerpts from April 17, 1965 speech, published in *National Guardian*, April 29, 1965, reprinted in *The New Left: A Documentary History* by Massimo Teodori (Indianapolis, IN: Bobbs-Merrill, 1969), 228–230.

168. William P. Bundy, "Address by William P. Bundy, Assistant Secretary for Far Eastern Affairs, Before the Faculty Forum of the University of California at Berkeley on May 27, 1965, 'A Perspective on U.S. Policy in Viet-Nam,' Department of State Bulletin, June 21, 1965, p. 1001," Vietnam Task Force, Office of the Secretary of Defense, [Part V. A.] Justification of the War. Public Statements. Volume II: D—The Johnson Administration, D-48, National Archives, Washington, D.C., accessed October 11, 2012, http://www. archives.gov/research/pentagon-papers/.

169. Bundy, "Address by William P. Bundy, Assistant Secretary for Far Eastern Affairs, Before the Faculty Forum of the University of California at Berkley on May 27, 1965 . . . "

170. Lyndon B. Johnson, "Address by President Johnson in Chicago, Illinois on June 3, 1965, 'The Peace of Mankind,' Department of State Bulletin, June 21, 1965, p. 987," Vietnam Task Force, Office of the Secretary of Defense, [Part V. A.] Justification of the War. Public Statements. Volume II: D—The Johnson Administration, D-48-49, National Archives, Washington, D.C., accessed October 11, 2012, http://www.archives.gov/research/ pentagon-papers/.

171. McMaster, *Dereliction of Duty*, 290–291; Karnow, *Vietnam*, 433.

172. New York Times, "Ground War in Asia," *New York Times*, June 9, 1965, 46.

173. I.F. Stone, "Lyndon Johnson Lets the Office Boy Declare War," *I. F. Stone's Weekly*, June 9, 1965, reprinted in *The Best of I. F. Stone*, by I.F. Stone, ed. By Karl Weber (New York: Public Affairs, 2006), 258.

174. Lippmann, "Asians Resent White Man's Intrusion in Viet War."

175. Stone, "Lyndon Johnson Lets the Office Boy Declare War."

176. John W. Finney, "U.S. Adding 21,000 to Vietnam Force, M'Namara Says," *New York Times*, June 17, 1965, 1; New York Times, "U.S. Troops Open First Big Attack Against Vietcong," *New York Times*, June 30, 1965, 1; Fred S. Hoffman, "New Air Mobile Units

May Fight in Vietnam," Associated Press, *Milwaukee Journal*, June 17, 1965, 2; Time, "The Airmobile Division," *Time*, June 25, 1965, accessed October 26, 2008, http://www.time.com/time/ magazine/article/0,9171,833759,00.html.

177. Oliver Quayle and Company, "A SURVEY OF THE POLITICAL CLIMATE IN MINNESOTA, Study #255," Bronxville, NY, June 1965, box 80 [1 of 2], folder PR16 PUBLIC OPINION POLLS (April 1964–June 1965) [1 of 4], Central File, Lyndon B. Johnson Presidential Library (Austin, TX).

178. Oliver Quayle and Company, "A Survey of the Political Climate in New York City, Post Election Wave II, Study #251," Bronxville, NY, June 1965, box 80 [1 of 2], folder PR16 PUBLIC OPINION POLLS (April 1964–June 1965) [1 of 4], Central File, Lyndon B. Johnson Presidential Library (Austin, TX).

179. Gallup Organization, *Gallup Poll #712* (Williamstown, MA: The Roper Public Opinion Research Center, June 4–9, 1965), 8–9.

180. Hayes Redmond, note containing unpublished Harris Poll numbers for Vietnam, June 17, 1965, box 71 [1 of 2], folder ND 19-CO 312 Vietnam (Situation In) (1964–1965) [4 OF 4], Central File, Lyndon B. Johnson Presidential Library (Austin, TX).

181. National Opinion Research Center, *NORC Amalgam Study #857* (Williamstown, MA: The Roper Public Opinion Research Center, June 1965), 18–20.

182. Gallup, *Gallup Poll #712*, 6–8.

183. Langguth, *Our Vietnam*, 367–369; Cooper, memorandum for Jack Valenti, "SUBJECT: The American Friends of Vietnam Program."

184. Chester L. Cooper, memorandum for McGeorge Bundy on a possible second "Teach-In," "SUBJECT: Teach-In, Chapter 2," 4 June 1965, Files of McGeorge Bundy, box 18, McGeorge Bundy May-June 1965 Teach-In, National Security File, Lyndon B. Johnson Presidential Library (Austin, TX).

185. Langguth, *Our Vietnam*, 367–369.

186. Harry Sions, Little, Brown and Company, letter to J. William Fulbright about foreign policy debate, 14 May 1965, Series 48 Foreign Relations Committee, 48-1 General 1965, Box 7, Folder 2, Fulbright Papers, University of Arkansas Library (Fayetteville, AR); J. William Fulbright, letter to Harry Sions of Little, Brown and Company about foreign policy debate, June 2, 1965, Series 48 Foreign Relations Committee, 48-1 General 1965, Box 7, Folder 2, Fulbright Papers, University of Arkansas Library (Fayetteville, AR); Harry Sions, Little, Brown and Company, second letter to J. William Fulbright about foreign policy debate, June 15, 1965, Series 48 Foreign Relations Committee, 48-1 General 1965, Box 7, Folder 2, Fulbright Papers, University of Arkansas Library (Fayetteville, AR).

187. Carl Marcy, "SUBJECT: Your Vietnam speech and appearance on the Today program," internal memo from Carl Marcy to Senator J. William Fulbright about public response to the Senator's *Today* appearance, U.S. Senate Committee on Foreign Relations, Washington, DC, June 22, 1965, Series 48 Foreign Relations Committee, 48-3 Committee Administration, Box 16, Folder 2, 1964-1965, Fulbright Papers, University of Arkansas (Fayetteville, AR).

188. Gallup Organization, *Gallup Poll #713* (Williamstown, MA: The Roper Public Opinion Research Center, June 24–29, 1965), 8–9.

189. Gallup, *Gallup Poll #713*, 8–9.

190. Gallup, *Gallup Poll #713*, 10–11.

191. Gallup, *Gallup Poll #713*, 12.

192. Gallup, *Gallup Poll #713*, 10–11.

193. Dean Rusk, "Secretary Rusk's Interview re Vietnam on 'Issues and Answers,' American Broadcasting Company Radio and Television on July 11, 1965, With ABC Correspondents William H. Lawrence and John Scali, Department of State Bulletin, August 2, 1965, p. 188," Vietnam Task Force, Office of the Secretary of Defense, [Part V. A.] Justification of the War. Public Statements. Volume II: D—The Johnson Administration, D-49-50, National Archives, Washington, D.C., accessed October 11, 2012, http://www.archives.gov/research/pentagon-papers/

194. E. W. Kenworthy, "Johnson's Policy in Vietnam—Four Positions in Congress," Washington, DC, New York Times, July 25, 1965, E3, ProQuest Historical Newspapers: New York Times (1851–2009).

195. Kenworthy, "Johnson's Policy in Vietnam—Four Positions in Congress."

196. NBC, "American White Paper": A Report on U.S. Foreign Policy (1945–1965) [flier for NBC News program to air on September 7, 1965], NBC News, [July 1965], in Series 48 Foreign Relations Committee, 48-1 General 1965, Box 7, Folder 2, Fulbright Papers, University of Arkansas Library (Fayetteville, AR).

197. NBC, "American White Paper."

198. NBC, "American White Paper."

199. National Opinion Research Center, NORC Amalgam Study #857 (Williamstown, MA: The Roper Public Opinion Research Center, June 1965), 14–17.

200. John Kenneth Galbraith, memorandum for President Johnson, "How to Take Ninety Percent of the Political Heat out of Vietnam," [July 1965], box 71 [1 of 2], folder ND 19-CO 312 VIETNAM (Situation In) (1964-1965) [3 OF 4], Central File, Lyndon B. Johnson Presidential Library (Austin, TX).

201. Galbraith, "How to Take Ninety Percent of the Political Heat out of Vietnam."

202. Galbraith, "How to Take Ninety Percent of the Political Heat out of Vietnam."

203. Galbraith, "How to Take Ninety Percent of the Political Heat out of Vietnam."

204. Galbraith, "How to Take Ninety Percent of the Political Heat out of Vietnam."

205. Galbraith, "How to Take Ninety Percent of the Political Heat out of Vietnam."

206. Kenworthy, "Johnson's Policy in Vietnam—Four Positions in Congress."

207. Kenworthy, "Johnson's Policy in Vietnam—Four Positions in Congress."

208. Kenworthy, "Johnson's Policy in Vietnam—Four Positions in Congress."

209. Mike Mansfield, letter to Lyndon B. Johnson, "SUBJECT: Meeting on Viet Nam," July 27, 1965, box 71 [1 of 2], folder ND 19-CO 312 VIETNAM (Situation In) (1964-1965) [3 OF 4], Central File, Lyndon B. Johnson Presidential Library (Austin, TX).

210. Mansfield, letter to Lyndon B. Johnson, "SUBJECT: Meeting on Viet Nam."

211. Mansfield, letter to Lyndon B. Johnson, "SUBJECT: Meeting on Viet Nam."

212. Robert S. McNamara, letter to Lyndon B. Johnson with responses to Senator Mike Mansfield's '18 points,' July 28, 1965, box 71 [1 of 2], folder ND 19-CO 312 VIETNAM (Situation In) (1964-1965) [3 OF 4], Central File, Lyndon B. Johnson Presidential Library (Austin, TX).

213. Lyndon B. Johnson, letter to Senator Mike Mansfield with attached responses to Senator Mansfield's '18 points,' July 28, 1965, box 71 [1 of 2], folder ND 19-CO 312 VIETNAM (Situation In) (1964-1965) [3 OF 4], Central File, Lyndon B. Johnson Presidential Library (Austin, TX).

214. Gallup Organization, Gallup Poll #714 (Williamstown, MA: The Roper Public Opinion Research Center, 16-21 July 1965), 6–8.

215. Gallup, Gallup Poll #714, 9–10.

216. Langguth, *Our Vietnam*, 383-384; Herring, *LBJ and Vietnam*, 2–3, 6; Helsing, *Johnson's War/Johnson's Great Society*, 1; Hunt, *Lyndon Johnson's War*, 98; Roselle, *Media and the Politics of Failure*, 33; McMaster, *Dereliction of Duty*, 321–322; Karnow, *Vietnam*, 441; Kimball, *To Reason Why*, 42.

217. U.S. Army, Video, "Why Vietnam," U.S. Army Audiovisual Center, Office of the Deputy Chief of Staff for Operations, Department of the Army, Washington, DC [1965], National Archives, accessed July 26, 2015, https://catalog.archives.gov/id/2569861?q=why%20vietnam.

218. Lyndon B. Johnson, "We Will Stand in Viet-Nam," *Department of State Publication 7937, Far Eastern Series 137*, U.S. State Department, Office of Media Services, Bureau of Public Affairs (Washington, DC: U.S. Government Printing Office, August 1965), accessed October 19, 2012, http://www.history.navy.mil/library/special/stand_vietnam.htm.

219. Lyndon B. Johnson, "Statement by President Johnson at White House News Conference on July 28, 1965, 'We Will Stand in Viet-Nam,' Department of State Bulletin, August 16, 1965, p. 262," Vietnam Task Force, Office of the Secretary of Defense, [Part V. A.] Justification of the War. Public Statements. Volume II: D—The Johnson Administration, D-50-51, National Archives, Washington, DC, accessed October 11, 2012, http://www.archives.gov/research/pentagon-papers/.

220. Johnson, "Statement by President Johnson at White House News Conference on July 28, 1965 . . . "

221. Johnson, "Statement by President Johnson at White House News Conference on July 28, 1965 . . . "

222. Johnson, "Statement by President Johnson at White House News Conference on July 28, 1965 . . . "

223. Johnson, "Statement by President Johnson at White House News Conference on July 28, 1965 . . . "

224. Johnson, "Statement by President Johnson at White House News Conference on July 28, 1965 . . . "

225. Johnson, "We Will Stand in Viet-Nam."

226. Johnson, "We Will Stand in Viet-Nam."

227. Johnson, "We Will Stand in Viet-Nam."

228. McNamara, letter to Lyndon B. Johnson with responses to Senator Mike Mansfield's '18 points,' July 28, 1965.

229. Herring, *LBJ and Vietnam*, 2; Roselle, *Media and the Politics of Failure*, 33.

230. Helsing, *Johnson's War/Johnson's Great Society*, 1.

231. Lewiston Morning Tribune, "There's No Change in Viet Nam Policy," *Lewiston Morning Tribune*, Lewiston, ID, July 29, 1965, 4.

232. Joseph Alsop, "Matter of Fact, Question: Does LBJ Really Mean Business?" Washington, Lewiston Morning Tribune, Lewiston, ID, July 29, 1965, 4.

Chapter 3

1. Oliver Quayle and Company, "A Survey of the Political Climate in Pennsylvania, Study #285," Oliver Quayle and Company, Bronxville, NY, August 1965, box 80 [2 of 2], folder PR16 Public Opinion Polls (August–December 1965) [2 of 2], Central File, Lyndon B. Johnson Presidential Library (Austin, TX).

2. Gallup Organization, *Gallup Poll #715* (Williamstown, MA: The Roper Public Opinion Research Center, 5-10 August 1965), 5–7.

3. White House, "Why Vietnam?" Pamphlet distributed to the Washington Press Corps, White House, Washington, DC, 20 August 1965, reprinted in *Congressional Record—Senate*, US Congress, Washington, DC, 25 August 1965, 20857, Series 48 Foreign Relations Committee, 48-1 General 1965, Box 7, Folder 3, Fulbright Papers, University of Arkansas (Fayetteville, AR).

4. White House, "Why Vietnam?"

5. White House, "Why Vietnam?"

6. White House, "Why Vietnam?"

7. White House, "Why Vietnam?"

8. Ernest Gruening, draft floor speech, "Draftees Should Not Be Sent to Southeast Asia Involuntarily without Congressional Approval," [August 1965], box 71 [1 of 2], folder ND 19-CO 312 Vietnam (Situation In) (1964-1965) [2 OF 4], Central File, Lyndon B. Johnson Presidential Library (Austin, TX), 39–41.

9. Lyndon B. Johnson, letter to Senator Ernest Gruening about his proposed amendment to prevent draftees from being involuntarily sent to Vietnam, [after 20 August 1965], box 71 [1 of 2], folder ND 19-CO 312 VIETNAM (Situation In) (1964-1965) [2 OF 4], Central File, Lyndon B. Johnson Presidential Library (Austin, TX).

10. Evening Bulletin, "Contradiction Seen: Guns, Butter Bother Chafee," *Evening Bulletin*, Philadelphia, PA, 11 August 1965, 34, found in box 71 [1 of 2], folder ND 19-CO 312 Vietnam (Situation In) (1964-1965) [2 OF 4], Central File, Lyndon B. Johnson Presidential Library (Austin, TX), 39–41.

11. Edward J. Meeman, "'National Honor' Is Romantic View: We Face Hopeless Cause in Vietnam, and Should Quit While There's Time," *Memphis Press-Scimitar*, August 2, 1965, in Series 48 Foreign Relations Committee, 48-1 General 1965, Box 7, Folder 3, Fulbright Papers, University of Arkansas Library (Fayetteville, AR).

12. Steven J. Rosenthal, *Vietnam Study Guide and Annotated Bibliography* (San Francisco, CA: Students for a Democratic Society, 1965), 2, 3.

13. Robert S. McNamara and Dean Rusk, "Interview with Secretary Rusk and Secretary McNamara on a Columbia Broadcasting System television program by Peter Kalischer, Alexander Kendrick, and Harry Reasoner, on August 9, 1965, 'Political and Military Aspects of U.S. Policy in Viet-Nam,' Department of State Bulletin, August 30, 1965, p. 342," Vietnam Task Force, Office of the Secretary of Defense, [Part V. A.] Justification of the War. Public Statements. Volume II: D—The Johnson Administration, D-53-58, National Archives, Washington, DC, accessed October 11, 2012, http://www.archives.gov/research/pentagon-papers/.

14. McNamara and Rusk, "Interview with Secretary Rusk and Secretary McNamara . . . "

15. Louis Liebovich, *The Press and the Modern Presidency: Myths and Mindsets from Kennedy to Election 2000* (Westport, CT: Praeger, 2001), 58; Kathleen J. Turner, *Lyndon Johnson's Dual War: Vietnam and the Press* (Chicago: University of Chicago, 1985), 152; A. J. Langguth, *Our Vietnam: The War 1954–1975* (New York: Simon & Schuster, 2000), 385.

16. McNamara and Rusk, "Interview with Secretary Rusk and Secretary McNamara . . . "

17. Alice Widener, "Why Ho Misses Message," New York, newspaper editorial [October 1965], Series 48 Foreign Relations Committee, 48-1 General 1965, Box 7, Folder 4, Fulbright Papers, University of Arkansas (Fayetteville, AR).

18. Oliver Quayle and Company, "A Survey of Public Opinion in New Haven, Connecticut, Wave IV, Study #288," Oliver Quayle and Company, Bronxville, NY, September 1965, box 80 [2 of 2], folder PR16 PUBLIC OPINION POLLS (August–December 1965) [2 of 2], Central File, Lyndon B. Johnson Presidential Library (Austin, TX).

19. Gallup Organization, *Gallup Poll #716* (Williamstown, MA: The Roper Public Opinion Research Center, August 27–September 1, 1965), 8–11.

20. Langguth, *Our Vietnam*, 394; Stanley Karnow, *Vietnam: A History* (New York: Penguin, 1997), 495.

21. Paul L. Montgomery, "Diverse Groups Join in Protest: Participants Range From Pacifists to Far Leftists," *New York Times*, November 28, 1965, ProQuest Historical Newspapers: *New York Times* (1851–2010) with Index (1851–1993), 86.

22. Students for a Democratic Society, "America and New Era," October 1965, in *The New Left: A Documentary History* by Massimo Teodori (Indianapolis, IN: Bobbs-Merrill, 1969), 159.

23. Students for a Democratic Society, "America and New Era," 164.

24. Pierre Bellocq, "Recruitment," political cartoon, *Philadelphia Inquirer*, October 21, 1965, 10, Series 48 Foreign Relations Committee, 48-1 General 1965, Box 7, Folder 4, Fulbright Papers, University of Arkansas (Fayetteville, AR).

25. Unknown, "Recruitment."

26. Gallup Organization, *Gallup Poll #719* (Williamstown, MA: The Roper Public Opinion Research Center, 29 October-2 November 1965), 16–17.

27. Gallup, *Gallup Poll #719*, 5–7, 8–9.

28. Gallup Organization, *Gallup Poll #716* (Williamstown, MA: The Roper Public Opinion Research Center, 27 August-1 September 1965), 8–11.

29. Gallup, *Gallup Poll #719*, 8–9.

30. Paul Harvey "Fulbright Changing His Views," [July 1966]. Series 48 Foreign Relations Committee, 48-1 General 1966–1967, Box 8, Folder 3, Fulbright Papers, University of Arkansas (Fayetteville, AR).

31. Jack Valenti, memorandum for President Johnson containing Senator Mike Mansfield's statement before traveling to Vietnam, 10 November 1965, box 12, folder CO 312 Vietnam (1964–1965), Central File, Lyndon B. Johnson Presidential Library (Austin, TX).

32. George Jenks, "Young Advises Pause in Raids On Vietnamese," Washington, DC, *Toledo Blade*, Toledo, OH, November 25, 1965, 2.

33. William B. Collins, "Vietnam War Isn't Worth the Cost of Lives, Clark Says," *Philadelphia Inquirer*, December 15, 1965, 2, Series 48 Foreign Relations Committee, 48-1 General 1965, Box 7, Folder 4, Fulbright Papers, University of Arkansas (Fayetteville, AR).

34. Pine Bluff Commercial, "Peace in Our Time," *Pine Bluff Commercial*, Pine Bluff, AR, 6 December 1965, Series 48 Foreign Relations Committee, 48-3 Committee Administration, Box 16, Folder 3, 1966, Fulbright Papers, University of Arkansas (Fayetteville, AR).

35. James "Scotty" Reston, "United States And Asia: Whose Move Next?" *New York Times*, Tokyo, *St. Petersburg Times*, St. Petersburg, FL, December 23, 1965, 10A.

36. Chester L. Cooper, memorandum for Messrs. Bundy, Moyers and Valenti and Cater, "SUBJECT: The American People, Vietnam and Us," December 14, 1965, box 71 [1 of 2], folder ND 19-CO 312 VIETNAM (Situation In) (1964–1965) [1 OF 4], Central File, Lyndon B. Johnson Presidential Library (Austin, TX).

37. Cooper, "SUBJECT: The American People, Vietnam and Us."

38. Cooper, "SUBJECT: The American People, Vietnam and Us."

39. Cooper, "SUBJECT: The American People, Vietnam and Us."

40. Gallup Organization, *Gallup Poll #721* (Williamstown, MA: The Roper Public Opinion Research Center, 11-16 December 1965), 12–13.

41. Cooper, "SUBJECT: The American People, Vietnam and Us."

42. Cooper, "SUBJECT: The American People, Vietnam and Us."

43. Gallup, *Gallup Poll #721*, 14.

44. Gallup Organization, *Gallup Poll #1966-0722: Television/Politics* (Williamstown, MA: The Roper Public Opinion Research Center, December 31, 1965–January 5, 1966), 13.

45. Walt Rostow, memorandum for President Johnson about explaining his Vietnam policy, January 26, 1966, box 71 [1 of 2], folder ND 19-CO 312 VIETNAM (Situation In) (January–March 1966), Central File, Lyndon B. Johnson Presidential Library (Austin, TX).

46. I. F. Stone, "Time to Tell the Truth for a Change," *I. F. Stone's Weekly*, November 22, 1965, reprinted in *The Best of I. F. Stone* by I. F. Stone, ed. By Karl Weber (New York: Public Affairs, 2006), 265.

47. Jack Valenti, memorandum for President Johnson about John Secondari's observations of press operations in Vietnam, December 10, 1965, box 71 [1 of 2], folder ND 19-CO 312 VIETNAM (Situation In) (1964-1965) [1 OF 4], Central File, Lyndon B. Johnson Presidential Library (Austin, TX).

48. Maxwell D. Taylor, letter to President Johnson on goals for Vietnam in 1966, 27 December 1965, box 71 [1 of 2], folder ND 19-CO 312 Vietnam (Situation In) (1964–1965) [1 of 4], Central File, Lyndon B. Johnson Presidential Library (Austin, TX).

49. Lyndon B. Johnson, "Annual Message to the Congress on the State of the Union, January 12, 1966," in *Public Papers of the Presidents of the United States: Lyndon B. Johnson, 1966.* Volume I, entry 6 (Washington, DC: Government Printing Office, 1967), 3–12, accessed January 6, 2013, http://www.lbjlibrary.net/collections/selected-speeches/1966/01-12-1966.html.

50. Lyndon B. Johnson, "The State of the Union Address of President Johnson to the Congress (Excerpts), January 12, 1966; Department of State Bulletin, January 31, 1966, p. 153," Vietnam Task Force, Office of the Secretary of Defense, [Part V. A.] Justification of the War. Public Statements. Volume II: D--The Johnson Administration, D-64, National Archives, Washington, D.C., accessed October 11, 2012, http://www.archives.gov/research/pentagon-papers/.

51. Johnson, "The State of the Union Address of President Johnson to the Congress (Excerpts), January 12, 1966."

52. Karnow, *Vietnam*, 500; Gary Hess, *Presidential Decisions for War: Korea, Vietnam, the Persian Gulf, and Iraq* (Baltimore, MD: Johns Hopkins University, 2009), 121–122.

53. Kevin Williams, "Vietnam: The First Living Room War," in *The Fog of War: The Media on the Battlefield* by Derrik Mercer, Geoff Mungham, Kevin Williams, and Sir Tom Hopkinson (London: Heinemann, 1987), 227–228.

54. Richard A. Brody, Paul Ekman, Edwin B. Parker, Nelson W. Polsby, Peter H. Rossi, Paul B. Sheatsley, Sidney Verba, *Public Opinion and the War in Vietnam* (Inter-University Consortium for Political Research, Winter 1966), 4–5, 14–15.

55. Brody et al., *Public Opinion and the War in Vietnam*, 18.

56. James G. Hershberg, "Peace Probes and the Bombing Pause: Hungarian and Polish Diplomacy During the Vietnam War, December 1965–January 1966," *Journal of Cold War Studies*, Vol. 5, No. 2 (Spring 2003): 32–67.

57. Time, "U.S. Peace Offensive," *Time*, January 14, 1966, cover.

58. Rowland Evans, Robert Novak, "Shelepin: Viet Nam Peace Key?" *St. Petersburg Times*, St. Petersburg, FL, January 4, 1966, 11-A.

59. Research Council, Inc., "Public Opinion Poll on the 'Peace Offensive' and Steel Prices," Princeton, NJ, January 6 [1966], box 80 [1 of 2], folder PR16 Public Opinion Polls (April 1964–June 1965) [1 of 4], Central File, Lyndon B. Johnson Presidential Library (Austin, TX).

60. Research Council, "Public Opinion Poll on the 'Peace Offensive' and Steel Prices."

61. Karnow, *Vietnam*, 459.

62. US Army, "US Army Staff Film Report 66-7A," National Archives, Washington, DC, accessed April 27, 2014, https://www.youtube.com/watch?v=sKAG6ywn01Y.

63. Lyndon B. Johnson, "Statement by President Johnson, U.S. and South Vietnamese leaders meet at Honolulu, February 6, 1966; Department of State Bulletin, February 28, 1966, p. 303," Vietnam Task Force, Office of the Secretary of Defense, [Part V. A.] Justification of the War. Public Statements. Volume II: D—The Johnson Administration, D-64, National Archives, Washington, D.C., accessed October 11, 2012, http://www.archives.gov/research/pentagon-papers/.

64. Walter Cronkite, Harry Reasoner, Lyndon B. Johnson, Hubert Humphrey, "LBJ meets VP Humphrey On return [sic] from Hawaii," *CBS Special Report*, CBS, February 8, 1966, Video #MP565, "Meeting with Vice President Humphrey upon return from Hawaii, February 8, 1966,"Motion Pictures, Audiovisual Materials, Lyndon B. Johnson Presidential Library (Austin, TX).

65. New York Post, *New York Post*, February 9, 1966, Vietnam Task Force, Office of the Secretary of Defense, [Part IV. C.] Evolution of the War. Direct Action: The Johnson Commitments, 1964–1968, Volume VIII—Re-emphasis on Pacification: 1965–1967, 49, National Archives, Washington, DC, accessed October 11, 2012, http://www.archives.gov/research/pentagon-papers/.

66. Gallup Organization, *Gallup Poll #1966-0723: Politics/Alcohol* (Williamstown, MA: The Roper Public Opinion Research Center, January 21–26, 1966), 8.

67. Gallup Organization, *Gallup Poll #1966-0724: Lyndon Johnson/Vietnam War* (Williamstown, MA: The Roper Public Opinion Research Center, February 10–15, 1966), 15–16.

68. Langguth, *Our Vietnam*, 420; Jack Valenti, note to Ambassador Henry Cabot Lodge on news story planted by Barry Zorthian, March 24, 1966, box 71 [1 of 2], folder ND 19-CO 312 VIETNAM (Situation In) (January-March 1966), Central File, Lyndon B. Johnson Presidential Library (Austin, TX); Henry Cabot Lodge, note to Jack Valenti on news story planted by Barry Zorthian, March 19, 1966, box 71 [1 of 2], folder ND 19-CO 312 Vietnam (Situation In) (January–March 1966), Central File, Lyndon B. Johnson Presidential Library (Austin, TX).

69. Ward Just, "Debate in U.S. Dismays Officials at Saigon," Saigon, *Washington Post*, February 27, 1966, A18, in box 71 [1 of 2], folder ND 19-CO 312 Vietnam (Situation In) (January–March 1966), Central File, Lyndon B. Johnson Presidential Library (Austin, TX).

70. Alan McIntosh [Publisher, *Rock County Herald*, Luverne, Minn.], "I Am a Tired American," *U.S. News & World Report*, February 14, 1966, 120, Series 48 Foreign Relations Committee, 48-1 General 1966–1967, Box 8, Folder 1, Fulbright Papers, University of Arkansas (Fayetteville, AR).

71. McIntosh, "I Am a Tired American."

72. U.S. Senate Committee on Foreign Relations, announcement of meeting on February 21, 1966, and agenda, [February 1966], Series 48 Foreign Relations Committee, 48-1 General 1966–1967, Box 8, Folder 1, Fulbright Papers, University of Arkansas (Fayetteville, AR).

73. E. W. Kenworthy, Special to *the New York Times*, "Gavin Warns U.S. China May Fight: Says a Build-Up in Vietnam Would . . . ," *New York Times*, February 9, 1966, ProQuest Historical Newspapers: *The New York Times* (1851–2010) with Index (1851–1993), 1.

74. U.S. Senate Historical Office, Photo, 1966 Senate Foreign Relations Committee, hearings on the war in Vietnam, Washington, DC, [February] 1966, Senate History, Art & History, U.S. Senate, accessed July 26, 2015, http://www.senate.gov/artandhistory/history/common/image/FulbrightForeignRelationsComm1966.htm.

75. E. W. Kenworthy, Special to *the New York Times*, "Kennan Bids U.S. 'Dig In' and Await Talks in Vietnam: Diplomat . . . ," *New York Times*, February 11, 1966, ProQuest Historical Newspapers: *The New York Times* (1851–2010) with Index (1851–1993), 1.

76. Dean Rusk, "Statement by Secretary Rusk Before the Senate Committee on Foreign Relations, February 18, 1966, 'The U.S. Commitment in Viet-Nam: Fundamental issues'

(Broadcast Live on Nationwide Television Networks); Department of State Bulletin, March 7, 1966, p. 346," Vietnam Task Force, Office of the Secretary of Defense, [Part V. A.] Justification of the War. Public Statements. Volume II: D—The Johnson Administration, D-65-69, National Archives, Washington, DC, accessed October 11, 2012, http://www. archives.gov/research/pentagon-papers/.

77. John Chamberlain, "These Days: Nixon Makes a Terrific Impact on Bull Elephants," King Features Syndicate, *Park City Daily News*, Bowling Green, KY, March 10, 1966, 3, 4.

78. Hubert Humphrey, "Vice President Humphrey Reports to President on Asian Trip, White House Press Release of March 6, 1966; Department of State Bulletin, March 28, 1966, p. 490," Vietnam Task Force, Office of the Secretary of Defense, [Part V. A.] Justification of the War. Public Statements. Volume II: D—The Johnson Administration, D-72-73, National Archives, Washington, DC, accessed October 11, 2012, http://www.archives. gov/research/pentagon-papers/.

79. Hubert Humphrey, "Address by Vice President Humphrey at National Press Club, Washington, D.C., March 11, 1966, 'United States Tasks and Responsibilities in Asia'; Department of State Bulletin, April 4, 1966, p. 523," Vietnam Task Force, Office of the Secretary of Defense, [Part V. A.] Justification of the War. Public Statements. Volume II: D—The Johnson Administration, D-73-74, National Archives, Washington, DC, accessed October 11, 2012, http://www.archives.gov/research/pentagon-papers/.

80. C. L. Sulzberger, "Foreign Affairs: Power and the Unloved One," Washington, DC, *New York Times*, February 27, 1966, E10, ProQuest Historical Newspapers: *The New York Times* (1851–2009).

81. Sulzberger, "Foreign Affairs: Power and the Unloved One."

82. Sulzberger, "Foreign Affairs: Power and the Unloved One."

83. Holmes Alexander, "How to Live with a Giant," Washington, DC, *Rome News-Tribune*, Rome, GA, April 13, 1966, 4.

84. Drew Middleton, "The U.N. Peace Outcry: U.S. Likely to Face Rising Criticism if Bombing Starts," United Nations, New York, *New York Times*, January 28, 1966, 12, ProQuest Historical Newspapers: *the New York Times* (1851–2009).

85. Commercial Appeal, "Too Little, Too Late," *Commercial Appeal*, Memphis, TN, 22 April 1966, 6, in Series 48 Foreign Relations Committee, 48-3 Committee Administration, Box 16, Folder 3, 1966, Fulbright Papers, University of Arkansas (Fayetteville, AR).

86. Commercial Appeal, "Too Little, Too Late."

87. Hayes Redmond, memorandum to Bill Moyers on public awareness of Fulbright Hearings, February 27, 1966, box 71 [1 of 2], folder ND 19-CO 312 Vietnam (Situation In) (January–March 1966), Central File, Lyndon B. Johnson Presidential Library (Austin, TX).

88. Robert Bernstein [President, Random House], letter to Senator J. William Fulbright expressing gratitude for deciding to publish 1966 Vietnam hearings and agreeing to write the forward, February 28, 1966, Series 48 Foreign Relations Committee, 48-1 General 1966–1967, Box 8, Folder 1, Fulbright Papers, University of Arkansas (Fayetteville, AR).

89. J. William Fulbright, letter to Vice President Humphrey inviting him to appear before the Senate Foreign Relations Committee, Washington, DC, 25 February 1966, Series 48 Foreign Relations Committee, 48-3 Committee Administration, Box 16, Folder 3, 1966, Fulbright Papers, University of Arkansas (Fayetteville, AR); US Senate Committee on Foreign Relations, press release on visit of Vice President Humphrey with Senate Foreign Relations Committee, US Senate Committee on Foreign Relations, Washington, DC, March 1, 1966, Series 48 Foreign Relations Committee, 48-3 Committee Administration, Box 16, Folder 3, 1966, Fulbright Papers, University of Arkansas (Fayetteville, AR).

90. Felix Belair Jr., "Russell Favors a Poll in Vietnam on U.S. Presence: Says 'We Can't Possibly Win' Against Vietcong If People Oppose American Help," *New York Times*, April 26, 1966, 1, ProQuest Historical Newspapers: *New York Times* (1851–2009).

91. Max Frankel, "Russell's Appraisal of War Will Have Bearing on Future," Washington, *New York Times, Press-Courier*, Oxnard, CA, April 27, 1966, 8.

92. Belair, "Russell Favors a Poll in Vietnam on U.S. Presence."

93. Frankel, "Russell's Appraisal of War Will Have Bearing on Future."

94. Frankel, "Russell's Appraisal of War Will Have Bearing on Future."

95. John M. Hightower, "Just How Did U.S. Get into Present Viet Fix?" Washington, DC, Associated Press, *Tuscaloosa News*, Tuscaloosa, FL, February 3, 1966, 1–2.

96. Hightower, "Just How Did U.S. Get into Present Viet Fix?"

97. Hightower, "Just How Did U.S. Get into Present Viet Fix?"

98. Carl Marcy, "Points to Make on Sense of Congress Amendment," point paper [from Carl Marcy to Senator J. William Fulbright], Washington, DC, February 28, 1966, Series 48 Foreign Relations Committee, 48-3 Committee Administration, Box 16, Folder 3, 1966, Fulbright Papers, University of Arkansas (Fayetteville, AR).

99. Marcy, "Points to Make on Sense of Congress Amendment."

100. Joseph A. Fry, *Debating Vietnam: Fulbright, Stennis, and Their Senate Hearings* (Lanham, MD: Rowman & Littlefield, 2006), 80.

101. Gallup Organization, *Gallup Poll #1966-0727: Vietnam/Politics/UFOs/Safety Standards in Automobiles* (Williamstown, MA: The Roper Public Opinion Research Center, April 14–19, 1966), 6–8, 22–25.

102. Gallup Organization, *Gallup Poll #1966-0728: Politics/Vietnam/Political Parties/Recreation* (Williamstown, MA: The Roper Public Opinion Research Center, May 5–10, 1966), 17–19.

103. Belair, "Russell Favors a Poll in Vietnam on U.S. Presence."

104. Belair, "Russell Favors a Poll in Vietnam on U.S. Presence."

105. Richard Helms, memorandum for Bill Moyers on seeking a second Congressional Resolution, 23 February 1966, box 71 [1 of 2], folder ND 19-CO 312 VIETNAM (Situation In) (January–March 1966), Central File, Lyndon B. Johnson Presidential Library (Austin, TX).

106. Leonard C. Meeker, "Legal Memorandum Prepared by Leonard C. Meeker, State Department Legal Adviser, for Submission to the Senate Committee on Foreign Relations, March 4, 1966, 'The Legality of United States Participation in the Defense of Viet-Nam'; Department of State Bulletin, March 28, 1966, pp. 15–16," Vietnam Task Force, Office of the Secretary of Defense, [Part V. A.] Justification of the War. Public Statements. Volume II: D—The Johnson Administration, D-70, National Archives, Washington, DC, accessed October 11, 2012, http://www.archives.gov/research/pentagon-papers/.

107. Dean Rusk, "Statement of Secretary Rusk Before the Senate Committee on Foreign Relations on May 9, 1966, 'Background of U.S. Policy in Southeast Asia'; Department of State Bulletin, May 30, 1966, p. 830," Vietnam Task Force, Office of the Secretary of Defense, [Part V. A.] Justification of the War. Public Statements. Volume II: D—The Johnson Administration, D-78-81, National Archives, Washington, DC, accessed October 11, 2012, http://www.archives.gov/research/pentagon-papers/.

108. Dean Rusk, "Address by Secretary Rusk Before the Council on Foreign Relations at new York, New York on May 24, 1966, 'Organizing the Peace for Man's Survival'; Department of State Bulletin, June 13, 1966, p. 926," Vietnam Task Force, Office of the Secretary of Defense, [Part V. A.] Justification of the War. Public Statements. Volume II: D—The

Johnson Administration, D-81-83, National Archives, Washington, DC, accessed October 11, 2012, http://www.archives.gov/research/pentagon-papers/.

109. *New York Times*, "Saigon's Air Base Shelled; 8 Dead and 160 Wounded: Saigon's Air Base Shelled by Reds," *New York Times*, April 13, 1966, ProQuest Historical Newspapers: *New York Times* (1851–2010) with Index (1851–1993), 1.

110. Charles Mohr, Special to *The New York Times*, "KY Goes to Danang with a Regiment to Reassert Rule: 1,500 Men Flown to U.S. Base Troops in City Set Up Roadblocks Protest Marches Grow Tear Gas Fired in Capital Demonstrators in Dalat Burn Radio Station KY Is in Danang with Regiment," *New York Times*, April 5, 1966, ProQuest Historical Newspapers: *New York Times* (1851–2010) with Index (1851–1993), 1.

111. John D. Pomfret, Special to *New York Times*, "Johnson Deplores Buddhist Suicides: At Arlington, He Says Tragic Protest in Vietnam Clouds Gains toward Stability," *New York Times*, May 31, 1966, ProQuest Historical Newspapers: *The New York Times* (1851–2010) with Index (1851–1993), 1.

112. Gallup Organization, *Gallup Poll #1966-0728: Politics/Vietnam/Political Parties/ Recreation* (Williamstown, MA: The Roper Public Opinion Research Center, May 5–10 1966), 12–13.

113. The Gallup Organization, *Gallup Poll #1966-0729: Vietnam/1968 Presidential Election* (Williamstown, MA: The Roper Public Opinion Research Center, May 19–24, 1966), 5–11.

114. Gallup, *Gallup Poll #1966-0729: Vietnam/1968 Presidential Election*, 5–11.

115. Rusk, "Address by Secretary Rusk Before the Council on Foreign Relations . . . on May 24, 1966 . . . "

116. George Herman, Lyndon B. Johnson, "President Johnson speaks at Arlington Cemetery," *CBS Special Report*, CBS, black and white with sound, May 30, 1966, Video #MP568, "President Lyndon B. Johnson speaks at Arlington cemetery," Audiovisual Material, Motion Pictures, Lyndon B. Johnson Presidential Library (Austin, TX).

117. Hubert Humphrey, "Address by Vice President Humphrey at Commencement Exercises at the United States Military Academy, West Point, New York on June 8 1966, 'Perspective on Asia'; Department of State Bulletin, July 4, 1966, p. 2," Vietnam Task Force, Office of the Secretary of Defense, [Part V. A.] Justification of the War. Public Statements. Volume II: D—The Johnson Administration, D-84-85, National Archives, Washington, DC, accessed October 11, 2012, http://www.archives.gov/research/pentagon-papers/.

118. St. Louis Globe-Democrat, "Sukarno—Going, Going, Soon Gone," *St. Louis Globe-Democrat*, July 18, 1966, in Series 48 Foreign Relations Committee, 48-3 Committee Administration, Box 16, Folder 3, 1966, Fulbright Papers, University of Arkansas (Fayetteville, AR).

119. Gallup Organization, *Gallup Poll #1966-0730: Johnson/1968 Presidential Election/ Vietnam/Race Relations/Political Parties* (Williamstown, MA: The Roper Public Opinion Research Center, June 16–21, 1966), 10–13.

120. Lyndon B. Johnson, "Address by President Johnson at Omaha Municipal Dock on June 30, 1966, "Two Threats to Peace: Hunger and Aggression'; Department of State Bulletin, July 25, 1966, p. 115," Vietnam Task Force, Office of the Secretary of Defense, [Part V. A.] Justification of the War. Public Statements. Volume II: D—The Johnson Administration, D-85-86, National Archives, Washington, DC, accessed October 11, 2012, http://www. archives.gov/research/pentagon-papers/.

121. Gallup Organization, *Gallup Poll #1966-0731: Vietnam* (Williamstown, MA: The Roper Public Opinion Research Center, July 8–13 1966), 5, 7–11.

122. Associated Press, "North Viet Nam Does Escalating, Rusk Says," Canberra, Australia, Associated Press, *Toledo Blade*, June 30, 1966, 6.

123. St. Louis Globe-Democrat, "Answer for Soviet Protest," *St. Louis Globe-Democrat*, 18 July 1966, 12A, in Series 48 Foreign Relations Committee, 48-3 Committee Administration, Box 16, Folder 3, 1966, Fulbright Papers, University of Arkansas (Fayetteville, AR).

124. Milward L. Simpson [US Senator], letter to John T. McNaughton [Assistant Secretary of Defense] requesting release of transcript of hearing on Gulf of Tonkin incident, 14 June 1966, Series 48 Foreign Relations Committee, 48-1 General 1966–1967, Box 8, Folder 2, Fulbright Papers, University of Arkansas (Fayetteville, AR).

125. J. William Fulbright, letter to Milward L. Simpson [US Senator] about his request to John McNaughton [Assistant Secretary of Defense] for release of transcript of hearing on Gulf of Tonkin incident, June 17, 1966, Series 48 Foreign Relations Committee, 48-1 General 1966-1967, Box 8, Folder 2, Fulbright Papers, University of Arkansas (Fayetteville, AR).

126. John T. McNaughton [Assistant Secretary of Defense], letter to Milward L. Simpson [US Senator] rejecting his request for release of transcript of hearing on Gulf of Tonkin incident, June 20, 1966, Series 48 Foreign Relations Committee, 48-1 General 1966-1967, Box 8, Folder 2, Fulbright Papers, University of Arkansas (Fayetteville, AR).

127. Milward L. Simpson [US Senator], letter to Senator Fulbright accompanying John T. McNaughton's [Assistant Secretary of Defense] refusal to release of transcript of hearing on Gulf of Tonkin incident, June 29, 1966, Series 48 Foreign Relations Committee, 48-1 General 1966–1967, Box 8, Folder 2, Fulbright Papers, University of Arkansas (Fayetteville, AR).

128. United Press International, "Fulbright Attacks LBJ 'Escalation' of Commitments," United Press International, Washington, DC, *Arkansas Gazette*, July 22, 1966, Series 48 Foreign Relations Committee, 48-1 General 1966-1967, Box 8, Folder 3, Fulbright Papers, University of Arkansas (Fayetteville, AR).

129. Gallup Organization, *Gallup Poll #1966-0733: Politics/Vietnam* (Williamstown, MA: The Roper Public Opinion Research Center, August 18–23, 1966), 15–22.

130. Lyndon B. Johnson, "Address by President Johnson before the Navy League at Manchester, N.H., August 20, 1966, 'Our Objective in Vietnam'; Department of State Bulletin, September 12, 1966, p. 158," Vietnam Task Force, Office of the Secretary of Defense, [Part V. A.] Justification of the War. Public Statements. Volume II: D—The Johnson Administration, D-88-89, National Archives, Washington, DC, accessed October 11, 2012, http://www.archives.gov/research/pentagon-papers/.

131. Gallup Organization, *Gallup Poll #1966-0734: Vietnam/Communist China/Civil Rights/Presidential Election* (Williamstown, MA: The Roper Public Opinion Research Center, September 8–13, 1966), 11–15.

132. Gallup, *Gallup Poll #1966-0734: Vietnam/Communist China/Civil Rights/Presidential Election*, 11–15.

133. The White House, "Presidential Diary" (Washington, DC: The White House, October 20, 1966), Lyndon B. Johnson Presidential Library (Austin, TX), accessed January 9, 2013, http://www.lbjlibrary.net/assets/lbj_tools/daily_diary/pdf/1966/19661020.pdf.

134. White House, "Text of the Joint Communiqué Issued at the Manila Summit Conference, Manila, The Philippines," White House, Washington DC, October 25, 1966, from Vietnam Task Force, Office of the Secretary of Defense, [Part VI. C.] Settlement of the Conflict. Histories of Contacts. Volume IV—Negotiations, 1967–1968, 70–74, National Archives, Washington, DC, accessed October 11, 2012, http://www.archives.gov/research/pentagon-papers/.

135. Frank Wolfe, Photo, Manila Conference of SEATO nations on the Vietnam War: Nations leaders, Manila, Philippines, 24 October 1966, Photo Archive, Lyndon B. Johnson Presidential Library (Austin, TX), accessed July 26, 2015, http://www.lbjlibrary.net/collections/photo-archive.html.

136. CBS, "The President in Asia: Vietnam Visit" (Fifth in a series), *CBS News Special Report*, October 27, 1966, Video #MP582, Audiovisual Materials, Motion Pictures, Lyndon B. Johnson Presidential Library (Austin, TX).

137. Charles Collingwood, David Schoumacher, Eric Sevareid, "The President in Asia: Eve of Manila Conference," *CBS News Special Report*, CBS, October 23, 1966, Video #MP580, "The President in Asia: The Eve of the Manila Conference," Audiovisual Material, Motion Pictures, Lyndon B. Johnson Presidential Library (Austin, TX).

138. Collingwood, Schoumacher, Sevareid, "The President in Asia: Eve of Manila Conference."

139. CBS, "The President in Asia: Vietnam Visit" (Fifth in a series).

140. CBS, "The President in Asia: Vietnam Visit" (Fifth in a series).

141. CBS, "The President in Asia: Vietnam Visit" (Fifth in a series).

142. Gallup Organization, *Gallup Poll #1966-0737: Vietnam/Elections* (Williamstown, MA: The Roper Public Opinion Research Center, November 10–15, 1966), 5.

143. Michael J. Towle, *Out of Touch: The Presidency and Public Opinion*, (College Station, TX: Texas A&M University, 2004), 103.

144. Gallup, *Gallup Poll #1966-0737: Vietnam/Elections*, 12–16.

145. Lyndon B. Johnson, "Annual Message to the Congress on the State of the Union, January 10, 1967," in *Public Papers of the Presidents of the United States: Lyndon B. Johnson, 1967*. Volume I, entry 3 (Washington, DC: Government Printing Office, 1968), 2–14, accessed January 6, 2013, http://www.lbjlibrary.net/collections/selected-speeches/1967/01-10-1967.html.

146. Johnson, "Annual Message to the Congress on the State of the Union, January 10, 1967."

147. Lyndon B. Johnson, "The State of the Union Address of President Johnson to the Congress (Excerpts), January 10, 1967; Department of State Bulletin, January 30, 1967, p. 158," Vietnam Task Force, Office of the Secretary of Defense, [Part V. A.] Justification of the War. Public Statements. Volume II: D--The Johnson Administration, D-98-99, National Archives, Washington, DC, accessed October 11, 2012, http://www.archives.gov/research/pentagon-papers/.

148. Congress of the United States, "Text of Joint Resolution, August 7, Department of State Bulletin, 24 August 1964, p. 268," Vietnam Task Force, Office of the Secretary of Defense, [Part V. A.] Justification of the War. Public Statements. Volume II: D—The Johnson Administration, D-16-17, National Archives, Washington, DC, accessed October 11, 2012, http://www.archives.gov/research/pentagon-papers/.

149. Carl Marcy, memorandum [for Senator J. William Fulbright] about role of Committee and hearings, US Senate Committee on Foreign Relations, Washington, DC, March 23, 1966, Series 48 Foreign Relations Committee, 48-3 Committee Administration, Box 16, Folder 3, 1966, Fulbright Papers, University of Arkansas (Fayetteville, AR).

150. Carl Marcy, letter [for Senator J. William Fulbright] suggesting the Senate Foreign Relations Committee take up less controversial topics, US Senate Committee on Foreign Relations, Washington, DC, March 30, 1966, Series 48 Foreign Relations Committee, 48-3 Committee Administration, Box 16, Folder 3, 1966, Fulbright Papers, University of Arkansas (Fayetteville, AR).

151. U.S. Senate Committee on Foreign Relations, draft press release about NATO and Europe hearings, U.S. Senate Committee on Foreign Relations, Washington, DC, June 1966,

Series 48 Foreign Relations Committee, 48-3 Committee Administration, Box 16, Folder 3, 1966, Fulbright Papers, University of Arkansas (Fayetteville, AR).

152. Norvill Jones [U.S. Senate Committee on Foreign Relations staffer], memorandum for Carl Marcy suggesting hearings on the role of the Senate in making foreign policy, US Senate Committee on Foreign Relations, Washington, DC, November 12, 1966, Series 48 Foreign Relations Committee, 48-3 Committee Administration, Box 16, Folder 3, 1966, Fulbright Papers, University of Arkansas (Fayetteville, AR).

153. Carl Marcy, "SUBJECT: Committee Hearings in the Next Session 'The United States as a Great Power,'" memorandum for Senator J. William Fulbright on potential topics of 1967 hearings, US Senate Committee on Foreign Relations, Washington, DC, 2 November 1966, Series 48 Foreign Relations Committee, 48-3 Committee Administration, Box 16, Folder 3, 1966, Fulbright Papers, University of Arkansas (Fayetteville, AR).

154. Marcy, "SUBJECT: Committee Hearings in the Next Session 'The United States as a Great Power.'"

155. Marcy, "SUBJECT: Committee Hearings in the Next Session 'The United States as a Great Power.'"

156. Carl Marcy, "Subject: Hearings in 90th Congress," memorandum for Senator J. William Fulbright on potential topics of 1967 hearings, US Senate Committee on Foreign Relations, Washington, DC, 29 November 1966, Series 48 Foreign Relations Committee, 48-3 Committee Administration, Box 16, Folder 3, 1966, Fulbright Papers, University of Arkansas (Fayetteville, AR).

157. Marcy, "Subject: Committee Hearings in the Next Session 'The United States as a Great Power.'"

158. Marcy, "Subject: Hearings in 90th Congress."

159. Dean Rusk, letter to Senator J. William Fulbright accepting invitation to testify in 1967 hearings, Office of the Secretary of State, Washington, DC, 30 December 1966, Series 48 Foreign Relations Committee, 48-3 Committee Administration, Box 16, Folder 3, 1966, Fulbright Papers, University of Arkansas (Fayetteville, AR).

160. Carl Marcy, "Subject: Hearings with Secretary Rusk and Committee Business," memorandum for members of the Senate Foreign Relations Committee about upcoming meetings, January 3, 1967, Series 48 Foreign Relations Committee, 48-3 Committee Administration, Box 16, Folder 3, 1966, Fulbright Papers, University of Arkansas (Fayetteville, AR).

161. J. William Fulbright, letter to Senator Richard B. Russell about Secretary of Defense Robert McNamara refusing to testify in 1967 hearings before Foreign Relations Committee until he testifies before the Armed Services Committee, January 4, 1967, Series 48 Foreign Relations Committee, 48-3 Committee Administration, Box 16, Folder 3, 1966, Fulbright Papers, University of Arkansas (Fayetteville, AR).

162. The Radical Education Project, "An Introduction And An Invitation," in *The New Left: A Documentary History* by Massimo Teodori (Indianapolis, IN: Bobbs-Merrill, 1969), 370.

163. Carol Stevens, "SDS re-examined at Dec. Conference," *SDS New Left Notes*, Vol. 1, No. 1 (January 21, 1966), 1.

164. Carl Oglesby, "Liberalism and the Corporate State," *SDS New Left Notes*, Vol. 1, No. 1 (January 21, 1966), 3.

165. Oglesby, "Liberalism and the Corporate State," 2.

166. Oglesby, "Liberalism and the Corporate State," 2–3.

167. Gregory Calvert, "In White America: Radical Consciousness and Social Change," Princeton Conference Speech, February 1967, published in *The National Guardian*,

March 25, 1967, reprinted in *The New Left: A Documentary History* by Massimo Teodori (Indianapolis, IN: Bobbs-Merrill, 1969), 380.

168. Calvert, "In White America: Radical Consciousness and Social Change," 380.

169. Douglas Robinson, "100,000 Rally at U.N. Against Vietnam War: Many Draft Cards Burned . . . ," *New York Times*, April 16, 1967, ProQuest Historical Newspapers: *New York Times* (1851–2010) with Index (1851–1993), 1.

170. Robinson, "100,000 Rally at U.N. Against Vietnam War: Many Draft Cards Burned . . . "

171. Paul Hofmann, Special to *New York Times*, "50,000 at San Francisco—Peace Rally," *New York Times*, April 16, 1967, ProQuest Historical Newspapers: *New York Times* (1851–2010) with Index (1851–1993), 3.

172. Douglas Robinson, "Throngs to Parade to the U.N. Today for Antiwar Rally: ANTIWAR THRONGS TO PROTEST TODAY," *New York Times*, April 15, 1967, ProQuest Historical Newspapers: *New York Times* (1851–2010) with Index (1851–1993), 1.

173. New York Times, "Nixon Says Asians Back U.S. on War," Tokyo, *New York Times*, April 8, 1967, ProQuest Historical Newspapers: *New York Times* (1851–2010) with Index (1851–1993), 3.

174. Tom Buckley, Special to *New York Times*, "NIXON URGES HALT: Says, in Saigon, That Division of Opinion Prolongs Fight," *New York Times*, April 15, 1967, ProQuest Historical Newspapers: *New York Times* (1851–2010) with Index (1851–1993), 2.

175. Robinson, "100,000 Rally at U.N. Against Vietnam War: Many Draft Cards Burned . . . "

176. Hofmann, "50,000 at San Francisco—Peace Rally."

177. New York Times, "Nixon Assails Protests," United Press International, Saigon, *New York Times*, April 17, 1967, ProQuest Historical Newspapers: *New York Times* (1851–2010) with Index (1851–1993), 9.

178. Tom Buckley, Special to *New York Times*, "Nixon Indicates He Seeks Step-Up in War Effort: Says Defeat of Foe in . . . ," *New York Times*, April 18, 1967, ProQuest Historical Newspapers: *New York Times* (1851–2010) with Index (1851–1993), 2.

179. Associated Press, "Accuses 2 Senators," Associated Press, Saigon, *New York Times*, April 18, 1967, ProQuest Historical Newspapers: *New York Times* (1851–2010) with Index (1851–1993), 2.

180. Tom Buckley, Special *to the New York Times*, "Nixon Indicates He Seeks Step-Up in War Effort: Says Defeat of Foe in . . . ," *New York Times*, April 18, 1967, ProQuest Historical Newspapers: *New York Times* (1851–2010) with Index (1851–1993), 2.

181. Gallup Organization, *Gallup Poll #1966-0743: Politics/Vietnam* (Williamstown, MA: The Roper Public Opinion Research Center, March 30–April 4, 1967), 5.

182. The Gallup Organization, *Gallup Poll #1966-0744: Presidential Johnson/1968 Presidential Election/George Wallace* (Williamstown, MA: The Roper Public Opinion Research Center, April 19–24, 1967), 6–12.

183. Gallup, *Gallup Poll #1966-0744: Presidential Johnson/1968 Presidential Election/George Wallace*, 6–12.

184. Langguth, *Our Vietnam*, 433–435; Karnow, *Vietnam*, 503–504.

185. Harrison E Salisbury, Special to *New York Times*, "A VISITOR TO HANOI INSPECTS DAMAGE LAID TO U.S. RAIDS: A Purposeful . . . ," *New York Times*, December 25, 1966, ProQuest Historical Newspapers: *New York Times* (1851–2010) with Index (1851–1993), 1.

186. Salisbury, "A Visitor to Hanoi Inspects Damage Laid to U.S. Raids: A Purposeful . . . "

187. Salisbury, "A Visitor to Hanoi Inspects Damage Laid to U.S. Raids: A Purposeful . . . "

188. Salisbury, "A Visitor to Hanoi Inspects Damage Laid to U.S. Raids: A Purposeful . . . "

189. Salisbury, "A Visitor to Hanoi Inspects Damage Laid to U.S. Raids: A Purposeful . . . "

190. Associated Press, "'Considerable Civilian Casualties' Heavy Damage Caused by Bombings on Hanoi," Associated Press, New York, *Gasden Times*, Gasden, Alabama, December 26, 1966, 1.

191. Harrison E. Salisbury, Special to *New York Times*, "U.S. Raids Batter 2 Towns; Supply Route Is Little Hurt: U.S. Raids in . . . ," *New York Times*, December 27, 1966, ProQuest Historical Newspapers: *The New York Times* (1851–2010) with Index (1851–1993), 1.

192. Salisbury, "U.S. Raids Batter 2 Towns; Supply Route Is Little Hurt: U.S. Raids in . . . "

193. Salisbury, "U.S. Raids Batter 2 Towns; Supply Route Is Little Hurt: U.S. Raids in . . . "

194. Associated Press, "'Hanoi Towns Devestated' Civilian Bombings Described," Associated Press, New York, *Miami News*, Miami, FL, December 27, 1966, 1.

195. Neil Sheehan, Special to the *New York Times*, "Washington Concedes Bombs Hit Civilian Areas in North Vietnam: Civilians' Areas Hit, U.S. Admits," *New York Times*, December 27, 1966, ProQuest Historical Newspapers: *New York Times* (1851–2010) with Index (1851–1993), 1.

196. E. W. Kenworthy, Special to the *New York Times*, "Eisenhower Says U.S. Aims Only at Military Targets: Eisenhower Calls Targets Military," *New York Times*, December 28, 1966, ProQuest Historical Newspapers: *New York Times* (1851–2010) with Index (1851–1993), 1.

197. Associated Press, "U.S. Intends to Continue Bombing Enemy Targets," Associated Press, Washington, D.C., *Nashua Telegraph*, Nashua, NH, December 28, 1966, 30.

198. Kenworthy, "Eisenhower Says U.S. Aims Only at Military Targets . . . "

199. Kenworthy, "Eisenhower Says U.S. Aims Only at Military Targets . . . "

200. *New York Times*, "Targets Military, Johnson Believes: He Is Satisfied that Orders . . . ," *New York Times* (1923–Current file), December 29, 1966, ProQuest Historical Newspapers: *The New York Times* (1851–2010) with Index (1851–1993), 1.

201. Neil Sheehan, Special to the *New York Times*, "Raids' Precision Seen in Reports: Pentagon Says Hanoi's Data Indicate Low Toll Rate," *New York Times*, December 30, 1966, ProQuest Historical Newspapers: *New York Times* (1851–2010) with Index (1851–1993), 2.

202. Sheehan, "Raids' Precision Seen in Reports: Pentagon Says Hanoi's Data Indicate Low Toll Rate."

203. New York Times, "A Flier Disputes Report on Raids: Navy Man Calls Dispatch on Namdinh Unbelievable," *New York Times*, December 29, 1966, ProQuest Historical Newspapers: *The New York Times* (1851–2010) with Index (1851–1993), 2.

204. Hanson W. Baldwin, "Pentagon Says Raids on North Vietnam Cut U.S. Casualties," *New York Times* News Service, New York, Nashua Telegraph, Nashua, NH, December 30, 1966, 1.

205. Baldwin, "Pentagon Says Raids on North Vietnam Cut U.S. Casualties."

206. United Press International, "Pravda Cites Hanoi Dispatches," United Press International, Moscow, *New York Times*, December 30, 1966, ProQuest Historical Newspapers: *New York Times* (1851–2010) with Index (1851–1993), 5.

207. New York Times, "Hanoi Dispatches to Times Criticized," Washington, DC, *New York Times*, 1 January 1967, ProQuest Historical Newspapers: *New York Times* (1851–2010) with Index (1851–1993), 3.

208. Harrison E. Salisbury, Special to *New York Times*, "Hanoi Premier Tells View; Some in U.S. Detect a Shift: Pham Van Dong . . . ," *New York Times*, January 4, 1967, ProQuest Historical Newspapers: *New York Times* (1851–2010) with Index (1851–1993), 1.

209. *New York Times*, "Hanoi Dispatches to Times Criticized."

210. Langguth, *Our Vietnam*, 436.

211. Salisbury, "Hanoi Premier Tells View; Some in U.S. Detect a Shift: Pham Van Dong . . . "

212. *New York Times*, "Obstacle to Peace Talks," *New York Times*, January 5, 1967, ProQuest Historical Newspapers: *New York Times* (1851–2010) with Index (1851–1993), 36.

213. General Assembly of the National Council of Churches, "Text of Appeal by National Council to Its Member Churches on the Vietnam War," *New York Times*, December 10, 1966, 8, ProQuest Historical Newspapers: *New York Times* (1851–2009).

214. Hedrick Smith, Special to *New York Times*, "U.S. Doubts Hanoi Has Given a Sign It Wants Parley," *New York Times*, January 7, 1967, ProQuest Historical Newspapers: *New York Times* (1851–2010) with Index (1851–1993), 1.

215. New York Times, "Sylvester Critical of Times Article," *New York Times*, January 20, 1967, ProQuest Historical Newspapers: *New York Times* (1851–2010) with Index (1851–1993), 2.

216. The White House, "Presidential Diary" (Washington, DC: The White House, February 11, 1967), Lyndon B. Johnson Presidential Library (Austin, TX), accessed January 9. 2013, http://www.lbjlibrary.net/assets/lbj_tools/daily_diary/pdf/1967/19670211.pdf.

217. Don Hesse, "'See—He's Making Peace Gestures,'" McNaught Syndicate, *Springdale News*, Springdale, AR, February 7, 1967, 2, Series 48 Foreign Relations Committee, 48-1 General 1966-1967, Box 8, Folder 4, Fulbright Papers, University of Arkansas (Fayetteville, AR).

218. Hesse, "'See—He's Making Peace Gestures.'"

219. Gallup Organization, *Gallup Poll #1966-0739: 1968 Presidential Election/Vietnam* (Williamstown, MA: The Roper Public Opinion Research Center, January 7–12, 1967), 5–6, 8.

220. Gallup Organization, *Gallup Poll #1966-0740: 1968 Presidential Election/Powell/Income Taxes* (Williamstown, MA: The Roper Public Opinion Research Center, January 26–31, 1967), 5–8, 13.

221. Gallup, *Gallup Poll #1966-0739: 1968 Presidential Election/Vietnam*, 5–6, 8.

222. Gallup Organization, *Gallup Poll #1966-0741: 1968 Presidential Election/US-China Relations* (Williamstown, MA: The Roper Public Opinion Research Center, February 16–21, 1967), 5, 9–11.

223. Drew Middleton, "Thant Disagrees with U.S. On War: Disputes Strategic Value of Vietnam to West—Says Domino Theory Is Invalid," *New York Times*, January 11, 1967, 1, 4, ProQuest Historical Newspapers: *The New York Times* (1851–2009).

224. Drew Middleton, "Thant Is Disputed by 7 Asian Envoys on His View of War," United Nations, New York, *New York Times* (1923–Current file), 14 January 1967, 1, 8; ProQuest Historical Newspapers: *New York Times* (1851–2009).

225. Dean Rusk, "Secretary Rusk Interview on 'Today' Program, January 12, 1967, With Hugh Downs from new York and Joseph C. Harsch in Washington; Department of State Bulletin, January 30, 1967, p. 168," Vietnam Task Force, Office of the Secretary of Defense, [Part V. A.] Justification of the War. Public Statements. Volume II: D— The Johnson Administration, D-99-101, National Archives, Washington, DC, accessed October 11, 2012, http://www.archives.gov/research/pentagon-papers/.

226. Middleton, "Thant Is Disputed by 7 Asian Envoys on His View of War."

227. *New York Times*, "Brezhnev Decries Bombing," Moscow, *New York Times*, January 14, 1967, 8.

228. Gallup, *Gallup Poll #1966-0741: 1968 Presidential Election/US-China Relations*, 5, 9–11.

229. Gallup Organization, *Gallup Poll #1966-0742: Vietnam War/1968 Presidential Election* (Williamstown, MA: The Roper Public Opinion Research Center, March 9–14, 1967), 9.

230. Vietnam Task Force, "Chronology," Vietnam Task Force, Office of the Secretary of Defense, [Part IV. C.] Evolution of the War. Direct Action: The Johnson Commitments, 1964–1968. Volume VIIII: B—U.S.-GVJN Relations. Volume 2: July 1965–December 1967, xvi, National Archives, Washington, DC, accessed October 11, 2012, http://www. archives.gov/research/pentagon-papers/.

231. White House Naval Photographic Unit [Navy Films], "The President: April 1967. MP883," video, (Washington, DC: US Department of the Navy, 1967), Lyndon Johnson Presidential Library, accessed February 28, 2015, https://www.youtube.com/ watch?v=QleuhyR1vPQ.

232. James Marlow, "James Marlow Reports," Washington, DC, Associated Press, *Gettysburg Times*, Gettysburg, PA, April 27, 1967, 15.

233. Lyndon B. Johnson, "Address by President Johnson before a Joint Session of the Tennessee State Legislature at Nashville, Tennessee on March 15, 1967; 'The Defense of Viet-Nam: Key to the Future of Free Asia,' Department of State Bulletin, April 3, 1967, p. 534" Vietnam Task Force, Office of the Secretary of Defense, [Part V. A.] Justification of the War. Public Statements. Volume II: D—The Johnson Administration, D-107, National Archives, Washington, DC, accessed October 11, 2012, http://www.archives.gov/ research/pentagon-papers/.

234. William P. Bundy, "Address by William P. Bundy, Assistant Secretary of State for East Asian and Pacific Affairs, before the national Executive Committee of the American Legion at Indianapolis, Indiana on May 3, 1967; 'Seventeen Years in East Asia,' Department of State Bulletin, May 22, 1967, p. 790," Vietnam Task Force, Office of the Secretary of Defense, [Part V. A.] Justification of the War. Public Statements. Volume II: D—The Johnson Administration, D-107-109, National Archives, Washington, DC, accessed October 11, 2012, http://www.archives.gov/research/pentagon-papers/.

235. Gallup Organization, *Gallup Poll #1966-0745:Johnson/Vietnam/Education/Elections* (Williamstown, MA: The Roper Public Opinion Research Center, May 11–16, 1967), 11–12.

236. Gallup, *Gallup Poll #1966-0745:Johnson/Vietnam/Education/Elections*, 11–12.

237. Value Line Investment Survey, "The Containment of Communism—a Possible Change in U.S. Policy," *Value Line Investment Survey*, newsletter, New York, June 23, 1967, Series 48 Foreign Relations Committee, 48-1 General 1966–1967, Box 8, Folder 5, Fulbright Papers, University of Arkansas (Fayetteville, AR).

238. Associated Press, "World Today," Washington, DC, Associated Press, *Warsaw Times-Union*, Warsaw, IN, May 9, 1967, 16.

239. Gallup Organization, *Gallup Poll #1966-0746: Vietnam/Middle East/1968 Presidential Election* (Williamstown, MA: The Roper Public Opinion Research Center, June 2–7, 1967), 5.

240. Gallup Organization, *Gallup Poll #1966-0747: Vietnam War/Politics* (Williamstown, MA: The Roper Public Opinion Research Center, June 22–27, 1967), 6–9.

241. Gallup Organization, *Gallup Poll #1966-0748: Vietnam/Civil Rights/Presidential Election* (Williamstown, MA: The Roper Public Opinion Research Center, July 13–18, 1967), 5.

242. Gallup, *Gallup Poll #1966-0748: Vietnam/Civil Rights/Presidential Election*, 6–7.

243. Hammond, *Public Affairs, 1962–1968*, 297.

244. Vietnam Task Force, "Chronology," Vietnam Task Force, Office of the Secretary of Defense, [Part IV. C.].

245. Hedrick Smith [Special to The *New York Times*], "Army Chief Sees End of Build-Up: 'We're Winning,' Declares General," Washington, DC, *New York Times,* August 13, 1967, ProQuest Historical Newspapers: *New York Times,* 10.

246. Harry F. Rosenthal, Tom Stewart, "Tonkin Gulf," Associated Press, *Arkansas Gazette,* 16 July 1967, reprinted in *Congressional Record* by U.S. Congress, Washington, D.C., February 28, 1968, 4582.

247. Harry F. Rosenthal, Tom Stewart, "U.S. Involvement Started in Tonkin Gulf," Associated Press, *Post-Crescent,* Appleton, WI, July 16, 1967, 26.

248. Rosenthal, Stewart, "U.S. Involvement Started in Tonkin Gulf."

Chapter 4

1. Gallup Organization, *Gallup Poll #1966-0749: Race Relations* (Williamstown, MA: The Roper Public Opinion Research Center, 3–8 August 1967), 5–7, 9.

2. Gallup Organization, *Gallup Poll #1966-0750:Johnson/Vietnam/Religion/1968 Presidential Election* (Williamstown, MA: The Roper Public Opinion Research Center, August 24–29, 1967), 5–9.

3. Gallup, *Gallup Poll #1966-0750:Johnson/Vietnam/Religion/1968 Presidential Election,* 12.

4. James Marlow, "Interpreting the News: US Caught in Vietnam War Box," Washington, DC, Associated Press, *Kentucky New Era,* Hopkinsville, KY, August 21, 1967, 3.

5. Pittsburgh Post-Gazette, "Senate Reflects Agony of War," *Pittsburgh Post-Gazette,* October 4, 1967, 5.

6. Gallup Organization, *Gallup Poll #1966-0745:Johnson/Vietnam/Education/Elections* (Williamstown, MA: The Roper Public Opinion Research Center, May 11–16, 1967), 11–12.

7. Don Oberdorfer, "Noninterventionism, 1967 Style," *New York Times,* September 17, 1967, SM115, ProQuest Historical Newspapers: *New York Times* (1851–2009) with Index (1851–1993).

8. Oberdorfer, "Noninterventionism, 1967 Style."

9. Lyndon B. Johnson, "Address on Vietnam Before the National Legislative Conference, San Antonio, Texas," 29 September 1967, Reprinted online by Gerhard Peters and John T. Woolley, *The American Presidency Project.* http://www.presidency.ucsb.edu/ws/?pid=28460, accessed July 15, 2014.

10. Johnson, "Address on Vietnam Before the National Legislative Conference, San Antonio, Texas."

11. Lyndon B. Johnson, "Remarks by President Johnson to the National Legislative Conference at San Antonio, Texas on September 29, 1967; 'Answering Aggression In Viet-Nam,' Department of State Publication 8305, East Asian and Pacific Series 167, Released October 1967," Vietnam Task Force, Office of the Secretary of Defense, [Part V. A.] Justification of the War. Public Statements. Volume II: D—The Johnson Administration, D-120-123, National Archives, Washington, DC, accessed October 11, 2012, http://www.archives.gov/research/pentagon-papers/.

12. Johnson, "Address on Vietnam Before the National Legislative Conference, San Antonio, Texas."

13. Dean Rusk, "Secretary Rusk's News Conference of October 12, 1967; Department of State Press Release No. 227, October 12, 1967," Vietnam Task Force, Office of the Secretary of Defense, [Part V. A.] Justification of the War. Public Statements. Volume II: D—The Johnson Administration, D-123-126, National Archives, Washington, DC, accessed October 11, 2012, http://www.archives.gov/research/pentagon-papers/.

14. Dean Rusk, "Transcript of Secretary Rusk's News Conference on Foreign Affairs Questions," Washington, DC, *New York Times*, October 13, 1967, 14, ProQuest Historical Newspapers: *New York Times* (1851–2009) with Index (1851–1993).

15. Rusk, "Transcript of Secretary Rusk's News Conference on Foreign Affairs Questions."

16. Dean Rusk, "Interview with Secretary Rusk, Videotaped at USIA Studios in Washington, DC, on October 16, 1967 and Later Broadcast Abroad; 'Secretary Rusk Discusses Viet-Nam in Interview for Foreign Television,' Department of State Bulletin, November 6, 1967, p. 595," Vietnam Task Force, Office of the Secretary of Defense, [Part V. A.] Justification of the War. Public Statements. Volume II: D—The Johnson Administration, D-126-129, National Archives, Washington, DC, accessed October 11, 2012, http://www.archives. gov/research/pentagon-papers/.

17. Dean Rusk, "Address by Secretary Rusk (Excerpt) made at Columbus, Indiana, October 30, 1967; 'Firmness and Restraint in Viet-Nam,' Department of State Bulletin, November 27, 1967, p. 703," Vietnam Task Force, Office of the Secretary of Defense, [Part V. A.] Justification of the War. Public Statements. Volume II: D—The Johnson Administration, D-132-134, National Archives, Washington, DC, accessed October 11, 2012, http://www. archives.gov/research/pentagon-papers/.

18. James Marlow, "Interpreting the News: US Caught in Vietnam War Box," Washington, DC, Associated Press, *Kentucky New Era*, Hopkinsville, KY, August 21, 1967, 3.

19. Marlow, "Interpreting the News: US Caught in Vietnam War Box."

20. Marlow, "Interpreting the News: US Caught in Vietnam War Box."

21. Gallup Organization, *Gallup Poll #1966-0751: Labor Unions/Presidential Election* (Williamstown, MA: The Roper Public Opinion Research Center, 14–19 September 1967), 5.

22. A.J. Langguth, *Our Vietnam: The War 1954–1975* (New York: Simon & Schuster, 2000), 394; Stanley Karnow, *Vietnam: A History* (New York: Penguin, 1997), 495.

23. Gallup Organization, *Gallup Poll #1966-0752: Vietnam/1968 Presidential Election* (Williamstown, MA: The Roper Public Opinion Research Center, 6–October 11, 1967), 7, 9–12.

24. Gallup, *Gallup Poll #1966-0752: Vietnam/1968 Presidential Election*, 9–12.

25. Gallup, *Gallup Poll #1966-0752: Vietnam/1968 Presidential Election*, 9–12.

26. Langguth, *Our Vietnam*, 459.

27. Langguth, *Our Vietnam*, 460.

28. Frank Wolfe, Photo, Vietnam War protesters at the March on the Pentagon, October 21, 1967, Photo Archive, Lyndon B. Johnson Presidential Library (Austin, TX), accessed July 26, 2015, http://www.lbjlibrary.net/collections/photo-archive.html.

29. Newsday, "The Silent Center," *Newsday*, Long Island, NY, [October–November 1967], box 73 [2 of 2], folder ND 19-CO 312 Materials sent from John P. Roche, May 19, 1968– Vietnam, Committee to Support Administration Position, Central File, Lyndon B. Johnson Presidential Library (Austin, TX).

30. Canton Repository, "The Great Silent Center," *Canton Repository*, Canton, OH, [October– November 1967], box 73 [2 of 2], folder ND 19-CO 312 Materials sent from John P. Roche, May 19, 1968–Vietnam, Committee to Support Administration Position, Central File, Lyndon B. Johnson Presidential Library (Austin, TX).

31. Pete Hamill [Washington News], speech to the Emergency Civil Liberties Committee, New York, 8 December 1967, Series 48 Foreign Relations Committee, 48-1 General 1966–1967, Box 8, Folder 5, Fulbright Papers, University of Arkansas (Fayetteville, AR).

32. Hamill, speech to the Emergency Civil Liberties Committee, New York, December 8, 1967.

33. Louis Harris, "Reaction to War Protesters Rises," *Washington Post*, December 18, 1967, in Series 48 Foreign Relations Committee, 48-3 Committee Administration, Box 16, Folder 4, 1967, Fulbright Papers, University of Arkansas Library (Fayetteville, AR).

34. Gallup Organization, *Gallup Poll #1966-0753: Politics/Unions/Federal Poverty Programs* (Williamstown, MA: The Roper Public Opinion Research Center, October 27–November 1, 1967), 9.

35. Gallup Organization, *Gallup Poll #1966-0754: Politics/Vietnam* (Williamstown, MA: The Roper Public Opinion Research Center, November 16–21, 1967), 10.

36. Gallup, *Gallup Poll #1966-0753: Politics/Unions/Federal Poverty Programs*, 12.

37. The Movement, "We've Got to Reach Our Own People," *The Movement*, November 1967, reprinted in *The New Left: A Documentary History* by Massimo Teodori (Indianapolis, IN: Bobbs-Merrill, 1969), 280.

38. The Movement, "We've Got to Reach Our Own People," 285.

39. Staughton Lynd, "Resistance; From Mood to Strategy," *Liberation*, December 1967, reprinted in *The New Left: A Documentary History* by Massimo Teodori (Indianapolis, IN: Bobbs-Merrill, 1969), 287.

40. John Kenneth Galbraith, "The Galbraith Plan to End the War," *New York Times*, November 12, 1967, 263, ProQuest Historical Newspapers: *New York Times* (1851–2009).

41. Galbraith, "The Galbraith Plan to End the War."

42. Walter Trohan, "Bennett Analyzes War in Vietnam," Washington, DC, *Chicago Tribune* Press Service, *Spokesman-Review*, Spokane, WA, October 26, 1967, 4.

43. Washington Post, "Brewster Backs LBJ Viet Stand," *Washington Post*, October 26, 1967, box 73 [2 of 2], folder ND 19-CO 312 Materials sent from John P. Roche, May 19, 1968– Vietnam, Committee to Support Administration Position, Central File, Lyndon B. Johnson Presidential Library (Austin, TX).

44. United Press International, "UPI-135 (U.N.)," Washington, DC, United Press International, 30 November 1967, in Series 48 Foreign Relations Committee, 48-3 Committee Administration, Box 16, Folder 4, 1967, Fulbright Papers, University of Arkansas (Fayetteville, AR).

45. Washington Post, "Brewster Backs LBJ Viet Stand."

46. Richard Hughes, "Romney's Stand May Be War Issue," Lansing, MI, United Press International, *Times-News*, Hendersonville, NC, November 30, 1967, 16.

47. Richard Hughes, "Romney View on Viet War Told," Lansing, MI, United Press International, *Press-Courier*, Oxnard, CA, December 3, 1967, 24.

48. Randall Bennett Woods, *Fulbright: A Biography* (New York: Cambridge University, 1995), 49.

49. Paul Findley [Congressman], letter to J. William Fulbright accompanying a draft resolution demanding investigation of Tonkin Gulf Resolution, Washington, DC, August 15, 1967, Series 48 Foreign Relations Committee, 48-3 Committee Administration, Box 16, Folder 4, 1967, Fulbright Papers, University of Arkansas (Fayetteville, AR).

50. Paul Findley [Congressman], H. RES. 869, proposed resolution demanding investigation of Tonkin Gulf Resolution, US House of Representatives, Washington, DC, August 10, 1967, Series 48 Foreign Relations Committee, 48-3 Committee Administration, Box 16, Folder 4, 1967, Fulbright Papers, University of Arkansas (Fayetteville, AR).

51. Findley, H. RES. 869, proposed resolution demanding investigation of Tonkin Gulf Resolution.

52. Findley, H. RES. 869, proposed resolution demanding investigation of Tonkin Gulf Resolution.

53. William Conrad Gibbons, *The U.S. Government and the Vietnam War: Executive and Legislative Roles and Relationships: July 1965–January 1968* (Princeton, NJ: Princeton University, 1995), 810–811.

54. Carl Marcy, "SUBJECT: Committee Hearings in the Next Session 'The United States as a Great Power,'" memorandum for Senator J. William Fulbright on potential topics of 1967 hearings, US Senate Committee on Foreign Relations, Washington, DC, 2 November 1966, Series 48 Foreign Relations Committee, 48-3 Committee Administration, Box 16, Folder 3, 1966, Fulbright Papers, University of Arkansas (Fayetteville, AR).

55. Albert Levitt [judge], "Statement of Albert Levitt of Hancock, N. H. Before the Senate Committee on Foreign Relations on Senate Resolution 151," September 19, 1967, Series 48 Foreign Relations Committee, 48-3 Committee Administration, Box 16, Folder 4, 1967, Fulbright Papers, University of Arkansas (Fayetteville, AR).

56. Levitt, "Statement of Albert Levitt . . . before the . . . Committee on Foreign Relations."

57. New York Times, "Expert Says LBJ Can Ignore Senate," Washington, DC, New York Times News Service, *Miami News,* August 24, 1967, 9A.

58. Gibbons, *The U.S. Government and the Vietnam War,* 232.

59. United Press International, "UPI-94," wire service story about Congressional resolution on the use of force, November 16, 1967, Series 48 Foreign Relations Committee, 48-1 General 1966–1967, Box 8, Folder 5, Fulbright Papers, University of Arkansas (Fayetteville, AR).

60. J. William Fulbright, letter to Philip W. Quigg [managing editor, *Foreign Affairs*] about Senate Foreign Relations Committee report on "national commitments," US Senate Committee on Foreign Relations, Washington, DC, December 5, 1966, in Series 48 Foreign Relations Committee, 48-3 Committee Administration, Box 16, Folder 4, 1967, Fulbright Papers, University of Arkansas (Fayetteville, AR).

61. Carl Marcy, letter to Senator J. William Fulbright about potential topics and intent of hearings by the Senate Foreign Relations Committee in 1968, US Senate Committee on Foreign Relations, Washington, DC, 15 December 1967, in Series 48 Foreign Relations Committee, 48-3 Committee Administration, Box 16, Folder 4, 1967, Fulbright Papers, University of Arkansas (Fayetteville, AR).

62. Carl Marcy, "Educational Hearings for 1968," memorandum for Senator J. William Fulbright about potential hearings in the Senate Foreign Relations Committee on US as a world power, US Senate Committee on Foreign Relations, Washington, DC, 13 December 1967, in Series 48 Foreign Relations Committee, 48-3 Committee Administration, Box 16, Folder 4, 1967, Fulbright Papers, University of Arkansas (Fayetteville, AR).

63. Norvill Jones, memorandum for Carl Marcy about proposed Senate Foreign Relations Committee hearings on US as a world power, US Senate Committee on Foreign Relations, Washington, DC, December 14, 1967, in Series 48 Foreign Relations Committee, 48-3 Committee Administration, Box 16, Folder 4, 1967, Fulbright Papers, University of Arkansas (Fayetteville, AR).

64. Carl Marcy, letter to Senator J. William Fulbright about potential topics and intent of hearings by the Senate Foreign Relations Committee in 1968, US Senate Committee on Foreign Relations, Washington, DC, December 15, 1967, in Series 48 Foreign Relations Committee, 48-3 Committee Administration, Box 16, Folder 4, 1967, Fulbright Papers, University of Arkansas (Fayetteville, AR).

65. Randall Bennett Woods, *J. William Fulbright, Vietnam, and the Search for a Cold War Foreign Policy* (Cambridge: Cambridge University, 1998), 138, 166–167.

66. Don Henderson, memorandum for Carl Marcy disagreeing with proposed Senate Foreign Relations Committee hearings on US as a world power, US Senate Committee on Foreign

Relations, Washington, DC, 14 December 1967, in Series 48 Foreign Relations Committee, 48-3 Committee Administration, Box 16, Folder 4, 1967, Fulbright Papers, University of Arkansas (Fayetteville, AR).

67. Peter Riddleberger [staffer, US Senate Committee on Foreign Relations], memorandum for Carl Marcy disagreeing with proposed Senate Foreign Relations Committee hearings on US as a world power, US Senate Committee on Foreign Relations, Washington, DC, 19 December 1967, in Series 48 Foreign Relations Committee, 48-3 Committee Administration, Box 16, Folder 4, 1967, Fulbright Papers, University of Arkansas (Fayetteville, AR).

68. US Senate Committee on Foreign Relations, "Statement by Senator J. W. Fulbright, Chairman, Senate Foreign Relations Committee," press release about release of William P. Bundy's statement about Tonkin Gulf Resolution from September 1966, US Senate Committee on Foreign Relations, Washington, DC, [December 21, 1967], in Series 48 Foreign Relations Committee, 48-3 Committee Administration, Box 16, Folder 4, 1967, Fulbright Papers, University of Arkansas (Fayetteville, AR).

69. United Press International, "TUPI-68 (TONKIN)," wire news release, Washington, DC, United Press International, December 21, 1967, Series 48 Foreign Relations Committee, 48-1 General 1966–1967, Box 8, Folder 5, Fulbright Papers, University of Arkansas (Fayetteville, AR).

70. Carl Marcy, memorandum for Senator J. William Fulbright about recent mail volume and subjects, US Senate Committee on Foreign Relations, 16 January 1968, Series 48 Foreign Relations Committee, 48-3 Committee Administration, Box 16, Folder 5, 1968, Fulbright Papers, University of Arkansas Library (Fayetteville, AR).

71. United Press International, "Bombs May Force Reds to Increase Use of Cambodia," United Press International, Washington, DC, *Bulletin*, Bend, Oregon, 24 November 1967, 12.

72. Reuter, "U.S. About to Enter New Phase of War," Reuter, Washington, DC, *Sydney Morning Herald*, November 23, 1967, 2.

73. United Press International, "U.S. plans to strengthen weapon supply to S. Vietnam," United Press International, Washington, DC, *Bulletin*, Bend, Oregon, November 24, 1967, 12.

74. Reuter, "U.S. About to Enter New Phase of War."

75. Associated Press, "Pentagon Eyes Reduction of War Surplus," Associated Press, Washington, DC, *Morning Record*, Meriden, CT, November 25, 1967, 7.

76. Gallup, *Gallup Poll #1966-0754: Politics/Vietnam*, 6.

77. Gallup Organization, *Gallup Poll #1966-0755: Economy/Presidential Election/Vietnam/Most Admired People* (Williamstown, MA: The Roper Public Opinion Research Center, December 7–12, 1967), 9.

78. Gallup Organization, *Gallup Poll #1966-0755: Economy/Presidential Election/Vietnam . . .*, 18.

79. Reuter, "U.S. about to enter new phase of war."

80. Melvin Small, *Johnson, Nixon, and the Doves* (New Brunswick, NJ: Rutgers University, 1988), 118.

81. Langguth, *Our Vietnam*, 462–465.

82. Robert Dallek, *Flawed Giant: Lyndon Johnson and His Times, 1961–1973* (New York: Oxford University, 493–496.

83. Fry, *Debating Vietnam*, 143.

84. Transcript, Robert S. McNamara Oral History Interview I, January 1, 1975, by Walt W. Rostow, Internet Copy, Lyndon B. Johnson Presidential Library (Austin, TX), 58.

85. Dan Rather, Frank Reynolds, Lyndon B. Johnson, "Presiden [sic] Johnson interview with network correspondents," raw footage (poor quality), December 18, 1967, Video #VTR

100, "LBJ Interview with network correspondents," Motion Pictures, Audiovisual Materials, Lyndon B. Johnson Presidential Library (Austin, TX).

86. Roscoe Drummond, "Gains Are Being Made in the Western Pacific Area," Washington, DC, Publishers-Hall Syndicate, *Observer-Reporter*, Washington, PA, December 12, 1967, 4.

87. Gallup Organization, *Gallup Poll #1966-0756: 1968 Presidential Election* (Williamstown, MA: The Roper Public Opinion Research Center, January 4–9, 1968), 14.

88. Harry F. Rosenthal, "Tonkin Gulf Again in News; Doubts May Stir Inquiry," Washington, DC, Associate Press, *Arkansas Democrat-Gazette*, December 24, 1967, in Series 48 Foreign Relations Committee, 48-6 Sub-Committees, Hearings, Studies, Investigations, 1967–1969, Box 28. Folder 3, (HEARING-TONKIN BAY RESOLUTION) 1967–1968), 1967–1969, Fulbright Papers, University of Arkansas (Fayetteville, AR).

89. Paul Conrad, "'We Are Waiting for a Signal from Hanoi'" (political cartoon), Register and Tribune Syndicate, *Los Angeles Times, Lewiston Morning Tribune*, Lewiston, ID, January 11, 1968, 4.

90. Conrad, "'We Are Waiting for a Signal from Hanoi.'"

91. John Chamberlain, "War Financing May Trip LBJ," *St. Joseph Gazette*, St. Joseph, MO, January 4, 1968, 4.

92. Lester Markel, "How the No. 1 Power Should Use Its Power," *New York Times*, 14 January 1968, SM22, ProQuest Historical Newspapers: *The New York Times* (1851–2009) with Index (1851–1993).

93. Lyndon B. Johnson, "Annual Message to the Congress on the State of the Union, January 17, 1968," *Public Papers of the Presidents of the United States: Lyndon B. Johnson, 1968–69*. Volume I, entry 14 (Washington, DC: Government Printing Office, 1970), 25–33, accessed January 6, 2013, http://www.lbjlibrary.net/collections/selected-speeches/1968-january-1969/01-17-1968.html.

94. NBC, "The President's Message: A Troubled Year Ahead/Analysis of the State of Union Address," *NBC Special Report*, January 17, 1968, 1 hour, black and white with sound, Video #VTR126 "Analysis of State of the Union with Galbraith and Lindsay," Audiovisual Material, Motion Pictures, Lyndon B. Johnson Presidential Library (Austin, TX).

95. Special Committee on Bombing Policy of the Citizen's Committee for Peace with Freedom in Vietnam, "A Balance Sheet on Bombing," Citizen's Committee for Peace with Freedom in Vietnam, box 73 [2 of 2], folder ND 19-CO 312 Materials sent from John P. Roche, May 19, 1968–Vietnam, Committee to Support Administration Position, Central File, Lyndon B. Johnson Presidential Library (Austin, TX).

96. NBC, "The President's Message: A Troubled Year Ahead/Analysis of the State of Union Address."

97. Edwin Newman (host), Lawrence E. Spivak, Max Frankel (*New York Times*), Peter Lisagor (*Chicago Daily News*), Charles Murphy (NBC News), Sen. J. William Fulbright, *Meet the Press*, January 21, 1968, Color with sound, Video #VTR130, "*Meet the Press/CBS Special Report*, Vietnam Peace Talks," Audiovisual Material, Motion Pictures, Lyndon B. Johnson Presidential Library (Austin, TX).

98. J. William Fulbright, letter of response to Henry Steele Commager [Professor, Amherst College, MA] about his letter comparing the USS *Pueblo* and USS *Maddox* incidents, February 10, 1968, Series 48 Foreign Relations Committee, 48-1 General 1968–1969, Box 9, Folder 1, Fulbright Papers, University of Arkansas (Fayetteville, AR).

99. George H. Aldrich, "QUESTIONS OF INTERNATIONAL LAW RAISED BY THE SEIZURE OF THE U.S.S. *PUEBLO*," *Proceedings of the American Society of International Law at Its Annual Meeting (1921–1969)*, American Society of International Law, Vol. 63, Perspectives for International Legal Development (April 24–26, 1969), 2–6.

100. Don Oberdorfer. *Tet!* (New York, NY: Avon Books, 1971), 246–251

101. Robert Pisor. *The End of the Line: The Siege of Khe Sanh* (New York: W. W. Norton and Company, 1982), 170–177.

102. Langguth, *Our Vietnam*, 474; Karnow, *Vietnam*, 539.

103. Karnow, *Vietnam*, 546.

104. Langguth, *Our Vietnam*, 472–474.

105. Langguth, *Our Vietnam*, 475.

106. Langguth, *Our Vietnam*, 475; Karnow, *Vietnam*, 542.

107. Gallup Organization, *Gallup Poll #1966-0757: Crime/Presidential Election/Vietnam* (Williamstown, MA: The Roper Public Opinion Research Center, February 2–6, 1968), 21–22.

108. Sydney Lizzard, "Special on Vietnam and Other Current Events," NBC, recorded from Washington NBC 4, Sunday, February 4, 1968, Video #0157, "Special Weekend Report on Vietnam," Audiovisual Material, Motion Pictures, Lyndon B. Johnson Presidential Library (Austin, TX).

109. Lizzard, "Special on Vietnam and Other Current Events."

110. U.S. Congress, "Public Testimony Before the Foreign Relations Committee by the Secretary of State," *Congressional Record—Senate*, US Congress, February 7, 1968, S1071, Series 48 Foreign Relations Committee, 48-3 Committee Administration, Box 16, Folder 5, 1968, Fulbright Papers, University of Arkansas Library (Fayetteville, AR).

111. Associated Press, "Johnson Offers to Let Foe Set Parley Agenda," Washington, DC, Associated Press, *Blade*, Toledo, OH, February 13, 1968, 1.

112. Carl Marcy, memorandum for Senator J. William Fulbright through staffer Lee Williams about possible use of tactical nuclear weapons in Vietnam, US Senate Committee on Foreign Relations, February 5, 1968, Series 48 Foreign Relations Committee, 48-3 Committee Administration, Box 16, Folder 5, 1968, Fulbright Papers, University of Arkansas Library (Fayetteville, AR).

113. Carl Marcy, memorandum for Senator J. William Fulbright about public fears of tactical nuclear weapon use in Vietnam, US Senate Committee on Foreign Relations, February 14, 1968, Series 48 Foreign Relations Committee, 48-3 Committee Administration, Box 16, Folder 5, 1968, Fulbright Papers, University of Arkansas Library (Fayetteville, AR).

114. Dean Rusk, letter to Senator J. William Fulbright about potential use of tactical nuclear weapon in Vietnam, US Department of State, Washington, DC, 10 February 1968, Series 48 Foreign Relations Committee, 48-3 Committee Administration, Box 16, Folder 5, 1968, Fulbright Papers, University of Arkansas Library (Fayetteville, AR).

115. J. William Fulbright, "Statement by Senator J. W. Fulbright, Chairman, Senate Foreign Relations Committee," statement about Secretary of State Dean Rusk's response to inquiries about the potential use of tactical nuclear weapon in Vietnam, US Senate Committee on Foreign Relations, Washington, DC, 15 February 1968, Series 48 Foreign Relations Committee, 48-3 Committee Administration, Box 16, Folder 5, 1968, Fulbright Papers, University of Arkansas Library (Fayetteville, AR).

116. Joseph Bruce Hamilton, Faux Casus Belli: The Role of Unsubstantiated Attacks in the Initiation of Military Action for Domestic Political Purposes (Dissertation in International Relations, Fletcher School of Law and Diplomacy, March 2000), 141, 143–145, 150; Woods, *J. William Fulbright . . .*, 168.

117. U.S. Senate, Senate Foreign Relations Committee, *The Gulf of Tonkin, The 1964 Incidents: Hearing before the Committee on Foreign Relations, United States Senate, 20 February 1968* (Washington, DC: U.S. Government Printing Office, 1968), 9, 17, 18, 19.

118. U.S. Senate, *The Gulf of Tonkin, The 1964 Incidents*, 26, 27, 38, 104.

119. U.S. Senate, *The Gulf of Tonkin, The 1964 Incidents*, 29–30, 49–50, 96–97, 49–50, 38, 40, 82–83.

120. U.S. Senate, *The Gulf of Tonkin, The 1964 Incidents*, 47, 82–83.

121. U.S. Senate, *The Gulf of Tonkin, The 1964 Incidents*, 26, 42–43.

122. U.S. Senate, *The Gulf of Tonkin, The 1964 Incidents*, 41–42, 54–56, 58–59, 66–67, 74, 69–70, 81, 82–83.

123. U.S. Senate, *The Gulf of Tonkin, The 1964 Incidents*, 41–42, 54–56, 58–59, 66–67, 74, 69–70, 81, 82–83.

124. U.S. Senate, *The Gulf of Tonkin, The 1964 Incidents*, 41–42, 54–56, 58–59, 66–67, 69–70, 74, 81, 82–83.

125. U.S. Senate, *The Gulf of Tonkin, The 1964 Incidents*, 19, 20, 21–22, 23, 52, 83–84, 88, 86.

126. U.S. Senate, *The Gulf of Tonkin, The 1964 Incidents*, 80.

127. U.S. Senate, *The Gulf of Tonkin, The 1964 Incidents*, 80.

128. U.S. Senate, *The Gulf of Tonkin, The 1964 Incidents*, 79–80.

129. U.S. Senate, *The Gulf of Tonkin, The 1964 Incidents*, 91–92, 102–103.

130. U.S. Senate, *The Gulf of Tonkin, The 1964 Incidents*, 102–103.

131. U.S. Senate Committee on Foreign Relations, "Statement for Senator J. W. Fulbright," statement by Senator J. William Fulbright on Secretary McNamara's comments on Senate Foreign Relations Committee Gulf of Tonkin hearings, U.S. Senate Committee on Foreign Relations, Washington, DC, 21 February 1968, Series 48 Foreign Relations Committee, 48-6 Sub-Committees, Hearings, Studies, Investigations, 1967–1969, Box 28. Folder 3, (Hearing—Tonkin Bay Resolution) 1967–1968), 1967–1969, Fulbright Papers, University of Arkansas (Fayetteville, AR).

132. U.S. Senate Committee on Foreign Relations, "Statement for Senator J. W. Fulbright."

133. Woods, *J. William Fulbright . . .* , 170.

134. John W. Finney, Special to The *New York Times*, "M'Namara Says Destroyers in '64 Warned of Enemy: Tells Senators That . . . ," Washington, DC, *New York Times*, February 25, 1968, 1, in Series 48 Foreign Relations Committee, 48-6 Sub-Committees, Hearings, Studies, Investigations, 1967–1969, Box 28. Folder 3, (Hearing—Tonkin Bay Resolution) 1967–1968), 1967–1969, Fulbright Papers, University of Arkansas (Fayetteville, AR).

135. E. W. Kenworthy, Special to *The New York Times*, "Nine Senators Feel U.S. Overreacted on Tonkin: Members of Fulbright . . . ," Washington, DC, *New York Times*, 25 February 1968, 29, in Series 48 Foreign Relations Committee, 48-6 Sub-Committees, Hearings, Studies, Investigations, 1967–1969, Box 28. Folder 3, (Hearing—Tonkin Bay Resolution) 1967–1968), 1967–1969, Fulbright Papers, University of Arkansas (Fayetteville, AR).

136. Kenworthy, "Nine Senators Feel U.S. Overreacted on Tonkin: Members of Fulbright . . . "

137. Gallup Organization, *Gallup Poll #0758* (Williamstown, MA: The Roper Public Opinion Research Center, February 22–27, 1968), 8–10.

138. Mark O. Hatfield [Senator, Oregon], letter to members of Senate about proposed resolution to limit President Johnson's ability to expand Vietnam War beyond South Vietnam, U.S. Senate, Washington, DC, 27 February 1968, Series 48 Foreign Relations Committee, 48-1 General 1968–1969, Box 9, Folder 1, Fulbright Papers, University of Arkansas (Fayetteville, AR)..

139. Mark O. Hatfield, Senator, Oregon, "Concurrent Resolution," draft resolution referred to Senate Foreign Relations Committee intended to limit President Johnson's ability to expand Vietnam War beyond South Vietnam, U.S. Senate, Washington, DC, [February

1968], Series 48 Foreign Relations Committee, 48-1 General 1968–1969, Box 9, Folder 1, Fulbright Papers, University of Arkansas (Fayetteville, AR).

140. Lloyd Shearer, "The Baby Doctor and the Chaplain," *Parade*, March 3, 1968, in Series 48 Foreign Relations Committee, 48-3 Committee Administration, Box 16, Folder 5, 1968, Fulbright Papers, University of Arkansas Library (Fayetteville, AR).

141. Drew Pearson, "Washington Merry-Go-Round: Vietnam's the Issue in New Hampshire," Washington, DC, *Gadsden Times*, Gadsden, AL, March 12, 1968, 4.

142. Lloyd Shearer, "The Untold Story of 'OPERATION VULTURE,'" *Personality Parade Magazine, Palm Beach Post*, March 16, 1968, 40.

143. Gallup, "Gallup Poll #758," Gallup, February 22–27, 1968.

144. Walter Cronkite, "Walter Cronkite Vietnam 1968," CBS News, February 27, 1968, http://www.youtube.com/watch?v=Nn4w-ud-TyE, accessed August 2, 2014.

145. Karnow, *Vietnam*, 559.

146. Louis Liebovich, *The Press and the Modern Presidency: Myths and Mindsets from Kennedy to Election 2000* (Westport, CT: Praeger, 2001), 45; Karnow, *Vietnam*, 559.

147. Langguth, *Our Vietnam*, 483.

148. Karnow, *Vietnam*, 562, 571–572.

149. Woods, *J. William Fulbright* . . . , 164.

150. *Washington* Post, "Fulbright: "The Idea Is to Influence You into a Wiser Policy," *Washington Post*, March 13, 1968, A10.

151. Washington Post, "Fulbright: "The Idea Is to Influence You into a Wiser Policy."

152. Drew Pearson, "Washington Merry-Go-Round: Vietnam's the Issue in New Hampshire," Washington, DC, *Gadsden Times*, Gadsden, AL, March 12, 1968, 4.

153. Lyndon B. Johnson, "Remarks of the President to the Foreign Policy Briefing, the State Department," Office of the White House Press Secretary, White House, Washington, DC, 19 March 1968, Series 48 Foreign Relations Committee, 48-3 Committee Administration, Box 16, Folder 5, 1968, Fulbright Papers, University of Arkansas Library (Fayetteville, AR).

154. Johnson, "Remarks of the President to the Foreign Policy Briefing . . . "

155. John Chamberlain, "These Days: Domino Theory at Work Following Tet Offensive," King Features Syndicate, *Daily News*, Bowling Green, KY, March 17, 1968, 64.

156. Ronnie E. Ford, *Tet 1968: Understanding Surprise* (New York: Frank Cass, 1995), 132; Langguth, *Our Vietnam*, 493.

157. David Wise, "Remember the *Maddox!*" Esquire, April 1968, 123, in Series 48 Foreign Relations Committee, 48-6 Sub-Committees, Hearings, Studies, Investigations, 1967–1969, Box 28. Folder 3, (Hearing—Tonkin Bay Resolution) 1967–1968), 1967–1969, Fulbright Papers, University of Arkansas (Fayetteville, AR).

158. Wise, "Remember the *Maddox!*," 123

159. Wise, "Remember the *Maddox!*," 123

160. Wise, "Remember the *Maddox!*," 123

161. Wise, "Remember the *Maddox!*," 123

162. Wise, "Remember the *Maddox!*," 123

163. Langguth, *Our Vietnam*, 430, 427.

164. Michael H. Hunt, *Lyndon Johnson's War: America's Cold War Crusade in Vietnam 1945–1968* (New York: Hill and Wang, 1996), 113.

165. Lyndon B. Johnson, "The President's Address to the Nation Announcing Steps to Limit the War in Vietnam and Reporting His Decision Not to Seek Reelection, March 31, 1968," in *Public Papers of the Presidents of the United States: Lyndon B. Johnson, 1968–69*. Volume

I, entry 170 (Washington, DC: Government Printing Office, 1970), 469–476, accessed January 6, 2013, http://www.lbjlibrary.net/collections/selected-speeches/1968-january-1969/03-31-1968.html.

166. Lyndon B. Johnson, "Remarks of the President to the Nation," March 31, 1968, Vietnam Task Force, Office of the Secretary of Defense [Part IV. C.]. Evolution of the War. Direct Action: The Johnson Commitments, 1965–1968. Volume VI: C—U.S. Ground Strategy and Force Deployments: 1965–1967. Program 6, 80–81, 86–87, National Archives, Washington, DC, accessed October 11, 2012, http://www.archives.gov/research/pentagon-papers/.

167. Lyndon B. Johnson, "Remarks of the President to the Nation," March 31, 1968

168. Lyndon B. Johnson, "The President's Address to the Nation Announcing Steps to Limit the War . . . "

169. Langguth, *Our Vietnam*, 493.

170. Yoichi Okamoto, Photo, President Lyndon B. Johnson addresses the Nation, announcing a bombing halt in Vietnam and his intention not to run for reelection, March 31, 1968, Photo Archive, Lyndon B. Johnson Presidential Library (Austin, TX), accessed July 26, 2015, http://www.lbjlibrary.net/collections/photo-archive.html.

171. Edwin Newman, "NBC Coverage of President's 31 March 1968 Speech," *NBC Special Report*, NBC, New York, March 31, 1968, Video #0242, "POTUS talk on Vietnam; includes declaration not to run," Audiovisual Material, Motion Pictures, Lyndon B. Johnson Presidential Library (Austin, TX).

172. Edwin Newman, "Kennedy Comments on LBJ 31 March Speech," *NBC News Special Report*, NBC, 1 April 1968, Video #0246, "Robert Kennedy comments on POTUS speech," Audiovisual Material, Motion Pictures, Lyndon B. Johnson Presidential Library (Austin, TX).

173. Carl Marcy, memorandum for Senator J. William Fulbright with thoughts on President Johnson's decision not to run for reelection, U.S. Senate Committee on Foreign Relations, Washington, DC, April 3, 1968, Series 48 Foreign Relations Committee, 48-3 Committee Administration, Box 16, Folder 5, 1968, Fulbright Papers, University of Arkansas Library (Fayetteville, AR).

174. Jesse Peter Merlan, "Pay My Share," Moscow, ID, *Lewiston Morning Tribune*, Lewiston, ID, April 27, 1968, 4.

175. C. L. Sulzberger, "LBJ Vietnam Concessions Mark Domino Theory Death," Paris, *New York Times*, *Press-Courier*, Oxnard, CA, April 7, 1968, 6.

176. Gallup Organization, *Gallup Poll #1968-0760: 1968 Presidential Election/Vietnam* (Williamstown, MA: The Roper Public Opinion Research Center, April 4–9, 1968), 10.

177. Gallup, *Gallup Poll #1968-0760: 1968 Presidential Election/Vietnam*, 11–19.

178. John W. Kole, "Don't Miscalculate, Rusk Tells Hanoi," Washington, DC, *Milwaukee Journal*, Milwaukee, WI, April 18, 1968, 2.

179. Jim Lowenstein [Senate Foreign Relations Committee staffer], memorandum for Carl Marcy about status of negotiations in Paris, U.S. Senate Committee on Foreign Relations, Washington, DC, June 11, 1968, Series 48 Foreign Relations Committee, 48-3 Committee Administration, Box 16, Folder 5, 1968, Fulbright Papers, University of Arkansas Library (Fayetteville, AR).

180. SDS, *An Introduction* (Chicago, IL: Students for a Democratic Society, 1968), 4.

181. California Peace and Freedom Movement, "California Peace and Freedom Movement Program," Founding Convention, Richmond, CA, March 1968, reprinted in *The New Left: A Documentary History* by Massimo Teodori (Indianapolis, IN: Bobbs-Merrill, 1969), 408.

182. Carl Oglesby "An Open Letter to McCarthy Supporters," 1968, in *The New Left: A Documentary History* by Massimo Teodori (Indianapolis, IN: Bobbs-Merrill, 1969), 412.
183. Roger Mudd, Robert F. Kennedy, "Senator Robert F. Kennedy's Announcement to Run for the Presidency," *CBS News Special Report*, Live from Washington, March 16, 1968, Video #0214-A, "Coverage of Sen. Kennedy's candidacy announcement," Audiovisual Material, Motion Pictures, Lyndon B. Johnson Presidential Library (Austin, TX).
184. Mudd, Kennedy, "Senator Robert F. Kennedy's Announcement to Run for the Presidency."
185. Frank Reynolds (moderator), Bill Lawrence (ABC News Editor), Bob Clark, Robert F. Kennedy, Eugene McCarthy, "*Issues and Answers* with Kennedy vs. McCarthy," *Issues and Answers*, ABC, June 1, 1968, Video #0981, "Issues and answers: RFK vs. Sen. Eugene McCarthy," Audiovisual Material, Motion Pictures, Lyndon B. Johnson Presidential Library (Austin, TX).
186. Reynolds, et al., "*Issues and Answers* with Kennedy vs. McCarthy."
187. Roger Mudd, Robert F. Kennedy, "Senator Robert F. Kennedy's Announcement to Run For The Presidency," *CBS News Special Report*, Live from Washington, 16 March 1968, Video #0214-A, "Coverage of Sen. Kennedy's candidacy announcement," Audiovisual Material, Motion Pictures, Lyndon B. Johnson Presidential Library (Austin, TX).
188. Mudd, Kennedy, "Senator Robert F. Kennedy's Announcement to Run for the Presidency."
189. Barbara Coleman, Erwin Knoll, "*Here's Barbara*: Credibility Gap," *Here's Barbara*, WJLA (ABC), Washington, DC, June 28, 1968, Video #1331, "*Here's Barbara* on Credibility Gap," Audiovisual Material, Motion Pictures, Lyndon B. Johnson Presidential Library (Austin, TX).
190. David Frost, Bill Moyers (*Newsweek*), Dick Goodwin, "*Tonight Show* featuring guests: Bill Moyers & Dick Goodwin," *Tonight Show*, NBC, July 5, 1968, Video #1401, "*Tonight*, with Bill Moyers & Richard Goodwin on campaign 68," Audiovisual Material, Motion Pictures, Lyndon B. Johnson Presidential Library (Austin, TX).
191. Gallup Organization, *Gallup Poll #1968-0765: 1968 Presidential Election* (Williamstown, MA: The Roper Public Opinion Research Center, July 18–23, 1968), 9–14.
192. Gallup Organization, *Gallup Poll #1968-0766: 1968 Presidential Election/Birth Control* (Williamstown, MA: The Roper Public Opinion Research Center, August 7–12, 1968), 7–11.
193. Gallup, *Gallup Poll #1968-0765: 1968 Presidential Election*, 16.
194. John Chamberlain, "The Domino Theory Takes Over at Home," *Evening Independent*, St. Petersburg, FL, July 2, 1968, 12-A
195. Joseph Alsop, "Matter of Fact: Harsh Recall to Reality," *Washington Post*, Washington, DC, *Daytona Beach Sunday News-Journal*, Daytona Beach, FL, August 25, 1968, 2C.
196. Albert Parry, "Why Moscow Couldn't Stand Prague's Deviation," *New York Times*, September 1, 1968, ProQuest Historical Newspapers: *The New York Times* (1851–2009) with Index (1851–1993), SM5.
197. Don Maclean, "Capital Capers," Washington, *Reading Eagle*, Reading, PA, August 8, 1968, 22.
198. Karnow, *Vietnam*, 594–596.
199. Langguth, *Our Vietnam*, 515, 517.
200. Langguth, *Our Vietnam*, 515, 517.
201. Herring, *LBJ and Vietnam*, 260–261.
202. Karnow, *Vietnam*, 595.
203. Herring, *LBJ and Vietnam*, 262.
204. NBC Evening News, "Vietnam / Fulbright / McGovern / Nelson," *NBC Evening News*, August 20, 1968, Vanderbilt Television News Archive, Nashville, TN, http://tvnews.vanderbilt.edu/program.pl?ID=441560.

205. NBC Evening News, "Vietnam / Fulbright / McGovern / Nelson."
206. United Press International, "No Concessions, Rusk Urges Panel," United Press International, Washington, DC, *News and Courrier*, Charleston, SC, August 21, 1968, 3A.
207. Frank Reynolds, Howard K. Smith, Eugene McCarthy, George McGovern, Hubert Humphrey, "Sen. McCarthy, Sen. McGovern, and Vice President Humphrey Closing Statements to the California Delegation," *ABC Coverage of the Democratic Convention*, Part II, ABC, August 27, 1968, Video #1851, "HHH, Sen. George McGovern & Sen. Eugene McCarthy address California deleg.," Audiovisual Material, Motion Pictures, Lyndon B. Johnson Presidential Library (Austin, TX).
208. United Press International, "No Concessions, Rusk Urges Panel."
209. Transcript, Carl Albert Oral History Interview IV, August 13, 1969, by Dorothy Pierce McSweeny, Internet Copy, Lyndon B. Johnson Presidential Library (Austin, TX), 9–14.
210. Doug Rossinow, *The Politics of Authenticity: Liberalism, Christianity, and the New Left in America* (New York: Columbia, 1998), 211–248.
211. Frank Reynolds, "Republican National Convention / Nixon," *ABC Evening News*, Tuesday, August 6, 1968, Vanderbilt Television News Archive, Nashville, TN, http://tvnews.vanderbilt.edu/program.pl?ID=1553.
212. Richard Nixon, "Highlights of Nixon Speech Accepting GOP Nomination," Associated Press, Miami Beach, FL, *Evening News*, Newburgh, NY, August 9, 1968, 9A.
213. Robert W. Lucas, "Nixon May Unite Democrats," Global News Service, Miami Beach, FL, *Evening News*, Newburgh, NY, August 9, 1968, 9A.
214. Andrew Tully, "National Whirligig," Miami Beach, FL, *Reading Eagle*, Reading, PA, August 8, 1968, 22.
215. Gallup Organization, *Gallup Poll #1968-0767: 1968 Presidential Election/Vietnam* (Williamstown, MA: The Roper Public Opinion Research Center, September 1–6, 1968), 8–13.
216. Gallup, *Gallup Poll #1968-0767: 1968 Presidential Election/Vietnam*, 20.
217. Nixon, "Highlights of Nixon Speech Accepting GOP Nomination."
218. Gallup, *Gallup Poll #1968-0766: 1968 Presidential Election/Birth Control*, 15–16.
219. Gallup, *Gallup Poll #1968-0767: 1968 Presidential Election/Vietnam*, 21, 22–23.
220. Gallup Organization, *Gallup Poll #1968-0768: 1968 Presidential Election/Vietnam* (Williamstown, MA: The Roper Public Opinion Research Center, September 19–24, 1968), 8–11.
221. New York Times, "Not Much Help From L.B.J.," *New York Times*, September 14, 1968, ProQuest Historical Newspapers: *The New York Times* (1851–2009) with Index (1851–1993), 30.
222. Harry Reasoner, "Unruh / Government Criticism," *CBS Evening News*, Thursday, October 10, 1968, Vanderbilt Television News Archive, Nashville, TN, http://tvnews.vanderbilt.edu/program.pl?ID=197853.
223. Gallup Organization, *Gallup Poll #1968-0769: Presidential Election/Political Parties* (Williamstown, MA: The Roper Public Opinion Research Center, September 26–October 1, 1968), 15.
224. Organization, *Gallup Poll #1968-0768: 1968 Presidential Election/Vietnam*, 11–12.
225. Transcript, George Ball Oral History Interview II, July 9, 1971, by Paige E. Mulhollan, Internet Copy, Lyndon B. Johnson Presidential Library (Austin, TX), 28–30.
226. R. W. Apple, Jr. [Special to *The New York Times*], "Humphrey Vows Halt in Bombing If Hanoi Reacts: A 'Risk for Peace' . . . ," *New York Times*, October 1, 1968, ProQuest Historical Newspapers: *The New York Times* (1851–2010) with Index (1851–1993), 1.

227. Gallup, *Gallup Poll #1968-0768: 1968 Presidential Election/Vietnam*, 8–11.

228. John L. Fisher, "Humphrey Maneuver," *New York Times*, October 18, 1968, ProQuest Historical Newspapers: *The New York Times* (1851–2010) with Index (1851–1993), 46.

229. Gallup Organization, *Gallup Poll #1968-0770: Presidential Election/Political Party* (Williamstown, MA: The Roper Public Opinion Research Center, October 17–22, 1968), 19.

230. Max Frankel [Special to *The New York Times*], "Bomb Halt Buoys Humphrey but Effect Is Unclear," *New York Times*, November 2, 1968, ProQuest Historical Newspapers: *The New York Times* (1851–2010) with Index (1851–1993), 21.

231. Langguth, *Our Vietnam*, 514–527.

232. Morris McLemore, "'Nation Needs Broad Review of Foreign Policy,'" Tallahassee, FL, *Miami News*, May 17, 1968, 6-A.

233. Maurice Carroll, "O'Dwyer Calls for U.N. to Arrange a Cease-Fire," *New York Times*, July 10, 1968, 21, ProQuest Historical Newspapers: *The New York Times* (1851–2009) with Index (1851–1993).

234. Jim Burnes, Frank Reynolds, "Oregon Senate Race," *ABC Evening News*, October 14, 1968, Vanderbilt Television News Archive, Nashville, TN, http://tvnews.vanderbilt.edu/program.pl?ID=69.

235. Ernest Cuneo, "Tumbling Dominoes: Manila Signals End to Pacific Alliance," North American Newspaper Alliance, Washington, DC, *Youngstown Vindicator*, Youngstown, OH, January 11, 1969, 10.

236. *US News & World Report*, "'What's Expected of a New President: Nationwide Survey,'" *US News & World Report*, December 16, 1968, 32, Series 48 Foreign Relations Committee, 48-1 General 1968–1969, Box 9, Folder 3, Fulbright Papers, University of Arkansas (Fayetteville, AR).

237. NBC Evening News, "Nixon / Klein," *NBC Evening News*, November 25, 1968, Vanderbilt Television News Archive, http://tvnews.vanderbilt.edu.er.lib.k-state.edu/diglib-fulldisplay.pl?SID=2013010979528808&code=tvn&RC=440816&Row=1.

238. Gallup Organization, *Gallup Poll #1968-0771: Elections/Vietnam* (Williamstown, MA: The Roper Public Opinion Research Center, November 9–14, 1968), 17–18.

239. The Gallup Organization, *Gallup Poll #1968-0772: Richard Nixon/The Year 1969* (Williamstown, MA: The Roper Public Opinion Research Center, December 5–10, 1968), 6–11.

240. The Gallup Organization, *Gallup Poll #773* (Williamstown, MA: The Roper Public Opinion Research Center, January 1–6, 1969), 9.

241. Lyndon B. Johnson, "Annual Message to the Congress on the State of the Union, January 14, 1969," *Public Papers of the Presidents of the United States: Lyndon B. Johnson, 1968–69*. Volume II, entry 676 (Washington, D. C.: Government Printing Office, 1970), 1263–1270, accessed January 6, 2013, http://www.lbjlibrary.net/collections/selected-speeches/1968-january-1969/01-14-1969.html.

Chapter 5

1. John M. Shaw, *The Cambodian Campaign: The 1970 Offensive and America's Vietnam War* (Lawrence, KS: University Press of Kansas, 2005), 15; George C. Herring, *America's Longest War: The United States and Vietnam, 1950–1975* (Boston: McGraw-Hill, 2002), 267.

2. Herring, *America's Longest War*, 284–285.

3. Gallup Organization, *Gallup Poll #774: Israel and Middle East Nations/China/Environment* (Williamstown, MA: The Roper Public Opinion Research Center, 23–28 January 1969), 9.

4. Associated Press, "The Domino Theory," Associated Press, Bangkok, *Gettysburg Times*, Gettysburg, PA, January 25, 1969, 7.

5. Associated Press, "The Domino Theory."

6. Associated Press, "The Domino Theory."

7. Associated Press, "Had No Real Alternative in Vietnam, Writes LBJ," Associated Press, New York, *Spartanburg Herald*, Spartanburg, SC, January 28, 1969.

8. Associated Press, "Had No Real Alternative in Vietnam, Writes LBJ."

9. New York Times News Service, "Had to Stop Reds in Viet, LBJ Claims," *New York Times* News Service, Washington, *Miami News*, Miami, FL, January 29, 1969, 20-C.

10. Associated Press, "Had No Real Alternative in Vietnam, Writes LBJ."

11. Walter Cronkite, Eric Sevareid, "Analysis (Rogers' Speech)," *CBS Evening News*, Thursday, March 27, 1969, Vanderbilt Television News Archive, Nashville, TN, http://tvnews. vanderbilt.edu/program.pl?ID=202841.

12. Walter Cronkite, Marvin Kalb, "Anti-Ballistic Missile / Panofsky / Symington," *CBS Evening News*, Friday, March 28, 1969, Vanderbilt Television News Archive, Nashville, TN, http://tvnews.vanderbilt.edu/program.pl?ID=202847.

13. Harry Reasoner, Eric Sevareid, "Analysis (Nixon News Conference)," *CBS Evening News*, Friday, April 18, 1969, Vanderbilt Television News Archive, Nashville, TN, http://tvnews. vanderbilt.edu/program.pl?ID=203148.

14. John W. Finney, Special to *The New York Times*, "Vietnam Pullout Urged as Senate Resumes Debate: Moratorium on Criticism of Nixon Ends-Aiken Asks 'Orderly Withdrawal,'" Washington, DC, *New York Times*, May 2, 1969, ProQuest Historical Newspapers: *The New York Times* (1851–2009) with Index (1851–1993), 1.

15. I. F. Stone, "Same Old Formulas, Same Tired Rhetoric," *I. F. Stone's Weekly*, June 2, 1969, reprinted in *The Best of I. F. Stone* by I. F. Stone, ed. by Karl Weber (New York: Public Affairs, 2006), 290.

16. Gallup Organization, *Gallup Poll #1969-0776: Ratings of Leaders* (Williamstown, MA: The Roper Public Opinion Research Center, March 12–17, 1969), 10–11.

17. Gallup Organization, *Gallup Poll #1969-0781: Vietnam/Supreme Court* (Williamstown, MA: The Roper Public Opinion Research Center, May 22–27, 1969), 13–14.

18. Gallup Organization, *Gallup Poll #1969-0777: Food Stamps/Anti-Ballistic Missiles Program* (Williamstown, MA: The Roper Public Opinion Research Center, March 27–April 1, 1969), 6.

19. A.J. Langguth, *Our Vietnam: The War 1954–1975* (New York: Simon & Schuster, 2000), 544–545; William Beecher, "Raids in Cambodia by U.S. Unprotested," *New York Times*, May 9, 1969, 1.

20. Gallup, *Gallup Poll #1969-0781: Vietnam/Supreme Court*, 13–14.

21. William F. Buckley, "On The Right: Some Thoughts on Vietnam," *Morning Record*, Meriden-Wallingford, CT, April 1, 1969, 6.

22. Buckley, "On the Right: Some Thoughts on Vietnam."

23. Gaddis, *Strategies of Containment*, 274–308.

24. Richard Nixon, "Joint Statement Following the Meeting with President Thieu," June 8, 1969, Online by Gerhard Peters and John T. Woolley, *The American Presidency Project*, University of California San Bernardino, accessed March 8, 2015, http://www.presidency. ucsb.edu/ws/?pid=2089

25. United Press International, "Nixon to Withdraw 25,000 Troops within Thirty Days," United Press International, Midway Island, *Herald-Tribune*, Sarasota, FL, 1.

26. NBC Evening News, "Midway Meeting / Thieu / Withdrawal / Laird," NBC, June 9, 1969, Vanderbilt Television News Archive, http://tvnews.vanderbilt.edu/ program. pl?ID=446374, accessed April 23, 2009.

27. Gallup Organization, *Gallup Poll #1969-0783: Vietnam/Epilepsy* (Williamstown, MA: The Roper Public Opinion Research Center, June 19–24, 1969), 5–6.

28. J. Edward Lee and H. C. "Toby" Haynsworth, *Nixon, Ford and the Abandonment of South Vietnam* (Jefferson, NC: McFarland, 2002), 27.

29. Gallup Organization, *Gallup Poll #1969-0784: Vietnam/Views of Large Cities/ABM Program/ Racial Integration* (Williamstown, MA: The Roper Public Opinion Research Center, July 10–15, 1969), 5–7.

30. Stuart Symington, "Planned Senate Hearings on Laos," speech delivered on the floor of the Senate, Washington, DC, 19 September 1969, Series 48 Foreign Relations Committee, 48-3 Committee Administration, Box 17, Folder 1, 1969, Fulbright Papers, University of Arkansas (Fayetteville, AR).

31. Associated Press, "Nixon to Withdraw 35,000 U.S. Troops from Vietnam; 'Bring an End to The War,'" Associated Press, Washington, DC, *Gettysburg Times,* Gettysburg, PA, 1.

32. Gallup Organization, *Gallup Poll #1969-0786: Nixon/Presidential Election* (Williamstown, MA: The Roper Public Opinion Research Center, August 14–19, 1969), 10.

33. Gallup Organization, *Gallup Poll #788* (Williamstown, MA: The Roper Public Opinion Research Center, September 17–22, 1969), 6.

34. Gallup Organization, *Gallup Poll #0789: Nixon/Vietnam/Marijuana/Birth Control* (Williamstown, MA: The Roper Public Opinion Research Center, October 2–7, 1969), 5, 8.

35. Gallup Organization, *Gallup Poll #0792: The Future/Political Leaders* (Williamstown, MA: The Roper Public Opinion Research Center, October 30–November 4, 1969), 13.

36. Langguth, *Our Vietnam*, 554–555.

37. Walter Cronkite, Bruce Morton, "Vietnam Criticism / Cong.," *CBS Evening News*, October 6, 1969, Vanderbilt Television News Archive, Nashville, TN, http://tvnews.vanderbilt. edu/program.pl?ID=200956.

38. Walter Cronkite, Morton Dean, David Dick, Terry Drinkwater, George Foster, Murray Fromson, Phil Jones, Marvin Kalb, Bruce Morton, Roger Mudd, Ike Pappas, Ed Rabel, Robert Schakne, Bill Stout, "Vietnam / Moratorium / Massachusetts / New York City / Georgia / California / Kansas / Illinois / Wisconsin / Indiana / Iowa / Michigan / Washington, DC," *CBS Evening News*, Wednesday, October 15, 1969, Vanderbilt Television News Archive, Nashville, TN, http://tvnews.vanderbilt.edu/program.pl?ID=200619.

39. Cronkite et al., "Vietnam / Moratorium / Massachusetts / New York City / Georgia . . . "

40. Cronkite et al., "Vietnam / Moratorium / Massachusetts / New York City / Georgia . . . "

41. Cronkite et al., "Vietnam / Moratorium / Massachusetts / New York City / Georgia . . . "

42. Cronkite et al., "Vietnam / Moratorium / Massachusetts / New York City / Georgia . . . "

43. Cronkite et al., "Vietnam / Moratorium / Massachusetts / New York City / Georgia . . . "

44. Cronkite et al., "Vietnam / Moratorium / Massachusetts / New York City / Georgia . . . "

45. Langguth, *Our Vietnam,* 554–555.

46. Richard Nixon, "Support of Nation Sought in Search for Peace," Associated Press, Washington, DC, *Spokane Daily Chronicle*, Spokane, WA, November 4, 1969, 10.

47. Nixon, "Support of Nation Sought in Search for Peace."

48. Nixon, "Support of Nation Sought in Search for Peace."

49. Nixon, "Support of Nation Sought in Search for Peace."

50. Nixon, "Support of Nation Sought in Search for Peace."

51. Nixon, "Support of Nation Sought in Search for Peace."

52. Nixon, "Support of Nation Sought in Search for Peace."

53. Gallup Organization, *Gallup Poll #0793: Vietnam/Most Admired People* (Williamstown, MA: The Roper Public Opinion Research Center, November 12–17, 1969), 9–10.

54. Bill Downs, Tom Jarriel, Keith McBee, Howard K. Smith, "Vets Day / President / Washington, DC Activities / California," *ABC Evening News*, Tuesday, November 11, 1969, Vanderbilt Television News Archive, Nashville, TN, http://tvnews.vanderbilt.edu/program.pl?ID=2952.

55. Gallup Organization, *Gallup Poll #0791: Vietnam War/Finances/Politics* (Williamstown, MA: The Roper Public Opinion Research Center, October 17–22, 1969), 13.

56. Gallup, *Gallup Poll #0793: Vietnam/Most Admired People*, 5.

57. Gallup, "Gallup Poll #1969-0777: Food Stamps/Anti-Ballistic Missiles Program," Gallup, March 26–April 1, 1969; Langguth, *Our Vietnam*, 554.

58. Gallup, "Gallup Poll #1969-0795: Vietnam," Gallup, December 12–15, 1969.

59. Gallup, *Gallup Poll #0793: Vietnam/Most Admired People*, 6–9.

60. James Weinstein, "Weatherman: A Lot Of Thunder but a Short Reign," *Socialist Revolution*, January–February 1970, reprinted in *Weatherman* ed. by Harold Jacobs, (San Francisco: Ramparts, 1970), 223.

61. Doug Rossinow, *The Politics of Authenticity: Liberalism, Christianity, and the New Left in America* (New York: Columbia, 1998), 211–248.

62. Karin Asbley, Bill Ayers, Bernardine Dohrn, John Jacobs, Jeff Jones, Gerry Long, Home Machtinger, Jim Mellen, Terry Robbins, Mark Rudd and Steve Tappis, "You Don't Need a Weatherman to Know Which Way the Wind Blows," *New Left Notes*, June 18, 1969, reprinted in *Weatherman* ed. by Harold Jacobs, (San Francisco: Ramparts, 1970), 34.

63. Andrew Kopkind, "The Real SDS Stands Up," *Hard Times*, June 30, 1969, reprinted in *Weatherman* ed. by Harold Jacobs (San Francisco: Ramparts, 1970), 22.

64. Tom Hayden, "Justice in the Streets," in *Trial* by Holt, Rinehart, Winston, Tom Hayden, 1970, reprinted in *Weatherman* ed. by Harold Jacobs, (San Francisco: Ramparts, 1970), 173–174; Associated Press, "Moratorium Continues after Night of Violence," Associated Press, Washington, DC, *Free Lance-Star*, Fredricksburg, VA, November 15, 1969, 1.

65. David Horowitz, "Hand-Me-Down Marxism in the New Left," *Ramparts*, September 1969, reprinted in *Weatherman* ed. by Harold Jacobs, (San Francisco: Ramparts, 1970), 60.

66. Carl Oglesby, "1969," in "Notes on a Decade Ready for the Dustbin," *Liberation*, August–September 1969, reprinted in *Weatherman* ed. by Harold Jacobs, (San Francisco: Ramparts, 1970), 74.

67. Andrew Kopkind, "The Radical Bombers," *Hard Times*, March 23, 1970, reprinted in *Weatherman* ed. by Harold Jacobs, (San Francisco: Ramparts, 1970), 290.

68. Frank Reynolds, Howard K. Smith, "Commentary (Fulbright and Military)," *ABC Evening News*, May 19, 1969, Vanderbilt Television News Archive, Nashville, TN, http://tvnews.vanderbilt.edu/program.pl?ID=5271.

69. Frank Reynolds, Howard K. Smith, "Commentary (Vietnam Commitment)," *ABC Evening News*, June 17, 1969, Vanderbilt Television News Archive, Nashville, TN, http://tvnews.vanderbilt.edu/program.pl?ID=5750.

70. Transcript, Clark M. Clifford Oral History Interview II, 7/2/69, by Paige Mulhollan, Internet Copy, Lyndon B. Johnson Presidential Library (Austin, TX), 10–11.

71. Clark M. Clifford, "A Viet Nam Reappraisal: The Personal History of One Man's View and How It Evolved," *Foreign Affairs*, Council on Foreign Relations, Vol. 47, No. 4 (July 1969): 601–622.

72. Recording of Telephone Conversation between Lyndon B. Johnson and Richard Russell, June 11, 1964, 12:26PM, Citation #3681, Recordings of Telephone Conversations—White House Series, Recordings and Transcripts of Conversations and Meetings, Lyndon B. Johnson Presidential Library (Austin, TX).

73. Transcript, Dean Rusk Oral History Interview II, September 26, 1969, by Paige E. Mulhollan, Internet Copy, Lyndon B. Johnson Presidential Library (Austin, TX), 9–11.

74. Transcript, Dean Rusk Oral History Interview II, September 26, 1969, 9–11.

75. Transcript, Dean Rusk Oral History Interview II, September 26, 1969, 9–11.

76. Bob Clark, Howard K. Smith, "Vietnam / Tonkin Resolution / Protests / McGovern," *ABC Evening News*, Tuesday, 14 October 1969, Vanderbilt Television News Archive, Nashville, TN, http://tvnews.vanderbilt.edu/program.pl?ID=2521.

77. NBC Evening News, "Gulf of Tonkin Resolution," *NBC Evening News*, October 14, 1969, Vanderbilt Television News Archive, accessed January 9, 2013, http://tvnews.vanderbilt.edu.er.lib.k-state.edu/diglib-fulldisplay.pl?SID=2013010979528808&code=tvn&RC=442820&Row=97.

78. Clark, Smith, "Vietnam / Tonkin Resolution / Protests / McGovern."

79. US Senate Committee on Foreign Relations, "Termination of Southeast Asia Resolution," draft Committee report on Tonkin Gulf Resolution, U.S. Senate Committee on Foreign Relations, Washington, DC, 1 May 1970, Series 48 Foreign Relations Committee, 48-3 Committee Administration, Box 17, Folder 4, 1970, Fulbright Papers, University of Arkansas (Fayetteville, AR).

80. Beggs, *The Vietnam War Dissent . . .* , 250.

81. NBC Evening News, "Gulf of Tonkin Resolution."

82. U.S. Senate Committee on Foreign Relations, "Termination of Southeast Asia Resolution."

83. U.S. Senate Committee on Foreign Relations, "Termination of Southeast Asia Resolution."

84. Bob Clark, Frank Reynolds, "Vietnam / Mathias," *ABC Evening News*, Monday, December 8, 1969, Vanderbilt Television News Archive, Nashville, TN, http://tvnews.vanderbilt.edu/program.pl?ID=3689.

85. Clark, Reynolds, "Vietnam / Mathias."

86. Charles Mathias Jr. [US Senator], form letter to fellow senators asking for support of a resolution to repeal Tonkin Gulf and other resolutions, US Senate, Washington, DC, December 1, 1969, Series 48 Foreign Relations Committee, 48-1 General 1968–1969, Box 9, Folder 4, Fulbright Papers, University of Arkansas (Fayetteville, AR).

87. NBC Evening News "Senate Hearing / Agnew," *NBC Evening News*, February 5, 1970, Vanderbilt Television News Archive, accessed 9 January 2013, http://tvnews.vanderbilt.edu.er.lib.k-state.edu/diglib-fulldisplay.pl?SID=2013010979528808&code=tvn&RC=450106&Row=91.

88. NBC Evening News "Senate Hearing / Agnew."

89. Gallup Organization, *Gallup Poll #0795: Vietnam* (Williamstown, MA: The Roper Public Opinion Research Center, December 12–15, 1969), 12.

90. Stuart Symington, "Statement by Senator Stuart Symington (D-MO), Senate Floor, February 16, 1970: Laos," Washington, DC, February 16, 1970, Series 48 Foreign Relations Committee, 48-3 Committee Administration, Box 17, Folder 4, 1970, Fulbright Papers, University of Arkansas (Fayetteville, AR).

91. Walter Cronkite, Dan Rather, "Nixon's Credibility / Laos + Busing," *CBS Evening News*, Tuesday, March 10, 1970, Vanderbilt Television News Archive, Nashville, TN, http://tvnews.vanderbilt.edu/program.pl?ID=208614.

92. Stuart Symington, "Why the Long Delay in Releasing the Laos Testimony?" speech delivered on the floor of the Senate, Washington, DC, 26 March 1970, Series 48 Foreign Relations Committee, 48-3 Committee Administration, Box 17, Folder 4, 1970, Fulbright Papers, University of Arkansas (Fayetteville, AR).

93. Stanley Karnow, "Events Proving Out Thesis of a Second Indochina War," Hong Kong, *Washington Post*, March 30, 1970, A17, in Series 48 Foreign Relations Committee, 48-3 Committee Administration, Box 17, Folder 4, 1970, Fulbright Papers, University of Arkansas (Fayetteville, AR).

94. Howard K. Smith, George Watson, "Vietnam / Bunker," *ABC Evening News*, Tuesday, April 28, 1970, Vanderbilt Television News Archive, Nashville, TN, http://tvnews.vanderbilt.edu/program.pl?ID=10152.

95. Walter Cronkite, "Gulf of Tonkin Resolution," *CBS Evening News*, Friday, February 6, 1970, Vanderbilt Television News Archive, Nashville, TN, http://tvnews.vanderbilt.edu/program.pl?ID=208581.

96. Howard K. Smith, "LBJ / Vietnam," *ABC Evening News*, Friday, February 6, 1970, Vanderbilt Television News Archive, Nashville, TN, http://tvnews.vanderbilt.edu/program.pl?ID=9438.

97. Cronkite, "Gulf of Tonkin Resolution," Friday, February 6, 1970.

98. Smith, "LBJ / Vietnam," Friday, February 6, 1970.

99. Cronkite, "Gulf of Tonkin Resolution," Friday, February 6, 1970.

100. Cronkite, "Gulf of Tonkin Resolution," Friday, February 6, 1970.

101. Cronkite, "Gulf of Tonkin Resolution," Friday, February 6, 1970.

102. Smith, "LBJ / Vietnam," Friday, February 6, 1970.

103. Cronkite, "Gulf of Tonkin Resolution," Friday, February 6, 1970.

104. Cronkite, "Gulf of Tonkin Resolution," Friday, February 6, 1970.

105. Cronkite, "Gulf of Tonkin Resolution," Friday, February 6, 1970.

106. Tom Jarriel, Frank Reynolds, "Administration / Senate / Tonkin Resolution," *ABC Evening News*, Tuesday, June 23, 1970, Vanderbilt Television News Archive, Nashville, TN, http://tvnews.vanderbilt.edu/program.pl?ID=10836.

107. Walter Cronkite, "Vietnam / Gulf of Tonkin," *CBS Evening News*, Tuesday, October 14, 1969, Vanderbilt Television News Archive, Nashville, http://tvnews.vanderbilt.edu/program.pl?ID=200595.

108. NBC Evening News, "Vietnam Hearing," *NBC Evening News*, February 4, 1970, Vanderbilt Television News Archive, accessed January 9, 2013, http://tvnews.vanderbilt.edu.er.lib.k-state.edu/diglib-fulldisplay.pl?SID=2013010979528808&code=tvn&RC=450086&Row=92.

109. Howard K. Smith, "Tonkin Resolution / Repeal," *ABC Evening News*, Friday, April 10, 1970, Vanderbilt Television News Archive, Nashville, TN, http://tvnews.vanderbilt.edu/program.pl?ID=9897.

110. NBC Evening News, "Tonkin Resolution/Fulbright," *NBC Evening News*, March 13, 1970, Vanderbilt Television News Archive, accessed January 9, 2013, http://tvnews.vanderbilt.edu.er.lib.k-state.edu/tvn-video-view.pl?SID=2013010979528808&code=tvn&RC=450218.

111. NBC Evening News, "Tonkin Resolution / Repeal / Reactions," *NBC Evening News*, June 24, 1970, Vanderbilt Television News Archive, accessed January 10, 2013, http://tvnews.vanderbilt.edu.er.lib.k-state.edu/diglib-fulldisplay.pl?SID=20130110500030517&code=tvn&RC=451728&Row=74.

112. NBC Evening News, "Tonkin Resolution/Fulbright," *NBC Evening News*, March 13, 1970, Vanderbilt Television News Archive, accessed January 9, 2013, http://tvnews.vanderbilt.edu.er.lib.k-state.edu/tvn-video-view.pl?SID=2013010979528808&code=tvn&RC=450218.

113. Walter Cronkite, "Tonkin Gulf Resolution," *CBS Evening News*, Friday, March 13, 1970, Vanderbilt Television News Archive, Nashville, TN, http://tvnews.vanderbilt.edu/program.pl?ID=208686.

114. Howard K. Smith, "Tonkin Resolution / Repeal," *ABC Evening News*, Friday, April 10, 1970, Vanderbilt Television News Archive, Nashville, TN, http://tvnews.vanderbilt.edu/program.pl?ID=9897.

115. Harry Reasoner, "Senate / Tonkin Resolution," *CBS Evening News*, Friday, April 10, 1970, Vanderbilt Television News Archive, Nashville, TN, http://tvnews.vanderbilt.edu/program.pl?ID=209171.

116. NBC Evening News, "Senate / Tonkin Resolution," *NBC Evening News*, April 10, 1970, Vanderbilt Television News Archive, accessed January 10, 2013, http://tvnews.vanderbilt.edu.er.lib.k-state.edu/diglib-fulldisplay.pl?SID=20130110500030517&code=tvn&RC=450635&Row=82.

117. Gallup Organization, *Gallup Poll #797* (Williamstown, MA: The Roper Public Opinion Research Center, January 15–20, 1970), 8.

118. Gallup Organization, *Gallup Poll #800* (Williamstown, MA: The Roper Public Opinion Research Center, February 26–March 2, 1970), 5.

119. Joseph Alsop, "Nixon Would Be Wise to Heed Abram's Call for Pullout Pause," Bien Hoa, South Vietnam, *Los Angeles Times*, 30 March 1970, in Series 48 Foreign Relations Committee, 48-3 Committee Administration, Box 17, Folder 4, 1970, Fulbright Papers, University of Arkansas (Fayetteville, AR).

120. Herring, *America's Longest War*, 287–288.

121. Shaw, *The Cambodian Campaign*, 17–22, 267, 284–285.

122. Shaw, *The Cambodian Campaign*, 21–24; Herring, *America's Longest War*, 290.

123. Herring, *America's Longest War*, 288–290; Shaw, *The Cambodian Campaign*, 24–28.

124. Stuart Symington, letter to the editor of the *Washington Post* about administration delay in releasing transcript from Laos hearings, 28 April 1970, Series 48 Foreign Relations Committee, 48-3 Committee Administration, Box 17, Folder 4, 1970, Fulbright Papers, University of Arkansas (Fayetteville, AR).

125. Herring, *America's Longest War*, 290; Langguth, *Our Vietnam*, 562, 564–565.

126. NBC Evening News, "Cambodia / Congress / White House," NBC, April 30, 1970, Vanderbilt Television News Archive, http://tvnews.vanderbilt.edu/program.pl?ID=450931, accessed April 25, 2009.

127. Herring, *America's Longest War*, 290; Langguth, *Our Vietnam*, 562, 564–565.

128. Herring, *America's Longest War*, 292; Shaw, *The Cambodian Campaign*, 162.

129. Richard Nixon, "Address to the Nation on the Situation in Southeast Asia," April 30, 1970, online by Gerhard Peters and John T. Woolley, *The American Presidency Project*, University of California San Bernardino, accessed April 4, 2015, http://www.presidency.ucsb.edu/ws/?pid=2490.

130. Nixon, "Address to the Nation on the Situation in Southeast Asia," April 30, 1970.

131. Nixon, "Address to the Nation on the Situation in Southeast Asia," April 30, 1970.

132. Herring, *America's Longest War*, 291; Langguth, *Our Vietnam*, 566.

133. Associated Press, "Nixon Praises Troops, Contrasts Them with 'Bums' Blowing Up Campuses," Associated Press, Washington, DC, *Lewiston Evening Journal*, Lewiston-Auburn, ME, May 1, 1970, 1.

134. United Press International, "Students Protest College Slayings," *Beaver County Times*, Beaver County, PA, May 18, 1970, 22; Herring, *America's Longest War*, 293.

135. Herring, *America's Longest War*, 154.

136. Department of Justice, "Ohio National Guard Troops on the Kent State University Campus," 4 May 1970, Office of the U.S. Attorney for the Northern Judicial District of Ohio, from the United States of America v. Lawrence Shafer, James Pierce, William Perkins, James McGee, Barry Morris, Ralph Zoller, Matthew McManus, Leon Smith (Fire Bombing and Shooting at Kent State), National Archives at Chicago, (Chicago, IL), accessed September 19, 2015, https://catalog.archives.gov/id/18542766?q=kent%20state.

137. New University, flyer for the Washington student strike's New University, Seattle, WA, May 1970, Photo and Document Repository, Harry Bridges Center for Labor History, University of Washington, Seattle, WA, accessed March 31, 2015, http://depts.washington.edu/labpics/repository/main.php?g2_itemId=2551&g2_GALLERYSID=TMP_SESSION_ID_DI_NOISSES_PMT.

138. Strike organizing committee, "Statement about the Kent State killings and announcement of student strike," Chapel Hill, NC, May 5, 1970, Records of the Office of the Chancellor—J. Carlyle Sitterson series (#40022), University Archives, Wilson Library, University of North Carolina at Chapel Hill, http://exhibits.lib.unc.edu/items/show/874, accessed March 31, 2015.

139. NBC Evening News, "Washington, DC / Antiwar Lobbies," NBC, May 11, 1970, Vanderbilt Television News Archive, http://tvnews.vanderbilt.edu/program.pl?ID=451067, accessed April 25, 2009.

140. The Gallup Organization, *Gallup Poll #811* (Williamstown, MA: The Roper Public Opinion Research Center, July 31–August 2, 1970), 5–8.

141. Gallup, *Gallup Poll #811*, 5–8.

142. Gallup, *Gallup Poll #811*, 8.

143. Gallup Organization, *Gallup Poll #804* (Williamstown, MA: The Roper Public Opinion Research Center, April 17–19, 1970), 5.

144. Gallup Organization, *Gallup Poll #806* (Williamstown, MA: The Roper Public Opinion Research Center, April 29–May 3, 1970), 5–14.

145. Gallup, *Gallup Poll #806*, 5–14.

146. I.F. Stone, "Only the Bums Can Save the Country Now," *I. F. Stone's Weekly*, May 18, 1970, reprinted in *The Best of I. F. Stone* by I. F. Stone, ed. by Karl Weber (New York: Public Affairs, 2006), 293–294.

147. NBC Evening News, "Nixon / Cambodia Speech / Reactions," NBC, May 1, 1970, Vanderbilt Television News Archive, http://tvnews.vanderbilt.edu/program.pl?ID=451037, accessed April 25, 2009.

148. Thomas Carvlin, "Nixon Invites Senate and House Groups to Cambodia Meeting," Chicago Tribune Press Service, Washington, DC, *Chicago Tribune*, May 2, 1970, 3.

149. U.S. Senate Committee on Foreign Relations, "Termination of Southeast Asia Resolution," draft Committee report on Tonkin Gulf Resolution, US Senate Committee on Foreign Relations, Washington, DC, May 1, 1970, Series 48 Foreign Relations Committee, 48-3 Committee Administration, Box 17, Folder 4, 1970, Fulbright Papers, University of Arkansas (Fayetteville, AR).

150. U.S. Senate Committee on Foreign Relations, "Termination of Southeast Asia Resolution."

151. Bob Clark, Frank Reynolds, "Senate / Cambodia / President," *ABC Evening News* Monday, June 22, 1970, Vanderbilt Television News Archive, Nashville, TN, http://tvnews.vanderbilt.edu/program.pl?ID=10819.

152. Walter Cronkite, Bruce Morton, "Senate / Cambodia," *CBS Evening News*, Tuesday, June 9, 1970, Vanderbilt Television News Archive, Nashville, TN, http://tvnews.vanderbilt. edu/program.pl?ID=210779.

153. Clark, Reynolds, "Senate / Cambodia / President," *ABC Evening News* Monday, June 22, 1970.

154. NBC Evening News, "Tonkin Resolution / Repeal," *NBC Evening News*, June 23, 1970, Vanderbilt Television News Archive, accessed 10 January 2013, http://tvnews.vanderbilt. edu.er.lib.k-state.edu/diglib-fulldisplay.pl?SID=20130110500030517&code=tvn&RC=4 51705&Row=79.

155. Tom Jarriel, Frank Reynolds, "Administration / Senate / Tonkin Resolution," *ABC Evening News*, Tuesday, 23 June 1970, Vanderbilt Television News Archive, Nashville, TN, http://tvnews.vanderbilt.edu/program.pl?ID=10836.

156. Bruce Morton, Harry Reasoner, Tony Sargent, "Tonkin Resolution / Repeal," *CBS Evening News*, Wednesday, June 24, 1970, Vanderbilt Television News Archive, Nashville, TN, http://tvnews.vanderbilt.edu/program.pl?ID=210518.

157. Frank Reynolds, "Commentary (US)," *ABC Evening News*, Tuesday, June 23, 1970, Vanderbilt Television News Archive, Nashville, TN, http://tvnews.vanderbilt.edu/pro-gram.pl?ID=10850.

158. Reynolds, "Commentary (US)," Tuesday, June 23, 1970.

159. Reynolds, "Commentary (US)," Tuesday, June 23, 1970.

160. Bruce Morton, Harry Reasoner, Tony Sargent, "Tonkin Resolution / Repeal," *CBS Evening News*, Wednesday, June 24, 1970, Vanderbilt Television News Archive, Nashville, TN, http://tvnews.vanderbilt.edu/program.pl?ID=210518.

161. Bob Clark, Frank Reynolds, "Tonkin Resolution / Repeal," *ABC Evening News*, Wednesday, June 24, 1970, Vanderbilt Television News Archive, Nashville, TN, http:// tvnews.vanderbilt.edu/program.pl?ID=10852.

162. NBC Evening News, "Tonkin Resolution / Nixon," *NBC Evening News*, July 10, 1970, Vanderbilt Television News Archive, accessed January 10, 2013, http://tvnews.vanderbilt. edu/program.pl?ID=451966.

163. NBC Evening News, "Tonkin Resolution / Repeal / Reactions," *NBC Evening News*, 24 June 1970, Vanderbilt Television News Archive, accessed January 10, 2013, http:// tvnews.vanderbilt.edu.er.lib.k-state.edu/diglib-fulldisplay.pl?SID=20130110500030517 &code=tvn&RC=451728&Row=74.

164. Morton, Reasoner, Sargent, "Tonkin Resolution / Repeal," Wednesday, June 24, 1970.

165. NBC Evening News, "Tonkin Resolution / Repeal / Reactions," June 24, 1970.

166. NBC Evening News, "Tonkin Resolution," NBC Evening News, July 28, 1970, Vanderbilt Television News Archive, accessed 10 January 2013, http://tvnews.vanderbilt.edu/pro-gram.pl?ID=452320.

167. NBC Evening News, "Tonkin Resolution / Repeal / Reactions," June 24, 1970.

168. Morton, Reasoner, Sargent, "Tonkin Resolution / Repeal," Wednesday, June 24, 1970.

169. NBC Evening News, "Tonkin Resolution / Repeal / Gruening," *NBC Evening News*, July 12, 1970, Vanderbilt Television News Archive, accessed January 10, 2013, http://tvnews. vanderbilt.edu/program.pl?ID=451989.

170. NBC Evening News, "Tonkin Resolution / Repeal / Gruening," July 12, 1970.

171. NBC Evening News, "Tonkin Resolution / Repeal / Gruening," July 12, 1970.

172. Frank Reynolds, "Commentary (US, Cambodia)," *ABC Evening News*, Thursday, August 6, 1970, Vanderbilt Television News Archive, Nashville, TN, http://tvnews.vanderbilt. edu/program.pl?ID=11905.

173. Gallup, *Gallup Poll #811*, 8, 9.

174. Stephen Geer, Howard K. Smith, George Watson, "Cambodia / Fighting / Nol / United States Aid," *ABC Evening News*, Friday, 21 August 1970, Vanderbilt Television News Archive, Nashville, TN, http://tvnews.vanderbilt.edu/program.pl?ID=11697.

175. Howard K. Smith, "Commentary (Cong. and Vietnam)," *ABC Evening News*, Friday, December 11, 1970, Vanderbilt Television News Archive, Nashville, TN, http://tvnews. vanderbilt.edu/program.pl?ID=8717.

176. Associated Press, "Nixon Sees Impact On Criticism," Associated Press, Washington, DC, *Reading Eagle*, Reading, PA, 19 November 1970, 28.

177. Edward P. Morgan, "Commentary (Administration)," *ABC Evening News*, Friday, November 27, 1970, Vanderbilt Television News Archive, Nashville, TN, http://tvnews. vanderbilt.edu/program.pl?ID=8535.

178. Bill Lawrence, Frank Reynolds, "Commentary (White House Credibility)," *ABC Evening News*, Monday, November 30, 1970, Vanderbilt Television News Archive, Nashville, TN, http://tvnews.vanderbilt.edu/program.pl?ID=8570.

179. NBC Evening News, "Def. Secretary, Pentagon Statements," NBC, January 6, 1971, Vanderbilt Television News Archive, http://tvnews.vanderbilt.edu/program. pl?ID=454060, accessed April 25, 2009.

180. Vanderbilt, "Vanderbilt Television News Archive: Search," Vanderbilt University, http:// tvnews.vanderbilt.edu.er.lib.k-state.edu/tvn-displayindex.pl? SID=20090425768859863 &pagenumber=3&code=tvn, accessed April 25, 2009.

181. Howard K. Smith, "Commentary (Nixon / News Embargo)," *ABC Evening News*, Friday, February 5, 1971, Vanderbilt Television News Archive, Nashville, TN, http://tvnews. vanderbilt.edu/program.pl?ID=14503.

182. Gallup Organization, *Gallup Poll #821* (Williamstown, MA: The Roper Public Opinion Research Center, January 8–11, 1971), 7.

183. Washington Post, "Nixon Says War's End Is in Sight," *Washington Post* Wire Service, Washington, DC, *Palm Beach Post*, Palm Beach, FL, January 5, 1971, 1.

184. Richard Nixon, "Annual Message to the Congress on the State of the Union," January 22, 1971, online by Gerhard Peters and John T. Woolley, The American Presidency Project, University of California San Bernardino, accessed 6 April 2015, http://www.presidency. ucsb.edu/ws/?pid=3110.

185. Herring, *America's Longest War*, 267, 284–285.

186. Herring, *America's Longest War*, 297–298.

187. Walter Cronkite, Marvin Kalb, Bob Schieffer, "Laos Situation," *CBS Evening News*, Wednesday, 03 February 1971, Vanderbilt Television News Archive, Nashville, TN, http://tvnews.vanderbilt.edu/program.pl?ID=215189.

188. NBC Evening News, "Laos / South Vietnam Attack / United States Reaction," NBC, February 8, 1971, Vanderbilt Television News Archive, http://tvnews.vanderbilt.edu/ program.pl?ID=456306, accessed 25 April 2009.

189. NBC Evening News, "Laos / South Vietnam Attack / Situation Analysis," February 24, 1971.

190. NBC Evening News, "Laos / South Vietnam Attack / Situation Analysis," February 24, 1971.

191. NBC Evening News, "Laos / South Vietnam Attack / Situation Analysis," February 24, 1971.

192. Walter Cronkite, Marya McLaughlin, "Jackson / Muskie," *CBS Evening News*, Friday, March 26, 1971, Vanderbilt Television News Archive, Nashville, TN, http://tvnews. vanderbilt.edu/program.pl?ID=215742

193. Gallup Organization, *Gallup Poll #824* (Williamstown, MA: The Roper Public Opinion Research Center, 19–22 February 1971), 6.

194. Gallup, *Gallup Poll #824,* 6.

195. Kevin Williams, "Vietnam: The First Living Room War," in *The Fog of War: The Media on the Battlefield* by Derrik Mercer, Geoff Mungham, Kevin Williams, and Sir Tom Hopkinson (London: Heinemann, 1987), 213–260.

196. Joseph Wershba, "What *Really* Happened at Tonkin Gulf?" *60 Minutes,* March 16, 1971, Museum of Broadcast Communications Archive, http://archives.museum.tv/archives.

197. Wershba, "What *Really* Happened at Tonkin Gulf?"

198. Wershba, "What *Really* Happened at Tonkin Gulf?"

199. Wershba, "What *Really* Happened at Tonkin Gulf?"

200. 60 Minutes, "Tonkin Gulf/60 Minutes/CBS TV/3-16-71," *60 Minutes,* CBS, transcript, 16 March 1971, Series 96 Audiovisual Material, 96.4 Film and Slides (Transcriptions), Box 12. Folder 21, Fulbright, 60 Minutes, CBS TV, Tonkin Gulf, March 16, 1971, Fulbright Papers, University of Arkansas (Fayetteville, AR).

201. Wershba, "What *Really* Happened at Tonkin Gulf?"

202. Wershba, "What *Really* Happened at Tonkin Gulf?"

203. 60 Minutes, "Tonkin Gulf/60 Minutes/CBS TV/3-16-71."

204. 60 Minutes, "Tonkin Gulf/60 Minutes/CBS TV/3-16-71."

205. 60 Minutes, "Tonkin Gulf/60 Minutes/CBS TV/3-16-71."

206. Gallup Organization, *Gallup Poll #0795: Vietnam* (Williamstown, MA: The Roper Public Opinion Research Center, December 12–15, 1969), 5–11.

207. *New York Times Co. v. United States,* 403 U.S. 713 (1971); Herring, *America's Longest War,* 299–300.

208. Herring, *America's Longest War,* 298.

209. Melvin Small, *Johnson, Nixon, and the Doves* (New Brunswick, NJ: Rutgers University, 1988), 298.

210. NBC Evening News, "Washington, DC / Antiwar Demonstrations," NBC, April 18, 1971, accessed 25 April 2009, Vanderbilt Television News Archive, http://tvnews.vanderbilt.edu/ program.pl?ID=457147.

211. NBC Evening News, "Washington, DC / Antiwar Demonstrations," April 18, 1971.

212. Bruce Morton, Roger Mudd, Tony Sargent, "Washington, DC / Anti-War Protests," *CBS Evening News,* Sunday, April 18, 1971, Vanderbilt Television News Archive, Nashville, TN, http://tvnews.vanderbilt.edu/program.pl?ID=216190.

213. NBC Evening News, "Washington, DC / Antiwar Demonstrations," April 18, 1971.

214. Morton, Mudd, Sargent, "Washington, DC / Anti-War Protests," Sunday, April 18, 1971.

215. U.S. Senate, Senate Foreign Relations Committee, *Complete Testimony of Lt. John Kerry to Senate Foreign Relations Committee,* From the Congressional Record (92nd Congress, 1st Session) (Washington, DC: US Senate, April 22, 1971), 179–210.

216. U.S. Senate, Senate Foreign Relations Committee, *Complete Testimony of Lt. John Kerry . . . ,* 179–210.

217. U.S. Senate, Senate Foreign Relations Committee, *Complete Testimony of Lt. John Kerry . . . ,* 179–210.

218. U.S. Senate, Senate Foreign Relations Committee, *Complete Testimony of Lt. John Kerry . . . ,* 179–210.

219. U.S. Senate, Senate Foreign Relations Committee, *Complete Testimony of Lt. John Kerry . . . ,* 179–210.

220. U.S. Senate, Senate Foreign Relations Committee, *Complete Testimony of Lt. John Kerry . . .*, 179–210.

221. U.S. Senate, Senate Foreign Relations Committee, *Complete Testimony of Lt. John Kerry . . .*, 179–210.

222. Associated Press, "Nixon Plans Slight Boost in 1971 Troop Cut in Vietnam," Associated Press, Washington, DC, *Spokesman-Review*, Spokane, WA, 1.

223. Gallup Organization, *Gallup Poll #828* (Williamstown, MA: The Roper Public Opinion Research Center, April 23–26, 1971), 5–7.

224. Gallup, *Gallup Poll #828*, 7.

225. *New York Times Co. v. United States*, 403 U.S. 713 (1971); Herring, *America's Longest War*, 299–300.

226. CBS News, "The Pentagon Papers—What They Mean/CBS TV/ July 13, 1971," transcript, CBS News Special Report, July 13, 1971, Series 96 Audiovisual Material, 96.4 Film and Slides (Transcriptions), Box 12. Folder 45, 'The Pentagon Papers—What They Really Mean,' CBS TV, July 13, 1971, Fulbright Papers, University of Arkansas (Fayetteville, AR).

227. CBS News, "The Pentagon Papers—What They Mean/CBS TV/ July 13, 1971."

228. CBS News, "The Pentagon Papers—What They Mean/CBS TV/ July 13, 1971."

229. CBS News, "The Pentagon Papers—What They Mean/CBS TV/ July 13, 1971."

230. CBS News, "The Pentagon Papers—What They Mean/CBS TV/ July 13, 1971."

231. CBS News, "The Pentagon Papers—What They Mean/CBS TV/ July 13, 1971."

232. CBS News, "The Pentagon Papers—What They Mean/CBS TV/ July 13, 1971."

233. CBS News, "The Pentagon Papers—What They Mean/CBS TV/ July 13, 1971."

234. Roper Organization, *Roper Commercial #524: Political Questions* (Williamstown, MA: The Roper Public Opinion Research Center, October 18–27, 1971), 8–9.

235. Herring, *America's Longest War*, 300.

236. Roper Organization, *Roper Commercial #524: Political Questions*, 29.

237. Gallup, "Gallup Poll #821," Gallup, January 8–11, 1971.

238. Gallup, "Gallup Poll #830," Gallup, May 14–17, 1971.

239. Gallup, "Gallup Poll #833," Gallup, June 25–28, 1971.

240. Roper Organization, *Roper Commercial #524: Political Questions*, 8–10.

241. Center for Military History, "U.S. Army Campaigns: Vietnam," Center for Military History, United States Army, Fort McNair, DC, 20 November 2010, accessed September 22, 2014, http://www.history.army.mil/html/reference/army_flag/vn.html.

242. Eric Sevareid, "Analysis (Credibility Gap)," *CBS Evening News*, Wednesday, January 5, 1972, Vanderbilt Television News Archive, Nashville, TN, http://tvnews.vanderbilt.edu/program.pl?ID=220112.

243. Sevareid, "Analysis (Credibility Gap)," Wednesday, January 5, 1972.

244. Sevareid, "Analysis (Credibility Gap)," Wednesday, January 5, 1972.

245. Richard Nixon, "Address on the State of the Union Delivered Before a Joint Session of the Congress," 20 January 1972, online by Gerhard Peters and John T. Woolley, *The American Presidency Project*, University of California San Bernardino, accessed April 9, 2015, http://www.presidency.ucsb.edu/ws/?pid=3396.

246. Bob Clark, Howard K. Smith, "State of The Union / Democratic Response," *ABC Evening News*, Friday, January 21, 1972, Vanderbilt Television News Archive, Nashville, TN, http://tvnews.vanderbilt.edu/program.pl?ID=17628.

247. Clark, Smith, "State of The Union / Democratic Response," Friday, January 21, 1972.

248. Clark, Smith, "State of The Union / Democratic Response," Friday, January 21, 1972.

249. Harry Reasoner, Frank Reynolds, "Campaign '72 / Muskie," *ABC Evening News*, Friday, January 28, 1972, Vanderbilt Television News Archive, Nashville, TN, http://tvnews.vanderbilt.edu/program.pl?ID=17735.

250. Morton Dean, Roger Mudd, "New Hampshire / McCloskey," *CBS Evening News*, Sunday, September 5, 1971, Vanderbilt Television News Archive, Nashville, TN, http://tvnews.vanderbilt.edu/program.pl?ID=219564.

251. Clark, Smith, "State of the Union / Democratic Response," Friday, January 21, 1972.

252. Gallup Organization, *Gallup Poll #844* (Williamstown, MA: The Roper Public Opinion Research Center, February 4–7, 1972), 13–19.

253. Donn A. Starry, *Mounted Combat in Vietnam*, (Washington, DC: Department of the Army, 1989), 199.

254. Gallup, *Gallup Poll #844*, 13–19.

255. Michele Clark, Walter Cronkite, Morton Dean, Charles Osgood, Ike Pappas, "Campaign '72 / Nixon Peace Proposal," *CBS Evening News*, Friday, January 28, 1972, Vanderbilt Television News Archive, Nashville, TN, http://tvnews.vanderbilt.edu/program.pl?ID=220016.

256. Clark, et al., "Campaign '72 / Nixon Peace Proposal," Friday, January 28, 1972.

257. Clark, et al., "Campaign '72 / Nixon Peace Proposal," Friday, January 28, 1972.

258. Tom Jarriel, Roger Peterson, Howard K. Smith, "Vietnam / Tonkin Gulf," *ABC Evening News*, Wednesday, April 19, 1972, Vanderbilt Television News Archive, Nashville, TN, http://tvnews.vanderbilt.edu/program.pl?ID=20257.

259. Howard K. Smith, "Commentary / Nixon and South Vietnam," *ABC Evening News*, Tuesday, April 18, 1972, Vanderbilt Television News Archive, Nashville, TN, http://tvnews.vanderbilt.edu/program.pl?ID=20253.

260. Ted Koppel, Harry Reasoner, "Vietnam / Retrospective, Part 2," *ABC Evening News*, Friday, January 26, 1973, Vanderbilt Television News Archive, Nashville, TN, http://tvnews.vanderbilt.edu/program.pl?ID=23036.

261. Koppel, Reasoner, "Vietnam / Retrospective, Part 2," Friday, January 26, 1973.

262. Koppel, Reasoner, "Vietnam / Retrospective, Part 2," Friday, January 26, 1973.

263. Walter Cronkite, Bruce Dunning, Bob Schieffer, "Vietnam / Offensive," *CBS Evening News*, Monday, April 17, 1972, Vanderbilt Television News Archive, Nashville, TN, http://tvnews.vanderbilt.edu/program.pl?ID=222552.

264. Howard K. Smith, "Vietnam / Blockade-Candidates Reaction," *ABC Evening News*, Tuesday, May 9, 1972, Vanderbilt Television News Archive, Nashville, TN, http://tvnews.vanderbilt.edu/program.pl?ID=20931.

265. Smith, "Vietnam / Blockade-Candidates Reaction," Tuesday, May 9, 1972.

266. Howard K. Smith, Frank Tomlinson, "Campaign '72 / Vietnam Veterans," *ABC Evening News*, Friday, July 28, 1972, Vanderbilt Television News Archive, Nashville, TN, http://tvnews.vanderbilt.edu/program.pl?ID=21699.

267. Smith, Tomlinson, "Campaign '72 / Vietnam Veterans," Friday, July 28, 1972.

268. Douglas Brinkley and Luke Nichter, eds., *The Nixon Tapes* (New York: Houghton Mifflin Harcourt, 2014), 182.

269. NBC Evening News, "Campaign '72 / Vietnam-McGovern and Salinger," *NBC Evening News*, August 17, 1972, Vanderbilt Television News Archive, accessed January 9, 2013, http://tvnews.vanderbilt.edu.er.lib.k-state.edu/diglib-fulldisplay.pl?SID=2013010979528808&code=tvn&RC=465635&Row=19.

270. NBC Evening News, "Campaign '72 / Vietnam-McGovern and Salinger." August 17, 1972.

271. Eric Sevareid, "Analysis (Republican Spies and President)," *CBS Evening News*, Wednesday, October 25, 1972, Vanderbilt Television News Archive, Nashville, TN, http://tvnews.vanderbilt.edu/program.pl?ID=220411.

272. Sevareid, "Analysis (Republican Spies and President)," Wednesday, October 25, 1972.

273. Bernard Kalb, Dan Rather, Roger Mudd, Mike Wallace, John Hart, Bruce Hall, Richard Threlkeld, Bruce Morton, Bob Schieffer,; Sylvia Chase, Eric Sevareid, "Camapign '72: Two Days to Go," *CBS Special Report*, Sunday, November 5, 1972, Vanderbilt Television News Archive, Nashville, TN, http://tvnews.vanderbilt.edu/program.pl?ID=659060.

274. Robert L. Knudsen, "Paris Peace Talks Vietnam Peace Agreement Signing," January 27, 1973, White House Photo Office, Nixon White House Photographs, 1/20/1969–8/9/1974, White House Photo Office Collection (Nixon Administration), 1/20/1969–8/9/1974, Richard M. Nixon Presidential Library, (Yorba Linda, CA), accessed September 19, 2015, https://catalog.archives.gov/id/194482?q=vietnam.

275. Herring, *America's Longest War*, 318–319.

Chapter 6

1. Eugene R. Wittkopf, *Faces of Internationalism: Public Opinion and American Foreign Policy* (Durham, NC: Duke University, 1990), 6–10, 174–5; James Meernik, "Presidential Support in Congress: Conflict and Consensus on Foreign and Defense Policy," *The Journal of Politics*, Vol. 55, No. 3 (August 1993): 569–587; John Kane "American Values or Human Rights? U.S. Foreign Policy and the Fractured Myth of Virtuous Power," *Presidential Studies Quarterly*, Vol. 33, No. 4 (December 2003): 772–800; Milton J. Rosenberg, "The Decline and Rise of the Cold War Consensus," *Bulletin of the Atomic Scientists*, March 1981, 7–9; Randall Bennett Woods, "The Rhetoric of Dissent: J. William Fulbright, Vietnam, and the Crisis of International Liberalism," in *Critical Reflections on the Cold War: Linking Rhetoric and History* edited by Martin J. Medhurst and H. W. Brands (College Station, TX: Texas A&M University, 2000), 187; Campbell Craig, Fredrik Logevall, *America's Cold War: The Politics of Insecurity* (Cambridge, MA: Harvard University, 2009), 241–242; Allen H. Barton, "Fault Lines in American Elite Consensus," *Daedalus*, Vol. 109, No. 3 (Summer 1980): 1–24; Robert David Johnson, *Congress and the Cold War* (New York: Cambridge University, 2006), xv–xx; Linda B. Miller, "Morality in Foreign Policy: A Failed Consensus," *Daedalus*, Vol. 109, No. 3, (Summer, 1980): 143–158; Andrew Hunt "'When Did the Sixties Happen?' Searching for New Directions," *Journal of Social History*, Vol. 33, No. 1 (Autumn, 1999): 147–161; Jungkun Seo, "The Party Politics of 'Guns versus Butter' in Post-Vietnam America," *Journal of American Studies*, 45, 2 (2011): 317–336; Benjamin O. Fordham, "The Evolution of Republican and Democratic Positions on Cold War Military Spending: A Historical Puzzle," *Social Science History*, Volume 31, Number 4 (Winter 2007): 603–636; Simon Hall, "The Response of the Moderate Wing of the Civil Rights Movement to the War in Vietnam," *The Historical Journal*, Vol. 46, No. 3 (September 2003): 669–701.

2. Gallup Organization, *State of the Nation, 1974* (Williamstown, MA: The Roper Public Opinion Research Center, 20 April 1974), 33–34, 42–43, 91–92.

3. Gallup, *State of the Nation, 1974*, 112–117.

4. Gallup, *State of the Nation, 1974*, 112–117.

5. Gallup, *State of the Nation, 1974*, 112–117.

6. Gallup Organization, *State of the Nation: 1976* (Williamstown, MA: The Roper Public Opinion Research Center, June 1976), 3–28, 65–71, 76–78, 80–84.

7. Yankelovich, Skelly & White, *Yankelovich, Skelly & White Poll #1973-COLL:Youth Study, 1973—College Sample* (Williamstown, MA: The Roper Public Opinion Research Center, Late Spring 1973), 7, 21–33.

8. Yankelovich, Skelly & White, *Yankelovich, Skelly & White Poll #1973-COLL:Youth Study, 1973 . . .*, 21–33, 85–88.

9. Yankelovich, Skelly & White, *Yankelovich, Skelly & White Poll #1973-COLL:Youth Study, 1973 . . .*, 50–51.

10. Yankelovich, Skelly & White, *Yankelovich, Skelly & White Poll #1973-PUB: Youth Study, 1973 . . .*, 50–51.

11. Wittkopf, *Faces of Internationalism*, 6–10, 174–175.

12. Jon Cowans, "A Deepening Disbelief: The American Movie Hero in Vietnam, 1958–1968," *The Journal of American -East Asian Relations* Vol. 17, No. 4 (2010), 324; Craig, Logevall, *America's Cold War*, 241–242; Meernik, "Presidential Support in Congress."

13. Louis Harris and Associates, *Chicago Council on Foreign Relations Poll #1974-2436L: American Public Opinion and U.S. Foreign Policy, 1974: Leaders* (Williamstown, MA: The Roper Public Opinion Research Center, 10–29 December 1974), 5–8, 33–41, 44–70, 75–82.

14. Louis Harris and Associates, *Chicago Council on Foreign Relations Poll #1974-2436L . . .*, 5–8, 33–41, 44–70, 75–82.

15. Louis Harris and Associates, *Chicago Council on Foreign Relations Poll #1974-2436L . . .*, 5–8, 33–41, 44–70, 75–82.

16. Louis Harris and Associates, *Chicago Council on Foreign Relations Poll #1974-2436L . . .*, 5–8, 33–41, 44–70, 75–82.

17. Bob Clark, Tom Jarriel, Harry Reasoner, "Cambodia Bombing Halt / President Vetoes Bill," *ABC Evening News*, Wednesday, June 27, 1973, Vanderbilt Television News Archive, Nashville, TN, http://tvnews.vanderbilt.edu/program.pl?ID=26491.

18. NBC Evening News, "Cambodia / Offensive," *NBC Evening*, April 4, 1973, Vanderbilt Television News Archive, accessed 8 January 2013, http://tvnews.vanderbilt.edu/program.pl?ID=470068.

19. Clark, Jarriel, Reasoner, "Cambodia Bombing Halt / President Vetoes Bill," Wednesday, June 27, 1973.

20. John Chancellor, Richard Valeriani, "South Vietnam Aid / Debate," *NBC Evening News*, Thursday, 06 February 1975, Vanderbilt Television News Archive, Nashville, TN, http://tvnews.vanderbilt.edu/program.pl?ID=481605.

21. Chancellor, Valeriani, "South Vietnam Aid / Debate," Thursday, February 6, 1975.

22. NBC Evening News, "South Vietnam / United States Military Aid / Senate, President," *NBC Evening News*, March 18, 1975, Vanderbilt Television News Archive, accessed January 8, 2013, http://tvnews.vanderbilt.edu/program.pl?ID=481794.

23. NBC Evening News, "South Vietnam / United States Military Aid / Senate, President," March 18, 1975.

24. Steve Bell, Sam Donaldson, Ted Koppel, Harry Reasoner, "US, Saigon / Secret Agreements," *ABC Evening News*, Wednesday, 09 April 1975, Vanderbilt Television News Archive, Nashville, TN, http://tvnews.vanderbilt.edu/program.pl?ID=37054.

25. White House Photographic Office, Photo, Secretary of State Henry Kissinger interrupting a meeting between President Gerald R. Ford and senior advisers to relay the latest information on the U.S. evacuation of Saigon, April 29, 1975, White House Photographic Collection, Gerald R. Ford Library (Ann Arbor, MI), accessed August 13, 2015, https://catalog.archives.gov/id/7329679

26. NBC Evening News, "**South Vietnam Fall / Diplomatic Aftereffects / Philippines**," *NBC Evening*, 1 May 1975, Vanderbilt Television News Archive, accessed January 8, 2013, http://tvnews.vanderbilt.edu/program.pl?ID=482624.
27. Ken Kashiwahara, Harry Reasoner, "Thailand," *ABC Evening News*, Thursday, February 12, 1976, Vanderbilt Television News Archive, Nashville, TN, http://tvnews.vanderbilt.edu/program.pl?ID=41690.
28. Murray Fromson, Roger Mudd, "Thailand / United States Troop Withdrawal," *CBS Evening News*, Monday, 05 May 1975, Vanderbilt Television News Archive, Nashville, TN, http://tvnews.vanderbilt.edu/program.pl?ID=240287.
29. Ronald Reagan, "Republican National Convention (July 17, 1980)," Miller Center, University of Virginia, 17 July 1980, accessed September 14, 2014, http://millercenter.org/president/reagan/speeches/speech-3406.
30. Reagan, "Republican National Convention (July 17, 1980)."
31. Sam Donaldson, Barrie Dunsmore, Charles Gibson, Frank Reynolds, Max Robinson, "El Salvador," *ABC Evening News*, Tuesday, March 3, 1981, Vanderbilt Television News Archive, Nashville, TN, http://tvnews.vanderbilt.edu/program.pl?ID=70851.
32. Donaldson, et al., "El Salvador," Tuesday, March 3, 1981.
33. Barrie Dunsmore, Charles Gibson, Frank Reynolds, "El Salvador," *ABC Evening News*,Wednesday, 25 February 1981, Vanderbilt Television News Archive, Nashville, TN, http://tvnews.vanderbilt.edu/program.pl?ID=70271.
34. Morton Dean, Charles Kraus, "El Salvador," *CBS Evening News*, Sunday, 08 March 1981, Vanderbilt Television News Archive, Nashville, TN, http://tvnews.vanderbilt.edu/program.pl?ID=276383.
35. Sam Donaldson, Frank Reynolds, Max Robinson, John Scali, "CIA / Casey," *ABC Evening News*, Wednesday, July 15, 1981, Vanderbilt Television News Archive, Nashville, TN, http://tvnews.vanderbilt.edu/program.pl?ID=72626.
36. Dan Rather, Bob Simon, "El Salvador," *CBS Evening News*, Monday, February 1, 1982, Vanderbilt Television News Archive, Nashville, TN, http://tvnews.vanderbilt.edu/program.pl?ID=282030.
37. Rather, Simon, "El Salvador," Monday, February 1, 1982.
38. Robert Pierpoint, Dan Rather, "El Salvador," *CBS Evening News*, Thursday, March 4, 1982, Vanderbilt Television News Archive, Nashville, TN, http://tvnews.vanderbilt.edu/program.pl?ID=282965.
39. Pierpoint, Rather, "El Salvador," Thursday, March 4, 1982.
40. Peter Collins, Sam Donaldson, Charles Gibson, Frank Reynolds, "El Salvador / United States Aid," *ABC Evening News*, Thursday, 10 March 1983, Vanderbilt Television News Archive, Nashville, TN, http://tvnews.vanderbilt.edu/program.pl?ID=83041.
41. Ann Compton, Sam Donaldson, "Kohl / US-USSR Disarmament Talks / El Salvador," *ABC Evening News*, Sunday, March 13, 1983, Vanderbilt Television News Archive, Nashville, TN, http://tvnews.vanderbilt.edu/program.pl?ID=83090.
42. Compton, Donaldson, "Kohl / US-USSR Disarmament Talks / El Salvador," Sunday, March 13, 1983.
43. Collins, et al., "El Salvador / United States Aid," Thursday, March 10, 1983.
44. Anne Garrels, Charles Gibson, Peter Jennings, "Central America / United States Aid," *ABC Evening News*, Thursday, May 10, 1984, Vanderbilt Television News Archive, Nashville, TN, http://tvnews.vanderbilt.edu/program.pl?ID=89855.
45. Bill Lynch, Lesley Stahl, "El Salvador," *CBS Evening News*, Saturday, February 5, 1983, Vanderbilt Television News Archive, Nashville, TN, http://tvnews.vanderbilt.edu/program.pl?ID=288889.

46. Sam Donaldson, Mike von Fremd, John Quinones, "Central American / Moynihan Resignation," *ABC Evening News*, April 15, 1984, Vanderbilt Television News Archive, Nashville, TN, http://tvnews.vanderbilt.edu/program.pl?ID=89439.

47. Dan Rather, Robert Schakne, "Nicaragua / World Court / Casey Controversy," *CBS Evening News*, Wednesday, April 25, 1984, Vanderbilt Television News Archive, Nashville, TN, http://tvnews.vanderbilt.edu/program.pl?ID=296597.

48. David Martin, Dan Rather, Peter King, "Nicaragua / United States Policy," *CBS Evening News*, Thursday, 04 April 1985, Vanderbilt Television News Archive, Nashville, TN, http://tvnews.vanderbilt.edu/program.pl?ID=303355.

49. Bill Plante, Dan Rather, "Nicaragua / United States Intervention," *CBS Evening News*, Monday, 03 March 1986, Vanderbilt Television News Archive, Nashville, TN, http://tvnews.vanderbilt.edu/program.pl?ID=308975.

50. Sam Donaldson, Charles Gibson, Peter Jennings, "Nicaragua / United States Rebel Aid," *ABC Evening News*, Wednesday, March 5, 1986, Vanderbilt Television News Archive, Nashville, TN, http://tvnews.vanderbilt.edu/program.pl?ID=101783.

51. Dan Rather, "Nicaragua / United States Rebel Aid," *CBS Evening News*, Wednesday, March 5, 1986, Vanderbilt Television News Archive, Nashville, TN, http://tvnews.vanderbilt.edu/program.pl?ID=309047.

52. Sheilah Kast, Kathleen Sullivan, "Nicaragua / United States Military Aid," *ABC Evening News*, Saturday, March 8, 1986, Vanderbilt Television News Archive, Nashville, TN, http://tvnews.vanderbilt.edu/program.pl?ID=101847.

53. Dan Rather, Lesley Stahl, "Nicaragua / United States Military Aid," *CBS Evening News*, Thursday, March 13, 1986, Vanderbilt Television News Archive, Nashville, TN, http://tvnews.vanderbilt.edu/program.pl?ID=308720.

54. Phil Jones, Dan Rather, "Nicaragua / United States Military Aid," *CBS Evening News*, Friday, March 14, 1986, Vanderbilt Television News Archive, Nashville, TN, http://tvnews.vanderbilt.edu/program.pl?ID=308744.

55. Mike O'Connor, Bob Schieffer, "Nicaragua / Contra Aid," *CBS Evening News*, Saturday, June 28, 1986, Vanderbilt Television News Archive, Nashville, TN, http://tvnews.vanderbilt.edu/program.pl?ID=310571.

56. Edwin E. Moïse, *Tonkin Gulf and the Escalation of the Vietnam War* (Chapel Hill, NC: University of North Carolina, 1996), xi–xii, xiv, 203, 225, 240, 254–255.

57. Moïse, *Tonkin Gulf and the Escalation of the Vietnam War*, 226–227.

58. Bromely Smith, "Summary Record of the Meeting on Southeast Asia. Cabinet Room, June 10, 1964, 5:30 PM. Southeast Asia (without the President)," June 10, 1964, Files of McGeorge Bundy, box 18, folder Meetings on Southeast Asia, Vol. 1, National Security File, Lyndon B. Johnson Presidential Library (Austin, TX); Vietnam Task Force, "Chronology," Vietnam Task Force, Office of the Secretary of Defense, [Part IV. C.] Evolution of the War, Direct Action: The Johnson Commitments, 1964–1968. Volume II: A, Military Pressures Against NVN, February–June 1964, xx–xxvii, National Archives, Washington, DC, accessed October 11, 2012, http://www.archives.gov/research/pentagon-papers/; Transcript, George Ball Oral History Interview I, July 8, 1971, by Paige E. Mulhollan, Internet Copy, Lyndon B. Johnson Presidential Library (Austin, TX), 13–15.

59. Caroline F. Ziemke, "Senator Richard B. Russell and the 'Lost Cause' in Vietnam, 1954–1968," *Georgia Historical Quarterly*, Vol. 72, No. 1 (Spring, 1988) 30–71.

60. Wittkopf, *Faces of Internationalism*, 5–9.

61. Michael H. Hunt, *Ideology and US Foreign Policy* (New Haven: Yale University, 1987); Frederick Merk, *Manifest Destiny and Mission in American History: A Reinterpretation* (Cambridge, MA: Harvard University, 1995); Walter A. McDougall, *Promised Land, Crusader State* (Boston, MA: Houghton Mifflin, 1997).

INDEX

Photographs and illustrations are indicated by page numbers in *italics*.

ACKNOWLEDGMENTS

I would like to begin by thanking several fellow scholars for their invaluable contributions to this work. Professor Michael Krysko was the professor who challenged and pushed me to my first published work of history, starting me out on what has become a lifelong journey. Professor Louise Benjamin has so completely reshaped my perspective on the interaction between the public and the media that her influence has touched every work I have produced since that first day in her class. Professor Kristin Mulready-Stone likewise fundamentally reshaped my perspective on East and Southeast Asia and the Western experience in both regions. Professor Derek Hoff showed me an entirely different way to look at the currents of radicalism in the 1950s and 1960s that has had a profound impact not just on this work but on my entire understanding of the Cold War era. And this book would not exist without the patient guidance of Professor Donald Mrozek, the man who set me on my path to a love of the discipline of history.

I would also like to thank the many others who made this work possible. First, I would like to thank Margaret Harman and the entire audiovisual archive team at the Lyndon B. Johnson Presidential Library for their help in making available hundreds of hours of rare television materials that were essential to the completion of this work. Likewise, I would like to thank Vera Ekechukwu and the staff in the Special Collections department at the University of Arkansas Library for their patience with me and diligence in preserving and making available the Fulbright Papers. Finally, I would like to thank the staff of the Vanderbilt Television News Archives at Vanderbilt University in Nashville; the service you provide is priceless.

I would also be remiss if I did not thank the members of the Graduate Admissions and Awards Committee of the history department at Kansas State University and the kind donors to the Robin Higham Military History Graduate Student Research and Travel

Fund. Without a generous grant from this fund I would not have been able to complete this work. I am humbled and honored to have been recognized with this grant, and I hope that this work is worthy of your trust in me.

As always, huge thanks go to my literary agent, Grace Freedson. Your patient hard work in seeing that my ideas reach the biggest possible audience is a big part of what keeps me writing.

And, of course, thank you to my beautiful wife, Aree; my patient and understanding children, Amy and Jonathan; and the newest members of my family, Matt and Mackenzie Millen, for suffering the long hours and tired mornings as I completed this book—not to mention the multiple military deployments in between! I am in perpetual awe of the patience and silent courage of America's military families, and my own is no exception.

And, finally, my thanks to God, through Whom all things are made possible.

ABOUT THE AUTHOR

Lieutenant Colonel Pat Proctor, PhD, is a U.S. Army veteran of both the Iraq and the Afghanistan wars with over twenty-two years of service in command and staff positions from Fort Hood, Texas, to Schofield Barracks, Hawaii. Lieutenant Colonel Proctor is currently the Senior Fire Support Trainer at the Joint Readiness Training Center in Fort Polk, Louisiana. He most recently deployed to Jordan, on the front lines of the war on ISIS, as the commander of the Gunner Battalion (4th Battalion, 1st Field Artillery). In 2012, Pat served as the Chief of Plans for Regional Command-East in Afghanistan, planning the transition of the war to Afghan security forces ahead of the withdrawal of American forces from Afghanistan. In 2009, Pat deployed to Iraq as operations officer for Task Force Patriot (2nd Battalion, 32nd Field Artillery), an artillery-turned-infantry battalion battling insurgents in Saddam Hussein's hometown of Tikrit. In 2007, Pat was drafted to work in Iraq as part of a handpicked, twenty-man team of soldiers, scholars, and diplomats commissioned by General Petraeus and Ambassador Crocker to create a new strategy for the war in Iraq. Pat worked with a State Department counterpart to write the strategic communication plan for what has since become known as the Iraq "surge."

Pat has written extensively on current affairs, military history, and military simulation topics. He is the author of *Task Force Patriot and the End of Combat Operations in Iraq* and co-author of *ASVAB AFQT Cram Plan*. Lieutenant Colonel Proctor has also written articles for the Phi Alpha Theta history honor society journal, *The Historian*, the U.S. Army War College journal, *Parameters*, Henley-Putnam University's *Journal of Strategic Security*, the U.S. Army Command and General Staff College journal, *Military Review*, and consumer magazines including *Armchair General* and *Military Simulations & Training*.

Lieutenant Colonel Proctor holds a doctorate in history from Kansas State University. He earned his first master's degree in military arts for strategy from the U.S. Army Command and General Staff College (CGSC). He also holds a second master's degree in military arts for theater operations from the highly selective School of Advanced Military Studies (SAMS). Pat holds a bachelor's degree in mechanical engineering from Purdue University.